*The Complete
Round-the-World
Cookbook*

The Complete Round-the-World Cookbook

Recipes gathered by
Pan American World Airways
from over 80 countries,
with food and travel comments by

MYRA WALDO

Greenwich House
New York

This 1982 edition is published by Greenwich
House, distributed by Crown Publishers, Inc.
by arrangement with Doubleday & Company.

Manufactured in the United States of America

**Library of Congress Cataloging
in Publication Data**
Main entry under title:

The Complete round-the-world cookbook.

Originally published: Garden City, N.Y.,
Doubleday, 1973.
Includes index.
1. Cookery, International. I. Waldo, Myra.
II. Pan American World Airways, inc.
TX725.A1C573 1982   641.59   82-3102
ISBN: 0-517-383500   AACR2

h g f e d c b a

BON VOYAGE AND BON APPÉTIT—
on this trip around the world to all those who love travel and fine food.

Preface

Brillat-Savarin, PHYSIOLOGIE DU GOÛT:
"In compelling man to eat that he may live, Nature gives him an appetite to invite him, and pleasure to reward him."

The past years have seen a tremendous awakening of interest in foreign foods and cookery. While the exact reason for this is not known, it undoubtedly includes such varying factors as the exposure of American G.I.s to a wide assortment of different cooking styles, the increasing number of Americans always on the move and touring in foreign countries, and, inevitably, the gradual maturity of our own country, gastronomically speaking.

The recipes in this book were gathered with the assistance of Pan American World Airways. Pan American agents in each of the more than eighty countries and territories served by the air line were requested to furnish recipes for local food specialties, eating and drinking customs, and other culinary information. The recipes came from all possible sources, including hotels, restaurants, local gourmet groups, and private citizens. Many of the recipes were in weights and measurements of the particular country, and these were converted into our normal usage. In certain other cases the dishes were not to the American taste or called for ingredients not normally available to us, and these were discarded.

The recipes were tested, and in only a very few instances was it found necessary to make some small changes in order to make them more acceptable to the American palate. In the interest of reproducing the cuisine of the various countries with the greatest possible accuracy, this was done only where it was found to be unavoidable. In general it may be said that where any dish is found to vary from the traditional method of preparation it is because the dish required ingredients not readily available to the American housewife, or was unwarrantedly difficult to prepare, or was not in accordance with American taste by reason of excessive sweetness, spiciness, and so forth.

The editor has taken a certain amount of liberty in the spelling of the names of certain foreign dishes in the interest of the greater simplicity. In addition there is almost always a degree of regional variance within the particular country involved as to the preparation of the dish itself as well as to the spelling and pronunciation of its name. This is particularly noticeable to those countries whose languages do not have Romanic backgrounds. Further, the translations supplied for many of the dishes are intentionally not always literal or exact, since many such translations would fail to explain the nature of the dish.

Occasionally it may be noted that a given dish is listed under a country other than the one in which the reader believes it should be placed. In certain groups of countries the food is quite similar; thus, in order not to repeat dishes and in the interest of a better balanced book, various other local specialties are substituted.

It is the intention of this book to make it possible for the reader to prepare complete dinners as served in any of the countries concerned. The book offers in order within each country selections of recipes for appetizers, soups, fish, meat, vegetables, desserts, etc. There are large numbers of casserole and stew preparations which represent complete meals in one dish. Therefore it is not necessary to prepare all of the dishes to reproduce the foreign flavor of a given country at your own dinner table or at a party.

This book will not teach the reader how to cook. It has been assumed that such fundamentals of food preparation as the washing of vegetables, fruits, and poultry, etc., are known. In that vein, the simple everyday steps have been either merely mentioned or purposely omitted. Nevertheless, it is believed that any person who follows the instructions may prepare any of the recipes in this book.

Of course the opinions and comments expressed in the book are those of the author and do not necessarily represent those of Pan American World Airways. Many descriptive chapters herein refer to United States citizens as "Americans." The other peoples of North and South America also believe that they are Americans, as indeed they are. On the other hand, it has been found that no other word describes the people of this country so well, and we are called Americans all over the globe. Further, it is extremely cumbersome to refer to ourselves as United Statesians, or even as North Americans, because Mexicans, for example, rightly consider themselves North Americans. It is hoped that this explanation will satisfy those who object to the use of the word "American" on the grounds of inaccuracy or unwarranted monopoly.

To those who find that many of the recipes contain onions, garlic, dried peppers, rice, and similar ingredients, it can only be said that the recipes represent the local cookery customs of the country involved. It is also true that in many countries vegetables and salads are not served as separate courses, and therefore these omissions may be noted. The reader's attention is invited to the back of the book, which contains cooking hints and terms, tables of weights and measurements, etc., a gourmets' glossary, and sources of foreign ingredients in the United States.

The world of travel, the observation of the life and ways of others, the spirit of inquiry, the willingness to eat what others eat, and fundamentally and primarily the maintaining of an open mind on all subjects is the surest way for us to learn something about the rest of the world. Whether we wanted it or not, world leadership has come to the United States. We can no longer sit back and let the world think what it will of us, nor can we fail to learn as much as possible about our neighbors who inhabit the globe. In this atomic age our neighbors *are* the Patagonians, the Zulus, and the people next door.

Myra Waldo

Contents

Europe Austria
Belgium and Luxembourg
Czechoslovakia
Denmark
England, Wales, and Northern Ireland
Finland
France
Germany
Holland (The Netherlands)
Hungary
Ireland
Italy
Norway
Poland
Portugal
Russia
Scotland
Spain
Sweden
Switzerland
Yugoslavia

AUSTRIA

Austria is a ghost of its former political self, having lost most of its territories through invasions, wars, and treaties. At one time or another, the fantastic Hapsburg Empire controlled vast land areas, including parts of Switzerland, Hungary, Bohemia, Moravia, Italy, Slovakia, Artois, Alsace, Burgundy, Franche-Comté, the Netherlands, Poland, not to mention Mexico (at least momentarily). Unhappily, by historical accident rather than choice, Austria is located in the center of Europe, and troops have marched across its land, looted and ravaged the lovely countryside, and ultimately left the nation a shadow of itself, geographically speaking.

Gastronomically, Austria is better than ever. In the process of absorbing other areas and nations while it was growing into a full-sized empire, and later, as it shrank, the nation learned the cooking style of those about them. Therefore the Austrian cuisine and the menus of its restaurants are studded with dishes of Germany, Italy, Czechoslovakia, and Hungary.

The food is basically solid and substantial. Although there are a few light and frothy preparations, almost everything from soup to dessert tends to be filling, hearty, and high in calories. Austrians are said to be eating somewhat less than before (and perhaps this is true for the very young), but the majority of people eat as frequently as six times a day. Of course, there's breakfast, lunch, and dinner (although sometimes the two may switch places, with the heavier meal consumed in the middle of the day); in addition, many people eat a midmorning snack (a sandwich perhaps), plus afternoon tea, which is more likely to consist of coffee and pastry, and also a little something before retiring! Because not too many hours go by without a bite of something to eat, appetizers aren't too important and most meals begin with soup. But even the lightest consommé is served with noodles or perhaps tiny or large dumplings.

Most of the main courses are like those served in Germany—meats come with sauces, perhaps as a stew. Rarely is a plain meat offered, merely broiled, in the American style. In fact, an American-style steak may be had only at a hotel catering to foreigners. The strongest emphasis is upon veal, which the Austrians prefer to beef. Poultry is good, and there are some fine fresh-water fish preparations; because Austria lacks a coastline, ocean fish aren't too common.

But the desserts of Austria! It's been said that Austrians read a menu starting with the dessert section and working backward. In no other country in the world are desserts and pastries available in such a wide range; generally speaking, they are also the best in the world. There are perhaps several hundred different kinds of cakes and pastries. Skeptics are invited to visit Vienna's leading *konditorei*, a revered establishment called Demel's, in order to observe the enormous variety available. It takes a will of iron to resist the confections, and most tourists will leave Demel's very happy and a pound or two heavier.

The beers of Austria are somewhat disappointing, but there are quite a few excellent white wines to be had. These include Gumpoldskirchner, perhaps the best. In Grinzing, a suburb of Vienna, there are scores of informal wine houses serving pitchers of fresh young wine, plus simple meals, where visitors can spend an extremely pleasant, unsophisticated evening, listening to delightful music.

BROWN SOUP

BRENNSUPPE

4 tablespoons butter	2 eggs
4 onions, sliced thin	3 tablespoons heavy cream
3 tablespoons flour	2 tablespoons chopped parsley
6 cups beef broth	1 teaspoon chopped chives
1 cup dry red wine	

Melt the butter in a deep saucepan. Add the onions and sauté until very brown, about 15 minutes, stirring frequently. Sprinkle with the flour and stir well. Gradually add the broth, stirring constantly until the boiling point is reached. Add the wine and cook over low heat for 1 hour. Correct seasoning.

Beat together in a bowl the eggs, cream, parsley, and chives. Gradually add 1 cup of the hot soup, stirring constantly to prevent curdling. Return to the saucepan, mixing well. Heat thoroughly but do not allow to boil. *Serves 8–10.*

SOUR CREAM SOUP

STEIRISCHE SUPPE

6 cups chicken broth	1 tablespoon flour
½ teaspoon freshly ground black pepper	1 cup sour cream
	1 cup heavy sweet cream
½ teaspoon salt	4 boiled potatoes, peeled
1 teaspoon cumin seed	and cubed

Combine the broth, pepper, salt, and cumin seed in a saucepan. Cook over high heat for 10 minutes. In a bowl mix the flour and sour cream to a smooth paste. Add 1 cup of the broth gradually, beating constantly. Return to the broth in the saucepan and beat well. Add the sweet cream and potatoes. Cook over low heat for 10 minutes but do not allow to boil. Correct seasoning. Serve hot. *Serves 8–10.*

PAPRIKA FISH

PAPRIKA FISCH

6 fillets of sole	½ teaspoon freshly ground
4 tablespoons butter	black pepper
2 cups sliced onions	¾ cup water
2 tablespoons sweet paprika	¾ sour cream
2 teaspoons salt	

Wash and dry the fillets; cut in half crosswise. Melt the butter in a large skillet; sauté the onions 10 minutes, stirring frequently. Mix in the paprika, then arrange the fillets in the skillet. Sprinkle with the salt and pepper, and add the water. Bring to a boil, cover, and cook over low heat 20 minutes. Carefully transfer the fish to a serving dish. Stir the sour cream into the skillet and heat, but do not let boil. Pour over the fish. *Serves 6.*

VEAL CUTLET, VIENNA STYLE

WIENER SCHNITZEL

½ cup flour	2 eggs, beaten
1 teaspoon salt	¾ cup dry bread crumbs
½ teaspoon freshly ground black pepper	¼ pound butter
	3 tablespoons lemon juice
2½ pounds veal steak, pounded thin and cut into 6 pieces	3 tablespoons chopped parsley

Combine the flour, salt, and pepper. Dip the veal in the mixture. Then dip each piece in the beaten egg and finally in the bread crumbs. Melt half the butter in a large frying pan and place the veal in it. Cook over low heat until tender and well browned on both sides, about 15 minutes. Remove the veal and place on a heated platter in a warm place. Brown the remaining butter in the frying pan. Add the lemon juice and parsley and stir well. Pour over the veal and serve. *Serves 6.*

VIENNESE STEW

WIENEREINTOPF

2 pounds shoulder of pork	3 (1 pound) potatoes, peeled
2½ teaspoons salt	and sliced thin
1 teaspoon freshly ground	2 carrots, julienne cut
black pepper	2 cups chopped cabbage
6 tablespoons butter	2 teaspoons caraway seeds
1½ cups finely sliced onions	1 cup beef broth

Cut the pork into 1½-inch cubes. Season the cubes with 1 teaspoon of the salt and ¼ teaspoon of the pepper.

Melt the butter in a skillet; sauté the onions, until golden brown, remove with a slotted spoon, and reserve. Reserve the butter in the skillet.

In a greased 2-quart casserole, arrange half of the potato slices. Sprinkle with a little of the salt and pepper. Make successive layers of the pork, carrots, onions, and cabbage. Sprinkle with half the caraway seeds and a little more of the salt and pepper. Cover with the remaining potato slices, and sprinkle with the remaining caraway seeds, salt, and pepper. Pour the reserved butter over the top, then add the broth. Cover the casserole and bake in a 375° oven 1½ hours. Remove the cover and bake 15 minutes longer. Served directly from the casserole. *Serves 6.*

CHICKEN PAPRIKA

PAPRIKA HÜHNER

2 3½-pound frying chickens,	4 tablespoons butter
disjointed	6 onions, peeled and sliced thin
2 teaspoons salt	1½ tablespoons sweet paprika
1 teaspoon freshly ground	½ pint sour cream
black pepper	

Wash and dry the chicken. Season with salt and pepper, rubbing in well, both inside and out. Melt the butter in a heavy saucepan. Add the sliced onions and the paprika, and cook for 3 minutes, stirring constantly.

Add the chicken and brown over high heat. Lower the heat and cover the pan. Cook for 30 minutes, stirring occasionally. Add a little water if the pan becomes too dry. Add the sour cream, stir well, and let simmer for 15 minutes. Serve with *Nockerl*, the popular dumplings of the Austrians. (See recipe in this section.) Pour a little of the sauce over the dumplings. *Serves 6–8.*

POTATOES WITH MUSTARD SAUCE

SENF KARTOFFELN

6 large potatoes, unpeeled	¾ teaspoon salt
6 tablespoons butter	½ teaspoon freshly ground
1 cup chopped onion	black pepper
3 tablespoons flour	¼ cup prepared mustard
1½ cups beef broth	¼ cup dry bread crumbs

Scrub the potatoes well. Place in a saucepan and cover with water. Boil until tender, about 30 minutes. Drain, peel, and cut into ½-inch slices.

While the potatoes are cooking, melt half of the butter in a saucepan. Add the onions and sauté for 5 minutes, stirring frequently. Add the flour and mix well until light brown in color. Add the broth, salt, and pepper, stirring constantly until the boiling point is reached. Cook over low heat for 10 minutes. Strain. Add the mustard, mixing well.

Arrange the potatoes in a buttered pie plate in uniform rows, with each slice of potato resting on the adjacent slice. Pour the strained sauce over the potato slices. Sprinkle with the bread crumbs and dot with the remaining butter. Bake in a 375° oven for 15 minutes, or until delicately browned on top. *Serves 6–8.*

NOODLES AND CABBAGE

KRAUT FLECKERL

1 large head cabbage	½ teaspoon freshly ground
1 tablespoon salt	black pepper
½ pound (2 sticks) butter	2 8-ounce packages broad
2 teaspoons sugar	noodles

Wash the cabbage and cut it as fine as possible, discarding all imperfect leaves and the core. Place the shredded cabbage in a bowl and add the salt, mixing well. Allow to stand for 2 hours. Rinse and drain well, squeezing out all the liquid. Melt half the butter in a skillet. Add the cabbage, sugar, and pepper. Cook over low heat for 1½ hours, or until browned,

stirring frequently. Add the remaining butter at intervals until all has
been used. Correct seasoning.

Break the noodles in half, so that each piece is flat. Boil in salted water
for 8 minutes. Drain well. Add to the cabbage and stir together until
mixed. Heat for a few minutes. Serve with roast meats or poultry. *Serves
6–8.*

DUMPLINGS, AUSTRIAN STYLE

NOCKERL

¼ pound (1 stick) sweet butter	1¾ cups sifted flour
4 eggs	½ teaspoon salt

Cream the butter until light and fluffy. Add the eggs one at a time, beating well after each addition. Sift the flour and salt together, and add to
the previous mixture. Mix well and shape into a long, thin roll. Set aside
for 15 minutes. Break off very small pieces and drop into either boiling,
salted water or boiling soup. Remove the *Nockerl* as they come to the
top, which should be in about 3 minutes. Place in a colander to drain.
Serve hot, in place of potatoes, with any dish having a gravy. Pour some
of the gravy over the *Nockerl*. If desired, the boiled *Nockerl* may be
fried in butter and served in this fashion. *Serves 6–8.*

SOUFFLÉED OMELET

SALZBURGER NOCKERLN

4 egg yolks	6 egg whites
2 tablespoons flour	¾ cup sugar
½ teaspoon vanilla extract	Confectioners' sugar
4 tablespoons butter	

Beat the egg yolks very well, then beat in the flour and vanilla.

Preheat the oven to 350°.

Use an oblong, flat, flameproof pan about 12 inches long, or an 11-inch
skillet. Put the butter into it, and let melt over low heat. Meanwhile, beat
the egg whites until peaks begin forming, then very gradually beat in
the sugar. Continue beating until very stiff. Fold the yolk mixture into
the egg whites. When the butter is foamy, pick up about one sixth of the
mixture at a time with a ladle, and gently drop it into the prepared pan,
making six mounds. With a spoon, smooth the top and sides of each.
Cook over direct heat for 1 minute, then transfer the pan to the middle
level of the oven. Bake 10 minutes, or until *nockerl* are golden. Serve
at once, sprinkled with confectioners' sugar. *Serves 6.*

As served at the Vienna Inter-Continental Hotel.

SACHER'S CHOCOLATE CAKE

SACHER TORTE

5 ounces sweet chocolate	1 cup superfine sugar
1 tablespoon water	6 egg whites
½ pound (2 sticks) sweet butter	1¼ cups sifted cake flour
6 egg yolks, beaten	

Preheat oven to 325°.

Break the chocolate into small pieces and place in the top of a double boiler with the tablespoon of water. Cook over hot water until the chocolate melts. Add the butter and stir until melted. Add the beaten egg yolks, beating constantly. Add the sugar and beat steadily until well mixed. Cool for 10 minutes. Beat the egg whites until stiff but not dry. Fold in the chocolate mixture and the flour alternately, thoroughly but gently. Butter an 8-inch-square pan and dust with flour. Pour the mixture into it. Bake for 30 minutes, or until a cake tester comes out clean. Remove from the pan and allow to cool. Now prepare:

⅓ cup apricot jam	2 tablespoons hot water
3 ounces (squares) unsweetened chocolate	1 egg
	1 egg yolk
¾ cup confectioners' sugar	5 tablespoons sweet butter

Put the jam in a cup and place it in hot water. Stir until melted. Spread on top of the cake and allow to set, about 20 minutes. Melt the chocolate over hot water. Remove from the heat, add the sugar and water, and beat until well blended. Add the egg, beating briskly. Add the egg yolk and continue to beat. Add the butter, a tablespoon at a time, beating steadily. Spread on top of the cake. Cool. Cut into oblong pieces to serve. *Serves 8–10.*

BELGIUM AND LUXEMBOURG

At dawn each weekday, there's a fascinating outdoor food market held in Brussels, an exciting gathering behind the main post office building. It's all over by about eight each morning, so obviously late sleepers will miss this colorful event. From all over the small nation of Belgium, the finest of foods are shipped, and the display is nothing short of overpowering. Because this country is almost miniature in size, there isn't any spot which is more than four hours away from the capital city. Therefore, only the freshest of fruits and vegetables reach the market, sometimes only hours from the ground or tree.

Dressed in everyday clothes, with comfortable shoes, you will find it quite diverting to wander through the old part of town adjacent to the outdoor food market. Even the streets here are named for foods–Turnip Street, Cabbage Street (in French of course), and so on. Now is a good time for a second breakfast, where you can have steaming hot coffee or chocolate, together with *cramique,* a delicious type of raisin bread, or perhaps a bit of honey cake.

There's no doubt that the food of Belgium has remained in the shadow of that of France. Within reason this makes a degree of sense, for France is a large country, whereas Belgium is small, and there's no doubt but that the respective cuisines are similar. This applies particularly to that served in the hotels and restaurants of the de luxe category. However, in the countryside it's still possible to dine upon Belgian specialties, which are often quite extraordinary.

Much of the country is devoted to agriculture. As a result, meal hours follow the pattern of people around the world who work in fields. Breakfast is simple, eaten early in the morning. At midmorning, perhaps a snack. The principal meal of the day is around noon, and it might well be heavy and substantial. The evening meal begins early, typically 6 P.M., and is lighter than the midday repast, consisting of sausages, cold meats, eggs, or the like. Of course this doesn't apply to Antwerp or Brussels, which follow a quite different way of urban life; in those cities, an evening dinner is often the large meal of the day, usually served much later in the evening than 6 P.M.

Belgium, because of its cool northern location, produces no wines but drinks those of France and Germany with enthusiasm. However it does have some excellent beers—Faro, Kriek-Lambic, and Gueuze, for example—which are excellent, and have rather more bubbles than usual, produced by the manner of fermentation. With the beers, it's customary to nibble on fried potatoes, fried mussels, or *pottekees,* a kind of fresh white cheese prepared with onions.

Among the novelties in this cuisine, at random, are such items as buttermilk soup, eel pie, *carbonnade Flamande* (a beef stew prepared with beer), duck or goose prepared with a creamy garlic sauce, and waffles made with beer.

In Luxembourg, a miniature country with loads of charm, soups are especially popular. Perhaps the best known are the bean, onion, sorrel, lentil, and leek soups. For whatever reason, soups are enormous favorites and appear at almost every meal, occasionally even at second breakfasts in the rural areas. The chief meat of the country is pork, something easily noticed from the highways, for it appears that every farm has its own supply of pork on the hoof. Among the dessert specialties, clearly cakes have the upper hand in Luxembourg. It also features a very frothy, semi-dry white wine, which many people drink as if it were water, which it's not. Definitely not.

EELS IN GREEN SAUCE

LES ANGUILLES AU VERT

3 pounds small eels	⅛ teaspoon tarragon
2 teaspoons salt	⅛ teaspoon sage
½ teaspoon white pepper	⅛ teaspoon chervil
6 tablespoons butter	2 shallots, chopped
1 cup finely chopped sorrel	1½ cups dry white wine
1 cup finely chopped spinach	3 egg yolks
¼ cup chopped parsley	¼ teaspoon lemon juice

Have the skin removed and the eels cleaned. Wash, dry, and cut crosswise into 2-inch pieces. Season with the salt and pepper.

Melt the butter in a skillet; lightly brown the eel in it. Add the sorrel, spinach, parsley, tarragon, sage, chervil, shallots, and wine. Bring to a boil and cook over low heat 10 minutes.

Beat the egg yolks and lemon juice in a bowl. Gradually beat in the liquid from the skillet. Return to skillet and cook, stirring gently until thickened, but do not let boil. Taste for seasoning. Serve hot or cold. *Serves 8–10.*

CHICKEN SOUP-STEW

WATERZOOÏ DE POULET

2 2-pound broilers
Chicken livers, gizzards, hearts,
  feet, veal bones
6 cups water
2 parsley roots
3 sprigs parsley
2 stalks celery

2 teaspoons salt
½ teaspoon white pepper
1 lemon, peeled and sliced thin
2 cups dry white wine
4 tablespoons butter
½ cup fresh bread crumbs

Clean the chickens carefully, singeing the skin to remove all pinfeathers. Combine the chicken livers, gizzards, hearts, and feet and the veal bones in a saucepan. Add the water, parsley roots, parsley, celery, salt, pepper, and lemon. Bring to a boil and skim the top thoroughly. Cover and cook over low heat for 2 hours. Strain.

Place the chickens in a casserole. Pour the soup stock and the white wine over them. Add the butter. Cover and cook over low heat for 45 minutes, or until tender. Remove the chickens and cut into serving pieces. Add the bread crumbs to the soup. Return the chickens to the soup and stir well. Serve hot, directly from the casserole, placing a piece of chicken in each soup plate and pouring the soup over it. *Serves 4-6.*

CREAM OF ASPARAGUS SOUP

CRÈME D'ASPERGES

1½ pounds asparagus or
  2 packages frozen
1½ quarts chicken broth

3 egg yolks
1 cup light cream
3 tablespoons minced parsley

If possible, buy white asparagus, the type used in Belgium. If only the green type is available, peel off the outer green portions. Cut off about 16 tips and reserve. Cut the remaining asparagus into small pieces and combine with the broth. Bring to a boil and cook over low heat 30 minutes. Purée in an electric blender, then strain, or force through a sieve. Cook the asparagus tips 10 minutes (5, if frozen), then drain.

Beat the egg yolks in a bowl; mix in the cream. Gradually add the hot soup, stirring steadily to prevent curdling. Return to the saucepan. Taste for seasoning. Sprinkle with parsley. Heat, but do not let boil. Add asparagus tips. *Serves 6-8.*

BEEFSTEAK, FLEMISH STYLE

BOEUF À LA FLAMANDE

4 tablespoons butter
6 large onions, sliced
4 pounds beef, about 1 inch
thick, cut into 12 pieces
2 tablespoons flour
1 cup water
2 cups beer
2 tablespoons wine vinegar

2 teaspoons salt
½ teaspoon freshly ground
black pepper
1 teaspoon sugar
3 tablespoons chopped parsley
2 bay leaves
½ teaspoon thyme

Melt the butter in a Dutch oven or casserole. Add the onions and sauté until brown, stirring frequently. Remove the onions and set aside. In the fat remaining, brown the beef on both sides and remove. Sprinkle the flour on the pan juices and mix until smooth. Add the water, stirring constantly. Return the onions and beef to the saucepan. Add the beer, vinegar, salt, pepper, sugar, parsley, bay leaves, and thyme. Cover and cook over low heat for 2 hours. Serve hot with boiled potatoes. *Serves 6–8.*

PURÉE OF BRUSSELS SPROUTS

PURÉE DES CHOUX DE BRUXELLES

2 pounds brussels sprouts
4 tablespoons butter
1 tablespoon flour
1 tablespoon meat extract

1 cup water
2 egg yolks, beaten
¼ cup heavy cream

Boil the sprouts in salted water for 10 minutes. Drain well. Melt the butter, add the sprouts, and toss gently for 2 minutes. Sprinkle the flour on them, add the meat extract and the cup of water, mixing well. Cover and cook over low heat for 15 minutes. Force the sprouts through a sieve. Beat the egg yolks and cream together in a bowl. Gradually stir in the puréed sprouts. Correct seasoning. Heat but do not allow to boil. *Serves 6–8.*

CARROTS, FLEMISH STYLE

CAROTTES À LA FLAMANDE

3 tablespoons butter
12 small carrots, scraped
1 teaspoon salt

¼ teaspoon white pepper
1 teaspoon sugar
¼ cup heavy cream

Melt the butter in a heavy saucepan. Add the carrots, salt, pepper, and sugar. Cover and cook over low heat for 20 minutes, or until tender. Add the cream, stir, and cook 2 minutes longer. *Serves 4–6.*

FRUIT TART, LIÉGE STYLE

TARTE LIÉGEOISE

1 cup flour	4 tablespoons butter
¼ teaspoon salt	1 egg yolk
2 teaspoons sugar	1 tablespoon cold water

Sift the flour, salt, and sugar together into a bowl. Cut in the butter with a pastry blender or two knives. Combine the egg yolk and water and add to the previous mixture, tossing lightly with a fork until a ball of dough is formed. Preheat oven to 375°.

Roll out the dough about ⅛ inch thick on a lightly floured surface. Line a 9-inch pie plate with the dough and prick in several places with a fork. Cover with a piece of wax paper and pour some beans or rice on the paper to keep the dough down. Bake in a 375° oven for 15 minutes, or until lightly browned. Discard the beans or rice. Now prepare the filling:

3 egg yolks	1 tablespoon brandy
1 teaspoon flour	1 cup heavy cream, whipped
4 tablespoons sugar	2 cups blueberries or seedless
⅛ teaspoon salt	grapes
1 cup scalded milk, cooled	¼ cup melted raspberry jelly

Beat the egg yolks, flour, sugar, and salt together in the top of a double boiler. Gradually add the milk, beating constantly for 2 minutes. Place over hot water and stir with a wooden spoon until the mixture begins to thicken. Remove from the heat and place pan in cold water. Stir until the mixture becomes cool and thick. Add the brandy. If the mixture is not completely smooth, force it through a sieve. Fold in 4 tablespoons of the whipped cream. Spread half of the custard on the bottom of the tart shell. Combine the fruit and jelly and pour half of the mixture on the custard. Cover with the remaining custard, then add the remaining fruit and jelly. Cover with the remaining whipped cream. If desired, the whipped cream may be forced through a pastry tube for additional effect. Chill for 2 hours. *Serves 6–8.*

CZECHOSLOVAKIA

This is a country where fine food and its preparation are given serious consideration. In any event that was the situation before the war. Everywhere the people consumed vast quantities of good food accompanied by heroic beakers of one of the world's finest beers, the *Plzeňské pivo,* the Pilsener beer of Czechoslovakia. Many beer drinkers consider Pilsener the finest beer in the world, but a certain amount of difference of opinion on the subject, supported by national partisanship, makes an ultimate decision rather difficult. The country also produces local wines and some fairly good brandies, but beer is unquestionably the national beverage.

The Czechs like fresh-water fish dishes, of which *ryba na cerno,* or fish made with a black sauce, is one of the best. It has many ingredients, and the resulting flavor is superb. Undoubtedly the favorite main dishes are those made with pork or goose. These are inevitably served with sauerkraut and dumplings, but the meat or poultry is treated in a variety of ways. A favorite Czech manner of preparing sauerkraut is to serve it hot with caraway seeds. Pork products are prepared in countless manners, but the favorite of all is sausage in one shape or another. No other country has such a variety, and sausages really constitute a cult among the Czechs. People will argue fiercely the relative merits of one pork butcher as against another across the street. The most famous of Czech ways with ham is undoubtedly the renowned Prague-style ham, which is canned and shipped all over the world.

The one feature of Czechoslovakian food that cannot be dismissed lightly is the matter of the ever present *knedlíky,* or dumplings. This is not to be taken humorously, for the local dumplings are very light indeed. These come in every conceivable size and shape, round and small, egg-shaped, nut-shaped, heavy, light, doughy, spongy, rich, unsweet, and so on endlessly. To date, no one has come up with a triangular one, but it is always possible. They are served in soups, with meats or poultry, and of course there is a tremendous array of desserts built around sweet *knedlíky.* The only possible limit is the imagination of the maker. Housewives treasure dumpling recipes and refuse to trade them with their best friends; discussions rage endlessly as to which housewife makes better *knedlíky.* A good *knedlíky* recipe is regarded as part of every young girl's dowry.

This is not to indicate that the local cuisine is completely dependent upon pork sausages, beer, and dumplings. There are also famous rabbit, chicken, and game dishes, and above all the Czech way with goose is unsurpassed. Of all vegetables, probably the only one that appeals to the people is the mushroom in its many varieties, a fondness shared with their Polish neighbors.

Hovězí maso is another important part of the local cooking style; it is similar to the French *pot au feu*, a type of boiled beef in the pot. Various sauces are served with it, recalling the Austrian ways with boiled beef. Thus, while the cuisine resembles those of neighboring countries, it retains its own individuality even when borrowing from them.

BEER SOUP

PIVNÍ POLÉVKA

1 quart beer	1 tablespoon butter
1 quart water	3 egg yolks
2 tablespoons sugar	1 cup heavy cream

Combine the beer and water in a saucepan. Bring to a boil and add the sugar and butter. Cook over heat for 30 minutes. Beat the egg yolks in a bowl. Add the cream and again beat well. Very gradually add the beer mixture to the egg and cream mixture, beating constantly to prevent curdling. Pour the mixture back into the saucepan and heat again but do not allow to boil. *Serves 6–8.*

FISH IN BLACK SAUCE

RYBA NA CERNO

2 cups water	¾ cup water
1 cup vinegar	2 cups beer
2 onions, sliced	2 tablespoons lemon rind
2 sprigs parsley	4 slices rye bread, cut into small
1 stalk celery	cubes
2 cloves garlic, minced	6 gingersnaps
2 bay leaves	½ cup seedless raisins
⅛ teaspoon thyme	½ cup almonds, sliced
2 tablespoons pickling spice	2 tablespoons lemon juice
½ teaspoon powdered ginger	¼ cup sugar
6 slices (¾ inch thick) pike,	2 tablespoons butter
whitefish, carp	2 tablespoons flour
1 pound prunes, presoaked	

Combine in a saucepan the 2 cups of water, vinegar, onions, parsley, celery, garlic, bay leaves, thyme, pickling spices, and ginger. Bring to a boil and cook over medium heat for 30 minutes. Add the fish and cook 30 minutes longer.

Cook the prunes in ¾ cup of water until soft, about 25 minutes. Drain reserving the juice. Remove the pits and chop the prunes very finely. Return the chopped prunes to the juice, and add the beer, lemon rind, bread cubes, gingersnaps, raisins, almonds, lemon juice, and sugar and mix well. Cook over medium heat for 10 minutes. Place the fish on a platter, reserving the stock.

In a separate saucepan melt the butter and add the flour, stirring constantly until brown. Gradually add the fish stock to this saucepan, stirring constantly until the boiling point is reached. Add the prune and beer mixture and stir well. Cook for 5 minutes. Pour the sauce over the fish and serve. *Serves 6.*

Note: Although the quantity of fish listed in this recipe will serve 6, it may be increased to serve up to 12 merely by adding additional slices of fish. It will not be necessary to increase the quantity specified for any other ingredient, since the sauce will be sufficient to serve 12.

GOOSE WITH APPLE STUFFING

HUSA S JABLKOVOU NÁDIVKOU

10- to 12-pound goose
3 teaspoons salt
1 teaspoon freshly ground
  black pepper
2 teaspoons caraway seeds

3 cups sliced apples
2 tablespoons water
1 cup fresh bread crumbs
1 small onion, minced
⅛ teaspoon cayenne pepper

Wash the goose and carefully remove any remaining feathers. Dry thoroughly. Combine the salt, pepper, and caraway seeds and rub into the skin and inside of the goose. This is best done at least 8 hours before using, to allow the seasoning to be absorbed.

Place the sliced apples in a saucepan with the water. Cook over low heat until very soft, about 20 minutes. Mash the apples with a fork and add the bread crumbs, minced onion, and cayenne pepper. Mix well. Stuff the goose with the apple mixture and fasten the opening with skewers or with thread. Roast on a rack in a shallow pan in a 350° oven for 3 hours. Pour off the fat as it accumulates. At the end of 2 hours, carefully pour over the skin 1 cup of ice water. Baste a few times during the final hour of roasting. The skin should be crisp and brown when the goose is completed. *Serves 6–8.*

STEWED MUSHROOMS

DUŠENÉ HOUBY

2 pounds mushrooms	2 teaspoons caraway seeds
4 tablespoons butter	1 tablespoon flour
3 tablespoons chopped parsley	1 teaspoon vinegar
½ teaspoon salt	3 tablespoons sour cream

Wash the mushrooms thoroughly under cold water. Drain. Peel them, if the skin is heavy, and slice. Melt the butter in a large skillet and add the mushrooms, parsley, salt, and caraway seeds. Sauté lightly for 15 minutes. Add the flour and mix well until smooth. Add the vinegar and sour cream. Cook 15 minutes longer, stirring occasionally. Serve as a vegetable or on slices of buttered toast. *Serves 4–6.*

FARINA DUMPLINGS

KRUPIČNÉ KNEDLÍKY

2 eggs	1 teaspoon salt
1 egg yolk	½ cup farina
½ cup melted butter	¼ cup dry bread crumbs

Beat the eggs and the yolk in a bowl. Add 2 tablespoons melted butter, the salt and farina. Mix well. Set aside for 1 hour. Drop by the teaspoon into boiling salted water. Boil for 30 minutes. Drain well but carefully. Serve with remaining melted butter and bread crumbs. *Serves 4–6.*

POTATO NOODLES

BRAMBOROVÉNUDLE

4 large potatoes, unpeeled	2 tablespoons flour
3 cups water	3 eggs
2 teaspoons salt	4 tablespoons butter

Place the unpeeled potatoes in a saucepan with the water and cook until soft. Peel them while hot and mash in a bowl. Add the salt, flour, and eggs. Mix well and knead into a dough. If the mixture is too thin to roll, add a very little additional flour. Place on a lightly floured board and roll as thin as possible. Cut into strips about ¼ inch wide by about 4 inches in length.

Butter a baking dish and place the strips of dough in it, preferably in a crisscross arrangement. Dot the top of the noodles with little pieces of butter. Bake in a 375° oven for 30 minutes, or until browned on top. Serve with meat or poultry dishes. *Serves 6–8.*

POPPY SEED CAKE

MAKOVÝ DORT

½ pound poppy seeds
8 egg yolks
1¼ cups sugar
¼ cup seedless raisins

1 teaspoon grated lemon rind
1 teaspoon cinnamon
8 egg whites

Preheat oven to 325°.

Grind the poppy seeds thoroughly in a food chopper, electric blender, or grinder and set aside. Beat the egg yolks in a bowl until thick. Gradually add the sugar, a tablespoon at a time, until well blended and very thick. Add the raisins, lemon rind, cinnamon, and ground poppy seeds. Mix well. Beat the egg whites until stiff but not dry, and fold them gently and carefully into the previous mixture.

Butter a spring-form pan and dust with a little flour. Pour the mixture into it. Bake in a 325° oven for 50 minutes, or until a cake tester comes out clean. Cool, then carefully remove the spring form. The cake may be served with whipped cream on top. It will keep fresh and moist for several days. *Serves 8–10.*

DENMARK

By and large, American visitors to this tiny nation find its food exactly to their taste. To begin with, the cooking style is not unlike that of our own country (some differences will be discussed subsequently), and the ingredients are typically very fresh. Furthermore, the Danes are a delightful people, with a sense of humor almost identical to ours.

As a rule, Danes begin their day with a very light breakfast, although children may eat some porridge. In the middle of the day, many people have *smørrebrød,* literally "buttered bread," a type of open-faced sandwich. Typically they eat several of them, as you will when in Denmark. There are two principal types—the flat ones and the high ones. A flat one is easily imagined, but the high open sandwiches are beautifully arranged, artistically designed, and are a delight to both the eye and the palate. Often, some of these creations are really salads or main courses, theoretically classified as open-faced sandwiches merely being served on buttered bread. Some of the possibilities of *smørrebrød* are considered in the recipe section that follows. Dinner is somewhat early in the evening, and may consist of a simple meat dish, followed by dessert. In families, it's customary to offer second portions.

In this country, you'll find the soups to be worthy of note. Perhaps the national soup is made of yellow split peas, and made in sufficient quantity so there's inevitably enough for the following day. Of course, this is primarily a cold weather soup. In addition to the usual ones, Denmark features sweet fruit soups such as *sødsuppe* (made of various fruits), and also a preparation made of elderberries called *hyldebaersuppe*, as well as a creation prepared with apples and lemon peel. Also a soup made with buttermilk, served cold. Finally, the most controversial of all, a beer soup made with rye bread and beer, called *øllebrød*. This is definitely an acquired taste.

One of the great specialties of Denmark is its pastry, which bears the somewhat strange name of *Dansk Wienerbrød*, that is, Danish Vienna bread! However, the reason for its strange name is lost in conflicting tales and folklore. In any event, it's the basis for our own Danish pastry, except that it's far better in Denmark than is our own "prune Danish," for example. The lightness and delicacy of this pastry on its home grounds is guaranteed to astonish anyone. It's a trifle troublesome to prepare the dough, but the results are definitely worthwhile.

Danish drinking habits are interesting. It is customary for a host to lift his glass and say, "Welcome," with everyone present expected to take a drink. Subsequently, if a guest wishes to have a drink he must first raise his glass, greet the other guests, every person present must drink, and so on. The entire ceremony is repeated each and every time with each drink that follows. The local beers are outstanding, among the finest in the world, and are perfect with *smørrebrød*. *Snaps*, a potent clear white drink, is served ice cold, and is stronger than you think. Wines are imported, and served on special occasions. Cherry Heering, the famous cherry brandy, is produced here, and makes a fine after-dinner drink.

Denmark is a land of abundance, filled with good things to eat. The people fancy themselves as among the leading gastronomes of Europe, although they are hotly disputed by the French and the Belgians. No matter, for whoever wins the contest, visitors will find much to enjoy at a Danish table. Under no circumstances should a tourist miss the delicious fish, fresh or smoked, and the shellfish, which may be described only by that hackneyed and moth-eaten word, fabulous! The oysters, shrimp, and lobsters of Denmark are worth the trip to Europe in the opinion of many gourmets.

OPEN SANDWICHES

SMØRREBRØD

Open-faced sandwiches–that is, one slice of bread–are as a Danish cult, a phenomenon, and a way of life almost impossible to describe. *Smørre-brød* is eaten by almost everyone in Denmark for lunch every single day. The reason for their popularity is easily understood, once they have been seen and tasted.

The Danes are great believers in exciting as well as satisfying the appetite, and thus the preparation of the open-faced sandwiches follows a tradition. First, the bread should be very thinly sliced, not so thickly as it is normally supplied to us by commercial bakeries. If possible, obtain unsliced bread and cut thin slices by hand, using a knife with a serrated edge. Try not to use just plain white bread. Instead, try whole-grain, sour rye, pumpernickel, or other unusual types of bread.

Next, spread very small amounts of butter (preferably sweet butter if available) on each slice of bread; when whipped butter is obtainable, it should be used. If meat sandwiches are planned, mix a little mustard in with the butter and spread the bread with the mixture.

Now we come to the question of eye appeal. If hard-cooked eggs are used, slice them as thin and as uniform as you can. Spread the egg slices on the buttered bread as evenly as possible, in two or three equal rows. Place a sardine diagonally across the sandwich. Place a paper-thin slice of lemon over the sardine.

Shrimp are definitely the most popular single type of *smørrebrød*. Use the smallest cooked shrimp you can obtain and place them evenly on the buttered bread, so that each shrimp rests on the one behind it. The main thing to remember is that the shrimp should be arranged as carefully as possible to create an even pattern. Place 1 teaspoon of mayonnaise in the center of the sandwich and sprinkle a little parsley on top.

Place a slice of crisp, washed and dried lettuce on the buttered bread and put a piece of cold, cooked fish on the lettuce. Cut a paper-thin slice of lemon. Hold a piece of paper over one half of the lemon slice and sprinkle with paprika. Now cover the side that has the paprika on it and sprinkle minced parsley on the other side. Place the decorated lemon slice on top of the fish. (When using pieces of cold fish, make sure that there are no bones in the fish.)

For meat sandwiches, cut away any possible fat. Place the meat so that it hangs over the sides of the bread. If desired, prepare a special butter by melting 4 tablespoons of butter and, when cool, combining it with 2 tablespoons of grated horseradish.

Cheese sandwiches may be imaginatively prepared too. If Swiss cheese is used, have the edges hang over the sides of the bread; this is the type of sandwich in which the bread should be spread with mustard butter. Cheese may be combined with slices of meat or with lettuce.

These delicious and appealing sandwiches may be served for lunch or late suppers. The bread should not be sliced thick, regardless of when it is served. If several different types of open-faced sandwiches are served, the fish sandwiches should be served first, followed by the meat, and lastly the cheese.

YELLOW PEA SOUP

GULE AERTER

1 pound yellow split peas	4 leeks
3½ quarts water	2 onions
3 pounds pork	3 carrots
¼ pound salt pork	3 sprigs parsley
1 parsley root	½ teaspoon thyme
1 celery root	1 pound potatoes
1 parsnip	Salt

Wash the split peas well, then soak in 1½ quarts of the cold water for 2 hours. Bring to a boil in the same water, then cook over low heat 1¼ hours or until tender.

While the peas are soaking, combine in a large pan the pork, salt pork, parsley root, celery root, parsnip, leeks, onions, carrots, parsley, thyme, and potatoes with the remaining 2 quarts of water. Bring to a boil. Cover and cook over low heat 3 hours. Strain the stock and add enough to the peas to make it the consistency you like. Cut the vegetables into small pieces and add them to the peas. Add salt to taste. The meat can be served as a separate course with mustard sauce. *Serves 8–10.*

FISH MOUSSE WITH ONION SAUCE

FISKEFARS AND LØGSOVS

3 pounds cod or pike fillets	2 teaspoons salt
¼ cup butter, softened	½ teaspoon white pepper
2 eggs, beaten	½ cup heavy cream
2 tablespoons potato flour	

Preheat oven to 350°.

Wash and dry the fillets. Grind or chop very fine in a food mill or chopper. Add the softened butter and beat together with the ground fish until thoroughly blended. Add the beaten eggs, the potato flour, salt, and white pepper and mix well. Correct seasoning.

Butter a 7- or 9-inch ring mold carefully. Whip the cream until stiff. Fold into the fish mixture. Pour the mixture into the mold and cover it. If you do not have a pot cover sufficiently large, use a piece of aluminum foil. Place the mold in a pan of hot water. Bake for 50 minutes. Meanwhile prepare the following sauce:

¼ pound butter	1½ cups heavy cream, scalded
2 large onions, chopped fine	1 teaspoon salt
3 tablespoons flour	¼ teaspoon white pepper

Melt the butter in a saucepan. Add the chopped onions and cook over low heat about 10 minutes, or until golden brown, stirring occasionally to prevent the onions from burning. Add the flour, stirring constantly until smooth. Add the scalded cream and continue stirring until the boiling point is reached. Add the salt and pepper and cook 5 minutes.

Run a knife around the edge of the mold, tap the sides gently, and unmold the fish onto a platter. Serve with the sauce in a separate dish. *Serves 8–10.*

ROAST PORK WITH APPLES AND PRUNES

STEGT SUINEKAM MED AEBLER OG SVEDSKER

1 pound prunes, pitted	1 teaspoon salt
1 cup water	½ teaspoon pepper
6 apples	
6-pound loin of pork or 2 racks spareribs	

Place the prunes in a saucepan with the water and bring to a boil. Remove from the heat and allow to soak for 5 minutes. Peel and core the apples and cut them into ¼-inch slices. Place them in the saucepan with the prunes.

If a loin of pork is used, ask your butcher to prepare it as a crown. If spareribs are used, have them cracked in the middle of each strip. Combine the salt and pepper and rub it into the meat. Place the pork in a roasting pan.

Drain the water from the prunes and apples. If the crown of pork is used, fill the center with this mixture and cover with a piece of aluminum foil. If spareribs have been selected, place half of the prune and apple mixture on each of the two strips of spareribs. Fold the spareribs over, at the places where the ribs have been cracked in the middle. Fasten with skewers. Roast in a 350° oven for 25 minutes per pound. Add small amounts of hot water to the pan if it becomes too dry.

About 15 minutes before the pork is done, prepare the following sauce:

3 tablespoons pan drippings	1 cup beef broth
2 tablespoons flour	¼ cup milk, scalded

Carefully remove 3 tablespoons of drippings from the roasting pan and put it in a small saucepan. Add the flour, stirring constantly until the mixture is smooth. Slowly add the broth, stirring steadily, and then the scalded milk, again stirring well. Bring to a boil and remove from the heat. Serve separately in a sauceboat. *Serves 4–6.*

SPAGHETTI WITH SWEETBREADS

SPAGHETTI MED BRISLER

3 pairs calves' sweetbreads	¼ pound (1 stick) butter
2 cups boiling water	2 tablespoons flour
2 tablespoons vinegar	½ cup heavy cream
2 teaspoons salt	2 cups sliced mushrooms
1 bay leaf	2 8-ounce packages thin
1 onion	spaghetti

Wash the sweetbreads carefully and soak in cold water for ½ hour. Drain thoroughly. Combine the sweetbreads, boiling water, vinegar, salt, bay leaf, and onion in a saucepan. Cook over medium heat for 15 minutes. Drain; reserve 1 cup of the stock. Remove the membrane from the sweetbreads and cut into small cubes.

Melt half the butter in a saucepan. Add the flour, stirring until smooth. Gradually add the reserved stock and the cream, stirring constantly until the boiling point is reached. Cook over low heat for 5 minutes, stirring occasionally. Melt the remaining butter in a frying pan. Add the mushrooms and sauté for 10 minutes, stirring frequently. Combine the sweetbreads, sauce, and mushrooms and mix well. Correct seasoning. Place over low heat.

Cook the spaghetti in boiling, salted water for 10 to 12 minutes. Drain thoroughly and rinse with cold water. Put the spaghetti on a platter, pour the sauce over it, and serve immediately. *Serves 4–6.*

POTATOES, DANISH STYLE

KARTOFLER

3 tablespoons butter
1 onion, sliced
6 cold boiled potatoes, peeled
2 teaspoons sugar

2 teaspoons vinegar
1 teaspoon salt
¼ teaspoon freshly ground
   black pepper

Melt the butter in a large frying pan. Add the sliced onion and sauté for 5 minutes, stirring occasionally. Slice the potatoes and add to the onion. Sauté for 5 minutes, turning the potatoes over to brown on both sides. Add the sugar, vinegar, salt, and pepper and mix. Cook 5 minutes longer. *Serves 6–8.*

SWEET AND SOUR RED CABBAGE

AADKAAL

3 pounds red cabbage
¼ cup butter
4 tablespoons vinegar
½ cup water

2 tablespoons currant jelly
1 tablespoon sugar
1 teaspoon salt

Wash the cabbage thoroughly, discarding the core and all imperfect leaves. Cut or shred into thin strips. Drain well. Melt the butter in a deep saucepan. Add the cabbage and toss it around with a large spoon so that it becomes evenly coated with butter. Add the vinegar and water. Cover and cook over low heat for 1½ hours. Add the jelly, sugar, and salt and mix well. Cook for 20 minutes. Correct seasoning. This dish is best prepared a day in advance and then reheated. *Serves 6–8.*

DANISH PANCAKES

PANDEKAGER

¼ pound (1 stick) sweet butter
1½ cups flour
1 teaspoon sugar

½ teaspoon ground cardamom
1½ cups milk
4 eggs, beaten

Melt half the butter and let it cool. Mix the flour, sugar, and cardamom in a bowl; add the milk gradually, mixing until smooth. Beat in the eggs, then the cooled butter. Let the batter stand for 1 hour.

Melt a little butter in a 5-inch skillet. Pour in about a tablespoon of batter, turning the pan quickly to cover the bottom thinly. When the edges of the pancake begin to brown, lift the pancake, put a little more butter in the pan, and turn pancake to brown other side. Serve rolled up or folded into quarters with jam or lemon juice and sugar. *Serves 6–8.*

DANISH PASTRY

DANSK WIENERBRØD

1 cake or package yeast
1¼ cups milk, scalded and cooled
¼ cup sugar
2½ cups sifted flour
¼ cup melted butter

2 eggs, beaten
½ teaspoon salt
½ pound (2 sticks) sweet butter
½ cup melted butter

Place the yeast in a bowl. Add the cooled milk and dissolve the yeast. Beat in the sugar and ½ cup of the flour. Cover and allow to rise for 30 minutes in a warm place.

In a separate bowl mix together the melted butter, beaten eggs, and salt. Add the remaining flour alternately with the yeast mixture. Knead the dough on a floured surface for about 5 to 10 minutes, or until smooth in texture and elastic. If the dough is too spongy, add a very little more sifted flour. Place in a bowl, cover with a cloth, and put in a warm place to rise for about 1 hour, or until double in bulk. When risen, roll out about ¼ inch thick on a floured surface. Break ¼ pound of the butter into small pieces and place them in the center of the dough. Fold the sides of the dough over, wrap in wax paper, and place in the refrigerator for 30 minutes.

Remove from refrigerator. On a floured surface, roll the dough ½ inch thick. Break the remaining ¼ pound of sweet butter into small pieces and again place in the center of the dough. Fold the sides of the dough over again, wrap in wax paper, and return to the refrigerator for 30 minutes. Remove once again, roll out again ½ inch thick, fold over again. Wrap in wax paper and return to the refrigerator for 30 minutes. Remove from refrigerator, place in a bowl, cover, and allow to rise for 45 minutes in a warm place. Preheat oven to 425°. Roll ¼ inch thick on a floured surface. Cut into 4-inch squares and fill with either of the following mixtures:

FILLING 1

1 cup chopped nuts
¼ cup sugar
2 teaspoons cinnamon

FILLING 2

1 cup cottage cheese
1 egg yolk, beaten
¼ cup sugar
½ teaspoon vanilla

For either filling, combine the ingredients and place a portion in the center of each square of dough. Fold the dough over in any desired shape. Brush with a little melted butter. Place on a buttered baking sheet. Bake in a 425° oven for 20 minutes. *Makes about 30–36 pastries.*

Note: If desired, use only part of the dough, keeping the balance in the refrigerator. It will keep about a week.

ENGLAND, WALES, AND NORTHERN IRELAND

What can possibly be said about England's food that hasn't been said before? It has been criticized by almost every foreign visitor as lacking in imagination, deficient in preparation, and always as unexciting. The statement is true. But, like many other generalizations, it is true only as far as it goes. England *does* have good food, though many scoffers would have you believe otherwise. It should also be remembered that England is an island and is not self-sufficient. It must of necessity import the largest proportion of its food–staples, not merely luxuries. If fruits and green salads are rarities it is because most of these items must be imported.

France is separated from England only by the few miles that make up the English Channel, but a million light-years separate the cuisines of France and England. It has been previously said but it is worth repeating that France is a land of one religion and a hundred sauces, whereas England has one sauce and a hundred religions. Both statements are incorrect, because France has a thousand sauces, and England doesn't have a hundred religions. The ultimate insult in France is to tell a cook that he is fit to cook only for the English. *Tiens! Alors!*

For their own protection, visitors to England should understand British food habits. Breakfast is the best meal of all, with delicious and substantial local specialties such as kippers, hot cereals, broiled ham or bacon, and the like. Lunch, at about 1 P.M., and dinner, served late in the evening, are the meals that bring forth those hollow groans from the tourists. They find the fish and meat dull and the desserts impossibly sweet, and as for the vegetables, there are only two words for them–brussels sprouts. The time to stoke up is at teatime, in the late afternoon. The British have many delicious cakes, delicate sandwiches, and tea specialties such as bath buns and crumpets. Crumpets are really good, in spite of all the P. G. Wodehouse-style jokes about them. Scones are often served, but these are probably Scotch in origin. The visitor to England can eat well, if only he will learn to emphasize breakfast and tea rather than lunch and dinner. If you get hungry between times there's always fish and chips, England's answer to the American hot dog. This favorite dish of all classes of people is nothing more or less than slices of fish, deep-fat fried, with potato chips. Foreign food in restaurants is good.

No discussion of John Bull's food should omit England's contribution in the way of dairy products. Devonshire cream, thick and rich, is a treat. Cheeses are a British tradition and are among the finest in the world. Those with an international reputation include Cheshire, Stilton, and Cheddar cheeses.

Everyone knows about the famous pubs of England—the workingmen's clubs. Here it is that one finds the famous beers of the country in a variety that will startle the beer drinker from the States. There is stout (a powerful black brew), bitter ale (made with an extra quantity of hops), old ale, lager, and many more. The Briton likes to order a combination of two beers, and this is known as "'alf and 'alf." Bourbon and rye are little known here, but scotch whisky is much appreciated, though somewhat short in supply. A much more traditional drink is English-style gin, known as London gin in certain parts of the world. It is a high-quality drink, made from barley and juniper berries. Gin is served straight, with Italian vermouth (shortened to "gin and it"), with quinine water (known as "gin and tonic"), or in various other ways.

Coffee is not the national drink of the country as any tourist will immediately tell you. The British must distrust coffee—why else would they treat it so badly? Espresso coffee machines and vacuum-packed coffee have helped the situation. Tea is the drink here, and tourists are cautioned not to vary from the norm. Properly made tea tastes much better than anyone ever thought it could, and the varieties of tea used by the English far exceed our own limited taste and knowledge on the subject. But there's good news for coffee drinkers. All over London, you'll find espresso bars, and these serve very good coffee.

GIN AND IT

   3 jiggers Italian vermouth   6 jiggers gin

Gently pour the vermouth and gin into a glass pitcher or other receptacle. Stir but do not shake. Pour into cocktail glasses and serve at room temperature in the English manner, or add ice, if you prefer. If desired, before pouring the liquor into a glass, a piece of lemon peel may be rubbed around the edges. *Serves 6.*

STAR GAZY PIE

4 tablespoons butter	2 tablespoons tarragon vinegar
4 mackerel fillets	4 egg yolks
1¼ cups bread crumbs	4 slices bacon, half cooked
3 tablespoons chopped parsley	1 cup sifted flour
½ teaspoon thyme	½ teaspoon salt
½ teaspoon marjoram	⅓ cup shortening
1 teaspoon salt	3 tablespoons water
½ teaspoon pepper	

Melt the butter in a skillet. Brown the mackerel on both sides. Butter a casserole and sprinkle it with half of the bread crumbs, coating the bottom heavily. Combine the parsley, thyme, marjoram, salt, and pepper. Arrange a layer of mackerel, top with the remaining bread crumbs, and sprinkle with the parsley mixture. Beat the vinegar and egg yolks together and add to the casserole. Arrange the bacon slices on top.

Sift the flour and salt together into a bowl. Cut in the shortening with a pastry blender or two knives until the consistency of coarse sand. Add the water, tossing lightly with a fork until a ball of dough is formed. Roll out on a lightly floured surface and place on top of the casserole, sealing the edges. Prick with a fork in a few places. Bake in a 325° oven for 1¾ hours. Serve hot or cold, directly from the casserole. *Serves 6–8.*

LANCASHIRE HOT POT

4 tablespoons butter	4 onions
6 loin or shoulder lamb chops	1 cup sliced mushrooms
3 teaspoons salt	½ cup string beans, cut in half
1 teaspoon freshly ground	1 cup beef broth
black pepper	½ cup light cream
6 (2 pounds) potatoes, peeled	
and sliced	

Melt 2 tablespoons of the butter in a skillet. Brown the chops well on both sides. Arrange the chops on the bottom of a casserole. Sprinkle with 1 teaspoon of the salt and ½ teaspoon of the pepper. Place half the potatoes on the chops in a layer. Add successive layers of onions, mushrooms, and string beans. Combine the stock, cream, and remaining salt and pepper. Pour over the vegetables. Arrange the remaining potatoes in an even, overlapping design. Dot with the remaining butter. Cover the casserole and bake in a 350° oven for 2½ hours. Remove the cover and bake for 20 minutes, or until potatoes brown on top. Serve hot, directly from the casserole. *Serves 6.*

BUBBLE AND SQUEAK

3 teaspoons salt	4 tablespoons butter
1 teaspoon pepper	1 boiled cabbage, chopped fine
12 slices cold roast beef or 1 cold	½ teaspoon nutmeg
chicken, sliced	2 tablespoons vinegar

Mix together half the salt and pepper. Sprinkle it over the beef or chicken. Melt 2 tablespoons of the butter in a skillet. Brown the slices of beef or chicken on both sides. Remove and set aside in a warm place. Melt the remaining butter in the skillet and add the cabbage, nutmeg, remaining salt, and remaining pepper. Cook over medium heat, stirring constantly, until the cabbage is lightly browned. Sprinkle the vinegar over it and cook 1 minute longer. Serve with the meat or chicken. *Serves 4–6.*

BRAISED VEAL

5 pounds rump of veal	2 onions, chopped
4 slices bacon	½ cup chopped celery
½ teaspoon thyme	2 cups broth
¾ teaspoon pepper	2 cups dry white wine
2 tablespoons oil	2 teaspoons salt
6 tablespoons butter	1 bay leaf
½ cup grated carrots	2 teaspoons arrowroot
2 tablespoons chopped parsley	

Have the veal tied into a nice firm shape. Pour boiling water over the bacon and simmer 10 minutes. Drain and dry. Cut each slice of bacon into 4 long strips. Season the strips with the thyme and ½ teaspoon pepper. Have the butcher lard the meat, or with a larding needle pull the strips through the meat.

Heat the oil and 4 tablespoons of butter in a Dutch oven. Add the carrots, parsley, onions, and celery. Cover and simmer 10 minutes. Add the veal and brown lightly on all sides. Add the broth, wine, salt, bay leaf, and remaining pepper. Bring to a boil and simmer 3 hours, or until the veal is tender.

Transfer the veal to a hot serving platter and keep warm. Strain the gravy, pressing through the vegetables.

Mix the arrowroot to a paste with a little water, and stir into gravy over low heat, then swirl in the remaining butter. Carve the veal and serve the gravy in a sauceboat. *Serves 8–10.*

As served at the Portman Square Hotel.

YORKSHIRE SALAD

3 tablespoons molasses	2 heads lettuce, shredded
6 tablespoons vinegar	3 scallions (green onions),
½ teaspoon freshly ground	sliced fine
black pepper	

Combine the molasses, vinegar, and pepper in a bowl and mix well. Combine the lettuce and scallions and mix well together. Pour the dressing over it. Toss until the lettuce is well coated with the dressing. Serve cool but not ice cold. *Serves 4–6.*

YORKSHIRE PUDDING

2 cups sifted flour	1 cup milk
1 teaspoon salt	4 eggs, beaten
1 cup light cream	1 cup beef drippings

Sift the flour and salt into a bowl. Gradually add the cream and milk, beating well. Add the eggs, beating vigorously. Cover and place in the refrigerator for 1 hour. Heat the drippings in an 8-inch square pan. Beat the batter for 1 minute and pour into the pan. Bake in a 450° oven for 15 minutes. Reduce oven temperature to 350° and bake for 15 minutes longer or until the pudding is crisp and brown. *Serves 6–8.*

Note: Yorkshire pudding is the traditional accompaniment to roast beef. No recipe is given for roast beef since it is cooked in the usual manner. The drippings called for in this recipe may be obtained from the pan in which the meat is roasted.

CRUMPETS

2 cakes or packages yeast	2 tablespoons melted butter
½ cup lukewarm water	½ teaspoon salt
2 eggs	1 teaspoon sugar
1½ cups lukewarm milk	3 cups sifted flour

Preheat oven to 400°.

Dissolve the yeast in the water. Beat the eggs, add the milk, butter, salt, and sugar. Add the yeast mixture and the flour, beating until smooth and well blended. Cover and set aside in a warm place for 15 minutes. Fill buttered muffin tins about half full. Bake in a 400° oven for 15 minutes. Serve hot with plenty of melted butter and raspberry jam. *Makes about 24.*

MARLBOROUGH PUDDING

1 cup flour	4 eggs
¼ teaspoon salt	2 tablespoons lemon juice
⅓ cup shortening	1 tablespoon grated lemon rind
4 tablespoons milk	¼ teaspoon nutmeg
4 tablespoons butter	2 cups applesauce
1 cup sugar	1 cup heavy cream

Preheat oven to 350°.

Sift the flour and salt into a bowl. Cut in the shortening with a pastry blender or two knives until the consistency of coarse sand. Add the milk, tossing lightly with a fork until a ball of dough is formed. Wrap in wax paper and place in the refrigerator, while preparing the filling.

Cream the butter, add the sugar, and beat well together. Add the eggs and beat until light and fluffy. Add the lemon juice, lemon rind, nutmeg, applesauce, and cream. Mix well.

Roll out the dough about ⅛ inch thick on a lightly floured surface. Place in a buttered 10-inch pie plate. Pour the filling into it. Bake in a 350° oven for 45 minutes, or until delicately browned and firm in texture. Serve hot or cold. If desired, whipped cream may be served with this pudding. *Serves 6–8.*

SEED CAKE

5 eggs	2 teaspoons caraway seeds
2 teaspoons water	1¼ cups sifted cake flour
1 teaspoon orange extract	2 tablespoons grated lemon rind
1 cup sugar	½ cup confectioners' sugar

Beat the eggs in a bowl. Place the bowl over hot water and continue beating until thick and lemon-colored. Add the water, orange extract, sugar, and caraway seeds. Beat with a rotary beater (still over hot water) for 10 minutes. Remove from hot water. Preheat oven to 350°. Sift the flour and combine with the lemon rind. Fold into the egg mixture thoroughly. Butter a 12-inch loaf pan or an angel-cake pan and dust lightly with flour. Pour the batter into it. Sprinkle the top with confectioners' sugar. Bake in a 350° oven for 50 minutes, or until a cake tester comes out clean. *Serves 8–10.*

CHICKEN LIVER AND ANCHOVY SAVOURY

4 tablespoons butter
6 chicken livers
½ teaspoon pepper
2 anchovy fillets
½ cup chicken broth

3 slices buttered toast, edges
   trimmed, and cut in half
2 tablespoons dry bread crumbs
2 tablespoons grated Parmesan
   cheese

Melt the butter in a skillet. Sauté the chicken livers in it. Chop the livers with the pepper and anchovy fillets until well blended. Return the mixture to the skillet and add the broth. Cook over medium heat for 5 minutes, stirring frequently. Place the mixture on the toast. Sprinkle with the bread crumbs and cheese. Place under the broiler for 1 minute to brown. Serve hot. *Serves 6.*

Note: Savouries occupy a unique position in England. They are served at the conclusion of a meal, after dessert.

FINLAND

If you mention Finland, most Americans are likely to respond with: "Oh yes, the only country that repaid its World War I loans." This simple fact is indicative of the Finnish personality, as is their stalwart (and successful) defense of the nation when invaded by Russia. The Finns are a most unusual people, inhabiting a beautiful country which has fresh pine-laden air during the summer months and very cold weather in wintertime. The coastlines, fronting on the Gulfs of Bothnia and Finland, are lovely, as are the lakes scattered about the countryside. Bear in mind, although it is similar to Scandinavian countries (Norway, Sweden, and Denmark) it is not a part of that classification.

As one might anticipate in this distinctive country, even the meal hours and food customs show a departure from the expected. Most people arise early, and, except for children, almost everyone has coffee and open sandwiches; hot food is rarely eaten. At lunch, they tend to have a number of appetizers (much like the Swedish *smörgåsbord*) called *voileipäpöytä* in Finnish. These typically include a number of salty foods, for their palate delights in such things as herring, smoked salmon, cured meats, and so forth. The Finns even have a word for this "hunger for salt," called *hiukasu*. The appetizer course is followed by a hot dish, plus coffee. Dinner comes very early, perhaps at 5 P.M. Later in the evening, typically by 9:30 or 10 P.M., open sandwiches are again served. Of course, tourist restaurants and hotels keep more normal hours, suitable for people who prefer their evening meal later than 5 P.M.

The Finns like hot soups, particularly in wintertime (as can be imagined!), notably beef broth, cabbage, and other hearty soups. They also have a fondness for fish soups, made of crayfish, salmon, or fresh-water lake fish. Incidentally, the only shellfish normally encountered here is the crayfish, at its best in late summer. As to lake fish, they're inevitably cooked with fresh dill, that most delightful of herbs; many types of fish (but particularly salmon) are smoked or salted, and they're quite delicious.

One interesting point to remember. Because the climate had generally been regarded as unsuitable, chickens were raised only in comparatively small numbers until quite recently. Modern methods have now substantially increased the number of chickens available, but many country people still refuse to eat them, much preferring the wilder taste of game birds, which they find far more interesting than the comparatively bland taste of the domestic bird. However, on one point, all Finns agree—the reindeer. It is served as an appetizer when smoked (and smoked reindeer tongue is marvelous), made into a soup, and eaten much like beef, in stews, potted, etc.

The cheeses are all right, but far from distinguished in quality. As a rule, they tend to imitate other western cheeses, with a fair degree of success. A great novelty is the arctic cloudberry, the *lakka*, which is a sort of yellow type of raspberry; it requires considerable sugar, and is delicious when served with cream or ice cream.

PICKLED HERRING

ETIKKASILKAT

4 salt herring	¼ cup sugar
3 onions, sliced	2 tablespoons pickling spices
½ cup hot water	2 bay leaves
1½ cups vinegar	

Wash the herring thoroughly. Place in a bowl with water to cover, and allow to soak for 24 hours. The water should be changed frequently, but at least twice. Drain, and cut off the heads of the herring. Cut each fish into 4 pieces. Place in a large jar or other container which can be covered. Add the sliced onions.

Combine the water, vinegar, sugar, pickling spices, and bay leaves. Stir until the sugar is dissolved. Pour over the herring. Cover and marinate in the refrigerator for at least 24 hours. Serve cold. This dish may be accompanied by parsley potatoes. *Serves 8–10.*

INDIVIDUAL CABBAGE PIES

KAALIPIIRAKKA

2 cups flour	¼ pound (1 stick) butter
1¼ teaspoons salt	5 cups finely shredded cabbage
¾ cup shortening	(about 1 large head)
2 egg yolks	2 teaspoons sugar
2 tablespoons cold water	

Sift the flour and ¼ teaspoon of the salt together in a bowl. Cut in the shortening with a pastry blender or two knives until it is the consistency of corn meal. Beat the egg yolks and water together and add to the flour, tossing lightly with a fork until a ball of dough is formed. Wrap in wax paper and place in the refrigerator while preparing the cabbage.

Melt the butter in a saucepan and add the shredded cabbage. Cook over low heat for 1 hour, stirring occasionally. Add remaining salt and the sugar and continue cooking over medium heat until the cabbage is delicately browned, about 5 minutes, stirring frequently. Set aside to cool for 30 minutes. Preheat oven to 375°.

Roll the dough ⅛ inch thick on a lightly floured surface. Cut out 4-inch circles. Place 1 tablespoon of the cabbage mixture in the center of each circle of dough. Fold over the edges and seal with a little water or egg white. Place on a lightly greased baking sheet. Bake in a 375° oven for 20 minutes, or until golden brown. *Makes about 36.*

OXTAIL SOUP

LIHAKEITTO

2 oxtails	2 pounds beef
2 tablespoons butter	1 tablespoon salt
½ cup sliced onions	6 peppercorns
1 carrot, sliced	1 clove
2 stalks celery, sliced	3 sprigs parsley
1 tablespoon flour	3 tablespoons dry sherry
4 quarts water	

Have the oxtails sawed into small pieces. Melt the butter in a kettle. Add the oxtail pieces, the onions, carrot, and celery. Cook 15 minutes. Sprinkle with the flour, stirring until browned. Add the water and meat. Bring to a boil. Add the salt, peppercorns, clove, and parsley. Cover and cook over low heat 3 hours. Strain and skim the fat.

Stir the sherry into the soup, and serve with tiny cubes of the meat. *Serves 10–12.*

As served in the Helsinki Inter-Continental Hotel.

CHICKEN LIVERS WITH APPLES

KANANMAKSAA OMENIEN KANSSA

¼ pound (1 stick) butter
6 apples, peeled, cored, and cut
   into sixths
4 tablespoons sugar
1½ pounds chicken livers
1½ teaspoons salt
1½ teaspoons freshly ground
   black pepper

¼ cup chicken broth
1½ tablespoons cornstarch
1 cup apple juice
2 tablespoons currant jelly
1 tablespoon lemon juice

Melt half the butter in a skillet. Add the apples and sprinkle them with the sugar. Cook over low heat for 10 minutes, or until the apples are soft. Turn them frequently but do not break the slices.

Melt the remaining butter in a skillet. Add the chicken livers and sauté for 5 minutes. Sprinkle with the salt and pepper. Add the stock and cook over medium heat for 5 minutes.

Mix the cornstarch and 2 tablespoons of the apple juice together in a cup to form a smooth paste. Combine this mixture with the remainder of the apple juice and add the currant jelly and lemon juice. Place the mixture in a saucepan and cook over low heat, stirring constantly, until the mixture thickens. Place the apples on a serving dish. Arrange the chicken livers over them. Serve the sauce separately. *Serves 4–6.*

FRESH SALTED SALMON IN DILL

VÄHÄNSUOLATTUA LOHTA

5 pounds fresh salmon, in one
   piece
2 tablespoons coarse salt

1 tablespoon sugar
1 tablespoon white peppercorns
12 sprigs fresh dill

Cut the salmon in half lengthwise and remove the bones. Rub insides of both halves with a mixture of the salt, sugar, and peppercorns. Spread the dill on the insides and press the two pieces together. Put the fish on a plate or board and weight it down. Chill for 12 hours or overnight. To serve, cut in thin diagonal slices. Sprinkle with chopped dill. *Serves 10–12.*

BAKED MUSHROOMS

SIENIMUREKE

6 tablespoons butter
2 onions, chopped fine
1 cup milk
1 cup light cream
2 cups bread crumbs
2 pounds mushrooms, chopped
fine

2 teaspoons salt
½ teaspoon freshly ground
black pepper
3 eggs, well beaten

Melt the butter in a skillet. Add the onions and sauté for 10 minutes, stirring frequently. Combine the milk, cream, and bread crumbs. Set aside for 10 minutes. Combine the sautéed onions, bread-crumb mixture, mushrooms, salt, pepper, and eggs. Mix well. Pour into a buttered 10-inch loaf pan. Bake in a 350° oven for 1 hour. Pour a little melted butter over the mushrooms and serve. *Serves 6–8.*

FINNISH PANCAKES

SUOMALAINEN PANNUKAKKU

1 cup sifted flour
1½ cups milk
2 egg yolks
3 tablespoons sugar

½ teaspoon salt
1 tablespoon melted butter
2 egg whites
4 tablespoons butter

Sift the flour into a bowl. Add the milk and mix until smooth. Set aside for 30 minutes. Beat the egg yolks, sugar, and salt together. Add to the flour mixture, together with the melted butter, and mix thoroughly. Beat the egg whites until stiff but not dry, and fold them into the previous mixture carefully. Melt half the butter in a plätter pan, frying pan, or griddle. When the butter is hot, drop the batter into it by the tablespoon to form small pancakes. Bake over medium heat until browned on both sides. Continue until all the batter is used up, using additional butter as required.

If desired, very thin slices of peeled apple may be placed in each tiny pancake while it is baking. Serve with preserved lingonberries. (These are available in cans or jars.) Cooked whole-cranberry sauce may be used as a substitute. *Makes about 36.*

STRAWBERRY PUDDING

MANSIKKATORTTU

5 egg yolks
¾ cup sugar
3 cups crushed strawberries,
  fresh or frozen
1 cup lady-finger crumbs or dry
  bread crumbs

1 teaspoon vanilla extract
5 egg whites
Whipped cream

Preheat oven to 375°.

Beat the egg yolks in a bowl. Add the sugar and beat until light and fluffy. Add the strawberries; if frozen berries are used, drain slightly. Add the crumbs and vanilla extract and mix together thoroughly. Beat the egg whites until stiff but not dry. Fold into the strawberry mixture carefully. Butter a glass or pottery baking dish and dust lightly with sugar. Pour the mixture into it. Bake in a 375° oven for 35 minutes, or until firm. Serve cold with whipped cream. If desired, a few sliced strawberries may be placed in the whipped cream. *Serves 6–8.*

FRANCE

France holds a unique place in the hearts of gourmets. To speak of French food is to speak of the world of food. If it is true that every country gets the food it deserves, certainly France deserves the finest food. In no other country do the pleasures of the table occupy such an important position, become the subject of so much conversation, and constitute so important a part of the national character. Tips about restaurants are considered as important as tips about the stock market. A Frenchman demands the best, will refuse anything else, and thus by elimination France has the greatest restaurants, chefs, and food, and French cooking has become the accepted and classic cuisine of the world.

The French are serious eaters. Breakfast is completely unimportant, consisting almost inevitably of coffee with a *brioche* or a *croissant*, little masterpieces of pastry. A businessman's quick lunch may take two or more hours, consist of four or five courses, a bottle or two of wine, followed by a brandy or several. While eating his dinner, a true son of France will often be planning next day's lunch or that of the day after.

French specialties? It would be necessary to list the thousands of dishes that make up the cuisine of the entire world. French cooking has made itself felt in almost every metropolitan community in the world, and French menus are known wherever civilization exists. There are two general styles of French cooking: the *bourgeoise* (middle-class) and the *haute cuisine* (high cuisine). The former is the home style of the average person, the way it is prepared by the peasants and by ordinary folk even in the large cities. The *haute cuisine* is the classic and traditional style of the great chefs, employing the famous sauces, elaborate rituals, and attention to detail that constitute the essence of French cooking. Of course French food may also be subdivided regionally, but in France there is a tremendous difference in this regard as compared with our own country. It is not unusual for volatile arguments to take place between Frenchmen concerning the excellence of one regional dish over another, whereas in our country the differences are really trivial. These discussions are conducted with a seriousness that most Americans would find difficult to comprehend.

France has so many unique food specialties that any listing would have to be inadequate and incomplete, but here are a few: truffles (a mysterious tuberlike growth used to flavor many dishes), *bar-le-duc* (the finest of all currant jellies), *bouillabaisse* (a Mediterranean fish soup), *pâté de foie gras* (goose livers ground to a fine paste), *fraises des bois* (tiny wild strawberries), *agneau pré sale* (lamb grown on salt marshes and possessing a unique flavor), and *escargots* (snails). Many of these specialties exist because Frenchmen are willing to forgo mass production of food in favor of excellence of quality. For example, veal is slaughtered at the age of six weeks in order to present the gourmet with snow-white meat and a more delicate flavor. Chickens, particularly those from Bresse, are hand-fed and not permitted to exercise, in order to preserve their succulence and tenderness.

Almost 250 varieties of cheese are produced in France, but comparatively few have reached this country. Everyone knows Port Salut, Pont Lévêque, Roquefort, Brie, Camembert; but not many people are familiar with the fine local cheeses produced in very small quantities and generally unavailable outside of France.

The drinking of wine occupies a unique position in France. Just as the gourmet's food is a matter of the utmost importance, so is the selection of the proper wine with his meal. But the average Frenchman does not worry too much about vintage wines or about what wine with what food, so long as wine is available. Most Frenchmen will not eat a meal unless it is accompanied by wine, even *vin ordinaire*–ordinary wine, either red or white. While many tourists concern themselves unduly with vintage years, the average Frenchman recognizes only two primary rules: white wine with fish or chicken, red wine with meats.

Champagne stands alone in the world of wines. It is the undisputed king in the eyes of the world. The bubbles that delight so many people are the result of many years of constant effort and attention, since the fermentation is produced individually in each bottle. To visit the great caves of Epernay or Rheims where the wines are made is one of the truly great tourist experiences of a visit to France.

But France is also the land of many other wines, including the red types, the whites, and the pinks (rosés). In addition there are many liqueurs, such as Chartreuse, Grand Marnier, and the different types of brandy. Almost without exception, the wine and liquor producers welcome visitors and will be pleased to show them through their establishments, often with complimentary tastings of their various products.

Paris is the center of the world of French restaurants. Many of these are frankly designed to attract tourists, specializing more in glamor, high prices, and décor than fine food. Parisians shake their heads mournfully and say that such places have "gone American." Others have resisted temptation, often at a substantial loss, and continue to serve the great dishes that have made their country the byword for fine food.

Although many leading restaurants continue to serve marvelous food in Paris and the surrounding provinces, it is a fact that fine restaurants have faded away, on occasion, to a shadow of their former greatness. It is equally true that new restaurants, presided over and owned by young chefs, have come to the fore. Rather than list and recommend particular restaurants, it is suggested that the thoughtful gourmet obtain a copy of the Michelin Guide, which lists restaurants in every community of France, grading them according to their degree of excellence. Although Michelin is far from infallible, it is an excellent and informative guide to the restaurants of this nation, which has many of the best dining places in the world.

By all means, rent a drive-yourself car and wander about the countryside, eating in provincial restaurants that feature (incidentally at far lower prices than Paris) some extraordinary and unusual food. Also, order local wines wherever available, for these represent excellent value and are typically young and fresh, rather than vintage and costly.

VERMOUTH CASSIS

3 jiggers Crème de Cassis, black currant, or blackberry syrup	6 large jiggers French vermouth
	12 ice cubes

Mix the vermouth and Crème de Cassis and pour into tall highball glasses. Place 2 ice cubes in each glass. Fill each glass with carbonated water and stir lightly. *Serves 6.*

ANCHOVY HORS D'OEUVRE

ANCHOIADE

2 tins anchovy fillets
2 cloves garlic, minced
1 teaspoon lemon juice

1 tablespoon olive oil
3 slices bread

Place the anchovies and the oil in which they were prepared in a bowl with the minced garlic. Mash with a fork until they are soft. Add the lemon juice and oil and mix well. Trim the crusts from the bread and cut each piece in half lengthwise.

To serve, fry the bread slices in some butter or oil. Spread with the anchovy mixture, then place on a buttered baking sheet and put under the broiler until heated. *Serves 6.*

ONIONS WITH RAISINS

OIGNONS À LA MONÉGASQUE

⅓ cup tarragon vinegar
1 cup water
2 tablespoons dry white wine
4 tablespoons olive oil
2 tablespoons tomato paste
⅓ cup seedless raisins
1 tablespoon sugar

1 teaspoon salt
¼ teaspoon freshly ground
    black pepper
2 tablespoons chopped parsley
1 bay leaf
1 pound small white onions,
    peeled

Combine the vinegar, water, wine, oil, tomato paste, raisins, sugar, salt, pepper, parsley, and bay leaf in a saucepan. Mix well. Add the onions. Bring to a boil. Cover and cook over low heat for 25 minutes, or until the onions are done. Cool, then chill in the refrigerator. Serve as an hors d'oeuvre. *Serves 4–6.*

CHICKEN LIVER SPREAD

PÂTÉ DE FOIE DE VOLAILLE

1 pound chicken livers
1 onion
¾ cup rendered chicken fat or
 melted butter
4 tablespoons grated onion
2 teaspoons salt

½ teaspoon freshly ground
 black pepper
¼ teaspoon mace
1½ teaspoons dry mustard
⅛ teaspoon anchovy paste
1 tablespoon brandy

Wash the livers carefully, removing any discolored areas. Place them in a saucepan with the onion and water to cover. Bring to a boil, cover, and cook over low heat for 10 minutes. Drain completely and discard the onion. Purée in an electric blender, or grind the livers in a food chopper three times, or until very smooth. Add the chicken fat, grated onion, salt, pepper, mace, mustard, anchovy paste, and brandy. Mix together until completely smooth. Place the pâté in a mold or other attractive dish, pressing it down until fairly firm. Chill for at least 3 hours. If in a mold, turn out onto a plate. Slice the pâté about ¼ to ½ inch thick and serve with crusty French bread. Freshly ground pepper may be sprinkled on top. This is delicious as a cocktail spread. *Serves 6–8.*

ONION SOUP

SOUPE À L'OIGNON

⅓ cup butter
3 cups diced onions
2 tablespoons flour
7 cups beef broth
½ teaspoon freshly ground
 black pepper

6 slices French bread, toasted
6 thin slices Gruyère or Swiss
 cheese
4 tablespoons grated Gruyère or
 Swiss cheese

Melt the butter in a heavy saucepan. Add the onions and sauté over very low heat until brown. Stir frequently. Add the flour and mix until smooth. Add the broth gradually, stirring constantly. Add the pepper. Cover and cook over low heat for 30 minutes. Correct seasoning. Put a slice of toast in each soup plate or individual tureen. Place a slice of cheese on the bread and pour the soup over it. Place under the broiler for 1 minute to melt the cheese, if desired. Sprinkle with grated cheese and serve. *Serves 6.*

LEEK AND CHEESE SOUP

SOUPE AU POIREAU ET AU FROMAGE

8 leeks	1 cup uncooked macaroni
1 onion, chopped	1 tablespoon salt
6 tablespoons butter	2 cloves garlic
6 cups chicken broth	1 cup grated Swiss cheese
1 quart boiling water	1 cup dry white wine

Wash the leeks thoroughly to remove any possible sand. Slice thin, using all of the white part and about half of the green portion. Combine with the chopped onion. Melt the butter in a deep saucepan and add the leek and onion mixture. Cook over low heat, stirring occasionally, for 10 minutes. Do not allow the leeks or onions to brown. Add the stock, cover, and cook over low heat for 45 minutes.

In a separate saucepan boil the water. Break the macaroni into small pieces and add to the water, together with the salt and garlic. Boil until the macaroni is tender, about 15 minutes. Drain. Add to the leek mixture and continue cooking over very low heat while preparing the cheese mixture.

Place the cheese in the top of a double boiler over hot water and add the wine. Stir frequently until the cheese melts. Pour the soup into individual plates and add 2 tablespoons of the cheese mixture to each portion. *Serves 6–8.*

FISH SOUP-STEW

BOUILLABAISSE

Stock:

3 pounds fish trimmings (head, skin, and bones)	4 sprigs parsley
3 tablespoons olive oil	½ teaspoon thyme
1 cup chopped onions	½ teaspoon rosemary
2 stalks celery and leaves, cut up	1 bay leaf
2 carrots, sliced	4 cups water
	2 cups dry white wine

Wash the fish trimmings. Heat the oil in a large saucepan; add the onions, celery, carrots, parsley, thyme, rosemary, and bay leaf. Cook over very low heat for 10 minutes, stirring frequently. Add the water, wine, and fish trimmings. Bring to a boil and cook over medium heat 1 hour. Strain, pressing down to extract all the liquid. Reserve the stock and keep hot.

Fish:

3 pounds assorted sliced fish	½ cup olive oil (about)
1 pound eel, sliced	3 leeks or 6 scallions (green
2 teaspoons salt	onions), sliced thin
½ teaspoon freshly ground	1½ cups peeled, seeded tomatoes
black pepper	2 pieces orange rind
½ teaspoon thyme	2 1½-pound lobsters, cut up
½ teaspoon rosemary	in the shells
½ teaspoon powdered saffron	Sliced, dried French bread
1 teaspoon crushed fennel seeds	

Wash and dry the fish and eel. Mix together the salt, spices, herbs, and
¼ cup of the oil. Pour the mixture over the fish, and turn the pieces to
coat them. Let stand 30 minutes.

In a large saucepan, heat the remaining oil. Add the leeks and cook
over low heat 5 minutes. Pour in the reserved boiling stock; add the
firmer pieces of fish, the tomatoes, orange rind, and lobsters. Bring to a
boil, and cook over high heat 5 minutes. Add the remaining fish and cook
15 minutes longer. Taste for seasoning.

While the fish is cooking, prepare the sauce.

Sauce:

2 cloves garlic, minced	¼ cup olive oil
½ teaspoon Tabasco	½ cup fish soup
½ cup fresh bread crumbs,	
soaked and drained	

Mix together the garlic, Tabasco, and bread crumbs; very gradually beat
in the olive oil, then the soup.

When ready to serve, put a slice or two of dried bread in each deep
soup bowl. Arrange the fish on a platter, and pour the soup into the soup
bowls. Serve the fish and soup simultaneously with a bowl of the sauce,
from which each person can help himself. *Serves 6–8.*

*Note: This version of bouillabaisse won't be exactly as it is on the Medi-
terranean, because the fish here aren't the same. Rascasse in particular is
not available here. But the stew will be delicious nevertheless.*

FISH MOUSSE BALLS

QUENELLES DE BROCHET

1 cup water
¼ pound (1 stick) butter
2¼ teaspoons salt
1 cup sifted flour
3 eggs
1½ pounds boneless pike or
other white meat fish

½ teaspoon white pepper
⅛ teaspoon nutmeg
¼ cup heavy cream
3 cups fish stock, or boiling
salted water

Bring the water, butter, and 1 teaspoon of the salt to a boil, and stir until the butter melts. Remove saucepan from the heat and with a wooden spoon beat in the flour all at once. Return to low heat and cook, beating steadily until mixture forms a ball and leaves the sides of the pan. Remove from the heat and beat in one egg at a time, continuing to beat until smooth and glossy. Transfer to a mixing bowl.

Grind the fish three times in a meat chopper or purée in an electric blender. Add to the flour mixture with the pepper, nutmeg, and remaining salt. Beat with an electric mixer or wooden spoon until very smooth and light. Taste for seasoning. Chill 2 hours. Beat in the cream very gradually.

Bring the fish stock to a boil in a large skillet, then reduce heat to low. Use two wet round soup spoons to shape the quenelles. Pick up a spoonful of the mixture and smooth the top with the other spoon. Carefully drop it into the skillet. Dip the spoons in cold water and work quickly to shape remaining quenelles. Don't crowd skillet, as the quenelles double in size when cooking. Cook over low heat 20 minutes. Remove with a slotted spoon and drain well on a napkin or kitchen towel.

Sauce:

½ cup cooked shrimp or lobster
2 tablespoons butter
2 tablespoons flour

1 cup hot fish stock or bottled
clam juice
¼ cup heavy cream

Chop half the shrimp to a paste, or purée in an electric blender. Coarsely chop the remaining shrimp. Melt the butter in a saucepan, blend in the flour, then remove from the heat. Beat in the fish stock with a wire whisk until smooth. Return to the heat and cook, stirring steadily, until the boiling point, then cook over low heat 5 minutes longer. Stir in the cream and all the shrimp. Taste for seasoning. Cook 5 minutes, but do not let boil.

Arrange the quenelles on a heated serving dish or individual plates, and pour the sauce over them. *Serves 6–8.*

FISH WITH BREAD SAUCE

POISSON À LA RESERVE DE BEAULIEU

6 fillets of trout, red snapper, or sole	¼ cup white wine
Fish heads and skin	10 slices white bread, trimmed
2 cups water	½ pound (2 sticks) butter
3 teaspoons salt	2 egg yolks
	2 teaspoons chopped chives

Combine the fish heads and skin with the water and 1 teaspoon of the salt in a saucepan. Boil for 30 minutes, or until only ½ cup of stock remains. Place the fish flat on a buttered baking dish. Sprinkle with the remaining salt. Pour the stock and wine over it. Soak the bread in boiling water, then squeeze dry. Cream the butter and add the egg yolks, chives, and bread, blending well. Spread this mixture about ½ inch thick over the fish. Bake in a 375° oven for 20 minutes, or until browned on top. Serve at once. Do not accompany this dish with lemon slices. *Serves 6.*

Note: When prepared at the Restaurant La Reserve de Beaulieu, it is made with the renowned Mediterranean fish, the loup, or wolf fish.

FILLET OF SOLE WITH LOBSTER SAUCE

FILET DE SOLE À L'AMÉRICAINE

4 tablespoons olive oil	½ cup water
1 lobster, cut in eighths, in the shell	4 tomatoes, peeled, seeded, and chopped
1 tablespoon butter	2 teaspoons salt
1 clove garlic, minced	½ teaspoon tarragon
3 shallots, chopped	Dash of cayenne pepper
¼ cup brandy	6 fillets of sole
1½ cups dry white wine	2 tablespoons chopped parsley

Heat the olive oil in a saucepan. Add the lobster and cook over high heat until it turns red. Add the butter, garlic, and shallots. Cook over low heat for 2 minutes. Add brandy and set it aflame. Let burn a few seconds. Add 1 cup of the wine, the water, tomatoes, 1 teaspoon of the salt, tarragon, and cayenne pepper. Cover and cook over low heat for 20 minutes. Strain the sauce. Remove the lobster meat from the shells and cut into ¼-inch cubes. Return to the sauce. Cook over very low heat while preparing the fillets.

Arrange the fillets in a buttered skillet. Sprinkle with the remaining salt and add the remaining wine. Cover with buttered wax paper and cook over low heat (without boiling) for 15 minutes. Place the fillets on a plat-

ter. Combine the sauces and pour over the fish. Sprinkle with parsley.
Serves 6.

BEEF, BURGUNDY STYLE

BOEUF BOURGUIGNONNE

4 pounds cross rib or chuck of
   beef
½ cup flour
2½ teaspoons salt
½ teaspoon freshly ground
   black pepper
3 tablespoons olive oil
6 tablespoons butter
¼ cup cognac
3 slices bacon, diced
2 cups diced onions

¾ cup grated carrots
2 cloves garlic, minced
3 cups dry red wine
2 tablespoons minced parsley
1 bay leaf
½ teaspoon thyme
16 small white onions
1 teaspoon sugar
16 mushroom caps
1 tablespoon arrowroot or
   cornstarch

Cut the meat into 2-inch cubes; roll in a mixture of the flour, salt, and pepper. Heat the oil and 3 tablespoons of butter in a skillet; brown the meat very well on all sides. Transfer to a casserole or Dutch oven; pour warm cognac over it and set aflame.

To the skillet, add the bacon, diced onions, carrots, and garlic. Cook over medium heat until vegetables brown. Add to the meat with the wine, parsley, bay leaf, and thyme. Cover and cook over low heat 2½ hours. While the meat is cooking prepare the vegetables.

Melt the remaining butter in a skillet; add the onions and sugar. Brown lightly. Remove the onions and sauté the mushrooms 5 minutes. Add to the meat after 2 hours of cooking. Mix the arrowroot with a little cold water and stir into the gravy. Cook 5 minutes longer. Taste for seasoning.
Serves 6–8.

FILLET OF BEEF WITH SWEETBREADS

FILET À LA LUCULLUS

¼ cup olive oil
¾ cup chopped onions
1 clove garlic, minced
¾ cup grated carrots
2 slices bacon, half cooked and
   drained
2 tablespoons flour
2 cups beef broth
¼ cup dry white wine
2 tablespoons tomato sauce

1 bay leaf
3 tablespoons chopped parsley
2 pairs sweetbreads, parboiled
⅓ cup dry bread crumbs
2 teaspoons salt
½ teaspoon freshly ground
   black pepper
6 tablespoons butter
2 egg yolks
6 fillets of beef, cut 1 inch thick

Heat the olive oil in a saucepan. Add the onions, garlic, carrots, and bacon. Sauté 10 minutes. Sprinkle with the flour, stirring until smooth. Add the broth, stirring constantly to the boiling point. Add the wine, tomato sauce, and bay leaf. Cover and cook over very low heat 1 hour. Taste for seasoning. Discard the bay leaf and stir in parsley. Cut each sweetbread in half.

Mix the bread crumbs with 1 teaspoon salt and ¼ teaspoon pepper. Dip 6 pieces of sweetbread in it. Heat half the butter in a skillet. Brown the breaded sweetbreads in it. Keep warm. Dice the remaining sweetbreads.

Beat the egg yolks. Gradually add the wine sauce, stirring constantly to prevent curdling. Return to heat and cook, stirring constantly until thickened. Do not allow to boil. Add the diced sweetbreads.

Heat the remaining butter in a skillet. Add the fillets and cook over high heat 4 minutes on each side. Sprinkle with remaining salt and pepper. Arrange the fillets on a heated serving dish with a sweetbread over each. Pour the sauce over them. *Serves 6.*

VEAL AND MUSHROOMS

VEAU AUX CHAMPIGNONS

½ pound (2 sticks) butter	⅛ teaspoon white pepper
1½ cups chopped onions	2 egg yolks
2 tablespoons flour	3 tablespoons heavy cream
1 cup chicken broth	24 mushrooms, stems removed
½ cup milk	12 slices veal cut ¼ inch thick
1 teaspoon salt	1 3-oz. can pâté de foie gras

Melt half the butter in a saucepan. Add the onions and cook over very low heat for 15 minutes; do not allow them to brown. Sprinkle with the flour and mix well. Gradually add the broth and milk, stirring constantly until the boiling point is reached. Add the salt and pepper. Cover and cook over very low heat for 40 minutes, stirring occasionally. Force the mixture through a sieve. Beat the egg yolks and cream together in a bowl. Gradually add the sauce, beating constantly to prevent curdling. Reheat but do not allow to boil.

Melt 4 tablespoons of the butter in a skillet. Add the mushrooms and sauté for 5 minutes, stirring occasionally. Melt the remaining 4 tablespoons of butter in a skillet. Add the veal slices and sauté for 5 minutes on each side. Spread the pâté de foie gras on 6 of the veal slices and cover with the remaining 6 slices.

Place the veal in an ovenproof dish that may be brought to the table. Arrange the mushrooms around the meat and pour the sauce over it.

Place under the broiler until delicately browned, about 5 minutes. Serve directly from the dish. *Serves 6.*

As served at the Paris Inter-Continental Hotel.

CHICKEN IN THE POT

POULE AU POT

5- to 6-pound chicken	2 egg yolks
Gizzard and liver	2 egg whites
¼ pound ham	2 pounds short ribs of beef
2 tablespoons butter	3 quarts water
1 onion, chopped	3 carrots, peeled and sliced
1¼ cups bread crumbs	1 bay leaf
¼ cup light cream	1 onion
2 tablespoons chopped parsley	3 sprigs parsley
4 teaspoons salt	¼ teaspoon thyme
1 teaspoon white pepper	1 cup rice

Wash and dry the chicken. Chop the gizzard, liver, and ham or grind in a food chopper. Melt the butter in a skillet. Add the onion and sauté for 5 minutes. Place the bread crumbs in a bowl and moisten with the cream. Add the sautéed onion, the ham mixture, parsley, 1 teaspoon of salt, ½ teaspoon of pepper, and the egg yolks. Mix well. Beat the egg whites until stiff but not dry and fold into the bread-crumb mixture. Stuff the chicken and carefully fasten the opening with skewers or thread. Truss.

Place the beef and water in a large heavy saucepan. Bring to a boil. Add the chicken, carrots, bay leaf, onion, parsley, thyme, and the remaining salt and pepper. Cover and cook over low heat for 2 hours, or until meats are tender. About 30 minutes before the cooking time is up, transfer 3 cups of the soup to another saucepan. Wash the rice in warm water and add. Cover and cook over low heat 20 minutes. The soup is usually served as a separate course, together with the carrots. The meats are served with the rice. *Serves 4–6.*

CHICKEN WITH DUMPLINGS

POULET NIVERNAIS

2 3-pound fryers, disjointed
4 teaspoons salt
½ teaspoon freshly ground
  black pepper
¼ pound (1 stick) butter
2 cloves
12 small white onions
1 cup sliced mushrooms
1 clove garlic, minced
¼ teaspoon thyme

½ teaspoon marjoram
1 bay leaf
1¼ cups dry white wine
½ teaspoon saffron
1 cup sour cream, scalded
1½ cups sifted flour
2 teaspoons baking powder
2 eggs, beaten
⅓ cup milk
1 tablespoon minced parsley

Season the chicken with 3 teaspoons of the salt, and the pepper. Melt the butter in a casserole or heavy saucepan; brown the chicken in it. Stick the cloves in an onion and add with all the onions and the mushrooms; cook over low heat 5 minutes. Stir in the garlic, thyme, marjoram, bay leaf, and wine. Cover and bake in a 375° oven 45 minutes or until almost tender. Remove from the oven and place over direct low heat. Stir the saffron and sour cream into the pan; taste for seasoning. Prepare the dumpling batter while the chicken is cooking.

Sift the flour, baking powder, and remaining salt into a bowl. Beat in the eggs and milk. Drop by the teaspoon around the edge of the casserole. Cover and cook 15 minutes without raising the cover. Sprinkle with the parsley. *Serves 8–10.*

DUCK WITH CHERRIES

CANARD À LA MONTMORENCY

5–6-pound duck
2 teaspoons salt
¼ teaspoon freshly ground
  black pepper
1 cup chopped onions
½ cup grated carrots
½ teaspoon thyme
1 cup cherry brandy

2 tablespoons arrowroot or
  cornstarch
1 cup chicken broth
3 tablespoons wine vinegar
4 tablespoons sugar
1 16-ounce can pitted black
  cherries, drained

Wash and dry the duck. Rub with the salt and pepper. Place on a rack in a roasting pan with the onions, carrots and thyme. Roast in a 450° oven 30 minutes. Reduce heat to 350° and roast 1½ hours longer or until tender. Transfer the duck to a heated platter. Pour off all the fat from the gravy. Add the cherry brandy to the pan, scraping the bottom of browned particles, then pour into a saucepan. Mix the arrowroot with the broth, then stir into the saucepan. Cook over low heat, stirring constantly until thickened.

Cook the vinegar and sugar until caramel-colored; stir a little of the brandy sauce into it, then return to the saucepan. Add the cherries; cook 2 minutes. Taste for seasoning. Arrange the cherries around the carved duck and pour sauce over all. *Serves 4.*

BAKED MUSHROOMS

CHAMPIGNONS AU GRATIN

1 clove garlic, minced	2 tablespoons wine vinegar
1 onion, grated	1½ pounds mushrooms, washed
2 tablespoons chopped parsley	and sliced
⅛ teaspoon basil	¼ pound (1 stick) butter
1 teaspoon salt	½ cup dry bread crumbs
¼ teaspoon freshly ground	1 tablespoon grated Parmesan
black pepper	cheese
⅓ cup olive oil	

Combine the garlic, onion, parsley, basil, salt, pepper, oil, and vinegar in a bowl. Add the mushrooms and allow to marinate for 3 hours, basting frequently. Drain. Melt half the butter in a skillet. Add the mushrooms, and cook over high heat for 1 minute. Reduce the heat to low and cook for 10 minutes, stirring frequently. Butter a baking dish very well and place the mushrooms in it. Sprinkle the bread crumbs and Parmesan cheese on top and dot with the remaining butter. Place under the broiler until browned. *Serves 4–6.*

POTATOES IN CREAM

GRATIN DAUPHINOIS

6 large potatoes, peeled and	½ teaspoon nutmeg
sliced very thin	1 cup light cream
2 teaspoons salt	3 tablespoons butter
½ teaspoon freshly ground	
black pepper	

Arrange layers of potatoes sprinkled with salt, pepper, and nutmeg in a buttered baking dish. Pour the cream over the top and dot with butter. Bake in a 300° oven for 1 hour, or until the cream is absorbed and the top lightly browned. *Serves 6–8.*

GREEN SALAD

SALADE VERTE

1 cup olive oil	1 clove garlic, crushed
¼ cup wine or tarragon vinegar	1 head romaine lettuce
1 teaspoon salt	2 endive
¼ teaspoon freshly ground	1 head escarole
black pepper	

Combine the olive oil, vinegar, salt, pepper, and garlic in a bowl. Beat vigorously with a rotary beater, or place the ingredients in a bottle and shake vigorously. Chill. Wash, drain, and chill the lettuce, endive, and escarole. Tear, do not cut, the lettuce into 2-inch pieces. Cut the endive into ½-inch pieces. Tear the escarole into small pieces. Combine the greens in a salad bowl. Add the dressing just before serving and toss lightly. *Serves 4–6.*

Note: Any combination of green vegetables may be used with this simple classic dressing.

DESSERT PANCAKES

CRÊPES

1¼ cups sifted flour	1 cup milk
1 teaspoon salt	1 tablespoon vegetable oil
2 eggs, beaten	4 tablespoons butter

Combine the flour and salt. Gradually add the eggs and the milk, beating steadily until the mixture is smooth and completely free of lumps. Add the oil and beat 1 minute longer. Chill for 2 hours. Place a small piece of butter in a 6-inch frying pan and when it begins to bubble pour 2 tablespoons of the batter into it, and turn from side to side, to spread the batter evenly and thinly. Cook over very low heat for 1 minute, then turn over and cook for about 30 seconds. Remove carefully to a plate. Repeat the process until the batter is used up. Be very careful not to tear the pancakes when removing them from the pan. With a little practice it is possible to work with two frying pans at the same time.

The pancakes may be filled with jam or jelly, and then rolled up. Serve about 3 to a portion. They may also be served with the following *Suzette* sauce:

3 tablespoons sugar
4 tablespoons butter
¾ cup orange juice
2 tablespoons grated orange
rind

2 teaspoons grated lemon rind
¼ cup curaçao or Grand Marnier
¼ cup brandy

Cream the sugar and butter together. Place in a skillet and add the orange juice and orange and lemon rind. Cook over very low heat until the sugar is completely melted, stirring occasionally. Add the liqueur. Fold each pancake in half then fold again so as to bring the opposite corners together, forming a pie-shaped wedge. Carefully place each folded pancake in the sauce and heat thoroughly. Place the pancakes and sauce in a serving dish. Heat the brandy, set it afire, then pour it over the pancakes and serve flaming. *Serves 6–8.*

CHOCOLATE MOUSSE

MOUSSE AU CHOCOLAT

2 tablespoons brewed coffee
3 ounces sweet chocolate
4 egg yolks

¼ cup sugar
4 egg whites
1½ cups heavy cream

Combine the coffee and the chocolate in the top of a double boiler. Place over hot water until the chocolate is completely melted. Remove from the heat and set aside to cool for 15 minutes.

Beat the yolks until light in color. Add the sugar and continue beating until light and fluffy. Add the cooled chocolate and mix well. Beat the whites until stiff but not dry and fold them slowly and carefully into the chocolate mixture. Whip the cream and gently fold it into the mixture. Pour into unbuttered individual dishes or into a 2-quart mold. Chill at least 4 hours. *Serves 8–10.*

LIQUEUR SOUFFLÉ

SOUFFLÉ AUX LIQUEURS

4 tablespoons butter
4 tablespoons flour
1½ cups light cream, scalded
⅓ cup sugar

5 egg yolks
½ cup brandy or fruit cordial
10 ladyfingers
6 egg whites

Preheat oven to 350°.

Butter a 2-quart soufflé dish and dust lightly with sugar.

Melt the butter in a saucepan. Add the flour and mix to a smooth paste. Gradually add the cream, stirring constantly until the boiling point is reached. Add the sugar and cook over low heat for 5 minutes, stirring frequently. Let cool for 5 minutes. Beat the egg yolks in a bowl. Gradually add the cream mixture, beating constantly. Add half the brandy. Cool for 10 minutes. Soak the ladyfingers in the remaining brandy. Beat the egg whites until stiff but not dry and fold into the cream mixture. Pour half the soufflé mixture into the prepared dish. Drain the ladyfingers and arrange them over it; cover with remaining soufflé. Bake in a 350° oven for 30 minutes. Serve at once. *Serves 6–8.*

Note: A soufflé must be served and eaten immediately when it is ready. A delay of a few minutes is enough to allow the soufflé to fall. Have your guests waiting for the soufflé, because it will not wait for them.

CHERRY CUSTARD PUDDING

CLAFOUTIS AUX CERISES

3 cups fresh or canned pitted black cherries	3 eggs
¼ cup cognac or cherry liqueur	¼ teaspoon salt
⅔ cup sugar	1 teaspoon almond extract
1¼ cups light cream	Confectioners' sugar

In a bowl, combine the drained cherries, cognac, and 2 tablespoons of the sugar. Let stand 1 hour. Preheat oven to 350°. Lightly butter a 2-quart baking dish.

In a blender bowl or electric mixer bowl, beat together the cream, eggs, salt, almond extract, and remaining sugar, until very light and smooth. Pour a little (about ½ inch) of the batter into the baking dish. Drain the cherries and spread over the batter. Pour the remaining batter over the cherries and smooth the top. Bake on the middle level of the 350° oven for 55 minutes, or until a knife inserted comes out clean. Serve hot or warm, with a light sifting of confectioners' sugar on top. Don't worry if the clafoutis falls a bit as it cools. *Serves 6–8.*

GERMANY

Although France and Germany are neighbors, their cuisines are as far apart as the poles. The French style of cooking may have become the accepted standard of the world, but it has made practically no progress whatsoever in Germany, nor is it likely that it ever will. Though both nations are extremely fond of good food, the differences in tastes are decisive.

The problem is exemplified in the national drinking habits. Though Germany produces and consumes some fine wines, the country is known primarily as a land of beer drinkers. In France, although beer is popular, wine is by all odds the drink of the country. Where lies the distinction between the two countries? It is suggested that the difference is so basic that any discussion must take into account the nationalistic differences in character. As a generalization, the French are given to that which is light and bright, whether in art, decoration, music, or food. The Germans are sober and grave; their expression in any form is more than likely to be serious, ponderous, and cautious. German buildings are stolid, German art is weighty, and inevitably their approach to any problem is stolid and thoughtful.

The two countries definitely express their national characteristics in their food. German food is always substantial; seldom does one encounter a dish that could possibly be described as frivolous, as is the case with a considerable number of French dishes. A Frenchman may work for hours to create a bit of fluff or pastry to tempt the appetite; a German chef would seldom waste his time unless the results were material. Even German desserts are substantial enough to constitute a light meal for an American. This is a land of outdoor people, of mountain climbers, skiers, and hikers; it is also a country where people usually come to the table seeking hearty fare. However, German cookery is not necessarily limited to plain dishes; it has one of the very few important cuisines of the world, with numerous noteworthy and outstanding dishes.

Germany has made a distinct impression on the food of the United States, although the full effect is little realized here. Our national favorite, the "hot dog," is definitely traceable to the German sausage. Sauerkraut, to be sure, is distinctly German. When frankfurters (from Frànkfurt, Germany) are combined with sauerkraut, it is easy to see that the favorite snack of millions of Americans is a direct descendant of German ancestors. Our second popular favorite is the hamburger, a chopped meat specialty reputed to have originated in Hamburg, Germany. And there can be no argument about the nationality of beer or the nationality of those who brought it to its present stage of popularity in the United States.

Not popular in our country but a national favorite in Germany is the famous *Aalsuppe* (eel soup), which is much better than it sounds. Cold and hot beer soups are immensely popular there, and are easily duplicated although they represent something of an acquired taste. Fruit soups are good but often too sweet for American tastes, except as light lunches. Another great German favorite is herring, prepared in bewildering variety and particularly esteemed when served with beer.

Sauerbraten, a sour pickled beef dish, is well known here. Goose stuffed with apples and onions is a national dish; chicken livers are also prepared with the same accompaniments. Sauerkraut is so important to some Germans that it is eaten two or even three times a day. It is served in diversified styles, hot or cold, with wine, with caraway seeds, with apples, etc. Dumplings, a part of almost every meal, are prepared in countless fashions; potatoes are of nearly equal importance.

A special section could be devoted to a discussion of the world-famous German *Delikatessen* (delicate eating). The word itself has moved into the English language almost intact as delicatessen. It includes the entire range of smoked and pickled meats, sausages, liverwurst, potato salad, pickles, and the like. Cheeses that have emigrated to our own country include Münster, Limburger, and Tilsiter; some of these have become naturalized, or have taken out first citizenship papers.

There is one style of German cooking called "sweet and sour" which has made little headway in this country, except in the area surrounding Milwaukee and in the Pennsylvania Dutch region near Lancaster. Since these areas were predominantly settled by Germans, this is not surprising. This style consists in combining in one sauce both sweet ingredients (fruit, sugar) and sour stuffs (vinegar, lemon juice). Meats, vegetables, and other dishes are prepared in the sweet and sour style.

Space limitations prevent any serious discussion of other great specialties, such as Westphalian ham, potato pancakes, mountain trout, and noodle dishes. Since the war, good food has returned to Germany, and most of the prewar food specialties are now available.

Most American visitors admire German beers but are not too fond of the German style of serving them at room temperature. The influx of G.I.s has encouraged some chilling of beer, but the custom is not yet widespread. Beer drinking is about two thousand years old in the region we call Germany today, and customs are not quickly changed. All German beer is of high quality in this land of beer connoisseurs, but some brews are exceptional, Munich being particularly renowned in this respect. The vineyards of Germany produce, among others, the Rhine and Moselle wines which are highly regarded by wine drinkers the world over. Germans drink enormous amounts of wine, which may come as a surprise to those who believe that only beer is important to the people.

LIVER DUMPLINGS IN SOUP

LEBERKNÖDEL SUPPE

¼ pound calf's or chicken liver	Pinch of thyme
½ small onion	4 teaspoons minced parsley
1 egg yolk	1½ slices bread, trimmed
¼ teaspoon salt	½ cup milk
⅛ teaspoon freshly ground black pepper	½ cup sifted flour (about)
	2 quarts chicken or beef soup

Purée in an electric blender or grind together the liver and onion, using the finest blade of a food grinder. Mix in the egg yolk, salt, pepper, thyme, and parsley.

Soak the bread in the milk, squeeze out the liquid, and mash smooth. Add to the liver. Add just enough of the flour to make a stiff batter.

Bring the soup to a boil. Dip a teaspoon in the soup, then fill it with liver batter and drop the batter into the soup. Redip spoon in broth before shaping each dumpling. Cover the pot and cook 12 minutes or until they rise to the surface. *Serves 8.*

As served at the Frankfurt Inter-Continental Hotel

FISH WITH CARAWAY SEED CABBAGE

FISCHE MIT KÜMMELKRAUT

¼ pound (1 stick) butter	1 cup boiling water
1 medium head cabbage, shredded	¾ teaspoon freshly ground black pepper
4 potatoes, sliced thin	6 slices pike, whitefish, or halibut
2 tablespoons caraway seeds	
3 teaspoons salt	

Melt the butter in a deep saucepan. Add the cabbage, potatoes, caraway seeds, 2 teaspoons of the salt, and boiling water. Cook over medium heat for 25 minutes. Stir well. Sprinkle the pepper and the remaining salt on the fish slices. Place the fish slices on top of the cabbage and do not stir. Cover and cook over low heat for 35 minutes. Correct seasoning. Serve carefully so as not to break up the slices of fish. *Serves 6.*

MEAT BALLS IN CAPER SAUCE

KLOPSE

4 tablespoons butter
3 onions, chopped
6 slices white bread
1 cup light cream
1½ pounds beef, ground
½ pound veal, ground
½ pound pork, ground
4 anchovy fillets
3 eggs
2 teaspoons salt

1 teaspoon freshly ground
    black pepper
½ cup ice water
3 cups boiling water
¼ teaspoon marjoram
3 sprigs parsley
3 stalks celery
2 tablespoons flour
2 tablespoons lemon juice
¼ cup capers, drained

Melt 2 tablespoons of the butter in a skillet and add the onions. Sauté
for 10 minutes, stirring occasionally. Soak the bread in cream for 10
minutes. Press the excess liquid from it. Grind the bread with the
sautéed onions, ground beef, veal, pork, and the anchovies in a food
chopper. Add the eggs, 1 teaspoon of the salt, ½ teaspoon of the pepper,
and the ice water. Mix together and shape into 2-inch balls. Combine in
a deep saucepan the boiling water, remaining salt and pepper, marjoram,
parsley, and celery. Drop the meat balls into it and boil for 20 minutes.

Melt the remaining butter in a saucepan. Add the flour and mix to
smooth paste. Strain the liquid in which the meat balls were cooked,
and add, stirring constantly until the boiling point is reached. Cook
over low heat for 5 minutes. Add the lemon juice and capers and stir
well. Place the meat balls on a platter and pour the sauce over them.
Serves 8–10.

MARINATED POT ROAST

SAUERBRATEN

6 pounds top round or breast of
    beef
2 cups thinly sliced onions
2 carrots, sliced thin
3 cloves
6 peppercorns, crushed
2 bay leaves
1 cup red wine vinegar
1 cup dry red wine
2½ cups water
2 teaspoons salt

½ teaspoon freshly ground
    black pepper
2 tablespoons vegetable oil
5 tablespoons butter
1 cup minced onions
½ cup grated carrots
2 tablespoons potato flour or
    cornstarch
1 tablespoon sugar
¾ cup gingersnap crumbs
1 cup sour cream

Put the meat in a bowl (not metal). Combine the sliced onions, sliced carrots, cloves, peppercorns, bay leaves, vinegar, wine, and water in a saucepan. Bring to a boil, then let cool. Pour the marinade over the meat. Cover and let marinate in the refrigerator 4 days. Turn meat once or twice a day.

Drain the meat, dry thoroughly, and sprinkle with the salt and pepper; strain and heat the marinade. Heat the oil and 1 tablespoon butter in a Dutch oven. Brown the meat in it on all sides. Remove the meat. In the fat remaining, sauté the minced onions and grated carrots for 5 minutes. Add 2 cups of heated marinade and return the meat. Bring to a boil, cover, and cook over low heat 2 hours, adding the remaining marinade, after 1 hour.

Melt the remaining butter in a skillet; blend in the flour, then the sugar until browned. Mix in a little gravy, then stir into the remaining gravy. Re-cover and cook 30 minutes longer, or until the meat is tender. Transfer the meat to a heated platter. Stir the gingersnap crumbs into the gravy; cook over medium heat 5 minutes. Stir in the sour cream. Slice the meat, pour some of the gravy over it, and serve the rest in a sauceboat. Serve with potato pancakes (see recipe this section). *Serves 10–12.*

PORK SAUSAGES IN BEER, BERLIN STYLE

BRATWURST IN BIER, BERLINER ART

2 cups boiling water	6 peppercorns
18 pork sausages (Bratwurst)	½ teaspoon salt
1 tablespoon butter	2 cups beer
4 onions, sliced	2 tablespoons water
1 bay leaf	2 tablespoons potato flour

Pour the boiling water over the sausages; drain and dry them. Melt the butter in a skillet. Add the sausages and brown on all sides. Remove the sausages from the pan and pour off all but 2 tablespoons of the fat. Add the onions; sauté 10 minutes. Return the sausages to the pan and add the bay leaf, peppercorns, salt, and beer. Cook over low heat 20 minutes. Mix the water and potato flour to a smooth paste and add to the sausages, stirring constantly until the boiling point is reached. Cook over low heat 5 minutes. Serve with mashed potatoes. *Serves 6–8.*

STEAK WITH PINEAPPLE AND CHERRIES

RINDFLEISCH MIT ANANAS UND KIRSCHEN

¼ pound (1 stick) butter	1 onion
1 fresh pineapple, peeled and cut into strips, or 1 16-ounce can sliced pineapple, drained	1¼ teaspoons salt
	Dash of cayenne pepper
	2 cups milk
1 cup canned sour red cherries, drained	1 cup dry bread crumbs
	6 slices toast, trimmed
1 cup port wine	6 fillets mignon, cut 1 inch thick
2 cloves	

Melt 1 tablespoon of the butter in a saucepan. Add the pineapple, cherries, and wine and simmer until glazed, about 20 minutes. While the fruit is simmering, place the cloves in the onion. Combine the onion, ¼ teaspoon of the salt, cayenne pepper, and milk in a saucepan. Bring to a boil and cook over medium heat for 5 minutes. Strain. Add the bread crumbs, stirring constantly until thick and smooth. Add this mixture to the fruit and mix well. Simmer over low heat while preparing the fillets.

Melt half of the remaining butter in a saucepan and place the toast in it. Fry for 30 seconds on each side. Remove and set aside. Melt the remaining butter in the same saucepan and place the fillets in it. Fry for 3 or more minutes on each side, depending on the degree of rareness desired. Place the toast on individual plates or a large platter. Put a fillet on top of each slice of toast and pour the sauce on top. *Serves 6.*

BAKED APPLES STUFFED WITH LIVER

ÄPFEL MIT LEBERFÜLLE

6 large baking apples	½ teaspoon salt
½ pound chicken livers	2 tablespoons butter
⅛ teaspoon thyme	½ cup cider

Wash and core the apples. Scoop out the interiors of the apples but do not discard. Grind the scooped-out apple pulp with the chicken livers. Add the thyme and salt and mix well. Stuff the apples with the mixture and dot the tops with butter. Place the apples in a well-buttered baking dish. Pour the cider over the apples. Bake in a 350° oven for 45 minutes, or until apples are tender. Serve as an accompaniment to roast turkey or chicken. *Serves 6.*

PIGS' KNUCKLES WITH SAUERKRAUT AND PEAS-PUDDING

EISBEIN MIT SAUERKRAUT UND ERBSEN PUREE

1 cup dried yellow peas
6 pounds pickled pigs' knuckles
2 bay leaves
8 peppercorns
2 eggs, beaten
2 tablespoons potato flour
2 teaspoons salt

½ teaspoon freshly ground
  black pepper
2 tablespoons lard or butter
3 onions, sliced
2 pounds sauerkraut, drained
3 slices bacon, cooked and
  crumbled

Soak the peas overnight in water to cover. Drain and again cover with water, boil until tender, about 1 hour. Drain and set aside. Soak the pigs' knuckles for 3 hours. Drain, cover with water, add the bay leaves and peppercorns. Boil 3 hours, or until tender.

Combine the peas, eggs, potato flour, salt, and pepper in a bowl. Pour into a buttered baking dish. Bake in a 375° oven for 30 minutes.

Melt the lard in a saucepan and add the onions. Sauté for 10 minutes, stirring occasionally. Remove 4 tablespoons of the onion and set aside. Add the sauerkraut, and cook over low heat for 15 minutes. Place the sauerkraut on a large platter. Drain the pigs' knuckles carefully and place them over the sauerkraut. Sprinkle the reserved sautéed onions and crumbled bacon on top of the peas-pudding. Serve together, with the peas-pudding in individual dishes. *Serves 6–8.*

CHICKEN FRICASSEE

HÜHNERFRIKASSEE

2 4-pound roasting chickens,
  disjointed
1 lemon
5 cups water
3 teaspoons salt
¼ pound (1 stick) butter

4 tablespoons flour
¼ pound mushrooms, chopped
½ cup dry white wine
½ teaspoon white pepper
3 egg yolks
⅓ cup heavy cream

Wash and dry the chickens. Cut the lemon in half, and with one half rub the chicken pieces. Bring the water and 2 teaspoons of the salt to a boil. Add the chicken; cook 5 minutes. Drain and dry the chicken; reserve the liquid.

Melt half the butter in a Dutch oven. Lightly brown the chicken in it. Add the reserved liquid. Bring to a boil and simmer 45 minutes or until chicken is tender. Remove the chicken, reserving the stock. Carefully pull off the skin of the chicken.

Melt the remaining butter in a saucepan; stir in the flour. Add the stock, stirring until thickened. Add the mushrooms, wine, juice of the other half lemon, the pepper, and remaining salt. Simmer 10 minutes. Beat together the egg yolks and cream. Stir in a little hot sauce, then return to balance of sauce, stirring steadily. Add the chicken. Place pan over an asbestos pad or hot water until hot. Serve with rice. *Serves 6–8.*

POTATO PANCAKES

KARTOFFELPUFFER

4 medium raw potatoes, grated	1 teaspoon salt
1 cup cooked, mashed potatoes	½ teaspoon white pepper
1 egg	Oil or butter for frying
1 egg yolk	

Press the liquid from the grated potatoes. Combine the grated potatoes with the mashed potatoes, egg, egg yolk, salt, and pepper. Shape into desired size pancakes and fry until brown and crisp on both sides. The pancakes are often served with *Sauerbraten* (see recipe in this section) or other substantial meat dishes, or as a luncheon dish with applesauce. *Makes about 18.*

STUFFED FILLET OF BEEF

GEFÜLLTE FILET

6-pound fillet of beef	2 tablespoons potato flour or
Salt	cornstarch
Pepper	½ cup Madeira
1 8-ounce can *pâté de foie gras*	1½ cups beef broth
6 tablespoons butter	

Make a deep cut in the meat lengthwise. Season the meat with salt and pepper. Mash the *foie gras* and stuff the fillet with it. Close the opening and tie the meat at 2-inch intervals.

Melt the butter in a shallow roasting pan; put the fillet in it, cut side up. Roast in a 425° oven 45 minutes, basting frequently. Transfer the fillet to a heated serving dish, cut away strings, and keep warm.

Place pan over direct heat. Mix the cornstarch with the wine and broth. Add to the pan. Cook, stirring until thickened. Taste for seasoning. Slice the fillet and serve with the sauce. *Serves 8–10.*

PLUM DUMPLINGS

ZWETSCHGENKNÖDEL

3 medium potatoes, boiled and cooled	1 egg, beaten
⅓ cup flour	12 small blue plums, pitted
½ cup potato flour	12 small cubes sugar
½ teaspoon salt	¼ pound butter, melted
	3 tablespoons dry bread crumbs

Peel the potatoes and put them through a ricer or sieve, or mash them until very smooth. Add the flour, potato flour, salt, and egg. Mix until a fairly firm dough is formed. Place on a lightly floured surface and shape the dough into a long roll, about the shape of a rolling pin. Cut into 12 pieces, as evenly as possible.

Place a cube of sugar in the center of each plum. Press each plum into a piece of dough, making sure that the plum is completely covered. Cook in rapidly boiling, salted water for 10 minutes. Drain well. Pour melted butter over the dumplings and sprinkle with the bread crumbs.

Note: This recipe provides for 12 dumplings, or 2 per person. If served as a dessert, or as an accompaniment to a main course, it will probably be sufficient. However, for healthy appetites, it may be advisable to double this recipe.

SWEET PASTRY

MÜRBETEIG

2 cups sifted flour	2 tablespoons white vinegar
⅛ teaspoon salt	1 tablespoon cold water
¾ cup sugar	3 tablespoons heavy cream
½ pound (2 sticks) sweet butter	1 cup blanched walnuts or
1 egg	almonds, chopped fine

Sift the flour, salt, and 2 tablespoons of the sugar into a bowl. Add the butter, using one hand to blend until smooth. Make a hollow in the center of the mixture and place the egg, vinegar, and water in it. Mix all together until a dough is formed. Wrap in wax paper and place in the refrigerator for at least 2 hours, overnight if possible.

METHOD 1: Roll out about ¼ inch thick on a lightly floured surface. Cut with a cooky cutter into desired shapes, brush with the cream, sprinkle with the remaining sugar and the chopped nuts. Place on a baking sheet.

Bake in a 375° oven for 15 minutes, or until lightly browned.

METHOD 2: Roll out about ¼ inch thick on a lightly floured surface. Place in an unbuttered pie plate or baking sheet. Place rows of thinly sliced fruits, such as apples or peaches, on the dough. Sprinkle remaining sugar and the chopped nuts on top. Bake in a 375° oven for 40 minutes. *Serves 10–12.*

Note: Mürbeteig *is the basic dessert pastry of Germany. It can be used in countless ways to make sweet pastries.*

HOLLAND (THE NETHERLANDS)

Only an hour after your Pan American plane lands at Schiphol Airport you will find yourself in Amsterdam, the capital. In that short hour it is possible to see enough of the Old World charm of the country to understand why tourists always find Holland a delight. It is an immaculate land, filled with canals, windmills, picturesque buildings, not a few wooden shoes, and a multitude of flowers, particularly tulips. These last are seen at their best during the month beginning about April 15 of each year at Haarlem. Holland sometimes looks like the stage setting for a road-company Schubert operetta.

The wealth of Holland goes back to its early colonial days, when fearless explorers and settlers hacked out the nation's claims in the new worlds. Dutch travelers, businessmen, and government officials have brought back to their small country the wealth and flavors of faraway places, especially those of the islands of Indonesia. Ginger, cinnamon, nutmeg, and curry are recognized examples of spices accepted in Holland. Cinnamon is used with considerable abandon by the Dutch, often in dishes where its use might well be questioned.

Hollanders who can afford it often eat six or more times daily. Breakfast is a real meal, usually based upon a hot cereal made of groats. Coffee and possibly some cake is the rule at eleven o'clock. Lunch is about 1 P.M. and dinner as early as six-thirty, but most people require a hearty tea at about four-thirty plus the addition of some small sandwiches and little cakes. Before retiring for the night, a large cup of cocoa and any cold meats or leftover cake are consumed. Apparently the ladies of Holland are not yet counting their calories, for the well-rounded female figure divine is still the Dutch ideal.

Seafood is one of the pivot points of the local cuisine. Such delicacies of the sea as shrimp, lobster, eel, mussels, the famous Zeeland oysters, and the herring are commonplaces of the table. Herring is particularly appreciated, as it is in the Scandinavian countries, and is served in almost every conceivable fashion. You may not believe it, but there is a little Dutch rhyme that may be paraphrased as "A herring a day keeps the doctor away!"

Substantial soups are the rule, and no Hollander considers a soup worthwhile unless it is rich and filling. Meat dishes also follow this pattern; instead of plain roast or broiled meat, they are often supplemented with garnishes, as typified by the recipes for *heete bliksem* (pork chops with apples) or *gevulde kalfsborst* (stuffed breast of veal). If a dish is good, the Dutch cook prefers to make it better by making it richer or more fattening. Also popular throughout the land are the well-known rice-table dishes of Indonesia; recipes for those East Indian specialties will be found in the Indonesian section.

Holland beers are famous all over the world, and the same is true of Dutch gin, *jenever*. Many people at first do not like its dry taste, but initiates proclaim it the world's best, providing it is chilled within an inch of its life. There are no locally produced wines, but after-dinner cordials are excellent, particularly those made by Bols, and the orange *curaçao* is probably the best of these; Advocaat is an apéritif made with eggs and liquor.

Dutch chocolates are exported everywhere, and the coffee candy known as *hopjes* is the standard confection. Of course no discussion about Holland and its food would be complete without mentioning the two outstanding cheeses of the nation, the rich, creamy Edam and the equally excellent Gouda. No gourmet in Holland fails to nibble at one of these cheeses at the conclusion of a substantial Dutch meal.

CARROT SOUP

PEENSOEP

4 tablespoons butter	3 tablespoons farina
6 carrots, sliced	½ teaspoon white pepper
1 onion, chopped	Dash of nutmeg
1 cup sliced celery root	2 tablespoons chopped parsley
2 quarts chicken broth	

Melt the butter in a saucepan. Add the carrots, onion, and celery root. Sauté for 15 minutes, stirring frequently. Add the broth and stir. Cover and cook over low heat for 45 minutes. Force the soup and vegetables through a fine sieve or purée in an electric blender. Return the soup to the saucepan. Add the farina, pepper, and nutmeg, stirring constantly. Cook over low heat for 20 minutes. Correct seasoning. Sprinkle parsley on each portion before serving. *Serves 6–8.*

FISH CAKES

VISCHKOEKJES

8 slices white bread, trimmed	2 teaspoons salt
1½ cups milk	1 teaspoon freshly ground
1 pound fish fillets	black pepper
½ pound butter	¼ teaspoon nutmeg
2 eggs, beaten	3 tablespoons chopped parsley

Soak the bread in the milk for 10 minutes. Mash until very smooth. Grind the fish twice in a food chopper and place in a bowl. Cream half of the butter until soft, and add to the fish, together with the bread, eggs, salt, pepper, nutmeg, and parsley. Mix well. Shape into small cro-quettes. If the mixture is too loose, a little cracker meal may be added. Melt the remaining butter in a frying pan. Fry the fish cakes over low heat until browned on both sides. Serve with small boiled potatoes. *Serves 6–8.*

PORK CHOPS WITH APPLES

HEETE BLIKSEM

5 potatoes, peeled and cubed	2 teaspoons pepper (see Note)
2 large onions, diced	2 teaspoons salt
5 apples, peeled and cubed	6 pork chops, 1 inch thick
4 cups beef broth	12 pork sausages

Combine the potatoes, onions, apples, and broth in a saucepan. Cook over medium heat for 45 minutes, or until the liquid is absorbed. Sprin-kle 1 teaspoon of the pepper and the salt on the pork chops. Heat a skil-let. Add the chops and fry until tender and well browned on both sides, about 30 minutes. In a separate frying pan, fry the sausages until browned. Drain well. Add the remaining pepper to the potato and apple mixture and stir. Form into a mound in the center of a platter. Arrange the pork chops and sausages around it. *Serves 6.*

Note: This dish is called heete bliksem *in Holland, which may be trans-lated as "hot lightning." The pepper suggested in this recipe is compara-tively little by Dutch standards but quite high by ours.*

STUFFED BREAST OF VEAL

GEVULDE KALFSBORST

½ pound ground beef
1 egg, beaten
4 teaspoons salt
2 teaspoons pepper
2 tablespoons chopped parsley
6 gherkins

2 hard-cooked eggs
1 breast of veal (with pocket
   for stuffing)
4 tablespoons butter
3 onions, sliced

Mix the ground beef, egg, 1½ teaspoons of the salt, ¾ teaspoon of the pepper, and the parsley together. Divide the mixture in half and shape each half to fit the pocket in the veal. On one of the halves arrange the gherkins and eggs. Cover with the remaining half. Place in the veal pocket and fasten the opening with skewers or toothpicks. Sprinkle the remaining salt and pepper on the veal. Melt the butter in a roasting pan. Place the veal in it, with the onions arranged around the meat. Roast in a 350° oven for 3 hours, or until the veal is brown and tender. Baste frequently. Slice carefully between the ribs and serve. *Serves 4–6.*

Note: If breast of veal is not available, thin veal steaks may be used. The stuffing should be placed on top of the veal, then rolled up and fastened.

HOT CURRIED SLAW

KERRY KOOL SLA

2 cups beef broth
1 bay leaf
1 clove garlic
4- to 5-pound head cabbage,
   shredded
2 cloves
1 onion
3 teaspoons salt

1 teaspoon freshly ground
   black pepper
4 tablespoons butter
3 tablespoons flour
1½ cups heavy cream
1 tablespoon curry powder
¼ cup ground nuts or bread
   crumbs

Combine the broth, bay leaf, garlic, and shredded cabbage in a saucepan. Place the cloves in the onion and add to the cabbage, together with 2 teaspoons of the salt and the pepper. Cook over medium heat for 10 minutes, stirring occasionally. Drain, discarding the bay leaf, garlic, and onion. Butter a baking dish and place the cabbage in it.

Melt the butter in a saucepan. Add the flour, stirring until smooth. Gradually add the cream, stirring constantly until the boiling point is reached. Place ½ cup of this sauce in a cup and add the curry powder, mixing until smooth. Return to the saucepan, stirring well. Add the remaining salt. Cook over low heat for 5 minutes, stirring frequently. Pour the sauce over the cabbage in the baking dish. Sprinkle either ground nuts or bread crumbs on top. Bake in a 425° oven for 15 minutes. Serve hot. This dish is particularly good with roast meats. *Serves 6–8.*

ROAST STUFFED CAPON

GEBRADEN KIP

Capon:

8-pound capon	½ teaspoon freshly ground
2 teaspoons salt	black pepper

Wash and dry the capon and rub the fowl inside and out with the salt and pepper.

Stuffing:

1 whole chicken breast	¼ teaspoon white pepper
¼ pound ground veal	Dash of nutmeg
¼ cup fresh bread crumbs	2 tablespoons minced parsley
¼ cup light cream	6 tablespoons melted butter
1 egg, beaten	1 cup heavy cream
1 teaspoon salt	

Discard the skin and bones of the chicken breast and grind meat in a food chopper. Add the veal and grind again.

Soak the bread crumbs in the cream, then mash smooth. Add to the ground meats with the egg, salt, pepper, nutmeg, parsley, and 2 tablespoons of the melted butter. Stuff the capon with the mixture and sew the opening. Tie to hold its shape.

Put the capon in a roasting pan and pour the remaining butter over it. Roast in a 375° oven 2½ hours, basting and turning to brown all sides. Transfer the bird to a platter and remove the strings. Stir the cream into the pan juices; place over high heat and bring to a boil, scraping the bottom of browned particles. Taste for seasoning and serve in a sauceboat. *Serves 6.*

BAKED ENDIVE

LOFSCHOTEL

6 endive or 6 small bunches celery	6 hard-cooked eggs, halved
	½ cup melted butter
6 slices ham	¼ teaspoon nutmeg

If celery is used, cut off the leaves, but each bunch should remain whole. Boil the endive in salted water for 10 minutes, or until tender. Drain. Wrap a slice of ham around each endive and place in a buttered baking dish. Arrange the eggs around the endive and add the melted butter. Sprinkle the nutmeg on top. Bake in a 400° oven for 10 minutes. *Serves 6.*

RAISIN PANCAKES

DRIE IN DE PAN

½ cake or package yeast	½ teaspoon salt
½ cup lukewarm milk	3 tablespoons seedless raisins
¾ cup sifted flour	4 tablespoons butter

Soften the yeast in ¼ cup of the lukewarm milk for 5 minutes. Stir until smooth. Sift the flour and salt into a bowl. Add the yeast mixture and mix well. Add the balance of the milk and beat well. Cover and place the bowl in a pan of warm water. Allow to rise for 1 hour. Wash and dry the raisins. If they are not very fresh and plump, soak them in hot water for 15 minutes. Add the raisins to the batter, mixing lightly.

Melt half of the butter in a frying pan. Drop a tablespoon of batter at a time into the pan, to form small pancakes. Bake over low heat until brown and well done on both sides. Serve sprinkled with sugar.

CHOCOLATE LAYER CAKE

CHOCOLADE TAART

6 tablespoons butter	2 cups sugar
3 ounces (squares) unsweetened chocolate	2½ cups sifted flour
	4 teaspoons baking powder
4 eggs	1 cup milk

Preheat oven to 350°.

Place the butter and chocolate in a saucepan over hot water. Stir until melted and smooth. Cool for 10 minutes. Beat the eggs in a bowl. Add the sugar, beating steadily until light and fluffy. Add the melted chocolate and mix well. Sift the flour and baking powder together. Add the milk and flour mixture alternately to the chocolate mixture, beating thoroughly after each addition. Butter two 9-inch layer cake pans and dust lightly with flour. Pour the batter into the tins as equally as possible. Bake in a 350° oven for 30 minutes, or until a tester comes out clean. Cool for 15 minutes and turn out. Now prepare:

¼ cup sugar	1 cup milk
2½ tablespoons cocoa, (Dutch style, if possible)	1 teaspoon vanilla extract
1 tablespoon cornstarch	2 cups heavy cream, whipped

Combine the sugar, cocoa, and cornstarch in the top of a double boiler. Gradually add the milk, stirring constantly until smooth. Cook over hot water over medium heat, stirring constantly until the mixture is thick. Add the vanilla. Cool for 30 minutes. Add ⅓ cup of the cocoa mixture to the whipped cream and stir lightly but thoroughly. Spread the remaining cocoa mixture between the layers. Cover the cake with the whipped cream. If desired, sprinkle a little shaved chocolate on top of the cake. *Serves 8–10.*

HUNGARY

Although once a part of the great monarchy of Austria-Hungary of pre-World War I days, Hungary has gone its own separate way. Just as Austria has always turned toward the west, Hungary has faced the east, and to this day its cuisine has always evidenced more or less a *magyar*, or Mongoloid, influence. While Vienna danced to Strauss waltzes, the people of Budapest preferred the wild gypsy music, unrestrained, unfettered. In its cuisine Austria has always been conservative, classic, and correct. In Hungary the food habits again indicate the character of the people, for caution has been abandoned, and unusual and exciting tastes and colors greet the diner.

The mere mention of Hungary means "goulash" to most people for it is the one particular dish that Hungary has exported to the world. Actually the word itself is a corruption from the Hungarian term, *gulyás*, but goulash it is and always will be to the average person. This dish is usually made of chicken or beef, plentifully laden with Hungary's favorite condiment, paprika, sweet or hot. The sweet paprika is a mild, beautiful shade of red which adds greatly to the taste and eye appeal of the dish, without burning the lips or palate. Unless it is used in unwarranted quantities, paprika can be a most satisfactory addition to the kitchen shelf. So fond are Hungarians of their beloved paprika that they make a paprika cheese, the *liptói*. Rather similar to the *gulyás* are two close relations, the *paprikás* and the *tokány*. For general purposes, it may be said that the meat in *tokány* is usually cut into smaller pieces than in the *gulyás*, and some vegetables are added. The *paprikás* dishes are similar but as a rule sour cream is used in preparing them.

Among Hungary's unique foods are the famous *Balaton fogas*, a variety of lake fish unlike any other known variety. Before the war tourists always made a point of having a *fogas* in one of Hungary's many fine restaurants. Another unique creation is the renowned "red bacon" of the peasantry. It is made by dipping extremely fat pieces of bacon into paprika. The coloring soaks into the bacon and creates the red effect. Bacon prepared this way has a rather interesting flavor but it is not recommended that it be eaten in the peasant fashion—raw!

Noodles, dumplings, and other doughy materials have been developed to a state of perfection closely resembling the Italian standard. These are used in soup, with meat and poultry, with desserts, in almost endless and inconceivable ways. Particularly good are the noodles with melted butter and poppy seeds; also the dumplings enclosing pitted fresh plums and covered with buttered bread crumbs. Strudels are high in popularity and are made with any filling that strikes the baker's fancy, such as cheese, *mohn* (poppy seed), cherries, nuts, and jams. While somewhat difficult to make, they are spectacular. Of course the national dessert of the country is undoubtedly the *dobos torta*, a very tricky cake to make. This many-layered confection of chocolate and caramel has been acclaimed by pastry fanciers throughout the world.

Hungarians are always acclaimed as gourmets, and they are undoubtedly very fond of good living. Part of their search for the better things of life has led to the development of unique liquors and brandies, mostly fruit-based. The best of these cordials is probably put out under the Zwack label, and these include some fine plum brandies.

The Tokay wine of the nation is unique in quality and acceptance and well deserves the position of honor it holds with knowing wine drinkers. Even Frenchmen who look condescendingly upon the wines of other countries have been heard to admit that Hungary possesses a fine wine in the Tokay. The very best of these is made from grapes that have been allowed to become overripe upon the vines. When the grapes have lost all their moisture and are shrunken and dried out, they are harvested. These raisins are known as the *formint*, which is carefully blended with normally harvested grapes. It is of interest to note that many Tokay "Essence" wines command fabulous prices in the world market, particularly in view of the fact that they are customarily sold in smaller than average bottles.

GOULASH SOUP

GULYÁSLEVES

1 pound beef	2 green peppers, diced
1 pound pork	2 tomatoes, diced
1 pound lamb	8 cups boiling water
½ pound ham	4 potatoes, peeled and cut into
3 tablespoons butter, lard, or	cubes
chicken fat	½ pound smoked sausage
6 onions, chopped	(Hungarian or German type,
2 tablespoons Hungarian paprika	if available)
1 teaspoon freshly ground	
black pepper	

Cut the beef, pork, and lamb into 1-inch cubes. Cut the ham into ¼-inch cubes. Melt the butter in a large saucepan. Add the chopped onions and the cubed meats and cook over high heat until brown, stirring frequently. Add the paprika and pepper and cook over low heat for 30 minutes, stirring occasionally. Add the green peppers, tomatoes, and water. Continue cooking for 1 hour. Add the potatoes and cook 30 minutes longer.

While the soup is cooking, cut the sausage into ½-inch slices and boil in a saucepan for 10 minutes. Drain and add to the soup immediately. Correct seasoning. No salt has been provided in this recipe because certain sausages have a great deal of salt. If necessary, add some now. *Serves 8–10.*

Note: This is a very thick soup.

BEAN SOUP AND DUMPLINGS

BABLEVES CSIPETKÉVEL

1 cup dried white beans	½ teaspoon freshly ground
2 quarts beef broth	black pepper
2 carrots, sliced	1 teaspoon paprika
1 parsnip, sliced	1 egg
4 tablespoons butter	2 tablespoons water
2 onions, chopped	3 frankfurters (Hungarian style,
1¼ cups sifted flour	if available), sliced
2 teaspoons salt	

Soak the beans overnight in water to cover. Drain. Place the beans in a saucepan with the broth, carrots, and parsnip. Cook over low heat for 2 hours. Remove 1 cup of the beans and force them through a sieve. Return the purée to the soup. Melt the butter in a saucepan. Add the onions and sauté until brown, stirring frequently. Sprinkle 2 tablespoons of the flour over them, stirring until smooth. Gradually add 1 cup of the soup, stirring constantly. Return the contents of the saucepan to the soup. Add the salt, pepper, and paprika. Cook over low heat for 1 hour.

Meanwhile, sift the remaining flour into a bowl. Make a well or depression in the center and add the egg and water. Mix to a smooth paste. Knead until the dough does not stick to the fingers. Roll out very thin on a lightly floured surface and allow to remain there for 45 minutes. Pinch off small pieces of the dough and drop them into the boiling soup. Cook until they float. Fry the frankfurter slices for 5 minutes. Drain. Add them to the soup. Serve hot. *Serves 8–10.*

STUFFED KOHLRABI

TÖLTÖTT KALARÁBÁ

Kohlrabi:

12 large kohlrabi	1 hard-cooked egg, chopped
2 tablespoons butter	¼ teaspoon freshly ground
½ cup chopped onion	black pepper
1 pound ground beef	⅛ teaspoon marjoram
¼ cup bread cubes	2 tablespoons olive oil
1 egg, beaten	1 cup beef broth

Peel the kohlrabi and cook in boiling salted water 5 minutes. Drain. Scoop out the centers and chop fine.

Melt the butter in a skillet; add the onion and beef. Cook over high heat 3 minutes, stirring almost steadily.

Soak the bread cubes in water 5 minutes. Drain well; add to the meat with the beaten egg, chopped egg, pepper, and marjoram. Mix well and taste for seasoning. Stuff the kohlrabi; you will not use all the mixture. Spread the remaining meat mixture on the bottom of a deep 11-inch pie plate. Arrange the kohlrabi over it and brush with the oil. Pour the broth around them. Bake in a preheated 350° oven 30 minutes, basting once or twice with the pan drippings. Prepare the sauce meanwhile.

Sauce:

3 tablespoons butter	1 cup sour cream
3 tablespoons flour	¼ cup grated Parmesan cheese
1 cup dry white wine	2 tablespoons minced dill

Melt the butter in a saucepan; blend in the flour, then gradually stir in the wine. Cook over low heat 5 minutes, stirring constantly until mixture thickens. Cool, then stir in the sour cream, cheese, and dill. Taste for seasoning. When the 30 minutes' baking time is up, spoon the sauce over the kohlrabi. Place under the broiler until browned. *Serves 6–12.*

As served at the Buda Inter-Continental Hotel.

HUNGARIAN GOULASH

GULYÁS

6 tablespoons butter	3 pounds beef (cross rib, chuck,
5 large onions, chopped	etc.)
2 tablespoons Hungarian	1 8-ounce can tomato sauce
paprika	1 clove garlic, minced (optional)
2 teaspoons salt	½ cup sour cream
½ teaspoon freshly ground	
black pepper	

Melt 4 tablespoons of the butter in a heavy saucepan. Add the onions and sauté for 15 minutes, stirring frequently. Remove the onions and set them aside. Combine the paprika, salt, and pepper. Cut the meat into 2-inch cubes and roll in the mixture. Melt the remaining butter in the saucepan. Add the meat and brown well on all sides. Return the onions to the saucepan. Add the tomato sauce and garlic and stir. Cover and cook over low heat for 3 hours, stirring occasionally. Add the sour cream and stir. Heat but do not allow the mixture to boil. Serve hot with boiled *nokedli* (see recipe in this section). *Serves 6–8.*

BRAISED STEAK, HUNGARIAN STYLE

ESTERHÁZY ROSTÉLYOS

⅓ cup flour
1½ teaspoons salt
¾ teaspoon freshly ground
 black pepper
6 individual steaks, about 1 inch
 thick
3 slices bacon, chopped
4 tablespoons butter

2 carrots, chopped
2 stalks celery, chopped
½ cup sliced mushrooms
3 tablespoons chopped parsley
1 bay leaf
½ cup water
1 cup sour cream
2 tablespoons capers, drained

Mix the flour, salt, and pepper together. Dip the steaks in it, coating well. Fry the bacon in a large skillet until half done. Drain the fat from the pan. Add the butter and brown the steaks on both sides over high heat. Add the carrots, celery, mushrooms, and parsley and cook over high heat for 2 minutes. Add the bay leaf and water. Cover and cook over low heat for 30 minutes, or until the steaks are tender. Remove the bay leaf and force the gravy and vegetables through a sieve. Return to the saucepan. Correct seasoning. Add the sour cream and capers, stirring constantly. Cook over low heat for 3 minutes. Serve hot. *Serves 6.*

DUMPLINGS

NOKEDLI

3 cups sifted flour
1 teaspoon salt
2 eggs
¾ cup water

1 tablespoon melted butter
2 quarts boiling, lightly salted
 water
¼ cup melted butter

Sift the flour and salt into a bowl. Beat the eggs in a separate bowl; add the ¾ cup water and the butter and mix. Combine the egg mixture with the flour, beating constantly until smooth.

Have the boiling, salted water in a deep saucepan and drop the batter by teaspoons into the water. The dumplings will come to the surface as they are done. Remove immediately. Drain well and pour the melted butter over them. They may be eaten in place of potatoes with a meat course, or served with Hungarian *gulyás* (see recipe in this section), pouring the *gulyás* sauce over the *nokedli.*

NUT STRUDEL

DIÓSRÉTES

2½ cups sifted flour	⅓ cup sugar
½ teaspoon salt	2 cups ground nuts
1 egg	1 tablespoon grated lemon rind
2 tablespoons salad oil	2 tablespoons lemon juice
⅔ cup warm water	½ cup seedless raisins (optional)
½ cup melted butter	4 egg whites
4 egg yolks	¼ cup bread crumbs

Sift the flour and salt into a bowl. Make a well in the center and put the egg and oil in it. Work the flour into it gradually, adding enough warm water to make a soft dough. Knead it well and pick it up and slap it down on a board several times. Continue until the dough loses its stickiness, about 10 minutes. Form into a ball and dust with a little flour. Cover with a warmed bowl and allow to remain for 45 minutes.

Spread a fresh tablecloth on a large table. Sprinkle the cloth freely with flour and roll the dough as thin as possible. Brush the dough with a little of the melted butter. Flour the hands and begin stretching the dough from underneath, using the backs of the hands, not the fingers. Go around the table slowly at least several times, gently pulling the dough toward you until it is as thin as possible, almost transparent. Brush the dough again with some of the melted butter.

Beat the egg yolks well. Add the sugar, beating until light and creamy. Add the nuts, lemon rind and juice, and the raisins. Beat the egg whites until stiff and fold into the mixture. Sprinkle the dough with the bread crumbs. Spread the nut mixture evenly over about one third of the dough on one of the long sides of the table. Lift up the tablecloth and slowly and carefully roll the dough over as for a jelly roll. Preheat oven to 400°. Butter or oil a baking sheet. Transfer the strudel carefully. Brush with the remaining butter. Bake in a 400° oven for 35 minutes, or until brown on top. Cut into slices while hot. Serve hot or cold. *Serves 8–10.*

Note: Frozen purchased strudel leaves make a good substitute for the dough.

APPLE CAKE

ALMA TORTA

2 cups sifted flour	½ cup sugar
Dash of salt	2 tablespoons cinnamon
¾ pound sweet butter	¼ cup melted butter
½ cup ice water	6 large apples, peeled, quartered,
1½ tablespoons vinegar	and sliced thin

Sift the flour and salt together into a bowl. Add the butter and, using one hand, blend the ingredients together. Combine the ice water and vinegar and add. Continue mixing until well blended. Form into a ball, place in a bowl, and cover. Store in the refrigerator overnight. Remove the dough from the refrigerator 15 minutes before using. Preheat oven to 375°. Roll out half the dough at a time as thin as possible on a lightly floured surface. If the dough should tear, patch it with additional thin pieces of dough.

Place each piece of the dough on unbuttered jelly roll pans. Arrange the apple slices on the dough in rows as uniformly and evenly as possible. Sprinkle the sugar and cinnamon on top. Pour the melted butter over the apples. Bake in a 375° oven for 25 minutes, or until delicately brown on top. Cut into squares or strips. Serve with whipped cream. *Serves 10–12.*

IRELAND

Ireland, which has made famous the wearing of the green, is also a land of green. Visitors are always surprised at the lush carpet of color that covers everything: it is as if Ireland were one big garden dedicated to the production of cholorophyll. Surrounded by the sea, it is a country of considerable interest to the tourist.

Fisheries play an important part in the life of the people, and much of the Irish diet is based upon the fisherman's catch. Herring, particularly, is one fruit (what a word to describe herring!) of the sea that is eaten regularly; halibut, cod, and haddock, as well, are of prime importance. The country also is proud of its trout and the world-famous salmon, both fresh and smoked. Fish soups are well made and deservedly popular.

Irish beef is exceptional, and the young, Irish lamb is also of high quality. But it is the locally cured hams and bacon that are the pride of the countryside. They are now being exported extensively, and one taste of these pork products will convince any skeptic. Poultry and game, too, are in the top category.

Everyone knows of Ireland's fondness for the potato, but comparatively few know of colcannon, made of potatoes and cabbage, or of Irish potato cakes. A favorite Irish way of handling vegetables is to boil cabbage, potatoes, and onions together with meat. Salads and greens are becoming more important but are still comparatively rare except during the summer season.

A staple food is porridge, which the country people eat almost every day of their lives. The coarse, full-grain oatmeal is so nourishing and filling that a pot of it is kept cooking all day long over the farmer's fire. An unusual Irish item is carrageen, a moss collected along the shore and used as the basis for sweet desserts and milk puddings. Coffee is much appreciated here, but tea has a strong traditional hold upon the people, and if you stop at an Irish country cottage you will almost always be offered tea rather than coffee.

Irish whisky has its adherents, for there are those who find it superior to scotch. It resembles scotch whisky but is not so thick or so smoky as that liquor. The world-renowned Guinness stout, an extremely rich dark beer, is produced here. Many people prefer to drink stout half and half— that is, mixed with ordinary beer in order to cut its heavy body.

Good food is easily obtained in Ireland, and at prices that please those who have unwillingly become accustomed to high prices. Ireland does not have night clubs but it does have pubs such as the Abbey Bar and the Buttery. Here you should try Celtic coffee made of hot, black coffee and Irish whisky, topped with a dollop of whipped cream.

Just a passing word about a rather weak, ineffectual drink called *poteen*, or tiny pot. It is said that the little Irish leprechauns distill a liquor from potatoes high up in the hills, and according to their own secret formula. Very little of this innocuous beverage reaches the outside world.

IRISH WHISKY HIGHBALL

6 jiggers Irish whisky   Ginger ale
6 thin pieces lemon peel

Place 2 ice cubes in each highball glass. Add 1 jigger Irish whisky and 1 piece of lemon peel. Fill each glass with ginger ale.

DUBLIN SHRIMP COCKTAIL

2 pounds large raw shrimp
2 cups water
1½ teaspoons salt
1 small onion
1 bay leaf
½ teaspoon dry mustard
¾ cup mayonnaise

½ teaspoon sugar
¼ cup tomato sauce
1 tablespoon malt or cider
  vinegar
3 drops red food coloring
Lettuce
Lemon wedges

Wash the shrimp, shell, and devein. Bring the water, salt, onion, and bay leaf to a boil. Add the shrimp and cook over low heat 5 minutes. Drain, cool, then chill.

Blend the mustard with a little mayonnaise, then combine with all the mayonnaise, sugar, tomato sauce, vinegar, and food coloring. Taste for seasoning, adding salt and pepper if necessary.

Arrange the shrimp on a bed of lettuce, with the lemon wedges as a garnish. Serve the sauce in a sauceboat. *Serves 8.*

IRISH POTATO SOUP

7 cups water
6 medium potatoes, peeled and
  sliced
2 onions, sliced
1 carrot, sliced
½ teaspoon thyme

1 bay leaf
1 clove
½ cup milk, scalded
½ cup cream, scalded
1½ teaspoons salt
½ teaspoon pepper

Boil the water in a saucepan. Add the potatoes, onions, carrot, thyme, bay leaf, and clove. Cook over low heat for 45 minutes. Force the mixture through a sieve. Add the milk, cream, salt, and pepper. Cook over low heat for 10 minutes. Correct seasoning. Serve hot. *Serves 8–10.*

ARAN SCALLOP SOUP

1½ pounds scallops
1 pound fillet of sole
1 onion
1 stalk celery
6 cups water
1½ teaspoons salt
½ teaspoon white pepper
2 slices bacon, diced
3 cups peeled diced potatoes

3 sprigs parsley
½ teaspoon thyme
3 cups peeled diced tomatoes
1 cup crushed pilot crackers
4 tablespoons butter
2 cups hot light cream
Mace
Chopped parsley

Wash the scallops, cover with boiling water, drain, and dice. Refrigerate until needed.

Cut the sole in pieces and combine with the onion, celery, water, salt, and pepper. Bring to a boil and cook over low heat 45 minutes. Strain the stock, and reserve.

Brown the bacon in a saucepan; add the potatoes and cook over low heat 5 minutes, shaking the pan frequently. Add the fish stock, parsley, and thyme. Bring to a boil and cook over low heat 20 minutes. Mix in the tomatoes and scallops; cook 20 minutes. Remove the parsley. Gradually stir in the crackers to thicken soup. Break the butter into small pieces and add to the soup, and when melted, stir in the cream. Taste for seasoning, adding salt and pepper if necessary. Serve sprinkled with mace and chopped parsley. *Serves 8–10.*

IRISH-STYLE CABBAGE AND POTATOES

COLCANNON

6 boiled potatoes	1 onion, chopped fine
¼ pound (1 stick) butter, melted	1 small head cabbage, boiled
1½ teaspoon salt	
½ teaspoon freshly ground black pepper	

Peel and mash the potatoes with half of the butter and the salt, pepper, and onion. Mix well together. Chop the cabbage coarsely. Add to the previous mixture and mix lightly but thoroughly. Heat in a buttered pan but do not allow the mixture to brown. Serve very hot. Heap in a mound. Make a well in the center and pour the remaining melted butter in it. *Serves 6–8.*

IRISH STEW

6 large potatoes, peeled and cut into 1½-inch cubes	6 large onions, sliced
2 teaspoons salt	3 pounds boneless lamb, cut into 1-inch cubes
½ teaspoon freshly ground black pepper	1 cup water

In a heavy saucepan place a layer of potatoes and sprinkle with a little of the salt and pepper. Add a layer of onions, and again season. Place a layer of lamb on top and season. Repeat until all of the ingredients are used up; the top layer should consist of potatoes. Pour the water over it and cover. Bring to a boil and cook over low heat for 1½ hours, or until the lamb is tender. *Serves 6–8.*

Note: This recipe is an authentic one for an Irish stew. In certain localities carrots, celery, and tomatoes are added in additional layers.

WHEATEN BREAD

4 cups whole wheat flour
1 teaspoon salt
1 teaspoon baking soda

½ teaspoon baking powder
1 teaspoon sugar
2 cups buttermilk

Preheat oven to 400°.

Mix together all the dry ingredients in a bowl. Make a well in the center and into it put the buttermilk. Work in the flour mixture until well blended. Turn out onto a lightly floured board and knead for 2 minutes, or until smooth. Shape into two loaves and place on a greased baking sheet. With the back of a knife, cut a deep cross in the center of each loaf. Bake 40 minutes or until golden brown. Cool on a cake rack.

IRISH POTATO PANCAKES

BOXTY

1½ pounds potatoes
1 cup flour
½ cup milk
1½ teaspoons salt

1 teaspoon baking powder
4 tablespoons vegetable oil
Butter

Peel and grate the potatoes. Mix in the flour, milk, salt, and baking powder.

Heat a griddle or heavy skillet and add 2 tablespoons of the oil. When oil bubbles drop the potato mixture into it by the tablespoon. Let cook over low heat, until browned on both sides, turning them only once. Spread with butter immediately, and keep hot while preparing the balance. *Makes about 24.*

CHOCOLATE POTATO CAKE

½ pound (2 sticks) butter
2 cups sugar
4 eggs, beaten
3 ounces (squares) unsweetened
  chocolate, melted
1 cup cold mashed potatoes

1 teaspoon cinnamon
¼ teaspoon nutmeg
2 cups sifted flour
1 teaspoon baking soda
1 cup buttermilk
1 cup coarsely chopped nuts

Preheat oven to 350°.

Cream the butter. Add the sugar gradually, beating until light and fluffy. Add the eggs and beat well. Add the chocolate, potatoes, cinnamon, and nutmeg. Sift the flour and baking soda together and add to the chocolate mixture alternately with the buttermilk. Beat well. Add the nuts, mixing lightly. Pour into a 9-inch buttered spring-form pan. Bake in a 350° oven for 45 minutes, or until a cake tester comes out clean. Cool in the pan, then turn out. *Serves 8–10.*

IRISH COFFEE

For each serving, carefully warm a stemmed whisky goblet. Into it put a jigger of Irish whisky and a small sugar cube. Fill with strong hot black coffee to within one inch of the rim. Stir to dissolve sugar. Top with lightly whipped cream to reach the rim. Don't stir after floating the cream.

ITALY

The word "cuisine" is used to describe a style of cooking. Seldom is the word employed in its most limited sense, that of a truly individual and nationalistic manner of preparing food. Certainly the word may be used in all honesty to describe the food of Italy, for here is a truly great cuisine.

Many Americans, particularly those who are not fond of garlic, mistakenly believe that all Italian food is based on tomatoes and garlic. In certain parts of Italy, particularly in the north, rice is a much more important and popular food than spaghetti, though one would hardly know this by eating the typical food served in Italian restaurants in the United States. The reason for this apparent contradiction is readily explained. Most Italian immigrants to our shores have come from the south of Italy, and from Sicily and Sardinia, rather than from the north. The southerners have brought with them their own style of cooking, which is based on olive oil, garlic, spices, tomatoes, and spaghetti. The northern preference for butter, rice, and the use of little or no garlic is not nearly as well known in this country.

Italians love good food and spend long hours eating their meals and drinking their wines. They seldom drink hard liquor, but almost every meal is taken with wine, most of which is comparatively inexpensive and of modest quality. Breakfast is a simple repast, usually coffee and hot milk with a crust of bread. The midday meal is fairly substantial, and of course the evening meal is very important, at least for city dwellers. It is eaten at a late hour and is as elaborate as the means of the family permit.

Seafoods of all kinds are a regular part of Italian food. Shellfish, in particular, are looked upon as great delicacies, which indeed they are in Italy. The people eat many things that are unattractive to Americans educated only to canned tuna fish but are really not so exotic when they are tasted. Squid in its ink and baby octopus are examples of what is exotic to Lincoln, Nebraska, but very ordinary to Naples, Italy. Best of all are the seafood soups of the small fishing villages, where the seafood practically leaps out of the fisherman's basket into the oil of the casserole. Surely the old proverb that fish live in water and die in oil holds true in the Mediterranean area.

Vegetables and salads are of great importance and are served at almost every lunch and dinner. To most Italians, it is the *pasta asciutta*, or dry dough, that makes the meal. This term refers to the various spaghettis, macaronis, and other starchy products that have become an accepted part of our own American eating habits. But the Italian people do not limit themselves to one or two varieties as we do, for there are dozens and dozens of different *pastas*. From the extremely thin strands, such as *vermicelli* (little worms) and *capellini d'angelo* (angel's hair), to the enormous varieties that are stuffed with meat and cheese, from the tiniest bits of dough used for baby foods to the most beautiful shell forms, the world of *pasta asciutta* is a wide one. To accompany this range of shapes and sizes, there is an equal variation in color for sauces to accompany these pastes, including white, yellow, green, and red mixtures.

Italian cheeses are excellent. Those known to us include the increasingly popular Bel Paese, Gorgonzola, Mozzarella, Provolone, and Ricotta. Worthy of mention are the comparatively little-known Caciocavallo, Lodigiano, and Robiolino.

Except on festive occasions, rich desserts and fancy cakes are little known. The custom is to end most meals with fresh fruit and cheese, eaten together. Coffee, black as a starless night, is the usual finish to a meal. *Caffé espresso,* made by forcing steam through finely pulverized coffee, is the favorite method of preparation.

Almost the only strong drink that the people like is the rather crude grape liquor, *grappa,* beloved of the G.I.s during the war. Wines are Italy's pride. *Chianti* is so much a part of the American concept of Italy that when an American tourist in that country orders wine without specifying the type, he will automatically be served with Chianti. But Chianti is only one of Italy's wines, and there are others deserving of notice.

Among the red wines there are Barbera, Bardolino, Barolo, Nebbiolo, and Valpolicella. The whites include Est! Est! Est! (certainly the most fascinating name in the world for a wine), Frascati, Lachryma Christi (the Tears of Christ), Marsala, Orvieto, and Zucco. Asti Spumante, a sparking wine, is delightful.

Most travelers regard Italian food as one of the high points of their trip. Famous restaurants in Rome include Hosteria dell'Orso, Capriccio's, and Alfredo's, which is almost exclusively a tourist restaurant. No two people agree as to Rome's best eating places, but many consider Giggi Fazzi and Passetto's to be the finest. In Venice, perhaps the best is La Fenice.

STUFFED PEPPERS

PEPERONI RIPIENI

6 large green or red peppers	½ cup peeled chopped tomatoes
1 7-ounce can tuna fish	2 tablespoons chopped capers
1 3-ounce can anchovies	1 clove garlic, minced
¼ cup fresh bread crumbs	½ cup olive oil
½ cup chopped black olives	

Wash and dry the peppers; cut a ½-inch piece from the stem end and scoop out the seeds and fibers. Drain the tuna and anchovies and chop; mix in the bread crumbs, olives, tomatoes, capers, garlic, and 2 tablespoons of the oil. Stuff the peppers. Arrange in an oiled baking dish and pour 1 tablespoon of oil on each. Cover and bake in a 350° oven 40 minutes. Serve hot or cold as an appetizer. *Serves 6.*

THICK VEGETABLE SOUP

MINESTRONE MILANESE

1 teaspoon olive oil	1 cup chopped celery
½ pound salt pork, chopped	3 carrots, sliced
½ cup chopped onions	2 potatoes, peeled and diced
½ teaspoon minced garlic	2 cups cooked or canned chick-
1 teaspoon chopped parsley	peas
¼ teaspoon sage	1½ cups shredded cabbage
1 teaspoon salt	½ pound zucchini, diced
½ teaspoon freshly ground	1 cup shelled peas
black pepper	1½ quarts beef broth
1 tablespoon tomato paste	1 cup elbow macaroni
1 cup water	Grated Parmesan cheese

Combine the oil and salt pork in a large saucepan. Cook over low heat 5 minutes. Pour off the fat. Add the onions, garlic, parsley, sage, salt, and pepper. Cook 10 minutes. Blend the tomato paste with the 1 cup of water and add. Bring to a boil and cook 5 minutes. Add all the vegetables and the broth. Bring to a boil and cook over low heat 45 minutes. Mix in the macaroni; cook 10 minutes longer or until the macaroni is tender. Taste for seasoning. Serve sprinkled with cheese. *Serves 6–8.*

FRESH GREENS SOUP

ZUPPA D'ERBE

1 large head lettuce
2 cups sorrel or spinach, fresh
or frozen
2 stalks celery, diced
6 scallions (green onions),
chopped

6 cups chicken broth
1½ teaspoons salt
3 tablespoons butter
6 slices toast (French-style
bread, if available)
¼ cup grated Parmesan cheese

Wash the lettuce and sorrel thoroughly. Drain. Tear the lettuce leaves into small pieces. Remove the stems from the sorrel and chop coarsely. Combine the lettuce and sorrel in a saucepan. Add the celery, scallions, broth, salt, and butter. Cook over medium heat for 30 minutes, stirring occasionally. Correct seasoning. If desired, the soup and vegetables may be forced through a sieve or puréed in an electric blender. Place a slice of toast in each soup plate. Pour the soup over it and sprinkle with the Parmesan cheese. *Serves 6.*

SHRIMP IN RED SAUCE

SCAMPI FRA DIAVOLO

2 pounds raw shrimp, shelled
and deveined
¼ cup olive oil
2 whole cloves garlic
¼ cup warm cognac
1 pound tomatoes, peeled and
chopped

½ cup dry white wine
1½ teaspoons salt
⅛ teaspoon crushed dried red
pepper
½ teaspoon orégano
¼ cup chopped parsley

Wash and dry the shrimp. Heat the oil in a casserole or deep skillet; add the garlic and shrimp. Cook 5 minutes, then discard the garlic. Add the cognac and set it aflame. When flames die, add the tomatoes, wine, salt, red pepper, and orégano. Cook over medium heat 5 minutes. Remove the shrimp and boil the sauce rapidly until reduced to half its original volume. Return the shrimp and heat. Sprinkle with the parsley, and serve with sautéed French or Italian bread. *Serves 6–8.*

GREEN NOODLES

LASAGNE VERDI

Bolognese Sauce:

6 tablespoons butter
1 cup finely chopped minced
    onions
½ cup grated carrots
1 pound ground beef
1 8-ounce can tomato sauce

4 cups beef broth or water
1½ teaspoons salt
½ teaspoon freshly ground
    black pepper
1 cup heavy cream

Melt the butter in a saucepan; sauté the onions and carrots 10 minutes. Add the beef; cook, stirring frequently, until no pink remains. Add the tomato sauce, broth, salt, and pepper; cover and cook over low heat 2 hours, stirring occasionally. Mix in the cream and taste for seasoning.

Noodles:

½ pound spinach
4 cups sifted flour
1½ teaspoons salt

3 eggs, beaten
4 tablespoons butter
½ cup grated Parmesan cheese

Wash and drain the spinach. Cook over low heat 5 minutes. Drain very well. Purée in an electric blender, force through a sieve or chop very fine. If spinach is wet, place over low heat until moisture evaporates.

Sift the flour and salt into a bowl. Make a well in the center and into it put the eggs and spinach. Work in the flour with the hands. Turn out onto a floured surface and knead until smooth and elastic. Form into a ball and cover with a bowl; let stand 20 minutes.

Divide dough into 4 pieces and roll out each piece paper thin, sprinkling with flour as you roll. Let dry 1 hour, then cut into 4-inch squares. Cook a few at a time in boiling salted water 2 minutes. Remove with a slotted spoon and drop into cold salted water. Drain and place on a cloth to dry.

In a buttered baking dish, spread a little sauce. Make as many successive layers as possible of the noodles, sauce, and grated cheese. End with sauce and cheese. Dot with the butter. Bake in a 375° oven 25 minutes. *Serves 6–8.*

Note: If you don't want to make the noodle dough, buy 1 pound green lasagne.

FISH, HOME STYLE

PESCI ALLA CASALINGA

3 tablespoons butter	1 tablespoon flour
2 tablespoons olive oil	½ cup bottled clam juice
3 onions, chopped	¼ teaspoon orégano
2 cloves garlic, minced	3 teaspoons salt
½ cup chopped mushrooms	¾ teaspoon freshly ground
¼ cup capers, drained	black pepper
3 tablespoons chopped parsley	6 slices bass, trout, or any other
¼ cup ground almonds	mild-flavored, white-meat fish

Combine the butter and olive oil in a large skillet. Add the onions and garlic and sauté for 10 minutes, stirring frequently. Add the mushrooms, capers, parsley, almonds, flour, stock, orégano, 1 teaspoon of the salt, and ¼ teaspoon of the pepper. Mix well. Cook over low heat for 10 minutes, stirring occasionally.

Combine the remaining salt and 1 teaspoon of pepper and sprinkle on the fish slices. Carefully place the slices on top of the vegetable mixture. Cover and cook over medium heat for 35 minutes. If desired, the fish may be baked, uncovered, in a 400° oven for 35 minutes. Serve immediately. *Serves 6.*

VEAL IN TUNA FISH SAUCE

VITELLO TONNATO

3 pounds rolled shoulder or leg of veal	1½ teaspoons salt
1 cup olive oil	½ teaspoon freshly ground black pepper
1 cup sliced onions	2 7-ounce cans tuna fish, drained
1 cup grated carrots	8 anchovy fillets
2 cloves garlic	1 egg yolk
2 bay leaves	2 tablespoons lemon juice
½ teaspoon thyme	2 tablespoons capers, rinsed
2 cups dry white wine	and drained
3 cups chicken broth	

Rinse and dry the veal.

Heat ¼ cup of the oil in a Dutch oven or heavy saucepan; lightly brown the veal in it. Pour off the fat. Add the onions, carrots, garlic, bay leaves, thyme, wine, broth, salt, and pepper. Cover and cook over low heat 2 hours, or until tender. Let the meat cool in the gravy. Remove the veal. Cook the gravy over high heat for 10 minutes. Strain ½ cup of the gravy.

If you have a blender, use it. Put the tuna fish, anchovies, egg yolk, lemon juice, and the remaining olive oil into the blender, and run at high speed until the mixture is puréed. Turn into a small bowl, and gradually mix in the reserved gravy. The sauce should now be the consistency of very heavy cream. Taste for seasoning and stir in the capers.

If you don't have a blender, mash the tuna fish and anchovies, then put through a fine sieve. Beat the egg yolk in a bowl with an electric mixer or whisk, and, still beating, add the lemon juice and tuna mixture. Add the oil by the half teaspoon, still beating, and when ¼ is used up, add it in a slow steady stream. Continue as directed for the blender method.

Cut the meat in thin slices. Cover the bottom of a serving dish with a thin layer of the sauce, and arrange the veal slices over it. Pour the rest of the sauce over it, and smooth it so as to cover each slice. Cover the dish with plastic wrap, and chill overnight, or for at least 4 hours. Let stand at room temperature for 30 minutes before serving. Garnish with lemon slices, black olives, and capers. *Serves 8–10 as a first course.*

FILLET OF BEEF WITH MARSALA

FILETTO AL MARSALA

2½ teaspoons salt	1 carrot, sliced
1 teaspoon freshly ground	¼ pound prosciutto ham,
black pepper	chopped
¼ teaspoon thyme	2 tablespoons flour
4-pound fillet of beef	1 cup beef broth
4 tablespoons butter	1 cup Marsala or sweet sherry
2 onions, chopped	2 tablespoons chopped parsley

Combine the salt, pepper, and thyme. Rub into the meat thoroughly. Melt the butter in a heavy pot or a Dutch oven, over direct heat. Add the meat and onions, and brown the meat on all sides. Add the carrot and ham. Sprinkle the flour on top of the meat and add the broth to the pan.

Place the meat in a 350° oven and roast for 45 minutes, basting occasionally. Remove the gravy, vegetables, and ham from the pan, and force through a sieve. Add the wine and combine with the puréed gravy. Pour over the meat. Continue roasting for 10 minutes, for rare meat, or 15 minutes for medium, 20 minutes for well done. Baste occasionally. Slice the meat and pour gravy over the slices. *Serves 6–8.*

STUFFED MEAT ROLLS

BRACIOLETTE RIPIENE

12 pieces sirloin steak, cut ¼ inch
   thick and about 3 by 5 inches
¾ cup minced parsley
½ cup blanched sliced almonds
2 tablespoons seedless raisins
2 tablespoons grated Parmesan
   cheese
1¼ teaspoons salt

¼ teaspoon freshly ground
   black pepper
12 thin slices prosciutto or
   cooked ham
4 tablespoons butter
¾ cup dry white wine
1 cup peeled chopped tomatoes

Pound the steak as thin as possible.

Mix together the parsley, almonds, raisins, and cheese. Season one side of each piece of steak with salt and pepper. On the unseasoned sides, place a slice of ham, cut to fit the meat. Put some of the parsley mixture on each, and roll up. Tie with thread or fasten with toothpicks.

Melt the butter in a skillet; brown the rolls on all sides. Add the wine and tomatoes, bring to a boil, cover, and cook over low heat 20 minutes. *Serves 4–6.*

SPAGHETTI WITH PORK-TOMATO SAUCE

SPAGHETTI ALL'AMATRICIANA

⅓ cup olive oil
½ pound lean raw pork, cut
   julienne
1½ pounds tomatoes, peeled and
   diced
1¼ teaspoons salt

¼ teaspoon crushed red pepper
1 pound spaghetti, cooked and
   drained
Grated Pecorino, Romano, or
   Parmesan cheese

Heat the oil in a skillet; brown the pork in it very well. Stir in the tomatoes, salt, and pepper. Cover and cook over low heat 20 minutes. Pour over the spaghetti and toss. Serve with grated cheese. *Serves 4–6.*

ROAST LEG OF LAMB

ABBACCHIO AL FORNO

3–4-pound leg of lamb
3 cloves garlic, cut in slivers
8 rosemary leaves or ½ teaspoon, dried
2 teaspoons salt

½ teaspoon freshly ground black pepper
4 tablespoons butter
1½ cups dry white wine

In Italy, *abbacchio* is newly born milk-fed lamb. Our hot house or baby lamb is not so young, but makes a good substitute. Make a few slits in the leg and into them insert some garlic and rosemary. Rub the leg with the salt and pepper. Place in a shallow roasting pan and dot with the butter. Roast in a 450° oven 25 minutes or until browned. Pour off the fat. Add the wine; reduce; reduce heat to 350° and roast 1 hour longer or until tender; baste frequently. *Serves 4–6.*

CHICKEN IN WHITE WINE

POLLO AL VINO BIANCO

2 teaspoons salt
1 teaspoon freshly ground black pepper
1 tablespoon flour
2 2½-pound chickens, disjointed
4 tablespoons olive oil
2 onions, chopped
1 cup white wine
1 tablespoon tomato paste

1 cup chicken broth
3 anchovies, mashed fine
¾ cup wine vinegar
2 cloves garlic, minced
1 tablespoon capers, drained
3 tablespoons chopped sweet pickles
2 tablespoons chopped parsley

Combine the salt, pepper, and flour. Rub into the chicken as thoroughly as possible. Heat the olive oil in a casserole or skillet. Add the onions and sauté for 5 minutes, stirring frequently. Add the chickens and brown well on all sides. Add the anchovies and wine; cook over high heat for 5 minutes. Mix the tomato paste and broth together and add, stirring well. Reduce heat to medium, cover, and cook for 45 minutes, or until chickens are tender.

In a small saucepan, bring the vinegar to a boil and cook over high heat for 2 minutes. Add the garlic, capers, pickles, and parsley and cook over low heat for 1 minute only. Pour over the chicken. Serve hot. *Serves 6–8.*

PEAS AND RICE

RISI E BISI

4 tablespoons butter	3½ cups hot chicken broth
3 tablespoons minced onions	1 pound fresh or 1 package
1 teaspoon salt	frozen green peas
¼ teaspoon white pepper	½ cup melted butter
1½ cups raw rice	¾ cup grated Parmesan cheese

Melt the 4 tablespoons butter in a saucepan; sauté the onions, salt, and pepper until yellow. Stir in the rice until yellow. Add half the hot broth. Cover and cook over low heat 10 minutes. Add the peas and remaining broth; re-cover and cook 10 minutes longer, or until rice and peas are tender. With a fork, stir in the melted butter and cheese. *Serves 6–8.*

Note: Since this is a rice dish, it should not be served when a thick soup or spaghetti is part of the meal.

CELERY, WITH CHEESE

SEDANI ALLA PARMIGIANA

3 bunches celery	¼ teaspoon white pepper
3 tablespoons butter	¼ cup grated Parmesan cheese
½ cup chicken broth	¼ cup grated Gruyère or
¼ cup chopped ham	American cheese
1 teaspoon salt	

Wash the celery thoroughly and remove the leaves. Cut into slices ½ inch thick. Melt the butter in a skillet. Add the celery and sauté for 5 minutes, stirring gently so as not to break up the slices. Add the broth, ham, salt, and pepper. Cover and cook over medium heat for 15 minutes. Drain carefully. Turn the celery into a buttered baking dish. Sprinkle the grated cheeses on top. Bake in a 425° oven for 15 minutes, or until the cheese is delicately browned. *Serves 6–8.*

TOMATO SAUCE FOR SPAGHETTI

SALSA DI POMODORO

¼ cup olive oil
3 onions, chopped
3 cloves garlic, minced
3 tablespoons chopped parsley
2 29-ounce cans Italian-style
  tomatoes

3 tablespoons dry white wine
2 teaspoons salt
½ teaspoon freshly ground
  black pepper
1 teaspoon orégano
¼ cup chopped mushrooms

Heat the olive oil in a saucepan. Add the onions and garlic and sauté for 10 minutes, stirring frequently. Add the parsley, tomatoes, wine, salt, pepper, and orégano. Stir well. Cover and cook over low heat for 2 hours. Add the mushrooms. Cover and cook over low heat for 2 hours. Force the mixture through a sieve. Correct seasoning. Serve over spaghetti or other Italian macaroni. A glass of Chianti, Barbera, or Bardolino wine is excellent with this sauce. *Makes about 1½ quarts.*

Note: The sauce improves with flavor as it cooks. If possible, make the sauce the day before it is used, and reheat before serving.

ANCHOVY SAUCE FOR SPAGHETTI

SALSA DI ACCIUGHE

½ cup olive oil
¼ pound (1 stick) butter
1 can anchovy fillets, undrained

8 cloves garlic, sliced
2 tablespoons chopped parsley

Combine the olive oil and butter in a saucepan. Cook over low heat until the butter melts. Mash the anchovies very fine. Add, with the oil from the can and the garlic, to the saucepan. Cook over medium heat for 1 minute, stirring constantly, or until garlic browns. Do not allow the garlic to burn. Add the parsley, stir well, and serve. The sauce may be poured over spaghetti. It may also be used as a dip or sauce for artichokes and broccoli. *Makes about 1 cup.*

Note: This sauce may be changed into the classic bagna cauda *sauce by adding 1 sliced truffle to the mixture when the anchovies are added.*

NOODLES WITH WALNUTS

GNOCCHI ALLA GRANERESE

1 cup ground walnuts
1 clove garlic, minced
1 pound Ricotta or cottage
   cheese
1 cup grated Parmesan cheese

2 teaspoons salt
½ teaspoon freshly ground
   black pepper
1 pound broad noodles

Roll or pound the walnuts and garlic on a board or in a mortar until a paste is formed. Place in a large bowl. Add the Ricotta and Parmesan cheeses, salt, and pepper. Mix well. Boil the noodles in salted water until tender, about 10 minutes. Drain. Add to the walnut mixture and toss lightly with two forks until the noodles are well coated. Place on a heated platter and serve. *Serves 4–6.*

POTATO BALLS

GNOCCHI

3 pounds potatoes (about
   8 large potatoes)
2 egg yolks, beaten
2 tablespoons salt

1 cup sifted flour
Boiling water
⅓ cup grated Parmesan cheese
¼ cup melted butter

Boil and mash the potatoes. Add the egg yolks and 2 teaspoons of the salt, beating well. Add the flour gradually, adding just enough so that a dough is formed; it may not be necessary to add all of the flour. Knead the dough until very smooth. Break off pieces and roll out ¾ inch in diameter and about 1½ inches long.

Add the remaining salt to a large saucepan of boiling water. Drop the *gnocchi* into it, about 10 at a time. When they come to the surface, remove them immediately, drain, and keep warm. Continue until all of the *gnocchi* have been cooked. Place the *gnocchi* in a serving dish and sprinkle with Parmesan cheese and melted butter. If desired, serve with a little hot tomato sauce. *Serves 8–10.*

SPAGHETTI WITH EGG AND BACON SAUCE

SPAGHETTI ALLA CARBONARA

4 tablespoons butter
2 tablespoons olive oil
½ cup julienne-cut ham
½ cup julienne-cut lean bacon
½ cup thinly sliced mushrooms
½ teaspoon freshly ground
   black pepper

¼ cup grated Pecorino or
   Parmesan cheese
2 eggs, beaten
1 pound spaghetti, cooked and
   drained

Heat the butter and oil in a skillet; sauté the ham, bacon, mushrooms,
and pepper 5 minutes, but do not let brown. Remove from the heat and
stir in the cheese, then the eggs. Toss with the spaghetti. *Serves 4.*

GREEN SALAD

INSALATA VERDE

1 cup chopped green pepper
1 cup chopped red pepper
2 teaspoons chopped parsley
½ cup chopped fresh tomatoes
2 tablespoons chopped celery
2 scallions (green onions),
   sliced
6 radishes, chopped

1 teaspoon chopped anchovies
2 tablespoons capers
½ teaspoon salt
¼ teaspoon freshly ground
   black pepper
3 tablespoons wine vinegar
½ cup olive oil

Combine the green pepper, red pepper, parsley, tomatoes, celery, scallions, radishes, anchovies, capers, salt, and pepper in a bowl. Add the
vinegar, mixing lightly. Add the olive oil very gradually, mixing thoroughly. Chill and serve. *Serves 4–6.*

ALMOND SPONGECAKE

BOCCA DI DAMA

5 egg yolks
5 tablespoons sugar
3 tablespoons sifted flour
3 tablespoons finely ground
   almonds

2 teaspoons grated lemon rind
5 egg whites
1 cup heavy cream
¼ cup confectioners' sugar
¼ cup sliced toasted almonds

Preheat oven to 300°.
Butter a 9-inch layer-cake pan and dust lightly with flour.

Beat the egg yolks in the top of a double boiler. Add 4 tablespoons sugar, beating well. Place over hot water and beat with a rotary beater for 5–10 minutes. Remove from heat. Combine the flour, almonds, lemon rind, and remaining sugar; add to the yolk mixture. Beat the egg whites until stiff but not dry. Fold them into the previous mixture carefully. Pour mixture into the pan. Bake in a 300° oven for 35 minutes, or until a cake tester comes out clean. Allow to cool in the pan, then turn out.

Whip the cream and add the confectioners' sugar. Cover the cake with it and sprinkle the sliced almonds on top. The cake is also very good with fruits instead of the sliced almonds. *Serves 6–8.*

NUT TART

TORTA DI NOCI

1¼ cups finely ground walnuts	1 teaspoon vanilla extract
¾ cup sugar	1 teaspoon grated lemon rind
⅓ cup unsweetened cocoa	4 egg whites
4 egg yolks, beaten	2 tablespoons dry bread crumbs

Combine the walnuts, sugar, and cocoa in a bowl. Gradually add the egg yolks, beating well. Add the vanilla extract and lemon rind and mix well. Preheat oven to 350°. Beat the egg whites until stiff but not dry and fold them into the mixture carefully. Butter a 9-inch glass baking dish and dust with the bread crumbs. Pour the mixture into it. Bake in a 350° oven for 30 minutes, or until a cake tester comes out clean. The tart may be served hot or cold. When eaten hot, the texture is somewhat like that of a soufflé. *Serves 6–8.*

NORWAY

Norway and Alaska have in common the fact that they are in similar latitudes, but differ in that Alaska has warmer winters and Norway has milder summers. At least this is true for the two cities of Oslo, Norway, and Juneau, Alaska.

Pan American planes land at Fornebu Airport, rather a long ride from Oslo, but one that will immediately give the visitor an opportunity to learn something of the country.

This is a tourist land and it is becoming more so with each successive year. Filled with scenery that may honestly be described as awe-inspiring, populated with sturdy, resourceful people, Norway attracts more and more tourists. The *fjords*, the coastal chasms of the western part of the country, and the North Cape, the land of the Lapps, are must-sees for every visitor. From May until September, Norway has practically no darkness at all; in the northern portion of the country it is not only light but quite bright every hour of the day. It requires an effort to go to bed with the sun shining, even though your watch tells you it is after midnight, but it is a wonderful experience.

The very things that make Norway so exciting for the visitor, such as the mountains, the scenery, and the rugged countryside, also militate to the nation's disadvantage, for only a small part of the land, estimated to be as little as three per cent, is suitable for agriculture. By force of circumstances, the people have turned to grazing cattle and to the sea for their food.

Herring is the principal fish, though cod and mackerel are almost equally important. Herring is eaten fresh, dried, smoked, salted, spiced, pickled, and even made into *sildegryn* (herring soup)! There are apparently no dishes calling for whipped cream and herring, but there are several made with sour cream. In a country where fish is such an important part of the diet, it is understandable that the Norwegians should excel in fish cookery. To the housewife's way of thinking, fresh fish must be really fresh, and she will often buy her fish only from the boat from which it was actually caught, particularly at the renowned Bergen market. Smoked fish is much appreciated here; a local specialty is an overripe fish dish, *rakørret-raketrout*, or salted trout kept for a month or longer until it is ripe. To those who would turn up their nose, it is only necessary to remind them of our fine cheeses, kept until they have reached the desired state of moldiness—pardon, ripeness.

The Norwegians love codfish, and eat it regularly. Of course it's served boiled, but also smoked, creamed, pressed between two wooden boards, prepared with potash lye, and so forth. Another favorite—this time, meat —is mutton, that is, mature lamb with a strong taste as opposed to the young lamb popular in the United States. It's used sometimes to make *lapskaus*, a mutton stew; also *fenalår*, which is smoked cured leg of mutton; not to mention *pinnekjøtt*, dried salted mutton; *puss pass*, mutton cooked with potatoes and vegetables and heavily peppered; and possibly the favorite of all, *faar i kaal*, which is mutton and cabbage.

Although most of the usual meat dishes are eaten with appreciation, Norway has for the intrepid eater more unusual fare, such as elk, bear, and especially reindeer steak (*rensdyrstek*), all of which are eaten fresh, dried, and salted. Grouse, elk, and hare are other common game sources.

Breads follow the Scandinavian pattern, and the *flattbröd,* wafer-thin, is unusually good. Dairy products are excellent and the local cheeses outstanding. *Gjetost,* the chocolate-colored goat's milk cheese, and *gammelost,* made of fermented cow's milk, may be singled out for comment. Desserts follow the Swedish style, although there are exceptions.

Norwegians drink a considerable quantity of hard liquor; a little too much, by their own admission. The favorite is *dram,* similar to *snaps* in Sweden. Beer is very good, and the local fruit wines, *fruktvin,* are worth trying.

There is much good food to be had in Norway, particularly in the restaurants of Oslo. The Kongen and Dronningen restaurants are the apparent leaders, but the Speilen and Telle are both high on any list for fine meals.

LIVER LOAF

LEVERPOSTEI

1½ pounds calf or beef liver	1 cup fresh bread crumbs
¼ pound salt pork	2 tablespoons grated onion
2 anchovy fillets	2 teaspoons salt
3 eggs, beaten	½ teaspoon freshly ground
2 tablespoons milk	black pepper

Preheat oven to 350°.

Wash the liver carefully and remove any membranes. Grind it 3 times with the salt pork and anchovies. Place in a bowl and add the eggs, milk, bread crumbs, grated onion, salt, and pepper. Mix until very smooth. Butter a 9-inch loaf pan and pour the mixture into it. If desired, the pan may be lined with very thin slices of salt pork. Place the loaf pan in a pan of hot water. Bake in a 350° oven for 1½ hours. Let the pan cool for a while at room temperature, then place it in the refrigerator to chill. Cut into ½-inch slices and serve cold as an appetizer with thin slices of buttered rye or pumpernickel bread. *Serves 8–10.*

HERRING SOUP

SILDEGRYN

½ cup dried yellow peas	¼ teaspoon salt
½ cup barley	½ teaspoon pepper
3½ quarts water	3 potatoes, peeled and sliced
1 turnip, sliced	¼ teaspoon thyme
1 carrot, sliced	2 salt herring, filleted and
1 onion, chopped	sliced ½ inch thick

Soak the peas overnight in water to cover, if a presoaked variety is not used. Drain well. Combine the peas, barley, and water in a saucepan. Cook over medium heat for 45 minutes. Add the turnip, carrot, onion, salt, and pepper. Cover and cook for 45 minutes. Add the potatoes and thyme and stir well. Cook for 25 minutes. Add the herring slices and cook 5 minutes longer. Correct seasoning. Serve hot. *Serves 8–10.*

POACHED BAKED SALMON

FORLORNE LAKS

3 1-inch-thick slices salmon
2 teaspoons salt
½ teaspoon freshly ground
   black pepper
2 tablespoons flour
3 tablespoons butter

1½ cups hot heavy cream
1 bay leaf
3 tablespoons chopped onions
2 tablespoons minced dill or
   parsley

Cut the salmon slices in half through the bone and rub with a mixture of the salt, pepper, and flour. Melt the butter in a baking dish; lightly brown the fish on both sides. Add the cream, bay leaf, and onions. Bake in a 400° oven 30 minutes, or until fish flakes easily when tested with a form. Baste frequently. Discard bay leaf and sprinkle with the dill or parsley. *Serves 6.*

ROAST FRESH HAM

SKINNESTEK

1½ tablespoons salt
1½ teaspoons freshly ground
   black pepper
1 teaspoon nutmeg
1 fresh ham

1½ cups boiling water
2 tablespoons butter
2 tablespoons flour
½ teaspoon dry mustard

Combine the salt, pepper, and nutmeg; rub into the ham thoroughly. Score the fat in several places with a knife. Place the ham in a roasting pan. Roast in a 450° oven for 30 minutes. Add the boiling water, reduce the oven temperature to 350°, and roast 25 minutes a pound.

Remove the gravy from the pan and skim off all the fat. Add water if necessary to make 1½ cups of gravy. Melt the butter in a saucepan. Add the flour and mustard, stirring until smooth. Add the gravy, stirring constantly until the boiling point is reached. Cook over low heat for 5 minutes. Correct seasoning. Carve the ham and serve the gravy separately. *Serves 8–10.*

CAULIFLOWER WITH SHRIMP SAUCE

BLOMKÅL MED REKESOS

3 tablespoons butter
1 cup fresh bread crumbs
1½ cups milk
1 teaspoon salt
1 teaspoon sugar

1 cup coarsely chopped cooked
   shrimp
1 tablespoon brandy
1 whole cauliflower

Melt the butter in a saucepan. Add the bread crumbs, mixing well. Add the milk, stirring constantly until the boiling point is reached. Add the salt, sugar, and shrimp and cook over low heat for 5 minutes. Remove from heat and add the brandy. Place a whole head of firm cauliflower in a large saucepan of boiling, salted water. Cook for 20–25 minutes but do not allow to overcook. Place the sauce over low heat and allow to thicken for 2 minutes. Drain the cauliflower completely and place on a serving platter. Pour the sauce over it and serve at once. *Serves 6–8.*

RAW POTATO DUMPLINGS

KUMLER

6 (2 pounds) potatoes, peeled
1 teaspoon salt
⅛ teaspoon thyme
⅓ cup cracker meal

2 tablespoons flour
¼ pound pork, diced
6 cups beef broth

Grate the potatoes into a bowl. Add the salt and thyme and stir. Mix in the cracker meal and flour. The mixture should be fairly stiff; add a little more cracker meal if necessary. Wet the palms of the hands and form the mixture into 1-inch balls. Press a cube or two of pork into the center of each ball and roll in the hands so that the pork is completely covered. Place the broth in a saucepan and bring it to a boil. Drop the dumplings into it and cook over low heat for 1 hour. Serve with soup, boiled meats, or sausages. *Serves 8–10.*

CHRISTMAS CAKE

JULEKAKE

2 cakes or packages yeast
½ cup sugar
1⅓ cups lukewarm milk
3¾ cups sifted flour
½ teaspoon ground cardamom
seeds

¼ cup melted butter
¼ pound butter
¾ cup chopped candied fruit
¼ cup seedless raisins

Place the yeast in a bowl with 1 tablespoon of the sugar and ¼ cup of the milk. Mix until smooth. Add 3 tablespoons of the flour and mix again. Cover and allow to rise in a warm place for 20 minutes. Combine the remaining sugar, remaining flour, and the cardamom seeds in a bowl. Add the melted butter and the remaining milk. Mix well and beat in the yeast mixture. Cover and allow to rise in a warm place for 30 minutes.

Cut the butter into small dots and knead into the dough. Place the dough on a lightly floured surface and knead for 5 minutes. Add the candied fruit and the raisins and knead until they are well distributed. Butter two 12-inch loaf pans and dust lightly with flour. Divide the dough in half, shape into loaves, and place in the pans. Brush the top of each loaf with a little milk. Cover with a cloth and allow to rise for 20 minutes. Preheat oven to 375°. Bake for 35 minutes, or until lightly browned. *Serves 10–12.*

BUTTER MERINGUE CAKE

TÅRTA

½ pound (2 sticks) sweet butter
2½ cups sugar
6 egg yolks
¾ cup sifted flour
2 teaspoons baking powder

⅔ cup milk
2 teaspoons vanilla extract
8 egg whites
¾ cup finely ground walnuts
1½ cups heavy cream

Preheat oven to 325°.

Cream the butter well. Add 1 cup of the sugar and continue creaming until light and fluffy. Add the egg yolks and beat well. Sift the flour and baking powder together and add to the butter mixture alternately with the milk. Beat well. Mix in the vanilla. Butter two 9-inch layer-cake pans. (Use pans with removable or slip bottoms, or spring-form pans, if possible.) Dust lightly with flour. Divide the mixture evenly and place half in each pan.

Beat the egg whites until stiff but not dry. Gradually add the remaining sugar, beating well. Spread this mixture on top of the cake batter to within 1½ inches of the outside edges of the pans. Sprinkle with the walnuts. Bake in a 325° oven for 40 minutes. Cool on a cake rack for 1 hour.

Whip the cream. Remove the layers from the tin, meringue side up. Spread the whipped cream on top of the meringue and put layers together, meringue sides up. Sprinkle a few walnuts on top, if desired. *Serves 8–10.*

POLAND

Poland, which has seen so much unhappiness in the past centuries, is filled with many conflicting ways of life. Surrounded by two larger and more powerful neighbors, Russia to the east and Germany to the west, the nation has never been at peace with itself or with the world for any great length of time.

Since Poland was once part of Russia, the Russian influence on Polish food is strongly felt. The great beet soup of Poland, its *barszcz,* is a first cousin to Russia's *borscht,* although there are differences. Poles, however, are great individualists, and there are many talented amateur cooks and chefs in Poland; most Poles fancy themselves as gourmets, and possibly they are correct in their belief. Certainly it cannot be denied that they evince great interest in food, and Polish food is well recognized for its fine qualities.

The cuisine of the country is largely based upon the following: freshwater fish, ham and pork, sour cream, dark breads, mushrooms, cucumbers, game dishes, sauerkraut, noodles and dumplings, rich cakes, and buckwheat groats, *kasza,* as they are called in Poland.

A great national favorite is the mushroom, of which the Poles are excessively fond. For the most part these fungi grow wild in Poland's forests, are gathered by the peasants and brought to the markets, fresh and moist. Dried mushrooms find their way into homes all over the globe. Cucumbers are also enormously popular and are prepared in many ways, often with sour cream.

The people's reason for loving such growing things of the fields and forests as cucumbers, radishes, scallions, and mushrooms is not hard to discern. Winter in Poland bears little resemblance to our own. In America, snowplows immediately clear the roads, television breaks the monotony for the few people who are snowbound, and those who can, go to Florida for two weeks. In Poland, when winter begins the people are forced into a state of semihibernation. Snow covers the landscape, there is little sun, and Florida is a long way off. When spring comes and the earth permits the tender green shoots to emerge, the people rejoice in a way that we, who live around the corner from a supermarket that has strawberries in February, will find hard to comprehend.

Because of these cold winters the people are interested in solid and substantial fare rather than in delicacies which would tempt a jaded palate. That is not to say that Polish food is not exciting or stimulating to the appetite, because it certainly is that. However, it does mean that much of the cuisine is based upon filling and satisfying ingredients.

By the same token, Poles are very fond of rich desserts, particularly cakes. *Babka,* more or less the national cake, is made of a yeast dough, often filled with many kinds of candied fruits, raisins and nuts, and covered with a sugar glaze.

To correct one misunderstanding about Polish drinking habits: they do not drink *vodka,* as you might have thought previously; they drink *woudka.* There's a great difference, for the Polish drink has a *w* instead of a *v,* and somehow a *u* sneaked in. It must be admitted that, other than the difference in spelling, both drinks taste exactly the same. The people prefer coffee to tea (when they can afford it), and beer to wine.

BEET SOUP

BARSZCZ

½ cup dried lima beans
8 large beets, peeled and halved
2 pounds stewing beef, cut into
    2-inch cubes
    (Beef bones if available)
1 cup canned tomatoes
3 quarts water

2-pound head cabbage, shredded
1 apple, peeled and quartered
2 teaspoons salt
1 teaspoon freshly ground
    black pepper
Sour cream

Wash the beans carefully. Soak in water to cover overnight. Cook in the same water 2 hours until tender. Drain and reserve. Combine the beets, meat, tomatoes, and water in a deep saucepan. Bring to a boil and skim the top. Cook over medium heat for 1½ hours. Add the cabbage, apple, salt, and pepper. Cook for 30 minutes. Add the lima beans. Correct seasoning. Cook 15 minutes. Grate the beets and return to the saucepan. Serve very hot, with a tablespoon of sour cream and a few pieces of meat in each plate. *Serves 8–10.*

PIKE WITH EGG SAUCE

SANDACZ

3 (1 pound) onions, sliced
1 carrot, sliced thin
1 slice lemon
2 cups water
2 teaspoons salt
1 teaspoon freshly ground
    black pepper

6 slices (2 inches thick) pike or
    other fresh-water, white-meat
    fish
2 tablespoons salt butter
4 hard-cooked eggs, chopped
3 tablespoons lemon juice

In a large saucepan place the onions, carrot, lemon, water, salt, pepper, and fish. Bring to a boil. Cook over medium heat for 40 minutes. Melt the butter in a separate saucepan and add the chopped eggs and lemon juice. Cook 2 minutes. Arrange the drained fish on a platter and pour the egg sauce over it. *Serves 6.*

Note: If fresh-water fish isn't available, use sole.

SAUERKRAUT WITH PORK

KAPUSTA Z WIEPRZOWINA

2 tablespoons vegetable oil or
    butter
3 pounds spareribs, cut into
    individual pieces, or 6 pork
    chops
1 cup coarsely chopped onions
2 cloves garlic, minced
1 teaspoon salt

½ teaspoon freshly ground
    black pepper
1 bay leaf
1½ cups boiling water
1 pound sauerkraut
1 apple, peeled and chopped
2 tablespoons barley
1 teaspoon caraway seeds

Heat the oil in a large saucepan, add the pork and cook over high heat, turning the meat frequently until it is brown on all sides. Add the onions and garlic, cook over medium heat until the onions and garlic are browned. Mix in the salt, pepper, bay leaf, and water and cook for 30 minutes, stirring occasionally. Add the undrained sauerkraut, apple, barley, and caraway seeds and mix well. Continue cooking for 1 hour, or until meat is tender. Correct seasoning and remove the bay leaf. Serve the pork and sauerkraut together. *Serves 6.*

STUFFED DOUGH POCKETS

USZKA

2 cups sifted flour	1 onion, chopped
1 teaspoon salt	1½ pounds mushrooms, chopped
2 eggs, beaten	¼ teaspoon freshly ground
⅓ cup water	black pepper
2 tablespoons butter	

Sift the flour and ½ teaspoon of the salt into a bowl. Beat in the eggs and water. Knead until smooth, cover, and set aside while preparing the filling.

Melt the butter in a skillet. Add the onion, mushrooms, pepper, and remaining salt. Sauté for 10 minutes, stirring frequently. Cook over high heat for 1 minute to evaporate any liquid. Cool for 15 minutes.

Roll out the dough ⅛ inch thick on a lightly floured surface. Cut into 3-inch squares. Place a tablespoon of the mushroom mixture in the center and fold over the dough, sealing the edges carefully. Cook in boiling salted water for 12 minutes. Drain well. If desired, after the *uszka* are boiled, they may be fried in butter. Serve in soups, or as an accompaniment to meat dishes. *Makes about 30.*

POTATO DUMPLINGS

KARTOFLANE KLUSKI

1 cup cold mashed potatoes	½ teaspoon baking powder
3 eggs, beaten	3 slices white bread
1 teaspoon salt	¼ cup butter
1 cup sifted flour	

Place the mashed potatoes in a bowl. Add the beaten eggs and the salt. Beat well. Add the flour and baking powder and again beat well. Cut the bread into small cubes. Melt the butter in a saucepan, and brown the cubes of bread on all sides.

Take a heaping tablespoon of the potato mixture and wrap it around several fried cubes of bread, forming them into 2-inch balls. Place them carefully in boiling, salted water. Cover and cook for 15 minutes. Drain well. Serve with meat dishes. *Makes about 12.*

POLISH COFFEECAKE

BABKA

¼ pound (1 stick) butter
½ cup sugar
1 teaspoon salt
3 egg yolks, beaten
1 cake or package yeast
¼ cup lukewarm water
2 tablespoons grated lemon rind
½ cup seedless raisins

2 cups sifted flour
½ cup light cream, scalded and cooled
3 tablespoons crushed zwieback crumbs
1 tablespoon cinnamon
3 tablespoons chopped almonds

Cream the butter, then add the sugar. Continue creaming until well blended. Add the salt and egg yolks and beat. Place the yeast in the ¼ cup lukewarm water and stir until dissolved. Add the previous mixture. Add the lemon rind and raisins and stir well. Gradually add the flour and the ½ cup cream alternately, beating well after each addition. Turn out onto a lightly floured surface and knead the dough until it becomes elastic and does not stick to the fingers. Place it in a bowl, cover, and put in a warm place to rise for 1 hour. At the end of this time punch the dough down firmly, re-cover, and allow to rise for 2 hours longer.

Butter a 12-inch loaf pan and dust with the zwieback crumbs. Place the dough in the pan, brush with a little milk, and sprinkle with the cinnamon and almonds. Bake in a 350° oven for 30 minutes. *Makes one 12-inch loaf.*

PORTUGAL

This comparatively small but resolute nation, facing upon the Atlantic Ocean, draws its livelihood primarily from the sea. Thus you would expect the cuisine of the country to be based upon seafood. The visitor expects to see fish, his mind accepts the possibility of seeing tremendous quantities of fish, and he anticipates eating all sorts of delectable fish dishes. The realization is here greater than any possible anticipation, for the mind cannot cope with the enormous catches made by the fishermen; a visit to the fishing docks may often be described as stupefying.

Shellfish are prepared in hundreds of different ways, but oysters and crabs are notably of the highest rank. Oysters from Portugal are highly regarded in France, that land of forty million gourmets. Any possible excess in the population of France over forty million is undoubtedly composed of infants under one year of age and visiting Americans.

For those who have not examined the mark of origin on a can of sardines in recent months, it should also be pointed out that this is the home base of that amazingly fertile fish, which reproduces itself by the billions. The Portuguese prefer them fresh or dried rather than canned. Another pillar of the local cuisine is the humble cod, the *bacalhau*. Soups and chowders are often made of seafood and are uniformly excellent.

But it must not be assumed that seafood is the sum total of all that is noteworthy in Portugal. There are excellent meat dishes of which *iscas* (calf's liver) and *carne de vinha* (spicy pickled meat) are merely representative examples. Many desserts are rich, sticky pastries of astronomical caloric value. Far better than the pastries and egg-based puddings that usually end meals are the fresh fruits, which are superb when in season. Perhaps accompanied by a Portuguese cheese, the meal will then close on a high note. The Portuguese will tell you that the leading cheese is *serra*, which is rich and creamy, with a slightly salty aftertaste; it's a cheese you won't forget too easily. In addition, *serpa* cheese is somewhat like *serra*, but a bit drier, a touch less salty, with a very pleasant aftertaste. Although there are other good cheeses, it's always a good idea when dining to ask if they have any fresh locally made white cheese, typically called *queijo fresco*, and they may be eaten plain, with sugar or preserves, or with fruit or berries. Indeed, the flavor is so delicate that they're equally good as a first course, perhaps sprinkled with salt and pepper.

Most people remark how close a resemblance Portuguese food bears to that of its neighbor, Spain, but the Portuguese version is likely to have garlic in it, which is used much more sparingly next door. French influence on the local cuisine is also strong, but actually, and somewhat irrationally, the food seems closer to that of Italy than any other country, especially in the use of garlic, oil, tomatoes, and onions. In fact the French expression *à la portugaise* means that those ingredients appear in a given dish.

Until recently the Portuguese people strongly criticized their own port wine. Their objection was based upon the fact that, before being marketed, the wine received many additives: about twenty per cent brandy, artificial red coloring, and elderberries were introduced into the product. A good deal of substandard wine was shipped out of the country only to run into additional adverse criticism. At the present time Portuguese legislation prohibits many of these practices and the great name of port is slowly regaining its former eminence. Formerly the bulk of this wine was shipped to Britain, where it was highly regarded. In recent years the British palate has changed and the demand has dwindled somewhat; Portuguese wine merchants are finding it extremely difficult to locate a substitute market.

Tawny and ruby port are the best known, but one of the most interesting types is the so-called "crusted" port, in which a sort of crusted deposit forms on the inside of the bottle. Madeira is well thought of by experts but has found a rather small audience in the competitive world market. It is available both as a dry wine, suitable for use before dinner, and also in a sweet type for desserts or after-dinner consumption. The best known of these are the Sercial and the Malvasia.

As to table wines, Portugal has a fair enough selection, none of them outstanding or world-renowned, but delicious with lunch or dinner and quite inexpensive. Unique to the country are its *vinhos verdes,* which translates as "green wines." The term does not mean that the wine is green in color, but rather that it's young and "green" in that sense. *Vinhos verdes* come in white and red types, but the vast majority of it is available as a dry red wine; the white type is semisweet. These very young wines have a little bite to them, and are somewhat sparkling. The bubbles are natural, and not produced by a secondary fermentation as is the practice with champagne. *Vinhos verdes* are quite delicious, easy to drink on a warm day, but carry a considerable amount of power, which may be noted when consumed in quantity.

GREEN SOUP

CALDO VERDE

2½ quarts water	½ teaspoon freshly ground
4 tablespoons olive oil	black pepper
4 potatoes, peeled and diced	2 pounds kale or 1 pound
2 teaspoons salt	spinach and 1 pound cabbage

Combine the water, olive oil, and potatoes in a saucepan. Cook over medium heat for 30 minutes. Force the potatoes through a sieve or mash them as fine as possible. Return them to the liquid in the saucepan. Add salt and pepper and cook over low heat for 1 hour. Wash the kale (or the spinach and cabbage if they are substituted for the kale) and remove the tough fibers. Shred finely and drain well. Add to the potato mixture and cook over medium heat for 15 minutes, stirring occasionally. Correct seasoning. Serve hot or cold. *Serves 8–10.*

PORTUGUESE FISH SOUP

SOPA À PORTUGUESA

3 tablespoons olive oil
3 fillets of sole or other
  white-meat fish
1 pound shrimp, peeled and
  cleaned
3 cups water
3 cups bottled clam juice
6 sprigs parsley
½ teaspoon basil
6 white onions

5 slices bread, trimmed
6 hard-cooked egg yolks,
  mashed
1 cup ground almonds
1½ teaspoons salt
1 teaspoon freshly ground
  black pepper
6 slices toast (French bread, if
  possible)

Heat the olive oil in a frying pan. Add the fillets and brown on both
sides. Set aside. Combine the shrimp, water, clam juice, parsley, basil,
and onions in a saucepan. Cook over medium heat for 10 minutes. Add
the fried fillets, bread, and egg yolks. Cook over medium heat for 15 minutes. Force the mixture through a sieve and return it to the saucepan.
Add the almonds, salt, and pepper. Cook over low heat, stirring constantly, until hot, but do not allow the mixture to boil. Place a slice of
toast in each soup plate and pour the soup over it. The result is so thick
that it might well be considered as a stew but it is an old Portuguese
soup recipe. *Serves 6–8.*

CODFISH, PORTUGUESE STYLE

BACALHAU À GOMES DE SÁ

2 pounds dried codfish
6 potatoes
1 cup olive oil
3 large onions, sliced
4 cloves garlic, minced

1 teaspoon freshly ground
  black pepper
½ cup dry white wine
6 hard-cooked eggs
¼ cup chopped parsley

Wash the fish thoroughly, in several changes of water. Soak the fish overnight in water to cover. Drain well. Add fresh water to cover. Cook
over medium heat for 20 minutes. Drain, reserving the liquid. Remove
the skin and bones carefully. Shred the fish coarsely. Cook the unpeeled
potatoes in the fish stock until tender, about 30 minutes. Peel and slice
thin.

Heat the olive oil in a frying pan. Add the onions and garlic and sauté
for 5 minutes. Add the fish and potatoes. Cook over high heat for 2 minutes, stirring constantly. Add the pepper and white wine and stir. Place

the mixture in a buttered baking dish or casserole. Bake in a 425° oven for 15 minutes. Chop 3 of the eggs coarsely and slice the other 3. Garnish with the eggs and parsley. Serve directly from the baking dish or casserole. *Serves 8–10.*

CALF'S LIVER IN WINE

ISCAS

12 thin slices calf's liver	1 bay leaf
2 cloves garlic, minced	1 cup dry white wine
1 teaspoon salt	¼ cup olive oil
½ teaspoon freshly ground	
black pepper	

Wash the liver carefully. Combine the garlic, salt, pepper, bay leaf, and wine in a bowl. Add the liver and marinate overnight in the refrigerator. Baste occasionally. Heat the olive oil in a frying pan until it smokes. Add the liver slices and wine mixture all at once. Stir gently, but constantly for 5 minutes. Serve immediately. *Serve 4–6.*

TRIPE, OPORTO FASHION

TRIPAS À MODA DO PORTO

2 cups dried white beans	2 tablespoons olive oil
2 pounds tripe	3 large onions, chopped
1½ quarts water	4 tomatoes, peeled and chopped
2 chicken breasts, removed from bone and cubed	2 teaspoons salt
½ pound ham, cubed	1 teaspoon freshly ground black pepper
½ pound sausage (Portuguese or Spanish type, if possible), sliced	

Soak beans in water to cover overnight. Drain. Add fresh water to cover. Cook over medium heat until tender, about 1½ hours. Drain. Cut the tripe into small pieces and combine in a large saucepan with the water. Cook over medium heat 2 hours. Add the chicken, ham, and sausage and cook over low heat 1 hour longer. Drain, reserving the stock.

Heat olive oil in a saucepan. Add the onions and sauté for 10 minutes, stirring frequently. Add the tomatoes, beans, cooked meat, 2 cups of the stock, salt, and pepper. Stir well and cook over low heat for 30 minutes. Correct seasoning and add a little more stock if necessary. The dish should have the consistency of a thick stew. Serve hot. *Serves 8–10.*

SPICY PICKLED PORK

CARNE DE VINHA

2 cups vinegar
1 tablespoon salt
½ teaspoon thyme
1 teaspoon dried ground chili
    peppers
3 cloves garlic, minced

2 bay leaves
3 cloves
3 pounds boneless pork loin
2 tablespoons olive oil
6 slices stale bread

Combine the vinegar, salt, thyme, chili peppers, garlic, bay leaves, and cloves in a large bowl. Place the pork in it and baste for 5 minutes. Marinate in the refrigerator for 2 days. Turn the pork several times.

Place the pork and marinade in a saucepan, cover, and cook over medium heat for 45 minutes. Drain the pork but reserve the marinade. Heat the olive oil in a frying pan and brown the pork in it on all sides. Continue frying for 35 minutes, or until the pork is tender. Dip the bread in the marinade and fry in the oil in which the pork was browned. Fry until the bread is browned on both sides. Slice the pork and serve it with the fried bread slices. *Serves 6–8.*

STUFFED CAPON

GALUIHA RECHIADA

7-pound capon
1½ tablespoons salt
2 teaspoons freshly ground
    black pepper
3 cups dry white wine
¼ pound (1 stick) butter
4 onions, chopped
½ teaspoon nutmeg

1 teaspoon cinnamon
2 cups fresh bread crumbs
1½ cups sliced green olives
6 hard-cooked eggs, coarsely
    chopped
1 teaspoon vinegar
½ cup milk, scalded

Wash and dry the capon, reserving the gizzard and liver. Combine 1 tablespoon of the salt and 1½ teaspoons of the pepper and rub it into the capon inside and out. Place the capon in a large bowl or pan and pour the wine over it. Marinate overnight in the refrigerator. Baste occasionally.

Place the gizzard in a saucepan with water to cover and boil for 30 minutes. Add the liver and boil 5 minutes longer. Drain. Cut up the gizzard and liver finely. Melt the butter in a skillet. Add the onions and sauté for 10 minutes, stirring frequently. Combine the sautéed onions with the nutmeg, cinnamon, remaining salt and pepper, bread crumbs, olives, eggs, vinegar, milk, and the gizzard and liver. Mix well.

Drain the capon but reserve the wine. Stuff the capon with the previous mixture, fastening the opening with skewers or with thread, or cover with a piece of aluminum foil. Roast the capon in a 350° oven for 2½ hours or until tender. Add 1 cup of the reserved wine after the first 30 minutes of roasting time. Baste frequently, adding more wine if required. *Serves 4–6.*

FRIED BREAD DESSERT

RABANADAS

3 cups milk	4 eggs, beaten
⅓ cup honey	1 cup vegetable oil
⅓ cup sugar	¼ cup confectioners' sugar
2 tablespoons grated lemon rind	¼ cup cinnamon
½ cinnamon stick	
⅛ teaspoon salt	
12 slices French bread (½ inch thick) or 6 slices white bread, cut in half	

Combine the milk, honey, sugar, lemon rind, cinnamon stick, and salt in a saucepan. Bring to a boil and cook over low heat for 1 hour. Remove from the heat. Dip the bread slices in this mixture and then in the beaten eggs. Heat ½ cup of the oil in a frying pan. Fry the bread in it until light brown on both sides. Add additional oil as required. Cool the fried bread for 30 minutes. Serve with the confectioners' sugar and cinnamon. *Serves 6.*

MERINGUE IN CUSTARD

LEITE CREME CON FARÓFIAS

2 cups milk	1 cup sugar
1½ cups light cream	3 egg yolks
2 teaspoons vanilla extract	2 tablespoons cornstarch
3 egg whites	1 teaspoon cinnamon

Combine the milk, cream, and vanilla in a saucepan and bring to a boil slowly over low heat. Beat the egg whites until stiff but not dry. Add ½ cup of the sugar gradually, beating well. Drop a tablespoon of the egg whites into the boiling milk mixture. Turn continuously with a fork until firm. Remove each meringue carefully and drain. Continue until all of the egg whites are used up. Reserve the milk.

Beat the egg yolks, cornstarch, and remaining sugar in a saucepan. Gradually add the reserved milk, stirring constantly until the boiling point is reached. Pour the mixture into a large serving bowl and place the meringues carefully on top. Sprinkle with the cinnamon. Chill for at least 2 hours. This dessert may be served hot, but if so desired, it is advisable to pour the hot milk mixture into individual dishes, with the meringues on top of each portion. *Serves 6–8.*

RUSSIA

It is difficult to consider the food and eating habits of Russia, because there is the unresolved question of whether to discuss the problem as of today or yesterday. Certainly it will be agreed that the excessively lavish meals of the czarist regime are gone, and that the native cuisine has been greatly simplified. However, recent visitors to Russia have attested to the fact that state banquets honoring diplomats or distinguished persons are almost as lavish as ever, though food in such quantity and quality is unavailable to the general public.

Vodka is the national drink. It is taken straight for the most part, accompanied by herring or some other appetizer. Most foreigners think of *vodka* as a clear white liquid, usually about 100 proof. There is, however, a red variety known as *riabinovka*, and a more or less yellowish type called *zubrovka*. *Vodka* should be taken in tiny glasses and never tasted or sipped. The correct procedure is to throw the fiery liquid to the back of the throat and hope for the best.

The Russians are fond of *zakuska* (appetizers). Probably the popular favorite is herring, but caviar would undoubtedly be the national choice except for its price and scarcity. It is now too expensive for all but a few.

The French, recognized as the leading gourmets of the world, have proclaimed that Russia's contribution to the world of serious eaters–that is connoisseurs–is the Russian soup. This is quite true, and an example is supplied here, the sauerkraut soup known as *schchi* (why suffer?–it's pronounced chee), just the thing to warm you up after a hard day on the steppes of Russia. The famous Russian beet soup, *borscht,* is known all over the world.

Cotletki pojarski (chicken cutlets) are appreciated the world over; *koulebiaka,* a meat or fish pie, is another fine dish; these are merely highlights, for Russia's cuisine is extensive. An interesting feature of Russian cooking is the lavish use of sour cream. It must be remembered that refrigeration is a comparatively recent innovation, and without it cream spoils quickly. The sour taste has always appealed to the Russians, and it is used whenever possible: in almost all soups, in many of the meat dishes, and particularly on the many different kinds of pancakes that constitute a unique feature of Russian food. Cereals, particularly whole-grain types, are much appreciated in this cold land. *Kashoi*, or buckwheat groats, are exceptionally good and may be obtained in the United States in foreign groceries and specialty shops. Heavy, whole-grain breads are eaten by everyone; American-style white breads are unknown.

There are many unique features in the cuisine, characterized by an inordinate love of mushrooms and cucumbers, by a fondness for smoked fish, sauerkraut, dark breads, and sour milk and cream. Sturgeon, when it is available, is Russia's favorite fish.

Dinner is always an early meal in Russia, usually about 5 P.M. Recent industrialization, which entails changed working hours, has revised meal hours to a certain degree but not completely. Normally, and by choice, the Russians like an early breakfast and prefer to lunch about noon. The favorite meal, for those who can manage it, is undoubtedly the late evening snack, served family style at about 10 P.M. This is the time for family and friends to gather, the time for conversation, and for eating the dainties that the Russians love so dearly. Tea is consumed in unbelievable quantities by our own one- or two-cup standards. A good Russian can drink a dozen glasses of tea; glasses, not cups, are used, reputedly because the people like to warm their hands on the hot glasses. To a Russian, tea never tastes so good as when the water is boiled in a samovar, a large brass or copper vessel made expressly for that purpose. Tea is not made in the samovar; water is boiled in it, and then the tea, which differs considerably from the varieties sold in this country, is steeped in a teapot.

Although the U.S.S.R. is one political unit, it consists of numerous nations of which a principal one is the Ukraine, which has its own representative at the United Nations. Little Russia, the Ukrainians call their considerable area located just north of the Black Sea and immediately to the east of Poland. With a population of more than 30,000,000, whose capital city is located at Kiev, the Ukraine has a fine cuisine which differs considerably from that of Russia itself, though at the same time the two share many dishes in common.

Because the Ukraine is located on the Black Sea, fish is fairly important. Like the Russians, the Ukrainians also have a great liking for certain foods such as cucumbers, black breads, sour cream, and sauerkraut. Vodka, as in Russia, is the regional liquor. Tea is the beverage of the country, both winter and summer.

The type of food that is usually thought of as being Jewish-style was originally Ukrainian in origin. At one time the Ukraine had a very large Jewish population. About 1890 the Jews began to leave in large numbers and come to the United States to escape religious persecution. They brought with them the Ukrainian food customs, and these have been accepted as Jewish-style cooking, particularly in the New York City area. Such delicacies as *blintzes* and *varenikis* (little stuffed dough pockets) are now considered to be both Ukrainian and Jewish.

EGGPLANT CAVIAR

RUBLNNYI BAKLAZHAN

1 large eggplant
1 onion, sliced
2 tomatoes, peeled
3 tablespoons vinegar
1 slice white bread, trimmed

1½ teaspoons salt
½ teaspoon freshly ground black pepper
2 teaspoons sugar
4 tablespoons vegetable oil

Wash the eggplant and cut off the stem. Place the eggplant on a baking sheet or wrap it loosely in aluminum foil. Bake in a 325° oven for 1 hour. Cool for 30 minutes. Peel and set aside. Place the onion in a chopping bowl and chop fine. Add the tomatoes and eggplant and chop fine. Pour the vinegar on the bread, soaking it well. Add to the eggplant with the salt, pepper, sugar, and oil. Continue chopping until well blended. Correct seasoning; the mixture should be fairly spicy. Chill for at least 1 hour. Serve with slices of thin pumpernickel bread. *Makes about 3 cups.*

HERRING CROQUETTES

KOTLETI SLEDZIOWE

3 salt herring
¼ pound (1 stick) butter
1 onion, chopped
1 cup dry bread crumbs

1 egg, beaten
⅛ teaspoon freshly ground black pepper

Wash the herring thoroughly. Soak them overnight in water to cover, changing the water several times. Remove the skins and bones carefully. Chop fine. Melt 3 tablespoons of the butter in a skillet. Add the onion and sauté for 10 minutes, stirring frequently. Add ½ cup of the bread crumbs. Cook for 15 minutes, stirring occasionally. Remove from heat. Add the egg, pepper, and chopped herring and mix well. Shape into croquettes of any desired size and dip in the remaining bread crumbs. Melt the remaining butter in a skillet. Fry the croquettes until brown on both sides. Serve with boiled potatoes. *Serves 4-6.*

SAUERKRAUT SOUP

SCHCHI

3 pounds short ribs of beef
A few marrow bones
3 cloves garlic, minced
2 onions, chopped
3 quarts water
1 19-ounce can tomatoes
1 large head cabbage
3 teaspoons salt

1 teaspoon freshly ground
  black pepper
¼ cup lemon juice
¼ cup sugar
2 tablespoons flour
2 tablespoons water
1 pound sauerkraut
½ cup sour cream

Wash the meat and bones and place in a deep pot. Add the garlic, onions, water, and tomatoes. Bring to a boil and skim the top of any foam. Shred the cabbage coarsely, discarding the core. Add to soup with salt and pepper. Cook for 1½ hours. Add the lemon juice and sugar. Cook 30 minutes. Mix the flour and water to a smooth paste and add to soup, stirring constantly. Add the sauerkraut and cook until meat is tender. Correct seasoning. The soup may need more sugar or lemon juice, depending on the tartness of the sauerkraut.

Serve in deep soup plates, garnished with sour cream. The meat may be served at the same time, on a separate platter. When served with *piroshki,* it is almost a complete meal. *Serves 8–10.*

MEAT PASTRY

PIROSHKI

1 cup flour
⅛ teaspoon salt
¼ pound (1 stick) butter
3 tablespoons sour cream
4 tablespoons melted butter

4 chicken livers or 1 slice calf's
  liver
½ cup sliced mushrooms
½ teaspoon salt
⅛ teaspoon pepper

Sift the flour and ⅛ teaspoon salt into a bowl. Add the ¼ pound butter and work together with the hand until well blended. Add the sour cream and mix again until smooth. Wrap in wax paper and chill at least 2 hours, overnight if possible.

Place the 4 tablespoons melted butter in a saucepan and add the livers, mushrooms, salt, and pepper. Cook over low heat for 10 minutes. Chop fine and cool for 15 minutes.

Roll out the dough ⅛ inch thick on a lightly floured board. Cut rounds with a cooky cutter. Place a heaping teaspoon of the liver mixture on each and fold over the dough, sealing the edges carefully. Place on a baking sheet. Bake in a 375° oven for 20 minutes. Serve hot. *Piroshki* are usually served with *schchi*. However, they may be served as hot hors d'oeuvres. *Makes about 20.*

FISH STEW

SELIANKA

10 dried mushrooms	1 teaspoon freshly ground
2 pounds fresh-water fish, sliced, and head	black pepper
	2 quarts water
1 stalk celery, sliced	3 tablespoons butter
2 carrots, peeled and sliced	1 onion, chopped
1 parsnip, peeled and sliced (optional)	4 tablespoons tomato paste
	1 tablespoon capers, drained
2 teaspoons salt	10 ripe olives

Soak the mushrooms in water to cover for 2 hours. Drain carefully. Rinse and slice.

Wash the fish and head. Place the head in a deep saucepan, reserving the fish itself. Add the celery, carrots, and parsnip, salt, pepper, and water. Boil for 45 minutes. Strain. Melt the butter in a large saucepan. Add the chopped onion and sauté for 10 minutes, stirring frequently. Add the fish and brown lightly on both sides. Add the tomato paste, capers, olives, and strained fish stock. Cook over medium heat for 40 minutes, or until fish is cooked. Correct seasoning. Serve in deep soup plates garnished with lemon slices and parsley. *Serves 6–8.*

MEAT PIE

KOULEBIAKA

1 cake or package yeast	2 eggs, beaten
½ cup lukewarm water	½ teaspoon salt
4 cups sifted flour	1½ cups light cream, scalded
1 tablespoon butter	and cooled

Place the yeast in a cup with the water. Mix to a paste and allow to soak for 5 minutes. Add 1 cup of the flour and stir well. Place in a warm place, cover with a cloth, and allow to rise until double in size, about 1 hour. Add the butter, eggs, salt, cream, and the remaining flour. Knead into a dough. If necessary, add a little more flour to form the dough. Place in a bowl, cover with a cloth, and allow to rise in a warm place for 2 hours. While it is rising, prepare the filling:

¼ pound (1 stick) butter
2 onions, chopped
2 pounds veal or beef, chopped
½ pound mushrooms, chopped
2 hard-cooked eggs, chopped

2 teaspoons salt
1 teaspoon freshly ground
   black pepper
4 tablespoons cream
1 egg yolk, beaten

Melt the butter in a saucepan. Add the onions and sauté for 10 minutes, stirring frequently. Add the meat and mushrooms and cook for 20 minutes over medium heat, stirring occasionally. Add the chopped eggs, salt, pepper, and cream; mix well. Correct seasoning.

Preheat oven to 375°.

Roll out the dough about ½ inch thick on a lightly floured surface. Butter a 12-inch loaf pan thoroughly. Place the dough in the pan so that it extends over the sides. Place the meat mixture in the center and fold over the dough so that it meets in the middle. Allow to rise for 15 minutes. Brush the top of the dough with the beaten egg yolk. Bake in a 375° oven for 35 minutes, or until browned on top. If desired, melted butter may be brushed across the top before serving. The loaf may be sliced in the pan or turned out onto a plate. *Serves 8–10.*

CHICKEN CUTLETS

COTLETKI POJARSKI

4 slices white bread
½ cup light cream
4 whole chicken breasts
1½ teaspoons salt
¼ teaspoon white pepper
1 pound butter
1 egg, beaten

½ cup bread crumbs
½ pound mushrooms, sliced
1 tablespoon flour
¼ cup chicken broth
1½ tablespoons lemon juice
3 egg yolks, beaten
Dash of cayenne pepper

Soak the bread in the cream. Remove the meat from the raw chicken breasts and grind in a food chopper as fine as possible. Add 1 teaspoon of the salt and the pepper. Melt 2 tablespoons of the butter and add with the bread. Chop the mixture until very smooth. Shape into 6 large or 12 small cutlets. Dip in the beaten egg and then in bread crumbs. Chill 1 hour. Melt 4 tablespoons of butter in a skillet and fry the cutlets in it over low heat, until browned on both sides. Add more butter as necessary. Remove and keep warm.

Melt 2 tablespoons of butter in the same skillet. Add the mushrooms and sauté for 5 minutes. Sprinkle the flour on top, stirring until smooth. Gradually add the broth, stirring until the boiling point is reached. Cook over low heat for 5 minutes, stirring frequently. Set aside.

Divide the remaining butter into three pieces. Place one piece in the top of a double boiler; add the lemon juice and egg yolks. Place over hot, not boiling, water. Beat constantly with a wire whisk or wooden spoon. When the first piece of butter melts, add the second. When the mixture thickens, add the third piece, still beating constantly. Cook over low heat so that the water never boils. Continue cooking and beating for 2 minutes after the last piece of butter melts. Remove from the heat. Add the remaining salt and the cayenne pepper. If the mixture curdles, add 1 tablespoon of heavy cream and beat vigorously. Add the mushrooms. Serve the sauce on top of the cutlets. *Serves 6.*

FRUIT JELLY DESSERT

KISSEL

1 pound sugar	1 pound fresh or dried apricots
1½ cups water	¼ cup potato flour

Combine the sugar and ½ cup of the water in a saucepan. Boil until the mixture is syrupy, about 15 minutes. Wash and pit the fresh apricots; if dried apricots are used, wash them and soak for 2 hours in water. Add to the syrup and cook until very soft. Force through a sieve. Combine the remaining 1 cup of water and the potato flour in a saucepan. Mix until smooth. Add the puréed apricots and cook until very thick over low heat, about 20 minutes. Pour into individual dishes. May be served either hot or cold, with heavy sweet cream. *Serves 6–8.*

CHEESE PASTRIES

VATROUSHKIS

2 cups sifted flour	2 eggs
½ pound salt butter	2 tablespoons melted butter
1 cup plus 4 tablespoons sour cream	½ teaspoon salt
1 pound cream cheese	1 teaspoon sugar
	1 egg yolk, beaten

Sift the flour into a bowl. Cut the butter into the flour with a pastry blender or two knives. Add 4 tablespoons of the sour cream and mix together into a ball. Wrap in wax paper and place in the refrigerator overnight, or at least for 2 hours.

Preheat oven to 375°.

Cream the cheese until soft, add the eggs, and beat together until light and fluffy. Add the remaining sour cream, the melted butter, salt, and sugar. Mix well. Roll out the dough ⅛ inch thick on a lightly floured surface. Cut out 3-inch circles. Place 2 teaspoons of the cheese mixture in the center of each circle of dough. Pinch the sides together but do not pinch the dough together in the center; the effect should be that of a cup. Brush each piece of pastry with the beaten egg yolk. Place on a baking sheet. Bake in a 375° oven for 20 minutes, or until delicately browned. *Makes about 30.*

WALNUT CAKE

MAZOURKA

9 egg yolks	1 pound walnuts, ground
2 cups sugar	½ pound candied fruit peel,
9 egg whites	ground
3 cups flour	2 tablespoons lemon juice

Preheat oven to 325°.

Beat the yolks in a bowl; add the sugar and beat well. Beat the whites in a separate bowl until stiff but not dry and fold into the yolk mixture carefully. Add the flour, walnuts, candied fruit, and lemon juice, mixing lightly. Butter a jelly roll pan, about 11 by 17 inches, and dust lightly with flour. Pour the mixture into it. Bake for 30 minutes, or until a cake tester comes out clean. Dust with powdered sugar. The resulting cake will be about 1 inch high and should be served in long, thin slices. *Serves 8–10.*

SCOTLAND

Here is a region where the temperature seldom warms the visitor, but where the friendship and hospitality of the people make up for it. Scotland is hard and barren, and full of rugged scenery, but the people are not the dour folk that they have been made out to be; rather, they may be described as reserved in nature. Scotch hospitality comes as a surprise to those visitors who know Scotland only as the land of Scotch jokes. This section will contain no Scotch jokes whatsoever.

Scotland's contributions to the world of the gourmet may be limited in number, but those few are impressive in their importance. For example, the scotch whisky that has found acceptance the world over is produced here. No one knows whether it is the local water, the ingredients, or the method of manufacture, but it is certain that scotch whisky has never been successfully duplicated anywhere else in the world. While the people are justifiably fond of their own local product, there is very little scotch in Scotland. Most of it is exported, principally to the United States, in return for much-needed foreign credits.

Of the natural resources, Scotch salmon and trout are outstanding delicacies. Game birds are also exceptional, but not nearly so plentiful in numbers as they formerly were. Other local specialties include herring, Scotch bacon, locally grown mutton, and the staple food, porridge, or oatmeal as we call it. The porridge of Scotland is not the quick-cooking variety used by American housewives so that the family breadwinner can catch the 8:03. It is the slowly cooked, natural cereal that the Scots use, and their finished product is completely different from our anemic American-style oatmeal. It takes much longer to make Scotch oatmeal, and in the kitchens of the country people it is customary to see a pot of porridge cooking over a low fire at any hour of the day. The raw oatmeal is also used for dipping and coating raw fish before cooking; fresh herring dipped in Scotch oatmeal is unusually good. To duplicate the recipes contained in this section, be sure to use the Scotch type of oatmeal, which may be had at many fine groceries or delicacy shops.

The one dish that typifies Scotland is haggis. Unfortunately most visitors do not care to eat it after learning that it is a kind of pudding prepared from the sheep's heart, liver, and lungs and cooked with oatmeal in the lining of the sheep's stomach. It is better than it sounds, but it still is not a dish for everyone. The recipe for pot haggis is much more to our taste.

Tea is a fine meal, because the Scotch are particularly adept at cakes and pastries. Scotland has produced its own shortbread, and of course there are the famous scones. As in England, most visitors enjoy breakfast and tea more than lunch and dinner. This need not be so if, instead of making fruitless attempts to find international food, the tourist will eat local specialties.

HOT PINT

| 4 cups ale | 4 tablespoons sugar |
| 1 egg, beaten | ½ cup scotch whisky |

Heat the ale to the boiling point. Combine the egg, sugar, and scotch and mix well. Gradually add the boiling ale, stirring constantly to prevent curdling. Pour into mugs from a height, so as to create a froth. If the drink is poured into glasses, be sure to place a spoon in each glass. Drink immediately while the froth remains.

TRADITIONAL CHICKEN AND LEEK SOUP

COCKY-LEEKY

5-pound stewing chicken, disjointed	½ teaspoon white pepper
2½ quarts water	12 fresh leeks or 18 scallions (green onions), sliced
2 teaspoons salt	1½ cups rice, half cooked

Wash the chicken thoroughly. Place in a saucepan with the water. Cook for 2 hours, or until tender. Add the salt and pepper at the end of the first hour of cooking. Remove the chicken and keep warm. Add the leeks and rice to the soup and cook for 25 minutes. Remove the chicken from the bones and add to the soup. Cook 5 minutes longer. This soup makes an excellent meal in one dish. *Serves 6–8.*

FISH BALLER

2 fillets of sole	½ teaspoon white pepper
2 cups water	¼ teaspoon thyme
1 pound shrimp, shelled and cleaned	1 egg
1 tablespoon chopped parsley	1½ cups fresh bread crumbs
1¼ teaspoons salt	1 egg yolk, beaten
	Fat for deep-fat frying

Combine the fillets and water in a saucepan. Bring to a boil and cook over medium heat for 10 minutes. Remove the fillets and set aside to cool. Place the shrimp in the same liquid in which the fish was cooked, and cook for 7 minutes. Drain and set aside to cool for 10 minutes. Grind the fillets and shrimp three times in a food chopper. Place in a bowl and add the parsley, salt, pepper, thyme, egg, and 1 cup of the bread crumbs. Beat the mixture until smooth and light, using an electric mixer if desired. Correct the seasoning. Shape into 1-inch balls. Dip them into the egg yolk and remaining bread crumbs. Heat the fat to 380°. Fry several of the fish balls at a time until they are golden brown, about 2 minutes. Drain. Serve hot. *Serves 4–6.*

HAMBURGER, SCOTCH STYLE

MINCE

3 tablespoons butter	1 teaspoon freshly ground black pepper
2 pounds beef, ground	1 cup chopped onions
3 tablespoons boiling water	
2 teaspoons salt	

Melt the butter in a saucepan and add the meat, stirring constantly to prevent lumps from forming. When the meat is brown, add the water, salt, pepper, and onions. Cover and cook over very low heat for 35 minutes, stirring frequently. Serve with skirl in the pan (see recipe in this section). *Serves 6–8.*

CHICKEN STOVIES

4 teaspoons salt
1½ teaspoons white pepper
6-pound chicken, disjointed
6 large potatoes, peeled and cut
    into sixths

4 onions, sliced
4 tablespoons butter
1½ cups chicken broth

Combine 2 teaspoons of the salt and 1 teaspoon of pepper and rub into the chicken thoroughly. Butter a casserole and arrange a layer of chicken on the bottom, followed by successive layers of potatoes and onions. Dot each layer with a little of the butter and sprinkle the remaining salt and pepper on the layer of potatoes. Pour the broth over the contents of the casserole. Cover. Bake in 325° oven for 3 hours, or until tender. Serve hot, directly from the casserole. *Serves 4–6.*

POT HAGGIS

1 pound liver
3 cups water
3 large onions
¼ pound raw beef fat

1½ cups oatmeal (Scotch
    oatmeal, if possible)
1½ teaspoons salt
1 teaspoon freshly ground
    black pepper

Combine the liver and water in a saucepan. Bring to a boil and cook over medium heat for 10 minutes. Add the onions and cook for 20 minutes. Remove the liver and onions, reserving the liquid. Grind the liver, onions, and beef fat together.

Place the oatmeal in a hot frying pan and stir continuously until lightly browned. Be sure the pan is completely dry, and be careful not to burn the oatmeal. Add the oatmeal to the liver mixture, together with the salt and pepper, and 1¾ cups of the reserved liquid. Mix well. Pour into a greased casserole. Cover the top, using a piece of aluminum foil if the cover does not fit tightly. Place in a deep pan of boiling water on top of the stove and steam for 2 hours. *Serves 8–10.*

Note: The above recipe differs considerably from the Scotch method. The traditional recipe is to use the stomach bag of a sheep and fill it with the liver, heart, and other assorted parts of a sheep.

SKIRL IN THE PAN

⅓ cup butter	½ cup boiling water
2 onions, chopped fine	2 teaspoons salt
½ cup oatmeal (Scotch oatmeal, if possible)	⅛ teaspoon freshly ground black pepper

Melt the butter in a saucepan. Add the onions and sauté until brown, about 10 minutes, stirring frequently. Add the oatmeal, stirring constantly. Add the water, salt, and pepper and mix well. Cook over low heat for 20 minutes, or until soft. Serve with mince (see recipe in this section) or with other meats.

CREAM SCONES

2 cups sifted flour	6 tablespoons butter
⅛ teaspoon salt	1 egg
1 teaspoon baking powder	3 tablespoons heavy cream

Preheat oven to 400°.

Sift the flour, salt, and baking powder into a bowl. Cut in the butter with a pastry blender or two knives until the consistency of coarse sand. Beat the egg and cream together and add to the mixture, tossing lightly with a fork until a dough is formed. Roll the dough out about ¾ inch thick on a lightly floured surface. Do not roll more than once. Butter a baking tin and dust lightly with flour. Place the dough on the tin and cut into 2-inch squares with a knife. Brush the top with a little milk. Bake in a 400° oven for 15 minutes. Recut the squares. Serve hot. Reheat before serving, if the scones are served again. Serve with butter and preserves or jelly. *Serves 6–8.*

SCOTCH SHORTBREAD

½ pound (2 sticks) sweet butter	1 cup sifted cake flour
1 cup confectioners' sugar	2 tablespoons cornstarch

Combine the butter and sugar together on a board. Blend together with the hands. Sift the flour and cornstarch together and gradually work it into the previous mixture until well blended. Preheat oven to 425°. Butter an 8-inch square pan and dust lightly with flour. Pat the dough into the pan with the hands, as this dough cannot be rolled. Prick the top with a fork in several places. Bake in a 425° oven for 5 minutes; then reduce the heat to 350° and bake 10 minutes longer, or until lightly browned. Cut into squares immediately. *Serves 8–10.*

SPAIN

Spain is a brilliant red cape, a hot, yellow sun; it is gay music and unrestrained flamenco dancing. These characteristics of the country and of the people are observable in the national cuisine, with its strong flavor combinations and unusual dishes. Just as the conservative British eat bland and colorless food, so the flaunting Spaniards prefer lively and colorful fare. Gastronomically speaking, the two nations are a world apart, but just to confuse the issue, the contradictory English are extremely fond of Spanish sherry.

The food of Spain is based upon certain principal ingredients: olives and olive oil; the flavorings of garlic, saffron, and paprika; seafood, rice, beans, chick-peas, and smoked sausages. Fresh fruits and melons are often superb, and of course there are the renowned wines of the country.

Those who can afford it eat a light breakfast but make up for it with two enormous meals—lunch from 1 to 3 P.M., and dinner at ten in the evening, or even slightly later. The Spanish people love good food, and dining is a fine art. Tourists may have to adjust themselves to the late meal hours, but little adjustment is required to the delicious food. *Olla podrida* is the meat stew of the peasantry, but the tourist favorite is *paella valenciana*, a delicious combination of rice, chicken, lobster, and shrimp. *Angulas* (baby eels) may sound exotic, but they won't after you've tasted them. *Zarzuela de mariscos* (literally meaning a musical comedy of seafood) is also very good, but neither of these two last preparations can readily be duplicated in this country.

With all their wonderful fresh fish, the Spaniards are inordinately fond of dishes made with sun-dried codfish. The usual meats are to be had, including goat and kid, but these are merely adequate and not equal to the seafood. *Gazpacho* is served either as a cold vegetable soup or as a salad, though a valid criticism might be that it is too dry for a soup and too wet for a salad. There are literally scores of recipes for making *gazpacho*, and it may well be that no two Spanish cooks have the same recipe, for it appears in many different colors and textures, and is served in varying fashions.

The chief basis of much of Spain's cookery involves the use of olive oil in cooking. It's used instead of butter, because this is primarily a hot-weather country, and when the nation's cuisine was developing many centuries ago, there was no refrigeration. Unfortunately, the olive oil may be used far too liberally for American tastes, but not necessarily always. It should be mentioned that Spanish food is bland and not spicy; however, garlic and onions may be added liberally.

There is an entire series of dishes based upon rice. Perhaps the best known is the *paella*, often an elaborate creation based upon yellow rice (colored by saffron) with chicken and seafood. Similar preparations made with chicken alone, or with just seafood, are typical. However, rice dishes are also made with almost anything available, including (but not limited to) clams, beans, artichokes, duck, and so on.

The cocktail hour often starts here at 8:30 P.M. and even nine-thirty is not unusual! Red, white, and pink wines are produced in abundance almost everywhere in the nation, several of them being quite well known, particularly the Marqués de Riscal brand. The wine of Málaga, a sweet, dessert type, is justly accepted as a fine wine by the world. Interestingly enough, this wine is produced only by the third harvest of the vines, the first being used for drying into raisins, and the second for a white wine.

But it is the wine of Xeres de la Frontera region for which Spain is famous. Xeres is also Jerez, and the British anglicized their favorite drink into "sherris," and over the centuries it has become the familiar word "sherry." It is a unique wine, admittedly inimitable, dry or sweet, pale or dark, and suitable for use as an appetizer or as a dessert wine depending upon the type. The sweet, darker types usually have brandy added; the drier varieties are pale and unchanged. The principal divisions include the golden or sweet sherry, the *oloroso* or medium, and the finest of all, the dry *amontillado*. The Spanish people love the *manzanilla* wine produced in Andalusia, but its perfumed, aromatic flavor does not immediately receive everyone's approval.

In soft drinks, *horchata*, a cold, milky drink, is the warm-weather favorite. Hot chocolate for breakfast, and black coffee at other meals, are the other beverages of importance.

COLD SOUP-SALAD

GAZPACHO

2 onions, chopped
2 cloves garlic, minced
4 green peppers, chopped
5 tomatoes, chopped
2 teaspoons salt
½ teaspoon pepper
2 teaspoons Spanish paprika

⅓ cup olive oil
⅓ cup wine vinegar
1½ cups water
Garnishes: Croutons, diced cucumbers, onions, tomatoes, and green peppers

Combine the onions, garlic, green peppers, and tomatoes. Purée a little at a time in an electric blender or force through a food mill. Add the salt, pepper, and paprika. Add the olive oil gradually, beating steadily. Add the vinegar and water and stir well. Place in the refrigerator to chill for at least 2 hours, using a wooden or glass bowl; do not use a metal bowl. Add the cucumber slices before serving.

This dish may be served as either a cold soup or as a salad, though it will seem to be quite a wet salad. When *gazpacho* is served, no other soup or salad should be served. *Serves 6–8.*

CHICK-PEA SOUP

COCIDO MADRILEÑO

1 pound dried chick-peas (*garbanzos*)	1¼ pounds bacon strips, half cooked, and cut in half
3 quarts water	2 carrots, sliced
1½ pounds beef	1 onion, chopped
2 marrow bones	2 leeks, sliced
1 pound smoked ham, cubed	2 teaspoons salt
¼ pound smoked sausage (Spanish sausage, if available), sliced	6 potatoes, peeled and cut in shoestring lengths

Wash the chick-peas and discard any imperfect ones. Soak them overnight in water to cover. Drain and rinse. Boil the water in a large saucepan. Add the chick-peas and cook for 30 minutes. Add the beef and bones and cook over medium heat for 30 minutes. Add the ham, sausage, and bacon. Cover but allow the steam to escape, and cook over low heat for 1 hour. Add the carrots, onion, and leeks and cook for 30 minutes. Add the salt and potatoes and cook for 30 minutes. Correct seasoning. Strain the stock and serve. The meat and vegetables should be served on a separate plate. *Serves 8–10.*

FISH PIE

PASTEL DE PESCADO

3 tablespoons olive oil	1 teaspoon freshly ground black pepper
½ cup ground almonds	
2 cloves garlic, minced	5 tomatoes, peeled and chopped
4 onions, chopped	5 fillets of sole or other white-meat fish
1 bay leaf	
2 teaspoons salt	
3 cups mashed potatoes, seasoned with salt and pepper	

Heat the oil in a saucepan. Add the almonds and sauté for 5 minutes, stirring frequently. Remove the almonds and set aside. Place the garlic and onions in the saucepan and sauté for 10 minutes, stirring frequently. Add a little more olive oil if necessary. Add the bay leaf, salt, pepper, and tomatoes and cook over low heat for 10 minutes, stirring occasionally. Grind 1 of the fillets in a food chopper. Cut the remaining fillets in thirds. Reserve one-third of the tomato mixture as a sauce. Force the balance of the mixture through a sieve. Add the ground fish and the almonds. Cook over low heat for 10 minutes, stirring frequently.

Butter a 9-inch casserole. Line the bottom and sides carefully with the mashed potatoes but reserve some for the top of the casserole. Arrange layers of the tomato mixture and of the fish fillets until they are all used up. Cover the top with mashed potatoes. Bake in a 425° oven for 30 minutes. Serve directly from the casserole with the reserved tomato sauce, which should be heated. *Serves 6–8.*

FISH WITH WALNUTS AND GREEN PEPPERS

PESCADO A LA ANDALUCIA

6 slices sea bass, snapper, or other firm fish	2 cloves garlic, minced
2 teaspoons salt	2 cups finely chopped onions
½ teaspoon freshly ground black pepper	2 tablespoons minced parsley
½ cup ground walnuts	3 tablespoons olive oil
	3 tomatoes, peeled and quartered
	2 green peppers, cut julienne

Rub the fish with the salt and pepper. Mix together the walnuts, garlic, onions, and parsley. Pour half the oil into a baking dish and spread half the nut mixture in it. Arrange the fish in the dish in a single layer and cover with the remaining nut mixture. Arrange the tomatoes and pepper over it and sprinkle with the remaining oil. Cover the dish and bake in a 325° oven 45 minutes, removing the cover for the last 10 minutes. *Serves 6.*

LOBSTER, CATALAN STYLE

LANGOSTA CATALANA

3 live lobsters, split	1½ cups chicken broth
½ cup olive oil	1 bay leaf
5 onions, chopped	½ teaspoon orégano
2 teaspoons salt	¼ teaspoon thyme
½ teaspoon dried ground chili peppers	½ cup chopped parsley
	1 teaspoon saffron
½ cup brandy	2 cloves garlic, minced
2 tablespoons tomato paste	½ ounce unsweetened chocolate

Remove the coral and liver from the lobsters and reserve. Heat the olive oil in a large casserole or Dutch oven. Add the onions and sauté for 15 minutes, stirring occasionally. Add the lobsters, salt, chili peppers, and brandy. Set the brandy aflame and cook over high heat until the brandy stops burning. Add the tomato paste, broth, bay leaf, orégano, thyme, and parsley. Mix. Bake in a 375° oven for 20 minutes.

Pound the saffron, garlic, chocolate, coral, and liver to a smooth paste. Add a little sauce from the casserole, mixing well. Return the mixture to the casserole and stir. Cook over low direct heat for 5 minutes. Correct seasoning and discard bay leaf. Place the lobsters on a platter. Pour the sauce over them and sprinkle with remaining parsley.

Note: If the lobster is to be served as a main course for 6 people, double the recipe.

SPANISH NATIONAL STEW

OLLA PODRIDA

2 cups dried chick-peas (*garbanzos*)	3 cloves garlic, minced
	2 teaspoons salt
3 quarts water	1 teaspoon freshly ground black pepper
3 tablespoons olive oil	
1 pound stewing beef, cubed	2 cups shredded cabbage
1 pound veal (breast preferably), cut into 2-inch strips	1 pound fresh or ½ package frozen peas
1 pound lamb, cubed	½ pound fresh or ½ package frozen string beans
½ chicken, disjointed	
1 pound smoked ham, cubed	2 cucumbers, peeled and sliced
4 smoked sausages (Spanish *chorizos*, if possible), sliced	1 head lettuce, coarsely shredded
2 onions, chopped	

Soak the chick-peas overnight in water to cover. Drain. Place in a large saucepan with the water. Cook over medium heat for ½ hour. Heat the olive oil in a large frying pan. Sauté the beef, veal, lamb, and chicken in it until browned on all sides. Add the browned meats, ham, sausages, onions, garlic, salt, and pepper to the chick-peas. Cover and cook over low heat for 1½ hours, or until the meats are tender. Remove 2 cups of the stock and place it in a separate saucepan. Add the cabbage, peas, and string beans and cook for 10 minutes, Add the cucumbers and lettuce and cook 10 minutes longer.

Place the meat and chick-peas on a platter, reserving the stock. Drain the vegetables, again reserving the stock, and place on a separate platter. Combine the stocks. This constitutes a complete meal: soup, meat, and vegetables. *Serves 6–8.*

SWEETBREADS IN SHERRY

MOLLEJAS DE TERNERA AL OLOROSO

3 pairs sweetbreads	3 onions, chopped
1½ teaspoons salt	1 cup sweet sherry
1 tablespoon vinegar	6 shallots or sliced scallions
2 cups water	(green onions)
¼ pound (1 stick) butter	

Wash the sweetbreads. Combine in a saucepan with the salt, vinegar, and water. Bring to a boil, cover, and cook over low heat for 10 minutes. Drain. Cover with cold water. Allow to cool for 30 minutes. Drain and remove the membranes. Dice coarsely. Melt the butter in a saucepan. Add the sweetbreads and sauté for 5 minutes, stirring frequently. Add the onions and sauté for 10 minutes, stirring frequently. Add the sherry. Cook over low heat for 5 minutes, then add the shallots. Cook over low heat 5 minutes longer. Correct seasoning. Serve with buttered green peas. If served as a main course, double the number of sweetbreads. *Serves 6 as a first course.*

MARINATED ROAST BEEF

CARNE ASADO

3-rib roast of beef or 5-pound rolled roast	⅓ teaspoon orégano
3 cloves garlic, minced	2 cups chopped onions
2½ teaspoons salt	3 cups dry red wine
1 teaspoon freshly ground black pepper	2 cups chopped tomatoes
	½ cup sliced mushrooms
	2 tablespoons cornstarch

Rub the meat with a mixture of the garlic, salt, pepper, and orégano. Place in a large bowl and let stand 30 minutes. Add the onions and 2½ cups wine. Cover and let marinate in the refrigerator 24 hours, basting and turning the meat a few times.

Remove the meat from the marinade and place the meat in a shallow roasting pan. Reserve the marinade. Roast in a 450° oven 15 minutes. Pour off the fat and reduce the heat to 350°. Add the tomatoes, mushrooms, and the marinade, and roast a total of 15 minutes a pound for rare meat, or to desired degree of rareness. Baste occasionally. Transfer the meat to a hot platter. Purée the gravy in an electric blender, or force through a sieve; skim the fat. Mix the cornstarch with the remaining wine; add to the gravy, stirring steadily to the boiling point, then cook 5 minutes longer. Carve the meat and serve with the gravy. *Serves 6–8.*

CHICKEN, RICE, AND SEAFOOD

PAELLA VALENCIANA

2 dozen clams
2 1½-pound live lobsters
1 3-pound chicken, disjointed
½ cup lard or olive oil
2 *chorizos* (Spanish sausages) cut in 1-inch pieces
3 tomatoes, peeled and diced
2 sweet red peppers, cut julienne
½ pound scallops

4 cups long grain rice
½ teaspoon powdered saffron
8 cups boiling chicken broth or water
1 clove garlic, minced
2½ teaspoons salt
½ teaspoon black pepper
1 cup canned green peas
8 cooked or canned artichoke hearts

Wash and scrub the clams. Cut the lobsters into small pieces, in the shell. Wash and dry the chicken.

Heat the lard or oil in a skillet, brown the chicken pieces in it. (A *"paellera,"* a shallow, large two-handled metal pan, is customarily used for making paella.) Any large shallow pan can be used.

Arrange the chicken in the greased pan, then around it the clams, lobster, *chorizos*, tomatoes, peppers, and scallops. Spread the rice over all. Mix together the saffron, broth, garlic, salt, and pepper; pour the mixture into the pan. Cover, bring to a boil and cook over high heat 10 minutes. Arrange the peas and artichokes on top of the rice. Re-cover and bake in a 375° oven 15 minutes longer, or until the rice is tender. Remove the cover for the last 5 minutes. Serve directly from the dish. *Serves 8.*

DUCK AND RICE

PATO Y ARROZ

¼ pound (1 stick) butter
2 4-pound ducks, disjointed
6 cups stock or 2 cans consommé
and 2 cans water
4 tablespoons tomato paste
4 teaspoons salt
1½ teaspoons freshly ground
black pepper
1 teaspoon Spanish paprika

1½ cups rice
1 cup cooked or canned green
peas
¼ cup grated Gruyère cheese
½ cup sliced, sautéed mushrooms
⅛ pound ham, sliced in julienne
strips
2 pimentos, sliced thin

Melt 3 tablespoons of the butter in a casserole or saucepan. Add the ducks and brown well on all sides. Add 1½ cups of the stock, 2 tablespoons of the tomato paste, 2 teaspoons of salt, 1 teaspoon of pepper, and the paprika. Cover and cook over low heat for 1¼ hours, or until the ducks are tender. Skim the fat from the gravy.

Melt the remaining butter in a saucepan. Add the rice and brown lightly. Add the remaining stock, tomato paste, salt, and pepper. Cover and cook over low heat for 20 minutes. Add the peas and cheese. Cook for 5 minutes. Correct seasoning. Add the mushrooms, ham, and pimentos. Mix lightly. Place the ducks in the center of a platter with the rice around it. Pour the gravy over the ducks. Serve with a chilled white wine. *Serves 8.*

CAULIFLOWER

COLIFLOR

1 medium head cauliflower
3 cups boiling water
3 teaspoons salt
4 tablespoons olive oil or butter
1 onion, chopped

2 cloves garlic, minced
2 tablespoons vinegar
¼ teaspoon freshly ground
black pepper

Wash the cauliflower thoroughly, remove the leaves, and separate into flowerets. Place in a saucepan with the water and 2 tablespoons of the salt. Boil for 10 minutes. Drain. Heat the oil in a saucepan. Add the onion and garlic and sauté for 5 minutes, stirring frequently. Add the vinegar, cauliflower, pepper, and remaining salt. Cover and cook over low heat for 10 minutes. Serve hot or cold. *Serves 4.*

POTATO-ALMOND CASSEROLE

PATATAS EN CAZUELA

6 potatoes, peeled and sliced ¼ inch thick
2 eggs, beaten
1½ teaspoon salt
¾ cup sifted flour
⅓ cup olive oil
2 slices white bread, trimmed

¼ cup milk
1 onion, chopped
2 cloves garlic, minced
½ cup blanched ground almonds
3 tablespoons chopped parsley
1½ cups water

Dip the potato slices in the eggs. Mix the salt and flour together and dip the potato slices in it, coating them thoroughly. Heat the olive oil in a frying pan. Brown the potatoes in the oil quickly over fairly high heat. Remove and place in a buttered casserole.

Soak the bread in the milk for 5 minutes. Squeeze out all the liquid and crumble the bread. Place the bread, onion, garlic, and almonds in the same frying pan and sauté for 5 minutes, stirring frequently, until the mixture is quite smooth and lightly browned. If necessary, add a little more olive oil. Add the parsley and water and mix together. Pour the mixture over the potatoes. Bake in a 325° oven for 50 minutes. Serve hot, directly from the casserole. *Serves 6–8.*

RICE SALAD

ENSALADA DE ARROZ

2 cups cooked rice
2 green peppers, sliced fine
2 pimentos, sliced fine
4 tomatoes, peeled and cubed
2 tablespoons chopped onion
2 tablespoons chopped parsley

¾ cup olive oil
¼ cup wine vinegar
1½ teaspoons salt
½ teaspoon freshly ground black pepper
1 clove garlic, minced

Combine the cooked rice, green peppers, pimentos, tomatoes, onion, and parsley in a bowl. Mix lightly with two forks. Beat together the olive oil, wine vinegar, salt, pepper, and garlic. Pour over the rice mixture and again toss lightly. Chill and serve very cold. *Serves 6–8.*

WALNUT DESSERT PANCAKES

BALTASARES DE NUENCE

2 eggs	3 tablespoons sifted flour
1 egg yolk	3 tablespoons brandy
½ cup sugar	¼ pound (1 stick) butter
2 teaspoons grated lemon rind	¼ cup sifted confectioners' sugar
¾ cup finely ground walnuts	

Beat the eggs and egg yolk in a bowl. Add the sugar and beat until light. Add the lemon rind, walnuts, and flour and beat until well blended. Add the brandy. Mix. Melt half the butter and add to the walnut mixture, mixing lightly.

METHOD 1: Melt a small piece of the remaining butter in a 7-inch skillet. Pour a tablespoon of the mixture into it and turn the pan from side to side to coat the bottom. Make the pancakes as thin as possible. Bake over low heat until lightly browned on both sides; remove from pan and roll up immediately. Repeat until all the batter is used up. Sprinkle with confectioners' sugar.

METHOD 2: Melt the remaining butter in a baking pan. Pour into the pan by the tablespoon to form small circles. Bake in a 450° oven for 5 minutes. Turn each pancake and bake for 3 more minutes, or until browned. Remove from the pan and roll up immediately. Sprinkle with confectioners' sugar.

Serve hot or cold. The second method will produce a crisper pancake. *Serves 4–6.*

BANANA CAKE

TORTA DE BANANA

4 tablespoons butter	3 bananas, peeled and halved
½ cup sugar	lengthwise
2 eggs, beaten	2 tablespoons lemon juice
1 cup sifted flour	¼ cup dark brown sugar
½ teaspoon salt	¼ cup fresh or dried grated
1 teaspoon baking powder	coconut (optional)

Preheat oven to 350°.

Cream the butter. Add the sugar and beat until light and fluffy. Add the eggs and beat well. Sift the flour, salt, and baking powder together and add to the previous mixture, mixing well. Butter an 8-inch square

pan and dust lightly with flour. Pour the batter into the pan, spreading
it as evenly as possible. Arrange the banana slices on top. Sprinkle with
the lemon juice, brown sugar, and coconut. Bake for 30 minutes, or until
a cake tester comes out clean. Remove from the oven and cool. Turn out
carefully. Serve with whipped cream, if desired. *Serves 8–10.*

SWEDEN

There can be no denying the enormous attraction of England, France,
and Italy for American tourists. A recent survey shows that the vast majority of visitors head for those three countries. Recently, however, some
of the Scandinavian nations have shown an increase in the number of
American visitors, and Sweden deserves to have its fair share. It's a nation
with good food, excellent accommodations, and unbelievable scenery.
Perhaps the day will come when Sweden will receive the number of
tourists it deserves.

Here is the home of the *smörgåsbord,* the table loaded with dozens of
plates filled with varying hors d'oeuvres. Often the choice involves not
dozens but fifty or even a hundred different appetizing fish, meat, and
cheese dishes. The etiquette of the *smörgåsbord* involves at least three
visits to the table, in order not to mix the varying flavors of the different
foods. The Swedes always start with the fish and herring, then go on to
meat, hot dishes, and cheese. The amount of food consumed as a first
course by many Swedish people would constitute a full meal for an average American, but the average Swede is a hearty eater and continues
through a full dinner. How did the *smörgåsbord* come into existence?
Many centuries ago, particularly in rural areas, when there was a party
or gathering, everyone brought some food. It was arranged on a long table, and the assembled guests helped themselves from the large arrangement of assorted dishes.

Cocktails and other alcoholic beverages are not normally served before
dinner, but there is a considerable amount of skoaling, or toasting, which
takes place during the dinner itself. It is considered extremely discour-
teous not to respond to a toast, but this works a great hardship on people
who are not used to drinking. The usual drink with *smörgåsbord* is *snaps,*
a type of brandy. *Snaps* is served ice cold, and is not tasted or sipped but
swallowed in a gulp; it is very potent. The *snaps* bottle is often frozen
into a small block of ice and brought to the table that way, an attractive

way of serving it. Beer is extremely good and is considered essential, a normal conclusion in view of the large amount of salty fish dishes that the Swedish people love to eat. Wine is of limited importance except among the more sophisticated city inhabitants. The famous Swedish Christmas drink known as *glögg* has traveled all over the world and is almost as important a part of that holiday as the tree.

Meal hours follow the pattern that we are familiar with, except for a few slight variations. Upon arising coffee and rolls are served in one's hotel room; those who wish it may obtain a larger breakfast. Lunch and dinner are at normal hours, except that dinner is usually available from 5 P.M. The Swedes, in company with all Northern peoples, are hearty eaters and think much of good food. The finicky eater is not a part of the Swedish way of life, and ladies who eat heartily are more likely to get married than those who count calories.

Favorites of all the people are the rich, thick soups, of which the *vit-kålsoppa,* or cabbage soup, is a typical example. With its large seacoast, Sweden depends heavily upon the sea to support itself, and fish dishes are unusually good. There are such things as fish puddings, herring salads, and of course the famous salmon dishes such as *lax med citronsås,* for which a recipe appears in the following section. The people like meat dishes, and lamb, beef, and pork are common foods. Probably the outstanding favorite of the meat dishes would be the *köttbullar* (meat balls made with sweet cream).

The Swedish people love coffee, and with it they must have their many different kinds of coffeecake. They cannot be challenged on this subject, for they are undoubtedly the world champions. Another great specialty of the country is the flat breads—crunchy, delicious, and particularly suited to the national custom of the *smörgåsbord.* The flat rye bread is *knäckebröd,* which the country people eat in almost unbelievable quantities.

CAVIAR CUSTARD

KAVIARLÅDA

1⅓ cups heavy cream	½ cup minced chives
1⅓ cups fresh bread crumbs	6 ounces black or red caviar
8 eggs	4 tablespoons butter

Preheat oven to 325°.

Scald the cream, then pour it over the bread crumbs. Let stand 10 minutes. Beat the eggs and mix in the undrained bread crumbs. Stir in the chives and caviar. Spoon into six buttered custard cups or other individual baking dishes. Dot with butter. Bake 20 minutes, or until a knife inserted in the center comes out clean. Serve hot. *Serves 6.*

COLD FRUIT SOUP

BLANDAD FRUKTSOPPA

1 pound assorted dried fruit (other than prunes)	2 apples
½ pound prunes	1 cinnamon stick or 2 teaspoons powdered cinnamon
8 cups water	2 tablespoons cornstarch
¾ cup sugar	2 tablespoons cold water

Wash the dried fruit and prunes thoroughly. Place in a saucepan with the water and sugar. Soak overnight. Peel and core the apples. Cut into eighths. Leaving the dried fruit in the same water in which it was soaked, place the saucepan over medium heat. Add the apples and cinnamon. Cook over medium heat for 45 minutes, or until the fruit is very soft. Remove the fruit and force through a sieve, discarding any pits. Return the fruit pulp to the soup and continue cooking over medium heat. Combine the cornstarch with the water in a cup and stir until smooth. Gradually add to the soup, stirring constantly until the boiling point is reached. Continue cooking for 5 minutes. Chill and serve ice cold. *Serves 8–10.*

Note: This soup is quite sweet to American taste. It is therefore better suited to lunches or late suppers than as a part of large dinners. The cinnamon taste is very distinctive and may be reduced, if desired.

CABBAGE SOUP WITH DUMPLINGS

VITKÅLSOPPA MED KROPPKAKOR

4 tablespoons butter	2 quarts chicken broth
3-pound head cabbage, coarsely shredded	2 teaspoons salt
2 tablespoons dark brown sugar	½ teaspoon freshly ground black pepper

Melt the butter in a saucepan. Add the cabbage and sauté until brown, stirring frequently. Add the sugar and cook over medium heat for 3 minutes, stirring constantly. Add the broth, salt, and pepper. Cover and cook over low heat for 45 minutes. Correct seasoning. Serve with the following dumplings:

4 tablespoons butter	¼ cup sifted flour
2 onions, chopped	1 teaspoon salt
¼ pound ham, diced	2 egg yolks, beaten
3 (1 pound) boiled potatoes, peeled	

Melt the butter in a saucepan. Add the onion and sauté for 5 minutes, stirring frequently. Add the ham and sauté for 10 minutes. Set aside. Mash or rice the potatoes. Add the flour, salt, and egg yolks and mix together. Knead into a dough and shape into a long roll about 1 inch in diameter. If mixture doesn't hold together, add a little more flour. Break off pieces of dough about 1 inch long and flatten with the hand on a lightly floured surface. Place a heaping teaspoon of the ham mixture on each and shape into round dumplings, pressing the edges together. Drop into boiling, salted water and cook for 15 minutes. Drain. The dumplings may be placed in the cabbage soup or they may be served in a separate dish. *Serves 8–10.*

SALMON WITH LEMON SAUCE

LAX MED CITRONSÅS

3 onions, sliced	2 tablespoons white vinegar
2 carrots, sliced	4 tablespoons chopped dill
2 teaspoons salt	4 cups water
1 teaspoon white pepper	4 pounds fresh salmon (in one
1 bay leaf	piece) or 6 slices

Combine the onions, carrots, salt, pepper, bay leaf, vinegar, 2 tablespoons of the dill, and the water in a saucepan. Bring to a boil and add the salmon. Cover and cook over medium heat for 20 minutes. Remove cover and cook for 20 minutes. Remove the fish carefully and strain the stock. Sprinkle the fish with the remaining dill. Keep the salmon warm and prepare the following sauce:

3 tablespoons butter	¼ teaspoon white pepper
2 tablespoons flour	1 teaspoon sugar
¾ cup heavy cream, scalded	3 tablespoons lemon juice
1 teaspoon salt	2 egg yolks

Melt the butter in a saucepan. Add the flour and mix to a smooth paste. Gradually add the cream and 1 cup of the reserved fish stock, stirring constantly until the boiling point is reached. Cook over low heat for 5 minutes. Add the salt, pepper, sugar, and lemon juice, and mix well. Beat the yolks in a bowl. Gradually add 1 cup of the sauce, beating constantly. Return this mixture to the saucepan and cook over low heat for 1 minute, stirring constantly. Do not allow to boil.

Serve the fish and the sauce separately. Tiny boiled and buttered potatoes are often served with the salmon. If desired, the salmon may be served cold. In that event the sauce should also be cold. *Serves 6.*

SWEDISH MEAT BALLS

KÖTTBULLER

¼ pound (1 stick) butter
1 large onion, chopped
1 cup fresh bread crumbs
1 cup light cream
1 pound beef, chopped
1 pound pork, chopped
½ pound veal, chopped

2 teaspoons salt
¾ teaspoon freshly ground
   black pepper
2 eggs, beaten
2 tablespoons chopped parsley
1 tablespoon flour
1½ cups heavy cream, scalded

Melt 3 tablespoons of the butter in a skillet. Add the onions and sauté for 10 minutes, stirring occasionally. Soak the bread crumbs in the cream. Combine the beef, pork, and veal in a bowl. Add the sautéed onions, the bread crumbs, salt, pepper, eggs, and parsley. Mix well. Shape into 1-inch balls. Melt 3 tablespoons of the butter in a skillet and fry the balls in it until very brown, shaking the pan frequently. Be careful not to break the balls, and add butter as necessary. Remove the meat balls and keep warm.

Add the flour to the remaining butter in the skillet. Mix to a smooth paste. Gradually add the heavy cream, stirring constantly until the boiling point is reached. Cook over low heat for 5 minutes. Correct seasoning. Pour over the meat balls and serve. *Serves 8–10.*

SWEDISH POT ROAST

GRYTSTEK

3 teaspoons salt
1 teaspoon freshly ground
   black pepper
5 pounds beef of cut suitable
   for pot roast
4 tablespoons butter
3 large onions, chopped
2 cups boiling water
4 tablespoons molasses

2 bay leaves
½ teaspoon allspice
3 carrots, sliced
¼ cup brandy
3 anchovy fillets
1 tablespoon vinegar
2 tablespoons flour
1½ cups light cream

Mix the salt and pepper together and rub into the meat thoroughly. Melt the butter in a large Dutch oven. Brown the meat on all sides. Add the onions and continue browning for 5 minutes. Add the water, molasses, bay leaves, allspice, carrots, and brandy and stir. Mash the anchovies in a small bowl and add the vinegar, mixing well. Add this mixture to the meat and stir well. Cover and cook over low heat for 2½ hours, or until tender.

Remove the meat from the Dutch oven and set it aside. Mix the flour and cream together until smooth and add to the gravy, stirring constantly until the boiling point is reached. Correct seasoning. Cook over low heat for 5 minutes. Remove the bay leaves. Carve the meat and serve with the gravy separately. *Serves 8–10.*

ROAST LEG OF LAMB

LAMMSTEK

5-pound leg of lamb	2 cups beef broth
1 tablespoon salt	1 cup strong brewed coffee
½ teaspoon white pepper	¼ cup heavy cream
2 carrots, sliced	½ teaspoon sugar
2 onions, sliced	3 tablespoons flour

Rinse, trim, and dry the lamb; rub with the salt and pepper. Place the leg in a roasting pan and roast in a 450° oven 20 minutes, turning the leg to brown all sides. Pour off the fat. Add the carrots, onions, and 1 cup of the broth. Reduce heat to 350° and roast 45 minutes, basting occasionally. Add a mixture of the coffee, cream, and sugar; roast 45 minutes longer, basting occasionally.

Transfer the leg to a heated platter. Strain the pan juices and skim the fat. Mix the flour with a little of the remaining broth and stir into the pan juices, cooking and stirring over low heat until mixture boils. Add the remaining broth and cook 5 minutes longer. Taste for seasoning. Serve the gravy in a sauceboat. *Serves 8–10.*

SEAFOOD SALAD

SALLAD JONAS

2 cooked lobsters	¾ cup olive oil
1 pound boiled shrimp	¼ cup vinegar
12 mussels (optional)	2 tablespoons water
2 scallions (green onions), chopped or 4 tablespoons chopped chives	1 teaspoon salt
	⅛ teaspoon freshly ground black pepper
3 tomatoes, cubed	1 head lettuce, finely shredded
1 tablespoon prepared mustard	

Remove the lobster meat from the shells and cut into large pieces. Peel the shrimp and cut each one into four pieces. Combine the lobster meat, shrimp, mussels, onions, and tomatoes. Mix well. In a bowl mix the mustard and olive oil until smooth. Add the vinegar, water, salt, and pepper, and beat until well blended. Pour over the seafood mixture and mix carefully but thoroughly. Chill for 30 minutes. Arrange mounds of the seafood mixture on individual plates and cover with the shredded lettuce. *Serves 6–8.*

PUFF PASTE CREAM TART

TUSENBLADSTÅRT

Pastry:

1⅔ cups flour	¼ cup ice water
½ pound (2 sticks) sweet butter	3 tablespoons sugar

Sift the flour into a bowl; cut in the butter with a pastry blender or two knives until small particles are formed. With a wooden spoon, gradually mix in the ice water until a ball of dough is formed. Wrap in a damp towel and chill 30 minutes. Preheat oven to 450°.

Divide the dough into six equal pieces, and roll out each piece into a 9-inch circle. Place each circle on wax paper-lined baking sheets. Prick the tops all over with a fork, and sprinkle with sugar. Bake in a 450° oven 7 minutes, or until tops are golden brown. Cool, then remove carefully from the paper.

Filling:

3 egg yolks	5 tablespoons butter
1 tablespoon cornstarch	1 teaspoon vanilla extract
6 tablespoons sugar	2 cups applesauce
1⅓ cups heavy cream	

Beat the egg yolks in the top of a double boiler. Stir in the cornstarch and sugar until smooth, then mix in the cream and the butter. Place over hot water and cook, stirring steadily until thickened and smooth. Remove from the heat and add the vanilla. Cool, stirring occasionally.

Spread the pastry layers alternately with applesauce and cream filling, sandwiching them together. Leave the top layer plain.

Topping:

1 cup confectioners' sugar	1 teaspoon sugar
2 teaspoons lemon juice	½ cup ground toasted almonds
2 tablespoons water	Candied fruits
1 cup heavy cream	

Sift the confectioners' sugar into a bowl; stir in the lemon juice and water until it is a spreadable consistency. If too dry, add a little more water. Spread the mixture evenly over the top.

Whip the cream with the sugar and pipe around the sides of the tart. Sprinkle the almonds around the top edge of the tart and decorate with candied fruits. *Serves 8–10.*

APPLE CAKE WITH VANILLA SAUCE

ÄPPLEKAKA MED VANILJSÄS

¼ pound (1 stick) sweet butter	4 egg yolks
3 cups stale spongecake crumbs or cracker crumbs	4 tablespoons sugar
2½ cups sweetened applesauce	2 cups heavy cream
2 teaspoons cinnamon	2½ teaspoons vanilla extract

Preheat oven to 350°.

Melt the butter in a skillet. Add the crumbs and cook over medium heat 5 minutes, stirring frequently. Butter an 8-inch square baking dish. Place a layer of crumbs on the bottom and add alternate layers of applesauce, cinnamon, and crumbs. Start and finish with the crumbs. Bake in a 350° oven for 30 minutes, or until set and delicately browned on top. Let cool, then turn out of the pan carefully.

Beat the egg yolks in the top of a double boiler. Add the sugar and beat well. Scald 1¼ cups of the cream and add it to the yolks, beating constantly. Place over hot water and cook until thick, stirring constantly. Remove from the hot water, add the vanilla, and let cool for 1 hour. Whip the remaining cream and fold it into the sauce. Cut the cake in squares and serve the sauce in a separate dish. *Serves 6–8.*

TRADITIONAL SWEDISH CHRISTMAS DRINK

GLÖGG

4 cups red wine (burgundy or claret)	5 cloves
4 cups port wine	¼ pound almonds, blanched
1 tablespoon finely chopped orange or lemon peel	¼ pound seedless raisins
5 cardamom seeds	¼ pound cube sugar
1 cinnamon stick (or 2 teaspoons powdered cinnamon)	2 cups brandy

A large copper kettle is the proper utensil for preparing *glögg*, but a large enamel or glass saucepan may be used. Combine the red wine and port in the saucepan over low heat. Take a piece of cheesecloth about

4 inches square and place in the center the orange peel, cardamom seeds, cinnamon, and cloves. Tie or sew the cheesecloth together securely, and place it in the wine mixture. Simmer for 20 minutes. Add the almonds and raisins and simmer for 10 minutes. Remove from the heat and discard the cheesecloth.

Place the cubes of sugar in a metal strainer and rest it on top of the saucepan if possible. Set the brandy aflame and pour it very gradually over the sugar. If there is any difficulty in lighting the brandy, warm it briefly. As the lighted brandy is poured over the sugar, it will caramelize. As an alternative, ½ cup of granulated sugar may be dissolved in the wine, and the brandy set aflame and poured into the wine. Serve hot in mugs. *Serves 12–14.*

SWITZERLAND

This silent, majestic country known the world over for snow, winter sports, tourists, hotels, scenery, watches, and cheese, is comparatively little known for its cuisine. Since tourists flock to this land in tremendous numbers, the Swiss hotelkeepers have succumbed to pressure and serve the inevitable and apparently inescapable imitation-French hotel food known everywhere. The average tourist, too busy with his sightseeing or skiing, leaves Switzerland under the impression that the Swiss people are the most hospitable in the world, are experts in putting holes in cheese, make the best watches in the world, but have practically nothing at all in the way of a national cuisine.

This is unfortunate because it is partially untrue. The Swiss do have their own food specialties, which may be tasted if the tourist will occasionally break away from the hotel *de luxe* and dine at a small village restaurant. There is much that will be of interest to the food-conscious visitor.

First, a brief explanation of Switzerland's background. It was formed principally from small segments of France, Italy, and Germany. These three languages are spoken to this day in Switzerland by a great number of persons. It is not surprising, therefore, to find that the cuisine has three distinct backgrounds—French in the west, Italian in the south, and German in the east and north.

Switzerland's contribution to the world of the gourmet consists largely of fine chocolates, cheese, wines, and liqueurs. The Swiss, like their neighbors the French, are very fond of wines and produce a substantial number of quite good types. The Neuchâtel and the Riesling-Sylvaner are probably the best known of these. The people prefer the dry white wines, and these are served as apéritifs, with food, and as refreshment any time during the day. Unfortunately many Swiss wines do not lend themselves to shipment, and may be fully enjoyed only in the country that produced them. Great favorites, too, are *kirsch,* a clear cherry brandy, and *marc,* a strong brandy made from the second pressing of the grape. Beer is well liked, particularly in the north and eastern portions of the country, which might be expected since those cantons are adjacent to Germany.

Although the Swiss cuisine is largely borrowed from its neighbors, the *fondue,* a melted cheese dish, may be said to be one of the truly national dishes. It is made with Swiss cheese, white wine, and *kirsch.* Etiquette decrees that pieces of toast be dipped into the *fondue. Râclette,* another national dish, is made by melting cheese before an open fire or stove, and is served with boiled potatoes. *Ramekins* are another cheese favorite.

Bern canton (province) has a local specialty in the *Berner Platte,* composed of assorted meats and sauerkraut; St. Gall canton boasts of a delicious veal sausage called *St. Galler Bratwurst;* Lucerne has a delicacy called *Kuegeli-Pastete,* a puff paste filled with sweetbreads, mushrooms, and other delicacies. The southern cantons feature Italian-style food.

Swiss chocolates are among the richest and smoothest in the world and are exported to the farthest corners of the earth.

GRAVY SOUP

GERÖSTETE MEHLSUPPE

5 tablespoons butter or chicken fat
5 tablespoons flour
7 cups hot beef broth

1 cup buttered croutons
¼ cup grated Swiss or Gruyère cheese

Melt the fat in a deep saucepan. Add the flour and stir well. Cook over low heat until a deep brown in color, stirring constantly to prevent burning. Gradually add the hot broth, stirring constantly until the boiling point is reached. Cover and cook over medium heat for 1½ hours, stirring occasionally. Correct seasoning. Serve with croutons on top and sprinkle grated cheese over each portion. *Serves 4–6.*

SALMON, BASEL STYLE

LACHS, BASELER ART

6 slices fresh salmon	¼ pound butter
2 teaspoons salt	2 onions, chopped
1 teaspoon pepper	3 tablespoons stock or water
4 tablespoons flour	

Sponge the salmon carefully but do not wash. Combine the salt, pepper, and flour and pat into the fish on all sides. Melt half of the butter in a skillet. Fry the salmon slices in it 5 to 8 minutes on each side or until golden brown. Place the fish on a heated platter and keep warm.

Melt the remaining butter in the same skillet. Sauté the onions over low heat for 15 minutes, stirring frequently, until they are soft and yellow but not browned. Pour the onions over the salmon. Place the stock or water in the same skillet, scraping any glaze or particles remaining in the pan. When the mixture boils, pour it over the fish. Sprinkle a little sweet paprika on the fish; chopped parsley may also be added. Serve with very thin slices of lemon. Although this is a comparatively simple dish, it is a great favorite of the Swiss. *Serves 6.*

MEAT PLATTER, BERNE STYLE

BERNER PLATTE

1 smoked beef tongue	1 cup dry white wine
2 pounds ham or pork, or	¼ pound Canadian bacon
1 pound of each	½ pound smoked sausage (in one
2 pounds short ribs of beef	piece, if possible)
3 pounds sauerkraut	

Place the tongue in a deep saucepan and cover with water. Bring to a boil and pour off the water. Cover with fresh boiling water. Cover and cook over medium heat for 1½ hours. Add the ham or pork and the short ribs of beef. Cover and cook for 2 hours, or until all the meats are tender. While the meats are cooking, combine the sauerkraut, wine, bacon, and sausage in a saucepan. Cover and cook for 1½ hours. Slice the cooked meats and arrange on a platter with the sauerkraut in the center. *Serves 10–12.*

ROAST BEEF, SOUTHERN STYLE

STUFFATO ALLA CHIASSESE

3 cloves garlic, minced
2 teaspoons salt
1 teaspoon freshly ground
black pepper
4 tablespoons flour
6- to 8-pound rib roast of beef
2 tablespoons butter

2 onions, chopped
¼ pound sliced bacon, half
cooked and drained
1 cup dry red wine
6 potatoes, peeled and quartered
3 tomatoes

Combine the garlic, salt, pepper, and flour and rub into the meat. Melt the butter in a large roasting pan on top of the stove. Add the onions and meat. Sear on all sides until well browned. Place the strips of bacon on top of the meat, fastening with toothpicks. Pour the wine over the meat.

Roast the meat in a 350° oven for 15 to 22 minutes per pound, depending on the degree of rareness desired. Baste occasionally. About 45 minutes before the meat is ready, add the potatoes and tomatoes. Small quantities of water may be added if required. Place the meat, potatoes, and tomatoes on a platter and serve hot. *Serves 8–10.*

FRIED POTATOES

RÖSTI

2 pounds potatoes
1 tablespoon vegetable oil
4 tablespoons butter
1 cup chopped onions

1 teaspoon salt
¼ teaspoon freshly ground
black pepper
2 tablespoons boiling water

Cook the unpeeled potatoes until tender but still firm. Drain and cool. Peel the potatoes, then cut into julienne strips, or grate on a long grater.

Heat the oil in a 9-inch skillet; add the butter and let it melt. Add the potatoes, onions, salt, and pepper. Cook over low heat, turning frequently with a spatula, for 5 minutes. With the spatula, smooth the potatoes into a cake. Sprinkle the top with the water. Cover the pan and cook 15 minutes, or until bottom is golden and crisp. Shake the pan frequently and add a little butter, if necessary. Turn out onto a hot platter, browned side up. *Serves 6–8.*

ONION SALAD

ZWIEBELN SALAT

4 tablespoons butter	1 tablespoon flour
4 large onions, sliced ½ inch thick	1 teaspoon salt
	2 tablespoons vinegar

Melt the butter in a saucepan. Add the onions and sauté until light brown, stirring frequently. Sprinkle with the flour and cook for 3 minutes. Remove from the heat. Add the salt and vinegar and mix well. Serve hot or cold. The salad is particularly good when served with small, buttered, boiled potatoes as a separate course.

THE SWISS NATIONAL CHEESE DISH

FONDUE

1 clove garlic	Nutmeg
1 cup dry white wine	2 teaspoons potato flour
½ pound Gruyère cheese, grated	2 tablespoons *kirsch* or dry sherry
Freshly ground black pepper	French bread, cut in cubes

Rub an earthenware casserole or chafing dish with the garlic, then discard it. Pour the white wine into it and cook over medium heat for 2 minutes. Add the grated cheese and bring to the boiling point, stirring occasionally. In a cup, mix the potato flour and *kirsch* or sherry to a smooth paste and add to the cheese mixture, stirring constantly for 3 minutes, or until the mixture is thick. Add pepper and nutmeg to taste. Bring the casserole to the table and place the bread cubes near it. Each guest spears a cube with a fork and dips it into the *fondue*. This dish makes an excellent luncheon dish, or it may be served at a late supper.

CHEESE TARTS

RAMEKINS

1 cup sifted flour	½ pound Swiss cheese
1 teaspoon salt	1 tablespoon flour
⅓ pound butter	4 eggs, beaten
¾ cup heavy cream	Dash of pepper

Sift the flour and ½ teaspoon of the salt into a bowl. Add the butter, reserving 1 tablespoon. Work in the butter with the hand. Add 3 tablespoons of the cream and continue mixing until a ball of dough is formed.

Wrap in wax paper and place in the refrigerator overnight, or for at least 2 hours. Roll out the dough ⅛ inch thick on a lightly floured surface. Line an unbuttered 9-inch pie plate or 6 small individual pie plates with the dough. Preheat oven to 375°.

Grate half of the cheese and cut the remaining half into tiny cubes. Combine the grated cheese, flour, remaining salt, remaining cream, eggs, and pepper in a bowl. Mix well and add the cubed cheese. Pour the mixture into the pie plate. Dot with the remaining butter. Bake in a 375° oven for 35 minutes if the 9-inch pie plate is used, or for 20 minutes if the smaller individual plates are used. Serve hot. *Serves 6.*

NUT MERINGUE TORTE

BROYAGE

Vegetable oil	¾ cup fine granulated sugar
Flour	1 teaspoon vanilla extract
3 egg whites	¼ cup blanched ground nuts
⅛ teaspoon salt	⅓ cup sifted cornstarch
⅛ teaspoon cream of tartar	

Preheat oven to 325°.

Grease and dust with flour the bottom of two 9-inch cake pans with removable bottoms. If you don't have cake pans with removable bottoms, grease and dust a baking pan with flour. As a guide, press a 9-inch layer cake pan onto it, to form circles over which you can spread the meringue.

Beat the egg whites, salt, and cream of tartar until soft peaks form. Beat in 1 tablespoon of sugar at a time until ½ cup is used up and meringue is very stiff. Stir in vanilla. Mix together the nuts, cornstarch, and remaining sugar. Fold into the meringue. Divide between the pans or spread on the baking pan. Smooth the top with a wet spatula.

Bake in a preheated 325° oven 25 minutes, or until dry to the touch. Carefully remove from the pan and cool on a cake rack. Put layers together with the following:

6 ounces semisweet chocolate	1 egg yolk
2 tablespoons strong coffee	1 tablespoon brandy
¼ pound (1 stick) sweet butter, softened	

Melt the chocolate in the coffee, stirring until smooth. Cool. Cream the butter until fluffy, then beat in the chocolate, egg yolk, and brandy. Spread between the layers. Chill. This torte is especially good if made the day before it is to be served. *Serves 8–10.*

PEAR CAKE

BIRNENBROT

1 pound dried pears	1 cup chopped walnuts
1 cake or package yeast	¼ cup seedless raisins
1 cup milk, scalded and cooled	1 cup sugar
¼ cup melted butter	2 tablespoons cinnamon
¼ cup sugar	1 tablespoon candied orange
1 egg	peel
3¾ cups sifted flour	1 teaspoon grated lemon rind
½ teaspoon salt	½ cup *kirsch* or brandy

Soak the pears in water to cover overnight. Combine the yeast and luke-warm milk in a bowl and mix until smooth. Set aside for 5 minutes. Add the butter, sugar, and egg and mix well. Sift the flour and salt to-gether twice. Add to the yeast mixture gradually, mixing steadily. It may not be necessary to add all of the flour in order to make a dough. Knead the mixture until a stiff dough is formed. Cover and put in a warm place to rise until doubled in size, about 1½ hours. Punch the dough down and again allow to rise for 45 minutes.

Drain the pears well. Add fresh water and cook in a saucepan over medium heat until tender, about 30 minutes. Drain well and chop the pears finely. Combine the chopped pears, walnuts, raisins, sugar, cinna-mon, orange peel, lemon rind, and *kirsch* or brandy and mix well.

Divide the dough into two parts, making one part half again as large as the other. Work the fruit and nut mixture into the smaller piece of dough. Roll out the larger piece of dough on a lightly floured surface so that it is sufficient to line and overlap a buttered 10-inch loaf pan. Place the dough-fruit mixture in the center of the pan and cover with the overlapping dough, sealing the edges well with a little water or egg white. Prick the top with a fork in several places. Preheat oven. Let rise for 20 minutes. Bake in a 375° oven for 45 minutes, or until lightly browned on top. The cake should keep well for more than a week. Serve hot or cold in slices. Although to American tastes this is suitable for serving as a cake, in Switzerland it is often used as a sweet bread. *Makes one 10-inch loaf.*

YUGOSLAVIA

Yugoslavia has many neighbors, its borders touching upon Italy, Austria, Hungary, Rumania, Bulgaria, Greece, and Albania. The Yugoslavs are rather antipathetic to the Italians, and the food of that country is not popular in Yugoslavia, but the others have contributed heavily to the local food customs. From Austria and Hungary the Yugoslavs have appropriated the many dishes flavored with paprika, such as *ribji guljaž*, a fish specialty made with paprika. In common with Rumania, the basic food of the peasant group is corn meal served in several different ways, but usually boiled and eaten as a porridge. As their neighbors, the Bulgarians, favor mutton, the Yugoslavs also appreciate lamb, often served with many different vegetables. The favorite of the Greeks, grape leaves stuffed with rice, veal, or lamb, is often seen in Yugoslav homes and restaurants. Even tiny Albania shares with her much larger neighbor to the north the custom of preparing vegetables in oil, as well as the frequent use of sour milk.

The people are simple and friendly, fond of good solid food and strong drink. The cuisine of the country has that great but swiftly disappearing virtue, simplicity. One cannot find here the intricate dishes of some of Yugoslavia's neighbors, but appetizing and wholesome food is usually available.

Plums grow particularly well in this agricultural land. In fact much of the national diet is based on plums, for they are used in many different ways. Some are dried, some are made into fine preserves. A favorite soft drink is a tablespoon of plum jam in a glass of ice-cold water. The people are also fond of plum brandies, known as both *šljiovica* and *slivovka*. There are endless varieties of prune brandy, but these are mostly consumed within the country itself. *Maraskino* is a liqueur of the highest quality. The country produces a wide variety of good red and white wines containing about twelve to sixteen per cent alcohol. There is good *pivo* (beer) to be had here, both light and dark.

The Yugoslavs are fond of onions, hot peppers, spicy pickles, and other relishes. A true Yugoslav can swallow hot red peppers one after the other without batting the proverbial eye. Visitors are well advised to approach the local "relishes" with a degree of caution.

A national favorite is the *čevapčići*, a beef and veal sausage that is eaten by everyone. These are customarily roasted on open fires, as are most other meats. Another fine dish is *ćurka na podvarku* (turkey and sauerkraut). Rather simple desserts of fruit or cheese are eaten, although occasionally a rich confection filled with nuts and honey is prepared. Strong black coffee prepared in the Balkan style is the usual finish to a meal.

This being a nation with thousands of small dairy farms, cheese plays an important part as an everyday food. In the Serbian portion of the country, cheese is frequently served as a first course, either plain or with *pršuta,* thin slices of smoked meat, accompanied by a small drink of plum brandy. This area makes *kačkavalj,* a crumbly hard cheese very popular throughout Yugoslavia. In addition, there are numbers of fresh, soft white cheeses, which are quite delicious although unsophisticated to the palate. In the province of Vojvodina, two important cheeses are produced; *skuta* is a fresh type of cottage cheese; *sombor* has a distinctive flavor and a yellow coloring. In the southern part of the country, Macedonia, cheeses are made with sheep's milk. *Kefalotir* is medium hard, suitable for grating, and resembles Parmesan. The whey which remains from making this cheese is pressed and shaped into a round mass, and is then called *mandur,* and is suitable for eating or cooking. A soft, rather white cheese called *travnički* made chiefly in Bosnia-Herzegovina, is slightly salty and a touch sour, but it has its adherents; it is something of an acquired taste, all things considered.

BEAN SOUP

ČORBA OD PASULJA

2 cups dried white beans	3 cloves garlic, minced
1 pound smoked ham, cut into 6 pieces	3 potatoes, peeled and diced
2½ quarts water	½ teaspoon freshly ground black pepper
3 tablespoons vegetable oil	1 teaspoon sweet paprika
3 onions, chopped	3 tablespoons chopped parsley

Soak the beans overnight in water to cover. Drain, and discard any imperfect beans. Cover with fresh water, bring to a boil, and drain. Add fresh water and cook for 1 hour, or until tender. In a separate saucepan cook the ham and the 2½ quarts of water over medium heat for 1½ hours, or until tender. Heat the oil in a frying pan and add the onions, garlic, potatoes, pepper, paprika, and parsley. Sauté 15 minutes, stirring frequently. Drain the beans and combine with the undrained ham. Add the sautéed vegetable mixture. Cook over low heat for 15 minutes, mixing well. Serve hot. Taste for seasoning, adding salt if necessary. *Serves 8–10.*

SPICY FISH, YUGOSLAV STYLE

RIBJI GULJAŽ

3 tablespoons olive oil	2 teaspoons tomato paste
2 tablespoons chopped onion	2 tablespoons water
2 teaspoons salt	1 bay leaf
1 teaspoon freshly ground black pepper	2 teaspoons vinegar
1 tablespoon sweet paprika	1 clove garlic, minced
6 slices sea bass, fillet of sole, or similar fish	

Heat the olive oil in a large skillet. Add the onion and sauté for 5 minutes. Combine the salt, pepper, and paprika. Rub into each slice of fish. Place the fish in the skillet and brown on both sides. Add the tomato paste, water, bay leaf, vinegar, and garlic. Cook over low heat for 15 minutes, turning the fish once. Stir the sauce occasionally and baste the fish. Serve hot or cold. *Serves 6.*

BEEF AND VEAL SAUSAGES

ČEVAPČIĆI

1 pound beef, ground	1 teaspoon freshly ground black pepper
1 pound veal, ground	1 cup finely chopped onions
⅛ pound beef fat, ground	
2 teaspoons salt	

Combine the ground beef, veal, and fat with the salt and pepper in a chopping bowl. Chop until well blended and fine in texture. Form into sausages about 2 inches long. Broil in a 500° oven fairly close to the heat. Turn frequently until the sausages are well browned. Serve with the chopped onions on the side. If served with the bean soup (see recipe in this section), it becomes a complete meal. *Serves 6–8.*

Note: In Yugoslavia these sausages are usually broiled over an open fire. They make an excellent appetizer at a barbecue when prepared over a charcoal fire.

If you prefer, all beef can be used.

PRIEST'S LUNCH

POPINA JANJA YANJE

3 pounds brisket of beef, cut
  into 1-inch cubes
4 potatoes, peeled and diced
1 cup diced celery
8 small white onions
3 tomatoes, quartered
4 tablespoons chopped parsley

3 cloves garlic, minced
1 teaspoon salt
2 tablespoons paprika
4 bay leaves
12 whole peppercorns
6 cups beef broth

Combine the beef, potatoes, celery, onions, tomatoes, parsley, garlic, salt, paprika, bay leaves, peppercorns, and broth in a deep casserole. Mix gently. Cover the casserole with a large piece of parchment paper or aluminum foil so that it slightly overhangs the outside edges of the casserole. Tie the paper with a string to make a tight seal. Place the casserole cover over the paper. Bake in a 350° oven for 2½ hours. Correct seasoning and serve directly from the casserole. *Serves 6–8.*

ROAST TURKEY AND SAUERKRAUT

ČURKA NA PODVARKU

3 tablespoons chicken fat or
  butter
2 pounds sauerkraut
2 potatoes, grated
2 onions, grated

2 teaspoons pepper
3 teaspoons salt
1 teaspoon sweet paprika
12-pound turkey

Melt the fat in a saucepan. Add the sauerkraut, potatoes, onions, and 1 teaspoon of the pepper. Cook over high heat for 5 minutes, stirring constantly. Combine the remaining pepper, salt, and paprika and rub it into the turkey inside and out. If possible, this should be done the day before the turkey is to be cooked.

Place the sauerkraut mixture in a large roasting pan and put the turkey on top of it. Roast uncovered in a 350° oven. Allow 20 minutes per pound for roasting time. Turn the turkey several times during the roasting period, but end with the breast upward during the last 30 minutes. Baste frequently. Serve hot with the sauerkraut. *Serve 8–10.*

HAZELNUT COOKIES

KOLAČI OD LJEŠNJAKA

3 eggs
½ cup sugar
1 teaspoon vanilla extract
2 tablespoons brandy

1 tablespoon zwieback crumbs
or bread crumbs
2 cups ground hazelnuts
(filberts)
½ cup hazelnuts, halved

Preheat oven to 300°.

Beat the eggs in a bowl until light. Add the sugar and continue beating. Add the vanilla, brandy, and crumbs. Mix well. Fold in the ground nuts carefully but thoroughly. Shape a teaspoon of dough into a small ball. Place half of a hazelnut on each ball. If desired, the dough may be pressed flat. Bake in a 300° oven for 20 minutes, or until lightly browned. *Makes about 36.*

HOME-STYLE STRUDEL

LANJA PITA

Pastry:

½ pound (2 sticks) butter
⅓ cup sugar
2 egg yolks

1 teaspoon vanilla extract
2⅔ cups sifted flour

Cream the butter, then beat in the sugar until light. Beat in the egg yolks and vanilla. Mix in the flour until a dough is formed. Chill while preparing the filling.

Filling:

6 (2 pounds) green apples
½ cup sugar
¼ cup vanilla cooky or dry bread
crumbs

1 tablespoon grated lemon rind
1 teaspoon cinnamon
1 egg, beaten
Confectioners' sugar (optional)

Preheat oven to 400°.

Peel and slice the apples very thin. Mix with the sugar, crumbs, lemon rind, and cinnamon. Divide the dough into two pieces, one slightly larger than the other. Roll out the larger piece into a 12-inch square. Fit it into an oiled 8-inch-square baking pan. Put the filling into it, and cover with the remaining rolled-out dough, sealing the edges. Brush the top with the egg. Bake in a 400° oven 15 minutes, then reduce heat to 350° and bake 30 minutes longer, or until browned. Serve warm, cut into squares and dusted with confectioners' sugar if desired. *Serves 8–10.*

WINE LIQUEUR

VINSKI LIKER

1 quart red wine	2 teaspoons vanilla extract
1¼ cups sugar	2 cups brandy

Combine the wine and sugar in a saucepan. Bring to a boil and cook over medium heat for 10 minutes. Cool for 1 hour. Add the vanilla and brandy. Chill and serve cold. *Serves 8–10.*

The Balkans, the Near and Middle East

Albania
Arabia, Iran, Iraq, and
Afghanistan
Bulgaria
Greece
Israel
Rumania
Syria, Lebanon, and Jordan
Turkey

ALBANIA

The present-day inhabitants of Albania are descended from hill tribes running back thousands of years. The people were once Christians but now are mostly of the Mohammedan faith. Since Mohammedans shun pork in any form, and inasmuch as few of the populace are Christians, the ham and other pork dishes of the Balkan countries to the north are seldom seen here. Under Turkish control for several centuries, the influence of that period has made itself strongly felt in the local culture and cuisine.

The nation's economy is largely agricultural, with a particular emphasis on dairy products, which are unusually high in quality. Yogurt and sour milk are probably more important in the country's diet than almost any other single item, and are consumed daily. A particular hot-weather favorite is a bowl of chopped raw vegetables filled with cold yogurt and sprinkled with some rough, coarse salt. It is similar in both appearance and taste to the Russian summertime specialty of sour cream (*smetana*) with chopped vegetables.

For some reason mint dishes appeal to the national palate to a rather surprising degree. Mint is quite popular all through the Near East and in the Arabic-speaking lands; the Albanians use mint in making meatballs, in lamb dishes, salads, and cold drinks.

The country is hardly a rich one, and progress is difficult because of poor road conditions, which hinder transportation. Filled with beautiful mountainous scenery and startling panoramas, the very things that have made the country beautiful have prevented its development. Good roads are always expensive, but good roads built on high mountains are clearly beyond the means of the country in the foreseeable future. The people therefore live from the soil and from the sea, taking full advantage of what nature has offered them. Actually they have little choice.

Vegetables and fruits grow in profusion, but the Albanian public has particular favorites such as okra, eggplant, peppers, and artichokes.

These are usually prepared in the so-called Greek fashion, with plenty of olive oil and sometimes with the addition of tomatoes.

Chicken dishes are good, particularly when prepared in the Albanian fashion and stuffed with certain ingredients, varied according to what is available to the housewife. Lamb and mutton are naturally the meat favorites, as might be expected in a country located in the Near East and populated by Mohammedans. The cuisine is not complicated and the average Albanian peasant does not have a wide choice, but his food is almost always simple and good.

The drinks of the country include *raki,* the odd-flavored mulberry brandy known also in Turkey in a slightly different form. Since the countryside is laden with large, beautiful grapes during the harvest period, there is always plenty of wine of adequate quality, though seldom of exceptional or top rank. Black coffee, similar to the Turkish version, is also a favorite beverage.

Most of the meat dishes of the Near East are eaten in Albania, although they are handled somewhat differently than they would be, for example, in Turkey or Syria. The names, too, differ, but the lamb taste is almost always present.

YOGURT SOUP

TANABOUR

½ cup pearl barley	1 cup sour cream
4 cups beef broth	1 egg
1 teaspoon salt	4 tablespoons melted butter
½ teaspoon pepper	2 tablespoons chopped parsley
2 cups yogurt	

Soak the barley overnight in water to cover. Drain well. Combine with the broth, salt, and pepper in a saucepan. Cook over low heat for 2 hours, or until the barley is soft. Beat the yogurt, sour cream, and egg in a bowl. Gradually add 1 cup of the soup, beating constantly to prevent curdling. Return this mixture to the balance of the soup, beating well while adding. Add the butter and parsley, and stir well. Correct seasoning. Heat but do not allow to boil. *Serves 6–8.*

LEEK AND COTTAGE CHEESE PIE

BUREK ME PRESH

12 leeks or 24 scallions (green onions)
½ pound (2 sticks) butter
¾ cup light cream
1½ pounds cottage cheese
3 eggs, beaten

1 teaspoon salt
¼ teaspoon freshly ground black pepper
3 tablespoons minced dill
2 packages strudel leaves

Wash the leeks or scallions thoroughly, then slice the white part only very thin; discard green portions. Melt 4 tablespoons of the butter in a skillet; sauté the leeks or scallions 5 minutes, stirring frequently. Stir in the cream. Melt the remaining butter in a separate pan. Cool. Beat together the cottage cheese, eggs, salt and pepper. Mix in the dill and sautéed leeks and taste for seasoning.

Preheat oven to 400°. Grease an 11- by 16-inch baking (jelly roll) pan. Separate the strudel leaves, a package at a time—they measure 16 by 22 inches. Cut each leaf in half, so that they measure 16 by 11 inches. Put 9 leaves in the pan, one on top of the other, brushing each with melted butter. Spread the cheese mixture over it, and cover with the remaining 7 leaves, again brushing each with melted butter. Press down the edges and brush top layers with melted butter. Bake in a 400° oven 30 minutes, then reduce heat to 325° and bake 15 minutes longer. Serve hot or cold, cut into squares or oblongs. *Serves 8–10.*

ROAST STUFFED CHICKEN

PULE MEDROP

⅓ cup butter
2 cups fresh bread crumbs
¼ cup seedless raisins
¼ cup currants
2 tablespoons chopped black walnuts
2 tablespoons chopped hazelnuts
2 tablespoons chopped pine nuts

2 tablespoons chopped almonds
¼ cup sugar
¼ cup chicken broth
2 teaspoons salt
¼ teaspoon pepper
1 large roasting chicken

Melt 4 tablespoons of the butter in a saucepan and add the bread crumbs. Sauté for 5 minutes, stirring occasionally. Add the raisins, currants, nuts, sugar, and broth. Mix well. If mixture appears too dry, add a little more broth.

Mix salt and pepper together and rub into the chicken both inside and out. Stuff the chicken and close the opening carefully with thread or with skewers. Brush the chicken with the remaining butter. Roast in a 350° oven for 2½ hours, or until tender. Add ½ cup hot water for 1 hour and baste the chicken frequently with pan drippings during the roasting period. *Serves 4–6.*

VEGETABLE CASSEROLE

GJELLE ME ZARZAVATA

6 (2 pounds) potatoes, peeled and sliced thin
4 tomatoes, chopped
3 carrots, sliced thin
¼ cup chopped celery
2 onions, chopped fine
2 cloves garlic, minced

3 tablespoons chopped parsley
1½ teaspoons salt
½ teaspoon freshly ground black pepper
2 cups water
¼ cup olive oil

Place the potatoes in a shallow, buttered baking dish. Mix together the tomatoes, carrots, celery, onions, garlic, parsley, salt, and pepper. Spread over the potatoes and add the water. Bake in a 375° oven for 45 minutes. Pour the olive oil over the vegetables. Continue baking for 15 minutes. This dish may be served hot or cold. *Serves 6–8.*

SWEET SESAME BISCUITS

ISMIR SIMIT

2 eggs
⅓ cup sugar
2 tablespoons milk ·
⅓ cup melted butter

1½ cups sifted flour
¾ teaspoon baking powder
¼ cup sesame seeds

Preheat oven to 350°.

Beat 1 egg in a bowl. Add the sugar and beat until light. Add the milk and melted butter, and mix well. Sift the flour and baking powder together. Gradually add to the previous mixture, kneading until a dough is formed. If the dough is too soft, add a little more flour. Divide into about 18 small balls, or break off 18 pieces of dough. Roll each ball between the hands into a 9-inch strip. Fold each strip in thirds. Pinch the ends together. Place them on a buttered baking sheet. Beat the remaining egg and brush some on each biscuit. Sprinkle with the sesame seeds. Bake in a 350° oven for 20 minutes, or until delicately browned. *Makes 18.*

ALMOND PUFF PASTRY

EMATOR

1 cup water	1 teaspoon almond extract
¼ pound (1 stick) butter	2 cups sifted flour
1 cup sugar	¼ cup blanched almonds

Combine the water, butter, sugar, and almond extract in a saucepan. Bring to a boil and cook until butter and sugar are completely melted. Add the flour all at once, beating vigorously. Cook over low heat for 5 minutes, beating constantly. Preheat oven to 325°. Spread the mixture on a greased jelly roll pan, about 10 by 15 inches, or use two 8-inch square pans. Cut into squares or diamonds with a sharp knife and place an almond in the center of each. Bake for 15 minutes, then place under the broiler for a minute to brown the top. Cool. *Serves 8–10.*

ARABIA, IRAN, IRAQ, AND AFGHANISTAN

These countries are joined together in this section for several reasons: they are neighbors, they are Arabic-speaking, they share the same religion, but primarily they are combined because their cuisines follow a very close pattern. It is the purpose of this section to point out the similarities and differences that exist.

Arabia is a dry, hot country, but filled with oases, palms trees, and sheiks. Recently the country has begun to encourage tourism, and now there are a number of suitable places at which to stay. Being rich in oil, the nation is engaged in making some giant strides forward in education, highways, and housing. The local food is frequently very interesting, although if dining at a luxury hotel, the "international-style" cooking will be similar to that of Des Moines or Sacramento.

What was once biblical Mesopotamia is known today as Iraq. The famous city of Bagdad, curiously unaltered, still exists. The market places are as facinating as they were two thousand years ago; only the ultra-critical will carp because Elizabeth Arden products have replaced the myrrh and incense of yesteryear, and the long-playing phonograph records on sale are more practical than lyres.

Fabulous Persia has been superseded by present-day Iran, but many of its former colorful ways and customs remain. Like a Fitzpatrick travel talk in color, the streets and market places are lively beyond our imagination.

Afghanistan, once a land of mystery, has moved gently into the twentieth century. There is now a luxury hotel in Kabul, the very atmospheric capital, and there's a great deal to see and do there. The nation has comparatively few roads, although those immediately surrounding Kabul are first rate. Also, there's no railroad, which means that sightseeing is chiefly accomplished by local airline flights. Not too far from Kabul is the world-famous Khyber Pass, which is as exciting a spot as there is in the world, if you have a sense of history and remember the famous leaders, travelers, and traders who have come this way during the past thousands of years.

The people of this region were historically nomads, almost always on the move with the exception of those in a few certain areas. Meat is usually prepared in the nomad fashion. Since pork is forbidden, lamb is almost always the meat of these countries–that is, when it is available. A prime favorite, even today, is a whole young lamb roasted over an open fire. A good trencherman can manage several pounds of meat at a time. The other usual treatment of lamb is the familiar *kebab*, or meat roasted on a skewer. Although *kebabs* may be made with fish or vegetables, lamb is preferred. Poultry and wild game, particularly in Afghanistan, are important to those lucky enough to afford such delicacies.

Certain regions have fish, but it is often out of reach of the general public because of the high price. Those who can afford it regard fish as a welcome change in their somewhat limited diet. In Iraq there is the fresh-water *chaboute*, similar to trout, and much of this comes from the Euphrates River. Shellfish are not highly regarded even where they are available.

With almost every dish there is rice, sometimes merely plain boiled, but often combined with spices, nuts, and other ingredients. The poor eat rice to stay their hunger, but the rich eat rice because they feel that no meal is complete without it. Semolina dishes are also appreciated here, notably the *couscous*, a recipe for which is in the section on Northern and Central Africa.

All fresh vegetables are in great demand, but eggplant evidently appeals to the local palate more than any other. Raw vegetables such as cucumbers, radishes, and green onions are made into cool salads to refresh those who have been out in the hot sun. In Iran the guest will find beautiful salads covered with dressings made of sugar and honey. Apparently sweet foods satisfy the taste of the people, for many dishes are unexpectedly found to be soaked in cloying sweetness, in contradistinction to the Western trend toward crisp, non-fattening foods.

Fruits and vegetables are often very good; in Afghanistan the melons, nuts, and grapes are worthy of their famous reputation. Of course figs and dates are of tremendous importance as foods throughout the region. Iraq is noted for its dates, the principal food of many peasants.

Cold drinks of all sorts are popular, particularly yogurt, the cultured milk, *doogh,* a buttermilk drink, and numerous fruit and ground nut drinks.

Almost everyone drinks tiny thimblefuls of sweet black coffee with the greatest frequency, but since the cups are so small, this is not too surprising. It is also interesting to report that tea is consumed on a large scale, often with the addition of mint.

ARABIC STUFFED PEPPERS

FLEIFELI MEHSHIA

12 green peppers, uniform size	½ teaspoon freshly ground
1½ pounds ground beef	black pepper
1 tomato, peeled and chopped	¾ cup rice, half-cooked and
2 onions, chopped	drained
3 tablespoons chopped parsley	½ cup canned tomato sauce
2 teaspoons salt	1 cup water

Cut a ½-inch piece off the top of each pepper. Scoop out the seeds carefully. Mix together the beef, tomato, onions, parsley, salt, pepper, and rice. Stuff the peppers with this mixture. Place them in a baking dish. Pour the tomato sauce and water over them. Bake in a 350° oven for 1¼ hours, basting frequently. Add water to the pan if necessary. *Serves 6–12.*

Note: If there is too much meat mixture for the peppers, form them into balls and place in the baking dish.

ARABIC LENTIL SOUP

SHOURABAT ADAS

½ cup chick-peas	2 onions, chopped
½ cup lentils (pink, if available)	2 teaspoons salt
½ cup *bourghol* (cracked wheat)	1 teaspoon freshly ground
2 quarts water	black pepper
3 tablespoons butter	

Soak the chick-peas and lentils overnight in water to cover. Drain well. Place them in a saucepan with the *bourghol* and the water. Cover and cook over low heat for 1½ hours, or until the ingredients are tender.

Melt the butter in a saucepan. Add the onions and sauté until brown, about 15 minutes, stirring frequently. Add to the soup, together with the salt and pepper. Cook for 10 minutes. Correct seasoning. To make a very smooth soup, run the mixture in an electric blender for 1 minute. Serve hot. *Serves 8–10.*

As served at the Teheran Inter-Continental Hotel.

STUFFED LAMB

KABOURGA

3 tablespoons butter	2 tablespoons chopped nuts or
1 cup rice, washed and drained	whole pine nuts
2 onions, chopped	1 cup boiling water
1 green pepper, chopped	2 cloves garlic, minced
3 tablespoons chopped parsley	4 pounds breast of lamb and
3 teaspoons salt	ribs, with pocket for stuffing
1½ teaspoons freshly ground	1 8-ounce can tomato sauce and
black pepper	1 can water

Melt the butter in a saucepan. Add the rice, onions, and green pepper, and sauté for 10 minutes, stirring frequently. Add the parsley, 1 teaspoon of the salt, ½ teaspoon of the pepper, the nuts, and the boiling water. Cover and cook over low heat for 10 minutes. Drain well.

Rub the lamb with the garlic and remaining salt and pepper. Stuff the pocket with the rice mixture. Place the lamb in a roasting pan and pour the tomato sauce and water over it. Roast in a 350° oven for 2 hours, basting frequently. *Serves 4–6.*

EGGPLANT STUFFED WITH LAMB AND NUTS

SHEIKH EL-MIHSHIE

⅓ cup vegetable oil	1 teaspoon freshly ground
3 eggplants, cut in half	black pepper
lengthwise	½ cup pine nuts or pistachios
2 pounds lamb, ground fine	1 can tomato soup
2 teaspoons salt	1 cup water

Heat 3 tablespoons of the oil in a skillet. Place the unpeeled eggplants in the oil and fry for 5 minutes on the cut side and for 10 minutes on the skin side. Heat the remaining oil in a separate skillet. Add the lamb, salt, and pepper; sauté for 10 minutes, stirring occasionally. Add the nuts and mix well.

Arrange the eggplants in a casserole. Slash each eggplant lengthwise in several places. Stuff the slashes with the lamb mixture. Combine the tomato soup and water and pour over the eggplants. Bake in a 350° oven for 1 hour. Serve hot. *Serves 6.*

ROAST CHICKEN WITH SWEET STUFFING

DUGGAG MUHAMMAR

¼ pound (1 stick) butter	1 cup pistachio nuts
3 onions, chopped	½ cup seedless raisins
Gizzard and livers of chicken	1½ tablespoons salt
1½ cups rice, half-cooked	1 teaspoon freshly ground
3 tablespoons chopped parsley	black pepper
2 hard-cooked eggs, chopped	2 5-pound roasting chickens

Melt the butter in a saucepan. Add the onions and sauté for 10 minutes. Grind the gizzard and livers and add to the onions. Cook over low heat 10 minutes, stirring frequently. Add the rice, parsley, eggs, nuts, raisins, 2 teaspoons of the salt, and ½ teaspoon of the pepper. Mix well.

Combine the remaining salt and pepper and rub into the chickens, inside and out. Stuff the chickens with the previous mixture and fasten the openings with skewers or thread. Roast in a 350° oven for 2 hours, or until tender. Baste frequently with the pan juices. *Serves 8–10.*

LENTILS AND RICE

MJDARA

2 cups dried lentils	½ teaspoon freshly ground
3 cups boiling water	black pepper
¾ cup rice	½ cup olive oil
2 teaspoons salt	2 onions, chopped

Wash the lentils carefully and remove any imperfect ones. Soak overnight in water to cover. Drain well. Place them in a saucepan with the boiling water. Bring to a boil and cook over low heat for 1¼ hours. Add the rice, salt, and pepper and cook for 15 minutes, stirring occasionally. Add water if necessary. Heat the olive oil in a saucepan. Add the onions and sauté for 15 minutes, stirring occasionally. Add to the lentils and cook for 5 minutes. Correct seasoning. *Serves 6–8.*

SQUASH CASSEROLE

MASBAHET ED-DARWEESH

2 pounds zucchini or yellow
    squash
2 teaspoons salt
1 cup grated American or
    Cheddar cheese
½ cup cottage cheese

4 eggs, beaten
¾ cup dry bread crumbs
3 tablespoons chopped parsley
½ teaspoon freshly ground
    black pepper
3 tablespoons butter

Grate the squash. Add the salt and set aside for 30 minutes. Squeeze all
the liquid from the squash and discard. Mix the grated cheese and
cottage cheese together. Add the squash, beaten eggs, bread crumbs,
parsley, and pepper and mix well. Pour into a buttered baking dish and
dot with butter. Bake in a 350° oven for 45 minutes. *Serves 4–6.*

STRING BEANS WITH OLIVE OIL

LUBEY BE-ZEIT

½ cup olive oil
4 onions, chopped
2 pounds fresh or 2 packages
    frozen string beans

1 cup tomato juice
1 teaspoon salt
½ teaspoon freshly ground
    black pepper

Heat the olive oil in a saucepan. Add the onions and cook over low heat
for 15 minutes, stirring frequently. Do not allow the onions to brown.
Add the beans. Cover and cook over low heat for 15 minutes, stirring
occasionally. Add the tomato juice, salt, and pepper. Cook over low
heat for 15 minutes. Let cool. Serve cold. *Serves 4–6.*

MIXED SALAD

FATTOUSH

3 tomatoes, cubed
2 cucumbers, peeled and diced
1 green pepper, chopped
8 scallions (green onions),
    sliced thin
4 tablespoons chopped parsley

4 sprigs fresh mint, chopped, or
    1 tablespoon dried mint
½ cup olive oil
¼ cup lemon juice
1 teaspoon salt
2 cups tiny bread cubes

Combine the tomatoes, cucumbers, green pepper, scallions, parsley,
and mint in a bowl. Mix the olive oil, lemon juice, and salt together.

Pour over the vegetables. Add the bread cubes and toss lightly. Chill for 1 hour before serving. *Serves 4–6.*

STUFFED BAKED APPLES

TEFFAH BIL-FORN

¼ cup seedless raisins	¼ cup melted butter
6 large baking apples	1½ teaspoons cinnamon
1 cup sugar	2 cups water
½ cup cooked rice	

Soak the raisins in hot water for 10 minutes. Cut a 1-inch-thick slice off the top of each apple and reserve the tops. Scoop out the centers of the apples carefully so as not to break the skin. Sprinkle 1 teaspoon of the sugar in each. Drain the raisins. Combine with the rice, butter, and ¼ cup of the sugar and mix well. Stuff the apples with the mixture and sprinkle each apple with the cinnamon. Replace the tops of the apples.

Place in a buttered baking dish. Sprinkle the remaining sugar over and around the apples. Add the water. Bake in a 325° oven for 45 minutes. Baste frequently. These may be served as a dessert, hot or cold. They may also be served with roast meats or poultry as a garnish. *Serves 6.*

FARINA NUT DESSERT

IMRIG HELVA

1 cup milk	1 cup uncooked farina
1 cup water	½ cup pine nuts or chopped
1 cup sugar	almonds
4 tablespoons butter	

Combine the milk, water, and sugar in a saucepan. Cook over low heat until the mixture boils. Remove from the heat. Melt the butter in a saucepan. Add the farina and nuts. Cook over low heat, stirring constantly, until the farina is light brown. Gradually pour the milk mixture over it, stirring constantly until the boiling point is reached. Cover and cook over low heat until the liquid is absorbed, stirring frequently.

When all the liquid is absorbed, remove from the heat and set aside for 15 minutes, covered. Serve warm but not hot. Cinnamon may be sprinkled on each portion. *Serves 6–8.*

BULGARIA

The food of Bulgaria bears considerable resemblance to that of its Balkan neighbors. This is not surprising in view of the troubled history of these nations during the past few centuries, during which the borders of the countries changed with great regularity. However, the diet of the Bulgarian peasant is more healthful than that of any other Balkan country if local chauvinists can be believed. According to proud Bulgarians, the average peasant eats raw onions and garlic, drinks fully of his beloved yogurt, and eats his bacon raw. This diet must be healthful, for it is apparently true that Bulgarians live longer than any other European group. Octogenarians are commonplace; to attract any attention in this land of sprightly oldsters you must be at least a centenarian.

Many people believe that yogurt is paramount in importance with regard to the health of the Bulgarians, for it is the one article in their diet that helps to explain their astonishing longevity. Yogurt, a cultured milk now quite common in the United States, probably originated in Bulgaria, though it is eaten in almost all the countries at the eastern end of the Mediterranean. The milk contains a beneficial bacillus which some experts think aids digestion and physical well-being. Certainly it must be admitted that Bulgarians consume fabulous quantities of this product, which resembles sour milk to a considerable extent. Yogurt appears at every meal, is used for almost every culinary purpose, and is apparently relished equally by the peasants and the city people.

The country is agricultural, and produces a large crop of grains of many different types. A rather poor nation in spite of its abundant soil, the people lean heavily on beans, lentils, rice, wheat, and other grains for the substantive basis of their food. The recipe for *fassoul yahnia* is typical of the bean dishes so popular in the nation.

Facing the Black Sea, the Bulgarians like the locally caught fruits of that sea and make some fine dishes of them, treating the fish in a manner similar to that employed by their neighbors. Raw salads are among the enthusiasms of the populace, and these, together with the local fondness for yogurt, support a nation of health faddists such as Gayelord Hauser might dream about. The recipe for *meshana salata,* or mixed salad with roast green peppers, is but one of many Bulgarian salads.

Meals end with dessert and black coffee. In season there will probably be fresh fruit; usually they serve dried fruit or fruit compote when fresh fruits are not available. The people also enjoy the rich, sticky, honey-laden dessert *baklawa*, which is a great favorite throughout the Near East.

Bulgarians drink freely of their local brandies, which are quite high in potency. Since the country is filled with vineyards, wines are a national pride. Most of these are good but not extraordinary, though a few vintages are exceptional. *Greyano vino*, a hot wine and spice drink, is much appreciated during cold weather.

SOUP WITH MEAT BALLS

SOUPA SUS TOPCHETA

1 pound short ribs of beef and several bones	1 pound chopped beef
3 quarts water	1 tablespoon vinegar
2 onions	2 tablespoons chopped parsley
1 stalk celery	3 eggs
2 sprigs parsley	½ cup flour
1 turnip or parsnip	1 cup uncooked rice
1 carrot	1 tablespoon butter
1⅓ tablespoons salt	3 tablespoons lemon juice
1 teaspoon freshly ground black pepper	

Combine the short ribs, bones, water, 1 onion, celery, parsley, turnip, and carrot in a saucepan. Bring to a boil and cook over medium heat for 3 hours. Strain the broth and add 3 teaspoons of the salt and ½ teaspoon of the pepper to it. Mix the chopped beef with the vinegar, chopped parsley, and remaining salt and pepper. Separate 1 egg and add the white to the meat mixture, reserving the yolk. Mix all together well. Shape into 1-inch balls and roll in the flour.

Bring the broth to the boiling point and add the rice. Cook for 10 minutes. Add the meat balls and cook 15 minutes longer. Chop the remaining onion. Melt the butter in a saucepan. Add the onion and sauté for 10 minutes, stirring frequently. Sprinkle 1 tablespoon of the flour on it, stirring constantly. Add 1 cup of the broth, again stirring constantly. Return this mixture to the balance of the broth. Cook over low heat for 10 minutes. Beat the eggs and the remaining yolk in a bowl. Add the lemon juice. Add 2 cups of the broth, stirring constantly. Return this mixture to the balance of the broth, mixing well. Correct seasoning. Serve hot. The reserved meat may be served in a separate dish with the soup or put aside for future use. *Serves 8–10.*

FRIED BRAINS CROQUETTES

KIUFTETA OT MOZAK

3 calves' brains	1 teaspoon salt
2 cups water	½ teaspoon freshly ground
1 tablespoon vinegar	black pepper
¼ pound (1 stick) butter	2 tablespoons chopped parsley
1 onion, chopped	3 eggs, beaten
1 slice white bread, trimmed	¼ cup flour
¼ cup milk	½ cup bread crumbs

Wash the brains. Place in a saucepan with the water and vinegar. Bring to a boil and cook for 10 minutes. Drain. Plunge into cold water and set aside for 30 minutes. Drain. Remove the membrane and chop fine. Melt 2 tablespoons of the butter in a saucepan. Add the onion and sauté for 10 minutes, stirring frequently. Soak the bread in the milk for 5 minutes. Squeeze all the liquid out of it. Combine the brains, sautéed onion, bread, salt, pepper, and parsley together, and chop until smooth. Add 2 of the eggs, mixing until well blended. Shape into small croquettes. Dip in flour, then in the remaining egg, and finally in the bread crumbs. Melt the remaining butter in a saucepan and fry until brown on both sides. Serve at once. *Serves 4–6.*

CHICKEN STEW

PILE YAHNIA

¼ pound (1 stick) butter	2 tablespoons flour
2 4½-pound chickens, disjointed	2 tablespoons tomato paste
3 onions, chopped	2 cups water
3 teaspoons salt	1 pound uncooked chestnuts,
1 teaspoon paprika	peeled

Melt the butter in a saucepan. Add the chicken and brown on all sides. Add the onions. Cover and cook over medium heat until the onions begin to brown. Add the salt, paprika, and flour, mixing well. Mix the tomato paste and water together and add to the previous mixture, stirring well. Add the chestnuts. Cover and cook over low heat for 2 hours, or until the chicken is tender. Stir occasionally. Add water if the saucepan becomes dry. Serve hot. *Serves 6–8.*

BEAN STEW

FASSOUL YAHNIA

2 cups dried white beans   2 teaspoons salt
1 cup olive or vegetable oil   ⅛ teaspoon thyme
4 onions, chopped   ½ cup vinegar
2 teaspoons paprika

Soak the beans overnight in water to cover. Drain. Add fresh water and boil for 1½ hours, or until tender. Drain. Heat the olive oil in a saucepan. Add the onions and sauté for 10 minutes, stirring frequently. Mix in the beans, paprika, salt, thyme, and vinegar. Cook over low heat for 15 minutes. Stir carefully a few times. Correct seasoning. Serve hot or cold. *Serves 6–8.*

CHEESE POTATOES

KARTOFI SUS SIRENE

6 (2 pounds) potatoes, peeled   1 teaspoon freshly ground
    and sliced thin   black pepper
1 pound cottage cheese   2 eggs
1½ cups melted butter   1 cup yogurt
2 teaspoons salt

Arrange a layer of potatoes in a buttered casserole dish. Mix together the cheese and butter and spread a layer over the potatoes. Sprinkle with some of the salt and pepper. Continue with layers of potatoes, salt, pepper, and the cheese mixture until the ingredients are used up. Bake in a 375° oven for 30 minutes. Beat the eggs and yogurt together and pour over the top layer of the casserole. Bake 20 minutes longer, or until the egg mixture is set and lightly browned. Serve hot, directly from the casserole. *Serves 6–8.*

MIXED SALAD WITH ROAST PEPPERS

MESHANA SALATA

4 green peppers   3 tablespoons vinegar
3 tomatoes, sliced   ½ cup olive oil
2 onions, sliced   1 teaspoon salt
2 cucumbers, sliced

Wash and dry the peppers. Broil as close to the heat as possible, turning them to brown all sides, or place them on a fork, one at a time, and hold over a flame until the skin turns brown. Peel off the skin and cut the peppers in 1-inch strips. Chill for 1 hour. Combine the peppers, tomatoes, onions, and cucumbers in a salad bowl. Mix together the vinegar, oil, and salt and pour over the salad. Toss carefully and chill. Serve cold. *Serves 6–8.*

BRANDIED FRUIT SALAD

FRUKTOVA SALATA

3 apples, peeled and sliced thin	1 cup melon balls
3 pears, peeled and sliced thin	½ cup sugar
2 oranges, peeled and sliced thin	2 cups sweet white wine
1 cup pitted cherries	½ cup brandy

Combine the apples, pears, oranges, cherries, and melon balls. Sprinkle with the sugar. Mix the wine and brandy together. Pour over the fruit and mix gently but thoroughly. Chill for at least 3 hours. Serve very cold. *Serves 6–8.*

HOT WINE AND SPICES

GREYANO VINO

6 cups red wine	3 cloves
3 apples, peeled and sliced thin	¼ cup sugar
2 teaspoons cinnamon	1 teaspoon lemon juice

Combine the wine, apples, cinnamon, cloves, sugar, and lemon juice in a saucepan. Bring to a boil and cook over low heat for 20 minutes. Strain. Return the strained mixture to the saucepan and reheat. Serve very hot. *Serves 6–8.*

GREECE

There is a great difference of opinion as to whether certain dishes are Greek, Turkish, or Armenian in origin. Since the borders of these countries have changed many times within the past century, it is impossible at this late date to determine the exact origin of any particular dish. Although certain dishes have become the particular favorites of a given country, this is not necessarily positive proof of the origin of the dish in question. This is especially true of the food of Greece and its neighbors, which in general is very similar. Each country, on the other hand, has a few items which are more or less confined to that country. Forgiveness is sought of those who feel that their national dishes have been misplaced.

In the morning, breakfast is a simple affair of bread and coffee. Lunch, eaten from 1 P.M. to 3, or even later in the summertime, is a large meal. In the early evening, beginning at 7 or so, people begin to gather in the cafés to drink *ouzo*, a clear white liquid, which has a distinctive taste of anise, or licorice; *ouzo* is fairly strong. With the drinks it's customary to have small snacks, *mezé*, which are a type of hors d'oeuvre. Much later on, say about 9 P.M., dinnertime comes and many people head for the *tavernas*, those very pleasant informal restaurants of Greece. In a large percentage of these, there's an informal open kitchen, and it's part of the local scene to look into pots and see what's cooking that particular evening. Then, perhaps pointing if words are lacking, the evening meal can be selected on the spot. It's just another delightful custom of this most interesting of countries.

The people are fond of fish dishes, customarily made with olive oil, garlic, and tomatoes, Shellfish is very popular, but usually the catch is not extensive. Octopus, squid, and mussels, in addition to the more usual varieties, are much appreciated by all the people. Rock lobsters are considered a great delicacy but are relatively scarce.

The favorite soups are fish stews, lentil soups, and what is probably the national soup, *soupa avgolemono*, a lemon-flavored chicken soup. This is a truly exceptional soup, popular far beyond the boundaries of the country.

Lamb is the principal meat, veal has some small importance, but beef is seldom seen. The recipe for *entrather* (lamb with artichokes) is typical of the lamb dishes of the country. Lamb is used for almost all meat dishes: broiled over an open coal fire, roasted, cut into pieces for tasty stews, and ground up into patties. *Moussaka* (eggplant stuffed with ground lamb) appears frequently at the table.

Greece produces beautiful, large, flavorful lemons, and the Greek housewife takes full advantage of them, using lemon juice on practically everything she serves. Preparing the salad is a ritual performed by the host himself at the table. Lemons are used in place of the customary vinegar, with pleasing and tart results.

Greek wines, many of which contain resin, are not palatable to our taste, but foreign residents in Greece find that a liking for this wine may be acquired. Greek brandy, on the other hand, though not quite up to French standards of excellence, is very fine and has been exported extensively. Metaxa is an especially well-known brand.

Feta, a white, goat-milk cheese, is not suitable for normal use by our standards, though the Greeks like to eat it plain with a crust of bread. A few pieces of *feta* cheese broken into a green salad give it a unique flavor.

CAVIAR SPREAD

TARAMASALATA

6 slices homemade-style white bread
1 cup milk
1 cup *tarama* (Greek dried red mullet roe)

1 cup sesame or safflower oil
¼ cup lemon juice
¼ cup grated onion

Trim away the crusts of the bread, then crumble the bread into the milk. Let soak 5 minutes. Drain the milk off, and put the bread in the bowl of an electric mixer. Beat until fairly smooth, then, still beating, add a tablespoon of the *tarama* at a time. Still beating, add the oil in a slow, steady stream until half is used up. Beat in the lemon juice, then gradually add the remaining oil. Add the onion and beat again until the mixture is light pinky rose. Heap in a bowl and chill. Serve with black olives and Arabic or French bread.

Note: Tarama is sold in 8-ounce jars in Middle East or specialty food shops.

BAKED FISH

PSARIA PLAKI

½ cup olive oil
8 large onions, sliced
2 cloves garlic, minced
2 tablespoons butter
6 slices (½ inch thick) sea bass, haddock, or mackerel

2 teaspoons salt
1 teaspoon freshly ground black pepper
6 tomatoes, sliced
2 lemons, sliced
¼ cup water

Heat the olive oil in a skillet and sauté the onions and garlic until golden brown. Melt the butter in a large baking dish. Arrange the slices of fish in the dish, leaving some space between each slice. Sprinkle with the salt and pepper. Spread the onions over and around the fish slices. Place a slice of tomato on each piece of fish and top with a piece of lemon. Spread the remainder of the tomato and lemon slices around the dish. Add the water. Bake in a 375° oven for 30 minutes. Serve with the sauce remaining in the baking dish. *Serves 6.*

LEMON SOUP

SOUPA AVGOLEMONO

1 pound chicken parts (necks, backs, feet)	3 quarts water
	½ cup rice
1 onion	2 egg yolks
1 stalk celery	2 tablespoons lemon juice
1 carrot	2 teaspoons salt

Wash the chicken parts well. Combine in a saucepan with the onion, celery, carrot, and water. Bring to a boil, then skim the top. Cook over medium heat for 2 hours. Strain and return to saucepan. Wash the rice in warm water and let soak for 15 minutes. Wash again and add to the stock. Cook over low heat for 15 minutes. Beat the egg yolks in a bowl. Add the lemon juice and salt. Gradually add the stock, beating constantly to prevent curdling. Return to saucepan, still beating constantly. Heat but do not allow to boil. Correct seasoning. Serve with a slice of lemon. *Serves 6–8.*

Note: If desired, canned chicken broth may be substituted for the homemade stock.

LAMB AND ARTICHOKES

ENTRATHER

¼ pound (1 stick) butter	1 bay leaf
3 pounds lamb, cut into 1-inch cubes	2 cups boiling water
	1 package frozen artichokes
2 onions, chopped	3 eggs
2 cloves garlic, minced	2 tablespoons lemon juice
2 teaspoons salt	12 ripe olives
1 teaspoon freshly ground black pepper	

Melt the butter in a saucepan. Add the lamb and brown well on all sides. Add the onions, garlic, salt, pepper, bay leaf, and boiling water. Cover and cook for 1½ hours, stirring occasionally.

Add the artichokes, and cook 20 minutes.

Beat eggs and lemon juice together in a bowl. Add 1 cup of the gravy from the saucepan very gradually to the contents of the bowl, beating steadily. Return this mixture to the saucepan, beating continuously. Add

the olives. Cook over low heat for 5 minutes but do not allow to boil.
Serves 6–8.

ORÉGANO CHICKEN

KATES RIGANATI

½ cup olive oil
3 teaspoons salt
4 tablespoons lemon juice
2 4½-pound roasting chickens
¼ pound (1 stick) butter

2 cups canned tomatoes
1 teaspoon freshly ground
  black pepper
1 tablespoon orégano

Combine the olive oil, 2 teaspoons of the salt, and the lemon juice. Rub
it into the chickens, inside and out. Place the chickens in a roasting pan.
Roast in a 375° oven for 1 hour. Melt the butter in a saucepan. Add the
tomatoes, remaining salt, pepper, and orégano. Cook over medium heat
5 minutes, stirring occasionally. Pour over the chickens and reduce the
heat to 350°. Roast for 1 hour longer, or until tender, basting frequently. *Serves 8.*

SPINACH ROLLS IN PASTRY

SPANAKOPETA

1¾ cups sifted flour
2 teaspoons salt
1 cup water
¾ pound butter, melted
1 onion, chopped
10 scallions (green onions),
  sliced
4 tablespoons chopped dill
½ cup chopped parsley

2 pounds fresh or 1 package
  frozen spinach, cooked,
  drained, and chopped
½ teaspoon pepper
3 eggs
½ pound *feta* cheese or cottage
  cheese
½ cup grated Parmesan cheese

Sift the flour and 1 teaspoon of the salt into a bowl. Add the water,
mixing well. Knead gently. Roll out on a lightly floured surface as thin
as possible. Cut into four squares. Spread each with some melted butter.
Stack the squares into layers. Set aside.

Combine ¼ cup melted butter and the onion in a skillet. Sauté for 10
minutes. Add the scallions, dill, and parsley. Sauté for 5 minutes. Add
spinach, pepper, and remaining salt. Mix well. Cool for 10 minutes. Beat
the eggs in a bowl. Add the *feta* or cottage cheese and Parmesan cheese.
Mix until smooth. Add the spinach mixture, mixing until well blended.
Correct seasoning. Preheat oven to 400°.

Roll the dough (still stacked) as thin as possible. Brush with half the remaining butter. Spread the spinach mixture over two thirds of the dough. Roll up as for a jelly roll. Place in a baking pan. Prick top in several places. Pour remaining butter over it. Bake in a 400° oven for 30 minutes, or until crisp and brown on top. Slice and serve hot. *Serves 8–10.*

Note: If you don't want to make the dough yourself use a package of strudel leaves.

EGGPLANT CASSEROLE

MOUSSAKA MELITZANES

3 tablespoons olive oil
2 onions, chopped
1 large eggplant, peeled and
cut into ½-inch cubes
2 tomatoes, chopped
2 teaspoons salt

1 teaspoon freshly ground
black pepper
1 egg yolk, beaten
½ cup milk
½ cup cottage cheese

Heat the olive oil in a saucepan and add the chopped onions. Sauté for 5 minutes. Add the eggplant and continue cooking for an additional 10 minutes over low heat. Add the tomatoes, salt, and pepper, and cook for 10 minutes, stirring occasionally. Butter a 2-quart casserole and place the mixture in it. Combine the egg yolk, milk, and cottage cheese, and mix well. Pour over the eggplant. Bake in a 375° oven for 45 minutes. *Serves 4–6.*

WALNUT CAKE WITH SYRUP

KARIDOPITA

¼ pound (1 stick) butter
1¼ cups sugar
4 eggs
½ cup uncooked farina
2 teaspoons baking powder
Dash of salt

1 cup ground walnuts
¼ cup milk
1 teaspoon vanilla
1 cup water
1 tablespoon lemon juice

Preheat oven to 350°.

Cream the butter. Add ¾ cup of the sugar and continue creaming until light and fluffy. Add the eggs, one at a time, beating well after each addition. Add the farina, baking powder, salt, walnuts, milk, and vanilla, beating steadily. Pour into a buttered 10-inch loaf pan. Bake in a 350° oven for 35 minutes, or until a cake tester comes out clean. While the cake is baking, prepare the syrup.

Combine the remaining ½ cup of sugar in a saucepan with the water and lemon juice. Bring to a boil and cook over low heat for 10 minutes or until thick and syrupy. Pour over the hot cake and serve from the pan. The cake may be served cold without the syrup if desired. *Serves 6–8.*

ISRAEL

This new land presents a strange series of culinary contradictions, of considerable interest to the student of gastronomy. Almost without exception, the cooking style, the favorite dishes, and the way of eating of a nation's inhabitants have developed gradually over many centuries; indeed, in many cases, over a thousand years or more. Israel is exceptional in that it is a very new country, having come into existence since World War II. Of course, Israel has a central group called *sabras*, people born in the country; however, hundreds of thousands of other people were born in Europe and came to Israel as immigrants, bringing with them their own culinary styles.

Israel has permitted almost unrestricted immigration, and the new land is filled with people who were born in Russia, Poland, Austria, and Germany. They were accustomed to eating heavy and rich soups and fatty meats, suitable to a cold weather background. But a hot thick soup may be welcome in subzero weather with snow in the country, and completely unsuitable to a hot sunny country with temperatures approaching 100 degrees. As a result, there has been a collision between the old dishes and the need for lighter cooling foods suitable to the climate. Furthermore, many (but not all) people follow the *kosher* style of cooking, which prohibits certain meats and shellfish, and involves the use of separate sets of dishes and pots for dairy and meat. Also, the people of Israel have tended to adopt many of the dishes from their Arab neighbors (clearly neighbors, not friends); thus, a great many dishes that appear in chapters for surrounding Moslem countries are commonly served.

An example of a popular Israeli favorite of Arabic origin is *falafel*, considered as Israel's "hot dog" and sold on all street corners. Also of interest are *leben* and *lebenia*, both similar to yogurt, which probably originated in Bulgaria but are popular all through the Near East countries. *Leben* is made from skimmed milk, whereas *lebenia* is thicker and has the consistency of sour cream. They are used as all-purpose foods, for desserts, for refreshments, and are often combined with jams or syrups to make cold drinks. No mention of Israel could by-pass the egg bread of the country, *challah*, but the various flat breads, such as *kibbetz*, are equally well liked. Of the locally produced foods, such as dates, almonds, figs, raisins, and grapes, the biblical pomegranate is a particular favorite.

From Central Europe come such familiar Jewish-style dishes as *borscht* (beet soup); *chulent* (a hearty preparation of beans and meat); *gefülte* (stuffed) *fisch; kugel* (potato pudding); *blintzes* (thin stuffed pancakes); and *challah* (the classic egg bread). These are still popular, but many are less so than before, because they are too heavy and substantial for the warm weather of Israel. In particular, the young people tend, more and more, to eat lighter and more suitable foods than do their parents.

Tourists frequently complain about the meals in Israel. It is quite true that if a visitor looks for American-style roast beef and steaks, he will be disappointed. However, by looking and asking for the specialties of the country, the tourist will dine happily and enjoyably upon well-prepared dishes.

ISRAELI "HOT DOGS"

FALAFEL

2 cups cooked chick-peas or 1 20-ounce can, drained
3 cloves garlic, minced
3 tablespoons cornstarch
1 egg, beaten
¼ cup cold water
½ teaspoon baking soda
¾ teaspoon salt

¼ teaspoon dried ground chili peppers
1 teaspoon ground cumin seeds
2 tablespoons chopped parsley
1 tablespoon sesame or vegetable oil
Flour
Vegetable oil for deep frying

Grind the chick-peas through the coarse blade of a meat grinder. Mix in the garlic, cornstarch, egg, water, baking soda, salt, pepper, cumin, parsley, and sesame oil. Let stand 10 minutes. Form the mixture (it will be soft, but if too soft to hold together, add a little flour) into 1-inch balls. Roll in flour, coating them completely.

Heat deep oil to 365°. Put four balls at a time into a frying basket or strainer and fry about 3 minutes, or until lightly browned and they come to the surface. Drain on paper towels. *Makes about 20.*

POT ROAST WITH PRUNES

BASAR TZALOOUIE

4 pounds brisket or eye round
  of beef
¼ cup flour
2 teaspoons salt
½ teaspoon freshly ground
  black pepper
¼ teaspoon ground ginger
2 tablespoons sesame or
  vegetable oil

1 cup chopped onions
1 cup orange juice
2 cups boiling water (about)
½ teaspoon ground coriander
  seeds
2 tablespoons honey
12 presoaked prunes

Rinse and dry the meat. Mix together the flour, salt, pepper, and ginger. Coat the meat with the mixture.

Heat the oil in a skillet; brown the onions and meat in it. Pour off the fat, and add the orange juice. Cover and cook over low heat 2¼ hours, adding water from time to time, if necessary. Add the coriander, honey, and prunes. Check the gravy at this point; there should be about 2 inches. If not, add a little more water. Re-cover and cook 30 minutes longer. *Serves 6–8.*

As served in the Jerusalem Inter-Continental Hotel.

COLD BEET SOUP

COLD BORSCHT

8 large beets, washed and
  peeled
1 onion, chopped fine
2½ quarts water
1 tablespoon salt

⅓ cup lemon juice
3 tablespoons sugar
2 eggs
1 cup sour cream

Combine the beets, onion, water, and salt in a saucepan. Bring to a boil and cook over medium heat for 1 hour. Add the lemon juice and sugar and cook for 30 minutes. Correct seasoning; the soup may require a little more sugar or lemon juice, depending upon the sweetness of the beets.

Beat the eggs in a bowl. Gradually add 3 cups of the soup, beating constantly to prevent curdling. Return this mixture to the balance of the soup, beating steadily. Remove all of the beets from the soup. Grate 5 of the beets and return them to the soup. The remaining beets may be

used in a cold salad. Chill the soup and serve very cold with a spoonful
of sour cream in each plate. *Serves 8–10.*

*Note: If a very thick soup is desired, place the remaining beets in an
electric blender with 2 cups of the soup and run the machine until the
mixture is smooth. Add the mixture to the soup.*

GROUND FISH BALLS

GEFÜLTE FISCH

3 pounds whitefish	3 eggs
3 pounds pike	¾ cup ice water
5 onions	½ teaspoon sugar
6 cups water	3 tablespoons matzo or cracker
4 teaspoons salt	meal
1½ teaspoons white pepper	3 carrots, sliced

Have the fish filleted but reserve the head, skin, and bones. You may
use any combination of fresh-water fish, although this combination is
most popular.

Combine the head, skin, bones, and 3 sliced onions with the 6 cups
water, 2 teaspoons of the salt, and ¾ teaspoon pepper. Cook over high
heat 45 minutes. Strain into a clean pan, and add 1 sliced onion.

Grind the fish and remaining onion. Use an electric blender if you
prefer. Place in a chopping bowl and add the eggs, ice water, sugar,
meal, and remaining salt and pepper. Chop until very fine and spongy.
Moisten hands; shape quarter cups of the mixture into balls. Carefully
drop into the boiling fish stock. Add the carrots. Cover loosely and cook
over low heat 1½ hours, removing the cover for the last ½ hour. Taste for
seasoning. Cool the fish 20 minutes before removing from pan. Pour the
stock over the fish balls and arrange the carrots around it. Chill. Serve
with horseradish. *Serves 12–16.*

SPICED CARROTS

TZIMMES

1 cup orange juice	1 cinnamon stick
2 cups water	1 clove
¼ cup honey	2 bunches carrots, peeled and
6 tablespoons fat	cubed
¾ teaspoon salt	½ cup seedless raisins

Combine the orange juice, water, honey, fat, salt, cinnamon stick, and
clove in a saucepan. Bring to a boil and cook over low heat 10 minutes.

Discard the cinnamon and clove. Add the carrots and raisins. Cover loosely and cook over low heat 45 minutes, or until carrots are soft and mixture thickened. *Serves 6–8.*

EGG BREAD

CHALLAH

1 cake or package yeast	1½ teaspoons salt
1 tablespoon sugar	2 eggs
½ cup lukewarm water	2 tablespoons vegetable oil
½ cup boiling water	1 egg yolk
Pinch of saffron	2 tablespoons poppy seeds
4½ cups sifted flour (about)	

Mix together the yeast, sugar, and lukewarm water. Let stand 5 minutes.

Combine the boiling water and saffron, let stand until cool, then strain.

Sift 3 cups flour and the salt into a bowl. Make a well in the center and into it put the 2 eggs, oil, saffron water, and the yeast mixture. Work in the flour mixture gradually, then add just enough of the remaining flour to make a soft dough. Knead on a floured surface until smooth and elastic. Place in an oiled bowl and brush the top with a little oil. Cover with a towel, set in a warm place and let rise 1 hour.

Punch down, cover again, and let rise until double in bulk. Divide the dough into three equal parts. Between lightly floured hands, roll the dough into three strips of even length. Braid them together and place in an oiled baking pan. Cover with a towel and let rise until double in bulk. Brush with the egg yolk and sprinkle with the poppy seeds. Bake in a 350° oven 50 minutes or until browned. Cool on a cake rack.

HONEY CAKE

LEKACH

3½ cups flour	4 eggs
¼ teaspoon salt	¾ cup brown sugar, packed
1½ teaspoons baking powder	3 tablespoons vegetable oil
1 teaspoon baking soda	1½ cups dark honey
½ teaspoon ground cloves	½ cup brewed coffee
½ teaspoon powdered ginger	
1½ cups shelled filberts or almonds	

Preheat oven to 325°.

Oil an 11- by 16- by 4-inch baking pan and line it with liner paper or aluminum foil.

Sift together 3¼ cups of the flour, the salt, baking powder, baking soda, cloves, and ginger. Mix the nuts with the remaining flour.

Beat the eggs and brown sugar until thick and light. Beat in the oil, honey, and coffee; then stir in the flour mixture until smooth. Mix in the nuts. Turn into the pan.

Bake 1 hour or until browned and a cake tester inserted in the center comes out clean. Cool on a cake rack before removing from pan.

RUMANIA

Corn meal, often considered a typical early American food, is Rumania's favorite dish and in that country it is called *mamaliga*. This is a comparatively recent development in Rumania, for corn meal was brought to Europe from the New World only a few hundred years ago. It has taken hold of the public fancy to an astonishing degree, and people in all walks of life eat *mamaliga* practically every day; with the peasantry it is rare for any meal to go by without it. *Mamaliga* is eaten plain, hot or cold, and often with onions, garlic, sausages, sauerkraut, or whatever the cook has on hand. The single favorite combination is *mamaliga* served with *brinza* cheese, made from sheep's milk. Incidentally, *brinza* is available in both the regular style (which is somewhat salty) and as a type of sweet cheese.

Ikra, the Rumanian version of caviar, is a favorite and highly regarded appetizer. It is usual to serve it both with drinks and as the first course to a dinner. Herring and eggplant are other popular appetizers, very much to the taste of the Rumanian palate.

Soups are something of a cult here, but not the ordinary varieties made from meat, poultry, or vegetables. The national soups of the nation are called *tchorbas* (sour soups) and are based upon a fermentation agent, usually wheat bran, but often lemons, vine leaves, or sauerkraut juice. The recipe for *tchorba* given here is one made with veal, a typical variation.

Fish dishes are well liked, but the selection is somewhat narrow in choice. Carp, prepared in many different fashions, is served most often. Rumanian meat dishes are not complicated, for the national preference leans toward spicy sausages and the famous Rumanian broiled meat, for which no recipe is required. It consists merely of a wide assortment of meat, such as steak, lamb chops, sausage, sweetbreads, liver, pork chops, and almost any other available meat, broiled over charcoal simultaneously. These are served with a large number of spicy relishes, pickles, hot red peppers, and sauerkraut. Stews of all sorts, such as *tocana de cartofi* (potato stew), are prevalent.

Ghivetch, a medley of vegetables, is another national dish. Sometimes it is made of vegetables only, but often it is combined with fish or meat. The important point for the Rumanian cook to remember is that there must be as many different vegetables as possible, and that they should be the freshest and best available. Green vegetables for salad and also mushrooms are particular favorites of the country people.

Desserts are of several types. There are sweet pancake desserts, strudels, and tarts. Rumania's oriental heritage is indicated by a large group of desserts consisting of fruit and nut preserves and rose petals in thick syrup, known generally as *dulceata*, which are excessively sweet to our taste. The cottage cheese recipe given here, *alivenca*, will not be too cloying to our palates.

As in the Balkan countries, brandy of local manufacture is the favorite drink of the country. Brandy in Rumania means plum brandy, *tsuica*, a fine distilled liquor with a curious blossomlike aroma. Wines are produced in many areas, but the quality is not extraordinary by European standards.

The Rumanians are fond of cheese, and produce several excellent varieties. Both outstanding types, the *urda* and the *branza de burduf*, are made from sheep's milk. The latter is shipped to market in a container of pine or fir whose aroma permeates the cheese.

CAVIAR, RUMANIAN STYLE

IKRA

1 pound carp or pike roe	1 tablespoon ice water
1 tablespoon salt	1 onion, chopped fine
½ cup sesame or olive oil	10 ripe olives, sliced thin
2 tablespoons lemon juice	

Wash the roe carefully and remove the veins. Place in a bowl and sprinkle with salt. Chill for at least 6 hours. Beat the roe with a fork for 5 minutes. Gradually add the oil drop by drop, beating constantly. Add the lemon juice and ice water. Beat all together until the mixture is firm and each egg is separate. Sprinkle the onion and olives over the roe. The caviar should be served cold, as an appetizer, with quarters of lemon. Thin slices of dark bread are the usual accompaniment. *Serves 6–8.*

SOUR SOUP

TCHORBA

1 tablespoon vegetable or olive oil	¾ pound ground veal
1 onion, chopped	1 egg, beaten
1 carrot, diced	1 slice bread, soaked in milk and crumbled
2 sprigs parsley	¾ teaspoon salt
2 stalks celery	½ teaspoon freshly ground black pepper
3 cups beef broth	1 tablespoon chopped parsley
2 tablespoons rice	
4 cups sauerkraut juice	

Heat the oil in a deep saucepan. Add the onion and carrot and sauté for 5 minutes, stirring occasionally. Add the sprigs of parsley, celery, and broth. Bring to a boil, then add the rice. Cook for 10 minutes. Add the sauerkraut juice and boil for 10 minutes.

Combine the veal, egg, bread, salt, pepper, and chopped parsley in a bowl. Mix until smooth. Shape into walnut-sized balls and drop into the boiling soup. Cook over medium heat for 30 minutes. Serve hot. *Serves 6–8.*

As served at the Bucharest Inter-Continental Hotel.

BAKED FISH WITH VEGETABLES

GHIVETCH

1 cup vegetable or olive oil	1 green pepper, sliced fine
2 medium potatoes, diced	2 large onions, chopped
2 carrots, sliced	2 cloves garlic, minced
½ pound fresh or ½ package frozen green peas	2 tomatoes, chopped
¼ pound fresh or ¼ package frozen string beans, cut into small pieces	½ pound okra, sliced (optional)
	⅛ teaspoon thyme
	1 bay leaf
½ small eggplant, peeled and diced	3 teaspoons salt
1 cup shredded cabbage	1½ teaspoons freshly ground black pepper
	6 slices fish (carp preferably)

Preheat oven to 350°.

Pour the oil in a casserole or deep baking dish and bring to a boil. Combine the potatoes, carrots, peas, beans, eggplant, cabbage, green pepper, onions, garlic, tomatoes, okra, thyme, bay leaf, 2 teaspoons of the salt, and 1 teaspoon of the pepper. Add to the oil in the casserole and stir well.

Bake in a 350° oven for 30 minutes. Place the fish on top of the vegetables and sprinkle with the remaining salt and pepper. Bake for 30 minutes, or until fish is done. Remove the bay leaf and serve directly from the casserole. *Serves 6.*

TONGUE WITH OLIVES

LIMBA CU MASLINE

1 fresh or pickled beef tongue	2 tablespoons vinegar
3 tablespoons butter	½ teaspoon freshly ground
2 onions, chopped	black pepper
1 clove garlic, minced	1 bay leaf
2 tablespoons flour	½ teaspoon powdered ginger
½ cup canned tomato sauce	1 cup ripe olives
½ cup dry white wine	

Place the tongue in a deep saucepan with water to cover and boil for 3 hours, or until tender. Drain, reserving 1½ cups of the stock. Remove the skin carefully and cut the tongue into ¼-inch slices. Set aside.

Melt the butter in a saucepan and add the onions and garlic. Sauté for 5 minutes, stirring frequently. Mix in the flour until smooth. Combine the reserved stock, tomato sauce, wine, and vinegar. Add to the onion mixture gradually, stirring constantly until the boiling point is reached. Add the pepper, bay leaf, ginger, olives, and the slices of tongue. Cook over low heat for 15 minutes. Correct seasoning, adding salt, if necessary. Serve hot with tiny boiled potatoes. *Serves 6–8.*

STUFFED CABBAGE

SARMALE UMPLUTA

1 head cabbage	1 slice uncooked bacon, chopped
1½ pounds ground pork	fine
¾ pound ground beef	1 pound sauerkraut
1 slice bread, soaked in water	3 slices bacon, half cooked and
and crumbled	drained
1 onion, chopped	2 cups tomato sauce
1 teaspoon salt	1 cup sour cream
½ teaspoon freshly ground	
black pepper	

Place the entire head of cabbage in a large bowl and pour boiling water over it. Let stand 10 minutes. Drain the cabbage and remove 18 leaves carefully. Mix the ground pork and beef, crumbled bread, onion, salt, pepper, and chopped bacon together in a bowl. Place a tablespoon of this mixture in the center of each cabbage leaf and roll it up, turning in the ends carefully.

Spread the sauerkraut on the bottom of an earthenware casserole or heavy pot. Arrange the cabbage rolls carefully on top of the sauerkraut. Cut each slice of bacon into 3 pieces and place them over the cabbage rolls. Pour the tomato sauce over all. Cover and bake in a 375° oven 2½ hours, removing the cover for the last 30 minutes or until lightly browned. Mix in the sour cream. Heat on direct low heat for 5 minutes. *Serves 6–8.*

Note: The flavor is improved by reheating, so prepare the cabbage the day before it is to be served, if possible.

BEANS, PEASANT STYLE

FASOLE STIL TARANESC

1 pound dried white beans	1½ teaspoons salt
3 cups water	1 teaspoon freshly ground
¼ cup vegetable oil	black pepper
1 onion, chopped	3 tablespoons chopped parsley
1 tablespoon flour	3 tablespoons vinegar
1 tablespoon tomato paste	12 small sausages (optional)

Wash the beans and place in a heavy saucepan with the water. Soak overnight. Cook in the same water until tender, about 2 hours, adding more water if necessary. Drain but reserve ½ cup of the liquid.

Heat the oil in a saucepan and add the chopped onion. Sauté for 10 minutes, stirring occasionally. Sprinkle with flour, add the tomato paste, salt, pepper, and parsley, and stir well. Add the reserved liquid and vinegar, mixing well. Add the beans and simmer for 15 minutes. Fry the sausages, drain, and add to the beans. *Serves 6–8.*

POTATO STEW

TOCANA DE CARTOFI

2 tablespoons chicken fat or butter	¼ teaspoon sweet paprika
2 tablespoons flour	1 cup beef broth
2 teaspoons salt	6 potatoes, peeled and cubed
½ teaspoon freshly ground black pepper	¼ cup heavy cream

Melt the chicken fat in a deep saucepan, add the flour, salt, pepper, and paprika, and stir until smooth. Add the stock gradually, stirring constantly until the boiling point is reached. Add the potatoes and stir. Cover and cook over medium heat for 15 minutes. Add the cream and cook for 5 minutes. There should be only a small amount of sauce remaining. Serve hot with a little of the sauce poured over the potatoes. *Serves 6–8.*

CORN MEAL, RUMANIAN STYLE

MAMALIGA

1 quart water	1 cup brinza, or feta, or ½ cup
1½ teaspoons salt	grated Parmesan and ½ cup
1 cup yellow corn meal	cottage cheese
¼ cup melted butter	

Bring the water and salt to a boil in a saucepan. Add the corn meal gradually, stirring constantly until thickened. Cook over medium heat for 20 minutes. Butter an 8-inch square pan and pour the corn meal into it. Chill until firm, about 2 hours. Turn out carefully onto a lightly floured surface. Cut into slices about ½ inch thick. Preheat oven to 375°.

Butter a baking dish thoroughly. Arrange the slices in layers, sprinkle the melted butter and spread the cheese between each layer and on top. Bake in a 375° oven for 20 minutes, or until delicately browned. *Serves 6–8.*

Note: Mamaliga is the great national dish of Rumania. It appears at practically every meal, and is often served in place of bread. It often accompanies ghivetch.

DOUGHNUTS WITH CHERRIES

GOGOSI CU CIRESE

2 cakes or packages yeast	½ cup milk, scalded and cooled
½ cup lukewarm water	1 teaspoon vanilla extract
3 tablespoons sugar	Pitted fresh or canned sour red
3½ cups sifted flour (about)	or black cherries
8 egg yolks	Vegetable oil for deep frying
¼ pound (1 stick) sweet butter,	
melted and cooled	

In a bowl, mix together the yeast, water, and sugar. Stir in enough of the flour to make a batter. Cover and let rise in a warm place for 1 hour.

Beat the egg yolks well. Stir in the melted butter, milk and vanilla. Beat in the yeast mixture, and then enough of the remaining flour to make a soft dough. Beat well, then knead until smooth and shiny. Cover the bowl and let rise in a warm place for 30 minutes.

On a floured surface, roll out the dough ½ inch thick. Cut into 2-inch circles with a cooky cutter. Place a cherry in the center of half the circles, pressing down gently, and cover each with another circle, pressing the edges together firmly. Arrange the doughnuts on a floured surface, allowing space between each to permit rising. Sprinkle the tops lightly with flour, cover, and let rise until double in size, about 1 hour.

Heat deep oil to 375°. Fry two or three doughnuts at a time, until light brown on all sides. Don't crowd the pan; see that doughnuts don't touch each other, and keep turning them. Remove with a slotted spoon, and drain on paper towels. Serve warm, sprinkled with confectioners' sugar. *Makes about 48.*

Note: If you prefer, omit the cherries. Roll dough 1 inch thick, and cut into 2-inch circles. Let rise and fry as directed.

PEAR COMPOTE
PERE ÎN COMPOT

8 large fresh pears, peeled and sliced	4 cups water
¾ cup dry bread crumbs	⅓ cup sugar
2 teaspoons cinnamon	3 tablespoons lemon juice
	¼ cup white wine

Combine the pears, bread crumbs, cinnamon, and water in a saucepan. Cover and cook over low heat for 1 hour. Force through a sieve. Add the sugar, lemon juice, and wine and cook for 20 minutes. Chill. Serve cold, with a plain cake, such as spongecake. *Serves 6–8.*

SYRIA, LEBANON, AND JORDAN

These three neighboring countries have so much in common in the way of language, religion, and background that it is only natural to find the people eating the same foods and following almost identical cuisines. The regions involved are historic ones, filled with many ruins of biblical times, and of great interest to the tourist. The Cedars of Lebanon, found in this area, are a rewarding sight and may be seen from the fine resort hotels in the region. These three countries are sometimes called the

Levant, a somewhat arbitrary geographical designation but one that is commonly accepted to denote the three neighboring nations.

The diets of all three countries are quite similar. The basic foods are rice, lamb, eggplant, and yogurt. Meals are served in a colorful and interesting manner, particularly in private homes. Though the hotels and restaurants usually serve in the European fashion at normal tables and chairs, the local population prefers to eat at very low tables, barely two feet high, and thus, since ordinary chairs are useless, the guests must sit on the floor or upon cushions. Food is presented with considerable ceremony in the homes of the more prosperous, and although a meal may be simple or elaborate, depending upon the resources of the host, there is always an atmosphere of cordiality and hospitality toward any guest.

The only liquor served before a meal is *arrack,* the locally produced strong drink. Tourist hotels and restaurants serve the usual Western-style cocktails and drinks, but these do not appeal to the local population. Sometimes wine is served during the meal as a concession to Western visitors, but this custom is not always followed. The diner is more likely to be served with iced fruit drinks of great sweetness, or possibly with a soured milk beverage.

A typical native meal might consist of a thick lentil soup, stuffed eggplant prepared with plenty of olive oil, and a baked lamb dish. Rice is the basis of many dishes, and poor people literally exist on it. A favorite cooking style is the practice of wrapping mixtures of ground meat and rice in grape leaves and baking them, although this custom is followed throughout the region. The *kebabs* (meats roasted on a skewer) are enormously popular with the people.

Figs, dates, and grapes are of the finest quality and many different varieties are available. Oversweet desserts are still the preference of most, and the usual rich pastries of commendable delicacy and lightness are unfortunately drenched in an overabundance of honey or fruit syrup. Calories do not interest the populace, for overweight is generally not considered to be important, and wives are often encouraged to gain and maintain excess poundage. Thus, more and more rich desserts are consumed.

The Turkish-style coffee, which is about one third sediment and two thirds thick liquid, is the choice of the people of the three countries. Men spend hours in the coffeehouses, business is transacted over coffee cups, and guests are always served coffee.

Sambousiks, or finger foods, much like our own hors d'oeuvres are served with *arrack. Arrack* is usually mixed with a little water, which makes it look like Grade C milk, but it is not recommended for milk shakes!

CURRIED PASTRY

SAMBOUSIKS

1¼ cups sifted flour	¾ cup milk, scalded
1 teaspoon salt	1 tablespoon curry powder
¼ pound (1 stick) butter	1½ cups chopped cooked chicken,
4 tablespoons yogurt	beef, or veal
2 tablespoons vegetable oil	

Sift the flour (reserving 1 tablespoon) and ½ teaspoon of the salt into a bowl. Cut in half the butter with a pastry blender or two knives. Add the yogurt, tossing lightly until a ball of dough is formed. Chill for 15 minutes. Roll out on a lightly floured surface. Flatten the remaining butter and place it on the center of the dough. Fold the dough in half and then in quarters. Wrap in wax paper and chill for 1 hour.

Heat oil in a saucepan. Mix in the reserved flour until smooth. Gradually add the milk, stirring until the boiling point is reached. Add the curry and remaining salt, and cook over low heat for 5 minutes, stirring occasionally. Add the chopped meat; mix lightly. Preheat oven to 375°.

Roll out the dough ⅛ inch thick on a lightly floured surface. Cut into 3-inch circles with a cooky cutter. Place a tablespoon of the meat mixture in the center and fold over the dough, sealing the edges well. Place on a baking sheet. Bake in a 375° oven for 15 minutes or until brown. These hot pastries are excellent hot hors d'oeuvres. *Makes about 20.*

EGGPLANT APPETIZER

BABA GANNOJ

2-pound eggplant	1½ teaspoons salt
3 tablespoons sesame *tahini*	1 tablespoon sesame or safflower
paste (available in Middle	oil
East stores)	½ cup finely minced onions
1 clove garlic, minced	¼ cup minced parsley
⅓ cup lemon juice	

Wash the eggplant, wrap in foil, and bake in a 450° oven for 45 minutes. Unwrap, and when cool enough to handle, peel it. While the eggplant is baking, put the *tahini* in a bowl. Beat in the garlic, then very gradually the lemon juice. Mix in the salt.

Purée the eggplant in an electric blender or chop very fine, then beat in the *tahini* mixture. Beat until a smooth paste is formed. Taste for seasoning. Turn the eggplant into a fairly flat dish. Sprinkle with the oil, onions, and parsley. Chill. Serve as a dip with Arabic bread or crackers. If you prefer, the eggplant can be served on individual plates. *Makes about 3 cups.*

FISH AND RICE, DAMASCUS STYLE

SAYADIET

6 fillets of fish	½ teaspoon pepper
3 tablespoons flour	4 tablespoons butter
1 teaspoon salt	

Wash and dry the fillets. Combine the flour, salt, and pepper. Dip the fish fillets in it. Melt the butter in a frying pan or casserole. Brown the fish on both sides. Spread Arabic rice (see recipe in this section) over the fish. Cover and cook over low heat for 15 minutes. Serve hot. *Serves 6.*

BAKED MEAT AND WHEAT

KIBBEH

Wheat Mixture:

1 pound *bourghol* (fine crushed wheat)	2 teaspoons salt
2 pounds lean twice-ground lamb	½ teaspoon freshly ground black pepper
½ cup grated onions	¼ teaspoon cinnamon
	¼ cup ice water

Soak the wheat in cold water to cover for 30 minutes, kneading it several times. Drain thoroughly, then mix in the lamb, onions, salt, pepper, and cinnamon. Knead for a few minutes, then put through the fine blade of a food chopper, adding ice water as you grind.

Filling:

2 tablespoons olive oil	¼ teaspoon freshly ground black pepper
1 cup chopped onions	
1 pound ground lamb	¼ cup pine nuts
1 teaspoon salt	½ cup melted butter

Heat the oil in a skillet; brown the onions in it. Add the meat, salt, and pepper. Cook over medium heat, stirring frequently, for 5 minutes. Add the nuts. Cook, stirring frequently until browned.

Pat half the wheat mixture into a greased 9- by 12-inch baking pan. Spread the filling over it. Cover with the remaining wheat mixture, pressing down until firm. With a sharp knife, cut diagonal lines across the top to form a diamond pattern. Pour the melted butter over the top. Bake in a preheated 400° oven 30 minutes. Reduce heat to 350° and bake 30 minutes longer. Cut into squares and serve. This dish may be eaten hot or cold. *Serves 8–10.*

STUFFED CHICKEN, SYRIAN STYLE

DGAJ MUHSHY

⅓ cup olive oil
1 pound ground beef or lamb
½ cup rice, half cooked
⅓ cup pine nuts
3 teaspoons salt
1 teaspoon freshly ground
   black pepper

¼ teaspoon nutmeg
Dash of thyme
6-pound roasting chicken
2 quarts water
1 onion
1 stalk celery

Heat 3 tablespoons of the olive oil in a skillet. Add the ground meat and sauté over medium heat for 10 minutes, stirring occasionally. Add the rice, pine nuts, 1 teaspoon of the salt, ½ teaspoon of the pepper, the nutmeg and thyme. Mix well. Stuff the chicken with the mixture, closing the opening carefully with thread or skewers. Place in a deep saucepan with the water, onion, celery, and remaining salt and pepper. Cover and cook over low heat for 2 hours.

Remove chicken from the saucepan and drain. Brush the chicken with the remaining olive oil. Roast in a 400° oven till brown and tender, about 30 minutes. Serve hot. *Serves 4–6.*

CHICK-PEA SPREAD

HOMMOS

1 pound dried chick-peas
½ teaspoon baking soda
3 teaspoons salt
¾ cup sesame *tahini* paste
   (available in Middle East
   stores)

½ cup lemon juice
3 cloves garlic, minced
3 tablespoons minced parsley

Wash the chick-peas and discard any imperfect ones. Cover with water, mix in the baking soda, and let soak overnight. Drain, wash under cold running water, place in a saucepan, and cover with water. Bring to a boil, and cook over low heat 3 hours, adding 1½ teaspoons salt after 1 hour of cooking time. Drain. Purée the chick-peas in an electric blender or put through a food mill.

Gradually add the *tahini* and lemon juice alternately. Crush the garlic with the remaining salt, and beat into the chick-pea mixture. Spread on a serving dish and sprinkle with the parsley. Serve with Arabic or French bread. *Makes about 4 cups.*

Note: If you prefer, use 2 cans of chick-peas, which will eliminate the cooking process.

OKRA STEW

BAMIYEH

¼ pound (1 stick) butter	2 cups tomato juice
2 3-pound chickens, disjointed	2 cups water
2 cloves garlic, minced	1 teaspoon salt
½ teaspoon crushed coriander	½ teaspoon freshly ground
seeds	black pepper
2 pounds okra, stems removed	

Melt 6 tablespoons of the butter in a Dutch oven or casserole. Add the chicken pieces and brown well on all sides. Add the garlic and coriander and mix well. Cover and cook over low heat for 30 minutes.

In a separate saucepan melt the remaining butter, add the okra, and fry for 5 minutes. Add to the chicken with the tomato juice, water, salt, and pepper and stir. Cover and simmer over low heat for 45 minutes. Stir carefully so as not to break the okra. Correct seasoning. Serve hot, being careful to lift the okra out of the saucepan gently. *Serves 6–8.*

Note: 2 packages frozen okra can be substituted for the fresh, but cook only 20 minutes.

ARABIC RICE

RIZ MAFALFEL

2 cups rice	¼ pound (1 stick) butter
5 cups boiling water	¼ cup pine nuts or pignolias
2 teaspoons salt	

Wash the rice in several changes of water. Place in a bowl and add half the boiling water. Soak for 2 hours. Rinse with cold water. Drain well. Bring the remaining water to an active boil. Add the rice, salt, and all but 2 tablespoons of the butter. Cover and cook until the water is absorbed. Melt the remaining butter in a skillet. Add the nuts. (If large nuts are used instead of the pine nuts or pignolias, chop them.) Sauté until lightly browned and sprinkle over the rice. *Serves 6–8.*

SALAD, DAMASCUS STYLE

TABOOLI

½ pound *bourghol* (cracked wheat)
4 tomatoes, cubed
8 scallions (green onions), sliced
½ cup chopped parsley

3 tablespoons sesame olive oil
¼ cup lemon juice
½ teaspoon salt
Lettuce leaves

Soak the cracked wheat in hot water to cover for 2 hours. Drain thoroughly. Combine the tomatoes, scallions, parsley, oil, lemon juice, and salt in a bowl. Toss together lightly. Add the cracked wheat and again toss lightly. Arrange beds of lettuce leaves on individual plates. Sprinkle a few drops of olive oil on each portion. Divide the mixture into even portions. Serve cold. *Serves 6–8.*

Note: In Lebanon a little minced garlic is added to the above ingredients. The vegetables are chopped very fine on a chopping board, combined with the other ingredients, then chilled. The salad is served in a bowl surrounded by individual scoops of crisp romaine lettuce leaves, and everyone helps himself. Served in this fashion, it makes a good cocktail accompaniment. In the absence of romaine lettuce, use potato chips.

ARABIC BREAD

1 package active dry yeast
1¼ cups lukewarm water
3 teaspoons sugar
3 cups unbleached flour

1½ teaspoons salt
Vegetable oil
Olive oil
Sesame seeds

Mix the yeast with ½ cup of the water and 1 teaspoon of the sugar. Put in a warm place for 15 minutes.

Put the flour, salt, and remaining sugar in a large bowl. Make a well in the center and pour in the yeast mixture and remaining water. Mix in the flour. The dough should be fairly soft—if it's not, add a little more lukewarm water. Knead the dough (if you have a dough hook attachment for your electric mixer, use it) until smooth and shiny. Form into a ball, and brush the top with a little vegetable oil. Cover and let stand in a warm place 1¼ hours, or until double in bulk.

Preheat oven to 475°.

Punch the dough down, knead several times, and divide into six pieces, forming each into a ball. Cover and let stand for 10 minutes. Roll out each ball into a 5-inch circle. Brush with olive oil and sprinkle with sesame seeds. Arrange on baking sheets and bake 10 minutes. Transfer loaves to a board. Cover with a towel and let cool. *Makes 6 loaves.*

FARINA DESSERT

HREEST AL LOWZ

1 cup sugar
½ cup water
¼ cup butter
3 cups cooked farina or cream of
    wheat

½ cup honey
½ cup chopped walnuts

Boil the sugar and water in a saucepan until thick and syrupy, about 15 minutes. Add the butter and farina and stir well until completely blended. The mixture should be quite thick. Pour into individual serving dishes. Sprinkle the honey and walnuts on top. Serve hot. *Serves 8–10.*

TURKEY

No longer a country of mystery, veiled women, and E. Phillips Oppenheim international-spy stories, Turkey has progressed immeasurably in recent years. It is rich in thousands of years of history, and the Byzantine architecture of Istanbul always delights visitors.

Eating is an important matter here, the gourmet is regarded with reverence, and homage is accorded his opinions. Shopping for food is a delight to the eye and nose, because not only is the market colorful but the air is always filled with the aroma of freshly brewed coffee and rare spices.

Fish is in great demand, for there is a great variety of it, and apparently the waters surrounding the country abound in some of the world's finest seafood. Swordfish, fresh or smoked in the local fashion, is excellent. *Hamsi,* best described as a sort of sprat or anchovy, is considered a great delicacy, particularly by the coastal residents. Caviar from the roe of the locally caught sturgeon is expensive but greatly prized, and used frequently by those who can afford it.

Scarcely a dinner begins without soup, of which the Turks have a wide variety, both hot and cold. The recipe for the traditional *düğün chorbasi* (wedding soup) is hardly typical but it is of classic stature.

The people are very fond of starchy foods, such as lentils, rice (which is made into *pilafs*), chick-peas, and dried beans. Even Italian spaghettis and macaronis are frequently served, and most dinners contain one course, in this category. The most popular vegetables are eggplant and okra, which are prepared with great regularity and in many different fashions.

Lamb and beef are the national meats, and *shish-kebab* (broiled meat on a skewer) probably originated with the Turks, though there is some doubt expressed by their neighboring countries regarding this, despite the fact that the words themselves are Turkish. Pork is eaten only by non-Moslems, who are in the minority. Poultry of all sorts, including some wild game birds, appear frequently on the menu.

A great local specialty is the *börek*, a fine pastrylike dough wrapped around cheese or meat and fried crisp. It is an excellent cocktail appetizer when made in a small version.

Desserts are immensely popular here, and all sorts of confections are prepared and eaten with great relish. Possibly only Vienna equals Istanbul in the love of desserts. Fresh fruits, particularly figs, cherries, grapes, and peaches, are of superb quality. Melons are very good, and there is a wide selection. Cheeses are extremely popular, but there are only a few of meritorious quality.

There are several distinctive features to Turkish cooking. The people are very fond of fresh herbs and spices, and these are used frequently; perhaps the best known are cumin, fennel, dill, and coriander. The average Turkish chef has a somewhat heavy hand with garlic, and sometimes it is used far too liberally. Strangely enough, in a garlic-laden stew, the diner will note certain sweet ingredients such as seedless raisins, currants, and nuts. Rice dishes are commonplace, whereas potatoes are quite rare. Vegetables are rarely cooked plain with a little water for a brief time, as is the American style; more likely, they will be cooked for an hour or two, until rather soft, with a consequent loss of texture. This is not necessarily a fault, but a somewhat different way of cooking, for the vegetables are prepared typically in a meat or poultry broth, and well seasoned.

Raki, a grape distillation tasting of anise, is the strong drink of the nation. It is not appreciated at first taste, and beginners are advised to dilute it half and half with water. Many after-dinner liqueurs are prepared in an assortment of fruit flavors. Wines are improving steadily in quality, and there is a wide selection available in red and white, sweet and dry, still and sparkling types. As yet, however, these have not become generally available for export.

LAMB AND EGG SOUP

DÜĞÜN CHORBASI

3 pounds lamb and bones
1 onion
1 carrot, peeled
2 teaspoons salt
Dash of cayenne pepper
2½ quarts water

4 tablespoons butter
4 tablespoons flour
3 egg yolks
3 tablespoons lemon juice
⅓ cup melted butter
½ teaspoon paprika

Combine the lamb, bones, onion, carrot, salt, cayenne pepper, and water in a saucepan. Bring to a boil; cover and cook over low heat for 3 hours. Strain the soup, reserving the meat. Mince the meat and return to the soup. Melt the butter in a separate saucepan. Add the flour and mix to a smooth paste. Gradually add the soup, stirring constantly until the boiling point is reached. Cook over low heat for 15 minutes. Beat the egg yolks and lemon juice in a bowl. Gradually add 2 cups of the soup, stirring constantly. Return to the balance of the soup, stirring constantly. Do not allow soup to boil after the eggs are added. Add 1 tablespoon of butter to each portion and sprinkle with paprika. *Serves 8–10.*

Note: This is the traditional "wedding soup" of Turkey.

SWORDFISH ON SKEWERS

KILIÇ BALIĞI SISDE

1½ pounds swordfish
2 tablespoons olive oil
¼ teaspoon paprika
2 tablespoons finely grated onion

1 teaspoon salt
1 tablespoon lemon juice
Bay leaves
Lemon slices

Wash and dry the fish. Remove the skin carefully and cut into 1½-inch cubes. Combine in a bowl the olive oil, paprika, onion, salt, and lemon juice. Stir well. Place the cubes of fish in it and see that each piece of fish is coated with the mixture. Marinate in the refrigerator for at least 5 hours, overnight if possible. Divide the fish in six parts and place pieces carefully on skewers, putting a bay leaf and lemon slice between each. Broil in a 450° oven for 12 minutes turning the skewers several times to brown on all sides. Serve with the following sauce:

6 tablespoons lemon juice
4 tablespoons olive oil

½ teaspoon salt
1 tablespoon chopped parsley

Combine the lemon juice, olive oil, salt, and chopped parsley. Stir all together. Serve at room temperature in a sauceboat. *Serves 6.*

Note: If swordfish is unobtainable, fresh tuna or halibut may be substituted.

MEAT PASTRY

KIYMAH BÖREK

2¾ cups sifted flour	1½ pounds chopped beef
1¾ teaspoons salt	3 onions, chopped
4 eggs, beaten	½ teaspoon freshly ground
3 tablespoons water	black pepper
4 tablespoons vegetable or olive	½ cup melted butter
oil	½ cup milk

Sift the flour and ½ teaspoon of the salt into a bowl. Combine the eggs and water and add, mixing well. Knead until the dough is smooth and elastic; it should be soft. If necessary, add water or flour to make the dough soft and pliable. Cover with a wet cloth while preparing the filling. Heat the oil in a skillet. Add the beef, onions, pepper, and remaining salt. Sauté over low heat 15 minutes, stirring occasionally. Cool 15 minutes.

Divide the dough into eight balls, seven of which should be of equal size and one half again as large. Roll out the smaller balls 10 inches in diameter, stacking them with wax paper between each layer. Roll the larger ball to fit a 10-inch pie plate but allow it to overhang the edge. Preheat oven to 375°. Place three layers of the dough in the lined pie plate, brushing each with melted butter and milk. Place the meat mixture over the layers and cover with the remaining layers, again brushing each one with melted butter and milk. Fold over the overhanging dough and press the edges together. Bake in a 375° oven for 35 minutes or until brown on top. Turn out onto a plate and cut pie-shaped wedges. *Serves 6–8.*

LAMB STEW

TAS KEBAB

3 pounds boneless lamb	3 tablespoons lemon juice
2 teaspoons salt	4 tablespoons butter
½ teaspoon freshly ground	¾ cup chopped onions
black pepper	1 20-ounce can tomatoes

Cut the lamb into 2-inch cubes. Sprinkle with the salt, pepper, and lemon juice. Toss well, then let stand 1 hour at room temperature, mixing a few times. Drain the meat, reserving any liquid.

Melt the butter in a Dutch oven or deep skillet. Brown the lamb and onions in it very well. Add the tomatoes and reserved liquid. Bring to a boil, cover, and cook over low heat 2 hours, or until the lamb is tender. *Serves 6–8.*

RICE WITH TOMATOES

DOMATESLI PILAF

2 cups rice	3½ cups beef broth
4 tablespoons butter	1 teaspoon salt
3 tomatoes, peeled and chopped	

Wash the rice in several changes of water. Place in a bowl and cover with boiling water. Soak for 15 minutes. Drain. Melt the butter in a saucepan. Add the tomatoes and cook over low heat 10 minutes. Mash the tomatoes. Add the broth and salt. Bring to a boil and add the rice, stirring steadily. Cook over medium heat until the stock is absorbed. Reduce heat to very low and cook 15 minutes, stirring occasionally. Correct seasoning. *Serves 6–8.*

CUCUMBER SALAD

JAJIK

4 cucumbers	1 tablespoon chopped dill
1 teaspoon salt	2 cups yogurt
1 tablespoon vinegar	3 tablespoons olive oil
1 clove garlic, minced	1 tablespoon chopped mint leaves

Peel the cucumbers and cut in quarters lengthwise. Slice very fine. Place in a bowl and sprinkle with the salt. Mix together the vinegar, garlic, dill, and yogurt. Pour over the cucumbers and mix well. Sprinkle the olive oil and chopped mint leaves on top of the salad. Serve cool, but do not refrigerate. *Serves 6–8.*

TURKISH FRUIT SALAD

MEYVE SALATA

2 teaspoons powdered ginger	1 cup fresh or canned pineapple, cubed
½ cup brandy	
2 oranges, peeled and sliced thin	1 cup strawberries, halved

Dissolve the ginger in the brandy. Combine the oranges, pineapple, and strawberries in a bowl. Pour the brandy over the fruits, basting them for a few moments. Cover the bowl and chill for 3 hours. Arrange the salad on lettuce leaves and serve. *Serves 4–6.*

Note: Any combination of three fruits may be used with the ginger-brandy dressing for an unusual fruit salad.

SHREDDED WHEAT PIE

TEL KADAYIF

1 package shredded wheat	2 cups coarsely chopped walnuts
3 cups boiling water	2 cups milk
½ pound (2 sticks) butter, melted	1¾ cups sugar

Dip the shredded wheat in the boiling water, and remove quickly. Drain well. Wrap in aluminum foil and place in the refrigerator overnight or for at least 4 hours. Preheat oven to 375°. Spread 3 tablespoons of the butter on the bottom and sides of a 10-inch pie plate. Cut the biscuits in half lengthwise and arrange half of them on the bottom of the pie plate. Spread with the walnuts and cover with the remaining biscuits. Pour the remaining butter over the top. Press down firmly with a plate, then remove the plate. Bake in a 375° oven for 25 minutes, or until brown.

Prepare the syrup while the pie is baking. Combine the milk and sugar in a saucepan. Bring it to a boil, mix well, and cook until syrupy. Pour the syrup over the pie as soon as it is baked. Cover with a plate and set aside to cool for at least 2 hours. Turn out onto a plate. *Serves 8–10.*

Africa   *Egypt*
           North and Central Africa
           Union of South Africa

EGYPT

Lying in the northeastern part of Africa, Egypt is a tremendous land of which the western half is almost entirely an uninhabited desert. Since only a tiny portion of its land is available for cultivation (a reasonable approximation being about three per cent), the nation is practically supported by the area surrounding the Nile River. The great stream of fabulous history overflows its banks about early September of each year and carries with it the thick silt of the river bed. As the water drains away, the life-sustaining soil remains, permitting the raising of crops which would otherwise be impossible.

Egyptians are famous for their heavy breakfasts and for their exotic choice of foods at this first meal of the day. For example, a favorite breakfast dish in Egypt is called *fool mudammas*, which consists of cooked beans served with halves of sliced hard-cooked eggs. What makes this surprising is that none of the other Mediterranean or Near Eastern peoples begin the day with a heavy meal. Dinner, usually enjoyed in the evening cool after the great heat of the day has abated somewhat, is likewise an important meal. Between breakfast and dinner, the people do not exactly starve, for in addition to lunch they nibble on little delicacies, such as nuts, fruits, dates, figs, and other oddments. The Egyptians love cool, refreshing soft drinks and there are numbers from which to choose. Both tea and coffee are popular here.

Some fish is eaten, but poultry and meat are more appreciated by the average person. In Egypt "meat" usually means mutton, which is preferred to the younger and more delicate meat of the sheep which we call lamb. The fat of the full-grown sheep is quite strong in flavor and most Westerners find it unappetizing, though it must be admitted that in Australia and New Zealand there is little objection to mutton. Egyptians prefer their meat practically swimming in fat, and this, too, is hardly to our taste. The hotels and restaurants that cater to tourists have learned to avoid an overabundance of grease in their cooking; authentic French cuisine is the rule.

Bread is of the flat type, usually a rather large, spongy, whole wheat mixture which takes the place of cutlery for the *fellah*, or peasant, who sops up his food with it. Most people cannot afford fancy fare, and filling food such as beans, chick-peas, and rice are preferred by the majority. *Couscous*, though probably Algerian in origin, is a great favorite here. It is a meat or poultry dish based on a coarse cereal and is very satisfying.

The sweet desserts beloved of all people of the Near East are in evidence here. Wheat flour, thick fruit syrups, and honey are combined with calorific pastries to form desserts far too sweet for our tastes. Candies, too, are of such sweetness and richness that one piece will cloy the palate.

Water—yes, water—is the national drink of Egypt since it is a Moslem country; after water comes Turkish-style sweet, muddy coffee. Beer and alcoholic drinks are available but are generally unimportant. At Mariout, wines are being grown with reasonable success, and the Clos Mariout, a white wine, is well received by wine drinkers. In addition several satisfactory red wines are in production.

BEANS, EGYPTIAN STYLE

FOOL MUDAMMAS

1½ cups dried white beans	¼ cup lemon juice
2 teaspoons salt	3 scallions (green onions),
2 cloves garlic, minced	sliced fine
½ cup olive oil	

Wash the beans thoroughly and soak in water to cover overnight. Drain, and cover with fresh water. Cook until the skins split, about 2 hours. Drain well and cool. Place the beans in a bowl. Add the salt, garlic, olive oil, and lemon juice, and mix well. Chill. Serve with the scallions on top as an appetizer. If desired, the beans may be served as a salad on a bed of romaine lettuce. *Serves 6–8.*

FISH AND LAMB MOLD

BAMIA AU GOMBOS

3 tablespoons olive oil	½ teaspoon freshly ground
2 onions, chopped	black pepper
1 pound ground lamb	1 cup dry sherry
3 tomatoes, chopped	6 fillets of sole
2 teaspoons salt	

Heat the olive oil in a frying pan. Add the onions, lamb, tomatoes, salt, and pepper. Sauté for 15 minutes, stirring frequently. Add the sherry and stir well. Cook over low heat for 15 minutes. Butter a 7- to 9-inch casserole or mold. Arrange the fillets so that they cover the bottom and sides of the casserole. Pour in the lamb mixture. If the fillets extend over the outside edge of the casserole, turn them inward to cover the lamb mixture. Bake in a 275° oven for 2 hours. Turn out onto a heated serving platter. *Serves 6.*

CHICKEN AND GREENS

MLOOKHIA

5-pound chicken, disjointed	1 teaspoon ground coriander
1 onion	3 cloves garlic, minced
1 carrot	2 teaspoons salt
1½ quarts water	¼ pound (1 stick) butter
2 pounds kale, spinach, or chard	

Combine the chicken, onion, carrot, and water in a saucepan. Cook over medium heat for 45 minutes, or until chicken is nearly tender. Wash greens carefully. Drain well and dry thoroughly. Chop coarsely. Pound the coriander, garlic, and salt to a smooth paste. Melt the butter in a saucepan. Add the paste and chicken. Sauté for 10 minutes. Add the spinach. Cook over medium heat for 10 minutes. Correct seasoning. Serve with boiled rice. The chicken broth may be served separately. *Serves 4–6.*

Note: Mlookhia is a unique and very popular Egyptian vegetable. The green vegetables substituted are similar in flavor, though not so bitter.

MEAT CROQUETTES

KUFTA

1 pound chopped beef	¼ teaspoon cayenne pepper
1 pound chopped lamb	¼ teaspoon orégano
1 onion, chopped fine	3 tablespoons chopped parsley
2 eggs, beaten	1½ cups dry bread crumbs
½ cup milk	¼ pound (1 stick) butter
1½ teaspoons salt	

Mix together the beef, lamb, onions, eggs, milk, salt, cayenne pepper, orégano, parsley, and 1 cup of the bread crumbs. Form into eight croquettes and dip in the remaining crumbs. Melt half the butter in a frying pan. Fry the croquettes in it slowly over low heat until browned on both sides, about 20 minutes. Add butter as required. *Serves 8.*

EGGPLANT AND LAMB CASSEROLE

BEDINGANE ABIAD

½ cup sesame oil or vegetable oil
1 medium eggplant, peeled and
 sliced ¼ inch thick
2 onions, chopped fine
2 pounds lean ground lamb

2 teaspoons salt
1 teaspoon freshly ground
 black pepper
1½ teaspoons cinnamon
2 cups cooked rice

Heat ¼ cup of the oil in a skillet. Brown the eggplant slices in it on both sides. Remove the eggplant and set aside. Add the remaining ¼ cup of oil to the skillet and heat. Add the onions, lamb, salt, pepper, and cinnamon. Sauté for 10 minutes, stirring frequently.

Butter or oil a casserole. Arrange a layer of rice on the bottom. Cover with about one third of the lamb mixture. Add layer of eggplant and successive layers of rice, lamb and eggplant until the ingredients are used up, ending with rice on top. Bake in a 375° oven for 35 minutes, or until browned on top. Serve directly from the casserole. *Serves 6–8.*

CHICKEN AND CRACKED WHEAT

HAREESIE

5-pound chicken, cut in half
2 onions, chopped fine
8 cups water
2 cups *bourghol* (cracked
 wheat)
2 teaspoons salt

½ teaspoon freshly ground
 black pepper
1 teaspoon cinnamon
⅛ teaspoon ground cloves
¼ pound (1 stick) butter

Combine the chicken, onions, and water in a saucepan. Bring to a boil and skim the top carefully. Cook over low heat for 30 minutes. Meanwhile, soak the *bourghol* in water to cover for 20 minutes. Drain the *bourghol* and add to the chicken, together with the salt. Cover and cook over low heat for 1½ hours.

Remove the chicken meat from the bones, cut into small pieces, and return to the saucepan. Add the pepper, cinnamon, cloves, and butter. Cook over low heat for 15 minutes. Mix well. Correct seasoning. Serve each portion in a large soup plate. The consistency of the dish should be that of a porridge. *Serves 6–8.*

RICE FLOUR PUDDING

MEHALLABIA

½ cup seedless raisins
1⅛ cups sugar
1 tablespoon cornstarch
⅓ cup rice flour

4 cups milk
1 tablespoon rose water, orange
flower water, or vanilla extract

Soak the raisins in water to cover for 15 minutes. Combine the sugar, cornstarch, and rice flour in a saucepan. Gradually add the milk, stirring constantly until smooth. Cook over medium heat, stirring constantly until the boiling point is reached. Cook for 10 minutes, stirring occasionally. Reduce to low heat and cook, without stirring, until the mixture caramelizes on the bottom of the pot. Add the flavoring. Drain the raisins thoroughly and add, stirring gently. Pour the mixture into a serving dish or into 8 individual dishes. Chill at least 4 hours. *Serves 8.*

NORTH AND CENTRAL AFRICA

The continent of Africa is far greater in land area than a glance at a map might indicate. It encompasses a vast area of desert, oases, jungle, flatlands, mountains, coastline, lake regions, and has all the temperature and scenic variations that one might expect of a giant continent. At one time, much—indeed, most—of Africa was under the direct control of European countries, but recent years have seen the emergence of what are called "developing nations." The old shackles and encumbrances have been thrown off, and the daily newspapers are regularly reporting new countries coming upon the scene. Some of these are tiny, measuring but a few hundred square miles; still others cover enormous territories.

Quite naturally, therefore, it is rather arbitrary to sum up the culinary styles of scores and scores of nations, including thousands of different tribes and groupings, all of which have a degree, more or less, of individual cooking styles.

Morocco, Libya, Tunis, and Algeria are inhabited chiefly by Mohammedan people, and therefore, the food customs tend to follow a certain pattern. As might be expected, their Islamic background effects the diet of the people to a considerable extent, even though they live in different countries. With certain foods prohibited, they tend to have a similar diet. For example, throughout this entire region, the hungry traveler will find *couscous*, a substantial and filling semolina dish. Each country claims to have invented the preparation, but at this stage no one can be sure, although the best available evidence points to Algeria as the source. There are recipes galore for *couscous*, and its preparation varies from place to place, usually being quite spicy. However, it may also be served as a sweet dish, prepared with fruits and nuts, for example. In the homes of prosperous merchants, *couscous* will be offered only at the conclusion of a substantial meal, to subdue any remaining pangs of hunger. The correct way to eat *couscous* is with the fingers, but a kindly hostess will usually provide a large soup spoon for the foreign guest, as do the restaurants.

At the northwest corner of Africa is the fascinating land of Morocco, of particular interest to tourists. Although it is very worthwhile for sightseeing, the food is outstanding and not wildly exotic, although the presentation may be startling on occasion. The single most popular first course is probably the *bstilla*, which consists of very flaky pastry, filled with a delicious mixture of minced pigeon and other ingredients, sweet and spicy at the same time, and then dusted lightly with a sprinkling of sugar. The other famous dish is *méchoui*, a whole roast lamb brought to the table piping hot, and eaten with the fingers. The proper etiquette is to dip morsels in a mixture of salt and cumin. Also, it's possible one might be served a *tajine*, made with lamb or chicken, and it's a kind of spicy stew. (In Tunis, contrarily, a *tagine* is more like a heavy soufflé.) Frequently, there's a salad, perhaps a vegetable such as cooked eggplant, and, for dessert, fresh fruit and one of the country's delicious pastries. The national beverage of Morocco is mint tea, that is, tea strongly flavored with mint, and it's both delicious and refreshing.

In north central Africa is the Sudan, which has been overlooked by the rest of the world, gastronomically speaking. No meal is complete without one of the country's rather tasty, although chewy, types of puffy flat bread called *khupz* and *kisra*. No matter what one is served (except for soup, of course), it's customary to use the bread as a sort of all-purpose spoon and fork combined. In addition to the bread, it's rare not to find white rice, served in enormous quantities. Although the various meats come in the guise of stews, and are a trifle spicy, it's usual to add surprisingly large amounts of *shata*, which is a burning, searing hot sauce. Afterwards, perhaps a salad may be served to cool the palate, and the meal usually ends with tea.

Over on the northeast coast of the continent is the ancient land of Ethiopia, where the food customs are nothing short of fascinating. A low table is brought in and positioned before the diners. At first glance it appears to be covered by a tablecloth; a more careful inspection reveals that it is an edible sort of covering, constituting a kind of large pancake. Actually it's the country's national bread, called *injera*, which is brown-beige in color. It cannot be made here, for we lack the special kind of grain, called *tef*. While the prospective diner is accustoming himself to this edible tablecloth, various spicy dishes are arranged in small portions on the top, in attractive arrangements. Then, pieces of the dough "table-cloth" are broken off, wrapped around one or more of the foods, and then transferred to the mouth. That is, hopefully. As a rule, some of the sauce will drip onto the diner, surely down his wrist. One word of warn-ing: Ethiopia has the spiciest food of the continent, far surpassing that of Mexico, for instance, in its sharp, burning quality. When you've eaten up the "tablecloth," your dinner is finished. As a beverage, you'd be wise to call for the local beer, *tella*, which may help you bear up during the meal. One Ethiopian dinner is equal to two handkerchiefs, as a rule, to wipe away the tears and mop the brow.

Senegal has Dakar as its chief city, which was built by the French when they controlled this land. As a result, not only does Dakar have the appearance of a provincial town in France, but its food is somehow still subtly French in nature. In one or more of the excellent restaurants of Dakar you can dine as well and as expensively as in Paris. On the other hand, there are several native dishes of interest. Shrimp appears as an appetizer, or stuffed in vegetables, or in spicy sauces. Chicken prepara-tions are popular, such as *yassa*, a dish made with hot red peppers, lemon, and onions, and served on a bed of boiled rice. No desserts are eaten by the local people except for fresh fruit, although a fine restaurant might offer European cakes and pastry in the Parisian style. The coffee is a natural conclusion to a Senegalese dinner, and it is served black, strong, and powerful.

Ghana likes to add peanuts to its dishes, and a typical item on most menus would be groundnut stew, consisting of chicken cooked with vegetables and peanuts. (Incidentally, the word "groundnut" is used frequently throughout the continent to denote peanuts.) In the same manner, peanuts are cooked into a soft liquid mass, to which a type of flour is added, creating a peanut sauce. This delicious mixture is gen-erally placed over cooked bananas and plantains, or similar starchy fruits. Or the cook may decide to make a groundnut soup, often spiced up with a dash of hot pepper sauce; it may be served hot or cold and is equally good, although terribly fattening.

Most people are aware of the fact that Liberia, on the west coast, was created by a number of freed American slaves. It has many indica-tions of the American background of its first settlers, not to mention that most people speak English. Indeed, the capital city, Monrovia, was named for President Monroe. The oil used for cooking, palm oil, is very distinctive, and brings a nutty and special flavor to many dishes. Perhaps the outstanding dish is country chop, in which an assortment of fish and meats, together with fresh vegetables, are sautéed in palm oil; it is not necessarily a dish for everyone, because of the somewhat unique combination of tastes. On the other hand, almost everyone would like *jolov,* a rice-and-chicken preparation. As a side dish, a combination of rice and okra, bearing the somewhat strange name of *check-rice,* is quite tasty.

Kenya, the great safari country, mostly consumes English-style food in the large cities. Only in the "bush" can one obtain anything resembling native cooking. Perhaps the basic food of the tribal people is *irio,* the ultimate starchy combination of corn, potatoes, and dried peas. *Irio,* although more than merely filling, is fairly good with plain roast meats or broiled fish.

Tanzania is a gloriously beautiful country, often spectacularly so. Perhaps the high point, scenically, is snow-covered Kilimanjaro. The tribesmen and their families subsist chiefly upon corn meal, cooked into a cereal, sometimes called *mealy-mealy,* and sometimes *ugali.* The cooking is not appealing to tourists except for the excellent fruits and melons. Of course, there are several stews made with meat and poultry, but they are not very unusual. In addition, coconuts, plantains, bananas, and similar fruits are used in cooking.

Mozambique, a Portuguese sphere of influence, shows a certain culinary impact of that Iberian nation. In Portugal, for example, a favorite dish is prepared using the somewhat unusual combination of clams and pork; although strange at first, the combination is quite satisfactory. In Mozambique, they make *matata,* in which small clams are cooked with peanuts, green vegetables, and port wine (from Portugal, quite naturally). With almost anything that's served comes a small bowl of the hottest imaginable red pepper sauce, called *piri-piri.* Another interesting item is occasionally called African chicken, or sometimes *frango a cafrial,* and consists of chicken rubbed with garlic and peppers, then barbecued; this is truly delicious.

Off the southeast coast of Africa lies a very large island, Madagascar, which is called the Malagasy Republic. The capital city, Tananarive, lively and bustling, is just beginning to encourage tourism, and a visit to the city, and the countryside as well, is quite rewarding. Because this island was the home of Arab and Indian traders, their influence may be noted in the local cuisine. In particular, the Indian love for spicy curries may be seen on almost every menu, and in the people's homes as well. On request, most cooks will withhold the red pepper, called *sakay,* so as to make it fit to eat, by Western standards. A typical meat dish is *varenga*, made from beef cut into narrow strips. Because vegetables grow so well on this island, every meal features them; equally, the fresh tropical fruits can hardly be surpassed.

CREAM OF PEANUT SOUP

UGANDA

2 tablespoons cornstarch
3 cups milk
3 cups hot chicken broth
2 cups ground peanuts

2 tablespoons grated onion
2 teaspoons salt
⅛ teaspoon cayenne pepper

In a deep saucepan blend the cornstarch with the milk, stirring until smooth. Add the broth, peanuts, onion, salt, and cayenne pepper, stirring constantly. Bring to a boil and cook over medium heat for 5 minutes. Beat with a rotary beater for 1 minute. Strain. Serve hot. *Serves 6–8.*

FISH STEW

MAÏKA, NORTH COAST OF AFRICA

¼ cup olive oil
3 onions, chopped
2 tablespoons flour
4 cloves garlic, minced
2½ teaspoons salt
1 teaspoon pepper
½ teaspoon dried ground chili peppers
¼ teaspoon ground coriander
7 cups milk

2 pounds sliced, assorted fish (3 different varieties)
½ pound shrimp, shelled and cleaned
2 lobsters, in the shell, chopped into small pieces
6 slices toast (French bread, if possible)
3 tablespoons grated lemon rind

Heat the olive oil in a large saucepan. Add the onions and sauté for 15 minutes, stirring frequently. Sprinkle with the flour and mix until smooth. Add the garlic, salt, pepper, chili peppers, and coriander. Gradually add the milk, stirring constantly until the boiling point is reached. Add the fish, shrimp, and lobster and cook over low heat for 25 minutes. Correct seasoning. Place a slice of toast in each soup bowl. Sprinkle with the lemon rind and pour the soup over it. Arrange the fish on a separate platter and serve. *Serves 6–8.*

MIXED MEATS AND SEMOLINA

COUSCOUS

3 cups *faufal* (see text)
3 cups water
1½ tablespoons salt
1 cup dried or 2 cups canned
drained chick-peas
¼ cup olive oil
½ pound butter
2 cups chopped onions
3 pounds boneless lamb, cubed
3 chicken breasts, each cut in
4 pieces
3 cups chicken broth

2 carrots, sliced
2 green peppers, sliced
3 tomatoes, peeled and cubed
¼ teaspoon saffron
1 teaspoon freshly ground
black pepper
½ teaspoon cayenne pepper
2 cups shredded cabbage
2 cups seedless raisins
1 pound fresh shelled or 1
package frozen green peas

If possible, use a *couscousière,* a special double-boiler type of pot, the upper portion of which has holes in it like a colander. If you don't have one, see substitute instructions in body of recipe.

Faufal are tiny pellets of wheat, and can be found in Near East or oriental food shops. If unobtainable, you may substitute cracked wheat, wheat semolina, or even farina.

Put the *faufal* in a bowl and stir in the water and 1 teaspoon salt. Rub mixture between the hands above the water, then let it fall back into bowl. Do this several times. Do not allow lumps to form. Let the *faufal* soak until all the water is absorbed.

(If you are using dried chick-peas, cover with water, bring to a boil and let soak 1 hour. Drain.)

Heat the oil and half the butter in the bottom of the *couscousière* or a large saucepan; brown the onions, lamb, and chicken in it. Add the broth and the soaked chick-peas (if canned chick-peas are used, add later with the green peas). Mix in the carrots, green peppers, tomatoes, saffron, black pepper, cayenne pepper, and remaining salt. Turn the *faufal* into the top of the *couscousière* or a large strainer or colander and place over the bottom pan. Cover as tightly as possible. Cook over low heat 1½ hours, then to the chicken mixture add the cabbage, raisins, green peas (and canned chick-peas). Re-cover and continue cooking 45 minutes longer, or until chicken is tender. Stir the remaining butter into *faufal* with a fork. Heap the *faufal* in the center of a platter with the chicken, lamb, vegetables, and sauce around it. *Serves 8–10.*

MARINATED LAMB WITH LEMONS AND OLIVES

TAJINE

8 shoulder lamb chops, cut 1 inch thick
3 cloves garlic, minced
2 teaspoons salt
1 teaspoon crushed cumin seeds
½ teaspoon ground ginger
1 teaspoon freshly ground black pepper
⅛ teaspoon saffron

1 teaspoon cinnamon
1 teaspoon crushed coriander seeds
¾ cup olive oil
4 cups chopped onions
1 cup chopped parsley
3 lemons, quartered
½ cup black olives

Cut the chops in half crosswise. Combine the garlic, salt, and all the spices. Rub the mixture into the lamb, place in a bowl, cover, and let stand at room temperature for 2 hours.

Heat the oil in a Dutch oven or heavy casserole. Add the meat; cover and cook over low heat 30 minutes, stirring several times. Remove the meat and keep hot. To the oil remaining, add the onions and parsley. Cover and cook over low heat 15 minutes. Return the lamb and cook 30 minutes longer, adding a little water if necessary. Add the lemons and olives just before serving. *Serves 8–10.*

SPICY TUNA AND VEGETABLE SALAD

MESHWIYA

3 green peppers
3 tomatoes, peeled and cubed
10 scallions (green onions) thinly sliced
2 7-ounce cans tuna fish, drained and flaked
3 hard-cooked eggs, sliced
¼ cup minced parsley

1 tablespoon capers
⅓ cup olive oil
3 tablespoons lemon juice
1 clove garlic, minced
1½ teaspoons salt
¼ teaspoon freshly ground black pepper
6 drops Tabasco

Broil the peppers as close to the source of heat as possible, using a long-handled fork, turning the peppers until all sides are browned. Peel off the skin and cut the peppers into narrow julienne strips. In a large bowl, toss together the peppers, tomatoes, scallions, tuna fish, eggs, parsley, and capers. Mix together the oil, lemon juice, garlic, salt, pepper, and Tabasco. Pour over the salad and toss lightly. Chill for 30 minutes. Toss again before serving as a first course or luncheon dish. *Serves 4–6.*

TUNISIAN MEAT CUSTARD

TAGINE MALSOUKA

3 tablespoons olive oil	½ teaspoon cinnamon
½ cup chopped onions	1½ teaspoons salt
1 pound lean lamb, or beef, cut in small dice	¾ teaspoon freshly ground black pepper
1 cup water	6 eggs
1 cup canned white beans	Dash of Tabasco

Preheat oven to 375°.

Heat the oil in a saucepan; brown the onions and meat in it. Add the water, beans, cinnamon, 1 teaspoon of the salt, and ½ teaspoon of the pepper. Cover and cook over low heat 1 hour. Cool slightly.

Beat together the eggs, Tabasco, and remaining salt and pepper. Mix the eggs with the meat stew. Turn into a greased 10-inch pie plate. Bake in a preheated 375° oven 35 minutes, or until firm and gently set. Cut into wedges and serve hot. *Serves 4–6.*

PIGEON PIE

BSTILA

The pastry for *bstila* is very difficult to make, but an adequate substitute is either *phyllo* leaves (available in Greek or Middle East food shops) or packaged strudel leaves. Buy sixteen *phyllo* leaves or four packages of strudel leaves.

1 cup water	½ teaspoon saffron
½ pound (2 sticks) butter	½ teaspoon crushed coriander
¾ teaspoon salt	½ cup minced onions
½ teaspoon ground cardamom seeds	¼ cup minced parsley
⅛ teaspoon mace	4 pigeons, squabs, or whole chicken breasts
¼ teaspoon ginger	6 eggs
Dash of cayenne pepper	¼ cup sugar
⅛ teaspoon cinnamon	½ pound shelled almonds
Dash of powdered cloves	2 teaspoons cinnamon
⅛ teaspoon powdered fennel	3 tablespoons confectioners' sugar
¼ teaspoon freshly ground black pepper	

Combine the water, half the butter, the spices, onions, parsley, pigeons and their gizzards and livers (or chicken breasts) in a saucepan. Bring to a boil, cover, and cook over low heat 2 hours. Remove the pigeons, discard the skin and bones, and cut the pigeon meat, gizzards and livers into small pieces.

Beat 4 eggs in a bowl; gradually add the hot stock, beating until thickened. Beat the remaining eggs. Melt the remaining butter and pour half into a baking pan about 10 by 14 inches.

Use 5 sheets of pastry for the bottom layer, piling one on top of the other, and brushing each with beaten egg. Leaving a 2-inch border, sprinkle the sugar over the top layer, then the almonds and 1 teaspoon cinnamon. Cover with 5 layers of pastry, brushing each with beaten egg. Leaving a 2-inch border, spread the pigeon meat and cover with the sauce. Cover with the remaining layers of pastry, brushing each with beaten egg yolk. Tuck in all the edges to seal. Pour the remaining melted butter over the top. Bake in a preheated 425° oven 25 minutes or until golden brown. Sprinkle the top with the confectioners' sugar and the remaining cinnamon. While hot, cut into squares. *Serves 6–8.*

AFRICAN CHICKEN-PEANUT STEW

MOAMBA

2 4-pound chickens, disjointed	1½ pounds sweet potatoes,
6 cups water	peeled and quartered
2 cups ground peanuts	8 hard-cooked eggs, shelled
1 cup chopped onions	4 cups hot cooked rice

Wash the chicken pieces and combine in a saucepan with the water. Bring to a boil and cook over medium heat 45 minutes. Add the peanuts, onions, and sweet potatoes. Cover loosely and cook over low heat 45 minutes longer, or until the chicken is tender.

The stew is served in deep plates. Place an egg in each, cover the egg with some rice, and put some chicken and gravy over the top. Serve with side dishes of diced cucumber, chutney, and sliced bananas. *Serves 8.*

SPICED NUT BALLS

EL MAJOUN

1 pound toasted blanched almonds	½ teaspoon cinnamon
½ pound shelled walnuts	½ teaspoon saffron
1 pound seedless raisins	¼ teaspoon fennel seeds
3 tablespoons preserved ginger	⅛ teaspoon cayenne pepper
6 cardamom seeds	½ pound honey
¼ teaspoon mace	¼ pound (1 stick) butter
¼ teaspoon nutmeg	1½ cups sesame seeds

Grind the nuts and chop the raisins and ginger fine. Pound together all the spices. Use a heavy-bottomed saucepan, and in it combine the nuts, fruits, spices, honey, and butter. Cook over low heat, stirring frequently, until mixture turns very thick, about 1 hour. Watch carefully to prevent burning.

Let stand until cool enough to handle, then form into walnut-size balls and roll heavily in the sesame seeds. Keep in a cool dry place. *Makes about 60.*

UNION OF SOUTH AFRICA

The word "Africa" usually brings to mind vast plains and wild animals, and while this is true to a certain extent, Capetown and Johannesburg (called Joburg by its inhabitants) are extremely modern cities filled with fine buildings and not a few skyscrapers. The visitor is always surprised by the pace and tempo of these cities.

Four principal groups in addition to numerous minorities are represented here: the Dutch, British, Indian, and native populations. The Dutch (Boers) were the earliest settlers of this land, and brought with them their own style of cooking, names of dishes, and eating habits. The British, as they have the world over, brought a little bit of England with them in their hearts, and they prefer English food and the English way of life, typified by elaborate teas and formal dinners. The Indians came originally to labor under the hot African sun but have become shopkeepers. They, too, brought their food customs with them. The Bantu, the principal group of aborigines, have few dishes of interest to us, except those based on the wild game of the region.

Unfortunately for the curious gourmet, hotels and restaurants limit themselves to the hotel-style food known the world over as "international," which customarily means taking little or no advantage of the area's fine foodstuffs. To enjoy an *Afrikander* dinner, it would probably be necessary to secure an invitation to the home of a long-time resident, as these dishes are seldom seen on menus in public dining places.

The native groups are particularly fond of their home brew, known as Kaffir beer, but comparatively few tourists ever get around to tasting it. South Africa produces in a moderate-size area numerous wines of good quality, particularly sweet types. Both still and sparkling wines are available, though they are not yet of export standard, except for the local sherry-type wine. Local brandies are quite satisfactory. Of course the usual imported liquors may be had. In passing, it may be noted that the cocktail party is the most popular of all social events.

Until recently the great shellfish specialty of South Africa was unknown to the rest of the world. However, since the advent of frozen foods, the *langouste,* marketed as the South African lobster tail, has been well received. These are eaten broiled, boiled, sautéed in butter, served on noodles, and in many other fashions. Rock oysters and salmon are also unusually fine.

Many dishes of Dutch origin or influence may be noted in South Africa. For example, the *swartsuur* is a mutton stew, the *hoender pastei* is a type of chicken pie, and *poffertjes,* a sort of fritter. A popular meat mixture made with ground beef is called *babottee,* and is really a type of curry, perhaps an Indian influence. *Sosaties* are something like *shish-kebabs,* marinated meats on a skewer, except that *sosaties* are curry-flavored. Cakes and pastries are very much a part of the local scene, being very popular; also, they're generally homemade, and seldom purchased in bakery shops, for the women of South Africa are still interested in home baking. It is often a point of pride, and housewives often try to outdo one another in homemade cakes.

PICKLED SALMON

12 thin slices salmon, cut in half
4 teaspoons salt
1 teaspoon freshly ground
  black pepper
¼ cup olive or salad oil
6 large onions, sliced in thin rings
3 tablespoons curry powder

¼ teaspoon dried ground chili
  peppers
1 cup seedless raisins
2 tablespoons sugar
1 teaspoon turmeric
3 cups cider vinegar

Wash and dry the salmon. Mix 1 teaspoon of the salt with the pepper and sprinkle the fish with it. Heat the oil in a skillet and brown the fish in it on both sides. Remove the fish and let cool. Add 4 of the onions to the oil remaining in the pan and fry until brown.

Combine 2 tablespoons of the curry powder, the chili peppers, raisins, sugar, and turmeric. Add 3 tablespoons of the vinegar and mix well. Arrange several successive layers of fish, fried onions, and the spice mixture in a bowl or jar. Combine the remaining onions, vinegar, salt, and curry powder in a saucepan. Boil for 15 minutes. Pour over the layers of fish and allow to cool for 1 hour. Cover and keep in the refrigerator for at least 2 days before using. Prepared this way, the fish will keep about 2 weeks. Serve cold as an appetizer. *Serves 10–12.*

CURRIED POTATO SOUP

3 tablespoons butter	2 teaspoons salt
1 pound stewing beef, cut into ¼-inch cubes	2 tablespoons curry powder
	2 bay leaves
3 onions, chopped	3 potatoes large sliced
8 cups water	1 tablespoon vinegar

Melt the butter in a deep saucepan. Add the beef and onions and sauté until brown. Add the water, salt, curry powder, and bay leaves. Cook over medium heat for 45 minutes. Add the potatoes and vinegar. Cook for 30 minutes. Correct seasoning. Discard bay leaves. Serve hot in deep soup plates. *Serves 6–8.*

STUFFED ROCK LOBSTER TAILS

6 8-ounce African lobster tails	¼ cup minced onions
1½ quarts water	2 tablespoons curry powder
½ teaspoon pickling spice	2 tablespoons flour
2 cloves garlic, sliced	½ cup dry white wine
3 teaspoons salt	1 cup light cream
3 tablespoons butter	¼ cup julienne-cut pimentos

Thaw the lobsters and, with scissors, cut the soft side of the shell through the center. Bring the water, pickling spices, garlic, and 2 teaspoons of the salt to a boil. Add the lobster tails and cook 10 minutes. Drain and cool slightly. Remove the meat carefully, reserving shells. Cut the meat crosswise into thin slices.

Melt the butter in a saucepan; sauté the onions 5 minutes. Blend in the curry powder and flour, then gradually add the wine and cream, stirring steadily to the boiling point. Cook over low heat 5 minutes. Add the lobster and remaining salt. Taste for seasoning. Stuff the shells with the mixture and arrange on a baking sheet. Bake on the upper level of a preheated 425° oven 10 minutes. Arrange the pimentos on top of each lobster and bake 2 minutes longer. *Serves 6.*

MEAT STEW, CAPE MALAY STYLE

CURRIED BEAN BREDEE

1½ cups dried white beans	¼ teaspoon dried ground chili
2 tablespoons vegetable oil or	peppers
butter	2 tablespoons curry powder
4 pounds mutton or lamb, cut	1 tablespoon sugar
into 2-inch cubes	¼ cup water
3 onions, chopped	2 tablespoons vinegar
8 tomatoes, peeled and chopped	1 cup chopped sour apples
2 teaspoons salt	½ cup seedless raisins

Place the beans in a saucepan with water to cover and soak overnight. Drain, cover with water again, and boil for 1 hour.

Heat the oil in a heavy saucepan with a tight-fitting lid. Add the onions and sauté for 5 minutes. Add the meat and brown well on all sides. Add the tomatoes, salt, and chili peppers. Cover and cook over very low heat for 30 minutes. Mix the curry powder, sugar, water, and vinegar together until smooth. Add to the meat and stir well. Drain the beans and add, together with the apples and raisins, again stirring well. Cover and cook over very low heat for 2½ hours, or until meat is very tender. Small amounts of water may be added if required.

The resulting stew should be quite thick and rich. Best results will be obtained if the saucepan is tightly covered and the meat cooked slowly. Serve with boiled rice. *Serves 8–10.*

STEAK AND MACARONI CASSEROLE

2 pounds steak	1 cup dry bread crumbs
3 teaspoons salt	2 eggs, beaten
½ teaspoon freshly ground	Vegetable oil for deep-fat frying
black pepper	4 cups cooked macaroni
1 cup grated cheese	

Cut the steak into 1-inch squares. Sprinkle with 1½ teaspoons of the salt and ½ teaspoon of the pepper. Reserve half the cheese and dip the steak pieces in the remaining half. Then dip the pieces in the bread crumbs, eggs, and once again in the bread crumbs. Heat the oil to 375° in a deep saucepan. Drop several pieces of the meat into the fat at a time, and fry for 1 minute. Drain.

Place the macaroni in a buttered casserole. Sprinkle with the remaining salt, pepper, and cheese. Place the steak pieces on top. Bake in a

450° oven for 10 minutes, or until browned on top. This dish is often served with broiled tomatoes. *Serves 6–8.*

GROUND BEEF PIE

BABOTTEE

3 tablespoons butter	2 tablespoons curry powder
3 onions, chopped	1 teaspoon salt
2 slices white bread	2 tablespoons plum jam
1 cup milk	3 tablespoons lemon juice
2 pounds ground beef	¼ cup ground almonds
2 eggs	3 bay leaves

Melt the butter in a saucepan. Add the onions and sauté for 10 minutes, stirring occasionally. Soak the bread in the milk and squeeze dry, reserving the milk. Mash the bread fine. In a bowl combine the beef, sautéed onions, bread, 1 egg, curry powder, salt, plum jam, lemon juice, and almonds. Mix well. Place the bay leaves on the bottom of a buttered 10-inch pie plate and spread the meat mixture over them. Beat the remaining egg with the reserved milk and pour it over the meat. Bake in a 350° oven for 1¼ hours. Serve hot from the dish. *Serves 6–8.*

FRIED CAKES

KOEK SISTERS

2 cups sifted flour	Vegetable oil for deep-fat frying
⅛ teaspoon salt	1½ cups sugar
1 teaspoon cream of tartar	⅓ cup water
6 tablespoons butter	½ teaspoon cinnamon
1 egg, beaten	

Sift the flour, salt, and cream of tartar together into a bowl. Cut in the butter with a pastry blender or two knives until the consistency of coarse sand. Add the egg and toss lightly with a fork until the mixture forms a ball of dough. Roll out ¼ inch thick on a lightly floured surface. Cut into 5-inch circles and roll up in the shape of cornucopias, so that one end is closed and the other open.

Heat the deep fat to 385°. Drop a few cornucopias at a time into the fat. Fry until they rise to the surface. Remove immediately and drain. Combine 1 cup of the sugar, the water and cinnamon in a saucepan. Boil until syrupy, about 5 minutes. Dip each cake into the syrup, then roll in the remaining sugar. *Makes about 30 cakes.*

Asia   *Burma*
                      China
                      Hong Kong
                      India
                      Indonesia
                      Japan
                      Korea
                      Pakistan
                      Singapore and Malaysia
                      Sri Lanka (Ceylon)
                      Thailand (Siam)

Burma is a fey sort of place, somewhat dreamlike and unreal. Life move slowly, and no one appears to work very hard, much preferring a life of comparative ease—perhaps it might be regarded as the simple life, as it has sometimes been called. The Burmese are fond of American products —now in rather short supply—but it has not succumbed to chromium, neon, elaborate shops, and color television.

Tourist folders often describe a country as being populated with smiling people, and the traveler will find this trite description to be true of Burma. The people actually smile. Very few countries can make that statement. They really seem happy, and are apparently satisfied with their lives. Of course they are a simple, trusting people who are unaware of ulcers, the stock market, high blood pressure, 3-D, inflation, and the other benefits of civilization. Foolishly, they go on their way, wearing the colorful *lungyi*, something like a skirt, indulging themselves in their delightful festivals, little dreaming of the more important things of life, such as social security, taxes, and unemployment insurance.

From the moment the Pan American plane puts down at Mingaladon Airport, you will be able to re-create Kipling's Burma, although it will have to be in your mind. It was on the road to Mandalay that his British soldier saw the Burma girl smoking a cheroot. (The dictionary says that a cheroot is a cigar with a truncated end. A truncated end is . . .)

The land itself is a good one, heavily irrigated by the rivers which rise almost fifty feet during the rainy season. This flooding of the adjacent fields makes them particularly suitable for the growing of rice, sugar cane, and the local tobacco, which is made into cigars with truncated ends called cheroots, which in turn are smoked by Burma girls, or are we confused and is it the other way round? Speaking of women, it is only in Burma, of all the Asian countries, that those of female persuasion are held in high esteem by the male contingent. The respect and deference to their opinions are unique in the Orient.

On rising, there is coffee or tea with bread. At about 9 A.M., a breakfast of rice, soup, and curry. The midday meal, called tiffin in the
British fashion, is a fairly simple meal of meat, bread, and fruit. Dinnertime is usually 6 P.M. The meal often begins with soup, although all the
dishes are placed on the table at the same time. Soups are of two kinds:
the regular type, *hingyo,* and the acid soup, *chin-ye-hin.* Everyone in the
family helps himself from the various bowls according to his appetite
and preferences. Except on special occasions, cakes and other sweet
desserts are not served. Fresh or preserved fruits are the rule, and these
often end the meal.

The Burmese cuisine is similar to those of India and Indonesia. Curries
are standbys, and curry powder itself is the favorite seasoning. Pickles
and relishes of all kinds are well liked by the people, and a great favorite
is the garlic-laden pickled cabbage. Noodle dishes, such as fried vermicelli and *panthay khowse* (noodles and chicken), are popular. Most of
this descriptive material as to the food habits of the people applies only
to those who can afford it; there are many who must be satisfied with
a bowl of rice flavored with a little *nga-pi-gyet,* a garlic and shrimp
sauce that may reasonably be described as noxious. In all fairness it must
be allowed that it is possible to learn to like this Burmese favorite; the
Burmese are tolerant about our fondness for our smelly cheese, which
they abhor.

A typical Burmese meal, served for guests rather than as an everyday
repast, might begin with a soup of one sort or another, described above.
Then perhaps a fish dish, a *lethoke,* made of cooked small fish balls with
fried onions. Possibly it might include a truly great favorite, *balachaung,*
which is prepared with ground shrimp, onions, garlic, and ginger. After
this, there would probably be a curry of one sort or another, for the
Burmese make curries out of almost anything—eggs, vegetable, fish,
poultry, meat, etc. And for a side dish with the curry, possibly the *ohn
htamin,* coconut-flavored rice. Dessert might be fresh or preserved fruit.

Although coffee is well liked, this is a tea-growing country. The
Burmese prefer their tea with an orange blossom or jasmine fragrance;
in addition, they like to thicken it with grains or cereals until it has a
gumbo-like consistency, whereupon it ceases to taste like tea. On second
thought, perhaps they don't like tea as much as we first believed.

CABBAGE SOUP

MON LA HINGYO

2 tablespoons sesame or peanut
oil
1 tablespoon anchovy or shrimp
paste
2 onions, chopped fine
3 cloves garlic, minced
1 teaspoon plum jam
1 teaspoon lemon juice
2 fresh chili peppers, chopped
fine, or ½ teaspoon dried
ground chili peppers

2 tomatoes, chopped
3 cups shredded cabbage
6 cups beef broth
1½ teaspoons salt
¼ teaspoon freshly ground
black pepper

Combine the oil, anchovy or shrimp paste, onions, garlic, jam, lemon juice, chili peppers, tomatoes, and cabbage in a deep saucepan. Cover and cook over low heat for 20 minutes. Add the broth, salt, and pepper. Bring to a boil. Cook uncovered over low heat for 20 minutes. Correct seasoning and serve. *Serves 6–8.*

Note: Plum jam and lemon juice are used in this recipe as a substitute for the usually unavailable tamarind.

CURRIED FISH BALLS

NGA SOK HIN

2 pounds fillets of any white-meat
fish
½ cup sesame oil or peanut oil
2 fresh chili peppers, ground,
or ½ teaspoon dried ground
chili peppers
3 onions, chopped fine

4 cloves garlic, minced
1 teaspoon grated lemon rind
1 teaspoon turmeric
2 teaspoons salt
¼ cup flour
3 tomatoes, chopped

Wash the fish thoroughly and remove any bones. Grind it twice in a food chopper, or chop very fine. Heat ¼ cup of the oil in a skillet. Add the chili peppers, onions, garlic, lemon rind, turmeric, and salt. Sauté for 10 minutes, stirring frequently. Remove one third of this mixture and add to the ground fish. Chop together until smooth. Form the fish mixture into walnut-size balls. Roll lightly in the flour.

Add the remaining oil to the mixture in the skillet and heat. Add the fish balls and brown on all sides, stirring frequently. Add the tomatoes and cook over low heat for 25 minutes. Serve hot with boiled rice. *Serves 6–8.*

GINGER BEEF

AHME HNAT HIN

5 onions, chopped fine
4 cloves garlic, minced
2 teaspoons turmeric
2 fresh chili peppers, chopped, or ½ teaspoon dried ground chili peppers
1-inch piece fresh ginger, chopped, or 2 teaspoons powdered ginger
2 teaspoons salt
3 pounds beef, cut into 1½-inch cubes
½ cup sesame oil or peanut oil
8 tomatoes, chopped, or 1 29-ounce can
2 cups beef broth

Combine the onions, garlic, turmeric, chili peppers, ginger, and salt. Chop or pound together until very fine. Place the beef in a bowl and add the spice mixture. Coat the meat as well as possible. Leave in the bowl for 3 hours, turning frequently. Heat the oil in a deep saucepan until it bubbles. Add the beef and spices and brown well. Add the tomatoes and cook over medium heat for 10 minutes. Add the broth. Cover and cook over low heat for 1 hour, or until the meat is tender. *Serves 8–10.*

NOODLES AND CHICKEN, BURMESE STYLE

PANTHAY KHOWSE

3 cups fresh or unsweetened dried grated coconut
4 cups milk
½ cup sesame oil or peanut oil
3 onions, chopped fine
6 cloves garlic, minced
1-inch piece of fresh ginger, chopped fine, or 2 teaspoons powdered ginger
1 tablespoon curry powder
4 whole raw chicken breasts, boned and cut into small cubes
1 cup boiling water
2 teaspoons salt
¼ cup cornstarch or potato flour
¼ cup cold water
3 8-ounce packages broad noodles, cooked and drained
2 fresh chili peppers, chopped fine, or ½ teaspoon dried ground chili peppers
4 hard-cooked eggs, chopped
6 scallions (green onions), sliced thin

Combine the coconut and the milk in a saucepan. Bring to a boil, remove from the heat, and soak for 30 minutes. Press all the liquid from the coconut and discard the pulp.

Heat the oil in a saucepan. Add the onions, garlic, and ginger and sauté for 10 minutes, stirring frequently. Add the curry powder; stir, and cook 2 minutes longer. Add the chicken and sauté for 15 minutes, stirring occasionally. Add 2 cups of the previously prepared coconut milk, the boiling water, and the salt. Stir well and cover. Cook over low heat for 30 minutes, or until the chicken is tender. Mix the cornstarch and water to a smooth paste in a cup. Add to the chicken mixture, stirring constantly until the boiling point is reached. Cook over medium heat for 10 minutes, stirring frequently. Add the remaining coconut milk and stir. Heat but do not allow the mixture to boil.

Arrange the boiled noodles on a large platter or divide into individual portions. Sprinkle the chili peppers, eggs, and scallions over them. Pour the chicken mixture on top. *Serves 6–8.*

COCONUT RICE, BURMA STYLE

OHN HTAMIN

3 cups fresh or unsweetened dried grated coconut	3 onions, sliced
4 cups milk	3 cups raw rice
2 tablespoons sesame oil or peanut oil	2 teaspoons salt

Combine the coconut and milk in a saucepan. Bring to a boil, remove from the heat, and soak for 30 minutes. Press all the liquid from the coconut and discard the pulp.

Heat the oil in a deep saucepan. Add the onions and sauté for 15 minutes, stirring frequently. Wash the rice in several changes of water. Drain well. Add to the onions and cook over high heat until lightly browned, stirring constantly. Add the coconut milk and salt and stir. Add enough water, if necessary, to cover the rice by ½ inch. Cover and cook over low heat until rice is tender, about 15 minutes. Stir the rice from the bottom at least several times during this period. The rice is ready when all of the liquid has been absorbed, but do not allow the rice to become dry. *Serves 8–10.*

COCONUT CAKE

OWN THEE MOANT

¼ pound (1 stick) butter
1 cup sugar
4 egg yolks
¾ cup raw farina
½ cup sifted flour

1 teaspoon baking powder
1½ cups fresh or dried grated
coconut
1 teaspoon vanilla extract
4 egg whites

Preheat oven to 350°.

Cream the butter; add the sugar and beat until light and fluffy. Add the egg yolks and beat again. Sift the farina, flour, and baking powder together and add to the butter mixture, beating well. Chop the coconut very fine and add with the vanilla. Mix well. Beat the egg whites until stiff but not dry and fold into the coconut mixture carefully. Pour into two buttered 8-inch layer-cake pans. Bake in a 350° oven for 20 minutes or until a cake tester comes out clean. *Serves 8–10.*

Note: In Burma the cake is served plain. It may be iced or decorated with whipped cream and grated coconut if desired.

CHINA

Probably the largest and most popular group of foreign restaurants in this country is Chinese. However, the majority of these specialize in dishes that are seldom representative of the cuisine of their country. So widespread is this practice that many Chinese restaurants advertise themselves only by the flashing neon sign *Chop Suey.* This dish does not even exist in China! The exact manner in which a non-existent dish became a part of the English language is lost in conflicting folklore, but it is certain that *chop suey* is practically unknown in China. *Chow mein,* on the other hand, is an authentic Chinese item and merely means fried noodles.

Most Americans limit themselves to a few simple things such as egg rolls, egg drop soup, and similar dishes. They miss a world of culinary adventure by doing so. It has been said that there are four great cuisines in the world—French, German, Italian, and Chinese—and the Chinese is probably not the least of these. Just as we have our own local styles of preparing American food, so may Chinese cooking be divided into Canton, Peking, Szechuan, Fukien, and Shanghai styles. The majority of Chinese immigrants to the United States had their origins in Canton or Peking, and naturally these two styles are the most popular here. In recent years, a great number of Szechuan-style restaurants have made their appearance, and been warmly received. These places cook in the style of their province, which is noted for spicy food produced by the liberal use of red hot peppers, a somewhat exceptional state of affairs in China. Many of the dishes are burning to the palate, but it is wise not to order a complete meal of Szechuan dishes, for then one dish begins to taste like another, because of the burning taste.

Many normally curious people hesitate to try anything other than the few Chinese dishes with which they are familiar. They have heard of such rare and unpleasant-sounding ingredients as sharks' fins, birds' nests, and ancient eggs. But these are exotic and expensive, and certainly not necessarily representative of Chinese food. It is more important to understand the theory of the Chinese cuisine, which is founded upon economy, complexity, and subtlety. Few people in China are prosperous enough to think in terms of a whole duck or a whole roast beef. Rather, their dishes are based on staple foods such as rice or noodles, to which are added vegetables and a sauce, the whole flavored with the addition of an ounce or two of meat or poultry. Having a long history of developing culinary arts, but lacking ingredients on a sufficient scale, the cooks of China have devised complex flavor patterns. Most of the recipes in this section contain meat or poultry in amounts which would ordinarily be reserved for holidays in China. Fish is often used in more generous quantities, but only along the coastline.

The Chinese, as a nation, tend to use certain foodstuffs—soy sauce, garlic, onions, scallions, noodles, gingerroot, rice, and a wine that resembles sherry. Rather surprisingly, they sometimes use sugar in many dishes. They tend to cook with peanut oil, although sesame oil is popular. On the other hand, certain Western-style foods rarely (if ever) appear. These include butter, cheese, milk, cream, bread, and coffee. Desserts are served only on very special occasions, and sometimes not even then. As to meats, pork is the outstanding favorite, although beef is frequently served; lamb and veal are not much used. Throughout the entire country, Chinese food is cut into small pieces before cooking, for the Chinese do not use knives and forks at the table, preferring to pick up their food with chopsticks. For this reason, anything resembling an American steak or roast beef is never served.

The Chinese have many favorite locally made wines and liquors, but these have little appeal to our Westernized palates. Possibly the one exception is the hot rice wine, which many persons of European or

American background have learned to appreciate. Tea, of course, is the national drink. But it is not the commercial tea with which we are familiar. Rather, it is the so-called "China" tea, comparatively little known in this country, where the Pekoe and Orange Pekoe varieties have captured the market. Chinese of all classes drink large quantities of hot, unsweetened tea from tiny cups without handles. If you plan to serve a Chinese dinner, buy some Chinese tea and steep it in a teapot. It should be served throughout the entire meal.

There are fine Chinese dishes, almost without number. Those included here represent a small sampling of the world of Chinese cookery. If you will examine the ingredients called for in the recipe, you will find that few of them are exotic. Rather, it is the method of preparation that is unusual. Vegetables are cooked briefly and are incorporated directly into the main dish; they are seldom served separately. Try to obtain the items required for a recipe instead of omitting them. Often it is a seemingly unimportant ingredient that gives a dish its unique flavor. Do not overcook Chinese food; serve it promptly when it is ready.

BARBECUED SPARERIBS

SHEW PYE GULT

6 tablespoons honey	⅛ teaspoon powdered ginger
6 tablespoons vinegar	1½ cups beef broth
1 tablespoon sugar	2 tablespoons sherry
6 tablespoons soy sauce	3 pounds spareribs
2 cloves garlic, minced	

In a bowl, combine the honey, vinegar, sugar, soy sauce, garlic, ginger, broth, and sherry. Mix well. Cut the spareribs into individual ribs and place them in the bowl. Spoon the sauce over the ribs several times. Marinate at room temperature for at least 3 hours, basting frequently. If possible, marinate overnight in the refrigerator. Remove the ribs from the marinade and place them on a shallow roasting pan. Roast in a 350° oven for 1 hour. Pour off the fat as it accumulates on the bottom of the pan, at least four times during the roasting period. At the same time, baste the ribs with the marinade. When properly roasted the ribs should be crisp but not dried out.

One 3-pound rack of spareribs is enough for 6 people as an appetizer. If it is to be served as a main course, use 2 racks of spareribs and serve with rice. The quantity of marinade in this recipe will be sufficient for 2 racks. *Serves 6.*

FRIED MEAT BALLS AND CRAB MEAT

CHAN FAR YOOK KUN

1½ pounds ground pork
¼ pound cooked or canned crab
  meat
½ cup chopped mushrooms
½ cup chopped canned water
  chestnuts
2 teaspoons salt

½ teaspoon freshly ground
  black pepper
1 teaspoon sugar
1 cup cornstarch
2 eggs, beaten
2 tablespoons water
Vegetable oil for deep-fat frying

Combine the pork, crab meat, mushrooms, water chestnuts, salt, pepper, and sugar in a chopping bowl. Chop until well blended and very fine in texture. Shape into 1-inch balls. Dip each ball in cornstarch and coat well. Combine the eggs and water and dip each ball in the mixture. Heat the fat to 360° and drop a few balls at a time into it. Fry for 15 minutes. Drain well. Serve with sliced cucumbers. These little balls are excellent as hors d'oeuvres; spear each one with a toothpick and a thin slice of cucumber. *Makes about 30.*

STUFFED POCKETS OF DOUGH IN SOUP

WON TON

2 cups sifted flour
1½ teaspoons salt
⅔ cup water
1½ cups cooked chopped beef,
  pork, or chicken
2 teaspoons soy sauce
¼ teaspoon freshly ground black
  pepper

2 scallions (green onions), sliced
  fine
Cornstarch
4 quarts salted boiling water
6 cups chicken broth
1 cup cooked, julienne-cut beef,
  pork, or chicken
½ pound raw spinach, shredded

Sift the flour and salt together twice. Add the water and mix until well blended. Knead until smooth. Cover with a towel and set aside for 30 minutes.

Mix the chopped meat, soy sauce, pepper, and scallions until well blended. Roll out the dough as thin as possible on a board sprinkled with cornstarch. Cut into 2-inch squares. Place a heaping teaspoonful of the meat mixture in the center of each square and fold over diagonally. Press the edges together, using a little water. Bring the salted water to the boiling point and drop the *won ton* into it. Boil for 12 minutes. Drain.

Heat the broth and add the sliced meat and the spinach. Cook for only 2 minutes. Place 3 *won ton* in each soup plate and pour the soup over them. If desired, the *won ton* may be served without soup. After boiling them, drain well and fry in hot fat. Serve hot. *Serves 6.*

SOUR AND SWEET FISH

CHO LOW YU

6 slices fish or 2 whole sea bass or carp (about 2 pounds each)	4 tablespoons peanut or vegetable oil
3 egg yolks, beaten	3 tablespoons sugar
5½ tablespoons cornstarch	6 tablespoons vinegar
½ teaspoon salt	2 tablespoons honey
4 tablespoons dry sherry	1 teaspoon minced ginger
¼ cup flour	¼ cup pickled tiny onions,
¼ cup dry bread crumbs	drained
1 cup shortening for frying	½ cup cold water

Wash and dry the fish. If whole fish are used, with a sharp knife make several gashes to the bone of the fish on each side. If pieces of fish are used, it is better if the skin remains on during the cooking process to hold the fish together. The authentic Chinese style is to use whole fish. Beat the yolks until light, add 4 tablespoons of the cornstarch, the salt and sherry, and mix well. Dip the fish in this mixture, turning many times to make sure that it is well coated. Combine the flour and bread crumbs and dip the fish in it, again being careful to coat all sides. Heat the shortening until it smokes, then reduce the heat to medium. Place the fish in it carefully and cook for 5 minutes on each side if slices are used; allow 8 minutes on each side for whole fish. Remove from heat and drain.

Heat the oil in a saucepan. Add the sugar, vinegar, honey, ginger, and onions. Cook over low heat for 2 minutes. Mix the remaining cornstarch and water to a smooth paste and add gradually, stirring constantly until smooth and thick. Pour the sauce over the fish and serve. *Serves 6–8.*

FRIED RICE WITH SHRIMP

HAR CHOW FON

1½ cups rice	1 pound raw shrimp, shelled,
2½ cups water	cleaned, and coarsely chopped
4 tablespoons peanut or salad oil	3 onions, chopped
3 eggs	¼ pound mushrooms, sliced
1 teaspoon salt	3 tablespoons soy sauce
½ teaspoon pepper	1 teaspoon sugar

Wash the rice thoroughly. Soak in warm water for 15 minutes. Drain and rinse again. Combine in a saucepan with the water. Cover and bring to a boil. Cook over low heat for 12 minutes, or until the water is absorbed. Heat the oil in a large heavy skillet. Break the eggs into it. Fry until firm, then turn over and fry 1 minute. Remove the pan from the heat and cut the eggs into very thin shreds, while still in the pan. Return the pan to the heat. Add the salt, pepper, shrimp, onions, and mushrooms. Cook over low heat for 5 minutes, stirring frequently. Add the rice, soy sauce, and sugar. Cook over medium heat for 5 minutes, stirring almost constantly. *Serves 4–6.*

FRIED CHICKEN WITH BROWN SAUCE

TSWEI PI DZA GEE

4 Chinese dried mushrooms
2 whole raw chicken breasts,
    boned and cut in small cubes
2 tablespoons cornstarch
2 tablespoons dry sherry
1 teaspoon salt
2¼ cups vegetable oil

2 bamboo shoots, cut in small cubes
¼ teaspoon dried ground red chili peppers or ¼ teaspoon Tabasco
4 tablespoons *chiang* (bottled Chinese brown sauce)

Soak the mushrooms in warm water 10 minutes. Drain and dice. Toss the chicken cubes with the cornstarch, sherry, and salt. Heat 2 cups oil in a skillet until it bubbles. Fry the chicken in it until browned. Drain. Heat the remaining ¼ cup oil in a skillet and sauté the mushrooms, bamboo shoots, and red peppers 2 minutes. Stir in the *chiang*. Add the chicken; mix well. Cook 2 minutes more. Serve hot. *Serves 4–6.*

SPICY BEEF AND NOODLES

GNOW LOW MEIN

½ pound fine noodles
3 tablespoons oil
1 pound ground beef
1 teaspoon salt
½ teaspoon freshly ground black pepper
⅛ teaspoon Chinese pepper oil or Tabasco

1 clove garlic, minced
1 cup bean sprouts
1 tablespoon sugar
1 cup beef broth
2 teaspoons cornstarch
2 tablespoons water
¼ cup sliced scallions (green onions)

Cook the noodles as package directs. Drain and rinse under cold water. Drain well and chill.

Heat the oil in deep skillet; brown the meat in it, stirring frequently to prevent lumps from forming. Add the salt, pepper, pepper oil, garlic, bean sprouts, sugar, and broth. Bring to a boil. Mix together the cornstarch and water; stir into the skillet until thickened. Mix in the noodles and heat. Sprinkle with the green onions. *Serves 4–6.*

SPICED CRISP FRIED DUCK, SZECHUAN STYLE

SIANG SUE YAH

5-pound duck	6 slices gingerroot, cut julienne
3 tablespoons dry sherry	4 anise seeds
2 teaspoons crushed dried red peppers or ½ teaspoon cayenne pepper	2 eggs, beaten
	6 tablespoons flour
	Vegetable oil for deep frying
1½ teaspoons sugar	2 teaspoons coarsely ground
6 teaspoons salt	black pepper
1 leek, sliced	

Clean, wash, and dry the duck. Rub inside and out with the sherry and let stand 30 minutes.

Roll the red peppers into a powder with a rolling pin (or use ½ teaspoon cayenne pepper). Mix together the red peppers, sugar, and half the salt. Rub into the duck. Put the duck in a heatproof bowl or pan with the leek, ginger, and anise seeds. Place on a rack in a large deep pot containing enough water to reach halfway up the sides. Cover the pot and cook over medium heat 1½ hours, or until duck is tender. Watch water level, adding more if it boils out.

Cool the duck. Mix the eggs with the flour and brush on the duck, coating it well. Heat to 365° enough oil to cover the duck and fry the duck in it until browned and crisp. Drain, and cut into small pieces through the bone, trying to retain the shape of the duck.

While the duck is cooking, put the remaining salt in a dry skillet, and cook until it begins to turn color. Mix it with the black pepper. This mixture is used as a dip for the duck, and is customarily served in tiny dishes. *Serves 4–6.*

PEKING DUST

LUT TZE DAN GO

1 pound chestnuts	8 preserved kumquats
2 tablespoons sugar	¼ cup sugared or glazed walnuts
⅛ teaspoon salt	1 orange, peeled and sliced
1½ cups heavy cream	

Make a crisscross cut on the top of each chestnut. Cover with water and boil for 45 minutes, or until soft. Shell the chestnuts, then purée in an electric blender or put through a ricer. Add the sugar and salt and stir. Cool for 15 minutes. Whip the cream. Fold ½ cup of the whipped cream into the chestnut mixture. Press gently into a bowl, then turn out onto a platter. Chill for 1 hour. Garnish with the remaining whipped cream, kumquats, walnuts, and orange slices. *Serves 6–8.*

HONG KONG

Many people think Hong Kong is the single most fascinating of all destinations in the entire world. It is magnificent in appearance with a glorious and exciting harbor; the shopping may be the most comprehensive of any city; the street scenes are never-ending wonders; but, perhaps most delightful of all, it has a marvelous assortment of restaurants, featuring Chinese cooking from all of the provinces of that vast land. Dining out becomes what the French call an embarrassment of riches, for the only problem involves choosing where to have lunch and dinner.

Hong Kong, a British Crown Colony (and not China, as many people tend to write) consists of Victoria Island, plus the city of Kowloon across the harbor from Victoria, and some additional land, mostly devoted to agriculture, called the New Territories. Although Victoria has some fine restaurants, most of the best are in Kowloon, and they are very good indeed. Instead of choosing from perhaps fifty items, as is the case with many Chinese restaurants in America, here one selects from page after page of offerings. To make matters even more attractive, prices are comparatively moderate.

The two-meal-a-day custom is still observed by most of the Chinese residents. These meals are usually served about eleven in the morning and shortly after 5 P.M. Breakfast is usually nothing but a little *congee,* or water in which a small amount of rice has been boiled. The Chinese are fond of between-meal snacks, and frequently eat little delicacies called *dim sim.* A favorite time for serving these dainties is about 1 P.M., when large quantities of them are eaten, usually accompanied by many small cups of unsweetened, perfumed China tea. Those with good appetites and those who stay up late in the evening usually have a large bowl of rice or possibly noodles before retiring. On the other hand, the

Western idea of eggs, toast, and coffee for breakfast, followed by lunch and dinner, has been making itself felt in Hong Kong. The young people in particular, strongly influenced by American motion pictures and magazines to the dismay of the British residents, are the strongest advocates of Westernized food habits; the older people still stand loyally by the food and customs of their ancestors.

Chinese liquors are popular here. Among the best known are Ng Gar Pei, Gay Gook, and Ching Moy.

It is thought that Chinese food reaches a particularly high point in Hong Kong. Bearing in mind the premise that the Chinese cuisine is a great one, and that the Chinese have had to improvise dishes based on tiny cut-up pieces of meat or poultry, we now find this great cuisine operating, with variations, on an island where food is fairly plentiful. Dishes which were good are now improved, since the refugee Chinese cooks are no longer limited to a few ounces of meat.

HONG KONG GIMLET

3 tablespoons powdered sugar   Juice of 5 lemons
6 jiggers gin

Place the powdered sugar, gin, and lemon juice in a cocktail shaker with plenty of cracked ice. Shake well. Strain and pour into cocktail glasses, about two thirds full. Fill each glass with carbonated water. Serve ice cold. *Serves 6.*

Note: This drink is popular with the foreign colony only; the Chinese seldom drink gin.

MEAT CAKE SOUP

TSU YUK BENG TONG

1½ pounds ground pork   ¼ teaspoon freshly ground
6 scallions (green onions),   black pepper
   chopped fine   3 eggs, beaten
1 teaspoon salt   6 cups beef broth
1 teaspoon soy sauce

Combine the pork, scallions, salt, soy sauce, pepper, and eggs in a bowl. Mix well. Shape into 2-inch balls. Place the broth in the top of a double boiler over hot water, or use a saucepan over an asbestos pad. Add the meat balls. Cover and cook for 1 hour. Parsley may be sprinkled on top before serving. *Serves 8–10.*

FLUFFY SHRIMP BALLS

YANG CHOW HAAH KOW

2 pounds raw shrimp, shelled
  and deveined
4 water chestnuts
¼ pound pork fat or bacon
4 egg whites
¾ teaspoon salt

¼ teaspoon white pepper
½ cup sifted flour
2 tablespoons ice water
⅓ cup cornstarch
Vegetable oil for deep frying

Combine the shrimp, water chestnuts, and fat (if bacon is used, cover with water, bring to a boil, cook 2 minutes; drain), and chop together until very fine. Stir in the unbeaten egg whites, salt, pepper, flour, and ice water, and mix with the hand until mixture starts to turn pink. Pick up and slap down mixture on a board until it holds together. Form into walnut-sized balls. Roll in the cornstarch. Heat deep oil to 360°. Fry a few balls at a time until puffed and golden brown. Drain. Serve as soon as possible, as the balls collapse in a few minutes. *Makes about 32 balls.*

PORK IN PEANUT-HOISIN SAUCE

SHUEH TSAI MAO DOW RO SI

2 pounds boneless pork
3 tablespoons vegetable or peanut
  oil
1 cup ground peanuts
¼ cup soy sauce

⅛ teaspoon dried ground chili
  peppers
3 tablespoons *hoisin* sauce
  (available in Chinese shops)

Cut the pork in bite-sized pieces. Heat the oil in a saucepan; brown the pork in it. Add the peanuts, soy sauce, and chili peppers. Cover and cook over low heat 20 minutes or until pork is tender. Stir frequently and add a little water if necessary. Mix in the *hoisin* sauce and heat. Taste for seasoning. *Serves 4–6.*

WALNUT CHICKEN

HOP PO GAI DING

4 whole chicken breasts
1 teaspoon salt
2 teaspoons sugar
3 tablespoons sherry
1 tablespoon soy sauce
3 tablespoons cornstarch
1 egg, beaten
⅓ cup peanut or salad oil
1 cup blanched walnuts

½-inch piece of fresh ginger,
   chopped, or 1 teaspoon
   powdered ginger
2 cloves garlic, minced
¾ cup boiling water
1 teaspoon monosodium
   glutamate
1 cup canned bamboo shoots,
   sliced thin

Cut the uncooked chicken off the bones in small cubes. Combine the salt, 1 teaspoon of the sugar, the sherry and soy sauce in a bowl. Place the chicken cubes in it and spoon the mixture over them. Marinate for 15 minutes. Remove the chicken from the marinade and place on wax paper, reserving half the marinade. Sprinkle the cornstarch over the chicken, coating it well. Dip each piece in the egg.

Heat the oil in a skillet until it bubbles; add the walnuts and sauté until brown. Remove the walnuts and set aside. Add the ginger, garlic, and chicken to the oil remaining in the skillet. Brown well. Add the boiling water, monosodium glutamate, the remaining sugar, and the marinade. Cover and cook over low heat for 20 minutes, or until chicken is tender, stirring occasionally. In a separate saucepan, cook the bamboo shoots in their own liquid for 10 minutes. Drain well. Add the bamboo shoots and walnuts to the chicken. Cook over medium heat for 5 minutes. Serve with boiled rice. *Serves 6–8.*

PORK-STUFFED ORANGES

MA HO (GALLOPING HORSES)

2 tablespoons peanut or
   vegetable oil
1 tablespoon minced garlic
1½ pounds ground pork
¼ cup chopped peanuts
1 teaspoon ground coriander

½ teaspoon dried ground chili
   peppers
2 teaspoons anchovy paste
1 teaspoon salt
8 large oranges

Heat the oil in a skillet; sauté the garlic 2 minutes. Add the pork, peanuts, coriander, chili peppers, anchovy paste, and salt. Cook over low heat, stirring frequently, for 15 minutes.

Cut the unpeeled oranges in four sections, leaving the skin connected at the bottom. Take out pits. Flatten the oranges as much as possible and stuff them with the pork mixture. Arrange in a baking pan; bake in a 350° oven 10 minutes. *Serves 8.*

STEAMED SPONGE CAKE

GAY DON GO

3 egg whites	¾ cup sifted flour
¾ cup powdered sugar	½ teaspoon baking powder
3 egg yolks, beaten	

Beat the egg whites until peaks form, then gradually beat in the sugar until very stiff. Beat in the egg yolks. Sift the flour and baking powder over the egg mixture and stir thoroughly. Divide the mixture among 12 paper cupcake cups or greased glass custard cups. Place on a rack in a large saucepan and add water to just below the level of the rack. Cover, bring to a boil, and let steam over low heat for 20 minutes or until cakes are set.

Serve hot or cold. *Makes 12.*

INDIA

The cuisine of India is historic, surrounded by religious rituals and customs, and it is likely that centuries ago the inhabitants ate food prepared in much the same fashion as it is today. But this does not mean that all Indians eat the same type of food. There are many racial, tribal, and religious groupings, for it is populated by differing and conflicting groups of Brahmins, Moslems, Buddhists, Sikhs, Parsis, and Hindus. One group will eat beef but not pork, another is completely vegetarian, and a third group will eat pork but not beef, looking upon all cattle as holy.

To a person who approaches the food without any restrictions, the cuisine of India is delightful and unusual. Many Americans who spend a short time in India become so fond of the curries and other specialties that these dishes become lifetime favorites. More than likely, any curries you may have had outside India were not authentic. Curries do not necessarily have to be hot and spicy, and many of them are very light and delicate in flavor. Almost completely unknown to Americans are the great dishes of India, such as chicken korma, the delectable *copra kana* (coconut rice), and many excellent desserts.

Indians have distinctive food customs. Since there are no particular names for the various meals, guests are invited to dine at a given hour, rather than for lunch or dinner. In general, only one substantial meal is eaten each day. As might be imagined in the land where tea grows, it is a national favorite. Indians do not drink wines or liquors; however, most visitors have found that beer is an excellent adjunct to a curry.

Many tourists are surprised at the local fondness for hot curries, in view of the high temperatures of India. This raises the question as to whether a person is better or worse off eating spicy foods during warm weather. The Indian theory is that spicy foods heat the body, thus making the surrounding air seem cooler. This is in accordance with the Russian idea of drinking boiling-hot tea during summer weather.

It cannot be denied that a great number of American tourists are somewhat shocked at conditions in Calcutta, that teeming city of millions. Hundreds of thousands of people are homeless, sleeping upon the sidewalks, and this is scarcely likely to produce a gay holiday mood. Nevertheless, this overcrowded city is part of one's education, and should not be omitted. Furthermore, as perhaps a consolation of sorts, the food in Calcutta is quite good, with a fair assortment of interesting restaurants, including those at the leading hotels, and also in the main part of town.

LENTIL SOUP

PURPOO MULLIGATUNNY

1½ cups dried lentils
7 cups water
2 tablespoons butter
3 tablespoons chopped onions
1 clove garlic, minced
¼ teaspoon dried ground chili
    peppers

2 tablespoons Indian curry
    powder
1 teaspoon lemon or lime juice
1 teaspoon salt

Wash the lentils and discard any imperfect ones. Drain well. Bring the water to a boil in a saucepan and add the lentils. Cook until soft, about 1½ hours. Melt the butter in a separate saucepan. Add the onions, garlic, chili peppers, and curry powder. Mix well and sauté for 3 minutes over low heat, stirring constantly. Add this mixture to the lentils. Add the lemon juice and salt and stir well. Cook 15 minutes. Purée the mixture in an electric blender, or force through a sieve. *Serves 6–8.*

FISH ROLLS, BENGAL STYLE

BENGAL MUCHLEE

8 fillets of fish	½ teaspoon cinnamon
3 teaspoons salt	½ teaspoon powdered ginger
1 teaspoon freshly ground	1 teaspoon ground coriander
black pepper	seeds
1 cup water	2 eggs
1 clove garlic, minced	1 cup dry bread crumbs
2 onions, chopped	Vegetable oil for deep-fat frying
3 tomatoes, chopped	

Combine 2 of the fillets, 1 teaspoon of the salt, ½ teaspoon of the pepper, and the water in a saucepan. Bring to a boil and cook for 10 minutes. Drain and chop the fish very fine. Add the garlic, onions, tomatoes, cinnamon, ginger, coriander, 1 teaspoon of the salt, and the remaining pepper. Mix well. Spread an equal amount of the mixture on each of the 6 remaining fillets. Roll up carefully and fasten with toothpicks or tie with string.

Beat the eggs in a bowl with the remaining salt. Dip the fish rolls in the eggs, then in the bread crumbs. Heat the oil to 360° in a deep saucepan. Drop the fish rolls in carefully. Fry until brown, about 10 minutes. Drain and serve hot. *Serves 6.*

SHRIMP PILAU

MACHCHI PILAU

2 cups long grain rice	6 tablespoons butter
4 cups water	1 cup blanched ground almonds
2 cups finely chopped onions	2 teaspoons ground coriander
2 teaspoons salt	seeds
½ teaspoon freshly ground	¾ cup water
black pepper	½ teaspoon cinnamon
½ cup yogurt	
2 pounds raw shrimp, shelled	
and deveined	

Wash the rice, and rub it between the hands to help remove the starch. Continue washing in cold water until the water runs clear.

Toss together the onions, salt, pepper, yogurt, and shrimp. Melt the butter in a skillet; cook the mixture in it over high heat 2 minutes, shaking the pan frequently. Stir in the almonds, coriander, and ¾ cup water. Cover and cook 2 minutes.

Spread half the rice in a buttered casserole. Arrange the shrimp (reserving the sauce) in the center. Cover with remaining rice and pour sauce over it. Sprinkle with cinnamon, cover, and bake in a 300° oven 15 minutes. *Serves 6.*

As served at the Taj Mahal Hotel in Bombay.

LAMB CURRY

ROGAN JOSH

2 pounds boneless lamb
6 tablespoons butter
2 cups onions
2 cloves garlic, minced
1 teaspoon powdered ginger
1 teaspoon ground cumin
2 teaspoons ground coriander
   seeds
2 teaspoons salt

¼ teaspoon ground dried chili
   peppers
1 teaspoon saffron
1 large tomato, chopped
¾ cup chicken broth
½ teaspoon mace
½ teaspoon nutmeg
½ cup heavy cream

Cut the lamb in ½-inch cubes. Melt the butter in a saucepan; add the onions, garlic, ginger, cumin, coriander, salt, and chili peppers. Cook over medium heat 5 minutes, stirring frequently. Add the meat and half the saffron; cook until meat browns. Add the tomato, broth, mace, and nutmeg. Cover and cook over low heat 1 hour or until meat is tender. Stir in the cream and the remaining saffron. *Serves 8.*

CHICKEN CURRY

MURGHI CURRY

2 cloves garlic, minced
1 tablespoon coriander seeds
1 tablespoon cumin seeds
4 tablespoons sesame seeds
2 teaspoons turmeric
¼ teaspoon dried ground chili
   peppers

½ teaspoon powered ginger
2 teaspoons salt
2 3-pound fryers, disjointed
6 tablespoons butter
2 cups thinly sliced onions
1 cup yogurt
1 cup water

Pound together with mortar and pestle (or run in a blender) the garlic, coriander, cumin, sesame seeds, turmeric, chili peppers, ginger, and salt. Rub into the chicken. Let stand 2 hours.

Melt the butter in a casserole or Dutch oven; brown the onions in it. Add the chicken and any leftover spices and brown. Stir in the yogurt; cover and cook over low heat 45 minutes, adding small amounts of water from time to time. Remove cover for last 10 minutes. *Serves 8.*

SPICY COCONUT RICE

COPRA KANA

1 cup fresh or dried grated coconut	3 tablespoons chopped onion
2 cups milk	1½ tablespoons Indian curry powder
2 cups water	2 cups rice
¼ pound (1 stick) butter	

Combine the coconut, milk, and water in a saucepan. Bring to a boil, remove from the heat, and soak for 15 minutes. Press all the liquid from the coconut and discard the pulp. Melt the butter in a saucepan. Add the onion and curry powder. Sauté over very low heat for 5 minutes, stirring occasionally. Wash the rice in several changes of water. Add the rice to the onion. Cook over medium heat for 3 minutes, stirring constantly. Bring the coconut milk to a boil and add to the rice. Cover and cook over low heat until all the liquid is absorbed. Stir frequently, as the milk is apt to burn. *Serves 4–6.*

LENTIL AND EGG CURRY

DHALL CURRY

1 cup dried lentils	¾ cup water
3 tablespoons butter	1 teaspoon salt
2 onions, sliced	6 hard-cooked eggs, sliced
1 tablespoon curry powder	

Wash the lentils until water runs clear. Drain well. Melt the butter in a saucepan. Add the onions and curry powder and sauté for 10 minutes, stirring frequently. Add the water and lentils. Cover and cook over low heat for 45 minutes, or until the lentils are tender. Add the salt and sliced eggs and mix gently. Correct seasoning. Cook over low heat for 5 minutes. Serve hot. *Serves 4–6.*

STEWED TOMATOES, INDIAN STYLE

THUCAHLEY FOOGATHS

4 tablespoons butter	4 tomatoes, peeled and chopped
1 onion, chopped	1 teaspoon salt
2 cloves garlic, minced	1 tablespoon fresh or dried grated coconut
¼ teaspoon powdered ginger	
¼ teaspoon dried ground chili peppers	

Melt the butter in a skillet. Add the onion, garlic, ginger, and chili peppers. Sauté for 5 minutes, stirring occasionally. Add the tomatoes, salt, and coconut. Cook over low heat for 15 minutes, or until the liquid is absorbed. Serve as a relish.

CUCUMBER BOORTHA

BOORTHA

3 medium cucumbers	⅛ teaspoon dried ground chili
1 cup water	peppers
1 onion	½ teaspoon salt
1 clove garlic	2 tablespoons olive oil
½ green pepper	2 tablespoons lemon juice
½ teaspoon powdered ginger	

Peel the cucumbers, and cut into thick slices. Place in the water and cook for about 10 minutes, or until soft. Drain thoroughly. Chop the onion, garlic, and green pepper as fine as possible. Add the cucumber and continue chopping. Add the ginger, chili peppers, salt, olive oil, and lemon juice. Mix well. Chill for at least 2 hours. Serve as a salad or relish.

FRIED BREAD

POORI

1½ cups whole wheat flour	2 tablespoons shortening
1½ cups all-purpose flour	⅔ cup water
⅛ teaspoon salt	½ pound (2 sticks) butter

Sift together the two flours and salt. With the fingers, blend in the shortening and enough of the water to make a firm dough. Knead for a few minutes, then cover with a damp cloth and let stand 30 minutes. Knead again. Roll out thin and cut into 3-inch circles.

Melt the butter in a saucepan, then strain the butter into a skillet, discarding the white sediment remaining in the strainer. It is now "clarified" butter. Heat the clarified butter and drop the circles into it in a single layer. Immediately turn them over and press each one down with a spatula. Fry until golden brown and puffed. Drain on paper towels and serve hot. *Serves 8.*

SWEET BANANA PUFFS

MEETA KAYLA PUSTHOLES

2 cups sifted flour	3 ripe bananas
Dash of salt	4 tablespoons fresh or dried
¼ pound (1 stick) butter	grated coconut
¼ cup buttermilk or sour milk	Vegetable oil for deep frying

Sift the flour and salt into a bowl. Cut in the butter with a pastry blender or two knives. Add the buttermilk and mix well. Knead together. Roll out the dough ¼ inch thick on a lightly floured surface. Cut with a 5-inch round cooky cutter.

Mash the bananas, add the coconut, and mix well. Place a spoonful of this mixture in the center of each round of dough. Fold over and seal the edges, using a little water. Heat the fat to 360° and drop the pastries into it carefully. Fry until golden brown. Drain well. Serve hot or cold. If desired, the pastries may be baked on a buttered baking sheet in a 400° oven for 20 minutes. *Makes about 24.*

INDONESIA

The Republic of Indonesia consists principally of Java, Bali, Borneo, Sumatra, and various other beautiful small islands, most of which were formerly a part of the Dutch East Indies. Gastronomically speaking, the most interesting of these is undoubtedly Java.

Rice is the principal food and overshadowing any other dish is the world-renowned rice table, or *rijsttafel.* This was originally a Javanese dish, but the Dutch colonists took to it with such gusto that they have adopted it for their own, somewhat modifying its preparation. It is a great experience and one that almost everyone enjoys. Many local residents who have lived for years in the islands eat *rijsttafel* every day of the year, and declare that they look forward to eating it the next day.

Rijsttafel is a little hard to describe, for it consists of many different foods composed upon a bed of boiled rice. Each person is served with a large soup plate filled with rice. In the better hotels of the islands and on formal occasions, a dozen or more waiters line up, each carrying a single dish from which the diner helps himself. In your own home a buffet-style dinner may be served, each person helping himself to the various side dishes. There are usually combinations of fish, shrimp, chicken, or beef, as well as an occasional vegetable dish. Many of these are quite spicy and should be cautiously tested by those unacquainted with *rijsttafel*. Each helping from the side dishes is carefully placed upon the mound of boiled rice and eaten separately. It is not cricket to mix everything together.

To temper the spicy food, it is customary to serve tiny side dishes of palate refreshers, such as sliced cucumbers, grated coconut, chopped peanuts, and the like. The only beverage served with *rijsttafel* is cool beer, but resident Europeans usually begin with a drink or two of Holland dry gin (*jenever*). In this section will be found one of the favorite *rijsttafel* recipes, *nasi goreng*. For those who might wonder why the Javanese should have reason to honor the tragicomic figure of World War II, it might be in order to point out that *nasi* means boiled rice.

Since the local cuisine is built so solidly around the rice table and its accompaniments, it is natural that soups and other unnecessary dishes should be unimportant, although soups are served on occasion. Desserts, which are seldom served, are usually fresh fruit or based on fruit. Of increasing importance in the islands are the Chinese, who have taken over control of much of the commerce and industry; similarly, the Chinese influence on cookery is being felt, for the islanders enjoy Chinese dishes, particularly those containing noodles, a great local favorite.

Of course the many peasants and villagers live very simply on rice, with the possible addition of fish, coconuts, or vegetables and with an occasional treat of chicken or meat. No matter how poor or primitive the people are, the food is usually well prepared, seasoned with the high spicing that the people enjoy, and appetizingly served.

The word "Java" itself has become a part of the English—or is it the American?—language to signify coffee, and Java does produce much fine coffee. This is always served black and drunk with plenty of sugar. Alcoholic beverages are unimportant, for most Javanese are Mohammedans. Tea is also an important local drink.

At breakfast, Indonesians drink their local coffee, usually with some kind of bread, plus perhaps eggs. In the more rural areas, instead of bread, the people might have some boiled green bananas or cassava roots. Because the weather and humidity are tropical, most people do their work early in the day, going straight through the normal lunch hour. They tend to have lunch beginning at about two in the afternoon. This is always a meal built around boiled rice, with anywhere from three to six side dishes enjoyed with the rice. Then comes a siesta of a few hours, and upon awakening, a cup of tea, with some sort of snack, possibly light, possibly a substantial dish. Much later, when the heat of the day has gone and the evening cool encourages the appetite, the evening meal is served, and it's generally similar to lunch. For dessert, it's usual to offer a selection of delicious, cooling tropical fruits of which Indonesia has an almost overwhelming selection.

EAST INDIES COCKTAIL

1 cup brandy	1 teaspoon bitters
1 tablespoon curaçao	6 slices lemon peel
1 tablespoon pineapple juice	
2 teaspoons maraschino, or cherry brandy	

Combine the brandy, curaçao, pineapple juice, maraschino or cherry brandy, and bitters in a cocktail shaker. Add cracked ice and stir well. Pour into chilled cocktail or champagne glasses and place a twist of lemon peel in each.

Note: This recipe is not regionally authentic but was very popular with the foreign colony.

CHICKEN-GINGER SOUP

SOTO AJAM

5-pound chicken	3 tablespoons vegetable oil
2 stalks celery	3 onions, sliced
1 carrot, peeled	1 cup bean sprouts, drained
2½ quarts water	3 hard-cooked eggs, sliced
2½ teaspoons salt	6 slices lemon
1-inch piece fresh or preserved ginger, sliced fine	

Wash the chicken thoroughly. Place in a saucepan with the celery, carrot, and water. Bring to a boil; skim the top. Cook over medium heat for 2½ hours, or until chicken is tender. Add salt after the first hour. Strain the stock, add the ginger, and set aside. Cut the chicken into slivers. Heat the oil in a skillet. Add the onions and sauté for 15 minutes. Add the bean sprouts and cook over low heat for 5 minutes. Place onions, bean sprouts, sliced eggs, and chicken in a bowl. Serve the soup in individual plates, with a slice of lemon on top. It is customary for each person to help himself from the bowl of chicken. *Serves 6–8.*

FRIED NOODLES

BAHMI GORENG

½ pound *mie* (Chinese
  vermicelli), vermicelli, or fine
  egg noodles
2 eggs, beaten
¾ cup sesame or vegetable oil
1 pound raw pork, cut julienne
1½ cups thinly sliced onions
2 cloves garlic, minced
2 teaspoons minced gingerroot
3 cups shredded Chinese or
  green cabbage

1 cup bean sprouts
1 cup diced cooked shrimp
¼ cup chopped scallions (green
  onions)
1 tablespoon soy sauce
2 tablespoons peanut butter
½ teaspoon freshly ground
  black pepper

Cook the noodles in boiling salted water until almost tender. Drain and spread on a flat surface to cool and dry. If possible, chill for 2 hours. Make an omelet of the eggs. Roll up and slice fine.

Heat 2 tablespoons of oil in a skillet; sauté the pork for 10 minutes. Remove and keep warm. Heat 2 tablespoons of oil in the same skillet; sauté the onions, garlic, and ginger for 3 minutes. Remove and keep warm. Heat 2 tablespoons oil in the same skillet; sauté the cabbage and bean sprouts 3 minutes. Add the shrimp and sauté 2 minutes. Return all the sautéed ingredients and add the scallions, soy sauce, peanut butter, and pepper. Cook 2 minutes.

In a separate skillet, heat the remaining oil; turn the noodles into it and fry until browned. Drain. Heap the noodles on a platter and turn out the pork mixture over them. Sprinkle with the sliced omelet. *Serves 4–6.*

As served at the Bali Beach Hotel.

BAKED SPICY FISH

IEKAN BANDANG PANGGANG

1 teaspoon salt
¼ teaspoon freshly ground
  black pepper
2 cloves garlic, minced
4-pound shad or other fat fish,
  split and boned

½ cup melted butter
3 tablespoons lemon juice
¼ cup soy sauce
¼ teaspoon ground dried chili
  peppers

Mix the salt, pepper, and garlic to a smooth paste. Rub into the fish, inside and out. Place the fish in a buttered baking dish. Bake in a 375° oven for 10 minutes. Meanwhile, combine in a bowl the butter, lemon juice, soy sauce, and chili peppers and mix well. At the end of 10 minutes of baking time, pour one third of the sauce over the fish. Baste and turn the fish several times while baking for an additional 25 minutes. Heat the remaining sauce. Place the fish on a platter and pour the sauce over it. Serve with boiled rice. *Serves 4–6.*

BROILED CHICKEN ON SKEWERS

SATE AJAM

4 whole chicken breasts	2 cloves garlic, minced
½ cup ground peanuts	1½ teaspoons salt
½ cup chopped onions	¼ cup lime or lemon juice

Cut the meat of the raw chicken breasts into bite-size pieces. Pound or chop to a paste the peanuts, onions, garlic, and salt. Blend in the lime juice. Toss the chicken with the mixture and let stand 1 hour. Thread the chicken on 8 skewers. Arrange on an oiled broiling pan and broil 10 minutes, or until tender, turning the skewers frequently. Serve with the following sauce:

3 tablespoons vegetable oil	1 teaspoon salt
1½ cups thinly sliced onions	2 tablespoons soy sauce
2 cloves garlic, minced	1 cup water
½ teaspoon dried ground chili peppers	2 tablespoons lime or lemon juice
1 cup peanut butter	

Heat 2 tablespoons oil in a skillet; sauté 1 cup onions until browned and crisp. Remove. Pound or chop to a paste the remaining onions, the garlic, chili peppers, peanut butter, and salt. Heat remaining oil in the skillet; sauté the mixture 3 minutes. Blend in the soy sauce, water, and lime juice. Cook over low heat 5 minutes. Pour into a bowl and sprinkle reserved onions on top. Serve with the chicken. *Serves 8.*

Note: Cubes of pork may be substituted for the chicken.

CHICKEN LIVERS IN COCONUT MILK

SAMBAL HATI HATI

1 cup fresh or unsweetened dried
  grated coconut
1 cup milk
4 tablespoons butter
1 onion, chopped
3 cloves garlic, minced
2 chili peppers, sliced thin, or
  ½ teaspoon dried ground chili
  peppers

1½ pounds raw chicken livers,
  cut in quarters
¼ cup ground almonds
2 tablespoons grated lemon rind
2 tablespoons orange juice
1 tablespoon lemon juice
1 tablespoon plum jam
1 teaspoon sugar
1 teaspoon salt

Combine the coconut and milk in a saucepan. Bring to a boil, remove from heat, and soak for 30 minutes. Press all the liquid from the coconut and discard the pulp.

Melt the butter in a saucepan. Add the onion, garlic, and chili peppers. Sauté for 5 minutes, stirring frequently. Add the chicken livers and sauté for 5 minutes, stirring occasionally. Add the coconut milk, almonds, lemon rind, orange juice, lemon juice, plum jam, sugar, and salt. Cook over low heat for 10 minutes, stirring occasionally. Serve hot with boiled rice. *Serves 4–6.*

Note: Lemon juice and plum jam are used as a substitute for tamarind, usually unavailable.

CARAMEL PUDDING

KUWE SIRKAJA

1½ cups sugar
2 tablespoons butter
4 tablespoons sifted flour
6 egg yolks, beaten

1¼ cups milk
2 tablespoons grated orange rind
1 teaspoon vanilla extract
6 egg whites

Preheat oven to 350°.

Melt ¾ cup of the sugar in a heavy saucepan. Cook over low heat until browned and caramelized. Divide the mixture among 6 individual, buttered ovenproof dishes. Set aside.

Cream the butter. Add the remaining sugar and beat well. Add the flour and beat again. Add the egg yolks and beat until light and fluffy. Add the milk, orange rind, and vanilla, mixing well. Beat the egg whites until stiff but not dry. Fold into the milk mixture gently. Divide among the prepared dishes. Place the dishes carefully in a pan of hot water.

Bake in a 350° oven for 45 minutes, or until the puddings are set. Remove and allow to cool, then chill for at least 6 hours. Serve directly in the dish or run a knife around the edges of each dish and turn out onto a plate. *Serves 6.*

JAPAN

A great many mistaken ideas regarding Japanese food have become a part of the American credo. These are based primarily upon that bit of American mythology which firmly holds that the Japanese eat raw fish, seaweed, and rice exclusively. As to the raw fish, it is a fact that most of us eat raw oysters and clams; and the raw fish dish of Peru, *seviche*, is quite similar in preparation to the *sashimi* of Japan. Soup made from seaweed does not taste substantially different from our own clam broth; and there certainly is nothing very exotic about eating rice.

The Japanese are great perfectionists in the fine art of preparing and serving a meal. While the cuisine is not extensive—is even somewhat limited from the Western point of view—the attractive appearance of Japanese food goes a long way toward equalizing any possible deficit in that regard. Every dish is presented to the best possible advantage and is pleasing to the eye as well as the palate. With this in mind, the food is carefully arranged in colorful, dainty dishes, small portions are artistically arranged, and receptacles are carefully selected to blend and harmonize with the particular food being served.

Japanese food may be divided into the following rough groups: soups, including both *suimono* (clear soup) and *miso-shiru* (soup made with a fermented malt); *nimono* (boiled food), of which an example might be a boiled chicken dish; *yakimono* (broiled food), such as the great favorite *kabayaki* (broiled eels); *agemono* (fried food), the best known being *tempura*, deep-fat-fried shrimps; *mushimono* (steamed food), of which there are many steamed egg dishes; and the most renowned of all, *nabemono* (open frying-pan food), especially the famous *sukiyaki*, which is particularly attractive to watch while it is being made at your table. In addition, there are various other types of dishes, but rice is the common denominator of all Japanese food.

The use of certain flavorings gives Japanese food much of its unique character. Among these are *shoyu* (soy sauce), which more or less eliminates the need for salt; *miso*, a type of fermented paste made from malt;

mirin, a rather sweet variety of rice wine; and *ajinomoto,* already well known in this country as monosodium glutamate, used to bring out the flavoring in various foods.

The favorite beverages of the nation are beer and *sake.* Japanese beers are very much like the European types and are exceptionally good. *Sake,* the so-called rice wine, is actually as much a beer as it is a wine. White or golden yellow in color, it is usually made from white rice but occasionally from other grain, and tastes something like Spanish sherry. The Japanese prefer to drink it hot for reasons known only to themselves. The recent production of Japanese Western-style whisky is worthy of mention, and is in accordance with the well-known Japanese ability to mimic. Of course Japan is the land of tea, in this case green tea, which is the basis for a ritualistic ceremony, partly religious and partly symbolic, called *tscha-no-yu.*

The cuisine is built upon a few basic items such as rice, green tea, seafood, *shoyu* sauce, and the colorful local vegetables. Most visitors to Japan usually find themselves drawn to two dishes, the *tempura* (fried shrimp) and *sukiyaki.*

Just one fascinating bit of nonsense about the impact of the Western world upon the imperturbable Japanese. Into a formal and stately language has come a new Japanese word meaning appetizers. That word is, and we hesitate to use it, *o'dobre.* Oh, Admiral Perry, little did you know what you were doing to Japan when you opened her to trade with the Western world!

SHRIMP TOAST

HA DO SHI

2 tablespoons peanut or salad oil
1 onion, chopped fine
1 pound raw shrimp, peeled,
   cleaned, and chopped fine
1 teaspoon salt
½ teaspoon sugar
½ teaspoon white pepper
½-inch piece fresh ginger,
   chopped fine or 1 teaspoon
   powdered ginger

1 egg white
12 slices dry bread, trimmed
   and cut in triangles
2 eggs, beaten
1 cup dry bread crumbs
Peanut or vegetable oil for
   deep-fat frying

Heat the 2 tablespoons of oil in a skillet; sauté the onion for 10 minutes, stirring frequently. Combine the sautéed onion, shrimp, salt, sugar, pepper, and ginger in a bowl. Beat the egg white until it begins to stiffen and fold it into the shrimp mixture.

Dip the bread triangles into the beaten eggs. Spread the bread with the shrimp mixture and dip these into the beaten eggs again, then into the bread crumbs, coating all sides well. Heat deep oil to 360°. Drop each bread triangle carefully into the fat. Fry until golden brown. Drain and serve hot. *Makes 36.*

JAPANESE EGG ROLL

TAMAGO-YAKI

½ pound halibut or white-meat fish	4 tablespoons water
3 tablespoons sugar	2 tablespoons soy sauce
½ teaspoon salt	3 tablespoons *sake* or dry sherry
6 eggs, beaten	1 tablespoon vegetable oil

Remove the skin and bones from the fish carefully. Grind or chop it very fine. Add the sugar and salt and mix well. Beat the eggs, water, soy sauce, and sherry together. Combine with the fish mixture and mix well. Heat half of the olive oil in an 8-inch-square pan, or use an oblong pan of similar size (not a round one). Pour half of the mixture into it. Fry until lightly browned on both sides, turning it over carefully. Turn out onto a piece of wax paper, aluminum foil, or a napkin, and roll up like a jelly roll. If desired, fasten the ends with toothpicks. Repeat this procedure with the balance of the ingredients. Set aside for 30 minutes. Cut into slices about ½ inch thick. These are very good as hors d'oeuvres. *Serves 4–6.*

FISH BALL SOUP

UWO DANGO NO SHIRU

1 pound fillet of sole	½ teaspoon powdered ginger
½ pound raw shrimp, shelled and deveined	2 teaspoons cornstarch
3 scallions (green onions)	2 tablespoons vegetable oil
1 teaspoon salt	3 cups beef broth
⅛ teaspoon freshly ground black pepper	3 cups bottled clam juice
	½ pound spinach, shredded

Grind together the sole, shrimp, and scallions; blend in the salt, pepper, ginger, cornstarch, and oil. Shape into walnut-size balls.

Bring the broth and clam juice to a boil; carefully drop the fish balls and the spinach into it. Cook over medium heat 10 minutes. *Serves 6.*

FRIED FISH AND VEGETABLES

TEMPURA

18 raw shrimp	2 lobster tails
2 fillets of sole	2 carrots
6 sea scallops	18 string beans

Remove shell from shrimp, leaving the tail. Slit, and discard vein. Pound shrimp open. Cut the sole crosswise in 3-inch pieces. Slice scallops crosswise. Remove the meat of raw lobster tails and slice crosswise. Cut carrot in lengthwise slices. Leave string beans whole. Dry all ingredient carefully.

Tempura Batter:

2½ cups sifted flour	2 cups cold water
3 egg yolks	1 quart vegetable oil

Sift the flour 3 times. Beat together the egg yolks and water. Gradually add the flour, stirring lightly from the bottom with chopsticks or a spoon. Don't overstir—flour should be visible on top.

Heat the oil to 325°—a constant temperature is important for good tempura. Hold shrimp by the tail and dip each one in the batter; drop into the oil and fry until lightly browned. Dip other ingredients into batter, using a spoon, and gently drop into oil. Serve foods as soon as they are cooked, with the tempura sauce and coarse salt.

Tempura Sauce:

¾ cup clam juice	3 teaspoons sugar
¼ cup soy sauce	3 tablespoons grated white
¼ cup *sake* or dry sherry	radish or turnip
½ teaspoon freshly ground	1 teaspoon grated ginger
black pepper	

Mix together the clam juice, soy sauce, *sake*, pepper, and sugar. Divide among 6 small bowls. Just before serving place a little radish and ginger in each bowl. *Serves 6.*

As served in the Keio Plaza Inter-Continental Hotel.

BEEF IN SOY SAUCE

SUKIYAKI

2 pounds fillet of beef or sirloin
  steak
4 tablespoons sesame or
  vegetable oil
½ cup beef broth
¾ cup soy sauce
¼ cup sugar
2 tablespoons *sake* or dry sherry
2 cups thinly sliced onions

1 cup sliced celery
1 cup sliced bamboo shoots
½ pound mushrooms, sliced
  thin
1 cup shredded spinach
½ cup sliced scallions (green
  onions)
1 pound vermicelli, cooked and
  drained

Have the steak cut paper thin and into pieces about 2 by 3 inches. (If you do it yourself, partially freeze the meat to facilitate cutting.)

Heat the oil in a large skillet. Add the meat and brown on all sides. Combine the broth, soy sauce, sugar, and wine in a bowl. Add half of this mixture to the meat. Push the meat to one side of the skillet. Add the onions and celery; cook over low heat for 3 minutes. Add the remaining soy mixture, the bamboo shoots, mushrooms, and spinach. Cook over low heat 3 minutes. Add the scallions and cook for 1 minute. Heap the vermicelli on one side of a platter and the sukiyaki on the other, and serve immediately.

This dish is particularly suited for preparation at the table in a chafing dish. *Serves 4–6.*

CHICKEN AND SHRIMP

YAKI-TORI TO KO-EBI

¼ cup dried mushrooms
12 shrimp, peeled and cleaned
2 cups chicken broth
1 teaspoon salt
4 tablespoons sugar

3 tablespoons soy sauce
2 whole raw chicken breasts
⅓ cup *sake* or dry sherry
6 spears canned white asparagus

Wash the mushrooms thoroughly. Soak them in cold water for 1 hour. Drain. Combine the shrimp, broth, salt, sugar, and soy sauce in a saucepan. Bring to a boil and cook over medium heat for 7 minutes. Remove the shrimp and keep warm. Add the chicken cubes, sherry, and mushrooms to the broth mixture and cook over medium heat for 10 minutes, or until chicken is tender. Do not overcook. Remove the chicken and mushrooms and keep warm. Place the asparagus in the broth and cook for 2 minutes. Arrange the shrimp, chicken, mushrooms, and asparagus in separate mounds on a platter. Pour the sauce over it and serve. The sauce should be moderately thick; if it is not, boil it rapidly, uncovered, for a few minutes in order to thicken it. *Serves 4–6.*

CHICKEN AND EGG CUSTARD

CHAWAN MUSHI

8 dried mushrooms	2 cups chicken broth
2 whole chicken breasts	3 tablespoons soy sauce
3 tablespoons peanut oil	1 tablespoon *sake* or dry sherry
20 chestnuts, cooked and shelled	12 spinach leaves
(optional)	4 eggs, beaten
1 onion, sliced thin	6 thin slices lemon
3 scallions (green onions), sliced	

Wash the mushrooms thoroughly. Soak them in cold water for 1 hour. Drain. Slice thin. Remove all the meat from the uncooked chicken and cut into narrow strips. Heat the oil in a skillet. Add the chicken and cook over low heat for 5 minutes, stirring frequently. Add the chestnuts, onion, scallions, 4 tablespoons of the broth, soy sauce, sherry, and mushrooms. Bring to a boil over low heat for 2 minutes. Do not overcook.

Divide the mixture among 6 individual custard cups or place in a large bowl. Beat the eggs together with the remaining broth. Pour over the chicken mixture. Cover with spinach leaves. Place the cups or bowl in a pan of hot water and cover the pan. Steam for 25 minutes, or until the egg mixture is set. Serve hot with slices of lemon. *Serves 6.*

JAPANESE HONEY CAKE

KASUTERA

5 eggs	½ cup sifted flour
½ cup honey	2 tablespoons confectioners' sugar
¾ cup sugar	

Preheat oven to 350°.

Beat the eggs, honey, and sugar until very thick. Add the flour, beating well. Pour into a greased oblong 9- by 12-inch baking pan and bake in a 350° oven 35 minutes, or until a cake tester inserted comes out clean. Cool in the pan. Serve cut into strips and dusted with confectioners' sugar. *Serves 6.*

TURNIP PICKLE

DAIKON

2 pounds white turnips	1 cup sugar
1 cup water	¼ cup coarse salt
¼ cup rice wine vinegar or white vinegar	

Wash the turnips, peel, and cut in thin slices. Combine and bring to a boil the water, vinegar, sugar, and salt. Cool, then pour over the turnips. Cover and let pickle in the refrigerator 3 days before serving. *Makes about 1½ pints.*

KOREA

A generation ago, the majority of people would have found it difficult to locate Korea with any degree of accuracy. Recent events have focused world attention upon Korea and its name has become a household word. It is unlikely that the world will soon forget Korea, just as it is improbable that the impact of foreign nations on the Korean people will be overlooked.

Until quite recently the Koreans lived their own lives, and ate the rice, barley, wheat, and soy of their fields, and caught the abundant fish of the surrounding waters. The coming of the Japanese many years ago also changed Korean life substantially; not the least of the changes was the introduction of dairy products and many Japanese foodstuffs. Peculiarly enough, Korean food resembles Chinese food as much as it does Japanese, though there are certain distinguishing features which make it differ from either of them.

Korean food has this in common with Chinese: it is usually prepared in cut-up form so that it may be readily handled with chopsticks; flavoring is often reminiscent of Chinese sauces, particularly those containing soy sauce and ginger; and rice is the basic staple. A Japanese custom of letting each diner prepare his own food on small, individual charcoal burners at the table is also a part of the Korean food style, and Koreans like several dishes that are favorites with the Japanese.

The people are extremely fond of *kooks* (soups), which are prepared in many different fashions. They are all so rich and hearty that they would make a meal for many people. The peninsula of Korea juts into waters teeming with fish, and peacetime fisheries are of great importance. Clams and other seafood are greatly appreciated by the inhabitants, and the people living along the coast take full advantage of the large catches of fish.

As previously mentioned, the many meat dishes of Korea are both different and yet similar to their Chinese equivalents. Koreans are particularly fond of mixtures of pork and chicken, or of fish and meat; they also like food in which there are distinctive and sharply different flavors. Few Chinese dishes are spicy, but many Korea preparations are very highly seasoned with pepper and garlic. The recipe for broiled pork (*ton yuk kui*) is a fine Korean dish containing sesame seeds. These seeds are a national favorite. Rice and beans (*pah jook*) is a dish that may appear at almost any Korean meal.

One of the nation's most popular preparations is called *bul-googi* (sometimes also spelled as *bul-koogi*). It consists of meat or chicken marinated in soy sauce, onion, garlic, and ginger, then broiled quickly over an open flame; it may take the form of an outdoor barbecue, or be served indoors cooked over special fire pots. When larger chunks of meat are used, rather than slices, it's called *kalbi-kui,* and it's also delicious, although which is the better is a matter of personal choice. Also in the same general style is *jang-po,* except that here it's prepared with sugar and pine nuts. The Koreans have a dish called *san-juk,* which is much like *shish-kebab,* that is, cubes of meat on skewers broiled over an open fire; however, the local style involves threading on rice cakes (*tuk*) as well as meat, onions, and vegetables. Most meals have at least one noodle dish, sometimes served cold, sometimes hot; in fact, noodles are a standard lunch for a large portion of the population. This is true, even though they very often have rice for breakfast and dinner.

A unique feature of Korean food is *kim chee,* probably the most commonly seen dish. It is a sort of pickle, usually made of Chinese cabbage but often prepared with turnips, cucumbers, celery, or whatever is available at the particular season of the year. Most Koreans consider that they have not eaten a meal unless *kim chee* appears at the table. It is practically a standard food, and its peculiar odor greets(?) the person who approaches a Korean village even before he sees the people.

Cha (strong tea), taken plain, is the drink of the country.

MEAT BALL SOUP

KOOK SOO

4 tablespoons peanut or vegetable oil
1 onion, sliced
3 cloves garlic, minced
6 scallions (green onions), chopped
4 tomatoes, chopped
6 cups beef broth
½ teaspoon freshly ground black pepper
2 tablespoons soy sauce

¼ pound vermicelli, half cooked and drained
1 pound ground beef
1½ teaspoons salt
Dash of cayenne pepper
½ teaspoon ground ginger
3 tablespoons ground sesame seeds
¼ cup flour
1 egg, beaten

Heat 2 tablespoons of the oil in a saucepan. Add the onion, garlic, and scallions. Sauté 10 minutes. Add tomatoes, beef broth, and pepper. Cook over low heat 20 minutes. Mix in the soy sauce and vermicelli. Cook 10 minutes.

Mix together the ground beef, salt, cayenne pepper, ginger, and sesame seeds. Form into ½-inch balls. Dip in the flour and then the egg.

Heat the remaining oil in a skillet. Fry the meat balls until browned on all sides shaking the pan frequently. Add the meat balls to the soup. *Serves 6–8.*

SHRIMP-STUFFED GREEN PEPPERS

KO-CHOOH-JUHN

1 pound raw shrimp, shelled and deveined
4 green peppers
3 tablespoons soy sauce
½ teaspoon salt
¼ teaspoon dried ground chili peppers

3 tablespoons minced onions
2 cloves garlic, minced
½ cup flour
2 eggs, beaten
2 cups vegetable oil

Chop the raw shrimp.

Cut the peppers in half lengthwise, and scoop out the fibers and seeds. Pour boiling water over them, let stand 5 minutes, then drain. Cool.

Mix together the shrimp, soy sauce, salt, chili peppers, onions, and garlic. Stuff the pepper halves firmly, and smooth off level. Dip in the flour and then the eggs. Heat the oil until it bubbles. Fry the peppers in it until browned and tender. Drain and serve hot. *Serves 4–8.*

KOREAN DUMPLINGS

MANDOO

3 cups flour
1 teaspoon salt
1 cup water
1 cup cooked diced pork
½ cup bean sprouts
½ cup diced water chestnuts

¼ cup chopped scallions (green onions)
¼ cup chopped watercress
2 tablespoons soy sauce
½ teaspoon dried ground chili peppers

Sift the flour and salt into a bowl; work in the water, mixing until a stiff dough is formed. Knead for a few minutes; cover with a damp towel and let stand 30 minutes.

Mix together the pork, bean sprouts, water chestnuts, scallions, watercress, soy sauce, and chili peppers. Taste for seasoning. Roll out the dough as thin as possible. Cut into pieces 3 by 2 inches. Place a teaspoon of the mixture on each and fold over the dough. Seal the edges with a little water. Cook in boiling salted water 10 minutes. Drain and serve in soup, or drain and brown lightly in oil. Serve as an hors d'oeuvre, too. *Makes about 36.*

PORK STRIPS WITH SESAME SEEDS

TON YUK KUI

2 1-pound pork tenderloins
¾ cup soy sauce
5 tablespoons sugar
¼ cup beef broth
½ teaspoon freshly ground
black pepper

1 teaspoon grated ginger
2 cloves garlic, minced
½ cup sesame seeds

Trim the pork of all fat. (If tenderloins are not available, loin of pork, boned and cut in long, narrow strips, may be used.)

In a bowl, combine the soy sauce, sugar, broth, pepper, ginger, garlic, and sesame seeds. Marinate the pork in the mixture for 3 hours at room temperature. Turn and baste the meat frequently. Lift meat out and place on a rack in a baking pan. Roast in a 350° oven 45 minutes, turning and basting meat frequently. Cut in thin diagonal slices. To serve as an hors d'oeuvre, pierce each slice with a cocktail pick or toothpick. *Serves 6–8.*

SALTED GREENS

KIM CHEE

6 pounds celery cabbage, green
   cabbage, or cucumbers
3 tablespoons coarse salt
2 cups sliced scallions (green
   onions)
4 cloves garlic, sliced

1 tablespoon gingerroot, minced,
   or 2 teaspoons powdered
¾ teaspoon dried ground chili
   peppers
Water

Shred the cabbage into strips 1 inch wide, or slice the unpeeled cucumbers. Mix with half the salt and let stand 30 minutes. Wash and drain. Mix the scallions, garlic, ginger, chili peppers, cabbage or cucumbers, and remaining salt. Pack into a crock or glass jars. Add enough cold water to cover the vegetables. Cover the container and set aside in a cool place for 5 days. Taste to see if vegetables are pickled sufficiently–if not, let stand 2 more days. Chill and serve. *Makes about 2 quarts.*

HONEY NUT COOKIES IN SYRUP

YAK-KWA

1⅓ cups water
1¼ cups sugar
½ teaspoon ground ginger
¼ cup honey
2½ cups sifted flour

¼ cup sesame or vegetable oil
Vegetable oil for deep frying
½ cup pine nuts or slivered
   almonds

Combine 1 cup of the water and 1 cup of the sugar in a saucepan. Bring to a boil, stirring steadily until the sugar melts, then cook over high heat for 5 minutes. Mix in the ginger and cool.

Combine the remaining sugar and water with the honey. Bring to a boil and cook 1 minute. Cool.

Sift the flour into a bowl; make a well in the center and into it put the honey syrup and the ¼ cup oil. Gradually mix the flour into the well with the hand until a dough is formed. Form tablespoons of the dough into balls, then press each into a ¼-inch-thick circle.

Heat the fat to 375°. Fry a few circles at a time until light brown, turning them frequently. Drain and place in the sugar-ginger syrup; let soak 2 minutes, then remove and sprinkle one side with the nuts. *Makes about 36.*

PAKISTAN

Pakistan, no longer a divided country, is chiefly influenced by the cuisines of its neighbors, India and Iran. If anything, there are more dishes resembling those of India than otherwise. For example, the Pakistanis eat almost all of the types of curries found in India, which they eat with chutneys and similar relishes. They also eat the typical—and delicious—breads of India, including *puri* and *paratha*. However, Pakistan, with a climate somewhat resembling that of California, tends to produce a greater variety of fruits and vegetables.

The people eat all sorts of meat except pork, which is forbidden to them by their religion. Also, they are not often given to vegetarianism as are many Indians. Lamb and chicken dishes are appreciated here, and they appear frequently in the diet. An example of the influence of the Near and Middle East on West Pakistan is *murgh-i-musallam* (spicy baked chicken), which is the type of dish often found in neighboring Iran. *Huzoor pasand pulao,* made from lamb, fruit, and rice, also fits this description. Incidentally, the *pulao* dishes of this area have become a standard part of the cuisine of the world; in our country, *pulao* has become pilau, the herbs and seasoning have been changed, but the basic idea of the dish is the same.

Spicy food is the rule in Pakistan: chili peppers, dry mustard, ginger, and other spices form a part of almost every dish. Coconuts, raisins, nuts, and fruits of all sorts, and especially the delicious melons, help to round out the cuisine. However, these are all superstructure and trimmings resting upon the firm base of rice and wheat, the primary foods of the multitudes.

Fruits are the subject of great local pride. They are delightful for breakfast, for dessert, or at any time of the day. Many drinks, both alcoholic and non-alcoholic, are made from these fruits but most Pakistanis would rather drink tea. The national preference is for iced, sweet soft drinks; beers and wines are unimportant. Western-style liquors are available, but the majority of the people never touch alcohol and much prefer a glass of cold milk in the best tradition of the health-food stores of our own country.

The local desserts are quite interesting. For example, there is our old friend, rice pudding, here called *firni,* which tastes like ours but has pistachio nuts added, and is lightly dusted with silver foil (it's edible). Even bread pudding, *shahi tukra*, is served, but again with nuts, and flavored with rose water essence. Best of all, possibly, is the carrot *halwa*, a sweet carrot pudding which is miles better than it sounds.

One pleasant point to remember about visiting Karachi is that there is practically no rainfall; the weather is almost always pleasant, but November to March are the very best months for a visit. Carved articles made of ivory are outstanding values here.

MEAT PASTRIES

SAMOSAS

2 cups flour	1½ cups chopped onions
1½ teaspoons salt	2 green chilies, minced, or
½ cup melted butter	¼ teaspoon Tabasco
½ cup yogurt	¼ teaspoon minced fresh or
1 tablespoon vegetable oil	preserved gingerroot
½ pound ground beef	Vegetable oil for deep frying

Sift the flour and half the salt into a bowl; stir in the melted butter and yogurt until a dough is formed. Cover and let stand while preparing the filling.

Heat the 1 tablespoon oil in a skillet. Add the meat, onions, chilies, ginger, and remaining salt. Cover and cook over low heat 15 minutes, stirring frequently. Cool.

Roll out the dough on a lightly floured surface very thin. Cut into 3-inch squares. Put a little filling on one side, and fold over into triangles, sealing the edges with a little water or egg white.

Heat the oil to 370°. Fry a few pastries at a time until golden brown. Drain and serve hot. *Makes about 24.*

SHRIMP CURRY

CHINGRA KORMA

2 pounds raw shrimp, shelled and deveined	2 teaspoons powdered cumin
1 cup minced onions	1 teaspoon ground ginger
1 teaspoon salt	6 tablespoons butter
¼ teaspoon crushed dried red peppers	2 cups fresh tomato sauce
1 teaspoon ground coriander seeds	¼ teaspoon crushed cardamom seeds
	10 black peppercorns, crushed

Wash and dry the shrimp; toss with the onions, salt, red peppers, coriander, cumin, and ginger. Let stand 10 minutes.

Melt the butter in a casserole or deep skillet. Add the shrimp mixture and cook over low heat 15 minutes, stirring occasionally. Add the tomato sauce; cook and stir until sauce turns brown. Stir in the cardamom and peppercorns. *Serves 6–8.*

As served in the Inter-Continental Hotels.

LAMB AND FRUIT

HUZOOR PASAND PULAO

3 cups raw rice
¼ pound (1 stick) butter
3 pounds boneless lamb, cut
  into 1-inch cubes
3 onions, sliced thin
4 cups yogurt
2 cloves garlic, minced
1 teaspoon ground coriander
  seeds
1-inch piece fresh ginger,
  chopped, or 2 teaspoons
  powdered ginger
½ teaspoon freshly ground
  black pepper
2 cloves
3 cardamom seeds, crushed
1 tablespoon salt
½ teaspoon saffron
2 tablespoons boiling water
½ cup sliced, mixed nuts
  (almonds, pistachios, etc.)
2 oranges, peeled, segmented,
  and pitted
½ cup seedless grapes

Wash the rice thoroughly in several changes of water. Soak in cold water for 15 minutes. Drain well. Melt the butter in a saucepan. Add the lamb and onions; brown well on all sides. Add the yogurt, garlic, coriander, ginger, pepper, cloves, cardamom, and salt and stir well. Place the rice over it. Dissolve the saffron in the boiling water and mix into the saucepan. Arrange the sliced nuts, oranges, and grapes on top. Cover and cook over medium heat for 10 minutes. Reduce heat to low and cook for 25 minutes, or until the lamb and rice are tender. *Serves 6–8.*

CURRIED LENTILS

MASUR DHAL

1 pound lentils (red, if available)
6 cups water
2 tablespoons minced fresh or
  preserved gingerroot
¾ teaspoon turmeric
2 teaspoons ground cumin seed
1 teaspoon ground coriander
  seeds
1 bay leaf
1 cup chopped onions
2 teaspoons salt
4 tablespoons butter
2 tablespoons chopped coriander
  leaves or Chinese parsley

Pick over and wash the lentils until the water runs clear, then soak in water to cover for 1 hour. Drain. Combine the lentils in a saucepan with the 6 cups water, the ginger, turmeric, cumin, coriander, bay leaf, and half the onions. Bring to a boil, cover, and cook over low heat 45 minutes or until the lentils are tender, adding the salt after 30 minutes' cooking time. Drain if any water remains and discard the bay leaf.

Melt the butter in a skillet; sauté the remaining onions until golden brown. Stir in the drained lentils; cook and stir for 2 minutes. Serve sprinkled with the coriander leaves and accompanied by rice. *Serves 6–8.*

BROILED SPICED CHICKEN

MURGHI-I-MUSALLAM

2 2½-pound broilers, quartered	1½ teaspoons cinnamon
2 cups yogurt	1 teaspoon ground coriander
2 cloves garlic, minced	seeds
2 teaspoons salt	1 teaspoon dried mint
1 teaspoon freshly ground	½ teaspoon ground ginger
black pepper	3 tablespoons lemon juice
2 teaspoons ground cumin seed	2 drops red food coloring
½ teaspoon ground cardamom	(optional)
seeds	

Wash and dry the chickens, then marinate in a mixture of all the remaining ingredients for 3 hours at room temperature. Be sure the chicken quarters are well covered with the yogurt mixture, spreading it on if necessary.

Arrange the chicken on an oiled broiling pan, and broil on the lowest rack for 30 minutes on each side, basting frequently. *Serves 6–8.*

POTATOES AND RICE, PAKISTANI STYLE

ALU-KI-TARI

2 cups raw rice	2 cloves garlic, minced
¼ pound (1 stick) butter	½-inch piece fresh ginger,
2 onions, sliced thin	chopped, or 1 teaspoon
4 potatoes, peeled and quartered	powdered ginger
2 teaspoons salt	Dash of cayenne pepper
1 teaspoon turmeric	4 cups boiling water
1 teaspoon ground coriander	
seeds	

Wash the rice thoroughly in several changes of water. Soak in cold water for 30 minutes. Drain well. Melt the butter in a saucepan. Add the onions and sauté for 15 minutes, stirring frequently. Add the rice, potatoes, salt, turmeric, coriander, garlic, ginger, cayenne, and boiling water. Bring to a boil. Cover and cook over low heat for 30 minutes, or until the potatoes are tender. *Serves 8–10.*

NUT CANDY

HALVA

½ pound (2 sticks) butter
2 cups farina or semolina
2 cups confectioners' sugar
½ cup ground almonds

½ cup ground pistachio nuts
½ teaspoon ground cardamom
  seeds
4 tablespoons light cream

Melt the butter in a saucepan. Add the farina or semolina, stirring constantly with a wooden spoon until lightly browned. Remove from the heat. Add the sugar, almonds, pistachio nuts, and cardamom and mix well. Add the cream and cook over low heat, stirring constantly, until the mixture forms a ball and leaves the sides of the saucepan.

Butter an oblong baking dish. Pour the mixture into it and spread evenly. Cut into desired shapes and allow to cool. When cool, cut out the shapes completely. This dessert will keep very well in the refrigerator for more than a week. *Serves 8–10.*

SINGAPORE AND MALAYSIA

Singapore, a most exciting and diverting place for a visit, is a modern city, busy and lively, but with extremely hot and humid weather. It is completely independent, and no longer a British Crown Colony; the population is a mixture of British, Indians, Chinese, and Malayans, plus a smattering of other nationalities. In general, there are three principal styles of cooking offered in Singapore—Chinese, Malayan, and Western "international-style" food, found chiefly in hotels catering to tourists. In recent years, the number of new and elaborate hotels, elaborate skyscrapers in many cases, has been staggering. In any event, tourists should not lack a choice of luxurious, air-conditioned accommodations.

But there can be no denying that, lying close to the equator, Singapore is about as hot and damp as any major metropolis, although definitely worth a stop for any tourist. The shopping here is remarkably interesting and bargain-priced. But equally worthwhile, perhaps even more than equally, is the opportunity to sample the two foreign cuisines. The recipes in this section are from Malaya; the Chinese dishes served in Singapore may be found in both the China and the Hong Kong sections of this book. Malayans dearly love spicy foods; however, the quantity of red peppers normally used has been toned down to match Western palates.

Since Singapore is in the tropics and practically at sea level, the climate may not be disregarded with impunity. Business must be transacted early in the day, before the lunch hour and before the heat becomes unbearable. Most people stay indoors during the middle of the day, particularly during the hot months from June to September—except mad dogs and certain foreign residents. Activity commences once again at teatime, which in turn leads to a rather late dinner hour. There is a considerable amount of drinking, particularly of scotch whisky, by the foreign residents rather than by the local population. The Singapore gin sling originated here, of course.

Turning to Malaysia, a country lying immediately to the north of Singapore, we find a novel culinary style, based chiefly upon rice dishes, a wide selection of spices and herbs, and possibly the greatest selection of fresh fruits in the world. By all means, when there and particularly when in Kuala Lumpur (the capital city), a visit to a food market is a recommended tourist attraction. Of course, the usual display of familiar fruits are available, although the apples are imported. Even the familiar banana is here, although in a wide range of color, from almost pure white to darkest brown-black. The bananas may be purchased in a type that is the size of one's finger, up to giant specimens weighing quite a few pounds. Wandering through the market the visitor (if accompanied by one who knows the nation's fruits) sees *blimbing, carambola,* Chinese pears, *sapodilla,* jack-fruit, custard apple, *duku,* soursop, *jambu,* Chinese persimmons, rose apples, hog plums, fresh *lychees,* passion fruit, *pomelos, rambutans, rokams,* and a variety of tomato that grows on trees and is quite naturally called the tree-tomato.

The Malayans are small people as a rule, and their capacity for food is somewhat limited, but they are extremely fond of dishes seasoned with their own selections of spices and herbs. The basis of most Malay dishes is rice, which is a mainstay at almost every meal. Sometimes it is served plain but usually it is the foundation for a meat or fish dish. Two favorite spicing agents are ginger (both fresh baby shoots and the dried variety) and red chili peppers. These are used for flavor and color. Other frequently used spices include turmeric (which lends a yellow color), cloves, coriander (for its spicy aroma), garlic (no comment), tamarind, and fenugreek.

Malays do not drink alcoholic beverages as a general rule, although some of the younger people are breaking away from the old customs. Plain water is considered a very satisfactory drink, and Malayans seldom drink anything else before or during a meal.

Unquestionably the best desserts are the many fresh fruits of this region, some of which are familiar to us. The more unusual ones include many rare types of bananas, the mangosteens, and an evil-smelling but delicious fruit known as *durian*. This fruit has a prickly exterior, is quite large (the general size of a basketball), and is quite expensive. There are those who dearly love the *durian,* and thousands of people from Southeast Asia head for this country during the season when the fruit is at its best. When cut open, it emits an odor which is nothing short of nauseating, redolent of a combination of rotten eggs, garlic, and garbage. Many first-class hotels refuse to serve it in their dining rooms, for the odor fills the dining area, forcing the foreign guests to flee. In truth, the odor is sickening for those who are not used to it. During the *durian* season, the airlines carefully examine the hand baggage of every passenger, searching for concealed *durians,* because in the closed quarters of a plane in flight the odor spreads quickly because of the air-conditioning system. If the *durian* is cut open and eaten during the flight, many foreign tourists have to sit with cologne-dampened handkerchiefs over their faces. On the other hand, there must be a reason for all the excitement about *durians;* there can be little doubt but that it has a marvelous and exotic flavor, unique in the world of fruits (assuming one can bear the odor). Eating a *durian* has been described as spooning honey into one's mouth while riding on a garbage truck.

SINGAPORE GIN SLING

2 tablespoons powdered sugar	6 maraschino cherries
6 jiggers gin	6 finger-length slices fresh
1 jigger cherry brandy	pineapple
Juice of 2 lemons	

Mix the powdered sugar, gin, cherry brandy, and lemon juice together in a cocktail shaker. Half fill 6 tall highball glasses with cracked ice. Place a cherry and a slice of pineapple in each glass. Add the liquor and fill each glass with carbonated water. Serve ice cold. Add a fresh strawberry or paper-thin slices of lemon or orange, if available. *Serves 6.*

CHICKEN LIVER AND PEA SOUP

CHENG TAU, HU CHI

1 pound pork and several pork bones (see Note)	1 teaspoon powdered ginger
2 teaspoons salt	1 16-ounce can green peas, drained
2 quarts water	1 tablespoon soy sauce
½ pound chicken livers	½ teaspoon freshly ground black pepper
½ cup chopped mushrooms	

Combine the pork, bones, salt, and water in a saucepan. Bring to a boil and cook over medium heat for 2 hours. Strain the stock and reserve it. Chop the livers coarsely. Place them in a saucepan with the mushrooms, stock, ginger, and green peas. Cook over low heat for 10 minutes. Add the soy sauce and pepper. Bring to a boil and remove from heat. Serve very hot. The pork may be used for another dish, or may be served separately. *Serves 6–8.*

Note: If desired, 4 cans of beef or chicken broth may be used instead of making a pork stock.

FISH AND STRING BEANS

IKAN MASAK ASAM

1 teaspoon turmeric	4 tablespoons butter
1-inch piece of fresh ginger, chopped, or 1 teaspoon powdered ginger	½ pound fresh or ½ package frozen string beans
½ teaspoon dried ground chili peppers	2 cups water
	3 tablespoons lemon juice
6 cooked shrimp, peeled and chopped fine	2 tablespoons plum jam
	4 fillets of mackerel
5 onions, chopped	2 teaspoons salt

Combine the turmeric, ginger, chili peppers, shrimp, and onions. Chop or pound the ingredients to a smooth paste. Melt the butter in a large saucepan. Add the previous mixture and sauté for 5 minutes, stirring frequently. Add the beans and sauté for 3 minutes. Add the water. Mix the lemon juice and plum jam together, and add, stirring well. Cook over medium heat for 5 minutes. Add the mackerel and salt and cook over low heat for 20 minutes. Correct seasoning. Serve hot, over boiled rice. *Serves 6–8.*

Note: Lemon juice and plum jam are used as a substitute for tamarind, which is not readily available.

SPICY STEAK BITS

DONDENG

½ teaspoon dried ground chili
   peppers
Coarsely chopped almonds
3 tablespoons grated lemon rind
1-inch piece fresh ginger, ground,
   or 1 teaspoon powdered ginger
3 onions, chopped
4 cloves garlic, minced
3 pounds steak (about ½ inch
   thick), cut into strips 1×2
   inches

¼ pound (1 stick) butter
2 cups boiling water
1 teaspoon sugar
2 teaspoons salt
4 tablespoons lemon juice
3 tablespoons plum jam

Combine the chili peppers, almonds, lemon rind, ginger, onions, and garlic and mix well. Roll the steak pieces lightly in the mixture. Melt the butter in a saucepan. Add the meat and cook over high heat for 5 minutes, stirring constantly.

Combine the water, sugar, salt, lemon juice, and plum jam and add to the meat, mixing well. Cook over low heat for 15 minutes, or until the meat is tender. Stir occasionally. Correct seasoning. Serve with boiled rice and pour the sauce over the rice and meat. *Serves 6–8.*

FISH, STRAITS CHINESE FASHION

OTAK OTAK

1½ cups fresh or dried grated
   coconut
1 cup milk
2 tablespoons butter
2 pounds fish fillets
¼ cup ground almonds
3 tablespoons grated lemon
   rind
1-inch piece fresh ginger, grated,
   or 1½ teaspoons powdered
   ginger

1 teaspoon turmeric
½ teaspoon basil
1 teaspoon salt
3 onions, chopped fine
2 cloves garlic
2 eggs, beaten

Combine 1 cup of the coconut and the milk in a saucepan. Bring to a boil, remove from the heat, and soak for 30 minutes. Press all the liquid from the coconut and discard the pulp. Melt the butter in a skillet; add the remaining coconut and sauté until lightly browned, stirring constantly. Grind the fish in a food chopper or chop it. Add the almonds, lemon rind, ginger, turmeric, basil, salt, onions, garlic, and eggs; mix well. Add the sautéed coconut and the coconut milk. Mix well.

Cut squares (about 6–8 inches) of aluminum foil or parchment paper and butter them lightly. Place 2 tablespoons of the mixture on each square and fold the edges of the paper over carefully to keep the liquid from leaking out. Place on a buttered baking sheet. Bake in a 375° oven for 35 minutes. Serve the fish in its wrapping and have each person open his at the table. *Serves 8–10.*

Note: A smaller version may be used as a hot hors d'oeuvre.

SINGAPORE LOBSTER CURRY

3 cups milk	2 teaspoons salt
2 cups fresh or dried grated coconut	2 tablespoons curry powder
	2 tomatoes, chopped
¼ pound (1 stick) butter	2 tablespoons flour
5 onions, chopped	1 cucumber, peeled and cubed
2 cloves garlic, minced	Meat from 2 boiled lobsters or
⅛ teaspoon cumin seed, crushed	1 pound lobster meat, cubed
2 teaspoons powdered ginger	2 tablespoons lemon juice
Dash of cayenne pepper	1 tablespoon plum jam

Combine the milk and coconut in a saucepan. Bring to a boil, remove from the heat, and soak for 30 minutes. Press all the milk from the coconut and discard the pulp.

Melt the butter in a saucepan and add the onions and garlic. Sauté for 10 minutes, stirring frequently. Add the cumin seed, ginger, cayenne pepper, salt, curry powder, and tomatoes. Cover and cook over low heat for 10 minutes, stirring frequently. Add the flour, stirring constantly. Add the coconut milk slowly, stirring steadily until the boiling point is reached. Add the cucumber and lobster meat and cook over low heat for 15 minutes. Mix the lemon juice and jam together and add to the lobster mixture. Correct seasoning. Mix well. Serve hot, with boiled rice. *Serves 4–6.*

Note: Singapore is famous for the fieriness of its curries. Additional cayenne pepper may be added if desired.

COCONUT-GINGER CHICKEN

RENDAN SANTAN

2 cups fresh or unsweetened dried
  grated coconut
1½ cups light cream
2 tablespoons butter
1 tablespoon ground coriander
1 teaspoon ground anise
½ teaspoon saffron
1-inch piece fresh ginger, ground,
  or 1 teaspoon powdered ginger
2 cloves garlic, minced

2 tablespoons grated lemon rind
1 fresh chili pepper, sliced fine,
  or ½ teaspoon dried ground
  chili peppers
3 tablespoons lemon juice
1 tablespoon plum jam
1 teaspoon sugar
1 teaspoon salt
3 onions, sliced
3 whole chicken breasts

Combine 1½ cups of the coconut and the cream in a saucepan. Bring
to a boil, remove from the heat, and soak for 30 minutes. Press all the
liquid from the coconut and discard the pulp. Melt the butter in a
saucepan. Add the remaining coconut and fry until brown. Combine the
coriander, anise, saffron, ginger, garlic, lemon rind, chili peppers, lemon
juice, plum jam, sugar, and salt. Mix well. Add the sliced onions and
browned coconut.

Remove the chicken meat from the bones and cut into small pieces.
Place the chicken, the spice mixture, and the coconut cream in a saucepan. Place over high heat and cook, stirring constantly, until the mixture
boils actively. Reduce the heat and cook for 10 minutes, or until chicken
is tender. Serve hot with boiled noodles or rice. Pour the sauce over the
chicken and noodles. *Serves 4–6.*

COCONUT CUSTARD

SARIKAUJA

1½ cups fresh or dried grated
  coconut
1½ cups milk

4 eggs
1½ cups sugar

Combine the coconut and milk in a saucepan. Bring to a boil, remove
from the heat, and soak for 20 minutes. Press all the milk from the
coconut. Strain, and discard the pulp. Beat the eggs well. Add the sugar
and beat until light and fluffy. Add the coconut milk and beat well.
Preheat oven to 350°. Pour into six individual buttered custard cups.

Place them in a pan of water and cover each cup. Bake for 20 minutes in a 350° oven, or until the custard is set. Sprinkle a little grated coconut on top of each portion. *Serves 6.*

SRI LANKA (CEYLON)

The large island once known as Ceylon has changed its name to Sri Lanka, although the two names are both in use at the present time. Located almost directly south of India, this is an island consisting of about twenty-five thousand square miles, with food customs rather similar to those of her giant neighbor to the north. The island is still agricultural, devoted in large measure to the growth of tea, making the countryside beautiful beyond measure.

Until recently, hotel accommodations and facilities for tourists were extremely limited. But now there are fine hotels, air-conditioned and luxurious, at least in the colorful capital city of Colombo. In the outlying regions, there's a governmental network of rest houses, which are really cottages set aside for travelers, with pleasant rooms, gracious service, and surprisingly good food, all available at bargain prices.

Much of the food in Sri Lanka (or Ceylon, if you prefer) follows that of India, as mentioned above, but there are certain local specialties and some differences. Rice is the mainstay of the diet, and most foods are served with a curried flavor. Some of the curries, such as those made with chicken, are completely to American taste. Others, including those prepared with dried fish and garlic, are simply too much for the uninitiated. Curries are also made with just about every conceivable ingredient, including *katurumurunga* flowers, and every possible vegetable, as well as from eggs, and so forth.

One of the novel preparations here is called *āppas*, although they're better known as hoppers, which can be roughly described as a baked coconut-flavored pancake. An egg hopper is the same pancake containing an egg, baked on a special pan.

Sweet dishes are particularly well liked in this most interesting country. For example, you could choose from *seenakku, pasong, pittu, konda kavum, wandu āppa;* surely you get the idea. Of course your choice might well be some of the fresh fruit or melons, or, even better, the ice creams made from them, which have rare and unusual tropical flavors.

The local beer is excellent, and just about the perfect drink with the local food, which can be very very spicy. Wines are quite unimportant, and the imported vintages have a tendency to spoil quickly in the heat and humidity of Sri Lanka. Perhaps that's why the people much prefer to drink *arrak*, sometimes made from coconut flowers. It's a strong, strong liquor.

SPICED CHICKEN SOUP

MULLIGATAWNY

4-pound chicken, disjointed
2 quarts water
6 peppercorns
1 tablespoon salt
6 mustard seeds
1 teaspoon turmeric
½ teaspoon ground cumin

2 teaspoons ground coriander
2 teaspoons lemon juice
2 tablespoons butter
1 cup thinly sliced onions
¼ teaspoon dried ground red
    peppers

Wash the chicken and combine in a saucepan with the water, peppercorns, and salt. Bring to a boil, cover loosely, and cook over low heat 1½ hours or until tender. Skim the fat.

Pound to a paste the mustard seed, turmeric, cumin, coriander, and lemon juice. Melt the butter in a skillet; sauté the onions and red peppers over very low heat for 10 minutes without browning. Stir the spice paste into the onions and cook 5 minutes. Add to the soup and cook 10 minutes. Taste for seasoning. The chicken may be removed from the bones and served in the soup or served on the bone separately. *Serves 6.*

RICE WITH FISH

BURIANI

2 cups yogurt
1 cup finely chopped onions
⅛ teaspoon ground cloves
2 teaspoons tumeric
2 teaspoons salt
2 teaspoons ground coriander
¼ teaspoon saffron

4 slices fish (salmon, sea bass,
    etc.)
½ cup melted butter
3 cups half-cooked and drained
    rice
2 tomatoes, thinly sliced
2 pimentos, cut julienne

Combine the yogurt, onions, cloves, turmeric, salt, coriander, and saffron; marinate the fish in the mixture 1 hour.

Heat 2 tablespoons butter in a casserole; lightly brown the drained fish (reserve the marinade). Add half the marinade and 2 tablespoons butter. Cover with the rice. Arrange tomatoes and pimentos over it and add the remaining marinade and melted butter. Cover tightly and bake in a 350° oven 30 minutes. Shake the casserole occasionally. *Serves 4–6.*

As served in the Colombo Inter-Continental Hotel.

POTATO CURRY

BADUN

1 cup fresh or dried grated coconut
1 cup milk
2 tablespoons vegetable oil
1½ cup sliced onions
1½ pounds potatoes, cooked, peeled, and sliced

¼ teaspoon dried ground chili peppers
2 teaspoons curry powder
½ teaspoon minced gingerroot
3 cloves garlic, minced
1 teaspoon salt

If dried coconut is used, rinse it under cold running water. Combine the coconut and milk in a saucepan; bring to a boil, remove from the heat, and let stand 30 minutes. Press all the liquid from the coconut and discard the pulp.

Heat the oil in a saucepan, sauté the onions 10 minutes. Add the coconut milk and all the remaining ingredients. Cover and cook over low heat 10 minutes. Serve with meat or fish dishes. *Serves 6–8.*

CURRY WITH DUMPLINGS

KURUMA IRAICHCHI

2½ cups chopped onions
3 cloves garlic, minced
1 teaspoon ground cumin
2 teaspoons ground coriander
1½ teaspoons turmeric
½ teaspoon powdered ginger
½ teaspoon dried ground chili peppers
2½ teaspoons salt

2 pounds lamb, cut in 1-inch cubes
4 tablespoons butter
2 cups water
2 egg yolks
2 tablespoons melted butter
½ cup cracker meal
2 egg whites, stiffly beaten

Pound or chop to a paste the onions, garlic, cumin, coriander, turmeric, ginger, chili peppers, and 2 teaspoons salt. Toss with the meat. Melt the 4 tablespoons butter in a casserole or Dutch oven; cook the meat in it, stirring frequently until browned. Add the water; cover and cook over low heat 45 minutes.

Beat the egg yolks, melted butter, and remaining salt; stir in the cracker meal. Fold in the egg whites. Chill 10 minutes and shape into walnut-size balls. Arrange around the top of the meat; cover and cook over low heat 25 minutes. *Serves 6–8.*

EGGPLANT RELISH

BRINJAL SAMBOL

1 medium eggplant	1½ teaspoons salt
½ cup finely chopped onions	¼ teaspoon dried ground chili
¼ cup finely chopped green	peppers
peppers	3 tablespoons heavy cream
1 tablespoon oil	2 tablespoons lemon juice
¼ cup flaked coconut	

Bake the eggplant in a 350° oven 1 hour. Cool and peel. Sauté the onions and green peppers in the oil for 5 minutes.

Rinse the coconut under cold water. Chop together the eggplant, sautéed vegetables, coconut, salt, and chili peppers. Blend in the cream and lemon juice and chop until very fine. Taste for seasoning and chill. Serve as a relish. *Makes about 3 cups.*

SEMOLINA DESSERT

PAYASAM

2 tablespoons seedless raisins	2 cups boiling water
4 tablespoons butter	2 cups hot light cream
½ cup cashew nuts	½ cup sugar
½ cup semolina or farina	⅛ teaspoon ground cardamom

Soak the raisins in water to cover for 20 minutes. Drain and dry.

Melt 2 tablespoons of the butter in a skillet. Lightly brown the nuts in it. Remove the nuts. Stir the raisins into the butter remaining in the skillet and sauté 1 minute, stirring almost constantly.

Melt the remaining butter in a saucepan; stir in the semolina until golden. Add the boiling water, stirring constantly to the boiling point. Cook over low heat 5 minutes, stirring frequently. Add the cream and sugar. Bring to a boil, stirring constantly, then cook 5 minutes longer. Mix in the nuts, raisins, and cardamom. Serve warm or very cold. *Serves 6–8.*

THAILAND (SIAM)

Thailand, once known as Siam, is surely one of the most rewarding of all countries for the tourist. It has just about everything—including hot weather—that visitors look for. Although much of Bangkok's architecture is nondescript and routine, there are temples, shrines, and ancient buildings in the old style. The Thais themselves are generally a very pleasant, smiling nation of people, and although most of them now wear Western clothes, in the countryside it's common to see men and women wearing the national costume.

Bangkok, the throbbing, teeming capital city, is on the general order of Venice, for it is crisscrossed by a network of canals and waterways. But whereas Venice has fourteenth-century buildings facing onto the canals, here one finds tropical foliage and the moist air of the jungle. People of the rivers live their entire lives on their boats, and a trip through the canals will not be soon forgotten. There is even a floating market, though this is seen at its best rather early in the morning.

Thailand's food is influenced by its neighbors, China and India, and both styles of cooking are practiced in addition to the local cuisine. Seafood is a basic part of Thailand's diet. Particularly good are the prawns, which are used to make *hae kün* (shrimp rolls). There is also a rather large fish, the *plakapon*, that has a fine flavor. *Namplā* is an enormously popular smelly seasoning, in the form of a sauce made from salted shrimp or fish.

Indian influence may be noted in the popularity of curries, often thought by local connoisseurs to be among the best in the world, although this claim is frequently made in Southeast Asia. The curries (*kaeng phed*) are quite hot and should be approached with caution and considerable respect. *Kaeng chüd* (soup) is served at the same time as the other dishes making up the meal. Rice is the staple food of the nation, eaten by rich and poor alike, for the locally grown rice is of the highest quality.

Vegetables of all sorts are great favorites, and are often served with *nam prik* sauce, which is made of varying ingredients but usually includes garlic, pounded dried shrimp, and chili peppers. It is a startling(!) taste(!!) sensation(!!!) to most tourists. Salads (*yams*) are popular and are made from almost any growing thing: green plants, vine leaves, shrubs, and even the tender shoots of young fruit trees. Fruits grow in superabundance and are often magnificent in both taste and eye appeal; there are not only familiar species but, as might be expected in this exotic country, many uncommon types as well. A novel end to a meal is the so-called liquid dessert, a sweet syrup made from coconut milk, tapioca, bananas, rice, flowers, and many other ingredients. *Saton* (the wood apple) is often used for this purpose. The more usual desserts are sweet confections based on rice or cassava flour, palm sugar, mung beans, taro, or tapioca, in addition to fresh fruits.

Thai food is well seasoned; often the rice is cooked without salt to accentuate and absorb the highly flavored curries and other spicy foods. Soup appears at the same time as the main dishes, plus several side dishes. The Thais are fond of midafternoon snacking, called *krüang wang*, and indeed love to nibble on small foods throughout the day.

Tea is truly the beverage of the country. Almost everyone drinks it frequently throughout the day. Often it is made with the addition of orange, lemon, or jasmine flavoring. A host would be derelict in his duty if he did not offer a guest some tea as soon as he arrived. *Arak*, made from the sap of palm trees or fermented rice, and *mekong*, a local rice whisky, are both popular strong drinks.

CHICKEN-MUSHROOM SOUP

KAENG CHÜD

4-pound chicken, including	8 coriander seeds
giblets	2 tablespoons chopped Chinese
3½ quarts water	parsley
2 teaspoons salt	1 teaspoon anchovy paste
4 peppercorns	½ pound mushrooms, sliced
2 cloves garlic	

Wash the chicken and giblets and put in a saucepan with the water. Bring to a boil and add the salt. Cover loosely and cook over low heat 1½ hours. Drain the chicken and giblets. Remove the skin of the chicken and cut the meat and giblets into small pieces. Place the pieces between two plates, weighting them down.

Return the skin and bones to the stock, and cook over low heat 1½ hours. Strain. Skim the fat and reserve.

Pound together the peppercorns, garlic, coriander, and parsley until fine. Heat 2 tablespoons of the reserved fat in a skillet. Add the pounded ingredients and fry 3 minutes, stirring frequently. Blend in the anchovy paste, then add the chicken pieces and giblets. Cook 2 minutes, stirring. Add to the stock and bring to a boil. Add the mushrooms, cover, and cook 5 minutes. Serve very hot in Chinese soup cups or bouillon cups. *Serves 8–10.*

STEAMED FISH CURRY

MOR-MOK

3 pounds fish fillets	6 coriander seeds
2 tablespoons anchovy paste	1 teaspoon grated lemon rind
2 teaspoons minced garlic	3 tablespoons chopped shallots
1½ cups unsweetened shredded	or onions
packaged coconut	1 egg, beaten
3 cups milk	10 large cabbage leaves
1 tablespoon salt	½ cup thinly sliced green onions
¾ teaspoon dried ground chili	4 tablespoons minced Chinese
peppers	parsley
8 peppercorns	

Wash the fish and cut into paper-thin julienne strips. Add the anchovy paste and garlic. Mix well and refrigerate while preparing the coconut milk.

Rinse the coconut under cold running water, then combine in a saucepan with the milk. Bring to a boil, remove from the heat, and let stand 30 minutes. Run the coconut and milk in an electric blender, or strain. Add the milk to the fish, mixing well.

Pound together the salt, chili peppers, peppercorns, coriander seeds, lemon rind, and shallots until a paste is formed. Add to the fish and mix well. Mix in the egg with a wooden spoon.

Cut ten pieces of aluminum foil or parchment paper about 8 inches long. On each, place a cabbage leaf. Divide the fish mixture among them, pouring any excess liquid on top. Sprinkle the tops with the green onions and parsley. Fold over the leaves, then make envelope-type packages with the foil. (In Thailand, banana leaves are used in place of the foil.)

Put a rack in a deep pan, and add hot water to reach the rack. Arrange the packages on the rack. Cover the pan and cook over medium heat 45 minutes, adding boiling water from time to time to maintain the water level. Unwrap the packages and serve the fish in the cabbage leaves. *Serves 10.*

As served in the Siam Inter-Continental Hotel.

SHRIMP SALAD

YAM KOONG

1 cup milk
1 cup fresh or dried grated
  coconut
2 pounds raw shrimp, peeled
  and cleaned
2 cups water
2 teaspoons salt
1 bay leaf

1 tablespoon olive oil
2 cloves garlic, minced
2 shallots, minced, or ½ onion,
  grated
2 green peppers, chopped
2 tablespoons soy sauce
1 apple, peeled and grated
3 tablespoons chopped peanuts

Combine the milk and coconut in a saucepan. Bring to a boil, remove
from the heat, and soak for 30 minutes. Press all the milk from the
coconut and discard the pulp. Combine the shrimp, water, salt, and bay
leaf in a saucepan. Boil for 8 minutes. Drain, and split the shrimp
lengthwise. Chill for 1 hour.

Heat the olive oil in a saucepan. Add the garlic and shallots and sauté
for 2 minutes, stirring frequently. Remove from the heat. Add the green
peppers, soy sauce, grated apple, and peanuts and mix well. Combine
this mixture with the coconut milk and chill for at least 1 hour. Arrange
the shrimp on a platter, pour the sauce over them, and serve cold.
Serves 8–10.

COCONUT CHICKEN

KAI P'ANAENG

2 cups heavy cream
1½ cups fresh or unsweetened
  dried grated coconut
4 whole chicken breasts
3 cloves garlic, minced
2 shallots, minced, or ½ onion,
  grated
½ teaspoon dried ground chili
  peppers

3 tablespoons ground peanuts
1 tablespoon grated lemon rind
6 coriander seeds
1 teaspoon sugar
1 tablespoon mushroom essence
  or soy sauce

Combine the cream and coconut in a saucepan. Bring to a boil, remove
from the heat, and soak for 30 minutes. Press all the liquid from the
coconut and discard the pulp. Combine the coconut cream and the
chicken breasts in a saucepan. Cover and cook over medium heat for 30
minutes. Add the garlic, shallots, chili peppers, peanuts, lemon rind,
coriander seeds, sugar, and mushroom essence. Stir until well mixed.

Cook for 15 minutes or until chicken is tender. Turn the chicken frequently to coat with the sauce. Correct seasoning. If soy sauce is used, probably no salt will be required; if mushroom essence is used, it may be necessary to add about 2 teaspoons of salt. Serve with boiled rice. *Serves 6–8.*

SWEET AND PUNGENT SQUAB

NAM CHIM PRIA WAN

6 squabs of rock Cornish hens, quartered
3 teaspoons salt
¾ teaspoon freshly ground black pepper
¼ cup peanut or vegetable oil
4 cloves garlic, minced
3 tablespoons cornstarch
2 tablespoons sugar

½ cup water
¾ cup cider vinegar
4 tablespoons soy sauce
8 crushed coriander seeds
1½ cups thinly sliced onions
2 cups diced tomatoes
1½ cups diced green peppers
2 cucumbers, peeled and diced

Season the squabs with the salt and pepper. Heat the oil in a deep skillet; sauté the squabs and garlic until squabs brown. Cover and cook over low heat 20 minutes.

Mix together the cornstarch, sugar, water, vinegar, soy sauce, and coriander. Add to the squabs, stirring steadily until thickened. Add the onions, tomatoes, green peppers, and cucumbers. Cover and cook 7 minutes. *Serves 3–6.*

SIAMESE CRULLERS

KHANŎM SAI KAI

½ teaspoon saffron
1 tablespoon boiling water
2 cups sugar
1½ cups water

1¼ cups sifted flour
1 teaspoon baking powder
⅛ teaspoon salt
Vegetable oil for deep-fat frying

Soak the saffron in boiling water for 5 minutes. Combine the sugar and 1 cup of the water in a saucepan and cook until thick and syrupy.

Sift the flour, baking powder, and salt into a bowl. Add ½ cup of water and the saffron mixture, mixing until very smooth. Heat the fat to 370° in a heavy saucepan. Pour the batter through a narrow funnel into the fat in 2-inch lengths. After a little practice it will be possible always to pour the correct amount. Make only a few of the crullers at a time. Drain them, then place in the sugar and water mixture. Turn them a few times and remove to a platter to cool. *Serves 6–8.*

The
Pacific   *Australia*
Fiji Islands
Hawaii and the Polynesian Islands
New Zealand
The Philippines

AUSTRALIA

The land "down under" has many surprises for visitors. They are always astounded at the vast distances—often hundreds of miles—between communities, most of which are located along the east coast. It should be remembered that Australia is the only country in the world that occupies an entire continent. Australian back country today is very much like the western United States of two hundred years ago, with one important exception. The airplane is that exception; it has cut the traveling time between habitations from weary days to short hours.

The Australians are hearty eaters; they like large, substantial meals. The meal-hour pattern follows our own, except that dinner may be served a little earlier than we are accustomed to. Most of Australia's cuisine has come by way of England and has been adopted by the people. A typical example is toad-in-the-hole, originally an English item and now an everyday dish in Australia. Meat, of course, is greatly favored, as might be anticipated in this land of hundreds of thousands of grazing acres. Lamb is the first choice, but beef is almost equally popular. Since Australia is surrounded by the sea, fish dishes are almost always of high quality and well prepared. Fruits are very good, and there are many fruit desserts. No meal is complete without tea, for here, too, the tea habit is as strong as in England.

Australians are fairly heavy drinkers, particularly of the locally produced beer. This is a meritorious product and has a higher alcoholic content than our usual brews. Beer drinking has been described as the national pastime, and beer parties are common. Liquor laws are puzzling to the stranger, and many places serve liquor only at particular hours. Australian wines are growing in importance, and deservedly so, for they are of top quality. Although various wines have their adherents, the best include the locally made champagne, and also the fine dry red wines.

Sydney has most of the country's better restaurants, although Melbourne has its fair share. The capital is Canberra, a rather small city of about 15,000, but most of the life of the country is elsewhere. The visitor to Australia will find much to interest him, including the tremendous area of slowly building up their own traditions. Melbourne can also offer many exciting little restaurants for the visitor. Canberra, the capital city of Australia is much smaller than either Sydney or Melbourne, and does not offer such a wide choice for dining out. But Australians are naturally friendly and an invitation home to eat is sincerely meant.

It is difficult for the visitor to realize that more than one third of the continent is unexploited land. Large areas in Western Australia, South Australia, and the Northern Territory are reservations or desert. But in spite of this, the Australian "bush" has never been richer or more productive than it is today. Food is plentiful and Australians enjoy the best of all fresh foods.

They like their meat to be grilled or roasted and their desserts simple. The joy of many housewives, however, is to bake scones, cakes and biscuits for their families and friends.

Australia welcomes immigrants, and as a result, literally hundreds of new restaurants have opened throughout the continent, featuring food of most of the countries of Europe. Nowadays, for example, visitors can dine upon Greek, German, Austrian, French, Yugoslavian, and other nationality dishes. However, in the section which follows, emphasis has been placed upon local dishes. Of course, it isn't possible to prepare dishes that are based upon uniquely Australian foods, such as the excellent shellfish, seafood, and also kangaroo tails (although available canned).

OYSTER SOUP

18 shucked oysters
4 tablespoons butter
4 tablespoons finely chopped
  onions
3 tablespoons flour

4 cups bottled clam juice
2 cups water
⅛ teaspoon cayenne pepper
1 teaspoon grated lemon rind

Coarsely chop the oysters. Keep refrigerated until ready to add.

Melt the butter in a saucepan; sauté the onions 5 minutes. Blend in flour, then gradually add the clam juice and water, stirring steadily to the boiling point. Cook over low heat 10 minutes. Add the cayenne, lemon rind, and oysters. Cook 3 minutes. *Serves 6.*

As served at the Southern Cross Hotel in Melbourne.

CARPET BAG STEAK

2 3-inch-thick shell (Delmonico) or rump steaks
2 tablespoons olive oil
Cayenne pepper
¼ cup fresh bread crumbs

12 oysters, coarsely chopped
¼ cup chopped mushrooms
½ teaspoon salt
¼ teaspoon freshly ground black pepper

Slit the steak horizontally, through the center, to make a pocket for the stuffing. Rub the surfaces with the olive oil and sprinkle lightly with cayenne pepper. Mix together all the remaining ingredients and divide the mixture between the pockets in the steaks. Fasten the edges with skewers or toothpicks. Broil to desired degree of rareness. Cut crosswise, to serve. *Serves 4–6.*

STUFFED LAMB

COLONIAL GOOSE

6-pound leg of lamb, boned
3 tablespoons flour
3 teaspoons salt
1 teaspoon freshly ground black pepper
2 cups fresh bread crumbs
¾ cup grated onions

1 egg, beaten
3 tablespoons melted butter
1 teaspoon crumbled thyme
2 teaspoons minced parsley
1 tablespoon grated lemon rind
2 tablespoons olive oil

Ask the butcher to remove the bone so that a cavity will be formed for the stuffing. Rub the lamb with the flour, 2½ teaspoons of the salt, and ¾ teaspoon of the pepper.

Mix together the bread crumbs, onions, egg, melted butter, thyme, parsley, lemon rind, and remaining salt and pepper. Stuff the cavity and sew the opening or fasten with skewers. Heat the oil in a shallow roasting pan. Put the lamb in it and roast in a 325° oven 2½ hours, basting frequently. *Serves 8–10.*

DAMPEN BREAD

2½ cups flour
¼ teaspoon salt
½ teaspoon baking soda
½ teaspoon cream of tartar

2 eggs, beaten
⅓ cup melted butter, cooled
¾ cup buttermilk

Preheat oven to 350°.

Sift together the flour, salt, baking soda, and cream of tartar. Stir

in the eggs, butter, and buttermilk. Put into an 8-inch greased loaf pan.
Bake 45 minutes or until browned, and a cake tester inserted comes out
clean. *Makes one 8-inch loaf.*

*Note: This old Australian bread was customarily baked over an open
fire in the bush, but it's equally good made in the oven. Serve it in the
traditional way with molasses, or with jam.*

CHEESE-CURRY BISCUITS

¾ cup flour	1 egg yolk
½ teaspoon baking powder	2 tablespoons milk
2 teaspoons curry powder	⅛ teaspoon dry English mustard
4 tablespoons butter	¼ teaspoon salt
⅔ cup grated cheddar cheese	Dash of cayenne pepper

Mix the flour, baking powder, and curry powder together. Cut in the
butter with a pastry blender or two knives. Add the cheese and continue
mixing. Combine the egg yolk, milk, mustard, salt, and cayenne pepper.
Add to the mixture, stirring with a fork until a dough is formed. Preheat
oven to 400°. Roll out ⅛ inch thick on a lightly floured surface. Cut in
any desired shape. Place on a buttered baking pan. Bake in a 400°
oven for 7 minutes. *Serves 6–8.*

NUT SPONGECAKE

WIENCO TOOTE

4 egg yolks	4 egg whites
¾ cup sugar	½ teaspoon cream of tartar
2 teaspoons vanilla extract	⅛ teaspoon salt
¾ cup sifted cake flour	¼ cup melted butter, cooled
¾ cup finely ground almonds	Confectioners' sugar

Grease a 9-inch layer cake pan and dust lightly with flour.

Beat the egg yolks, then gradually add all but 2 tablespoons of the
sugar, beating with an electric mixer or wire whisk until thick and light.
Beat in the vanilla. Gently fold in the flour and nuts.

Beat the egg whites, cream of tartar and salt until soft peaks form,
then beat in the reserved sugar until stiff but not dry. Fold half the egg
whites into the flour mixture, then fold in all the egg whites lightly.
Fold in the melted butter. Turn into the pan. Bake in a preheated 350°
oven on the middle rack 30 minutes or until browned and slightly
shrunk away from the sides of the pan. Cool in the pan 5 minutes;

run a spatula round the edge and turn out onto a cake rack. Turn right side up and let stand until cold. Sift confectioners' sugar over the top. *Serves 6–8.*

Now prepare the following icing:

4 tablespoons butter	2 ounces unsweetened chocolate
2 cups sugar	1 teaspoon vanilla extract
½ cup milk	

Melt the butter in a saucepan. Add the sugar and milk. Bring to a boil, stirring constantly, and cook over low heat for 10 minutes. Melt the chocolate over hot water and add gradually to the previous mixture, stirring well. Remove from the heat and beat with a rotary beater until the mixture thickens. Add the vanilla. Ice the top and sides of the cake as evenly as possible. If the icing hardens, it may be softened by placing it over hot water.

FIJI ISLANDS

Although there are almost three hundred islands in this British Crown Colony, the only one that most tourists see is Viti Levu. Suva, the capital, is on the eastern portion of the island and one of the standard tourist sights is the local police force, colorful and unique.

Here is the land of bushy-haired natives, the bluest ocean in the world pounding on the whitest beach, luxuriant tropical growth, and, of course, the calm, reserved British officials who govern the islands. Here, too, are the East Indians who now outnumber the native Fiji population ·and are gradually taking over the business life of the colony.

Fruits and vegetables grow to enormous size here; there are many both familiar and unfamiliar, such as the granadilla, mandarin, soursop, breadfruit, taro, and, of course, the Fiji asparagus, the *duruka*.

The food of the native Fijians is somewhat primitive and unappealing; of course this does not apply to tourist hotels which serve international-style dishes. Nonetheless, the islands have several fine native dishes that are much appreciated by visitors. Naturally, many of the more interesting fruits and vegetables are unobtainable in our part of the world, but several recipes representative of the local food style have been selected. For example, the yam fish balls, shrimp in coconut, and the spinach in coconut milk may all be made in our own country. Meals usually conclude with fresh fruit, particularly the fine pineapple grown on the islands.

Tea is a favorite with everyone, and this, too, is locally grown. The natives also drink a homemade firewater, *yaqona,* or *kava,* as it is more popularly called. It is prepared from the pounded or grated *yaqona* root and mixed with water. The Fijians serve it at all important festivals and ceremonials, and it is drunk in extreme quantities on these occasions. Although this beverage is supposed to have curative properties, this fact has yet to be proven. To date, the only recorded cures have been of the local thirsts. Most visitors do not find it to their liking, preferring their own customary drinks, which offer no cures whatsoever.

BANANA CUP

½ cup ketchup	3 teaspoons Worcestershire sauce
3 tablespoons lemon juice	6 small bananas, diced
2 tablespoons finely chopped celery	

Combine the ketchup, lemon juice, celery, and Worcestershire sauce. Mix well. Peel and dice the bananas. Pour the sauce over them and chill for at least 30 minutes. Serve as an appetizer. *Serves 6–8.*

YAM FISH BALLS

2 pounds fish fillets	1 pound yams or sweet potatoes
1 cup water	½ cup hot milk
1 onion, sliced	1 egg, beaten
2 teaspoons salt	½ cup flour
1 teaspoon freshly ground black pepper	Vegetable oil for deep-fat frying

Wash the fish and place it in a saucepan with the water, onion, salt, and pepper. Cook for 20 minutes, or until fish is flaky. Cool for 30 minutes.

Peel the yams and cut into quarters. Place in a saucepan with water to cover. Cook until soft, about 30 minutes. Drain well and mash until smooth. Add the hot milk and beat until very light and fluffy. Finely flake the fish and add it to the yam mixture. Add the beaten egg and stir. Correct seasoning. Roll the mixture into 2-inch balls. Dip each ball into flour. Heat deep oil to 375° and fry the balls until lightly browned on all sides. Drain on paper towels and serve hot. *Serves 8–10.*

MOCK TURTLE SOUP

BAIGAN SOUP

2 large eggplants
1 quart milk
3 cups beef broth
2 tablespoons flour
2 tablespoons water
1 tablespoon anchovy paste

2 tablespoons butter
½ teaspoon salt
¼ teaspoon freshly ground
   black pepper
3 tablespoons chopped parsley

Peel the eggplants and cut into 1-inch cubes. Combine in a saucepan with the milk and broth and bring to a boil. Cook over low heat for 45 minutes, or until the eggplant is very soft. Mix the flour and water to a smooth paste and add it to the eggplant mixture, stirring constantly. Cook for 5 minutes, stirring frequently. Purée the mixture in an electric blender or force through as sieve. Add the anchovy paste, butter, salt, and pepper. Correct seasoning. Heat again but do not allow to boil. Serve sprinkled with the chopped parsley. *Serves 8–10.*

SHRIMP IN COCONUT SAUCE

¾ cup milk
2 cups fresh or unsweetened dried
   grated coconut
2 pounds raw shrimp, shelled
   and deveined

2 onions, chopped fine
¼ teaspoon dried ground chili
   peppers
1 teaspoon salt
½ cup heavy cream

Combine the milk and coconut in a saucepan. Bring to a boil, remove from the heat, and soak for 30 minutes. Press all the liquid from the coconut and discard the pulp. Place the shrimp in a saucepan. Add the coconut milk, onions, chili peppers, salt, and cream. Cook over low heat for 20 minutes. Correct seasoning. Serve hot. *Serves 6–8.*

Note: If a fresh coconut has been used, the shrimp mixture may be served in the scooped-out shell.

FIJI BAKED FISH

2 cups fresh or unsweetened dried
   grated coconut
1½ cups heavy cream
3-pound sea bass, pompano, or
   snapper or 6 slices of any
   white-meat fish

2 teaspoons salt
½ teaspoon white pepper

Combine the coconut and cream in a saucepan. Bring to a boil, remove from the heat, and soak for 30 minutes. Press all the liquid from the coconut and discard the pulp. Wash, clean, and dry the fish. Sprinkle thoroughly with the salt and pepper. Arrange the fish in a buttered baking dish. Pour the coconut cream over the fish. Bake in a 350° oven for 50 minutes. *Serves 6.*

SPINACH IN COCONUT MILK

1 cup fresh or unsweetened dried
   grated coconut
1 cup milk
2 pounds or 2 packages frozen
   spinach

1 teaspoon lemon juice
1 teaspoon salt
½ teaspoon freshly ground
   black pepper
1 onion, sliced thin

Combine the coconut and milk in a saucepan. Bring to a boil, remove from the heat, and soak for 30 minutes. Press all the liquid from the coconut and discard the pulp. Wash the spinach thoroughly and drain well. Combine the spinach, lemon juice, salt, pepper, onion, and coconut milk in a saucepan. Cover and cook over low heat for 20 minutes. Serve hot. *Serves 4–6.*

HAWAII AND THE POLYNESIAN ISLANDS

Among the last remaining escapist outposts are the several Hawaiian Islands. Since they are so easily reached by Pan American planes from Seattle, San Francisco, and Los Angeles, the increasing popularity of Hawaii may be readily understood. Unfortunately many tourists find Honolulu something less than they expected; instead of tropical, languorous native villages, they find an island metropolis, humming, buzzing, vibrant, and about as exotic as South Norwalk, Connecticut. To those who are taken aback, a word of advice is offered, for all is not lost. The Hawaiian Islands are more than Waikiki Beach, hot dogs, and commercialized hula dancers. There are the other islands, easily reached by plane, such places as Maui, Kauai, and the most primitive of all, Molokai Island. On these islands flowers seem to have worked out a special arrangement with nature, for seldom does one see such magnificent giant ferns, torch ginger, the great favorite, silversword, which apparently grows only in Hawaiian volcano craters, and of course the famous local orchids.

The staple food of the islanders is *poi*, a pasty substance made from taro root that has a fascinatingly repulsive taste. It has somewhat unfairly been said that *poi* tastes like sour mucilage; but this is a gross canard. Actually it tastes much more like white library paste. *Poi* is so bad, many people say, that they have to keep on tasting it over and over again to see if it is really as bad as they first thought. It is. Peculiarly enough, many people grow to like it eventually. Etiquette requires that it be eaten with the fingers only, apparently on the theory that if you suffer enough you might learn to appreciate it. There is two-finger or three-finger *poi*, indicating the consistency of this delicacy and the number of fingers required for its manipulation. Other staple island foods include yams, coconuts, the local fish (some very good, others insipid), breadfruit, and, inevitably, pineapples. Usually fresh pineapple is eaten by the islanders, to the surprise of visitors nurtured on the canned fruit. Surely pineapple is Hawaii's contribution to the world of good eating; the word "Hawaiian," appearing on any menu, means "served with pineapple" anywhere in the world from Tallahassee to Tanganyika.

To appreciate the flavor of island food, it is necessary to eat at a *luau*, a festive dinner usually combined with some entertainment. *Lomi*, the favorite salmon dish, makes a good appetizer. *Laulau*, which combines meat and fish in the same dish, may sound exotic, but it is no more unusual than the classic Italian combination of veal and tuna fish. The shellfish specialties, particularly the local crabs, are worthwhile. Of course to most islanders a barbecued roast suckling pig is the high point in the art of good living. Desserts are usually quite simple. The melons are delicious; and the pomegranates, lichees, and other local fruits are not to be overlooked. Macadamia nuts are very popular and have an excellent flavor.

Tourists usually find that the hotels and restaurants serve unusual and elaborate drinks, such as those served in scooped-out pineapples or coconuts, foot-high rum drinks, or bowls of mixed liquors with gardenias floating in them. These concoctions are very pretty and usually harmless except to the final figures on the dinner check and to the state of mind of susceptible misses from the mainland. The islanders look with tolerance upon these foibles of their eccentric but welcome visitors, although they prefer their own homemade *okolehao*, a firewater of authority.

In addition to Hawaii, in the Polynesian group there are the Marshall, Gilbert, Caroline, Tonga, and Samoan islands, which are inhabited by people of similar ethnic origins. The inhabitants of these many and varying islands are dependent for their food chiefly upon natural resources. There is a great similarity in the diets of the people. Seafood is most important, for it is customarily available in large supply. Much of the warm-water fish has little flavor, but the shellfish is almost always excellent. Chickens are appreciated; beef and lamb are of little importance. For some reason, islanders all over the globe love pork, particularly piglets, preferably roasted over an open fire or wrapped in green leaves and placed over hot stones.

The staple foods are taro, breadfruit, yams, and bananas, which can usually be counted on even when the fishing fails, as it does on occasion.

Meals are habitually two in number: breakfast, consisting of fresh fruit, and a more substantial meal in the late afternoon or early evening.

Polynesian drinks vary according to the locality. Some make liquor from sugar cane, whereas others distill palm-tree nuts or fibers, or prepare alcoholic coconut beverages. The fabled drink of the islands is *kava*, made by chewing kava fibers (thus mixing it with the saliva) and spitting it into a bowl containing water. This is all told to you in the interests of your greater knowledge; it is an example of pure science at work. The concoction ferments quickly, and, although non-alcoholic, becomes extremely intoxicating in several hours. *Kava*, anyone?

HAWAIIAN SALMON

KAMANO LOMI

1 pound smoked salmon	½ teaspoon salt
12 scallions (green onions)	4 tomatoes, peeled and chopped
¼ cup ice water	

Soak the salmon in cold water for 1 hour. Drain well. Remove any skin and small bones. Shred the salmon finely. Chop the scallions as fine as possible, until they are almost a paste. Add the ice water and salt. Combine the salmon and tomatoes. Crush with a fork or a pestle and mortar until very smooth. Add the scallions and mix well. Chill. Serve in a deep bowl as an hors d'oeuvre. *Makes about 3 cups.*

HAWAIIAN LOBSTER AND COCONUT

2 cups milk	3 1¼-pound boiled lobsters or
2 cups light cream	1½ pounds lobster meat
3 cups fresh or unsweetened dried grated coconut	

Combine the milk, cream, and coconut in a saucepan. Bring to a boil, remove from the heat, and soak for 30 minutes. Press all the liquid from the coconut and discard the pulp. Cut the lobster meat into 1-inch pieces and combine with the coconut milk. Heat but do not allow to boil. Serve hot or cold in bowls. *Serves 6.*

SALMON AND PORK, HAWAIIAN STYLE

LAULAU

½ pound smoked salmon, sliced thin
2 pounds fat pork, cut into slices 1 inch thick

36 large spinach leaves

Soak the salmon in ice water for 3 hours. Cut the slices into 1-inch strips. Remove any bones. Cut the pork into 2-inch squares. Wash the spinach leaves thoroughly in running water until all traces of sand are gone. Separate the leaves, using only the largest, and remove the stems.

Prepare sheets of aluminum foil, about 6 inches square. Place several overlapping spinach leaves on the aluminum foil, so that it is completely covered. Place a piece of pork in the center of the spinach leaves, and a piece of salmon in the center of the pork. Fold over carefully, so that the pork and salmon are covered by the aluminum foil. Tie the foil with thread, so that it cannot come apart. Drop into boiling water. Cover and cook for 3½ hours, being careful not to let the water evaporate. Serve with hot sweet potatoes. *Serves 6.*

Note: This is an outdoor Hawaiian dish, made with taro leaves, which are not available here. The spinach leaves are used as a substitute for these.

MARINATED STEAKS ON SKEWERS

TARIYAKI

1 cup soy sauce
⅓ cup *sake* or dry sherry
1-inch piece fresh or 1 teaspoon powdered ginger
4 tablespoons dark brown sugar
3 tablespoons grated onion
1 clove garlic, minced

18 pieces sirloin steak, ½ inch thick
12 cubes canned pineapple
12 mushroom caps
1 tablespoon cornstarch
2 tablespoons water

Combine the soy sauce, *sake* or sherry, ginger, brown sugar, onion, and garlic in a bowl. Mix well. Cut the steak into 1-inch squares and marinate in the sauce for 2 hours. Drain the steak, strain the marinade and reserve.

Alternate the steak, pineapple, and mushrooms on 6 skewers, starting and ending with the steak. Mix the cornstarch and water to a smooth paste in a saucepan. Add the marinade gradually. Cook over low heat, stirring constantly until smooth and thick. Broil the skewers 5 minutes, turning to brown all sides. The *tariyaki* may be served hot or cold. Serve the sauce hot in any event. *Serves 6.*

CHICKEN AND COCONUT

MOA LUAU
A ME WAI NIU

1 cup fresh or unsweetened dried
  grated coconut
1 cup milk
2 tablespoons vegetable oil
3 whole chicken breasts, boned
  and cubed

2 teaspoons salt
½ cup water
1½ pounds fresh or 1 package
  frozen spinach
3 tablespoons butter

Combine the coconut and milk in a saucepan. Bring to a boil, remove from the heat, and soak for 30 minutes. Press all the liquid from the coconut and discard the pulp. Heat the oil in a saucepan. Add the chicken and brown well on all sides. Add 1½ teaspoons of the salt and the water. Cover and cook over low heat for 20 minutes, or until the chicken is tender.

Wash the spinach carefully in many changes of water, if fresh spinach is used. Remove any stems or tough fibers. Melt the butter in a saucepan and add the spinach and the remaining salt. Cover and cook over very low heat for 20 minutes. Drain well. Drain the chicken. Combine with the spinach and coconut milk. Bring to a boil over low heat, stirring occasionally, and serve. *Serves 4–6.*

SWEET POTATO PUDDING

KOELE PALAO

2½ cups fresh or dried grated
  coconut
2 cups light cream

4 (2 pounds) sweet potatoes
4 tablespoons sugar
2 tablespoons butter

Combine 2 cups of the coconut and the cream in a saucepan. Bring to a boil, remove from the heat, and soak for 30 minutes. Press all the liquid from the coconut and discard the pulp. Boil the sweet potatoes until they are soft. Peel and mash them. Add the coconut cream and the sugar. Beat until light and fluffy. Pour the mixture into a buttered, shallow baking dish. Bake in a preheated 400° oven for 25 minutes. Melt the butter in a frying pan. Add the remaining coconut and sauté, stirring constantly until the coconut is lightly browned. Sprinkle the sautéed coconut on top of the pudding. Serve hot or cold. *Serves 6–8.*

COCONUT PUDDING

HAUPIA

3 cups fresh or dried grated coconut	⅓ cup cornstarch
3 cups milk	⅓ cup sugar

Combine the coconut and milk in a saucepan. Bring to a boil, remove from the heat, and soak for 30 minutes. Press all the liquid from the coconut and discard the pulp. Combine the cornstarch and sugar in a saucepan. Gradually add the coconut milk, mixing until smooth. Cook over low heat, stirring constantly, until thick. Pour into an 8-inch buttered pan and cool. Place in the refrigerator until firm. Cut into squares and serve. *Serves 6–8.*

NEW ZEALAND

These islands, members of the British Commonwealth, are made of the stuff fishermen dream about, for the big ones usually get caught here. That rule holds equally true for the deep-sea varieties and the fresh-water trout and salmon. New Zealanders are very fond of sports, and outdoor life heads their list of pleasures.

Since this is the case, game and seafood dishes are in the foreground of the national cuisine. There is a variety of green clam, the *toheroa,* which is undoubtedly the giant of all edible clams. It forms the basis of many fine dishes which unfortunately cannot be duplicated since the *toheroa* is not available and there is no adequate substitute. Although it is canned, few export shipments are made. Also unusual are the *pipis,* a shellfish, and the *pauas,* a type of abalone. There are also oysters, crayfish, whitebait, and many others, familiar and unfamiliar. An island recipe for lemon fish is included in this section.

As in Australia, mutton dishes are popular. However, beef and pork are also appreciated. Since New Zealand is practically one enormous game preserve, pheasants, wild duck, and red deer are used in many fine regional specialties. Barbecued wild pig is a local dish, but since wild pig is seldom available to us, the recipe for it has been modified; the resulting dish will be excellent nonetheless.

Kumeras, a type of sweet potato, is a satisfying item when roasted; *kumi kumi* is something like pumpkin; and a fine salad is made from *rauriki,* a green leaf of the milkweed family.

With their English heritage, New Zealanders naturally prefer beer and ale, and drink it in fairly large quantities. Wines are appreciated, but beer is undoubtedly the national beverage. The martini is a popular cocktail, but in general straight drinks are preferred.

One meal on which emphasis is placed is tea. Morning tea is usually just a simple cup of tea, but afternoon tea is an event, usually accompanied by cakes, particularly scones, for which a recipe is supplied. When guests are invited for tea, it often turns out to be a substantial meal.

New Zealand is the land of the kiwi, the famous bird that cannot fly, which has become the national emblem. Another national bird, almost as interesting, is the mutton bird, which lives on cliffs alongside the sea and dines exclusively on fish. Since it is such a seafood addict, the mutton bird tastes like fish and is extremely oily. Before being prepared, the bird must be boiled in three or more changes of water to remove a fraction of its fishiness, but some fishy taste always remains. The Maoris, the native population of New Zealand, are particularly fond of this bird, and usually omit the three water changes because they like the oily flavor.

LEMON FISH

3 pounds flounder, halibut, or
   other white-meat fish, cut into
   6 thick slices
2 teaspoons salt
3 tablespoons butter
2 onions, sliced fine
½ teaspoon freshly ground
   black pepper
½ teaspoon powdered ginger

Dash of mace
2 cups water
⅓ cup lemon juice
2 tablespoons grated lemon rind
2 eggs
2 tablespoons flour
½ teaspoon saffron
2 tablespoons chopped parsley

Wash and dry the fish. Sprinkle with salt. Melt the butter in a skillet. Add the onions and sauté for 5 minutes. Add the fish slices and brown slightly. Add the pepper, ginger, mace, and water. Cover and cook over low heat for 30 minutes. Add the lemon juice and rind and stir.

Beat the eggs in a bowl and add the flour, saffron, and parsley, beating well. Add ½ cup of the fish stock, beating constantly. Return the contents of the bowl to the saucepan, again stirring constantly. Cook over very low heat, stirring constantly, until thick. Do not allow the mixture to boil. Place the fish on a platter and pour the sauce over it. Serve with boiled potatoes and green peas. *Serves 6.*

ROAST LEG OF LAMB

5-pound leg of lamb	2 stalks celery, sliced
3 cloves garlic, slivered	2 carrots, grated
2 teaspoons salt	¾ cup chopped onions
½ teaspoon freshly ground	¾ cup beef broth
black pepper	¾ cup dry sherry
½ teaspoon rosemary	12 small white onions, peeled
3 tablespoons butter	

Make several shallow cuts in the leg, and into them insert the garlic slivers. Season the meat with the salt, pepper, and rosemary. Place the leg in a greased roasting pan and dot with the butter. Surround the leg with the celery, carrot, and chopped onions. Pour beef broth into the pan. Roast in a 300° oven 25 minutes a pound. Baste and turn frequently, and add wine and onions 30 minutes before end of roasting time. Pour off the pan juices and skim the fat. Serve the gravy in a sauceboat with the carved lamb and onions. *Serves 6–8.*

As served at the Auckland Inter-Continental Hotel.

STUFFED STEAK, NEW ZEALAND STYLE

6 thin, boneless steaks	⅓ cup bread crumbs
2 teaspoons salt	6 tablespoons ketchup
½ teaspoon freshly ground	1½ cups beef broth
black pepper	3 tablespoons flour
2 onions, chopped	3 tablespoons water
4 slices bacon, half cooked,	3 tablespoons butter
chopped fine	

Pound the steak with a mallet or the flat side of a knife until very thin. Sprinkle with the salt and pepper. Combine the onions, bacon, bread crumbs, and ketchup in a bowl. Mix well. Place equal amounts of the mixture on each of the steaks. Roll up each steak and fasten with string or skewers. Place in a buttered casserole. Pour the broth over the steaks and cover the casserole. Bake in a 350° oven for 35 minutes. Mix the flour and water together to form a smooth paste. Add to the casserole, mixing well. Dot the steaks with the butter. Correct seasoning. Leaving the casserole uncovered, bake for 10 minutes longer. Serve hot, together with the sauce. *Serves 6.*

TOHEROA SOUP

1 15-ounce can toheroa concentrate	⅛ teaspoon nutmeg
3 cups milk	2 tablespoons butter
1 teaspoon sugar	2 tablespoons cornstarch
	½ cup water

Pour the toheroa concentrate into a heavy saucepan. Bring to a boil and cook over low heat 30 minutes. Pour into a clean saucepan, being careful to leave any sandy residue in the first saucepan. To the concentrate add the milk, sugar, nutmeg, and butter. Bring to a boil. Mix the cornstarch with the water. Add to the soup, stirring until smooth and thickened. Serve hot in soup cups. *Serves 6.*

Toheroa is a type of shellfish found only in New Zealand. The canned concentrate or condensed soup is available in the United States in many specialty food shops. (If you can't get it, the following will provide an adequate substitute.)

Toheroa Substitute:

2 10-ounce cans minced clams	1 tablespoon cornstarch
1 cup canned condensed pea soup	3 cups milk

Purée the undrained clams in an electric blender. Pour into a saucepan, bring to a boil, and cook over low heat 15 minutes. Mix the pea soup, cornstarch, and milk until smooth and stir into the clams. Cook, stirring steadily until mixture boils and is smooth and thickened. *Serves 6.*

DROP SCONES

1 egg	1 teaspoon baking powder
1 cup milk	Butter for frying
½ cup sifted flour	

Beat the egg and milk together in a bowl. Sift the flour and baking powder together and add to the previous mixture, mixing until smooth. The batter should be the consistency of thin cream. Add more flour if necessary. Grease a griddle or large frying pan lightly. Drop the batter by tablespoon, and bake over low heat until lightly browned on both sides. Serve with plenty of butter, and jelly if desired. This is a favorite teatime specialty. *Serves 4–6.*

Note: Although the drop scone originated in Scotland, the New Zealanders consider it a local specialty, owing to the large number of persons of Scottish descent living there.

TEA PANCAKES

PIKELETS

2 eggs	1½ cups flour
2 tablespoons sugar	1 teaspoon cream of tartar
1 teaspoon baking soda	2 tablespoons melted butter
1 cup buttermilk	Butter for frying

Beat together the eggs and sugar. Dissolve the baking soda in the buttermilk and add to the eggs. Sift the flour and cream of tartar into the mixture, stirring until blended. Mix in the melted butter.

Heat a griddle or heavy skillet, and drop the mixture onto it with a teaspoon, allowing space between each to allow for spreading. Let brown on both sides over low heat. Serve hot or cold with butter and jam, preferably raspberry. *Makes about 30.*

APRICOT AND ALMOND PASTRY

KOROMIKO FLAN

1¼ cups sifted cake flour	1 cup apricot jam
¼ teaspoon salt	¼ pound (1 stick) butter
¾ cup shortening	½ cup sugar
3 eggs	½ cup finely ground almonds

Sift the flour and salt into a bowl. Cut in the shortening with a pastry blender or two knives, until the consistency of coarse sand. Beat one egg and add to the flour mixture, tossing lightly until a ball of dough is formed. Wrap in wax paper and chill for 1 hour. Roll out the dough ¼ inch thick on a lightly floured surface and line a 9-inch pie plate with it. Spread the apricot jam over it. Preheat oven to 350°. Cream the butter and add the sugar, beating until light and fluffy. Add the remaining eggs and beat well. Add the nuts, beating well. Pour into the prepared pie plate. Bake in a 350° oven for 30 minutes, or until delicately browned on top. *Serves 6–8.*

ORANGEADE, NEW ZEALAND STYLE

1 large lemon	¼ teaspoon powdered ginger
5 oranges	¼ teaspoon cinnamon
1 cup honey	2 cloves

Wash the lemon and oranges. Grate the lemon and one of the oranges. Squeeze the juice from the lemon and oranges and place in a saucepan with the grated rind. Add the honey. Bring to a boil and add the ginger, cinnamon, and cloves. Boil for about 5 minutes, or until the mixture is reduced by half. Force the mixture through a very fine sieve, pour into a bottle or other covered container, and cool. Place in the refrigerator.

Place a tablespoon of the orange mixture in a tall glass and fill with cracked ice and water. If desired, carbonated water may be used. Decorate the glass with a maraschino cherry and with slices of orange and lemon. *Serve 8–10.*

THE PHILIPPINES

During the war the G.I.s were very much taken with Philippine beer, which they pronounced uniformly excellent. Whether or not the climate of the islands helps to improve the taste of the beer is difficult to determine, for the temperature in the Philippines makes frequent cold drinks almost a necessity. It seldom gets cool in Manila, which is a definite understatement, and most of the time it is quite hot; the cool season is during January and February, when the *average* temperature is about seventy-five degrees, which should give you a general idea. The favorite drink of the native population is *tuba*, a potent, fermented beverage made from the sap of palm trees. Although some wine is consumed, by and large it is not too important.

The cuisine of the islands is exceptionally interesting, because four different cultural forces are at work. They are the American, native, Spanish, and Chinese. The American influence is obvious since, though it is now a republic, the country was formerly a dependency of the United States and still has a pronounced degree of attachment for things American. The native feeling in cooking is also apparent, since the people are quite loyal to the old ways of doing things. With a Spanish colonial history, the Iberian cuisine has left a definite impression on the food of the islands. Finally, the Philippines are close to China, and large numbers of Chinese live here, many of them having become nationalized. Chinese food is particularly popular, and there are Chinese restaurants everywhere. Noodle dishes are greatly appreciated, and are really staples in the local diet.

Breakfast is a very large meal even by our standards; it usually consists of rice, with the addition of fish (fresh or dried) and possibly a meat dish, plus hot coffee or thick hot chocolate. Some people eat another breakfast later in the morning, but the American toast-and-coffee influence is making itself felt, particularly in the cities. Lunch and dinner are very similar, both in size and with regard to the type of food eaten. Soup is often served as a separate course, but it is frequently combined with the main dish. The *merienda* (teatime) custom is still carefully observed, particularly by the ladies of the islands, and it constitutes an informal but important social hour.

Philippine food requires an understanding of the terms involved. If a dish has the word *manok* in it, it contains chicken; *isda* means fish; *baboy* is pork; *carne* is beef. Since a *tortillang* is an omelet, a *baboy tortillang* would be an omelet with pork, and so forth.

The undoubted favorite of the people is pork. *Lechon,* a whole barbecued pig, is a national dish, as is *adobo,* a mixture of chicken and pork regularly served in the majority of Filipino homes, although the recipe given is just one of dozens of variations on this dish. When made with pork only it is known as *adobo baboy.* Rice is the staple food and is served with practically any dish.

The people of the islands are very fond of odd snacks which they eat between regular meal hours. Some of these tidbits would be considered quite odd to anyone who has never lived there, but in a little while they become commonplace. The visitor soon finds himself eating food that would have seemed exotic a few short weeks before.

MANILA COCKTAIL

½ cup canned pineapple juice   6 egg whites
3 jiggers sweet vermouth   2 tablespoons cherry brandy
6 jiggers gin

Boil the pineapple juice in a saucepan rapidly until only 2 tablespoons of juice remain. Cool for 3 minutes. In a cocktail shaker place the pineapple juice, vermouth, gin, egg whites, and cherry brandy. Add plenty of ice. Shake vigorously for at least 1 minute. Pour into chilled cocktail glasses. Decorate with a maraschino cherry. *Serves 6.*

MEAT SOUP

SOPA DE PICADILLO

3 tablespoons vegetable oil	2 quarts water
3 cloves garlic, minced	1 cup beef broth
4 onions, chopped	1 teaspoon salt
1½ pounds ground beef	1 teaspoon freshly ground
3 tomatoes, coarsely chopped	black pepper
4 potatoes, peeled and cubed	

Heat the oil in a saucepan. Add the garlic and onions and sauté for 10 minutes, stirring frequently. Add the beef and cook over high heat for 5 minutes, stirring frequently. Add the tomatoes and potatoes and continue browning for an additional 5 minutes. Add the water, broth, salt, and pepper. Reduce heat to medium and cook for 25 minutes. Correct seasoning. Serve hot. *Serves 8–10.*

FISH WITH EGG SAUCE

PESCADO CON SALSA DE HUEVOS

6 slices fish (sea bass, mackerel, snapper, etc.)	3 tomatoes, chopped
	1 onion, sliced thin
1 cup water	4 hard-cooked eggs
6 tablespoons olive oil	4 scallions (green onions), sliced
4 tablespoons vinegar	thin
1½ teaspoons salt	2 pimentos, chopped
1 teaspoon pepper	

Combine the fish, water, 2 tablespoons of the olive oil, 2 tablespoons of the vinegar, 1 teaspoon of the salt, ½ teaspoon of the pepper, 2 tomatoes, and the onion in a saucepan. Bring to a boil and cook over low heat for 30 minutes. Remove fish to a platter and reserve ½ cup of the stock.

Mash the yolks of the eggs but reserve the whites. Add the remaining oil, vinegar, salt, and pepper and mix to a smooth paste. Chop the egg whites and add to the mixture. Add the scallions and pimentos. Combine with the reserved stock. Bring to a boil. Pour the sauce over the fish and serve with the remaining tomato, cut in wedges. *Serves 6.*

MEAT ROLL

MORCÓN

½ pound ham, ground
½ pound pork, ground
4 tablespoons grated cheese
(Gruyère or American)
¼ cup chopped sweet pickles
¼ cup chopped black olives
2 tablespoons lemon juice
4 teaspoons salt
1½ teaspoons finely ground
black pepper
1 egg
3 pounds boneless sirloin, cut
¼ inch thick (in one piece, if
possible)

3 hard-cooked eggs, quartered
1 cup vegetable oil
2 cups water
¼ cup vinegar
½ cup tomato sauce
1 onion, sliced
3 cloves garlic, minced
1 bay leaf
2 tablespoons flour

Combine the ham, pork, cheese, pickles, olives, lemon juice, 2 teaspoons of the salt, ¾ teaspoon of the pepper, and the egg. Mix well. Place the steak on a flat surface and spread with the mixture. If several steaks are used, divide the mixture evenly. Arrange the quartered eggs on the mixture. Roll up the steak carefully and fasten in several places with thread.

Heat the oil in a Dutch oven or heavy saucepan. Brown the meat on all sides. Drain the oil. Add the water, vinegar, tomato sauce, onion, garlic, bay leaf, and remaining salt and pepper. Cover and cook over medium heat for 1 hour, or until tender. Mix the flour with an equal amount of cold water and add to the gravy, stirring until smooth. Cook over low heat for 5 minutes. Remove the meat roll carefully from the gravy and place on a platter. Cut the threads and discard them. Slice the meat at an angle and serve with the sauce. *Serves 6–8.*

As served at the Manila Inter-Continental Hotel.

CHICKEN AND PORK CASSEROLE

ADOBO

1 cup fresh or unsweetened dried
    grated coconut
1 cup milk
3 whole chicken breasts, cut
    into 2-inch cubes
¼ cup olive oil
3 pounds boneless pork, cut into
    ½-inch cubes

6 cloves garlic, minced
1 tablespoon salt
1 teaspoon pepper
4 whole peppercorns
2 bay leaves
½ cup beef broth
½ cup wine vinegar

Combine the coconut and milk in a saucepan. Bring to a boil, remove from the heat, and soak for 30 minutes. Press all the liquid from the coconut and discard the pulp.

Wash and dry the chicken pieces. Heat the olive oil in a Dutch oven or casserole. Add the chicken and pork and sauté until brown on all sides. Add the garlic, salt, pepper, peppercorns, bay leaves, broth and vinegar. Cover and cook over low heat for 1 hour, or until the chicken and pork are tender, stirring frequently. Add the coconut milk and cook for 10 minutes. Correct seasoning. Serve with boiled rice. *Serves 8–10.*

STUFFED DUCK

RELLENADO DE PATO

2 4-pound ducks
2 cloves garlic, minced
4 teaspoons salt
1½ teaspoons pepper
¼ cup lemon juice
1 tablespoon honey
1 pound smoked ham, ground

1 pound sausage meat or
    Spanish-style sausage
½ pound beef, ground
3 eggs, beaten
¼ cup capers, drained
2 tablespoons seedless raisins
1 onion, chopped fine

Wash and dry the ducks thoroughly. Combine the garlic, salt, pepper, lemon juice, and honey, and rub into the ducks at least 2 hours before roasting them.

Combine the ham, sausage (if Spanish-style sausage is used, remove the casings), beef, eggs, capers, raisins, and onion, and mix well. Correct seasoning, depending on the type of sausage used. Stuff the ducks with the mixture, fastening the openings with skewers or with thread. Place on a rack in a roasting pan. Roast in a 425° oven for 20 minutes. Reduce heat to 325° and roast 2 hours longer, pouring off fat from time to time as it accumulates. The duck should be crisp and brown. *Serves 8.*

RICE, LUZON FASHION

ARROZ À LA LUZONIA

¼ cup olive oil
3 cloves garlic, minced
1 onion, chopped
½ pound pork, cut into matchlike
strips
8 raw shrimp, peeled and cut in
half
2 teaspoons salt
1 teaspoon freshly ground
black pepper

1 teaspoon Spanish paprika
3 cups cooked rice
4 eggs, beaten
3 pimentos, sliced thin
2 hard-cooked eggs, sliced thin
3 tablespoons butter
6 bananas, sliced

Heat the oil in a frying pan. Add the garlic, onion, and pork and sauté
for 20 minutes, stirring frequently. Add the shrimp and sauté for 5 minutes. Add the salt, pepper, paprika, and rice and mix well. Cook for 15
minutes. Stir in the eggs. Correct seasoning.

Butter or oil a mold or casserole generously. Arrange pimentos and egg
slices on the bottom. Place the rice mixture on top. Cover with a piece
of aluminum foil and tie it securely around the edges. Place the mold or
casserole in a pan of water. Cook for 40 minutes.

Meanwhile, melt the butter in a skillet. Sauté the banana slices in it until lightly browned. Unmold the rice carefully onto a platter. Arrange the
banana slices around it. Serve immediately. *Serves 6–8.*

FILIPINO CUSTARD

LECHE FLAN

2 cups fresh or dried grated
coconut
2 cups light cream
1 cup dark brown sugar
3 tablespoons water

4 eggs
2 egg yolks
1 cup white sugar
2 teaspoons grated lemon rind

Combine the coconut and cream in a saucepan. Bring to a boil, remove
from the heat, and soak for 30 minutes. Press all the liquid from the coconut and discard the pulp.

Combine the brown sugar and water in a saucepan. Cook over medium
heat until a thick syrup is formed. Spread three fourths of the mixture on
the bottom of a buttered ½-quart mold or soufflé dish. Mix the remaining
syrup with the coconut cream. Cook over low heat, stirring constantly,
until the syrup is dissolved. Beat the eggs and egg yolks in a bowl. Add

the sugar and lemon rind, beating well. Gradually add the cream mixture, beating constantly. Pour into the mold. Place the mold in a pan of water. Cover. Cook over very low heat for 1½ hours, or until the custard is firm. Do not allow the water in the pan to boil. Place the custard under the broiler for 1 minute to brown the top. Serve hot or cold. *Serves 6–8.*

North America

Alaska
and the Eskimo Regions
Canada
Central America
Mexico
United States

ALAKSA (THE 49th STATE)
AND THE ESKIMO REGIONS

There are many misapprehensions about Alaska, particularly with reference to its population and climate. There are about 125,000 white residents, and roughly about 35,000 of the native population, including the Eskimos, Aleuts, and Indians. Alaska is growing at a tremendous pace and there are few apparent signs of any slackening in this direction. Certainly there is room for all this growth and even a little more, at least with regard to space, for Alaska alone is equal to one fifth of the total land area of the rest of the United States. The climate is not as severe as most people think, particularly near Juneau, the capital. The summers are usually quite delightful, and flowers, vegetables, and fruit often attain tremendous size during the short growing season.

With a background of old-fashioned movies, most of us think of Alaska as a land filled with golden-hearted dance-hall girls, hard drinkers, bottles on the bars of saloons, and all the usual stereotyped paraphernalia of the Far North. While Alaska has not yet swung over completely to the milk shake, there are definite signs in that direction. Smile when you drink that chocolate malted, pardner! Coffee undoubtedly surpasses hard liquor as the favorite drink, and is consumed steadily by the population from morning to night. Coffee is the standard greeting to a guest, and few Alaskan households fail to keep a coffeepot going most of the day; this hospitality cannot be criticized, but few coffee drinkers would subscribe to the practice of boiling coffee.

It cannot be denied that Alaska's cuisine is based largely upon that of the other states, but certain distinctions must be drawn. The people rely on their local foods, particularly the fish of Alaskan waters. Cod, halibut, herring, and salmon are the largest catches, but salmon is the great favorite as well as the most important catch dollarwise. Fine salmon dishes appear frequently on Alaskan menus, and the fish is a treat when merely broiled with butter. Baked salmon is popular, and the salmon doughnut recipe is an unusual variation. Alaska crab, a giant among crustaceans, is becoming quite important economically; considerable shipments of this delicacy have been made to the other states.

Everyone has heard of the Alaskan "sourdoughs," the gold prospectors of the early days. Since this hardy breed had no bread nor any store where bread could be bought when on the trail, it was the custom to make a batch of sour dough and keep it going from day to day. Although there are few prospectors left, many people in Alaska still make sour dough pancakes and breads. In fact all kinds of breads, pastries, and cakes are popular here, probably because the crisp weather intensifies the desire for starches and sweets. Doughnuts are special favorites, and the recipe for potato doughnuts is a good example.

Alaska has many oddities in the food line. Bulb kelp, a type of seaweed found along the shore, is made into pickles and jellies. Cranberries and blueberries are somewhat different from the varieties to which we are accustomed, and are used in many unusual ways: for relishes, puddings, and even a cranberry ketchup. Wild strawberries are found in the fields even near the snow line. There are many other berries, such as the salmonberry, a seeded yellow or red berry used for jellies; black and red huckleberries; black and purple gooseberries; yellow cloudberries; and juneberries, which are used for preserves.

Wild game is still available in Alaska, and the people make the most of their opportunity. There are wild ducks, geese, and ptarmigan (the last a particular favorite of the Eskimos), mountain goats and rabbits, and even beaver. Bear meat, caribou, moose, and reindeer are not rare and are used for steaks, chops, rib roasts, burgers, meat loaves, and pot roasts in the same way that a midwestern housewife might use beef. A "mooseburger" or barbecued venison dinner is typical of the Alaskan approach to game cookery.

The Eskimos have shown a great appreciation for the material goods of the white man and are slowly abandoning their old way of life. Canned fruits, wheat flour, and sugar have made a strong impression upon them. While they still cling to their principal diet of raw dish, seal meat, and hot tea, the younger generation shows signs of preferring the diet of the whites.

The feet of bears, seal livers, white whale meat, ducks, and ptarmigan are considered good eating by the Eskimos. One of the great favorites is Eskimo ice cream, made as follows: Reindeer fat is rubbed or grated as fine as possible. Seal oil is added gradually to the reindeer fat, and a little water added for consistency. The mixture becomes very pale in color and foamy in texture. Eskimo gourmets then add blueberries or other wild berries for flavor. It is a great delicacy—at least Eskimo children find it so. It is not likely to become a popular favorite along the highways of the United States.

SALMON DOUGHNUTS

2 7-ounce cans salmon, drained
and flaked
1 tablespoon lemon juice
1 teaspoon salt
½ teaspoon freshly ground
black pepper

2 tablespoons grated onion
½ cup mashed potatoes
1 egg, beaten
1 cup dry bread crumbs
Vegetable oil for deep-fat frying

Combine the salmon, lemon juice, salt, pepper, onion, potatoes, and egg in a bowl. Blend well and chill for 1 hour. Remove from refrigerator and place on a lightly floured surface. Pat the mixture flat until it is about ½ inch thick. Cut out with a doughnut cutter. Heat the fat in a deep saucepan to 375°. Place the doughnuts in the fat and fry until golden brown, about 5 minutes. Drain and serve hot. Miniature doughnuts make excellent hot hors d'oeuvres. *Serves 6–8.*

BAKED ALASKA SALMON

4 pounds fresh salmon (either
the whole fish or in one piece)
2 cups fresh bread crumbs
2 tablespoons finely chopped
onion
1 tablespoon chopped parsley
2 teaspoons salt

½ teaspoon freshly ground
black pepper
1 teaspoon sage
4 tablespoons melted butter
1 cup chicken broth
6 strips bacon

Wash and dry the salmon. Split the fish open, leaving the skin intact. In a bowl combine the bread crumbs, onion, parsley, salt, pepper, and sage. Mix well. Add the melted butter and the broth and mix. Stuff the fish with the mixture carefully; do not pack down, or the filling will become heavy. Fasten the edges with skewers or thread.

Place the fish in a large buttered baking dish. Arrange the slices of bacon across the top of the fish. Bake in a 350° oven for 1 hour, or until fish flakes easily when tested with a fork. *Serves 6–8.*

SOUR DOUGH BREAD

Starter:

1 package active dry yeast	2 cups lukewarm water
1 teaspoon sugar	2 cups flour

In a bowl (not metal), mix together the yeast, sugar, water, and flour. Put a piece of paper towel over the bowl loosely and let stand in a warm place for 48 hours. Mix occasionally and add a little warm water if mixture gets too thick. When ready to make the bread, remove ½ cup and refrigerate the remaining mixture in a loosely covered jar. To keep the starter active, add ½ cup flour and ½ cup warm water every two weeks, then let it stand in a warm place until bubbly before refrigerating again.

Bread:

5 cups flour (about)	1 tablespoon sugar
2 cups lukewarm water	1 package active dry yeast
½ cup starter	2 teaspoons salt

Mix together 2 cups of the flour, 1 cup of the water, the starter, and sugar. Beat hard until smooth. Cover tightly and let stand 18 hours, stirring a few times. Mix in the yeast, salt, and 2 cups of the remaining flour. Beat well, and add just enough of the remaining flour to make a stiff dough. Knead until shiny and smooth (if you have a dough hook, use it, for it takes about 10 minutes by hand).

Shape into 2 loaves and put into greased 9-inch loaf pans. Make lattice-shaped slashes on top. Cover and let rise in a warm place until double in bulk, about 1 hour. Brush the top with water. Place a pan of boiling water on the bottom of the oven. Bake the breads in a preheated 400° oven 40 minutes or until browned. Brush the top with water once during the baking time. Remove from the pan and cool on a cake rack.

SOUR DOUGH PANCAKES

½ cup starter	¾ teaspoon salt
1½ cups flour	2 eggs, beaten
2 teaspoons sugar	¾ cup milk
½ teaspoon baking soda	

Mix together all the ingredients and make pancakes on a greased griddle or heavy skillet. *Makes about 30 two-inch pancakes.*

CRANBERRY RELISH

6 apples	1 orange
2 cups raw cranberries	2 cups sugar

Wash and core the apples. Cut the unpeeled apples into small pieces. Wash and drain the cranberries. Wash the unpeeled orange; cut into small pieces, removing any seeds and membranes. Grind all the fruits in a food chopper. Combine in a saucepan with the sugar and bring to a boil. Place in a bowl or jar and refrigerate for 24 hours before serving. *Makes about 2 pints.*

POTATO DOUGHNUTS

1 cup hot mashed potatoes	½ cup milk
1 cup sugar	1¾ cups sifted flour
½ teaspoon salt	2½ teaspoons baking powder
2 eggs, beaten	½ teaspoon nutmeg
3 tablespoons melted butter	Vegetable oil for deep frying

Combine the mashed potatoes, sugar, and salt in a bowl. Mix well. Add the eggs, melted butter, and milk, beating until very light and fluffy. Sift the flour, baking powder, and nutmeg together. Add to the potato mixture. Knead into a dough. Roll out ⅛ inch thick on a lightly floured surface. Cut out with a doughnut cutter. Heat deep oil to 360°. Drop the doughnuts into it carefully. Do not fry too many at once. Fry until lightly browned on both sides. Drain. Dust with sugar before serving. These are especially good hot. *Makes about 20.*

CANADA

Canada is an immense country stretching from ocean to ocean and having a mixture of both English and French cultures. It is a young country but is becoming increasingly more cosmopolitan under the influence of the many Scots, Italians, Ukrainians, and other Europeans who have adopted Canada as their home. English is the predominant language, with French and English spoken in the province of Quebec, parts of the Maritimes, Ontario, and Manitoba.

The country's cuisine covers a wide range, varying from coast to coast, from province to province, with the changing concentration of population and its ethnic origin. English-style foods are eaten over a great part of the country, but of course, in the prevailing French-Canadian sections the French culinary influence prevails. Bounded as the country is by the Atlantic Ocean on the east, the Pacific Ocean on the west coast, and the Arctic in the north, seafood dishes are favorites in many areas. The Atlantic provinces, for example, are a gourmet's paradise for lobster, considered by many among the finest in the world, oysters, and for the famous Atlantic salmon from the Gaspé area. From the Pacific, there is the unchallenged coho salmon. Gaining in popularity across the country is Arctic char, a delicious trout treat. Another delicacy is Winnipeg goldeye, a fresh-water herring-like fish, caught in Lake Winnipeg but available in many parts of Canada.

Onion soup, habitant pea soup, meat ball stew, pork and beans, and minced pork pie are served throughout Quebec as part of the French-Canadian cuisine. There are, however, some traditional dishes dating back to the seventeenth century that are still being served, such as bear and buffalo steaks, roast venison, and beaver tail soup. Quebec is famous also for its distinctively Canadian cheeses and Canadian sugar pie.

Eastern beef from Ontario, and western beef raised in Alberta hold a high place, with roast beef and Yorkshire pudding being almost as popular here as in the United Kingdom. Canadian bacon is a national pride, and shares its popularity throughout the world.

Canadian apple pie, made from the excellent apples grown in the Georgian Bay district in Ontario, the Acadian area of Nova Scotia and Okanagan Valley of British Columbia, served hot or cold, is a delectable dessert favorite. Canada is famous for its fresh fruits and vegetables and is building a fine reputation in serving these, indeed all its food, in a deliciously different manner. While it may be said that there is no distinctively Canadian cuisine, the admixture of various national groups within the country is bringing together an interesting potential by adaption.

Hardy Canadian beers and ales are welcome companions to meals, as are the Canadian wines whose plump grapes are mostly grown on the famous Niagara escarpment, where every year is a vintage year. Canadian whiskys speak for themselves throughout the world.

A unique Canadian product is the Canadian bacon, well accepted all over the world, but particularly in the United States. Canada produces a fair amount of wine, but since none of it is unusual, it is almost never exported. Canadian beers and ales and the "Canadian whisky" are the preferred alcoholic drinks. Both coffee and tea are popular with the Canadian public.

CHEDDAR CHEESE SOUP

4 tablespoons butter
1 tablespoon grated onion
4 tablespoons flour
4 cups chicken broth
2 cups milk, scalded

2 cups grated Cheddar cheese
½ teaspoon salt
½ teaspoon freshly ground
   black pepper

Melt the butter in a saucepan; sauté the onion for 5 minutes. Blend in the flour until smooth. Gradually add the broth stirring constantly until the boiling point is reached. Add the milk, cheese, salt, and pepper. Mix well. Cook over low heat until the cheese is thoroughly melted and the soup bubbles. Stir occasionally. Correct seasoning. Serve very hot. *Serves 8–10.*

CANADIAN PEA SOUP

SOUPE AUX POIS CANADIENNE

2 cups dried yellow peas
8 cups water
2 onions, chopped
4 slices bacon, cut into 1-inch
   pieces

2 teaspoons salt
½ teaspoon freshly ground
   black pepper
⅛ teaspoon sage
2 tablespoons chopped parsley

Wash the peas thoroughly and discard any imperfect ones. Soak them in the water overnight. Cook the peas in a large saucepan, in the water in which they were soaked. Add the onions, bacon, salt, pepper, and sage. Cover and cook over low heat for 3 hours. Add more water if necessary, but the soup should be fairly thick. Correct seasoning. Sprinkle with parsley and serve. *Serves 6–8.*

LOBSTER, PICTOU STYLE

6 cooked lobsters
¼ pound (1 stick) butter
½ cup cider vinegar
2 teaspoons sugar
1½ teaspoons salt

⅛ teaspoon white pepper
¼ teaspoon nutmeg
Dash of cayenne pepper
1½ cups heavy cream
6 slices toast

Remove the lobster meat from the shell and cut into small cubes. Melt the butter in a saucepan. Add the lobster meat and cook over low heat for 5 minutes, stirring occasionally. Add the vinegar, sugar, salt, pepper, nutmeg, and cayenne pepper. Cook over very low heat for 5 minutes but do not allow the mixture to boil. Remove from the heat. Add the cream gradually, stirring constantly. Correct seasoning. Place a slice of toast in each soup plate and pour some of the lobster mixture over it. *Serves 6.*

Note: This is a main course, not a soup.

FISH SALAD

1 pound cod, haddock, or any
    other salt-water, white-meat
    fish
1½ cups water
1 onion
1 teaspoon salt
2 apples, peeled and diced

½ cup peeled, diced cucumbers
½ cup diced celery
2 teaspoons parsley
½ teaspoon Worcestershire sauce
½ teaspoon grated onion
3 tablespoons mayonnaise
2 hard-cooked eggs

Wash the fish and place in a saucepan with the water, onion, and salt. Bring to a boil and cook over medium heat for 20 minutes. Drain well, flake, and let cool in the refrigerator for 2 hours.

Place the fish in a large bowl. Add the apples, cucumbers, and celery; mix well. Add the parsley, Worcestershire sauce, grated onion, and mayonnaise. Toss the ingredients together lightly. Arrange the portions on individual beds of lettuce leaves. Chop the yolks of the eggs fine, and sprinkle on top of each serving. *Serves 4–6.*

CLAM PIE

1 cup sifted flour
¼ pound (1 stick) salt butter
3 tablespoons ice water
¼ pound salt pork, cubed
3 onions, chopped
4 carrots, diced fine
½ cup dry white wine
2 cups fresh or canned clam
    juice

4 potatoes, peeled and diced
3 tablespoons chopped parsley
1 clove garlic, minced
2 bay leaves
2½ dozen clams, coarsely chopped
½ teaspoon freshly ground
    black pepper
1 tablespoon cornstarch

Sift the flour into a bowl. Cut in the butter with a pastry blender or two knives. Add the water and toss lightly until a dough is formed. Chill for 1 hour.

Preheat oven to 375°.

Combine the pork, onions, and carrots in a saucepan. Cook over medium heat for 10 minutes, stirring frequently. Add the wine, clam juice, and potatoes and cook over low heat for 15 minutes. Add the parsley, garlic, bay leaves, clams, and pepper. Mix the cornstarch with a little water to a smooth paste and add, stirring steadily until the boiling point is reached. Correct seasoning and remove the bay leaves. Pour into a 1½-quart buttered casserole or baking dish.

Roll the dough on a lightly floured surface to fit the top of the casserole. Place the dough on top of the casserole and seal the edges well. Prick the dough with a fork in several places. Bake in a 375° oven for 30 minutes or until pastry is browned. Serve hot directly from the casserole. *Serves 4–6.*

PORK PIE

TOURTIÈRE

3 cups sifted flour	2 onions
1 teaspoon salt	1 clove garlic, minced
¾ cup lard or butter	½ cup boiling water
1 egg, beaten	1½ teaspoons salt
4 tablespoons cold milk	½ teaspoon freshly ground
3 pounds pork or 1½ pounds pork	black pepper
and 1½ pounds veal	Pinch of sage
3 slices bacon	3 tablespoons chopped parsley

Sift the flour and salt together. Cut in the shortening with a pastry blender or two knives until the consistency of corn meal. Combine the beaten egg and the milk and add to the flour mixture. Toss lightly with a fork until a ball of dough is formed. Wrap in wax paper and chill for at least 1 hour.

If possible, use both pork and veal, as the dish will have a better flavor. Grind the meat, bacon, and onions. Add the garlic and mix. Place in a heavy ungreased saucepan, and cook over medium heat for 5 minutes, stirring constantly. Add the water, salt, pepper, sage, and parsley. Cover and cook for 20 minutes. The mixture should not be allowed to become too dry, and small quantities of boiling water should be added if required. Cool for 15 minutes.

Remove the dough from the refrigerator and divide into four pieces, two of which should be slightly larger than the other two pieces. Preheat oven to 450°. Roll out the four pieces of dough on a lightly floured surface. Line two 8-inch pie plates with the larger pieces of dough. Fill them equally with the meat mixture. Cover each pie with the smaller pieces of dough. Make a few slits across the top of each pie. Bake in a 450° oven for 10 minutes. Reduce heat to 350° and bake for 25 minutes, or until well browned. *Serves 6–8.*

CANADIAN BOILED DINNER

BOUILLI

3 tablespoons butter
5-pound stewing chicken,
   disjointed
1 pound lean beef, cubed
½ pound lamb, cubed
½ pound salt pork, cubed
1 turnip, peeled
2 cloves
2 onions
8 cups boiling water
1 tablespoon salt

1 teaspoon freshly ground
   black pepper
¼ teaspoon thyme
2 bay leaves
6 carrots, peeled and halved
1 head cabbage, quartered
6 potatoes, peeled and quartered
1½ pounds fresh string beans,
   tied with thread in 8 individual
   bunches

Melt the butter in a large saucepan. Add the chicken, beef, and lamb
and brown well on all sides over high heat. Add the salt pork and turnip.
Place a clove in each onion and add, together with the boiling water,
salt, pepper, thyme, and bay leaves. Cover and cook over low heat for 2¼
hours. Add the carrots, cabbage, potatoes, and string beans and cook 45
minutes longer. Correct seasoning. Arrange the meats in the center of a
platter and place the vegetables around it. The soup should be served
separately. *Serves 6–8.*

MAPLE WALNUT PIE

TORTE AU SUCRE À LA CRÈME

Pastry as in Clam Pie (recipe in
   this section)
2 cups maple or brown sugar
⅓ cup sifted flour

½ cup heavy cream
1½ cups coarsely chopped
   walnuts
3 tablespoons butter

Preheat oven to 375°.

Line a 9-inch pie plate with the pastry, reserving any scraps to make
lattice strips for the top. Spread the maple sugar on it, and sift the flour
over the sugar. Sprinkle the cream over the flour. Spread the walnuts
over the mixture and dot with the butter. Put the lattice strips over it and
bake 35 minutes. Serve warm or cold. *Serves 6–8.*

*Note: If you use brown sugar, rather than maple sugar, add 1 teaspoon
maple flavoring to the cream.*

CENTRAL AMERICA—GUATEMALA, HONDURAS, EL SALVADOR, NICARAGUA, COSTA RICA, AND PANAMA

Guatemala has one of the most colorful Indian populations of any country in the Western Hemisphere, and has in addition a delightful year-round climate in the highlands. Tourists are invariably (and we use the word advisedly) thrilled with Chichicastenango, the Indian village located in the mountains: Chichi (the familiar name) is one of those rare places that is more exciting than the travel folder.

The country has many dishes in common with its neighbor to the north, Mexico, although Guatemala uses fewer spices and seasonings. There are the usual Mexican preparations, but these are handled with a somewhat more delicate hand; this is merely a generalization, it must be admitted. Bean dishes such as *boquitas de frijoles* are favorites. The *Guatemaltecos*, as they like to call themselves, celebrate All Saints' Day with a special meat dish that requires considerable advance preparation but is as much a part of the holiday as turkey is of Thanksgiving.

Coffee and hot chocolate are the national beverages, although they are prepared somewhat differently than in the United States. Guatemalan coffee is among the world's finest, since it grows in the highlands at carefully selected altitudes. Guatemalan coffee tends to be somewhat bland, when not combined with other coffees, for it is smooth to the taste but a trifle insipid. However, to make matters worse, many people tend to make or buy a coffee concentrate and then add hot water. The resulting drink is not one calculated to encourage tourists to drink the local coffee. When your Pan Am plane lands at Guatemala City airport, the chances are that you'll be greeted with a cup of steaming hot coffee.

Meal hours follow our customary pattern, except that lunch is a more substantial meal than its American equivalent. An unusual Guatemalan custom is that of stacking all of the dishes to be used for a meal in front of each diner. On top of the stack is the soup plate, as soup usually begins the meal.

Beer is good here, and wines are liked, but these last are imported and consumed only by the city folk. The general population much prefer their own rum, which is coarse, crude, and not subject to argument.

Honduras is quite another story, politically, historically, and in most other ways. Gastronomically speaking, the country resembles Mexico rather strongly, but with American and European variations. Most of the local food is based on the Mexican staple dishes: beans, rice, *tortillas*, *tamales*, and the like.

American influence is becoming steadily more important, since most of the canned goods and prepared products come from the United States. Eating is not the amusement in Honduras that it is in Costa Rica, and Hondurans eat regular meals very much in the ordinary, three-meal-a-day pattern. In the agricultural section of the country the food is very simple and the diet often quite limited.

El Salvador, on the other hand, likes to serve its big meal at midday, and it often consists of seemingly endless courses, at least to visiting Americans accustomed to an appetizer, main course, and dessert. *Chicha*, the national strong drink, is very popular with all classes of people. It is served straight, mixed into cocktails, and even used in cookery in the manner shown in the recipe for *gallo en chicha* (chicken in cider–hard, that is).

The people are fond of eating at odd times and places, and one is always tempted by between-meal snacks. In this vein there are many different and original cocktail appetizers. The nation produces some fair wine, of which *nancito* wine is the most interesting. It is made from a native fruit, *nance*, and is generally unavailable outside of El Salvador.

Nicaragua, the largest of the Central American republics, is swiftly losing its sleepy, banana-country atmosphere; improvements are being made at a rapid pace. The country's cuisine is closely akin to its neighbors', but with certain differences. The *sopa de mondongo* (tripe soup) is an unusual variation on a theme, and *maduro en gloria*, fascinatingly named "heavenly bananas," is likely to become your family favorite.

Having a large corn crop, the nation uses all the standard Mexican-style corn dishes. However, the local *tamales*, here called *nacatamales*, are a chicken- and pork-filled variety, a little too difficult to try at home. There are also *tamales* of shrimp, turkey, olives, and fish, and practically any other possible (or impossible) combination.

The country has several good soft drinks, such as *champola*, made from *guanábana*, a remarkable tropical fruit, and the enormously favored *tiste*, made of roast dried corn, pulverized cocoa, cold water, sugar, and cracked ice. *Tiste* is very palatable and refreshing in hot weather. Beer, locally made, is good, and there is also *aguardiente*, a crude type of brandy.

Costa Rica is a peaceful place, the people generally relaxed and easygoing. The countryside is filled with flowers and growing things, and although the nation is not rich, no one seems to mind. Frequent and unhurried dining is the rule here, with meals and refreshments seldom more than three hours apart. The city businessman of our own country, with his hastily gulped coffee for breakfast and a chicken sandwich for lunch, finds no counterpart in pleasure-loving Costa Rica.

A great favorite is *elote* (green corn boiled in the husks), which is a welcome change from the ever present rice. American influence is quite strong here, and American canned products, prepared breakfast cereals, and other food are well received.

Panama is divided into two parts by the Panama Canal. A tremendous international traffic in ships and men traverses the canal with great regularity, for Panama, like Singapore, is truly that cliché, the "crossroads of the world." Whereas Panama's neighbor to the north, Costa Rica, has an easygoing, *mañana* attitude, the Panamanians must be infected by that American virus, the urge to collect dollars; in any event, life in the cities of Panama moves at a swifter, more hustling pace than in any other Central American city.

Food is therefore much more cosmopolitan, since so many foreigners reach Panama's shores. Meals are Spanish, American, French, slightly international, and occasionally even Panamanian. The one favorite dish is the *sancocho*, the renowned soup-stew of all the Latin countries. Panama feature liquors extensively in its restaurants and hotels, since it caters to large numbers of seafaring visitors, who are seldom known to spend their shore leaves attending symphony concerts.

Panama City and Colón are great shopping spots, with some phenomenal values in French perfumes, imported china and crystal, liquors and wines from all over the world, plus a considerable amount of useless gimcracks at fancy prices.

NANCITO COCKTAIL

6 jiggers *nancito* wine or
   Dubonnet
½ teaspoon bitters

2 tablespoons lemon juice
Cracked ice
Ginger ale

Chill 6 tall glasses in the refrigerator for at least 1 hour. Combine the wine with the bitters and lemon juice and stir. Fill the glasses with cracked ice and divide the mixture evenly among the glasses. Fill with ginger ale, stir, and serve. *Serves 6.*

CLAM APPETIZER

PICANTE DE ALMEJAS

1 green pepper
1 onion
2 tomatoes, peeled
24 fresh clams, minced, or 2 cans
   minced clams, drained

2 teaspoons Worcestershire
   sauce

Remove the stem and seeds of the pepper. Chop in a bowl with the onion. Add the tomatoes and continue chopping until very fine. Add the clams and Worcestershire sauce. Chop until well blended. Correct seasoning. Serve cold, as a cocktail dip, or heap it on toast. *Makes about 2 cups.*

BLACK BEAN APPETIZER

BOQUITAS DE FRIJOLES

1 cup dried black beans
4 cups water
2 onions
3 cloves garlic
1 teaspoon salt

3 tablespoons olive oil
Vegetable oil for deep frying
Toast squares
Grated Parmesan cheese

Wash the beans thoroughly and discard any imperfect ones. Soak overnight in water to cover. Drain, and wash the beans again. Combine the beans, water, 1 onion, and the garlic in a saucepan; cook over medium heat until the beans are soft, about 2 hours. Purée in an electric blender or force through a sieve. Mix in the salt. Chop the remaining onion. Heat the olive oil in a skillet; add the chopped onion and the bean pulp, stirring constantly until the mixture is thick, about 5 minutes. Correct seasoning.

Heat deep oil to 375°. Drop tablespoons of the mixture into the fat and fry until they rise to the surface, about 2 to 3 minutes. Drain. Serve on individual slices of toast and sprinkle with grated cheese. In Guatemala, the *boquitas* are served on fried *tortillas,* a crisp, flat corn cake. *Makes about 30.*

SALVADORAN SEAFOOD SOUP

SOPA DE MARISCOS

¼ pound (1 stick) butter
1 stalk celery, sliced
3 onions, chopped
3 potatoes, cubed
2 quarts water
2 teaspoons salt
¼ teaspoon dried ground chili
    peppers

1 pound raw shrimp, shelled
    and deveined
1 dozen fresh clams, coarsely
    cut, or 1 can clams
¼ pound flaked crab meat

Melt the butter in a large saucepan and add the celery and onions. Sauté over low heat for 10 minutes but do not allow to brown. Add the potatoes, water, salt, and chili peppers. Cook for 15 minutes, stirring occasionally. Add the shrimp and clams and cook for 5 minutes. Add the crab meat and continue cooking for 5 minutes. Correct the seasoning. Serve with a very thin slice of lemon in each plate.

TRIPE SOUP

SOPA DE MONDONGO

4 pounds tripe
½ cup vinegar
1 calf's foot or 2 beef bones
4 quarts water
2 cloves garlic
3 onions, chopped
1 green pepper, sliced
2 cups cubed squash
3 ears of corn, cut into 1-inch
    pieces

2 sweet potatoes, peeled and cut
    into 1-inch cubes
2 white potatoes, peeled and cut
    into 1-inch cubes
2 cups coarsely shredded
    cabbage
⅓ cup raw rice
3 teaspoons salt
1 teaspoon freshly ground
    black pepper

Soak the tripe in vinegar, with water to cover, for 2 hours. Drain well, then rinse. Place the tripe, calf's foot, and 4 quarts of water in a saucepan. Bring to a boil and skim the top carefully of all foam. Cook over low heat for 4 hours. Strain the stock into a clean saucepan. Cut the tripe in small pieces and set aside.

Add the garlic, onions, green pepper, squash, corn, sweet potatoes, potatoes, cabbage, rice, salt, and pepper to the stock. Cook over medium heat for 45 minutes. Add the tripe and cook for 10 minutes. Correct seasoning. *Serves 8–10.*

Note: This is a very thick soup, almost suitable as a main course.

RED SNAPPER, CUSCATLECA STYLE

HUACHINANGO CUSCATLECA

5 tablespoons butter
3 tablespoons olive oil
3 medium onions, sliced
2 cloves garlic, minced
1 teaspoon salt
6 small red snappers or 6
  individual portions of snappers
  or 6 butterfish

1 tablespoon wine vinegar
½ cup dry white wine
½ teaspoon freshly ground
  black pepper

Heat the butter and olive oil in a large frying pan. Sauté the onions and garlic for 5 minutes over low heat, add the salt, and stir. Place the fish in the pan and brown well on both sides. Add the vinegar, wine, and pepper and cook over low heat for 15 minutes, turning the fish once. Serve hot with tiny boiled potatoes. *Serves 6.*

MEAT AND VEGETABLE STEW

SANCOCHO

2 onions, chopped
3 cloves garlic, minced
4 tablespoons chopped parsley
½ teaspoon crushed coriander
  seeds
1 bay leaf
3 tablespoons lemon or lime
  juice
1 tablespoon salt
1 teaspoon freshly ground
  black pepper
2 pounds pork, cut into 1-inch
  cubes

1 pound beef, cut into 1-inch
  cubes
2 ounces ham, cut into small
  cubes
1 tomato, chopped
3 potatoes, peeled and cubed
1½ cups cubed squash or
  pumpkin
1 Spanish-style sausage
  (*chorizo*), sliced ¼ inch thick
2 green bananas, sliced ½ inch
  thick

Combine the onions, garlic, parsley, coriander, and bay leaf in a bowl. Pound until very fine in texture. Add the lemon juice, salt, and pepper and mix to a smooth paste. Place the pork, beef, and ham in a saucepan and add water to cover. Add the onion mixture and stir well. Cover and cook over low heat for 1½ hours. Add the potatoes, squash, and sausage, and cook for 20 minutes. Add the banana slices and cook for 15 minutes. Correct seasoning. Serve in deep plates. *Serves 6–8.*

BLACK BEANS AND PORK

FRIJOLES A LA GUATEMALAN

3 cups dried black beans
4 teaspoons salt
6 pork chops, cut ¼ inch thick
¼ teaspoon freshly ground
   black pepper
2 cups boiling water
½ cup olive oil

2 cups chopped onions
2 cloves garlic, minced
½ teaspoon dried ground chili
   peppers
2 onions, thinly sliced
½ cup grated Cheddar cheese

Wash the beans. Cover with water and bring to a boil. Let soak 1 hour; drain, add fresh water to cover and bring to a boil. Cook over low heat 2 hours or until tender. Add 3 teaspoons salt after 1 hour. Drain if any liquid remains.

While the beans are cooking, season the chops with the pepper and remaining salt. Brown the chops lightly in a skillet; add the boiling water. Cover and cook over low heat 30 minutes. Cut the chops in half.

Heat the oil in a casserole; sauté the onions 10 minutes. Add the garlic, beans, undrained pork, and the chili peppers. Cover and cook over low heat 30 minutes. Arrange the sliced onions on top and sprinkle with the grated cheese. *Serves 6–8.*

ROAST YOUNG PIG

ASADO DE TEPESCUINTLE

3 cloves garlic, minced
2 teaspoons salt
1 teaspoon pepper
½ teaspoon thyme
6 pounds young loin of pork or
   1 very small suckling pig

3 onions, chopped
1½ cups red wine
½ cup olive oil
2 tablespoons flour
3 tablespoons butter
3 bananas, sliced

The day before the dish is to be served, combine the garlic, salt, pepper, and thyme. Rub into the pork very well. Place the pork in a bowl, or use a roasting pan for the suckling pig. Add the onions and 1 cup of the wine and place in the refrigerator overnight, basting as frequently as possible. Heat the olive oil in a roasting pan. Place the pork and marinade in it. Roast for 25 minutes per pound, basting frequently.

Remove the pan juices and place in a saucepan. Add the flour and stir until smooth. Add the remaining wine, stirring constantly until the boiling point is reached. Cook over low heat for 10 minutes, stirring

occasionally. Force through a sieve. Melt the butter in a skillet and fry
the bananas in it lightly. Carve the pork and arrange on a platter, with
the bananas around it. Pour the gravy over the meat and serve. *Serves
6–8.*

BRAISED RABBIT

CONEJO PINTADO

2 teaspoons salt	2 bay leaves
1 teaspoon freshly ground	½ cup wine vinegar
black pepper	Dash of tabasco sauce
2 cloves garlic, minced	2 small rabbits, disjointed
3 onions, chopped	4 tablespoons olive oil
2 tomatoes, chopped	1 cup beef broth
½ teaspoon thyme	¼ cup dry sherry

Combine the salt, pepper, garlic, onions, tomatoes, thyme, bay leaves,
vinegar, and tabasco sauce in a bowl. Mix well. Add the rabbit, turning
the pieces several times to coat them. Marinate in the refrigerator overnight.

Remove the rabbits from the marinade; reserve the marinade. Heat
the oil in a saucepan and add the rabbits. Brown well on all sides over
high heat. Add the marinade and broth. Cover and cook over low heat
for 1¼ hours, or until the rabbits are tender. Add the sherry and correct
seasoning. Cook over low heat for 10 minutes. Serve hot. *Serves 6–8.*

CHICKEN IN CIDER

GALLO EN CHICHA

¼ pound (1 stick) butter	3 tablespoons vinegar
3 onions, chopped fine	12 prunes, presoaked
2 teaspoons salt	12 pimento-stuffed olives
1 teaspoon freshly ground	3 tablespoons capers, drained
black pepper	12 small white onions
2 4-pound chickens, disjointed	4 potatoes, peeled and cut into
2 cloves garlic, minced	1-inch cubes
2 green peppers, sliced fine	6 sausages (Spanish style, if
¼ teaspoon dried ground chili	possible)
peppers	
2 cups hard cider, or 1 cup apple	
brandy and 1 cup cider	

Melt the butter in an earthenware casserole or a heavy pot. Add the
chopped onions and sauté until brown, stirring frequently. Remove

the onions and set aside. Combine the salt and pepper and rub into the chicken pieces. Place in the casserole and brown on all sides. Add the sautéed onions, garlic, green peppers, chili peppers, cider, and vinegar.

Cover and cook over low heat for 1 hour, or until chicken is almost tender. Add the prunes, olives, capers, and white onions and cook for 10 minutes. Cut the sausages into small pieces and fry in a separate saucepan for 5 minutes. Drain and add to the chicken. Cook for 10 more minutes, or until chicken is tender. *Serves 6–8.*

SQUASH IN BUTTER SAUCE

CALABAZA EN MANTEQUILLA

3 small yellow squash	¼ pound cream cheese
1 tablespoon salt	½ cup melted butter

Peel the squash and cut in half lengthwise. Be sure to use very small, young squash. Place them in a saucepan with water to cover and add the salt. Boil for 15 minutes and drain well.

Spread the cream cheese on each piece, then put them together again. Place the squash in a buttered baking dish. Pour the melted butter over them, turning to coat the squash on all sides. Bake in a 375° oven until lightly browned, about 20 minutes. Cut each squash in half at right angles to the previous cut. Serve hot. *Serves 6.*

TAMALE, COSTA RICAN MANNER

TAMALE TICOS

2 pounds boneless pork, cubed	1½ teaspoons freshly ground
2 cups water	black pepper
¼ pound (1 stick) butter	3 boiled potatoes, peeled
4 onions, chopped	4 slices fried bacon
5 cloves garlic, minced	2 cups corn kernels, drained
1 cup raw rice	1 cup canned chick-peas, drained
1½ cups boiling water	1 cup canned small green peas,
2 cups canned tomatoes	drained
2 green peppers, diced	¼ cup seedless raisins
4 teaspoons salt	3 pimentos, sliced thin

Combine the pork and water in a saucepan. Cook over medium heat for 1 hour. Melt half of the butter in a saucepan. Add half of the onions and garlic and sauté for 10 minutes, stirring frequently. Add the rice and cook over low heat for 5 minutes, stirring constantly. Add the boiling water, tomatoes, green peppers, 2 teaspoons of the salt, 1 teaspoon of the pepper, and the remaining butter. Cover and cook over low heat for 45 minutes.

Drain the pork and reserve the stock. Grind the pork, potatoes, bacon, and corn. Add the remaining onions, garlic, salt, and pepper. Add the reserved stock and mix well. Place in a saucepan and cook over low heat for 10 minutes, stirring almost constantly.

Add the chick-peas, peas, and raisins to the rice mixture and mix carefully. In a 3-quart buttered casserole or baking dish arrange successive layers of the pork mixture, followed by the rice mixture, until they are all used up. Arrange the pimentos on top. Cover the casserole. If the cover is not tight-fitting, cover with a piece of aluminum foil and then put the casserole cover on top. If a baking dish is used, tie a piece of aluminum foil over the top to make a tight seal. Place in a pan of hot water and bake in a 350° oven for 45 minutes. Serve hot. *Serves 6–8.*

Note: In Costa Rica tamales are made individually in plantain or banana leaves. If desired, wrap small quantities of the two mixtures in aluminum foil. Boil in salted water for about 30 minutes. A corn-meal dough similar to the hallacas of Venezuela may be used as a base, as well.

STRING BEANS WITH EGG

EJOTES ENVUELTOS EN HUEVO

2 pounds fresh string beans
2 cups water
1½ teaspoons salt

2 eggs, separated
Fat for deep-fat frying

Wash the string beans and cut off the ends, but leave them whole. Combine with the water and salt in a saucepan. Bring to a boil and cook over medium heat for 10 minutes, or until almost tender. Drain. Divide the beans into 6 bunches and tie each bunch together with white sewing thread.

Beat the egg yolks well. In another bowl, beat the egg whites until stiff but not dry and fold them into the yolks gently but thoroughly. Dip the bunches of string beans into the egg mixture, coating them on all sides. Heat fat in a deep saucepan to 375°. Drop the beans into the fat. Fry until light brown, about 2 minutes. Drain. Serve hot. *Serves 6–8.*

NICARAGUAN TROPICAL SALAD

ENSALADA TROPICAL

1 cup fresh or dried grated
  coconut
2 cups finely shredded cabbage

1 cup fresh pineapple cubes
1 cup mayonnaise

If dried coconut is used, soak it in cold water for 15 minutes before using. Drain well. Combine the coconut, cabbage, pineapple cubes, and mayonnaise. Mix well. Chill. Serve on lettuce leaves. *Serves 6–8.*

HEAVENLY BANANAS

MADURO EN GLORIA

6 firm bananas
4 tablespoons butter
¼ pound cream cheese

4 tablespoons sugar
1 teaspoon cinnamon
1 cup heavy cream

Peel the bananas and slice each one lengthwise. Melt the butter in a skillet. Brown the bananas quickly in the butter over high heat. Place half of the banana slices on the bottom of a buttered pie plate. Beat the cream cheese until very soft. Add the sugar and cinnamon, beating until light and smooth. Spread half of the mixture on the bananas. Place the remaining banana slices on top, then spread with the remainder of the cream cheese mixture. Pour the cream over the top.

Bake in a 375° oven for 20 minutes, or until almost all the cream is absorbed and the top is lightly browned. Do not allow all the cream to be absorbed, or the bananas will be too dry. Serve hot. If desired, some whipped cream may be served with the bananas. *Serves 6.*

ALMOND TART

TARTA DE ALMENDRAS

2 cups sifted flour
½ teaspoon salt
1 cup shortening
3 eggs
2 tablespoons ice water
¼ cup apricot or raspberry jam
4 tablespoons butter

4 tablespoons sugar
1 tablespoon cornstarch
⅓ cup ground almonds
1 teaspoon grated lemon rind
½ teaspoon almond extract
2 tablespoons brandy

Sift the flour and salt into a bowl. Cut in the shortening with a pastry blender or two knives. Beat 1 of the eggs and the ice water together, and add to the previous mixture, tossing lightly with a fork until a ball of dough is formed. Chill for at least 1 hour. Roll two-thirds of the dough about ¼ inch thick on a lightly floured surface. Place in a 9-inch pie plate. Spread with the jam. Preheat oven to 425°.

Cream the butter. Add the sugar and cornstarch, beating until light and fluffy. Add the remaining eggs, beating well. Add the almonds, lemon rind, almond extract, and brandy and mix well. Pour into the pie plate. Roll out the remaining dough. Cut into strips and arrange evenly on top of the pie. Bake in a 425° oven for 10 minutes. Reduce the oven temperature to 350° and bake 20 minutes longer, or until a cake tester comes out clean. Serve cold. *Serves 6–8.*

NICARAGUAN EGGNOG

ROMPOPE

2 egg yolks	½ stick cinnamon or ½ teaspoon
1 quart milk	powdered cinnamon
1 cup sugar	1 teaspoon grated lemon rind
1 tablespoon corn meal	1 teaspoon vanilla extract
½ cup rum or brandy	

Beat the egg yolks in a saucepan until light. Add the milk, sugar, and corn meal. Cook over low heat, stirring constantly, until the mixture is syrupy. Remove from the fire and beat until cool, about 10 minutes. In a bowl combine the rum, cinnamon, lemon rind, and vanilla and mix together. Set both mixtures aside for 3 hours. Strain the rum mixture. Combine with the milk mixture and chill. Serve ice cold. *Serves 8–10.*

MEXICO

Our good neighbor to the south has three rather unusual liquors—*pulque, mezcal,* and *tequila.* Interestingly enough, all three drinks are made from a cactus plant, the maguey. *Pulque,* truly the national strong drink, is a partially fermented beverage consumed in tremendous quantities by everyone. Most visitors do not appreciate its yeasty taste. Nonetheless, saloons are called *pulquerías. Mezcal* is a potent, distilled beverage. *Tequila* is the drink most liked by visitors. There is a ritual attached to drinking *tequila* that is still followed. The drink is swallowed by throwing it quickly to the back of the throat, a quartered lemon is sucked, and finally one licks at a mound of coarse salt previously placed on the back of the hand; there are those heretics who execute the process in reverse. It is not known whether this is done to improve the taste or to prevent the throat from catching on fire.

Mexico has a strong Indian heritage, and this is clearly indicated in the national cuisine. If we think of bread as a staple, consider Mexico, where *tortillas* (pancakes made of ground corn) form the basic item of practically every meal for almost the entire nation. When *tortillas* are deep-fat-fried they are called *tostados;* a *taco* is a *tortilla* filled with beans or meat and other spicy ingredients, and so on. Corn *tortillas* are a little too difficult to make at home, but they are often available in Mexican stores in the larger cities, and they may be purchased in cans in U.S. specialty food shops. Mexico is also the land of *frijoles* (beans), served in endless variations, hot and cold.

One of the high points of the cuisine is the famous *mole de guajolote* (turkey in a *mole* sauce). This dish contains many ingredients, but the most surprising one is chocolate! After you have tried it, you will understand why it has acquired a national character. Those who say that they couldn't possibly eat turkey with chocolate sauce are respectfully requested to sample this dish.

Many people do not realize that chocolate is native to Mexico and is enormously popular even today, although coffee has made strong inroads. Mexican chocolate, stirred to a froth with a specially designed wooden paddle, is quite different than our usual hot chocolate. There are many other soft drinks which are everyday affairs with the people, for they are fond of the habit of taking frequent refreshment. Beer of excellent quality is also important in Mexico.

Mexico City, a delightful capital with a wonderful climate, has many fine restaurants where food is served at reasonable prices. It must be admitted that few of them specialize in Mexican food, although there are exceptions. Many hotels serve at least a few popular Mexican dishes, featuring them as local specialties. Of course, throughout the city there are any number of restaurants offering Mexican dishes, although apparently the majority of the better places have succumbed to influences from the north, and serve American preparations.

Breakfast depends upon where you eat it; in Mexico City it is usually coffee and a roll, but the peasants like a substantial meal of beans and whatever else is available. The largest repast of the day is lunch, from 1:30 P.M. until about three-thirty or sometimes later. Dinner, often a smaller meal, practically never starts earlier than 8:30 P.M. and is in full swing in the better restaurants as late as ten-thirty! A familiar sight is that of a hungry American tourist in search of something to eat at about seven-thirty in the evening.

Not all of Mexico consists of Mexico City, Taxco, and Cuernavaca, though these are well worth seeing. Most Americans find Acapulco tremendously interesting, even though it is often quite hot. In recent years, Yucatán has become enormously popular with American visitors, and the area is growing swiftly. Although the area around Mérida is becoming better known to tourists, it's at the lovely beach resort of Cozumel that the tourists flock, for the swimming is unsurpassed, and the weather remarkably good from October through April.

SPICY TOMATO DRINK

SANGRITA

½ cup orange juice
½ cup tomato juice
3 tablespoons lemon juice
7 drops Tabasco

⅛ teaspoon salt
Dash of freshly ground
   black pepper

Mix all the ingredients together and chill. Serve alone or as a chaser for tequila. *Serves 2.*

AVOCADO DIP

GUACAMOLE

3 ripe avocados
6 scallions (green onions),
   chopped
¾ cup peeled chopped tomatoes
2 teaspoons chili powder
3 jalapeña peppers, finely
   chopped, or ¼ teaspoon
   Tabasco

1½ teaspoons salt
2 tablespoons lemon juice
2 teaspoons minced cilantro,
   fresh coriander, or Chinese
   parsley (optional)

Peel the avocados, and mash the pulp. Mix in the scallions, tomatoes, chili powder, jalapeñas, salt, lemon juice, and cilantro, if used. Taste for seasoning. If the mixture is not to be served at once, put the avocado pit in the center (to prevent the avocado from turning dark) and cover with plastic wrap.

Serve as a dip with corn chips, or on shredded lettuce as a first course or salad. *Makes about 3½ cups.*

TORTILLA SOUP

SOPA DE TORTILLAS

12 tortillas (available frozen or in cans)
¼ cup vegetable oil
1 cup chopped onions
¼ cup canned tomato sauce

2 quarts chicken or beef broth
1 teaspoon minced fresh coriander (Chinese parsley), or parsley
⅓ cup grated Parmesan cheese

Cut the tortillas into very narrow strips.

Heat the oil in a saucepan; fry the tortillas in it until crisp. Drain. To the oil remaining in the pan, add the onions; cook 5 minutes. Add the tomato sauce; cook 5 minutes. Mix in the broth, coriander or parsley, and tortillas. Bring to a boil and cook over medium heat 30 minutes. Serve in bowls sprinkled with cheese. *Serves 6.*

PICKLED SHRIMP

ESCABECHE DE CAMARONES

2 pounds raw shrimp, shelled and deveined
¾ cup olive oil
¾ cup chopped onions
2 cloves garlic, minced
½ teaspoon freshly ground black pepper
1 teaspoon paprika

2 teaspoons salt
½ cup wine vinegar
¼ teaspoon dry mustard
2 teaspoons crushed cumin seed
¼ teaspoon dried ground chili peppers
2 onions, thinly sliced

Wash and dry the shrimp. Heat ¼ cup of the oil in skillet; sauté the onions and garlic 5 minutes. Add the shrimp, pepper, paprika, and 1 teaspoon salt; sauté 5 minutes, stirring frequently. Cool 10 minutes.

Mix together the vinegar, mustard, cumin, chili peppers, and the remaining oil and salt. Arrange layers of the shrimp and sliced onions in a bowl or jar and pour the marinade over all. Marinate in the refrigerator 48 hours basting and turning several times. Serve on shredded lettuce. *Serves 6–8.*

COCONUT SOUP

SOPA DE COCO

2 cups shredded fresh or dried   4 cups chicken broth
  unsweetened coconut   2 egg yolks
2 cups milk   ¼ cup heavy cream

Combine the coconut and milk in a saucepan. Bring to a boil, remove
from the heat, and soak for 30 minutes. Strain and combine the coconut
milk with the broth. Cook over very low heat for 20 minutes. Beat the
egg yolks and the cream in a bowl. Gradually add 2 cups of the soup,
beating constantly to prevent curdling. Return to the balance of the
soup and beat well. Continue cooking for 5 minutes over low heat but
do not allow to boil. *Serves 8–10.*

STUFFED GREEN PEPPERS

CHILES RELLENOS

¼ cup olive oil   6 large green peppers
¾ pound ground beef   ¼ cup flour
3 tablespoons tomato paste   2 eggs, beaten
2 cloves garlic, minced   1 cup fine dry bread crumbs
2 teaspoons chili powder   Vegetable oil for deep-fat frying
1 teaspoon salt
3 tablespoons ground almonds
  or peanuts

Heat the oil in a skillet and add the beef, tomato paste, garlic, chili
powder, salt, and ground nuts. Sauté over low heat for 5 minutes,
stirring constantly. Correct seasoning. Set aside. Remove the stems and
seeds of the peppers, leaving an opening large enough to stuff. Place
the peppers in a saucepan with water to cover. Bring to a boil and cook
10 minutes. Drain and cool for 5 minutes.

Stuff the peppers with the meat mixture. Sprinkle the flour on the
tops of the peppers at the open ends. Dip each pepper in the beaten
eggs, so that it is completely moistened. Then dip in the bread crumbs,
once again in the eggs, and again in the bread crumbs. Heat deep oil
in a heavy saucepan to 375°. Place one or two peppers in the fat at a
time. Fry until browned, then drain. Serve hot. *Serves 6.*

ROAST PORK WITH PEPPERS AND SAUSAGES

LOMO DE PUERCO EN SALSA RAJA

8-rib loin of pork
2 teaspoons salt
½ teaspoon freshly ground
   black pepper
2 cloves garlic, minced
3 tomatoes, diced, or 1½ cups
   drained canned tomatoes
¾ cup chopped onions

2 cups beef broth
6 Spanish or Italian sausages,
   sliced
3 tablespoons olive oil
4 green peppers, sliced thin
   lengthwise
1 cup sliced onions

Rub the pork with a mixture of the salt, pepper, and garlic. Place on a rack in a roasting pan. Roast in a 425° oven 30 minutes. Pour off the fat and remove rack. Add the tomatoes, chopped onions, and broth. Reduce heat to 350° and roast 1½ hours longer. Baste frequently. Brown the sausages in a skillet; drain and add to the pork; roast 15 minutes longer. Heat the oil in the skillet; sauté the green peppers and sliced onions 10 minutes.

Carve the pork and skim fat from gravy. Pour the gravy over the pork and cover with the sautéed vegetables. *Serves 6–8.*

STUFFED TORTILLAS

ENCHILADAS DE POLLO

3 tablespoons olive oil
¾ cup chopped onions
2 cups peeled chopped tomatoes
1 cup chopped green peppers
1¼ teaspoons salt
⅛ teaspoon dried ground chili
   peppers
2 cups coarsely chopped cooked
   chicken

¾ cup chopped pimento-stuffed
   olives
16 tortillas (see recipe in this
   section, or canned or frozen)
3 eggs, beaten
1½ cups vegetable oil
Freshly grated Parmesan cheese

Heat the oil in a saucepan; sauté the onions 5 minutes. Add the tomatoes, green peppers, salt, and chili peppers. Bring to a boil and cook over low heat 15 minutes, stirring frequently.

Mix together the chicken and olives. Place a tablespoon of the mixture on one side of each tortilla, fold over, and fasten with toothpicks. Dip the tortillas, one by one, in the beaten eggs. Heat the oil in a 7-inch skillet, and fry each tortilla until browned on both sides. Drain, remove the toothpicks and arrange them in a baking dish. Pour the tomato sauce over them and sprinkle with the cheese. Bake on the middle level of a preheated 425° oven 10 minutes or until bubbly and the cheese melted and lightly browned. *Serves 8–16.*

TORTILLAS

3 cups instant Masa Harina	1⅔ cups water (about)
1¼ teaspoons salt	

Masa Harina is available in packages put up by Quaker Oats. If you can't find it, use half very fine corn meal, and half corn flour. (Put the corn meal in an electric blender to make it even finer, or sift it through a fine sifter.) Combine the Masa Harina and salt in a bowl. Gradually add 1¼ cups of the water, stirring constantly, then knead with the fingers, and, spoon by spoon, add just enough of the remaining water, until a firm but not sticky dough is formed. Break off walnut-size balls, press them into 5-inch circles between two sheets of wax paper. Stack between sheets of wax paper.

Heat a 7-inch heavy skillet, or griddle, and put one tortilla at a time on it. Cook over medium heat 2 minutes, turn over with a spatula, and cook 2 minutes longer. Stack the tortillas on foil, cover, and keep warm in a 250° oven while preparing the balance. *Makes about 16.*

Note: Frozen and canned tortillas are available, and can be used for making enchiladas.

TURKEY WITH SPICY SAUCE

MOLE DE GUAJOLATE

8-pound turkey, disjointed	2 cinnamon sticks
4 cups water	2 teaspoons black peppercorns
1 whole onion	½ cup seedless raisins
3 teaspoons salt	1 cup shelled peanuts
⅓ cup sesame seeds	2 tomatoes, chopped
½ cup lard or vegetable oil	2 bananas
½ teaspoon crushed dried chili	2 ounces (squares) unsweetened
peppers	chocolate
12 whole cloves garlic	3 cups chicken broth
1 cup chopped onions	

Clean and wash the turkey. In a saucepan, combine the turkey, water, whole onion, and half the salt. Bring to a boil, cover loosely, and cook over medium heat 45 minutes. Prepare the sauce meanwhile.

Put the sesame seeds in a small skillet and place over low heat until browned, shaking the pan frequently.

Heat the lard or oil in a skillet; add the chili peppers, garlic, chopped onions, cinnamon sticks, peppercorns, raisins, peanuts, tomatoes, and bananas. Cook 15 minutes, stirring frequently. Cool 15 minutes. Run the mixture in an electric blender with the chocolate and half the sesame seeds, or put through the fine blade of a food chopper.

Discard the whole onion from the turkey mixture. Pour the stock from the turkey and chicken broth into the chocolate mixture. Bring to a boil and cook over low heat 20 minutes. Add the turkey and remaining salt. Cook 15 minutes. Serve sprinkled with the remaining sesame seeds and with rice and *frijoles refritos* (see recipe in this section). *Serves 6–8.*

Note: If you like really spicy foods, a little more chili peppers can be added.

EGGS WITH SAUSAGE SAUCE

HUEVOS RANCHEROS

2 tablespoons olive oil	2 pimentos, cut julienne
¾ cup sliced onions	1½ teaspoons salt
¾ cup chopped green peppers	½ teaspoon freshly ground black
1 clove garlic, minced	pepper
1½ cups chopped tomatoes	4 eggs
3 chorizos (Spanish sausages), sliced	½ cup grated American cheese

Heat the oil in a skillet; sauté the onions, green pepper, and garlic 5 minutes. Mix in the tomatoes and sausages; cook over low heat 5 minutes. Mix in the pimentos (reserve a few pieces) and half the salt and pepper. Turn into a shallow greased baking dish or two or four individual shallow baking dishes. Break the eggs over the sauce. Season the eggs with the remaining salt and pepper, sprinkle with the cheese, and garnish with the reserved pimento strips. Bake in a 425° oven 10 minutes or until eggs are cooked the way you like them. *Serves 2–4.*

REFRIED BEANS

FRIJOLES REFRITOS

1 pound dried red or pink beans	½ teaspoon dried ground chili
6 cups water	peppers
1½ cups chopped onions	½ cup lard, bacon drippings, or
2 cloves garlic, minced	vegetable oil
2 teaspoons salt	

Wash the beans until the water runs clean. Put the beans in a heavy saucepan, cover with water, and bring to a boil. Remove from the heat, and let the beans soak 1 hour. Drain, and add the 6 cups water and half the onions and garlic. Bring to a boil, cover loosely, and cook over low heat 2 hours. Add the salt, chili peppers, and 1 tablespoon of the fat. Cook 30 minutes longer (mixing frequently), or until the beans are tender. If all the liquid isn't evaporated, drain them. Mash the beans with a potato masher.

Heat the remaining fat in a large skillet; add the remaining onions and garlic. Sauté 5 minutes. Stir in the beans and cook, stirring frequently for 10 minutes. Serve as an accompaniment to main dishes. *Serves 6–8.*

BAKED DOUGHNUTS

PUCHAS

6 egg yolks
¼ cup sifted sugar
1¾ cups sifted flour
¼ cup brandy

2 egg whites
2 tablespoons confectioners' sugar

Beat the egg yolks in a bowl until lemon-colored. Add the sugar and again beat well. Gradually add the flour and brandy alternately. Mix well. Roll the dough into a long thin strip and break off 3-inch pieces. Form each piece into a ring. Place on a greased baking sheet. Bake in a 350° oven for 20 minutes, or until lightly browned.

While the doughnuts are baking, beat the egg whites in a bowl until stiff but not dry. Fold in the confectioners' sugar gently. When the doughnuts are lightly browned, spread the egg-white mixture over the top of each doughnut. Bake 3 minutes longer. *Makes about 20.*

UNITED STATES

It is not a simple matter to explain the food of this country to a person who has never visited our shores. Most foreigners, particularly Europeans, complain exceedingly about the monotony of our meals, the lack of original dishes, the limited menus in our homes, and the few good restaurants where satisfactory meals may be obtained. Perhaps they are partially correct, because it is true that the average restaurant does not turn out inspired food and most menus stay close to the steak, chops, and chicken routine. Perhaps these visitors are also somewhat wrong, because there are many specialties in this country that are unexcelled anywhere in the world.

The cuisine of the United States may be divided into many different subdivisions, but a reasonable, albeit arbitrary, grouping might be: Eastern, Southern, New Orleans Creole, Southwestern, and Western. Naturally a substantial argument may be advanced by those who would, for example, extol the virtues of cooking in the style of Maine, the Pennsylvania Dutch, and the Middle West.

In the East, there are many fine specialties, such as clam fritters, clam chowder, blueberry pancakes, Philadelphia ice cream, Boston baked beans and brown bread, Indian pudding, New England boiled dinner, apple and mince pies, and cranberry sauce. Concerning clam chowder, a few words of explanation are undoubtedly in order. Apparently there is a long-standing war between the devotees of two different schools of thought—the Maine and the Manhattan styles. In Maine clam chowder is made with milk or cream, plus potatoes and salt pork. In New York it is prepared with tomatoes and usually without milk or cream. It is feared that the two warring factions will never be reconciled, although Maine has not seceded from the Union on this account, as was once reported.

In the South, advantage is taken of the natural resources of the sea and the soil. In Maryland and the Tidelands many delicious preparations are made of crab, such as crab bisques, crab stews, crab cakes, and so forth. In Virginia the local peanut-fed hams and bacon play an important part in the diet of the people. Aged country hams are a specialty of North Carolina. It is somewhat farther south that one finds the famous Southern dishes—fried chicken, hominy, black-eyed peas, spoon bread, corn dodgers, pecan pie, Brunswick stew, corn pone, and old-fashioned shortcake.

The Creole food of New Orleans is unlike anything else in the country. It is here that European visitors to our country more often than not find food to their liking, if indeed they ever do find any. New Orleans dishes bear little or no resemblance to those of any other part of the United States. Somehow this style of food survives in the state of Louisiana, with its headquarters in New Orleans. For those to whom the early history of the United States is hazy, it may be appropriate to recall that France once owned and settled what is now Louisiana; the food, customs, and language of France have survived to the present day. Good use is made of the local seafood, including shrimp, crabs, and oysters. This is the only place in the world where authentic gumbos, *filés*, and jambalayas are to be had, although these dishes have spread throughout the Caribbean. There are about a half dozen famous restaurants in New Orleans where Creole food may be enjoyed in the perfection of fresh ingredients and authentic spices, prepared by cooks who know what to do with them.

The southwestern part of the United States has a proud history. Texas, particularly, has contributed heavily to this country in many ways, and its cuisine has made almost as deep an impression on the nation as a whole as has its citizenry. Texas was once part of Mexico, and its food has been strongly influenced by this early Mexican heritage. However, chili con carne, generally thought to be Mexican in origin, is really a Texas dish, and is practically unknown in Mexico, except in border towns catering to food-conscious American tourists in search of authentic Mexican food. Arizona and New Mexico, too, have contributed to our national cuisine.

On the west coast, outdoor living has dictated the food customs of these healthy, vigorous people. Because of the general excellence of the climate (all hail, California Chambers of Commerce!) and the increasingly popular American custom of dining outdoors, great local emphasis is placed on fresh vegetables, fruits, melons, and charcoal-broiled steaks and chops. Equally as important as the barbecued meats are the local salads, one of which, the Caesar salad, has been nationally accepted. In California it is customary to serve the salad before the main course; thus it actually becomes an appetizer, which inevitably startles all foreign visitors who have just become reconciled to potato chips and cheeseburgers.

In the northwestern part of the country the giant crabs are highly regarded as a delicacy and are now being exported to the rest of the nation. The renowned money-shell, razor, and giant geoduck clams are truly excellent.

But all of the above omits the Middle West, which has contributed substantially to the national diet. The region has good fish from the Great Lakes. Particularly important are dishes based on corn, for it is here that corn is grown by the thousands of acres. Strangers to our country are astonished at corn on the cob, since in most countries corn is looked upon as food for cattle. Attention, all French skeptics: if the corn is very young and freshly picked, and boiled briefly in milk with a little sugar, it will be found to be a true gourmet's delight, so help us Brillat-Savarin.

This discussion has concerned itself thus far with what is good and right with our food. What of those visitors to our country who find things wrong with our food, our meals, and our restaurants? The usual complaints concern our factory-made white breads, which they find tasteless; possibly this complaint is justified, but there is certainly an increase in the number of whole-grain breads, and better-quality white breads. Another point usually mentioned is that our beef is excellent but our lamb and veal inferior. This position is probably well taken. Beef *is* better here; but our lamb and veal do not usually match the foreign cuts, mainly because of our laws regarding the age at which cattle may be slaughtered.

Our food is at its worst when it attempts to imitate French food; it is at its best when it is based on our own local specialties. Most foreign visitors look for French food and are inevitably disappointed except in a very few New York City restaurants. Most of our French restaurants are about as French as Paris, Kentucky. Foreigners would do better not to criticize our food until after they have tried our truly native dishes. Some few visiting gourmets have pronounced our specialties excellent, but they have nothing but scorn for the national habits of putting mayonnaise on everything cold and a floury white sauce on anything hot.

Not too long ago children were being told that it was impolite to discuss food; this was at a time when children in Europe were listening to endless dissertations on the arts of dining and the table. Times have changed in our country, and probably in this regard, for the better. It is now considered proper to discuss food, and there is a tremendous tidal wave of interest in food and its preparation. This awakening has not been limited to the big cities, for it is just as strong in the small communities that dot the nation.

Our meal habits are quite different from those of most of the rest of the world, and therefore call for a little discussion. In Europe and South America the average breakfast is merely coffee and a piece of bread. In the United States breakfast is often a substantial meal consisting of fruit juice, hot or cold cereal, eggs and bacon, toast, and coffee. But of late, particularly in the larger cities on the two coasts, breakfast has been simplified, on the order of the European breakfast, with the addition of fruit juice. Possibly the smallness of this meal has been responsible for the development of what is known as the "coffee break," now a widespread custom of many business houses at 11 A.M.

Lunch in the larger towns and cities is usually a sandwich and a cup of coffee, with the possible addition of ice cream or pie for dessert. The custom of eating a large meal in the middle of the day still survives in certain parts of the country; where this is so, the evening meal is referred to as supper. The so-called "cocktail hour" has spread all over the world, so that no further discussion of this custom is required. Dinner, the evening meal, comes anywhere from about 6 P.M. to 8:30 P.M.; in general, earlier in the smaller communities and later in the more populous ones. As a recent development, it should be reported that in the largest cities, notably in New York (but also in other communities), there has been a tendency to push the dinner hour to a later time, after 9 P.M. This trend, which follows that of the major cities of Europe, is particularly noticeable on weekend evenings, when restaurants are crowded as late as 11 P.M.

A fairly large quantity of hard liquor is consumed before meals, straight or in cocktails; after dinner it is taken in the form of highballs. While scotch whisky is a popular drink on the east coast, the rest of the nation apparently prefers rye or bourbon, both of which contain considerable alcohol; the principal difference between them is that rye is made from wheat, whereas bourbon is derived from corn.

Wines are growing steadily in importance in this country and are produced in abundance in the states of California, Ohio, and New York. Formerly the wine producers had the unfortunate habit of calling their products "New York State sauterne," "California burgundy," etc., which was unfair both to the sauterne and burgundy of Europe and to the unique products of our own vineyards. At the present time most wine producers and their customers have become educated to the fact that the wines of this country do not duplicate those of Europe but are often new and original wine creations in their own right. In general, however, it must be admitted that wine is not yet an everyday household item. Beer, on the other hand, is widely appreciated and well received throughout the land.

No description of food in the United States should omit those two products of our roadside stands—the "hot dog" and the hamburger. These popular snacks are consumed by the million in our smallest hamlets and our most sophisticated communities. They are truly a bit of Americana.

If the national drink of our country is not a glass of cold milk or a chocolate malted, then it must inevitably be a cup of coffee. Served with cream and sugar, in defiance of experts the world over who advocate only unsweetened, black coffee, it is the one beverage that almost everyone drinks for breakfast, lunch and dinner. To end on a note of complete confusion calculated to send our theoretical French gourmet screaming into the streets, in the Boston and New England area generally, coffee is served with the main course! Naturally no gourmet would permit such a mixture of flavors in his native France.

OLD-FASHIONED COCKTAIL

EASTERN

6 dots sugar	6 slices orange
6 dashes bitters	6 maraschino cherries
12 cubes ice	6 large jiggers rye or bourbon
6 pieces lemon peel	

Use the 5- or 6-ounce glass commonly known as an old-fashioned glass. Place a lump of sugar in each and splash the bitters on the sugar. Mash the sugar with a spoon. If desired, add a tablespoon of cold water to each glass; this will aid in mashing the sugar. Place 2 ice cubes in each glass. Add the lemon peel, orange, and cherry. Pour in the rye or bourbon and serve with a muddler or stirring rod. If desired, a stick of fresh pineapple may be added. *Serves 6.*

NEW ENGLAND CLAM CHOWDER

EASTERN

1 quart hard clams or 2
   10½-ounce cans minced clams
¼ pound bacon, diced
3 onions, chopped fine
1 cup boiling water

1 cup bottled clam juice
3 potatoes, peeled and diced fine
½ teaspoon white pepper
3 cups milk
2 cups heavy cream

Wash, scrub, and open the clams, reserving all the juice. Grind the clams in a food chopper, again reserving the juice. Fry the bacon in a large saucepan until half cooked; pour off most of the fat. Add the onions and sauté until brown. Add the boiling water, all the clam juice, potatoes, and pepper. Cover and cook over medium heat for 20 minutes. Add the clams, milk, and cream, mixing gently. Cook over low heat for 15 minutes but do not allow the soup to boil. Correct seasoning. No salt is provided in the recipe, as clams are usually salty. *Serves 8–10.*

MANHATTAN CLAM CHOWDER

EASTERN

1 quart hard clams
¼ pound salt pork, diced
4 onions, chopped
2 cups diced tomatoes or 2 cups
   canned tomatoes
1½ quarts water
2 cups bottled clam juice
¾ cup coarsely chopped celery

4 tablespoons chopped parsley
2 bay leaves
½ teaspoon thyme
2 small potatoes, peeled and
   diced
1 teaspoon freshly ground
   black pepper

Scrub the clams thoroughly and open them, reserving all the juice. Grind the clams, again saving all the juice. Place the salt pork in a large saucepan and cook until well browned. Discard the pieces of pork. Add the onions to the pork fat and sauté for 10 minutes. Add the tomatoes, water, clam juice, celery, parsley, bay leaves, and thyme. Cover and and cook for 2 hours. Add the potatoes and cook for 20 minutes. Add the clams and pepper. Cook for 5 minutes. Correct seasoning. No salt is included in this recipe, as clams are usually salty. *Serves 8–10.*

BOSTON BAKED BEANS

EASTERN

3 cups dried pea beans	¾ teaspoon dry mustard
½ pound fat salt pork, sliced	3 tablespoons dark brown sugar
1 teaspoon salt	2 tablespoons molasses

Wash the beans in several changes of water and discard any imperfect ones. Place in a deep saucepan and soak in water to cover overnight. Drain and cover with fresh water. Cook over low heat for 45 minutes. Drain well.

Pour boiling water over the pork and drain. Place a layer of pork on the bottom of a deep pot, preferably earthenware. Pour half the beans over the pork and place the rest of the pork on top. Add the remaining beans. Mix the salt, mustard, brown sugar, and molasses together with a little hot water. Pour the mixture over the beans and add enough water to cover the beans. Cover the pot. Bake in a 275° oven for 8 hours, removing the cover for the last hour of baking time. If beans appear to be too dry, add a little more water. *Serves 6–8.*

GRIDDLECAKES

EASTERN

2 cups sifted flour	2 eggs, beaten
3 teaspoons baking powder	1½ cups milk
1 teaspoon salt	4 tablespoons butter, melted
2 tablespoons sugar	

Sift the flour, baking powder, salt, and sugar together. Beat the eggs and milk and add to the flour mixture. Beat until very smooth. Add the melted butter and beat again.

Heat an unbuttered griddle or, if a griddle is not available, use a lightly buttered frying pan. Pour small amounts of the batter onto the griddle and cook until brown on the bottom and air spaces begin to form on the top. Turn the griddlecake over only once, and cook until done on the other side. Serve hot, with plenty of butter and warm maple syrup. *Serves 6–8.*

INDIAN BREAD

EASTERN

½ cup sifted flour	2 eggs, beaten
1½ cups yellow corn meal	1 cup sour cream
½ teaspoon salt	1 teaspoon baking soda
4 tablespoons sugar	1½ cups milk

Preheat oven to 400°.

Sift the flour, corn meal, salt, and sugar into a bowl. Add the eggs and sour cream and beat until very smooth. Dissolve the baking soda in the milk. Add to the previous mixture and stir well. Pour into a buttered 9-inch loaf pan. Bake in a 400° oven for 25 minutes, or until a cake tester comes out clean and the bread is lightly browned. *Makes one 9-inch loaf.*

CHEESECAKE, NEW YORK STYLE

EASTERN

½ pound (2 sticks) butter	¼ cup sugar
1 cup sifted flour	1 egg yolk
Dash of salt	

Place the butter in a bowl. Add the flour, salt, and sugar. Blend together, using one hand. Add the egg yolk and continue mixing with the hand until well blended. Wrap in wax paper and place in the refrigerator for 1 hour. Preheat oven to 400°. Roll out one third of the dough on a lightly floured surface, to form a 9-inch circle. Place on the bottom of a 9-inch spring-form pan. Bake in a 400° oven for 10 minutes.

Remove from the oven. Butter the sides of the spring form and fasten it in place over the base. Roll the remaining dough in long strips to fit the sides and press into place, joining the bottom edges. Preheat oven to 475°. Now prepare the filling:

2½ pounds cream cheese	1 teaspoon vanilla extract
1¾ cups sugar	6 eggs
2 tablespoons flour	½ cup heavy cream
¼ teaspoon salt	

Beat the cheese with a rotary beater until light and fluffy, using an electric mixer if available. Add the sugar, flour, salt, and vanilla gradually, beating well. Add the eggs one at a time, beating well after each addition. Add the cream and blend well. Pour into the prepared pan. Bake in a 475° oven for 10 minutes. At the end of 10 minutes, reduce oven temperature to 225° and bake 1 hour longer.

Turn off the oven and open the door. It is not advisable to have windows open in the vicinity of the stove, as they may create drafts and affect the cake. Allow to remain in the oven for 5 minutes. Remove from the oven carefully and allow to cool in a place completely free of drafts. The cake will take about 2 to 3 hours to cool completely. When cooled, run a knife around the edge carefully and remove the sides of the spring form. Do not remove the bottom.

This cake is extremely rich, and small portions may be served. It is often served with coffee late in the evening. It is too heavy for dessert with a dinner, unless the meal has been a very light one. *Serves 12–16.*

MINT JULEP

SOUTHERN

12 sprigs fresh mint	Cracked ice
6 dots sugar	12 jiggers bourbon
6 tablespoons water	

Use a 12- or 16-ounce silver goblet or a tall glass for each individual drink. Crush a sprig of mint against each glass or goblet, then discard the mint. Dissolve a lump of sugar in a tablespoon of water in each glass. Half fill each glass with cracked ice. Add 2 jiggers of bourbon and stir gently.

Garnish each glass with a sprig of fresh mint.

Note: Apparently no two people agree on the proper method of making a mint julep. However, the recipe above is a popular one.

OYSTER STEW

SOUTHERN

3 tablespoons butter	1 teaspoon salt
2 tablespoons flour	¼ teaspoon white pepper
4 cups milk, scalded	1½ quarts shucked oysters
1 cup heavy cream, scalded	

In the top of a double boiler melt the butter and flour over direct heat, stirring constantly until the mixture is smooth. Gradually add the milk and cream, stirring constantly until the boiling point is reached. Add the salt and pepper and stir. Remove from the heat. Drain the oysters and add the liquid to the milk mixture, mixing well. Place over hot water and cook for 15 minutes. Add the oysters, stir, and continue cooking until the oysters curl at the edges. Place a lump of butter in each individual soup plate and pour in the stew, dividing the oysters as evenly as possible. *Serves 4–6.*

BAKED HAM, SOUTHERN STYLE

SOUTHERN

10-pound smoked ham	2 cloves garlic
2 tablespoons whole cloves	1 onion
1 stick cinnamon or 2 teaspoons powdered cinnamon	1 cup dark brown sugar
	2 teaspoons dry mustard
1 cup sugar	¾ cup water
1¼ cups vinegar	

Wash and scrub the ham thoroughly and place in a large saucepan with water to cover. Add 1 tablespoon of the cloves, the cinnamon, sugar, 1 cup of the vinegar, the garlic, and onion. Bring to a boil, reduce heat to medium and simmer for 2½ hours. Remove from heat and let cool for 3 hours.

Remove the skin from the ham and then dry the ham. Place the remaining cloves on the fat side of the ham at more or less regular intervals. Combine the brown sugar and dry mustard and rub into the ham well. Place in a baking pan and add the remaining vinegar and the water. Bake in a 350° oven for 1 hour, basting frequently after the first 30 minutes. *Serves 8–10.*

SOUTHERN FRIED CHICKEN

SOUTHERN

2 3-pound frying chickens, disjointed	½ teaspoon freshly ground black pepper
2 eggs	1 cup flour
1 cup milk	Vegetable oil for deep-fat frying
2 teaspoons salt	

Clean the chickens carefully. Beat the eggs well, add the milk, salt, and pepper, and mix well. Place the chicken pieces in the mixture, making sure that each individual piece is coated. Allow to stand for 10 minutes in the mixture. Remove the chicken and roll in the flour. Heat the deep oil to 360°. Place a few pieces of chicken in a frying basket and lower it into the fat. Fry until golden brown on all sides. As the pieces are re-

moved, keep them hot in the oven until all of the chicken is fried. Serve
with a cream gravy prepared as follows:

2 tablespoons of the fat in which the chicken was fried	1 tablespoon flour
	1 cup light cream, scalded

Place the fat in a saucepan. Add the flour and stir until smooth. Very
gradually add the scalded cream, stirring constantly until the boiling
point is reached. Correct the seasoning. Serve on top of the pieces of
chicken. *Serves 6–8.*

BRUNSWICK STEW

SOUTHERN

5-pound stewing chicken, disjointed	3 potatoes, peeled and cubed
1 pound beef, cut into 1-inch cubes	2 tablespoons catsup
2 quarts water	2 stalks celery
3 large onions, chopped	2 fresh tomatoes, chopped
1 teaspoon salt	1 cup canned corn kernels, drained
½ pound fresh or 1 cup frozen lima beans	4 tablespoons butter
¼ pound fresh or frozen okra	4 tablespoons sugar
	2 tablespoons vinegar
	Dash of cayenne pepper

Clean the chicken carefully. Place in a large saucepan with the beef,
water, onions, and salt. Cook over medium heat for 2 hours. Remove
the chicken and meat. Cut the chicken from the bones and set aside.

Add the lima beans, okra, potatoes, catsup, celery, tomatoes, corn
kernels, and butter to the soup. Cook for 30 minutes, stirring occasionally.
Return the meat and chicken to the soup and cook until most, but not all,
of the liquid is absorbed. Add the sugar, vinegar, and cayenne pepper
and cook 5 minutes longer, stirring frequently. Serve in deep dishes.
Serves 4–6.

SPOON BREAD

SOUTHERN

1½ cups white or yellow corn meal	5 tablespoons butter
1½ teaspoons salt	1½ cups milk
1 teaspoon sugar	½ cup light cream
1½ cups boiling water	4 eggs
	1 tablespoon baking powder

Preheat oven to 350°.

Combine the corn meal, salt, and sugar. Bring the water to an active boil in a saucepan and add the corn meal mixture slowly and gradually, stirring constantly. Remove from the heat. Add the butter, milk, and cream and stir well. Beat the eggs until light in color and add, again stirring steadily. Add the baking powder and mix well. Butter a 2-quart ovenproof dish and pour the mixture into it. The dish should not be more than two thirds full, to allow for expansion. Bake in a 350° oven for 35 minutes. Serve in place of potatoes. *Serves 6–8.*

PECAN PIE

SOUTHERN

1¼ cups sifted flour	⅔ cup dark brown sugar
¼ teaspoon salt	¾ cup dark corn syrup
⅓ cup shortening	3 eggs, beaten
3 tablespoons ice water	1 teaspoon vanilla extract
¼ cup butter	1 cup shelled pecan halves

Sift the flour and salt together. Cut in the shortening with a pastry blender or two knives until the consistency of coarse corn meal. Add the ice water and stir together lightly. Shape into a ball, wrap in wax paper, and chill for at least 1 hour. Roll out the dough to fit a 9-inch pie plate. Place in the pie plate and flute the edges.

Preheat oven to 400°. Cream the butter and sugar together until light and fluffy. Add the corn syrup, eggs, and vanilla and beat well. Add the pecans and stir. Pour the mixture into the prepared pie plate. Bake in a 400° oven for 10 minutes. Reduce the heat to 350° and bake 30 minutes longer, or until a knife comes out clean. Cool. Serve with whipped cream, if desired. *Serves 6–8.*

POUNDCAKE

SOUTHERN

1 pound (4 sticks) butter	½ teaspoon salt
2 cups sugar	2 teaspoons baking powder
10 eggs, separated	1 teaspoon vanilla extract
4 cups sifted cake flour	½ teaspoon mace

Preheat oven to 325°.

Cream the butter and gradually add the sugar, continuing to cream the mixture until light and fluffy. Beat the egg yolks and add, beating steadily while adding them. Sift the flour, salt, and baking powder together 4 times. Add gradually to the butter mixture, mixing well. Add the vanilla and mace. Beat well, using an electric mixer if possible. Beat the egg whites until stiff but not dry and fold gently and lightly into the previous mixture.

Butter two 9-inch loaf pans and dust with flour. Pour half the mixture into each pan. Bake in 325° for 1 hour or until a toothpick or cake tester comes out clean. *Makes two 9-inch loaves.*

SAZERAC COCKTAIL

NEW ORLEANS

1 tablespoon Herbsaint (absinthe substitute)	¼ teaspoon bitters
	12 cubes ice
4 tablespoons water	6 jiggers bourbon
6 sugar dots	6 twists of lemon peel

Using old-fashioned glasses, place a little of the Herbsaint in each one. Revolve each glass so that it is coated as much as possible. Pour out any liquid. Place ½ teapoon of water and 1 piece of sugar in each glass, and mash the sugar with a muddler or spoon until the sugar is dissolved. Add a little of the bitters to each glass. Add 2 ice cubes and 1 jigger of whisky to each glass and stir well. Place a twist of lemon peel in each. If desired, the glasses may be iced in the refrigerator before preparing the drink. *Serves 6.*

SHRIMP REMOULADE

NEW ORLEANS

2 pounds raw shrimp	6 tablespoons olive oil
3 onions, sliced	3 tablespoons lemon juice
3 cloves garlic, minced	1 tablespoon chili sauce
1 teaspoon salt	3 tablespoons catsup
½ teaspoon freshly ground black pepper	1 tablespoon horseradish
1 bay leaf	1 tablespoon prepared mustard
1 stalk celery	½ teaspoon paprika
3 cups water	Dash of cayenne pepper
2 scallions (green onions), chopped fine	

Shell and clean the shrimp, reserving a few shells. Wash and drain well. Combine the shells, onions, 2 cloves garlic, the salt, pepper, bay leaf, celery, and water in a saucepan. Cook over medium heat for 30 minutes. Add the shrimp and cook over low heat for 5 minutes. Allow the shrimp to cool in the liquid. Drain well.

Combine the scallions, olive oil, lemon juice, chili sauce, catsup, horseradish, mustard, paprika, cayenne pepper, and remaining garlic in a bowl. Beat well and pour over the shrimp. Marinate the shrimp for at least 3 hours, or overnight in the refrigerator. *Serves 6–8.*

SOLE AMANDINE

NEW ORLEANS

1 teaspoon salt	4 tablespoons dry white wine or
¼ teaspoon white pepper	vermouth
⅓ cup flour	½ cup sliced blanched almonds
⅜ pound (1½ sticks) butter	1 tablespoon minced parsley
6 fillets of sole	

Mix the salt, pepper, and flour together. Dip the fillets in it lightly. Melt half the butter in a skillet until bubbles form. Place the fillets in it carefully. Sauté for 5 minutes on each side. Add the wine and cook 2 minutes longer.

In a separate skillet heat the remaining butter. Add the almonds and sauté until brown, stirring frequently. Add the parsley and stir. Place the fillets on a serving dish and pour the almonds and sauce over them. Serve with a thin slice of lemon on each fillet. *Serves 6.*

Note: This was originally a French dish but it has become a part of the New Orleans cuisine.

GUMBO FILÉ

NEW ORLEANS

5-pound chicken, disjointed	2 quarts water
2½ teaspoons salt	½ teaspoon thyme
1 teaspoon freshly ground black	½ teaspoon rosemary
pepper	¼ teaspoon dried ground chili
1 clove garlic, minced	peppers
3 tablespoons butter	1 cup canned tomatoes
2 onions, chopped	1 cup okra
½ pound boiled ham, cut into	24 oysters
strips	1 tablespoon filé powder

Clean the chicken carefully. Combine the salt, pepper, and garlic and rub into the chicken. Melt the butter in a large saucepan. Add the onions and chicken. Brown well. Add the ham, water, thyme, rosemary, chili peppers, and tomatoes. Cover and cook over low heat for 1½ hours. Add the okra and cook for 1 hour. Add the oysters, bring the mixture to a boil, and cook for 3 minutes.

Remove the saucepan from the heat and immediately add the filé powder. Mix well. Serve at once. Do not return the gumbo to the heat once the filé powder is added, or it will become stringy. Serve in soup plates with boiled rice. *Serves 4–6.*

CREOLE JAMBALAYA

NEW ORLEANS

1½ cups raw rice
1½ quarts water
2 teaspoons salt
2 tablespoons butter
½ pound uncooked ham, cut into small pieces
1 clove garlic, minced
½ pound spicy sausage, sliced thin

2 onions, chopped
2 green peppers, chopped
4 tomatoes, chopped, or 1 cup drained, canned tomatoes
2 cups beef broth
2 cups cooked shrimp, chicken, or turkey, sliced

Wash the rice carefully. Place in a large saucepan with the water and salt. Cover and cook over low heat until the boiling point is reached. Cook 5 minutes longer. Drain, and rinse with cold water. Drain again.

In a separate saucepan, melt the butter and add the ham, garlic, sausage, onions, and green peppers. Cook over medium heat for 10 minutes, stirring frequently. Reduce to low heat and add the tomatoes and broth. Add the rice. Cook until almost all the liquid is absorbed.

Since there are many types of jambalaya, they may be made with either shrimp, chicken, or turkey. Add the desired ingredient. Correct the seasoning, bearing in mind that the dish is normally quite spicy. Heat thoroughly and stir gently. *Serves 4–6.*

LEG OF LAMB, CREOLE

NEW ORLEANS

6 tablespoons chili sauce
2 tablespoons vinegar
½ cup dry red wine
2 tablespoons olive oil
1 teaspoon salt
½ teaspoon freshly ground black pepper

1 tablespoon sugar
2 onions, chopped fine
2 cloves garlic, minced
1 bay leaf
1 cup beef broth
6-pound leg of lamb

In a bowl combine the chili sauce, vinegar, wine, olive oil, salt, pepper, sugar, onions, garlic, bay leaf, and beef broth. Stir well. Trim as much fat as possible from the leg of lamb. Pour the marinade over the lamb. Marinate for a least 6 hours, overnight if possible. Baste frequently.

Place the lamb and marinade in a roasting pan and roast in a 400° oven for 15 minutes. Then reduce heat to 350° and roast for 20 minutes per pound of weight. Baste frequently during the roasting process. Should the liquid evaporate too rapidly, add small quantities of boiling water to the pan. Skim any fat from the gravy and serve in a sauceboat with the lamb. *Serves 6–8.*

CAFÉ BRÛLOT

NEW ORLEANS

1 tablespoon whole allspice	4 lumps sugar
1 lemon rind, cut into thin strips	¼ cup brandy
1 orange rind, cut into thin strips	3 cups espresso or double-strength
1 whole stick cinnamon	hot coffee

In the top of a chafing dish place the allspice, lemon rind, orange rind, and cinnamon. Place the sugar and brandy in a ladle or bowl and heat. Set the brandy afire and pour it over the spice mixture. Light the flame under the chafing dish and, using the ladle or a large spoon, keep pouring the brandy over the other ingredients until the sugar dissolves. When dissolved, immediately add the coffee, which should be freshly made and about fifty per cent stronger than usual. Keep ladling for a few moments to mix the coffee, then serve in demitasse cups. *Serves 6.*

BARBECUED SPARERIBS

SOUTHWESTERN

3 tablespoons butter	½ teaspoon dry mustard
1 cup cider vinegar	2 teaspoons sugar
1 cup water	1 teaspoon paprika
2 tablespoons Worcestershire	½ cup chili sauce
sauce	2 cloves garlic, minced
1 teaspoon Tabasco	2 onions, chopped fine
¼ teaspoon cayenne pepper	3 racks of small spareribs, cracked

Combine in a saucepan the butter, vinegar, water, Worcestershire sauce, Tabasco, cayenne pepper, mustard, sugar, paprika, chili sauce, garlic, and onions. Bring the mixture to a boil. Place the spareribs in a bowl

and pour the vinegar mixture over them. Marinate at room temperature
for at least 2 hours, basting frequently. Place the spareribs on a baking
sheet and roast in a 350° oven for 1 hour. Baste frequently with 1 cup
of the marinade. *Serves 6–8.*

CHILI CON CARNE

SOUTHWESTERN

2 cups dried red beans or 4 cups canned chili beans	2 pounds lean beef, cut in ¼-inch cubes
3 tablespoons olive oil	2 tablespoons flour
2 onions, chopped	3 cups canned tomatoes
3 tablespoons chili powder	2 tablespoons salt
3 cloves garlic, minced	

If dried beans are used, wash carefully and discard any imperfect ones.
Place in a saucepan, with water to cover, and soak overnight. Wash thoroughly again and cover the beans with fresh water. Cook over low heat
until the beans are tender, about 2 hours. Drain well.

Heat the oil in a separate saucepan and add the onions, chili powder,
garlic, and beef. Cook over high heat until the meat is very brown on all
sides. Reduce heat to low. Add flour, stirring constantly until well
blended. Add the tomatoes. Cover and cook for 1½ hours. Add the salt
and beans. Cook for 45 minutes. Correct seasoning. The chili will have
a better flavor if prepared a day in advance. *Serves 6–8.*

SWEET POTATO PIE

SOUTHWESTERN

1 cup sifted flour	¾ cup sugar
⅛ teaspoon baking powder	1½ cups grated raw sweet po-
¼ teaspoon salt	tatoes
⅓ cup shortening	⅓ cup milk
3 tablespoons ice water	¾ teaspoon ground ginger
¾ cup butter	2 tablespoons grated orange rind

Sift the flour, baking powder, and salt into a bowl. Add the shortening
and cut it into the flour with a pastry blender or two knives, until the
consistency of coarse sand. Add the water, drop by drop, tossing lightly
with a fork until a ball of dough is formed. Chill for at least 1 hour. Roll
out the dough on a lightly floured surface and line an unbuttered 10-
inch pie plate with it. Place the pie plate in the refrigerator while preparing the filling. Preheat oven to 300°.

Cream the butter, add the sugar, and continue creaming until light and fluffy. Gradually add the sweet potatoes and milk alternately, beating well. Add the ginger and orange rind and again beat well. Pour into the prepared pie plate. Bake in a 300° oven until delicately browned, about 45 minutes. Serve hot, with whipped cream on the side. *Serves 8–10.*

WESTERN OMELET

WESTERN

8 eggs	6 tablespoons cold water
¾ teaspoon salt	1 cup diced bacon
¼ teaspoon freshly ground black	½ cup chopped onions
black pepper	1 large green pepper, diced

Beat the eggs with the salt, pepper, and water until well blended. Place the bacon in a large skillet, and fry for 5 minutes. Pour off most of the grease and add the onions and green pepper. Cook for 10 minutes. Add the eggs and cook over very low heat, lifting the mixture with a spatula as it cooks on the bottom, and tipping the pan to allow the uncooked mixture to run under. Do not fold or cut through the omelet; keep it in one large piece. *Serves 4–6.*

CIOPPINO

WESTERN

½ cup dried mushrooms	2 teaspoons salt
½ cup olive oil	⅛ teaspoon cayenne pepper
2 onions, chopped	3-pound striped bass, cut into
2 cloves garlic, minced	slices
1 green pepper, chopped	1 lobster or 1 Dungeness crab,
3 tablespoons chopped parsley	cut in small pieces
1½ cups canned tomatoes	1 cup raw shrimp, shelled and
1½ cups dry red wine	cleaned
2 bay leaves	2 cups shucked clams

Soak the mushrooms in water to cover for 30 minutes. Drain and slice fine. Heat the oil in a deep, heavy saucepan. Add the onions, garlic, green pepper, parsley, and mushrooms. Sauté for 10 minutes, stirring occasionally. Add the tomatoes, wine, and bay leaves. Cover and cook over low heat for 1½ hours. Add the salt, cayenne pepper, striped bass, lobster, and shrimp and cook 20 minutes. Add the clams and cook 5 minutes. Correct seasoning. Serve in soup plates with toasted French bread. *Serves 4–6.*

CAESAR SALAD

WESTERN

1 cup olive oil	½ teaspoon dry mustard
6 slices white bread, trimmed and cubed	½ teaspoon coarsely ground black pepper
3 cloves garlic, minced	1 teaspoon salt
3 heads romaine lettuce, washed drained, and chilled	⅓ cup wine vinegar
	1 egg, boiled 1 minute
6 anchovies, minced	¾ cup grated Parmesan cheese

Heat ½ cup of the oil in a skillet. Add the croutons and garlic. Sauté until brown. Set aside. Break the lettuce into 2-inch pieces, discarding any discolored or tough pieces. Place in a large bowl. Add the anchovies, mustard, pepper, salt, and the remaining oil. Toss with two spoons until the lettuce is well coated. Add the vinegar and toss. Break the egg over the salad and toss. Add the cheese and toss. Add the croutons before serving *Serves 4–6.*

Note: Caesar salad is served as a first course.

The Atlantic

and the

Caribbean
    Bermuda
    Bahamas
    The Greater Antilles
      Cuba
      Dominican Republic
      Jamaica
      Haiti
      Puerto Rico
    The Lesser and Netherlands Antilles

BERMUDA

Many people think of the lovely island of Bermuda as being in the Caribbean; actually it's not a part of those island groups, being located far to the north. Although there are about three hundred islands (if tiny coral islets are included), the total land area is barely twenty square miles. Because of Bermuda's great physical beauty and its famous springlike climate, it has become a favorite resort and vacation spot.

Bermuda is plentifully supplied with de luxe hotels which, like luxury hotels the world over, serve the so-called "international cuisine." Not only in Bermuda, although the situation is acute there, but everywhere in the world there has been a gradual deterioration of interest in serving unusual dishes on the part of chefs and owners of luxury hotels. Instead guests are served "international" food, which by its very name indicates that it is not the national food of any particular country. It means thick, floury cream sauces, innocuous soups, steaks and chops with green peas dyed a horrible green color, ice cream for dessert, the complete avoidance of spices and herbs, and the appearance on the menu of only those dishes which are completely familiar to the diner.

Unfortunately most hotels claim that they are only giving their guests what they want. Apparently myths die slowly, particularly among hotel clans. Some few places in Bermuda do serve native dishes, but on the whole they are obtainable only in private homes.

Beer and wines are of comparatively little importance here, although they are generally available. Imported scotch and rye whiskies are commonplace. Rum drinks, on the other hand, are outstanding favorites, and the swizzle is probably the most usual type of rum drink. The recipe for the Bermuda swizzle cup is only one version of the many different swizzles made in the islands.

Bermuda imports the vast majority of its food, but fish is the great exception, for the surrounding waters are filled with a wide assortment of both commercial and game fish. Fish chowders, Bermuda lobsters, and even shark are typical local fish dishes. The renowned Bermuda codfish breakfast is becoming a rarity, but it is an interesting recipe.

Cassava, a heavy, whitish root similar to the potato, is used to make a crust for chicken or meat pie. Another local specialty is the Bermuda onion, probably the most delicately flavored of all onions, which is used in many ways. The recipe for baked Bermuda onions is a fine example of old-fashioned Bermuda cookery. Almost every bit of meat is imported and there are no unusual recipes in this category other than the previously mentioned cassava pie. Desserts are of the usual American or British variety, except that there are some old-fashioned cooky and fruitcake recipes.

A plea to Bermuda hotel owners: Why not try to revive the old Bermuda style of cooking, at least on one day per week? Or why not serve one native dish every evening?

BERMUDA SWIZZLE CUP

2 eggs	3 teaspoons bitters
4 tablespoons sugar	6 jiggers light rum

Combine the eggs, sugar, and bitters in a tall glass and mix with a swizzle stick. Divide among 6 tall glasses. Add 1 jigger of rum to each glass, fill with cracked ice, and stir until the ingredients are well mixed.

HAMILTON FISH CHOWDER

¼ pound salt pork or bacon, diced small	3 quarts water
1 onion, sliced	⅛ teaspoon thyme
1 pound halibut, sole, or other white meat fish, cut into 1-inch pieces	1 tablespoon chopped parsley
	2 tablespoons butter
	4 tablespoons flour
3 fish heads	½ cup sherry

Place the salt pork in a deep saucepan. Cook until there are about 3 tablespoons of fat in the saucepan. Add the onion and fish. Cook over high heat until the fish is browned, stirring occasionally. Remove the fish. Reduce to low heat. Add the fish heads, water, thyme, and parsley. Cover and cook for 2 hours. Remove the fish heads and any bones.

Melt the butter in a separate saucepan. Add the flour and stir constantly until the mixture is smooth and brown. Gradually add a cup of the fish stock, stirring constantly. Add to the balance of the fish stock, stirring constantly. Return the browned fish pieces. Correct seasoning. Add the sherry just before serving, and stir well. *Serves 6–8.*

BERMUDA CODFISH BREAKFAST

2 pounds salt cod	1 teaspoon prepared mustard
6 potatoes, peeled	1 hard-cooked egg, chopped fine
2 tablespoons chopped parsley	3 bananas, sliced
⅓ cup butter or olive oil	1 avocado, peeled and sliced
½ teaspoon Tabasco	

Soak the codfish overnight in water to cover. Drain and rinse thoroughly. Place in a saucepan with water to cover and cook over medium heat for 2 hours. Drain, remove skin and bones, and return fish to the saucepan. Add fresh water to cover and the whole potatoes. Cook over medium heat for 30 minutes, or until potatoes are tender. Drain well. Keep warm. Combine the butter, Tabasco, mustard, and egg in a saucepan. Bring to a boil and remove from the heat. Arrange the fish and potatoes on a platter, with the bananas and avocado around the outside. Pour the sauce over all and serve. *Serves 6–8.*

BAKED BERMUDA ONIONS

4 large, sweet Bermuda onions	1 cup milk
3 slices buttered toast	½ teaspoon salt
1 cup grated Cheddar cheese	3 tablespoons butter
3 eggs	

Peel the onions and place in a saucepan. Cover with water and bring to a boil. Cook for 5 minutes. Drain well and cool for 10 minutes. Slice the onions ½ inch thick. Cut the toast in half diagonally, so as to form triangles. Place the buttered side of the toast face down in a large, deep pie plate or casserole. Arrange the onion slices over the toast. Sprinkle the grated cheese on top.

In a separate bowl beat the eggs well and add the milk and salt. Again beat well, then pour the mixture over the onions. Dot with butter. Bake in a 350° oven for 30 minutes, or until the egg mixture is firm. *Serves 6.*

CASSAVA PIE

1½ pounds boneless pork, cubed
4-pound chicken, cut into pieces
1½ teaspoons salt
½ teaspoon thyme
4 cups water
2 pounds cassava or white
  potatoes, grated

½ cup dark brown sugar
4 eggs, beaten
¼ cup melted butter
¾ teaspoon baking powder

Combine the pork, chicken, salt, thyme, and water in a saucepan. Cook over medium heat for 1½ hours. Correct seasoning. Drain, reserving the liquid. Carefully remove the chicken from the bones. Combine the chicken meat with the pork and set aside.

Peel the cassava, removing the inner yellow skin. Grate on a fine grater. Wet the grated cassava, then wring it dry with the hands. Place in a bowl, add the sugar, eggs, and melted butter, and mix well. Add the baking powder and mix well again. Line the bottom and sides of a 2-quart buttered casserole with the cassava mixture, reserving enough to cover the top of the casserole. Fill the center with the pork and chicken, and pour 1½ cups of the previously reserved stock over it. Spread the remaining cassava mixture on top. Bake in a 325° oven for 2 hours, basting occasionally with ½ cup of the stock. Serve hot. *Serves 6–8.*

Note: Cassava is not generally obtainable in the United States except in cities having large Spanish-speaking groups. However, the taste may be imitated by using white potatoes, with the addition, for this recipe, of 2 tablespoons of either farina or instant tapioca.

BERMUDA FRUITCAKE

¼ pound (1 stick) butter
1 cup dark brown sugar
2 cups sifted flour
1½ cups buttermilk or sour milk
½ cup chopped candied lemon
  peel

1 cup seedless raisins
2 teaspoons ground cinnamon
1 teaspoon ground nutmeg
¼ teaspoon ground allspice
2 teaspoons baking soda

Preheat oven to 375°.

Cream the butter and add the sugar, beating well. Add the flour (reserving 2 tablespoons) and the buttermilk alternately, spoon by spoon, stirring steadily. Beat well. Dust the lemon peel and raisins with the reserved flour and add to the mixture. Add the cinnamon, nutmeg, allspice, and baking soda and beat together. Butter a 12-inch loaf pan generously. Dust with a little flour. Pour the mixture into the pan. Bake in a 375° oven for 1 hour, or until a cake tester comes out clean. *Makes one 12-inch loaf.*

OLD-FASHIONED BERMUDA COOKIES

6 tablespoons butter	2 cups sifted flour
4 tablespoons vegetable	⅛ teaspoon salt
shortening or lard	1 teaspoon nutmeg
½ cup sugar	⅛ teaspoon baking soda
1 egg, beaten	1 tablespoon brandy

Cream the butter and shortening together. Add the sugar and beat until well blended. Add the egg and continue beating. Sift the flour, salt, and nutmeg together and add to the butter mixture. Blend well. Dissolve the soda in the brandy and add to the mixture, stirring well. Preheat oven to 375°.

Dust the hands well with flour and form walnut-size balls of dough. Press flat with the hands and place on an unbuttered baking sheet leaving space between each to allow for spreading. Designs may be made on top of each cooky, if desired, or a pastry wheel may be run around the edges. Bake in a 375° oven for 15 minutes, or until brown. These cookies are quite rich. They will expand while baking, so use only small amounts of dough for each cooky. *Makes 48.*

BAHAMAS

Many hundreds of tiny bits of land, reefs, and soil form the British Bahama Islands. Many of these islands are uninhabited, some have a very few natives living on them, but others are comparatively well settled. To the majority of tourists, the Bahamas mean just one spot—the capital city of Nassau on New Providence Island. To another specialized breed, deep-sea fishermen, the Bahamas mean the famous Bimini Island, located adjacent to the Gulf Stream, and the scene of the annual tuna competitions. Eleuthera and Harbour islands are somewhat off the beaten track but offer excellent vacations to those who wish to dispense with night clubs, television, and other trappings of civilization. In recent years, the Out Islands, as they are called, have become quite popular with vacationers. Of special interest to fishermen, scuba divers, and escapists, the Out Islands offer solitude and quiet nights, following physically active days. It should not be assumed that visitors to these islands will have to rough it; on the contrary, many of the Out Island hotels are quite luxurious.

Nassau is filled with hotels, guesthouses, and other places offering accommodations to visitors, most of whom come from the States. The islands are nevertheless distinctly British in flavor and tempo, and extremely conservative. The food is more likely to be American style than British, in honor of the large number of tourists, or possibly in the international style beloved by hotelmen. Local food is hard to find except in private homes.

British drinking habits are followed to a certain extent, although the American-style cocktail hour (or hours) is a recognized part of the local scene. Social life is at a high point during the winter season, with a considerable amount of formal entertaining. All liquors are available in Nassau at comparatively low prices, but rum mixtures and whisky and soda are the local choices.

The islands find it difficult to produce enough food for the inhabitants plus the tourists, and thus a great deal of it is imported, mostly from the States. Actually the only foods available locally are vegetables, fish, and some fruit, with a few exceptions. Fish of all deep-sea species are plentiful, and the local people make various chowders and stews of the many varieties available. Nassau fish chowder is a local specialty, but this is merely one example. Conchs (pronounced conks) are large shellfish common in the area, used for soup, chowders, and the conch fritters for which a recipe is given. Crabs are particularly good here, and often very plentiful. If he can find it, no visitor to Nassau should leave without trying turtle pie, an interesting food specialty of the islands.

Meat is imported, and there are practically no unique meat dishes of importance. On the other hand, chicken dishes are well prepared, as are such game birds as the wild pigeons and ducks of the region. The famous song about "Mama don't want no peas an' rice an' coconut oil" describes in reverse the local passion for peas and rice, probably the favorite native dish.

NASSAU FISH CHOWDER

3 pounds assorted fish	½ teaspoon thyme
1 teaspoon salt	2 bay leaves
3 tablespoons lemon juice	2 sprigs parsley
¼ pound salt pork, diced	1 teaspoon peppercorns
3 onions, chopped	4 cups boiling water
1 19-ounce can tomatoes, strained	2 tablespoons Worcestershire sauce
4 potatoes, peeled and cubed	¼ cup dry sherry
12 pilot crackers	

Wash and dry the fish. Cut it into 2-inch cubes, removing all the skin and bones. Sprinkle with the salt and lemon juice. Place the salt pork in a saucepan and fry until brown. Remove the browned pork with a slotted spoon and reserve. Add the onions and sauté for 10 minutes, stirring occasionally. Add the tomatoes and cook over low heat for 25 minutes.

In a heavy saucepan or Dutch oven arrange layers of the tomato mixture, browned pork, fish, potatoes, and pilot crackers until all the ingredients are used up. Add the thyme, bay leaves, parsley, pepper, and boiling water. Cover and cook over medium heat for 40 minutes. Add the Worcestershire sauce and sherry. Cook 20 minutes longer. Serve hot. *Serves 8–10.*

Note: This is a very thick chowder.

CONCH FRITTERS

3 cups ground conch or clams, drained	½ teaspoon freshly ground black pepper
1 cup sifted flour	1 egg, beaten
1 teaspoon baking powder	2 tablespoons water
2 tablespoons chopped onion	Vegetable oil for deep-fat frying
½ teaspoon salt	

Combine the ground conch or clams, flour, baking powder, onion, salt, pepper, egg, and water. Mix well. Form into walnut-size balls. Heat the deep oil to 375°. Fry a few balls at a time until browned on all sides. Drain well. Serve hot, on toothpicks, as an appetizer. *Makes about 48.*

Note: Conch is a large shellfish of the Florida and West Indies region. Although clams do not taste exactly like conch, the texture is similar.

TURTLE PIE

2 cups sifted flour
1½ teaspoons salt
½ cup shortening
2 eggs
2 teaspoons cold water
3 pounds turtle meat (see Note)
¾ teaspoon thyme
½ teaspoon marjoram
2 cups hot water
4 tablespoons butter

3 onions, chopped
1 tablespoon cornstarch
½ cup tomato sauce
1 tablespoon melted butter
2 egg yolks
¼ teaspoon pepper
½ cup dry bread crumbs
4 tablespoons fat
1 cup sherry

Sift the flour and ½ teaspoon salt into a bowl. Cut in the shortening with a pastry blender or two knives until the consistency of coarse sand. Beat 1 egg and the cold water together and add, tossing lightly until a ball of dough is formed. Wrap in wax paper and place in the refrigerator while preparing the filling.

Divide the meat in half; cube one half and grind the other. Place the cubed meat in a saucepan and cover with water. Bring to a boil, drain, and rinse with cold water. Combine in the saucepan with the thyme, marjoram, and hot water. Cook over low heat for 45 minutes. Drain, reserving the stock. Set the cubed meat aside. Melt the butter in a saucepan; add 2 onions. Sauté for 10 minutes. Add the cornstarch, stirring well. Add the tomato sauce and the reserved stock and mix well. Cook over low heat for 30 minutes. Strain and combine with the cubed meat. Correct seasoning.

Combine the ground meat with the remaining onion. Add the melted butter, egg yolks, pepper, and remaining salt. Mix well. Shape into 2-inch balls. Beat the remaining egg and dip the balls in it, then into the bread crumbs. Heat the fat in a skillet and fry the balls in it until brown on all sides. Preheat oven to 350°.

Pour the cubed meat mixture into a 2-quart casserole. Place the balls on top and pour the sherry over it. Roll out the dough on a lightly floured surface to fit the top of the casserole. Place on top of the casserole, sealing the edges well. Brush the top with a little beaten egg or milk. Bake in a 350° oven for 35 minutes. *Serves 8–10.*

Note: Although turtle meat is available, either fresh or in cans, veal may be substituted. Veal doesn't taste exactly like turtle, but its texture and appearance are similar enough to justify its use.

BAHAMIAN ROAST CHICKEN

6-pound roasting chicken
3 teaspoons salt
1 teaspoon freshly ground
    black pepper
4 tablespoons butter
3 cups fresh bread crumbs
⅛ teaspoon thyme

2 onions, chopped fine
3 tablespoons melted butter
2 cups water
3 tomatoes, chopped
3 potatoes, peeled and halved
6 carrots, peeled

Wash and dry the chicken. Make a paste of 2 teaspoons of the salt, ½ teaspoon of the pepper, and the 4 tablespoons butter. Rub it into the chicken, inside and out. Combine the bread crumbs and the remaining salt and pepper, the thyme, onions, and melted butter. Mix well. Reserve 1 cup of the mixture and stuff the chicken loosely with the balance. Fasten the opening with skewers or with toothpicks. Place the chicken in a roasting pan. Spread the reserved bread-crumb mixture around the chicken. Add the water and tomatoes.

Roast in a 350° oven for 1¼ hours, basting occasionally. Add the potatoes and carrots and roast 45 minutes longer, or until the chicken is tender. Serve with boiled rice. The sauce remaining in the roasting pan should be poured over the chicken and rice. *Serves 4–6.*

PEAS AND RICE, BAHAMA STYLE

2 cups dried pigeon peas
3 tablespoons vegetable oil
1 onion, chopped
3 tomatoes, chopped
3 cups boiling water

2 teaspoons salt
¾ teaspoon freshly ground
    black pepper
1 cup rice, washed and drained

Soak the peas overnight in water to cover. Drain, add fresh water, and boil for 1 hour, or until soft. Drain and force through a strainer. Heat the oil in a saucepan and add the onion. Sauté for 10 minutes, stirring frequently. Add the tomatoes and cook over low heat for 5 minutes. Add the water, the bean purée, salt, and pepper. Bring to a boil. Add the rice and mix together lightly. Cover and cook for 25 minutes, or until rice is tender. Watch the liquid carefully, adding small additional quantities of boiling water if necessary to prevent burning. *Serves 6–8.*

Note: Canned cooked pigeon peas are available. If used, omit cooking and proceed as directed.

BANANA PUDDING

10 ripe bananas
⅓ cup flour
1 cup sugar

1 tablespoon melted butter
1 teaspoon nutmeg

Mash the bananas. Add the flour, sugar, butter, and nutmeg. Pour into a buttered 8-inch square pan. Bake in a 325° oven for 30 minutes, or until delicately browned on top. Cut into squares and serve hot or cold, dusted with powdered sugar. If desired, whipped cream may be placed on each portion. *Serves 6–8.*

CUBA

At the present time, Americans are not going to Cuba, although it was probably the most popular of all destinations for vacationers within recent memory. It has been reported that all of the elaborate hotels and tourist-oriented restaurants are now nothing but shadows of their former selves. Once luxurious hotels are run-down, somewhat seedy, with soiled carpets and air conditioning that no longer works. Similarly, restaurants which served excellent Cuban specialties are now gone from the scene, or merely offering routine meals.

Cuba has always been noted for its shellfish. The shrimp are excellent, the lobster fine, but the single outstanding item is stone crabs. These gaudily colored crabs with brightly marked claws may be the best crabs in the world; only the claws are edible, for all practical purposes. When merely boiled (rather than prepared with elaborate sauces) the stone crab is nothing short of exquisitely delicious. At any time, however, they were never bargain priced, and the demand for these shellfish inevitably exceeded the supply.

Although Cuba's weather is typically rather warm, the national taste is toward filling, solid soups, typified by bean soup, which is an every-day item for most families. Chicken is (or at least, was) a standard food for everyone. However, the Cubans rarely eat plain boiled or roasted chicken. They would much rather serve it with rice, or made into a stew.

Rum and cola, sometimes called *cuba libre,* may or may not have originated here, and no one knows certainly at this late date. Cuba is a sugar cane island, sugar cane being its chief agricultural harvest, and much of it is made into rum. Beer is quite popular here, for the climate is hot most of the time; it may well be that beer is actually a more usual drink than rum, but accurate statistics are rare in Cuba.

BACARDI COCKTAIL

6 jiggers Bacardi rum
2 teaspoons grenadine

Juice of 2 lemons or limes

Place the rum, grenadine, and lemon or lime juice in a cocktail shaker with cracked ice. Shake well. Strain into chilled cocktail glasses. *Makes 6 cocktails.*

BOLITAS DE CANGREJO

CRAB FRITTERS

½ cup fine grated coconut
4 tablespoons butter
½ cup chopped onions
1 clove garlic, minced
1 pound crab meat

1 egg
½ teaspoon salt
⅛ teaspoon Tabasco
½ cup dry bread crumbs
1 cup vegetable oil

Rinse the coconut under cold running water. Drain well and dry. Melt 2 tablespoons of the butter in a skillet; lightly brown the coconut in it. Remove.

Melt the remaining butter in the skillet, sauté the onions and garlic in it until browned.

Pick over the crab meat, discarding any cartilage. Chop together the crab meat, onions, and coconut. Mix in the egg, salt, and Tabasco. Taste for seasoning. Form teaspoons of the mixture into balls and roll in the bread crumbs.

Heat the oil in a skillet. Brown the balls in it. Drain. Pierce with cocktail picks or toothpicks and serve hot. *Makes about 30 fritters.*

BLACK BEAN SOUP

SOPA DE JUDÍAS COLORADAS

2 cups dried black beans
3 quarts water
½ pound ham, cubed
2 tablespoons olive oil
2 onions, chopped
2 cloves garlic, minced
¼ cup chopped celery
1 carrot, sliced
1 green pepper, chopped
2 tomatoes, chopped

1 bay leaf
2 teaspoons salt
¼ teaspoon dried ground chili
  peppers
1 teaspoon Spanish paprika
2 tablespoons butter
3 tablespoons rum
3 hard-cooked eggs, sliced
6 slices lemon

Wash the beans thoroughly. Soak in water to cover overnight. Drain completely and rinse again. Combine in a saucepan with the 3 quarts of water and the ham. Bring to a boil. Cover and cook over low heat for 3 hours.

Heat the olive oil in a frying pan. Add the onions, garlic, celery, carrot, and green pepper. Sauté for 15 minutes, stirring frequently. Add to the beans, together with the tomatoes, bay leaf, salt, chili peppers, and paprika. Cover and cook over low heat for 1 hour. Purée in an electric blender or force the mixture through a sieve and return to the saucepan. Correct seasoning. Add the butter and rum. Serve the soup garnished with slices of egg and lemon. *Serves 8–10.*

BAKED FISH WITH ALMONDS

PESCADO HORNEADO CON ALMENDRAS

3 tablespoons olive oil
2 onions, chopped fine
1 clove garlic, minced
1 cup ground almonds
3 tablespoons chopped parsley
1 tablespoon beef extract
2 tablespoons lemon juice
1 teaspoon salt

½ teaspoon freshly ground black
  pepper
6 fillets of pompano, snapper, or
  sole
4 tablespoons butter
2 onions, sliced
½ teaspoon thyme

Heat the olive oil in a skillet. Add the chopped onions and garlic. Sauté for 10 minutes, stirring frequently. Add the almonds and parsley and sauté for 5 minutes, stirring almost constantly. Add the beef extract and mix well. Cook over low heat for 5 minutes, stirring occasionally.

Combine the lemon juice, salt, and pepper in a cup. Rub into the fish thoroughly. Melt the butter in an ovenproof baking dish and spread the onion slices in it. Sprinkle with the thyme. Arrange the fish fillets over the onions. Bake in a 375° oven for 15 minutes. Pour the sauce over the fish. Bake 20 minutes longer. Serve with lemon or lime wedges. *Serves 6.*

FRIED STEAKS

VACA FRITA

4 tablespoons olive oil
3 onions, chopped
3 cloves garlic, minced
1 green pepper, chopped
1 carrot, diced
6 tomatoes, chopped, or 2 cups canned tomatoes, drained
2 slices half-cooked bacon, minced
1 bay leaf

2 cloves
2 teaspoons salt
¼ teaspoon dried ground chili peppers
1 teaspoon Spanish paprika
¾ cup dry bread crumbs
6 1-inch-thick shell steaks
3 canned pimentos, sliced
4 tablespoons chopped parsley

Heat the olive oil in a saucepan. Add the onions and garlic and sauté for 10 minutes, stirring frequently. Add the green pepper, carrot, tomatoes, bacon, bay leaf, cloves, salt, chili peppers, and paprika. Cover and cook over low heat for 30 minutes, stirring frequently. Add the bread crumbs, mixing well. Correct seasoning. Cook over the low heat while preparing the steaks. Discard bay leaf.

Heat a skillet. Add the steaks and fry over high heat for 3 minutes on each side, or to desired degree of doneness. Place the steaks on a platter and pour the sauce over them. Arrange the pimentos on top and sprinkle with the parsley. Serve immediately. *Serves 6.*

CHICKEN WITH RICE

ARROZ CON POLLO

1 cup olive oil
2 3-pound chickens, disjointed
3 onions, chopped
3 cloves garlic, minced
2 cups raw rice
1½ cups canned tomatoes
3 fresh tomatoes, chopped
2 cups chicken broth
2 teaspoons saffron

1 tablespoon salt
½ teaspoon freshly ground black pepper
1 fresh chili pepper, sliced, or ¼ teaspoon dried ground chili peppers
1 cup canned tiny green peas
3 canned pimentos, sliced

Heat ½ cup olive oil in a large casserole or saucepan. Add the chicken and brown well on all sides. Remove the chicken. Sauté the onions and garlic in the same casserole for 10 minutes. Remove. Add the remaining oil to the casserole. Brown the rice in it lightly, stirring constantly. Replace the chicken, onions, and garlic. Add the canned and fresh tomatoes, broth, saffron, salt, pepper, and chili peppers. Mix carefully. Cover.

Bake in a 325° oven for 1½ hours. Add the peas and pimentos, and a little water if the rice is dry. Bake for 20 minutes, or until chicken is tender. Serve hot, right from the casserole. A dry white wine is recommended for this classic dish. *Serves 6–8.*

CUBAN CHICKEN STEW

GUISADO DE POLLO

3 cloves garlic, minced
2 teaspoons salt
1 teaspoon freshly ground black pepper
2 teaspoons Spanish paprika
2 3-pound chickens, disjointed
¼ cup olive oil
3 onions, chopped

1 bay leaf
½ cup dry white wine
3 potatoes, peeled and cubed
1 16-ounce can French-style green peas
½ cup sliced green olives
½ cup sliced canned pimentos

Mix the garlic, salt, pepper, and paprika to a paste. Rub into the chickens thoroughly, inside and out. If possible, season the chickens the day before they are to be used.

Heat the olive oil in a saucepan or casserole. Add the onions and sauté for 15 minutes, stirring frequently. Remove the onions and set aside. Add the chickens and brown well on all sides. Return the onions to the saucepan. Add the bay leaf and white wine. Cover and cook over low heat for 1 hour. Add small additional amounts of water if needed. Add the potatoes and stir gently. Cover and cook over low heat for 20 minutes. Correct seasoning. Add the peas, olives, and pimentos and cook over low heat for 10 minutes. *Serves 6–8.*

AVOCADOS STUFFED WITH VEGETABLES

AGUACATES RELLENO

½ cup olive oil
2 tablespoons vinegar
1 teaspoon salt
½ teaspoon freshly ground black
  pepper
1 clove garlic, minced
1 cup diced boiled potatoes
½ cup sliced cooked carrots
½ cup canned or cooked green
  peas

6 canned or cooked asparagus
  spears, sliced
¼ cup canned or cooked diced
  beets
3 avocados, cut in half and
  sprinkled with lemon juice
1 cup mayonnaise
2 hard-cooked eggs, chopped

Combine the olive oil, vinegar, salt, pepper, and garlic in a bowl. Beat
until well blended. Combine the potatoes, carrots, peas, asparagus, and
beets in a bowl. Pour the dressing over the vegetables and mix well.
Marinate for 30 minutes, mixing frequently.

Divide the mixture evenly and stuff the avocados. Mask the stuffing
completely with mayonnaise. Sprinkle with the chopped egg. If desired,
decorate with lettuce leaves or pimentos. Chill for 1 hour. Serve cold.
Serves 6.

DOUBLE YOLK DESSERT

YEMA DOBLE

2 cups sugar
1 cup water
6 egg yolks

2 egg whites
1½ tablespoons flour
2 tablespoons sherry

Combine the sugar and water in a saucepan. Cook until thick and
syrupy. Remove half of the mixture and set it aside. In a bowl, beat the
egg yolks until light in color. In a separate bowl, beat the egg whites
until stiff but not dry. Sift the flour over the whites and fold in carefully. Fold in the egg yolks carefully.

Bring the syrup in the saucepan to a boil. Drop the egg mixture into it
by tablespoons, but do not have more than 3 tablespoons of the mixture
cooking at one time. When the little "omelet" floats on the top, fold it in
half with two forks and remove it to a platter with a slotted spoon. Continue until all of the egg mixture is cooked. If more syrup is needed for
cooking the egg mixture, add some from the reserved half. Add the

sherry to the reserved syrup and heat it. Pour over the little omelets.
Serves 6–8.

SPONGECAKE

PANATELA

1⅛ cups sifted cake flour   1½ cups sifted sugar
1 teaspoon cream of tartar   7 eggs, separated
¼ teaspoon salt   2 tablespoons brandy
1⅛ cups water

Preheat oven to 325°.

Sift together 4 times the flour, cream of tartar, and salt. Set aside.
Combine the water and sugar in a saucepan. Cook over low heat until a
thread forms when a fork is lifted from the syrup. Beat the egg whites
until stiff but not dry. Add the syrup very gradually, beating constantly until the mixture cools. Beat the egg yolks until thick. Add the
brandy and stir. Fold into the egg-white mixture. Fold the flour mixture
into the egg mixture gently but thoroughly.

Butter an angel-cake pan and dust lightly with flour. Pour the batter
into it carefully. Bake in a 325° oven for 1 hour, or until a cake tester
comes out clean. Invert the pan onto a cake rack and allow to cool in
that position. Remove from the pan and sprinkle with powdered sugar, if
desired. *Serves 10–12.*

DOMINICAN REPUBLIC

Even the poorest scholar cannot leave school without remembering one
historic date, that of 1492, the year in which Columbus discovered America. That intrepid explorer actually landed on the island of Hispaniola,
little realizing that his fate was inescapably linked with it, for Columbus'
body lies today in Ciudad Trujillo, the capital of the country. However,
it should be remembered that the same claim is made by Seville, in
Spain, and also by several other Latin cities. It does seem, according
to the best evidence, that he is probably buried here.

The island of Hispaniola is shared by two dissimilar nations, Haiti and
the Dominican Republic. The French overtones of Haitian cuisine are
not evident in the Dominican portion of the island; the emphasis is upon

local foodstuffs, although certain dishes have a generally Spanish background.

This is a country of fruits and vegetables, all easily grown in a warm land of considerable sunshine and fertile soil. Sugar cane, sweet potatoes, squash, coffee, bananas, and mangos are plentiful and are mainstays in the local diet. Lobsters and shrimp are available along the comparatively long coast line, and they are incorporated into the diet to good effect; *sopa hamaca*, a fish soup with vegetables, is an interesting example of making the most of what is available.

Roast pork in any form is considered the most delectable of all meats, a truism of all the islands of the West Indies. *Carne de cerdo* (browned pork strips) is a recognized Dominican specialty; of even greater popularity is roast suckling pig, preferably cooked outdoors over an open fire. The wonderful soup-stew of the Latin countries, *sancocho*, is undoubtedly the people's choice for a national dish. Although *sancocho* is often made with two dozen different ingredients, the Dominicans have a *sancocho de siete carnes*, made with seven different meats in addition to the usual items, which is undoubtedly the champion *sancocho* of all. To scare off any possible rival claimants, it is made with bitter orange juice and all sorts of odd ingredients, such as *longaniza, yucca, yautia, mapuey, rulos, platanos,* and other foods unavailable to us. A more readily duplicated recipe for *sancocho* is listed in the section on Central America.

Beans and rice, the staple foods of the peasantry, are eaten at least once almost every day, and often several times daily. The people are very fond of sweet desserts, principally based on coconuts, bananas, and pineapple.

Santo Domingo coffee is not only the normal end to a meal, it is also the standard refreshment offered to guests, both business and social. The number of cups of coffee consumed per person is probably surpassed only in Brazil, and even that statement might be the subject of a poll by Dr. Gallup.

A fair amount of rum of reasonable quality, although not outstanding enough for exportation, is produced locally. The local people do not quibble on this point but consume it straight and in mixed drinks. Possibly the beer is better than the rum; certainly everyone seems to drink it.

The country has very good weather the year around. It can be quite warm during the summer months, though not unpleasantly so. Actually the best season to visit the Dominican Republic is from November to March inclusively. Generally speaking, the hotels tend to serve international-style food, although occasionally they may feature a local dish on their menus. In Ciudad Trujillo there are several restaurants that serve completely authentic Dominican food, and it is definitely worthwhile to have a meal or two in one or two of the local restaurants.

PICKLED FRIED FISH

ESCABECHE DE PESCADO

6 slices mackerel, sea bass, or
  similar fish
¼ cup lemon juice
¾ cup flour
3 teaspoons salt
1½ teaspoons freshly ground
  black pepper

½ cup vegetable oil
2 tablespoons olive oil
2 onions, sliced thin
1 clove garlic, minced
3 tomatoes, cubed
1 tablespoon tomato paste
2 tablespoons vinegar

Wash and dry the fish. Sprinkle with the lemon juice. Mix the flour, 2 teaspoons of the salt, and 1 teaspoon of the pepper together. Dip the fish slices into the mixture, coating them well. Heat the vegetable oil in a frying pan. Add the fish and fry until well browned on both sides, about 15 minutes. Remove the fish from the pan and place in a shallow bowl.

Heat the olive oil in a skillet. Add the onions and garlic and sauté for 5 minutes, stirring frequently. Add the tomatoes, tomato paste, vinegar, and remaining salt and pepper. Cook over low heat for 5 minutes. Pour the sauce over the fish and cover the bowl. Place in the refrigerator for 24 hours before serving. Serve as an appetizer on a bed of lettuce leaves. *Serves 6.*

FISH AND VEGETABLE SOUP

SOPA HAMACA

½ cup olive oil
2 onions, chopped
2 cloves garlic, minced
2 pounds fish, cubed
1 raw lobster, removed from
  shell and cut into pieces
1 cup raw rice
4 potatoes, peeled and cubed
2 tomatoes, chopped

2 cups coarsely shredded cabbage
2 tablespoons tomato paste
2½ quarts boiling water
3 pimentos, sliced thin
2 teaspoons salt
½ teaspoon freshly ground black
  pepper
½ teaspoon orégano

Heat the olive oil in a large saucepan. Add the onions and garlic and sauté for 5 minutes, stirring frequently. Add the fish, lobster, and rice and cook over high heat for 5 minutes, stirring constantly. Add the potatoes, tomatoes, cabbage, tomato paste, boiling water, pimentos, salt, pepper, and orégano. Stir well and cook over medium heat for 30 minutes. Correct seasoning. Serve hot. *Serves 8–10.*

MARINATED CHICKEN

CARNE DE AVES

3 1½-pound broilers, quartered
½ cup wine vinegar
2 green peppers, chopped
4 tomatoes, chopped
3 onions, chopped
2 cloves garlic, minced
2 teaspoons salt

1 teaspoon freshly ground black
  pepper
1 teaspoon orégano
½ cup olive oil
2 tablespoons tomato paste
1 cup sliced stuffed green olives

Wash and dry the chickens. Sponge with the vinegar and place in a bowl. Add the green peppers, tomatoes, onions, garlic, salt, pepper, and orégano. Mix well. Cover and marinate for 2 hours. Remove the chicken from the marinade, reserving the marinade. Heat the olive oil in a large skillet. Brown the chicken on all sides. Add the reserved marinade, tomato paste, and olives. Cover and cook over low heat for 30 minutes, or until the chicken is tender. Correct seasoning. *Serves 6.*

BROWNED PORK STRIPS

CARNE DE CERDO GUISADA

4 tomatoes, chopped
3 onions, chopped
2 cloves garlic, minced
2 teaspoons salt
½ teaspoon freshly ground black
  pepper

4 pounds boneless pork, cut into
  pieces ½ by 2 inches, ½ inch
  thick
¼ cup olive oil
¾ cup water

Combine the tomatoes, onions, garlic, salt, and pepper in a bowl. Mix well. Add the pork strips and stir well. Cover and set aside for 1 hour. Remove the pork from the bowl, reserving the vegetables.

Heat the olive oil in a deep skillet until it smokes. Add the pork strips and cook over high heat without stirring for 5 minutes. Then cook over high heat for 5 minutes, stirring occasionally. Combine the reserved vegetables with the water. Add the pork. Cover and cook over low heat for 45 minutes. Correct seasoning. Serve with boiled or fried rice. *Serves 8–10.*

COCONUT CHEESE TART

TORTA DE COCO

1¼ cups sifted flour
⅛ teaspoon salt
⅔ cup shortening
3 eggs
1 tablespoon cold water
¼ cup sugar

1 cup milk, scalded
½ cup heavy cream, scalded
½ cup cottage cheese, drained
½ cup fresh or dried grated
  coconut

Sift the flour and salt into a bowl. Cut in the shortening with a pastry blender or two knives until the consistency of coarse sand. Beat 1 of the eggs with the water and add, tossing lightly until a ball of dough is formed. Chill for 1 hour.

Preheat oven to 350°.

Beat the remaining eggs in a bowl. Beat in the sugar. Gradually add the milk and cream, beating steadily. Add the cottage cheese and mix until smooth. Add the coconut and again mix well. Roll out the dough ⅛ inch thick on a lightly floured surface. Line a 9-inch pie plate with the dough. Pour the mixture into it. Bake in a 350° oven for 45 minutes, or until a cake tester comes out clean. Serve hot or cold. *Serves 6–8.*

JAMAICA

Jamaica is a large island, which still retains a certain British atmosphere in rather engaging fashion. At one time, most of the resort development was in the general area of Kingston, a surprisingly good-sized and busy city. More recently, however, the growth has been around Montego, Port Antonio, and Ocho Rios, where dozens of elaborate hotels have been built. The weather here is generally good, although Jamaica does have a fair amount of rain; however, when there's snow in northern states in wintertime, Jamaica is delightfully warm.

The climate is usually tropical, but a regular trade wind blows almost constantly. With weather such as this, the vegetation is lush and thick, and parts of the island have a junglelike quality. A perfect place to examine the island's plant life is at the Hope Botanical Gardens, a few miles from Kingston. The produce of the island consists principally of beans, corn, ginger, sugar, coffee, and fruit. At one time sugar cane was almost the only crop, but now there is a fair amount of diversification.

The waters surrounding Jamaica are filled with many kinds of seafood, and fish dishes are a daily part of the diet. In addition, the rivers and streams supply several types of fresh-water mullet, some of which are excellent. There are shellfish, and of these, the lobster is the most highly esteemed. The recipe for stuffed lobster is a good example of the local method of handling this delicacy.

Meat is of considerably less importance than fish in the everyday life of the people. On the other hand, pork, beef, and lamb are well liked, although possibly lamb is the island favorite. Of course it must be understood that the hotels and restaurants serve food of the type and style that have become standardized in luxury establishments the world over. Thus the preference for fish is primarily on the part of the people of the island. Jamaica pepperpot is an interesting local soup specialty.

Vegetables grow abundantly and are used regularly, although the islanders have certain favorites. Dried beans and peas are so overwhelmingly popular that they almost inevitably appear at every native meal in one style or another. Red peas are particularly important to the Jamaicans; these are used in making the famous red pea soup and also in the preparation of beef and red peas.

The best desserts are the fruits, either in their natural state or in ice creams and puddings. Baked bananas are a typical dessert.

The drink of the island is the local rum, which is quite different from the Martinique, Haiti, Barbados, Virgin Islands, and Cuban types. Rum is somewhat of a staple article, frequently used in cooking. The renowned Planter's Punch is the drink of the island, or at least the tourists like to believe that it is. This belief assists the sale of rum, which in turn pleases the producers of rum, thus making everyone happy.

PLANTER'S PUNCH

Cracked ice	9 ounces light Jamaica rum (1⅛
6 dashes aromatic bitters	cups)
Juice of 3 limes or lemons	6 half slices orange
6 teaspoons sugar	6 maraschino cherries

Fill 6 tall highball glasses with finely cracked ice. Sprinkle a dash of bitters into each glass. Add the lemon juice, sugar, and rum and shake or stir until cold. Garnish each glass with an orange slice and a cherry. Serve with a straw. *Serves 6.*

STAMP AND GO

1 pound dried salt cod	3 eggs, beaten
1 onion, chopped fine	¼ cup flour
½ cup chopped tomato	3 tablespoons butter
1 clove garlic, minced	

Soak the cod in cold water overnight. Drain completely. Place in a saucepan with water to cover and cook for 40 minutes. Drain and remove the bones carefully. Mince fine with a fork. Mix in the onion, tomato, and garlic. Beat the eggs and add. Mix well. Form into small fritters.

Dip each fritter in flour. Heat the butter in a frying pan and fry the fritters until golden brown on both sides. In Jamaica, this dish is served with boiled green bananas or with fried plantains. However, it may be accompanied by French fried potatoes. Small fritters make very good hot hors d'oeuvres. *Serves 4–6.*

JAMAICA PEPPERPOT

2 pounds kale or cabbage	2 cups coarsely chopped onions
2 pounds boneless beef, cut into 1-inch cubes	2 quarts water
½ pound dried chipped beef	½ teaspoon salt
1 cup fresh or dried unsweetened grated coconut	⅛ teaspoon cayenne pepper
12 okra, stems removed	½ teaspoon thyme
	2 scallions (green onions), sliced

Wash the kale or cabbage thoroughly and cut away any discolored or tough portions. Cut into large pieces and place in a saucepan with the cubed beef, chipped beef, coconut, okra, chopped onions, and water. Bring to a boil and cook over low heat for 1 hour. Remove the kale or cabbage and okra from the saucepan; force them through a sieve and return the pulp to the saucepan. Add the salt, cayenne pepper, thyme, and scallions. Cook for 15 minutes, or until meat is tender. Correct seasoning, bearing in mind that the soup should be fairly hot and spicy. *Serves 6–8.*

STUFFED LOBSTER, JAMAICA STYLE

6 live lobsters, split	1 teaspoon salt
¼ pound butter	¼ teaspoon pepper
2 onions, chopped	Dash of cayenne pepper
¼ pound mushrooms, chopped	½ cup dry bread crumbs
1 tablespoon flour	½ cup grated cheese
½ cup chicken broth	

Remove the meat from the lobsters and cut in small pieces. Reserve the shells. Set aside. Melt 3 tablespoons of the butter in a saucepan. Add the onions and mushrooms and sauté for 15 minutes. Blend in the flour. Add the broth, stirring until the mixture boils. Add the lobster meat, salt, pepper, and cayenne pepper. Cook for 15 minutes. Correct seasoning.

Divide the lobster mixture among the shells. Sprinkle with the bread crumbs and cheese. Dot with the remaining butter. Place on a baking sheet. Bake in a 350° oven for 15 minutes, or until lightly browned on top. Serve with lime or lemon wedges. *Serves 6–12.*

BEEF AND RED PEAS

2 cups dried red peas	½ cup beef broth
2 pounds dried chipped beef	2 scallions (green onions), sliced
½ teaspoon freshly ground black pepper	¼ pound (1 stick) butter
⅛ teaspoon dried ground chili peppers	3 eggs
	½ teaspoon salt
¼ teaspoon thyme	¾ cup sifted flour
	¾ cup milk

Soak the peas in water to cover overnight. Soak the chipped beef in water to cover for 4 hours. Drain the peas, rinse, and cover with fresh water. Cook over medium heat 1 hour. Drain. Drain the chipped beef, add fresh water, and cook over medium heat for 30 minutes. Drain. Combine the peas and beef in a saucepan and add the pepper, chili peppers, thyme, broth, and scallions. Cover and cook over low heat for 30 minutes.

Cream 3 tablespoons of the butter. Add the eggs and salt, beating well. Add the flour and milk alternately, beating well. Add the remaining butter to the bean mixture. Drop the batter into the saucepan by the tablespoon. Cover and cook 15 minutes.

Serve with salad, as a main course. *Serves 8–10.*

IRIS SALAD

1 clove garlic, minced
¼ cup wine vinegar
¼ teaspoon salt
⅛ teaspoon freshly ground black
  pepper
¼ teaspoon paprika
¾ cup salad or olive oil
1 tablespoon chopped green
  pepper
1 tablespoon chopped pimento

1 tablespoon chopped green olives
1 tablespoon chopped sweet
  pickles
2 heads romaine lettuce
3 tomatoes, peeled and sliced ½
  inch thick
3 hard-cooked eggs, sliced
¼ cup chopped blanched almonds
2 bananas, diced

Mix together the garlic and vinegar and let stand 30 minutes. Strain, discarding the garlic. Combine the salt, pepper, paprika, oil, and vinegar in a bowl. Mix all the ingredients thoroughly. Add the green pepper, pimento, olives, and pickles. Mix well and chill.

Wash and dry the lettuce thoroughly. Arrange the leaves on individual plates. Place 2 slices of tomato on each plate, and place egg slices on the tomatoes. Sprinkle some almonds on each. Add the diced bananas to each portion. Pour the salad dressing over each salad and serve. *Serves 6–8.*

BAKED BANANAS WITH COCONUT CREAM

1 cup heavy cream
1 cup fresh or dried grated
  coconut
6 large firm bananas

4 tablespoons melted butter
1 tablespoon cinnamon
½ cup sugar
½ cup lime or lemon juice

Combine the cream and coconut in a bowl, place in the refrigerator, and soak for 30 minutes. Peel the bananas and place in a buttered baking dish. Mix the butter, cinnamon, sugar, and lime juice together and pour over the bananas. Bake in a 350° oven for 25 minutes, basting occasionally. While the bananas are baking, strain the cream, squeezing all the liquid from the coconut. Whip the cream and serve with the hot bananas. *Serves 6.*

HAITI

Although most people think of Spanish as the language of the Caribbean, this does not hold true for Haiti, where French is the official language. Official or not, the actual means of communication for most Haitians is Creole, which may be roughly described as a strange mixture of French, English, Spanish, and African.

There is something definitely foreign about Haiti: the language, the people, the perfumed air (although this sounds as if it were stolen from a travel folder, it is correct in this case). Even the food is off the beaten path, although there are French overtones (or undertones?) to many dishes.

Rum, known as *rhum* in Haiti, is the national alcoholic drink; it is prepared from the locally grown sugar cane. There are numerous varieties, and the best of them is indeed a fine product. Barbancourt is the great name among the *rhums*. Rum is served straight or in mixed drinks and is inexpensive. Many restaurants serve sugar, ice, and limes with the rum, permitting the diner to mix the proportions to suit himself.

If there is one simple dish that typifies the food of the peasants, it is probably the rice and beans or peas of the country folk. It is eaten at almost every meal and as a separate course. Haiti is surrounded by the sea, and fish dishes are often outstanding. The recipe for *marinade de crevette* (shrimp fritters) is typical of the unusual ways fish or shellfish is prepared. There are numerous good beef, pork, and poultry dishes to supplement the seafood, which nevertheless forms the basis of much of Haiti's cuisine.

Desserts are great specialties here, for the people are fond of sweet foods. Ice creams made from locally grown fruit are of particular importance. The coconut ice cream is often unbelievably rich, far surpassing the commercial product to which we have become accustomed. Sweet potatoes, cheap and nourishing, are eaten everywhere in the country and are often combined with sugar and syrup to make puddings and pies.

Haitian fruits are among the finest in the world; however, it is not an exotic fruit that is the favorite, for the people's choice is the familiar orange. The recipe for an orange soufflé in this section is not a dish of the country people but an example of high cuisine in the larger cities.

Every meal in Haiti ends with small cups of the nation's fine coffee, served black and very sweet.

Having enjoyed a tremendous tourist boom, the island has large numbers of fine, modern hotels, serving good and often superb food. While the hotels occasionally prepare some native food, this is more easily obtained in the towns and villages. It is surprisingly difficult to locate Haitian food, except in the homes of the residents, assuming you're fortunate enough to know someone. If not, inquire locally, and the chances are that you'll locate a small restaurant serving local specialties.

There are people who enjoy a vacation only in a foreign country. For them, Haiti is ideal, for it has a degree of the exotic that is difficult to define. Put it this way: you never for a moment feel as if you're in Brooklyn or your own home town. In addition, it is quite close to the United States, so you have the maximum of foreignness and the minimum of traveling expense.

HAITIAN RHUM PUNCH

3 teaspoons sugar	Cracked ice
3 tablespoons lemon juice	3 cups rum
1 tablespoon nutmeg	Mint leaves

Combine the sugar, lemon juice, and nutmeg. Stir until the sugar is completely dissolved. Add cracked ice and fill each glass with the rum. Stir. Garnish with several fresh mint leaves or use a few drops of mint flavoring. *Serves 6.*

SHRIMP FRITTERS

MARINADE DE CREVETTES

1 cup flour	1 clove garlic, minced
½ teaspoon baking powder	2 tablespoons finely minced
2 cups water	parsley
1 egg yolk	3 tablespoons finely chopped
2 egg whites	scallions (green onions)
½ teaspoon salt	4 drops Tabasco
½ teaspoon freshly ground black	1 cup cooked shrimp, quartered
pepper	Vegetable oil for deep frying

Beat together to make a batter all the ingredients but the shrimp and oil. Fold in the shrimp.

Heat deep oil to 370°. Pick up a tablespoon of the batter, being sure there is a piece of shrimp in it, and drop it into the oil. Don't crowd the pan. Fry until golden brown. Remove the fritters with a slotted spoon and drain on paper towels. Serve hot. *Makes about 24.*

CRAB MEAT AND AVOCADO, VINAIGRETTE

CRABE ET AVOCATS, VINAIGRETTE

1 pound crab meat
3 avocados
¼ teaspoon dry mustard
½ teaspoon salt
¼ teaspoon freshly ground black
   pepper

⅓ cup olive oil
3 tablespoons wine vinegar
1 onion, chopped
1 clove garlic, minced

Pick over crab meat, removing any cartilage. Cut the avocados in half and carefully scoop out the meat, reserving the shells. Cut the avocado meat into small cubes and combine with the crab meat. Mix the mustard, salt, and pepper in a bowl. Gradually add the oil, mixing steadily until the spices are dissolved. Beat in the vinegar, onion, and garlic. Pour over the crab and avocado mixture and mix carefully. Fill the shells with the mixture. Serve as an appetizer. *Serves 6.*

CHICKEN SOUP, HAITIAN STYLE

SOUPE AU POULET

1 tablespoon salt
½ teaspoon freshly ground black
   pepper
4-pound chicken, disjointed
3 tablespoons butter
½ pound ham or a ham bone
3 quarts water
1 chili pepper, sliced, or ¼
   teaspoon dried ground chili
   peppers

2 onions, chopped
1 stalk celery
3 potatoes, peeled and cut into
   quarters
2 carrots, sliced
2 sweet potatoes, peeled and cut
   into quarters
2 tablespoons flour
2 tablespoons tomato sauce

Combine the salt and pepper and rub it into the chicken thoroughly. Melt the butter in a large saucepan and brown the chicken in it on all sides. Add the ham, water, chili peppers, onions, and celery. Bring to a boil and skim the top. Cover and cook over medium heat for 1 hour. Add the potatoes, carrots, and sweet potatoes. Cover and cook for 1½ hours. Mix the flour and tomato sauce to a smooth paste. Add 1 cup of the soup, mixing constantly. Stir this mixture into the balance of the soup. Bring to a boil and cook over low heat for 10 minutes. Correct seasoning. Serve hot. If desired as a one-course meal, use 2 chickens. *Serves 8–10.*

FLAMING LOBSTER

HOMARD FLAMBÉ

3 cooked lobsters, split in half	1 teaspoon freshly ground black
2 tablespoons olive oil	pepper
½ cup chili sauce	½ cup rum, heated
½ cup wine vinegar	

Remove the lobster meat carefully and cut into large pieces, reserving the shells of the body. Heat the olive oil, chili sauce, vinegar, and pepper in a saucepan. Add the lobster meat to the sauce and cook over low heat for 5 minutes. Correct seasoning. Fill the shells with the mixture. Place a half lobster on each plate. Just before serving pour the rum over it and set aflame. *Serves 6.*

VEAL WITH CASHEW NUT SAUCE

ESCALOPE AUX NOIX

2 teaspoons salt	2 cups cashew nuts
1 teaspoon freshly ground black	3 tablespoons tomato sauce
pepper	1½ cups water
2 cloves garlic, minced	2 onions, chopped
3 pounds boneless veal, cut into	1 teaspoon cornstarch
1-inch cubes	1 teaspoon Worcestershire sauce
4 tablespoons butter	

Mix the salt, pepper, and garlic to a smooth paste. Roll the veal in it. Melt the butter in a casserole or Dutch oven; brown the veal in it. Add the nuts, tomato sauce, water, and onions. Cover and cook over low heat for 1 hour. Mix the cornstarch and Worcestershire sauce together and add to the gravy, stirring constantly. Cook, uncovered, for 30 minutes, or until veal is very tender. Correct seasoning. Serve with boiled rice. *Serves 6–8.*

ORANGE SOUFFLÉ

SOUFFLÉ AUX ORANGES

4 tablespoons butter	5 egg yolks
4 tablespoons flour	5 tablespoons sugar
2 cups light cream, scalded	1 orange, peeled and sliced thin
3 tablespoons grated orange rind	2 tablespoons confectioners' sugar
2 teaspoons orange extract	6 egg whites
2 tablespoons curaçao or brandy	

Melt the butter in a saucepan. Add the flour and mix until smooth. Gradually add the cream, stirring constantly until the boiling point is reached. Cook over low heat for 5 minutes, stirring occasionally. Add the orange rind, orange extract, and the liquor. Remove from heat and cool for 10 minutes. Beat the egg yolks and sugar in a bowl. Gradually add the cream mixture, beating constantly to prevent curdling. Cool for 20 minutes. Preheat oven to 350°.

Butter a 2-quart soufflé dish (or other ovenproof dish, preferably one with straight-edge sides) and dust with sugar. Place the orange slices on the bottom of the dish and sprinkle with the confectioners' sugar. Beat the egg whites in a bowl until stiff but not dry and fold them into the orange mixture gently and carefully. Pour into the soufflé dish. Bake for 30 minutes in a 350° oven, or until lightly browned. Do not open the oven under any circumstances until at least 20 minutes have passed. The soufflé should be fairly well set, otherwise the center will be too moist. Serve immediately, or the soufflé will fall. *Serves 6–8.*

PUERTO RICO

With the closing of Cuba to American tourists, Puerto Rico, lying roughly between the Caribbean Sea and the Atlantic Ocean, has been the gainer. U.S. visitors to this sunny land, where there is some sunshine about 355 days out of every year, never fail to notice that although the atmosphere is Spanish, there is definitely a feeling of being at home because of the considerable amount of English spoken.

In addition to boasting of their weather, Puerto Ricans are entitled to be proud of their wonderful seafood. Deep-sea fishing is unusually good

here, and fine catches are made regularly, both by sportsmen and by
commercial fishermen. Lobsters are good, and the local waters are filled
with a wide variety of fish of all sorts. But although fresh fish is plentiful, it must be admitted that most people prefer to eat the dried salt
cod imported from Newfoundland and Spain. The shrimp (often of
unbelievable size) and crabs are more than good; they have been acclaimed by gourmets as among the finest in the world. Many excellent
local dishes are prepared from these delicately flavored crustaceans.
Asopao, really "soupy rice," is an important dish made of rice and either
seafood or chicken. The shrimp version of *asopao* is considerably more
interesting to the enterprising gourmet than the chicken *asopao.*

Rum is the favorite drink of the islands, and is inexpensive and high
in quality. It is the custom to prepare your own drink by mixing the
desired portions of rum, ice, limes, and sugar to suit the individual
taste.

The island is becoming industrialized at a fast pace but generally may
still be classified as an agricultural area. Sugar, tobacco, coffee, and all
sorts of fruits and vegetables are grown in abundance. At one time sugar
constituted almost the sole crop; at the present time a reasonable amount
of diversification exists although not enough to satisfy certain critics.

There is definitely a Spanish quality to the food and tastes of the
people, but certain American touches have been noted. In general, however, the people prefer such old favorites as *arroz con pollo* (chicken
and rice but with local modifications). Roast suckling pig is probably
the favorite dish of everyone, although it is usually reserved for holiday
occasions.

Desserts are not unusual here, being limited largely to a few familiar
standbys such as fresh fruit, ice cream, and guava jelly. There are a few
coconut and banana desserts, and of course the tourist hotels serve
American-style desserts. The Puerto Ricans prefer to eat their candies
as dessert; these are sold at all street corners and are probably better
than the usual desserts. Black coffee, usually served quite strong, is the
typical end to a fine dinner. At breakfast, however, it is always prepared
half and half with hot milk (*cafe con leche*). Puerto Rican coffee is of
good quality but has not yet found its true level in the world's coffee
markets.

An interesting habit of the Puerto Ricans is their love of little snacks
purchased at street corners throughout the day; of these, the leading
favorite is pork cracklings, possibly not too sanitary but very delicious.

FROZEN DAIQUIRI, PUERTO RICAN STYLE

2 tablespoons powdered sugar
5 tablespoons lime or lemon juice
6 large jiggers pale rum (Puerto
  Rican type)

Cracked ice

Place cocktail or champagne glasses in the refrigerator about 30 minutes before they are needed. Put the sugar, lime juice, and rum in an electric blender. Crack the ice very fine and add to the blender. Run the blender for about 2 minutes. Pour into the chilled glasses and serve immediately. Small straws may be served with this drink if desired. *Serves 6.*

Note: Although the daiquiri probably originated in Cuba, the frozen style has become a Puerto Rican specialty.

ONION-ALMOND SOUP

SOPA DE CEBOLLA Y ALMENDRAS

3 tablespoons butter
5 onions, chopped
1½ cups blanched almonds

8 cups beef broth
6 slices toast
1 cup grated Gruyère cheese

Melt the butter in a large saucepan. Add the onions and sauté for 20 minutes, stirring frequently. Grind the almonds as fine as possible. Add to the onions, together with the broth. Cover and cook over low heat for 30 minutes. Correct seasoning. Place a slice of toast on the bottom of each soup plate. Sprinkle some of the grated cheese on each slice. Pour the soup over it and serve. If desired, the soup may be strained. *Serves 6–8.*

ROAST PORK

CERDO ASADO

2 tablespoons lard or butter
2 cups orange juice
1 tablespoon grated orange rind
2 cloves garlic, minced
3 teaspoons salt

1 teaspoon freshly ground black
  pepper
Dash of cayenne pepper
⅛ teaspoon orégano
6 pounds loin of pork

Melt the fat in a saucepan. Mix in the orange juice and rind, garlic, 1 teaspoon of the salt, ½ teaspoon of the pepper, the cayenne pepper, and orégano. Rub the remaining salt and pepper into the pork. Place the piece of pork in a roasting pan.

Roast in a 350° oven for 3 hours; add the orange mixture after half the roasting time, and baste frequently thereafter. Serve thick slices of the pork with the gravy poured over them. *Serves 6–8.*

FISH STEW

PESCADO GUISADO

½ cup olive oil
2 onions, coarsely chopped
1 carrot, peeled and sliced thin
2 leeks, sliced
2 cloves garlic, minced
2 tablespoons chopped parsley
2 pounds white-meat fish, cut into cubes (use 2 or 3 varieties, if possible)
1 bay leaf

2 teaspoons salt
½ teaspoon freshly ground black pepper
2 tomatoes, cut into small cubes
1 cup water
1 pound raw shrimp, shelled and cleaned
¼ pound scallops (or conch meat)
½ teaspoon saffron

Heat the olive oil in a deep saucepan. Add the onions, carrot, leeks, garlic, and parsley and sauté for 10 minutes, stirring frequently. Add the fish, bay leaf, salt, pepper, tomatoes, and water and cook for 20 minutes. Add the shrimp, scallops, and saffron, and cook for 10 minutes. Serve in deep soup plates, with lime or lemon wedges on the side. If desired, rub garlic on toast and serve 1 slice with each portion. *Serves 6–8.*

Note: In Puerto Rico this dish is made with the meat of the conch, a large shellfish of the West Indies. Scallops have been substituted, but conch is available in certain parts of the southeastern United States, either fresh or in cans.

EGGS AND CORN

HUEVOS DE MAÍZ

3 tablespoons butter
2 onions, sliced
2 green peppers, coarsely chopped
1 cup chopped tomatoes
2 teaspoons salt
½ teaspoon freshly ground black pepper

½ teaspoon chili powder
1 cup canned corn kernels, drained
2 tablespoons olive oil
6 or 12 eggs (use 12 eggs if served as a main course)

Melt the butter in a saucepan. Add the onions and green peppers and sauté for 10 minutes, stirring frequently. Add the tomatoes, 1 teaspoon of the salt, ¼ teaspoon of the pepper, and the chili powder. Cover and cook over low heat for 2 minutes. Correct seasoning.

Spread the mixture on the bottom of a baking dish or divide among 6 individual baking dishes. Spread the corn evenly over the tomato mixture and sprinkle with the olive oil. Break the eggs carefully on top of the corn, as for poached eggs. Sprinkle with the remaining salt and pepper. Bake in a 375° oven for 10 minutes, or until the eggs are set. Serve directly from the baking dish. *Serves 6–12.*

SOUPY RICE, PUERTO RICAN STYLE

ASOPAO

2 onions	1 teaspoon salt
1 green pepper	1 teaspoon freshly ground black
¼ pound bacon	pepper
¼ pound salt pork	2 cups raw rice
1 8-ounce can tomato sauce	½ cup capers, drained
1 bay leaf	½ cup sliced stuffed olives
¼ cup olive oil	2 pimentos, sliced
4 whole chicken breasts, with	12 fresh or canned asparagus
meat removed from bones and	tips
cut into small pieces	1 cup small canned peas
8 cups chicken broth	

Chop the onions, green pepper, bacon, and salt pork very fine. Place in a saucepan and cook over low heat for 15 minutes, stirring frequently. Add the tomato sauce and bay leaf and cook 15 minutes longer.

Heat the olive oil in a large saucepan or casserole. Add the chicken and brown lightly on all sides. Add the onion mixture, broth, salt, and pepper. Cover and cook over low heat for 10 minutes. Add the rice and cook over low heat for 30 minutes, stirring frequently. Add the capers, olives, and pimentos and cook 5 minutes longer. As the dish should be quite soupy and liquid, add more broth if rice becomes dry.

Heat the asparagus tips and peas separately. Arrange the rice mixture in deep soup plates with all of the liquid, and place the asparagus and peas on top of each portion. *Serves 6–8.*

As served at the Ponce Inter-Continental Hotel.

COCONUT RICE

ARROZ CON COCO

1 cup fresh or dried grated   1½ quarts milk
   coconut   ¾ cup sugar
1½ cups light cream   2 egg yolks, beaten
2 cups rice, washed and drained   1 teaspoon cinnamon

Combine the coconut and cream in a saucepan. Bring to a boil. Remove
from the heat and cool for 20 minutes. Press all the liquid from the
coconut and discard the pulp.

Combine the rice in a saucepan with water to cover and bring it to a
boil. Drain immediately. Boil the milk in a large saucepan. Add the rice.
Cover and cook over low heat for 20 minutes. Add the coconut cream,
sugar, egg yolks, and cinnamon, beating well. Cook for 1 minute only
and remove from the heat. Pour into a bowl and chill. Serve ice cold. A
little whipped cream may be placed on top if desired. *Serves 6–8.*

ALMOND PUDDING

PUDÍN DE ALMENDRAS

½ cup seedless raisins   1 cup heavy cream
½ cup white wine   1 cup dry bread crumbs
2 eggs   1 cup finely ground almonds
1 cup sugar   2 teaspoons cinnamon
1 cup milk   1 teaspoon nutmeg

Preheat oven to 350°.

Soak the raisins in the wine for 15 minutes. Drain. Beat the eggs in a
bowl. Add the sugar, beating well. Add the milk and cream and mix
well. Add the bread crumbs, almonds, cinnamon, nutmeg, and raisins
and mix well. Butter 6 individual custard cups or other individual
dishes. Pour the mixture into it. Place the dishes in a pan of water.
Bake in a 350° oven for 25 minutes, or until delicately browned on top
and moderately firm. Serve hot or cold. Whipped cream may be placed
on each portion. *Serves 6–8.*

THE LESSER and NETHERLANDS ANTILLES

The Greater Antilles are composed of Cuba, Jamaica, Haiti, the Dominican Republic, and Puerto Rico. The Lesser Antilles are those delightful islands curving in a semicircle directly to the southeast of Puerto Rico and then southwest, stretching to the coast of South America. Without exception, the islands are all affiliated to a greater or lesser degree with either the United States, Britain, France, or the Netherlands.

The Virgin Islands were once Danish, but they now form a welcome part of the United States. Since this is a free port, good values are often obtainable, though prices are often not quite so reasonable as in Curaçao and Panama. The islands were once forgotten by everyone but conscientious State Department clerks. They were once known to barbershop patrons of the nineties as the source of supply of bay rum. The Yankee dollar has caused quite a few changes here—certainly enough to confound the solid and sensible Danish officials who once governed the islands. Luxury hotels, deep-sea fishing yachts, glass-bottom boats, and good bathing attract increasing numbers of visitors.

Fruits are important in the local diet and are used in fruit cocktails, salads, and desserts. *Fungi* (corn meal balls) are served with *mauffay* (a salt-pork dish) and are typical examples of the local food. The islanders have an interesting custom of calling breakfast "tea" and of referring to the noonday meal as "breakfast."

In a southeasterly direction from the Virgins (as they are familiarly called) is Saba, an island without a harbor. Since ships cannot come alongside a pier, getting ashore is a difficult operation, particularly when the sea is running. There is also plane service, using the new types of short-takeoff-and-landing (STOL) aircraft, which touch down quickly and come to an exciting, shuddering stop at the end of a *very* short runway.

Nevis and Antigua, after having been overlooked while other Caribbean islands were developed for tourism, have begun to show signs of tourist life; this is particularly true of Antigua, with its excellent bathing beaches.

Guadeloupe and Martinique, separated by about eighty miles, are unique among the islands of the West Indies. They, and several additional small islands, are all that remain today of the French West Indian colonial empire. Here is a small but charming bit of France. Guadeloupe, while interesting, does not offer as much to the visitor as does Martinique, which has achieved the status of a French province, roughly equivalent to statehood in our own country. They are properly known as the "fortunate islands," as they undoubtedly are.

The food is French but with local touches, emphasis being placed on what is available, mostly fish and fruit, since almost all other foodstuffs have to be imported. *Acra l'en mori* (codfish balls) is an example of a local dish in the French-Martinique manner. The wines and liquors of France are available here at reasonable prices. A local pride is Martinique *rhum*, quite different from the other West Indian products.

Dominica lies between Guadeloupe and Martinique, and is British and very quiet, particularly when compared to the Gallic excitability of its neighbors. It is known for its many rivers, of which there are several hundred.

Saint Lucia has comparatively few accommodations for tourists, for the island is not a regular tourist haunt. Wonderful and enormous lobsters are caught in the surrounding waters, and these are prepared in a variety of ways. No matter how they are prepared, they will be found to be a treat. Fruits, too, are often of exceptional quality.

Saint Vincent, a British colony, has a colorful capital in Kingstown. The fame of the island is directly connected with the notorious Captain Bligh, who commanded the good ship *Bounty*, with orders to obtain breadfruit plants in Tahiti and bring them to Saint Vincent, which was in need of a low-cost food. Charles Laughton was so stubborn—that is, Captain Bligh was so stubborn—that after the mutiny he obtained another ship and subsequently completed his assignment by actually bringing the breadfruit to Saint Vincent in 1793, about six years after the mutiny.

Barbados is one of the few islands of the West Indies that produces green vegetables, but of course sugar cane is the principal crop. Barbados rum is good and bargain-priced. In the way of food, there is nothing unusual except flying fish, which are very good eating.

Grenada is the famous "spice island" of the West Indies. The delightful aroma of nutmeg and clove is everywhere, often noticeable at a considerable distance offshore. Grenada has very few restaurants, but the hotels offer good and sometimes fine meals.

Tobago is likely to become an important tourist spot someday. It has beautiful beaches, excellent hotels often serving wonderful meals, and many other creature comforts.

Trinidad offers the exotic, for it has a polyglot population, loads of color, and much excitement. This is the home of the calypso and also of the steel band. Calypso competitions are held in January and are worth attending.

Very small oysters, a Trinidadian specialty, are noteworthy, as are the shellfish in general. Trinidad has a large East Indian population, and Indian food is an accepted part of the island fare. Chicken *pelau*, not pilau (U.S.) or *pulao* (Pakistan), is a transplanted dish from the homeland. Pepperpot, a spicy meat dish, is a great local favorite; many people keep the pepperpot going steadily, merely adding fresh meat as required.

Trinidad produces a rum in substantial volume; its retail price is extremely low, both by the bottle and by the drink. Angostura bitters originated and still is manufactured here.

No discussion of these islands could possibly omit Curaçao and Aruba, the principal islands of the Dutch West Indies. These islands, however, are not part of the Lesser Antilles and are more correctly referred to as the Netherlands Antilles. However formal the correct and official designation, the islands are still the same friendly places. Most tourists see only Curaçao, famous as one of the best shopping ports in the world, particularly for perfumes, watches, linens, and liquors. The local food is quite good and varied, with dishes from many different lands available.

TRINIDAD RUM PUNCH

⅓ cup water
⅓ cup sugar
1 cup cracked ice
⅛ teaspoon bitters

⅓ cup lime or lemon juice
1⅛ cups Trinidad rum
6 pieces lime or lemon rind

Combine the water and sugar in a saucepan. Bring to a boil and cook over low heat for 15 minutes. Set aside to cool for 1 hour. Place the cracked ice in a mixing glass or pitcher. Add the bitters, lime juice, rum, and sugar syrup. Mix well. Strain into 6 chilled glasses and decorate each with a twist of lime or lemon rind. *Serves 6.*

FISH CAKES

ACRA L'EN MORI

1 pound fish fillets
½ onion
2 cloves garlic, minced
½ teaspoon thyme
¼ teaspoon pepper

1 package active-dry yeast
1½ cups lukewarm water
2 cups sifted flour
1½ teaspoons salt
Vegetable oil, for deep-fat frying

Grind the fish and onion in a food mill or chopper. Add the garlic, thyme, and pepper, and mix well. Refrigerate while preparing the batter. Combine the yeast and ½ cup of the lukewarm water. Soak for 5 minutes. Mix until smooth. Combine with the balance of the lukewarm water. Sift the flour and salt into a bowl. Add the yeast mixture, stirring until a soft batter is formed. Add more water or flour if necessary to have a batter of pouring consistency. Cover and set aside in a warm place for 2 hours. Stir in the fish mixture.

Heat deep oil to 360°. Drop the mixture into it by tablespoon, but do not fry more than a few at a time. Fry until the fish cakes are browned. Drain well. Serve hot. A smaller version of these fish cakes makes an excellent hors d'oeuvre. *Serves 8–10.*

CREOLE PEA SOUP

½ cup split peas
3 tablespoons butter
1½ pounds beef, cubed small
1 onion, chopped
2½ quarts water
1 carrot
2 teaspoons salt
¼ teaspoon freshly ground black
  pepper

2 sprigs parsley
½ teaspoon thyme
⅛ teaspoon nutmeg
2 white potatoes, peeled and
  cubed
2 sweet potatoes, peeled and
  cubed
½ cup chopped spinach

Wash the peas and discard any imperfect ones. Drain well. Melt the butter in a large saucepan. Add the beef cubes and onion and sauté until brown. Add the split peas, water, carrot, salt, pepper, parsley, thyme, and nutmeg. Cover and cook for 1 hour. Add the white and sweet potatoes and the spinach. Cover and cook for 30 minutes, or until the beef and vegetables are tender. *Serves 6–8.*

CRAB GUMBO

2 onions, chopped
4 tomatoes, chopped, or 1 cup
  canned tomatoes
7 cups water
10 okra, sliced
2 bay leaves
3 sprigs parsley

1½ teaspoons salt
½ teaspoon thyme
¼ teaspoon dried ground chili
  peppers
4 tablespoons butter
1 pound fresh or canned lump
  crab meat

Combine the onions, tomatoes, water, okra, bay leaves, parsley, salt, thyme, and chili peppers in a saucepan. Cover and cook over medium heat for 30 minutes, stirring occasionally. Melt the butter in a frying pan. Add the crab meat and sauté lightly until delicately brown, stirring frequently. Add to the tomato mixture. Cover and cook over low heat for 30 minutes. Correct seasoning. Serve with boiled rice. *Serves 6–8.*

CURAÇAO STUFFED CHEESE

KEESHI KENÁ

1 whole 4-pound Edam cheese
2 tablespoons butter
1 cup minced onions
1 pound ground beef
1 teaspoon salt
Dash of cayenne pepper

1½ cups peeled chopped tomatoes
½ cup dry bread crumbs
2 eggs, beaten
½ cup chopped stuffed olives
½ cup seedless raisins

Leave the wax coating on the cheese. Cut a 1-inch piece off the top; reserve. Scoop out the cheese, leaving a ½-inch-thick shell. Cover shell with water and let soak 1 hour. Drain. Grate the scooped-out cheese and measure 2 cups.

Melt the butter in a skillet; sauté the onions 5 minutes. Add the meat; cook over medium heat 5 minutes, stirring frequently. Add the salt, pepper, and tomatoes; cook 5 minutes. Remove from heat and mix in the bread crumbs, eggs, olives, raisins, and grated cheese. Stuff the cheese and replace the top. Place in a greased baking pan. Bake in a 375° oven 1½ hours. Remove from pan and let stand 5 minutes. Peel off the outer wax skin and cut the cheese into wedges. *Serves 6–8.*

Note: If you prefer, you may slice the cheese and line a casserole with it. Put the filling in, and cover with cheese slices. Bake only 40 minutes. Cut in wedges to serve.

As served at the Curaçao Inter-Continental Hotel.

VIRGIN ISLANDS POT ROAST

DAUBE MEAT

4 pounds beef (top round or top sirloin), cut 1½ inches thick
2 teaspoons salt
1 teaspoon freshly ground black pepper
2 cloves garlic, minced
½ teaspoon thyme
½ teaspoon mace

½ teaspoon nutmeg
2 tablespoons chopped parsley
3 onions, sliced
2 tomatoes, chopped
¼ cup wine vinegar
2 tablespoons butter
½ cup boiling water

Wash and dry the meat. Combine the salt, pepper, garlic, thyme, mace, and nutmeg. Rub into the meat thoroughly. Place the meat in a bowl and add the parsley, onions, tomatoes, and vinegar; mix well. Cover and marinate for 2 hours. Remove the meat, reserving the marinade. Melt the butter in a saucepan. Brown the meat well over high heat. Reduce heat and add the boiling water and the reserved marinade. Cover and cook over low heat for 1 hour, or until the meat is tender. *Serves 8–10.*

TRINIDAD PEPPERPOT

4-pound chicken, disjointed
2 pounds pork, cubed
1 pound corned beef, cubed, or
  2 pounds pickled spareribs,
  with ribs cut apart
3 cups water
3 onions, sliced
1 clove garlic, minced

½ teaspoon dried ground chili
  peppers
½ teaspoon thyme
2 tablespoons dark brown sugar
2 tablespoons Worcestershire
  sauce
½ teaspoon freshly ground black
  pepper

Combine the chicken, pork, corned beef, and water in a saucepan. Cover and cook over medium heat for 2 hours. Add the onions, garlic, chili peppers, thyme, brown sugar, Worcestershire sauce, and pepper and mix together. Cover and cook over low heat for 1 hour, or until meats are tender. Correct seasoning. Serve hot. *Serves 8–10.*

VIRGIN ISLANDS PORK AND FISH

MAUFFAY

½ pound salt pork, cubed
3 onions, chopped
1 pound pork, cut into 1-inch
  cubes
1 pound beef, cut into 1-inch
  cubes
7 cups water
2 fillets of fish (snapper, sole,
  bluefish), cut into 1-inch pieces

1 teaspoon salt
½ teaspoon freshly ground black
  pepper
¾ teaspoon thyme
3 tomatoes, chopped
½ cup corn meal

In a saucepan cook the salt pork over low heat until some of the fat is melted. Add the onions, pork, and beef and brown well. Add the water and cook over medium heat for 30 minutes. Add the fish, salt, pepper, thyme, and tomatoes. Stir in the corn meal gradually, to prevent lumps. Cook over low heat for 30 minutes. Correct seasoning. Serve with *fungi* (see recipe in this section). *Serves 6–8.*

CHICKEN AND PORK, GUADELOUPE STYLE

COLOMBO CREOLE

½ cup olive oil
2 onions, chopped
3-pound chicken, disjointed
1½ pounds boneless pork, cubed
2 cloves garlic, minced
3 cups diced eggplant
6 carrots, sliced
6 potatoes, peeled and cubed
2 teaspoons salt
½ teaspoon freshly ground black pepper
¼ teaspoon dried ground chili peppers
½ teaspoon thyme
2 tablespoons curry powder
2 cups water

Heat the oil in a saucepan. Add the onions and sauté for 10 minutes, stirring frequently. Remove the onions and set them aside. Add the chicken and pork and brown on all sides. Return the onions to the saucepan. Cover and cook over low heat for 25 minutes, stirring frequently.

Add the garlic, eggplant, carrots, potatoes, salt, pepper, chili peppers, thyme, curry powder, and water. Mix gently. Cover and cook over low heat for 45 minutes, or until the chicken is tender. Correct seasoning. Serve hot. *Serves 6–8.*

Note: This dish is an adaptation of an Indian curry, with local variations, and is an example of two different cuisines combined in one dish.

TRINIDAD CHICKEN PELAU

¼ cup flour
4 teaspoons salt
1½ teaspoons freshly ground black pepper
2 3-pound chickens, disjointed
½ cup olive oil
2 onions, chopped
2 tomatoes, peeled and cubed
2 teaspoons sugar
½ teaspoon thyme
3 cups chicken broth
1½ cups raw rice
¼ cup chopped ripe olives

Combine the flour, 2 teaspoons of the salt, and 1 teaspoon of the pepper. Roll the chicken parts in it. Heat ¼ cup of the olive oil in a heavy saucepan or casserole. Add the chicken and brown well on all sides. Remove the chicken and set aside. Add the remaining olive oil and the onions and cook over medium heat for 5 minutes, stirring frequently.

Add the tomatoes, sugar, thyme, and the remaining salt and pepper and cook over medium heat for 5 minutes. Return the chicken to the saucepan and add the broth. Cover and cook over low heat for 45 minutes. Add the rice and mix gently. Cover and cook over low heat for

25 minutes, or until the chicken and rice are tender, adding a little more water if necessary. When cooked, there should be no liquid remaining but the rice should be moist. Correct seasoning. Sprinkle the olives on top and serve. *Serves 6–8.*

CORN MEAL BALLS

FUNGI

1 cup yellow corn meal	1½ teaspoons salt
1 cup cold water	3 tablespoons butter
2 cups boiling water	

Mix the corn meal and cold water to a smooth paste. Have the boiling water and salt in a saucepan. Add the corn meal paste gradually, stirring constantly until thick. Add the butter and cook over low heat for 20 minutes, stirring frequently. Grease a teacup thoroughly. Using a tablespoon of corn meal at a time, shape into balls in the cup, and turn out. Serve hot with *mauffay* (see recipe in this section). *Serves 6–8.*

CORN CAKES

¼ pound (1 stick) butter	¼ teaspoon cinnamon
½ cup sugar	¼ teaspoon nutmeg
¾ cup sifted flour	2 eggs
½ cup corn meal	½ cup milk
2 teaspoons baking powder	

Preheat oven to 350°.

Cream the butter until smooth. Add the sugar, beating until light and fluffy. Sift the flour, corn meal, baking powder, cinnamon, and nutmeg together. Add to the butter mixture, beating well. Add the eggs and milk, again beating well. Pour into buttered muffin pans. Bake in a 350° oven for 20 minutes, or until a cake tester comes out clean. Serve hot or cold. The corn cakes may be served as a dessert or as a sweet bread. *Makes about 12 cakes.*

GROUNDNUT MACAROONS

3 egg whites	1 cup finely ground peanuts
¾ cup sugar	1 teaspoon vanilla extract

Preheat oven to 300°.

Beat the egg whites until stiff but not dry. Add the sugar gradually, beating steadily. Fold in the peanuts and vanilla. Butter a baking sheet well. Force the mixture through a pastry tube or drop by the tablespoon onto the baking sheet. Do not place the macaroons too close together. Bake in a 300° oven for 20 minutes, or until firm and dry. *Makes about 36 macaroons.*

CONKIES

¼ pound (1 stick) butter	½ cup cooked or canned pumpkin
¼ cup sugar	½ cup milk
3 eggs	2 cups corn meal

Cream the butter until smooth. Add the sugar and beat together until light. Beat in the eggs. Add the pumpkin, milk, and corn meal and mix well until smooth in texture.

Form into 2-inch balls. Wrap each one in aluminum foil or parchment paper. If parchment paper is used, tie each one securely with white thread; this will not be necessary if aluminum foil is used. Drop into boiling water and cook for 1 hour. Drain well. Serve hot in the paper in which they were cooked. They make an unusual dessert. *Makes about 24.*

PEANUT PIE

1½ cups sifted flour	½ cup sugar
½ teaspoon salt	½ cup milk
½ cup shortening	½ cup molasses
4 tablespoons cold water	¾ cup coarsely chopped peanuts
2 eggs	½ teaspoon vanilla extract

Sift the flour (reserving 1 tablespoon) and salt into a bowl. Cut in the shortening with a pastry blender or two knives. Add the water, tossing lightly until a ball of dough is formed. Roll out on a lightly floured surface to fit a 9-inch pie plate. Fit into the plate and flute the edges. Preheat oven to 425°.

Beat the eggs in a bowl. Add the sugar and remaining flour and beat until light and fluffy. Beat in the milk and molasses. Add the peanuts and vanilla. Mix lightly. Pour into the lined pie plate. Bake in a 425° oven for 10 minutes; reduce heat to 350° and bake for 25 minutes longer, or until a knife comes out clean. Serve hot or cold, with whipped cream if desired. *Serves 6–8.*

ARROWROOT AND APPLE CUSTARD

3 tablespoons butter	2 eggs, beaten
4 apples, peeled and sliced	⅓ cup sugar
1 tablespoon arrowroot	2 tablespoons seedless raisins
2 cups milk	½ cup crushed cornflakes

Preheat oven to 350°.

Melt the butter in a saucepan. Add the apples and cook over low heat for 10 minutes, stirring occasionally. Mix the arrowroot and 3 tablespoons of the milk to a smooth paste. Add the eggs and sugar and mix well. Place the remaining milk in a saucepan and bring to a boil. Pour gradually into the arrowroot and egg mixture, stirring constantly. Return to the saucepan. Cook over low heat, stirring constantly until the mixture is thickened, about 2 minutes. Add the apples and the raisins and mix well.

Pour into a buttered pie plate and sprinkle with the cornflakes. Bake in a 350° oven for 20 minutes. Serve hot or cold, with whipped cream, if desired. *Serves 6–8.*

South America

Argentina
Bolivia
Brazil
Chile
Colombia
Ecuador
The Guianas
Paraguay
Peru
Uruguay
Venezuela

ARGENTINA

Air travelers to Buenos Aires are surprised to find the world's largest air-port, called Ezeiza, serving that great metropolis. But their surprise con-tinues to mount as they find Buenos Aires to be an amazingly sophisti-cated city, having a great deal in common with Paris in both appearance and atmosphere. The city has a population of more than 3,000,000 but greater Buenos Aires totals about 7,000,000.

Tourists must likewise adjust to the mealtimes. Although Argentinians conform to the general South American custom of the late dinner hour, the lateness of the hour reaches its extreme in Buenos Aires. Breakfast is a simple meal, inevitably served in your room. Lunch comes early, about noon, and is an extremely substantial meal of many courses. Food is quite cheap here, and the Argentinians love to eat well. Tea is served about 5 P.M. or so, and is usually much more satisfying than merely tea and cake; meat is often served at teatime! Dinner is not eaten until 10 P.M. and often much later than that, particularly in the smarter restaurants and hotels. The dinner rush hour in Buenos Aires is about 11 p.m., and possibly as late as midnight.

If there's any single food the Argentinians love, it's beef, and nothing but beef. At one time, beef was so plentiful that the poorest person could afford all the meat he wanted, but those days have gone. Al-though comparatively moderate in price (because of the favorable ex-change rate) for tourists, beef is quite expensive to those who live in the country. In recent years there have been several "beefless" days each week, to the consternation of the public, permitting meat to be shipped out for needed foreign exchange. Being optimistic, the Argen-tinians are hopeful that more beef will reach them, so they can broil a steak every day for lunch, which was once the local custom.

Most tourists are surprised at the frequency with which Italian dishes appear on the menus, but this is because of the large number of Italian immigrants. Argentinian favorites include the *puchero*, a meat and vege-table soup something on the order of a New England boiled dinner, but with more meat; beef stews, such as the *carbonada;* and sweet desserts, of which the *dulce de leche* is a typical example.

Beer is a fine local product, but Argentina is primarily a country of wine drinkers. Both red and white wines are produced here, among which the best known are Casa de Piedra and Bianchi Cabernet. Champagnes are relatively cheap and of high quality.

Shopping for leather and suede articles on Buenos Aires' famous, narrow Calle Florida can be great fun, particularly in view of the bargains offered. When you get hungry, many of the city's best restaurants and hotels are nearby.

The real, native, and most widespread drink of all is *maté,* the so-called Paraguayan tea. *Maté* is prepared from the very young leaves of an evergreen tree, and the resulting infusion tastes much like tea but somewhat less astringent in flavor. Although efforts have been made to introduce the beverage in the United States, they have not been too successful, since most people do not like it until they become better acquainted with it.

ROSITA COCKTAIL

6 jiggers gin	1 jigger Crème de Rose
2 jiggers brandy	(optional)
2 teaspoons grenadine	6 maraschino cherries
1 teaspoon lemon juice	6 pieces lemon peel

Place the gin, brandy, grenadine, lemon juice, and Crème de Rose in a cocktail shaker with about 8 ice cubes. Shake well for at least 1 minute and pour into chilled cocktail glasses. Garnish each glass with a maraschino cherry and a slim twist of lemon peel. *Serves 6.*

Note: Crème de Rose is a French cordial made from rose petals and is difficult to obtain in the United States, although quite common in South America. It merely gives the drink an aroma. As a substitute, place a gardenia or rose petal in each glass.

PICKLED SQUABS

POLLITO EN ESCABECHE

3 squabs or rock Cornish hens,
  quartered
3 teaspoons salt
¾ teaspoon freshly ground black
  pepper
1 cup olive oil
4 large onions, sliced
2 cloves garlic, minced

2 pimentos, cut in julienne
  strips
4 bay leaves
½ cup tarragon vinegar
½ cup dry white wine
⅛ teaspoon dried ground chili
  peppers
3 tablespoons chopped parsley

Wash and dry the squabs, then rub inside and out with half the salt and pepper. Heat 2 tablespoons of the oil in a large skillet; lightly brown the squabs in it.

Spread half the onions in an earthenware or porcelain heatproof casserole. Arrange the squabs in the casserole and cover with the remaining onions. Mix together all the remaining ingredients and pour over the contents of the casserole. Cover and cook over low heat 45 minutes, or until squabs are tender. Remove the squabs with a slotted spoon. Cook the sauce over high heat until reduced to about half the quantity. Pour over the squabs and refrigerate overnight. Serve cold, as a first course or luncheon dish. *Serves 6–12.*

ARGENTINE BOILED DINNER

PUCHERO CRIOLLO

1 cup dried or 2 cups canned,
  drained chick-peas
2 pounds short ribs of beef
½ pound lean salt pork, sliced
3½-pound chicken, disjointed
3 spicy sausages (Spanish, if
  possible)
6 carrots, peeled
6 onions
6 cloves garlic, minced

1 small squash, peeled and
  sliced
6 tomatoes
1 cabbage, cut into eighths
1 green pepper, chopped
6 potatoes, peeled
6 leeks or scallions (green
  onions)
2 tablespoons chopped parsley

If dried chick-peas are used, soak overnight in water to cover. Drain. Measure 4 quarts of water into a large saucepan. Add the soaked chick-peas. (If canned chick-peas are being used, do not add until the vegetables are added.) Bring the water to a boil. Add the beef, pork, and chicken. Cover and cook over medium heat for 1½ hours. Add the sausages and carrots. Cook for 30 minutes. Add the onions, garlic, squash, tomatoes, cabbage, green pepper, potatoes, leeks, and parsley. Cook for 30 minutes, or until potatoes are tender. Correct seasoning. (No salt is provided in the recipe, because of the salt pork and sausage.)

Remove the meats and arrange on a platter. Place the vegetables around the meat. Serve the soup in individual plates at the same time. *Serves 6–8.*

FRIED STEAKS

CHURRASCO REBOSADO

4 egg yolks
1½ cups sifted flour
½ cup milk
1 clove garlic, minced
1½ teaspoons salt
½ teaspoon pepper

½ teaspoon marjoram
4 egg whites, stiffly beaten
8 fillets of beef or 8 individual
　boneless sirloin steaks
1 cup vegetable oil

Beat the yolks in a bowl. Add the flour, beating until smooth. Add the milk, garlic, salt, pepper, and marjoram and beat again until smooth. Fold in the egg whites carefully. Dip the steaks in the batter, coating them well. Heat the oil in a frying pan until it smokes. Fry the steaks in it for 5 minutes on each side. Serve with boiled rice and a crisp green salad. *Serves 8.*

FILLET OF BEEF, MAR DEL PLATA STYLE

LOMO, MAR DEL PLATA

3 tablespoons butter
4-pound fillet of beef (in 1
　piece)
4 slices bacon
2 hard-cooked egg yolks,
　chopped
½ cup chopped mushrooms
2 tablespoons chopped parsley
2 tablespoons olive oil
1 cup dry white wine

½ cup beef broth
1 onion, chopped
1 bay leaf
3 peppercorns
¼ teaspoon thyme
¼ cup dry bread crumbs
¼ cup grated Parmesan cheese
2 tablespoons flour
2 tablespoons water

Melt the butter in a skillet. Brown the fillet in it on all sides. Place the bacon on the bottom of a casserole or roasting pan, with the fillet over it. Mix the egg yolks, mushrooms, parsley, and olive oil together and spread it on the fillet. Add wine, broth, onion, bay leaf, peppercorns, and thyme.

Roast in a 350° oven for 30 minutes. Turn the fillet over, sprinkle with the bread crumbs and cheese, and continue roasting for 20 minutes. Remove the meat and keep warm. Mix the flour and water to a smooth paste and add to the gravy in the casserole. Place over direct heat and cook for 5 minutes, stirring constantly. Discard the bay leaf. *Serves 6–8.*

MEAT-CORN PUDDING

PASTEL DE CHOCLO

1 pound top sirloin of beef	1 cup chopped tomatoes
½ cup seedless raisins	¼ cup beef broth
3 tablespoons olive oil	¾ cup sliced stuffed olives
1 cup thinly sliced onions	½ teaspoon ground cumin seed
1 cup thinly sliced green pepper	2 tablespoons butter
1 tablespoon flour	½ cup chopped onions
3 teaspoons salt	2 cups canned corn kernels
¼ teaspoon dried ground chili peppers	2 egg yolks
	¼ cup heavy cream

Cut the meat in small dice.

Soak the raisins in hot water while preparing the meat. Heat the oil in a skillet; sauté the sliced onions and green peppers 5 minutes. Mix in the meat until browned. Sprinkle with the flour, 2 teaspoons of the salt, and the chili peppers. Stir in the tomatoes and broth. Cook over low heat 5 minutes, stirring frequently. Remove from heat and mix in the olives, cumin, and drained raisins. Turn into a 10-inch buttered pie plate.

Melt the butter in the skillet; sauté the chopped onions 5 minutes. Mix in the corn and remaining salt. Cook 5 minutes. Beat the egg yolks and cream; add to the corn mixture. Spread over the meat and bake in a 350° oven 20 minutes, or until the custard is firm. *Serves 4–6.*

BUTTER COOKIES

ALFAJORES

1¾ cups sifted flour	2 teaspoons grated lemon rind
⅛ teaspoon salt	4 egg yolks, lightly beaten
½ cup sugar	1 teaspoon vanilla extract
¼ pound (1 stick) butter	

Combine the flour, salt, and sugar in a bowl. Cut in the butter with a pastry blender or two knives. Work in the lemon rind, then mix in the egg yolks and vanilla. Shape into two balls and chill for 2 hours. Preheat oven to 325°.

Roll out one piece at a time on a floured surface to a thickness of ¼ inch. Cut into 2-inch rounds and, with a spatula, transfer the cookies to a cooky sheet. Bake 15 minutes or until browned. *Makes about 50 cookies—25 when sandwiched with Dulce de Leche* (see recipe in this section).

SWEET MILK DESSERT

DULCE DE LECHE

2 cups milk
¾ cup sugar
1 teaspoon vanilla extract

Dash of baking soda
1 cup fresh or dried grated
  coconut

Combine the milk, sugar, vanilla, and baking soda in a saucepan. Bring to a boil. Cook over very low heat 2½ hours, or until the mixture forms a soft ball when a small amount is dropped into cold water. Mix occasionally. Test the mixture once or twice to see whether the desired stage has been reached. Spread the *dulce de leche* between 2 *alfajores* (see recipe in this section). Sprinkle the coconut on a piece of wax paper and roll each cooky on its side so as to pick up the coconut.

Note: If desired, the Argentine custom may be followed, which is to use condensed milk, instead of regular milk and sugar. Shake 2 cans of condensed milk very well. Place in a saucepan and cover completely with water. Boil rapidly for 1½ hours, making sure that the cans are always covered with water. Cool under cold water. It is not necessary to add sugar, vanilla, or baking soda. Merely spread the alfajores with the contents of the can.

BOLIVIA

It is certain to be an exciting moment when your jet lands at the El Alto de la Paz Airport some 13,500 feet above sea level in extremely rarefied atmosphere. La Paz, the *de facto* capital of the country, is located at about 12,000 feet, and is therefore *below* the airport. Its only rival to the title of the highest capital in the world is Lhasa, Tibet, but La Paz is certainly the highest capital customarily reached by tourists.

Bolivia is not too far from the equator, and most people think of it as a tropical country; this is certainly true of the nation's lowlands, the Yungas, which are subtropical. In these narrow, steep valleys grow the delicious fruits of the country including the avocados, bananas, cherimoyas, and—particularly worthy of note—the local pineapples. La Paz itself is an amazing city, with an unbelievably colorful Indian population and sights that are sure to startle the tourist who believes that he has seen everything. Its altitude limits your movements for the first few days until some adjustment has been made to the great height, but after that it is possible to ski nearby at a mere 17,000 feet if that is your desire, and assuming that you know how to ski. The weather is extremely variable, and it is warm only in the middle of the day even during the summer.

Possibly because of the high altitude or the chilly weather, the Bolivians are fond of spicy foods, such as *picantes* (tiny pieces of chicken or other ingredients served in a very hot sauce). *Ají de carne* (actually a pepper meat) is a favorite treatment of beef and pork. The food eaten here is similar to that of Chile and Peru, but whereas in those countries red peppers are treated with a moderate amount of respect, in Bolivia all caution is cast aside.

Dinner is usually eaten when the temperature hovers in the low thirties, and hot, thick soups are justifiably popular. An interesting example is the *valdiviano con huevos* (a soup with eggs). Spaghettis and starchy foods of all sorts have become regular parts of the local diet, as heat-producing foods are much needed. *Parilladas* (meat roasted over open fires) are also greatly appreciated. Fresh fish is an unexpected treat in these high altitudes, since it comes from the world's highest navigable lake, Titicaca. A trip across this shallow lake is an unforgettable and very cold experience.

The Bolivians have a particular favorite in *chuño,* the frozen potato beloved of the Indian population. Owing to the altitude, local potatoes are fairly small at the beginning but then they are frozen, thawed, and frozen again. The process may be repeated several additional times, often ending with a potato the size of a golf ball. The net result is that almost all the moisture is removed from the poor little potato, leaving a small ball of practically pure starch. *Chuño* is then used in many different ways, often in Bolivian stews, but also with eggs or fish, to which it adds a rather unique, cheeselike flavor.

Although local wines and beer are available, the tourist is well advised to use them sparingly during the first few days of a visit because of the extreme altitude. The very best wine, it is agreed, comes from the Cochabamba region, the *muyurina.* Bolivian beer is indeed among the best in South America, if not the very best, as local chauvinists like to claim. Until a little adjustment has been made to the chilly evenings and the high altitude, most tourists are content to do without icy-cold beer, no matter how good it may be.

SOUP WITH EGGS

VALDIVIANO CON HUEVOS

½ cup olive or vegetable oil   2 quarts beef broth
4 cups chopped onions   ½ teaspoon marjoram
3 cloves garlic, minced   8 eggs
½ teaspoon achiote (optional)   4 tablespoons chopped parsley
½ pound dried beef, shredded   ⅛ teaspoon cayenne pepper

Heat the oil in a saucepan. Add the onions, garlic, and achiote and sauté
for 15 minutes, stirring frequently. Add the beef, broth, and marjoram
and cook over low heat for 30 minutes. Correct seasoning. Break the eggs
carefully into the soup. Cook for 3 minutes over medium heat. Place an
egg in each soup plate. Pour the soup over the eggs. Sprinkle with the
parsley and cayenne pepper. Serve immediately. *Serves 8.*

BAKED STUFFED FISH FILLETS

PESCADO AL HORNO

⅜ pound (1½ sticks) butter   3 teaspoons salt
2 onions, chopped   1 teaspoon freshly ground black
2 cups fresh bread crumbs   pepper
3 egg yolks, beaten   ¼ teaspoon nutmeg
2 tablespoons heavy cream   6 fillets of sole, snapper, or other
½ cup dry sherry   similar fish

Melt 1 stick of the butter in a frying pan. Add the onions and sauté for
10 minutes, stirring frequently. Add the bread crumbs and cook over low
heat for 2 minutes, stirring constantly. Remove the pan from the heat.
Add the egg yolks, mixing constantly. Mix in the cream, ¼ cup of the
sherry, 1½ teaspoons of the salt, ½ teaspoon of the pepper, and the nutmeg.

Divide the mixture evenly among the 6 fillets and roll each one up,
fastening them with toothpicks. Melt the remaining butter in a baking
dish. Place the fillets in it. Sprinkle with the remaining sherry, salt, and
pepper. Bake in a 400° oven for 30 minutes, basting frequently. Serve
with boiled potatoes and a dry white wine. *Serves 6.*

PEPPER PORK

AJÍ DE CARNE

½ cup olive oil
5 onions, chopped
3 cloves garlic, minced
3 tablespoons raw rice
3 pounds pork, cut into ½-inch cubes
4 tomatoes, chopped
¼ teaspoon saffron
2 teaspoons salt
½ teaspoon freshly ground black pepper

¼ teaspoon dried ground chili peppers
1 clove
¼ teaspoon cinnamon
2 cups beef broth
6 potatoes, peeled and quartered
2 green bananas, peeled and quartered
½ cup ground peanuts
½ cup heavy cream
1 tablespoon molasses

Heat the olive oil in a large saucepan. Add the onions and garlic and sauté for 5 minutes, stirring frequently. Add the rice and meat and cook over high heat until the meat is brown. Add the tomatoes, saffron, salt, pepper, chili peppers, clove, cinnamon, and broth. Cover and cook over low heat for 30 minutes.

Add the potatoes and bananas and cook 15 minutes longer. Add the peanuts, cream, and molasses. Cook for 15 minutes, or until the meat and potatoes are tender. Correct seasoning. Serve hot. *Serves 6–8.*

Note: This is a fairly spicy dish, and the Bolivians use considerably more chili peppers than called for in this recipe.

DUCK "DELICIOUS"

PATO DELICIOSO

2 4-pound ducks, disjointed
2 quarts water
5 carrots, sliced
3 stalks celery, sliced
3 cloves garlic, minced
5 leeks, sliced, or 2 onions, sliced thin
1 green pepper, sliced thin

1 tablespoon salt
1 teaspoon freshly ground black pepper
6 potatoes, peeled
3 tablespoons butter
2 cups dry bread crumbs
3 hard-cooked eggs, sliced

Remove as much fat as possible from the uncooked ducks. Combine the ducks in a large saucepan with the water, carrots, celery, garlic, leeks, green pepper, salt, and pepper. Bring to a boil and skim the top carefully. Cover and cook over medium heat for 45 minutes. Add the potatoes and cook for 30 minutes, or until the ducks and potatoes are tender.

Remove the ducks and set aside. Strain the stock and reserve the stock and vegetables separately.

Melt the butter in a saucepan. Add the bread crumbs and mix well. Add 2 cups of the reserved stock. Cook over low heat for 5 minutes, stirring frequently. Correct seasoning. Place the ducks on a platter, with the vegetables on top. Pour the bread-crumb mixture over and around the duck. Garnish with egg slices. Serve hot. *Serves 6–8.*

ALMOND COOKIES

ALFAJORES DE ALMENDRAS

½ pound (2 sticks) butter
1 cup sugar
3 eggs, beaten
3 tablespoons grated lemon rind
1 tablespoon brandy

⅛ teaspoon almond extract
1 cup sifted flour
2½ cups ground blanched
  almonds
1 egg white

Cream the butter. Add the sugar and beat until light and fluffy. Add the eggs, beating well. Add the lemon rind, brandy, almond extract, flour, and 2 cups of the ground almonds, again mixing well. Form the mixture into a ball, wrap in wax paper, and chill for at least 3 hours. Preheat oven to 375°.

Roll out the dough about ⅛ inch thick on a lightly floured surface. Cut into any desired shape, such as circles, strips, or squares. Brush with the egg white and sprinkle with the remaining almonds. Place on a buttered cooky sheet. Bake in a 375° oven for 12 minutes, or until lightly browned. *Serves 8–10.*

COCONUT TARTS

PASTELITOS DE COCO

2 cups sifted flour
½ teaspoon baking powder
1 teaspoon salt
½ cup shortening
4 tablespoons ice water
⅔ cup sugar

1½ cups fresh or dried grated
  coconut
¾ cup light cream
3 egg yolks, beaten
3 tablespoons butter

Reserve 1 tablespoon of the flour and sift the balance into a bowl with the baking powder and salt. Cut in the shortening with a pastry blender or two knives. Add the water, tossing lightly until a ball of dough is formed. Wrap in wax paper and place in the refrigerator while preparing the filling.

Mix the reserved tablespoon of flour with the sugar, coconut, and cream in a saucepan. Cook over low heat, stirring constantly, until the mixture is thick. Add 2 of the beaten egg yolks gradually, mixing constantly. Add the butter and cook over low heat for 3 minutes. Remove from the heat and cool. Preheat oven to 425°.

Roll out the dough about ⅛ inch thick on a lightly floured surface. Cut into 3-inch squares or circles. Place 1 tablespoon of the coconut mixture on half the pieces and cover with the remaining pieces, pressing the edges together carefully with a fork. Place on a baking sheet and brush the tops with the remaining egg yolk. Bake in a 425° oven for 12 minutes, or until lightly browned. *Makes about 30 tarts.*

BRAZIL

World travelers often debate as to which city has the most beautiful setting, and the winner is inevitably Rio de Janeiro. Since words have always failed those who attempt to describe the beauties of nature, no attempt will be made to describe Rio except to say that it must be seen in person. One of the greatest experiences of a lifetime is coming into Rio on a Pan American plane with the sea and the mountains as a background. São Paulo, the industrial city south of Rio de Janeiro, is growing so fast that no one can foresee the end of its phenomenal growth. As the Brazilians say, Rio for pleasure, São Paulo for work.

When you mention Brazil to a gourmet, his first thought is of coffee, and of course this is truly the land of coffee. But Brazil has many fine native dishes, many unique food creations, any number of rare fruits and, of course, fine seafood. The shrimp are particularly good, and you'll want to try them prepared in the local styles, particularly barbecued on a spit and the little shrimp pies (*empadinhas de camarões*) served as appetizers. Possibly "hash" is a horrible word to you, but that is because you have never eaten *picadinho,* the Brazilian version of hash, and probably the world's best. *Pato com môlho de laranja* (duck with orange sauce) is well worth searching for. Brazilians like meats broiled over coals, which they call *churrasco;* the meats are always sprinkled with a starchy flour called *mandioca,* which is made from the ground cassava roots found in Brazil.

If you asked a Brazilian what one dish typifies the country, he would probably select the *feijoada,* a bean dish made in different ways but usually containing meat, rice, and spices. Beans in any form are popular here and are served with practically any dish you might select.

Brazilians, in accordance with South American custom, have only coffee, usually served half and half with hot milk, for breakfast. During the rest of the day they drink ten, fifteen, twenty, or even more tiny thimblefuls of coffee, usually black and sweet, at one of the tiny coffee stands scattered throughout the city. Lunch is a large meal and so is dinner, which is eaten about 9 P.M. Teashops are very popular with everyone and are usually crowded in the afternoon, when the people stop for *chá* —that is, to drink their fourteenth, no, twenty-fourth cup of coffee.

One Brazilian specialty that has made its way around the world (in cans) is that great delicacy *palmitos,* or hearts of palm. They are obtained from the hearts of palm trees and have an exquisite flavor. Brazilians like them in salads, but they often appear surprisingly in many other dishes.

Other than coffee and *maté* (discussed in the sections on Paraguay and Uruguay), the Brazilians like their own *cachaça,* a raw rum that is pale only in color, for its effect is far from colorless. Most tourists do not approve of its unrefined taste, and prefer to drink the local beer, which is probably among the best in the world. Almost any given brand will be found to be excellent. While some wine is produced and imported, it cannot be said that wine drinking has assumed much importance in the land. There are many excellent bottled soft drinks, of which the best is probably *guaraná,* a popular favorite.

Oh yes, B----l nuts grow in Brazil. They are rather difficult to obtain in Rio de Janeiro, because most of them are shipped north to the United States, from Belém, in Pará.

BATIDA

6 jiggers rum or brandy	1 tablespoon honey
1 cup grapefruit juice	1 tablespoon fresh or dried grated
1 cup pineapple juice	coconut
1 ripe banana, cut into small	1 teaspoon almond extract
pieces	1 cup finely cracked ice
1 teaspoon grenadine	
1 tablespoon lemon or lime	
juice	

Place the rum, grapefruit and pineapple juice, banana, grenadine, lemon or lime juice, honey, coconut, almond extract, and cracked ice in an electric blender. Mix for at least 1 minute. Strain into chilled glasses. Decorate with a maraschino cherry or a fresh mint leaf. *Serves 6.*

Note: In Brazil, this drink is often made with cachaça, *a pale, underaged rum.*

SHRIMP HORS D'OEUVRE PASTRIES

EMPADINHAS DE CAMARÕES

1½ cups sifted flour
1½ teaspoons salt
¾ cup shortening
1 egg, beaten
¼ cup ice water
3 tablespoons olive oil
½ cup chopped onions
1½ cups chopped tomatoes

1 pound cooked cleaned shrimp, diced
½ teaspoon freshly ground black pepper
2 hard-cooked egg yolks, chopped
¼ cup chopped black olives
2 tablespoons minced parsley

Sift the flour and ¾ teaspoon of the salt into a bowl; cut in the shortening with a pastry blender or two knives. With a fork, stir in the egg and water until a ball of dough is formed. Wrap in foil or wax paper and chill 2 hours.

Heat the oil in a skillet; sauté the onions 10 minutes. Add the tomatoes; cook over low heat 10 minutes. Mix in the shrimp, pepper, and remaining salt; cook over low heat 5 minutes. Remove from heat and blend in the egg yolks, olives, and parsley. Taste for seasoning and cool.

On a lightly floured surface, roll out the dough ⅛ inch thick. Cut into 5-inch circles. Place a tablespoon of the shrimp mixture on each, and fold over the dough, sealing the edges with a little water. Arrange on a greased baking sheet. Bake in a preheated 400° oven 15 minutes, or until browned. Serve hot. *Makes about 2 dozen pastries.*

PUMPKIN SOUP

SOPA DE ABOBORA

3 tablespoons butter
½ cup minced onions
4 cups cooked or canned puréed pumpkin
6 cups chicken broth

1 teaspoon salt
Dash of cayenne pepper
2 cups light cream
Dash of nutmeg

Melt the butter in a saucepan; sauté the onions 5 minutes. Mix in the pumpkin, broth, salt, and cayenne pepper. Bring to a boil and cook over low heat 30 minutes. Mix in the cream; heat and taste for seasoning. Sprinkle with nutmeg. *Serves 6–8.*

SHRIMP-COCONUT STEW

VATAPA

1 cup unsweetened flaked
   coconut
2 cups milk
2 tablespoons olive oil
1½ cups finely chopped onions
2 cloves garlic, minced
½ teaspoon dried ground chili
   peppers
4 cups water
2 teaspoons salt

2 bay leaves
1 pound snapper or halibut,
   cut in 2-inch pieces
1½ pounds raw shrimp, shelled
   and deveined
½ pound dried shrimp, finely
   chopped (optional)
2 cups ground peanuts
½ cup yellow corn meal
3 tablespoons butter

Combine the coconut and milk; bring to a boil and let soak 30 minutes. Strain, squeezing out all the milk. Reserve the milk.

Heat the oil in a saucepan; sauté the onions, garlic, and chili peppers 10 minutes. Add the water, salt, and bay leaves. Bring to a boil; add the fish and raw shrimp. Cook over low heat 10 minutes. Remove the fish and shrimp; strain the stock. Combine the coconut milk with the dried shrimp and peanuts. Bring to a boil and cook over low heat 15 minutes. Strain.

Combine the reserved stock with the peanut mixture; bring to a boil, and stir in the corn meal. Cook over low heat 25 minutes, stirring frequently. Stir in the butter and return the fish and shrimp. Taste for seasoning. Serve in deep bowls. *Serves 6–8.*

CHICKEN WITH BROWN GRAVY

FRANGO AO MÔLHO PARDO

2 4-pound roasting chickens,
   disjointed
¼ pound chicken livers
2½ teaspoons salt
½ teaspoon freshly ground black
   pepper
2 tablespoons olive oil
2 tablespoons butter

1 cup chopped onions
1 bay leaf
1 stalk celery and leaves
2½ cups chicken broth
16 very small white onions
1 tablespoon flour
2 teaspoons Kitchen Bouquet
3 tablespoons water

Wash and dry the chicken pieces. Purée all the livers in an electric blender or chop to a paste. Refrigerate until needed. Season the chicken pieces with the salt and pepper.

Heat the oil and butter in a Dutch oven; brown the chicken in it very well. Add the chopped onions and let brown. Add the bay leaf, celery, and broth. Cover and cook over low heat 1 hour. Add the white onions and cook 30 minutes longer.

Mix the flour, Kitchen Bouquet, and water to a smooth paste. Stir into the gravy. Cook 5 minutes and taste for seasoning. Just before serving, stir the livers into the gravy. Heat, but do not let boil. Serve with rice. *Serves 8.*

ASSORTED MEATS AND BLACK BEANS

FEIJOADA

1 pound dried beef	1 cup chopped onions
3 cups dried black beans	2 cloves garlic, minced
1 pound raw corned beef	½ pound Spanish sausages,
¼ pound salt pork	sliced
4 pounds loin of pork	¼ teaspoon dried ground chili
1½ teaspoons salt	peppers
½ teaspoon freshly ground black	Rice
pepper	Sliced oranges
1 cup orange juice	Pickled onions
3 tablespoons olive oil	

Soak the dried beef in cold water for 2 hours. Drain, cover with fresh water, and bring to a boil. Cook 5 minutes. Drain and cut in small pieces.

Wash the beans, cover with water, and bring to a boil; let soak 1 hour. Drain, add fresh water to cover, and bring to a boil; add the dried beef; cook over low heat 2½ hours. While the beans are cooking, prepare the other meats. Combine the corned beef and salt pork in a saucepan. Add water to cover. Bring to a boil; cover and cook over low heat 2½ hours.

Season the pork loin with the salt and pepper; roast in a 375° oven 1¾ hours. When beans are tender, drain the corned beef and salt pork and add to the beans. Remove 1 cup beans and purée in an electric blender or mash to a paste. Return to the remaining beans with the orange juice. Cook over low heat 1 hour.

Heat the oil in a skillet; sauté the onions and garlic 5 minutes. Add the sausages and let brown. Add to the beans with the chili peppers. Cook 30 minutes. Taste for seasoning.

Slice the meats and arrange on a platter. Put the beans in a deep bowl. Serve with rice, sliced oranges and pickled onions. *Serves 10–12.*

DUCK WITH BRAZIL NUTS AND ORANGE SAUCE

PATO COM MÔLHO DE LARANJA

5-pound duck	¼ cup rum
6 cups orange juice	3 bananas, cut into 2-inch pieces
1 bay leaf	1 tablespoon cornstarch
2 teaspoons salt	½ cup slivered Brazil nuts
½ teaspoon freshly ground black	¼ cup Curaçao or Cointreau
pepper	½ cup currant jelly, cubed
2 tablespoons grated orange	
rind	

Wash and dry the duck; bring 4 cups of the orange juice and the bay
leaf to a boil in a saucepan. Add the duck; cook over low heat 30 minutes, turning the duck several times. Drain, skim the fat, and reserve 3
cups of the liquid. Season the duck with the salt and pepper; place in a
shallow roasting pan. Roast in a 450° oven 20 minutes. Add the grated
rind, the remaining orange juice and the rum. Reduce heat to 350° and
roast 30 minutes. Add the bananas and roast 15 minutes longer or until
duck is tender. Baste frequently. Transfer the duck and bananas to a
serving platter and keep warm. Skim the fat from the pan gravy, and
pour the gravy and reserved stock into a saucepan. Mix the cornstarch
with a little water to a smooth paste; stir into the gravy until thickened.
Add the Brazil nuts and Curaçao; cook over low heat 5 minutes.

Carve the duck and arrange the bananas and currant jelly around it.
Pour some gravy over it and serve the rest in a sauceboat. *Serves 4.*

TURKEY, BRAZILIAN STYLE

PERÚ A BRASILEIRA

10-pound turkey	4 green peppers, chopped
1½ tablespoons salt	½ cup chopped parsley
2 teaspoons freshly ground black	1½ cups wine vinegar
pepper	1 pound thinly sliced smoked
3 cloves garlic, minced	ham (Prosciutto or Parma
1 cup olive oil	type)
4 tomatoes, cubed	

The turkey should be seasoned the day before it is used. Mix the salt,
pepper, and garlic to a paste. Rub into the turkey thoroughly, both inside and out. Place the turkey in a roasting pan. Combine the olive oil,
tomatoes, green peppers, parsley, and vinegar. Pour over the turkey.
Place overnight in the refrigerator, basting occasionally.

Remove the turkey from the refrigerator 4 hours before it is to be roasted. Baste frequently during this 4-hour period. Place in a 350° oven and roast 2¾ hours, basting quite frequently. Carve the turkey into slices and arrange on a platter, alternating with a slice of ham after every third slice of turkey. Force the gravy through a sieve and serve separately in a sauceboat. *Serves 10–12.*

BRAZIL NUT CAKE

TORTA DE CASTANHA-DO-PARÁ

10 egg yolks	10 egg whites
1¾ cups powdered sugar	1½ cups heavy cream
3 cups finely ground Brazil nuts	2 tablespoons coffee essence
⅛ teaspoon salt	3 tablespoons confectioners'
2 tablespoons brandy	sugar
3 tablespoons dry bread crumbs	

Beat the egg yolks in a bowl. Gradually add the powdered sugar, beating until thick. Add the nuts, salt, brandy, and bread crumbs, mixing well. Preheat oven to 350°. Beat the egg whites until stiff but not dry and fold into the nut mixture.

Butter a 10-inch spring-form pan and dust lightly with bread crumbs. Pour the batter into it. Bake in a 350° oven for 45 minutes or until a cake tester comes out clean. Leave the cake in the oven with the heat off and the door open for 5 minutes after it is finished baking. Cool for 2 hours. Remove from the form. Split the cake.

Whip the cream and add the coffee essence and confectioners' sugar, mixing lightly. Spread some of the cream between the halves and place the rest on top. Chill. Some sliced or chopped Brazil nuts may be sprinkled on top if desired. *Serves 10–12.*

CHILE

Probably the most food-conscious nation of the South American countries is Chile, the (2900-mile) long land located on the southwestern portion of the continent. But while the shape of the nation is long and lean, a great deal of fat living is available there, particularly for those who enjoy seafood, game, fruits, and wines. Although the physical contours of Chile are like those of an anemic fashion model, with Chile's fine food, it is remarkable that any woman can remain slim.

It is advisable to eat only the typical breakfast of coffee and a bit of pastry or bread, for the meals that follow will make up for it. Lunch is always a substantial meal, and tea is a "must," a meal at which tea itself often plays an unimportant part, for it is actually a complete light meal usually served about 5:30 P.M. Custom decrees a brief pause, and then the "vermouth" hour begins at about six-thirty or so; it is so called because originally everyone drank a glass of vermouth, which has now been, to some extent, replaced by cocktails. Then everyone goes to see the latest motion picture at a performance advertised as the "Vermouth Showing," followed by a large dinner at ten in the evening.

The people are fond of thick, rich soups filled with meat and chicken, and these are important in the national diet. Corn, beans, and sausage are also in great demand and are used in numerous different fashions in cooking.

With its tremendous coast line facing the Pacific, Chile can fish in its own back yard for food, and out of the sea come many delicious and unusual fish. Running alongside the coast is that mysterious movement of water known as the Humboldt Current, a cold stream in the ocean moving northward from the Antarctic and carrying with it both fish and the food the fish live on. There are *congrio, corbina,* and swordfish—all extraordinarily fine-tasting. Chile has such unique shellfish as the *erizoa* (a sea urchin often served in a green sauce), *locos* (best described as a cross between an abalone and a scallop), *chorros* (giant clams), as well as oysters, shrimp, mussels, and many others. *Jaibas* (crabs) are excellent. The favorite treatment for shellfish is to prepare it as a *chupe,* or seafood chowder, sometimes mild but often very spicy. Seaweed found along the shore, *luche,* is used frequently. The pride of all Chilean seafood is probably the *langosta,* a delicately flavored lobster caught principally in the waters surrounding the Juan Fernández Islands off the coast of Chile. It is so good that it is usually just served boiled and cold with a little mayonnaise.

Game of all sorts is plentiful, and the Chileans make the most of their partridges, pigeons, plover, quail, and wild duck. Grilled meat is popular, but the national meat dish is a type of boiled dinner with many different vegetables. Fruits and vegetables are very fine, and the *paltas* (avocados) are of extraordinary richness. Desserts are usually of fruit, but *empanaditas de crema* (tiny cream pies) are seen everywhere.

The wines of Chile are unimpeachable and are often exported to the United States. The vineyards of Chile are considered the finest in South America and produce reds and whites, with a wide range of quality. The excellent local champagne costs a fraction of the price of an equivalent

French wine. *Chacolí* (a fermented grape cider) is a customary refreshment.

There are a handful of good restaurants which feature the delicious seafood of the country in Santiago, the capital city. Another group are dedicated to serving the truly national dishes of this country.

CHAMPAGNE-FRUIT COCKTAIL

CAZUELA EN CHAMPAÑA

½ cup chopped fresh pineapple
1 orange, peeled and sliced
½ cup strawberries

3 tablespoons sugar
¾ cup cognac
1 bottle champagne, well chilled

Chop together the pineapple, orange, and berries until very fine. Sprinkle with the sugar and pour the cognac over the mixture. Chill for at least 1 hour. Divide the mixture among 6 chilled champagne glasses. Fill with the champagne and serve immediately. *Serves 6.*

SEAFOOD CASSEROLE

CHUPO DE MARISCOS

3 1½-pound lobsters or 6 African lobster tails
1½ quarts water
2 teaspoons salt
2 pounds raw shrimp
24 clams
24 mussels
6 tablespoons butter

1 tablespoon Spanish paprika
¾ cup chopped onions
2 cups soft bread crumbs
1½ cups milk
½ cup cottage cheese
3 egg yolks
⅛ teaspoon cayenne pepper
4 hard-cooked eggs, cut in half

Wash the lobsters. Bring the water and salt to a boil. Drop the lobsters into them and cook 20 minutes. Drain the lobster. Drop the shrimp into the boiling liquid and cook 5 minutes. Drain, reserving the liquid.

Scrub the clams and mussels. Put in a pan with ½ cup of the reserved liquid. Cover and steam until the shells open. Drain and discard the shells.

Remove the meat of the lobsters and cut into 2-inch pieces. Shell and devein the shrimp. Put all the seafood in a 3-quart casserole.

Melt the butter in a saucepan; stir in the paprika and onions. Cook over low heat 5 minutes. Add the bread crumbs, milk, and 1½ cups of the reserved liquid. Bring to a boil and cook over low heat 10 minutes.

In a bowl, mix together the cottage cheese, egg yolks, and cayenne pepper. Add the hot sauce, stirring steadily to prevent curdling. Taste for seasoning. Pour over the seafood. Cover and bake in a 350° oven 10 minutes. Remove cover and place under the broiler until top browns. Garnish with the eggs. Serve with French bread and rice. *Serves 8.*

Note: In Chile, this dish is usually served much spicier, so add more cayenne, if you like.

CHILEAN FISH SOUP

CALDILLO DE PESCADO

1 cup olive oil	½ teaspoon freshly ground
4 onions, chopped	black pepper
2 cloves garlic, minced	4 potatoes, cubed
1 teaspoon marjoram	1 cup dry sherry
3 pounds fish, cut into 1-inch	4 tomatoes, peeled and sliced
pieces	3 egg yolks
7 cups water	4 tablespoons chopped parsley
2 teaspoons salt	

Heat the olive oil in a saucepan. Add the onions and garlic and sauté for 15 minutes, stirring frequently. Add the marjoram, fish, water, salt, and pepper. Cover and cook over medium heat for 30 minutes. Add the potatoes and sherry. Cover and cook over medium heat for 20 minutes. Add the tomatoes and cook 10 minutes longer. Correct seasoning.

Beat the egg yolks and parsley in a bowl. Gradually add 1 cup of the soup, beating constantly. Return the mixture to the balance of the soup, beating steadily. Heat but do not allow the soup to boil. Serve hot. *Serves 8–10.*

SQUABS STUFFED WITH NOODLES

POLLITA DE GRANO MENDEZ VIGO

1 pair sweetbreads	⅜ pound (1½ sticks) butter
1 cup water	1 onion, chopped
1 tablespoon vinegar	1 cup chopped mushrooms
3 teaspoons salt	2 cups medium-fine egg noodles,
1½ teaspoons freshly ground	boiled
black pepper	1 cup cream
2 cloves garlic, minced	¾ cup sherry
6 squabs or rock Cornish hens,	
with livers and gizzards	

Wash the sweetbreads in cold water. Place in a saucepan with the cup of water and the vinegar. Bring to a boil and cook over low heat for 10 minutes. Drain. Cover with cold water and set aside for 20 minutes. Drain. Remove the membrane and cut the sweetbreads into small cubes. Mix 2 teaspoons of the salt, 1 teaspoon of the pepper, and the garlic to a smooth paste. Rub into the squabs. Grind the livers and gizzards in a food chopper.

Melt 1 stick of the butter in a skillet. Add the onion and mushrooms and sauté for 5 minutes, stirring frequently. Add the noodles, sweetbreads, cream, sherry, and remaining salt and pepper. Mix carefully. Correct seasoning. Stuff the squabs with the mixture. Fasten the openings with skewers or with thread. Melt the remaining butter in a casserole or baking dish. Brown the squabs over direct heat on all sides. Roast in a 375° oven for 35 minutes, or until tender. Baste frequently. *Serves 6.*

BEEF STEW, CHILEAN STYLE

CARBONADA

4 tablespoons butter	¼ cup raw rice
4 pounds top sirloin, cubed	1 cup diced pumpkin or squash
1 onion, chopped	½ cup green peas
2 teaspoons paprika	½ cup corn kernels
4 potatoes, peeled and cubed	3 cups boiling water
2 teaspoons salt	2 egg yolks, beaten
½ teaspoon freshly ground black pepper	

Melt the butter in a large saucepan. Add the meat, onion, and paprika. Cook over high heat until the meat is browned on all sides. Add the potatoes and continue browning for 10 minutes, stirring occasionally. Add the rice, pumpkin or squash, peas, corn, and water. Cook over low heat for 1 hour, or until meat is tender. Stir occasionally. Correct seasoning. Place the beaten egg yolks in a deep serving dish or tureen. Pour the stew over it gradually, stirring well. Serve immediately. *Serves 8–10.*

TOMATO AND ONION SALAD

ENSALADA DE TOMATES Y CEBOLLAS

1 pound yellow onions	¾ teaspoon salt
3 tomatoes, peeled and sliced	¼ teaspoon freshly ground black pepper
¾ cup olive oil	
¼ cup red wine vinegar	⅛ teaspoon minced garlic

Peel the onions and cut into very thin slices lengthwise. Cover with boiling water and let stand 10 minutes. Drain, dry, and chill.

Arrange the tomatoes and onions on individual salad plates. Make a dressing of the oil, vinegar, salt, pepper, and garlic. Pour over the salad. Chill 1 hour. *Serves 8.*

CHICKEN AND CORN SALAD

BOCADO PRIMAVERA DE AVE

3 cups diced cooked chicken
2 cups cooked or canned corn
  kernels
6 tomatoes, cubed
3 green peppers, minced
2 cups mayonnaise

1 teaspoon salt
½ teaspoon freshly ground black
  pepper
Lettuce leaves
3 hard-cooked eggs, quartered

Combine the chicken, corn, tomatoes, green peppers, 1 cup of the mayonnaise, salt, and pepper. Mix gently but thoroughly. Arrange the lettuce leaves on a platter or individual plates. Heap the chicken mixture on it and smooth out as evenly as possible. Cover with the remaining mayonnaise, coating the salad mixture so that only the mayonnaise may be seen. Arrange the quartered eggs around it. If desired, radishes and olives may be placed around the salad. Chill and serve very cold. *Serves 6–8.*

CAKE ROLL

BIZCOCHO RELLENO

Cake:

4 egg yolks
⅓ cup sugar
2 teaspoons grated lemon rind
4 egg whites

⅛ teaspoon salt
¼ cup flour
¼ cup cornstarch
Cinnamon

Beat the egg yolks until thick. Gradually add half the sugar, beating until very light in color. Mix in the lemon rind. In another bowl beat the egg whites and salt until soft peaks form, then gradually beat in the remaining sugar until stiff. Fold ¼ of the egg whites into the yolks, then pour this mixture over the remaining whites. Sift the flour and cornstarch over the top and fold all together gently.

Grease an 11- by 16-inch jelly-roll pan, line with wax paper, and grease the paper. Pour the batter into the lined pan evenly. Bake in a preheated 400° oven 10 minutes, or until very lightly browned. Run a spatula under the paper and immediately turn out onto a towel-covered rack, paper side down. Cover with a moist towel until cool. Peel the paper off when cake cools and sprinkle with cinnamon.

Filling:

1 cup milk	⅛ teaspoon salt
1-inch piece cinnamon stick	4 egg yolks
1 teaspoon grated lemon rind	2 tablespoons butter
2 tablespoons cornstarch	Confectioners' sugar
¾ cup sugar	

Combine the milk, cinnamon stick, and lemon rind in a saucepan. Bring to a boil, remove from heat, and let stand 10 minutes. Strain.

Mix the cornstarch, sugar, and salt in the top of a double boiler. Stir in the milk mixture. Cook over low heat, stirring steadily, until mixture boils. Place over hot water and cook, stirring frequently, for 10 minutes.

Beat the egg yolks in a bowl; gradually add a little of the hot sauce, stirring steadily to prevent curdling. Return to double boiler, add the butter, and cook, stirring steadily for 2 minutes. Cool. Spread the cake roll with the filling and roll up. Sprinkle the top with confectioners' sugar. *Serves 8.*

COLOMBIA

Colombia has changed considerably in the past few decades and has become a much more prosperous and industrialized country. Accommodations for travelers, which were formerly only adequate, are now excellent. What hasn't changed about Colombia are the orchids, which apparently grow by the millions, and the world's finest emeralds, which, judging by their astronomical prices, do not grow with equal profusion.

But you can't eat emeralds or orchids, except for the pod of the *Vanilla planifolia* orchid, which produces the edible vanilla bean. You *can* enjoy Columbia's fine coffee and extraordinary fruits. A visit to a native market will disclose many fruits you have never seen before, in addition to the familiar tropical species. You'll want to try them all, particularly the *curubas* and the *guanábanas.*

Colombians are fond of high seasoning, and spicy dishes are to be expected, although occasionally a bland one will surprise you just when your palate has become accustomed to sharply spiced foods. Soups such as *cuchuco* (a wheat soup) and many more, almost all very filling and calorific, are great favorites. Seafood is very worthwhile here, since Colombia has two coast lines, one facing the Caribbean and the other fronting on the Pacific Ocean. The recipe for *arroz con pescado* (fish and rice) is simple but good.

Chicken dishes are well prepared and often contain fruits, corn, and various cereals. *Piquete*, almost always served outdoors, picnic fashion, contains chicken, pork, corn, and both white and sweet potatoes, and is typical of the country. *Ajiaco* (a pork and vegetable stew) is also important with both city and country people.

The food has Spanish overtones, but there is much in it that is purely local in character. The country is excessively fond of high seasoning, and beer is the favorite drink for neutralizing the spiciness of the food. Wines are of little importance, but the same cannot be said for the local firewater, *aguardiente*, which has almost no taste but considerable effect.

Of desserts there is little to say, other than that the very best are the country's fine fresh fruits, or ice creams made from them. No discussion of Colombia and its eating habits could afford to overlook the famous Sunday breakfast, which has assumed the importance of a great tradition. *Tamales* are the great Sunday morning treat, and it is a rare Colombian indeed who will forgo his *tamal*, usually accompanied by hot chocolate, bread, and the locally produced cheese.

Visitors to this lovely land find it easy to become adjusted to almost anything but the extremely late dinner hour. Ten o'clock is a normal dinnertime, but eleven or even midnight is not too extraordinary, particularly for a dinner party with many guests. Bogotá, the capital, is located up in the mountains, and before the coming of commercial aviation was quite inaccessible. It still retains a certain Shangri-La atmosphere, and the people like to think of their proud city as the Athens of the continent. Many citizens have cards printed which indicate their name and occupation, such as "Pedro Gomez, poet." Bogotá's pride for luxury and fine food is the new Hotel Tequendama.

EGG AND AVOCADO APPETIZER

PICANTE DE HUEVOS

6 hard-cooked eggs, chopped	1 onion, chopped fine
2 avocados, chopped fine	3 tablespoons chopped parsley
1 fresh chili pepper, chopped	2 tablespoons vinegar
fine, or ¼ teaspoon dried	1½ teaspoons salt
ground chili peppers	

Combine the eggs, avocados, chili pepper, onion, parsley, vinegar, and salt. Mix well and chop until smooth and well blended. Chill. Serve as an hors d'oeuvre on toast, or on lettuce leaves, as an appetizer. *Makes about 2½ cups.*

WHEAT SOUP

CUCHUCO

1 pound stewing beef	½ cup cracked wheat (cereal)
1 large beef bone	1 tablespoon salt
2½ quarts water	2 potatoes, peeled and cubed
1 onion	1 cup fresh or frozen green peas
1 clove garlic, minced	

Combine the beef, bone, water, onion, and garlic in a deep saucepan. Bring to a boil and skim the top carefully. Cook over medium heat for 1 hour. Add the cracked wheat, stirring constantly. Cook over low heat 30 minutes longer. Add the salt, potatoes, and peas. Cook for 20 minutes, or until the potatoes are tender. The meat should be cut into small pieces and served in the soup. *Serves 6–8.*

Note: This is a very substantial and filling dish, and should be followed ordinarily by a light main course.

FISH WITH RICE

ARROZ CON PESCADO

3 cups water	2 onions, chopped
3 teaspoons salt	1 clove garlic, minced
1½ cups raw rice	3 fillets of sole, shredded
4 tablespoons butter	½ teaspoon freshly ground black
2 tablespoons olive oil	pepper

Combine the water and 2 teaspoons of the salt in a saucepan. Bring it to a boil and add the rice. Cover and cook over medium heat for 15 minutes. Drain. Combine the butter and olive oil in a large skillet. Add the onions and garlic and sauté for 10 minutes, stirring frequently. Add the fish, pepper, and remaining salt; sauté 5 minutes. Add the rice and cook over high heat for 5 minutes, stirring frequently to prevent burning. Correct seasoning. Serve with a chilled dry white wine. *Serves 4–6.*

CHICKEN, HUNTER'S STYLE

POLLO AL CAZADOR

½ cup dried chick-peas or 1 cup
   canned chick-peas, drained
2½ teaspoons salt
½ teaspoon freshly ground
   black pepper
¼ cup flour
2 3-pound chickens, disjointed
⅓ cup olive oil
3 onions, quartered

3 tomatoes, peeled and chopped
1½ cups sliced mushrooms
2 green peppers, sliced
1½ cups dry red wine
¼ teaspoon dried ground chili
   peppers
¼ teaspoon orégano
1 bay leaf

Wash and soak the chick-peas overnight in water to cover. Drain well. Cook in water to cover for 1 hour. Drain well. (If canned chick-peas are used, omit these steps.) Combine the salt, pepper, and flour. Roll the chicken parts in it lightly. Heat the olive oil in a heavy saucepan. Add the chicken and brown well on all sides. Add the chick-peas, onions, tomatoes, mushrooms, green peppers, wine, chili peppers, orégano, and bay leaf. Cover and cook over low heat for 1 hour, or until the chicken is tender. Remove bay leaf and correct seasoning. *Serves 6–8.*

PORK AND CHICKEN, COLOMBIAN STYLE

PIQUETE

3 onions, chopped fine
2 cloves garlic, minced
3 tablespoons chopped parsley
2 teaspoons salt
½ teaspoon dried ground chili
   peppers
1 teaspoon ground cumin seed

3½-pound chicken, disjointed
2 quarts water
6 white potatoes
3 sweet potatoes, peeled
3 ears sweet corn, cut in half
6 pork chops

Combine the onions, garlic, parsley, salt, chili peppers, and cumin seed in a bowl. Pound together until quite smooth. Add the chicken, turning it for several minutes in the mixture until it is well coated. Cover and marinate overnight in the refrigerator. Place the chicken, spice mixture, and water in a saucepan. Bring to a boil, cover, and cook over medium heat for 1 hour or until chicken is tender. Remove the chicken, reserving the stock. Place the chicken in a buttered baking dish. Bake in a 450° oven for 15 minutes, or until the chicken is brown.

Add the white potatoes and the peeled sweet potatoes to the stock. Boil for 20 minutes. Add the corn and cook 10 minutes longer, or until the potatoes are tender. Place the pork chops in a hot skillet and fry for 15 minutes on each side, or until the pork is tender. Arrange the meats on one platter and the vegetables on another. Prepare the sauce while the meats are cooking.

½ cup dry bread crumbs	2 tomatoes, chopped
½ cup milk	½ cup grated Gruyère or
2 tablespoons olive oil	American cheese
2 onions, chopped	1 teaspoon salt

Soak the bread crumbs in the milk. Heat the oil in a skillet. Add the onions and sauté for 5 minutes. Add the tomatoes and cook over low heat for 10 minutes, stirring frequently. Add the bread-crumb and milk mixture. If the sauce is too thick, add a little additional milk. Cook over low heat for 2 minutes, stirring constantly. Add the grated cheese and salt. Cook, stirring constantly, until the cheese melts. Serve separately in a sauceboat. *Serves 6–8.*

BANANA OMELET

TORTILLA DE BANANA

4 tablespoons butter	¼ cup milk
4 bananas, sliced	6 egg whites
6 egg yolks	2 tablespoons chopped parsley
1 teaspoon salt	Dash of cayenne pepper

Melt the butter in a skillet. Add the bananas and sauté for 5 minutes, stirring frequently. Set aside. Beat the egg yolks, salt, and milk together in a bowl. Preheat oven to 350°. Beat the egg whites in a bowl until stiff but not dry. Fold into the yolk mixture carefully. Pour into a buttered baking dish and arrange the bananas on top. Bake in a 350° oven for 20 minutes, or until the omelet is set and delicately browned on top. Remove the omelet from the baking dish and fold it in half. Sprinkle with the parsley and cayenne pepper. Slice and serve as a luncheon or supper dish. *Serves 4–6.*

VEGETABLE SALAD

ENSALADA DE LEGUMBRES

3 Italian- or Spanish-style
   sausages, sliced thin, or ¼
   pound salami, in small pieces
½ cup cooked string beans
½ cup canned corn kernels
2 tomatoes, peeled and sliced
1 head of lettuce, *broken* into
   small pieces
¼ cup olive oil

⅓ cup wine vinegar
1 tablespoon chopped scallions
   (green onions)
1 tablespoon chopped parsley
1 clove garlic, minced
1 teaspoon salt
½ teaspoon freshly ground black
   pepper

Fry the sausages until lightly browned. Drain well and let cool. Combine the string beans, corn, tomatoes, lettuce, and sausages in a salad bowl. Mix together in a bowl the olive oil, vinegar, scallions, parsley, garlic, salt, and pepper. Pour over the salad. Toss lightly. Chill. Serve very cold. *Serves 4–6.*

TINY COCOA CAKES

PASTELES DE CACAO

¼ pound (1 stick) butter
1½ cups sugar
3 eggs
¾ cup unsweetened cocoa

1½ cups sifted flour
3 teaspoons baking powder
⅔ cup milk
1 teaspoon vanilla extract

Preheat oven to 375°

Cream the butter until soft. Add the sugar gradually, beating until light and fluffy. Add the eggs, beating well. Sift the cocoa, flour and baking powder together. Add to the butter mixture alternately with the milk, beating steadily. Add the vanilla and mix well. Preheat oven to 375°. Butter two muffin or cupcake pans and dust lightly with flour. Fill two thirds full. (The average pan has 8 cups.) Bake in a 375° oven for 20 minutes, or until a tester comes out clean. Serve hot or cold. *Makes about 16 cakes.*

ECUADOR

If those restless souls of several centuries ago in search of a land of per-
petual spring had found Ecuador, their search would have been termi-
nated. Few places in this world are blessed with so magnificent a climate
as are the highlands of this country. Although the word "Ecuador"
means equator, and although people automatically assume that any
country located on the equator must be hot and humid, it must also be
remembered that most of Ecuador is situated on the slopes of the
towering Andes. The coastline, including the seaport city of Guayaquil,
is usually tropical and steaming, but the beautiful mountain towns of
Ambato and Baños have a gardenlike atmosphere. Not to be missed by
any visitor is the unusual and colorful Indian market held for centuries
at Otavalo. Quito has about 9000 feet of altitude to contend with, but
most people aren't disturbed by it, and the city and the natives are
captivating in a way that is difficult to explain.

Ecuador is rich in fruits of all sorts, many of which are completely unfamiliar to us. There are dozens of varieties of bananas, ranging from the
very tiny ones to tremendous species. The *chirimoya*, with its green
exterior and snowy-white interior, is particularly delicious. Possibly the
most interesting fruit of all is the *naranjilla*, which may be described as a
type of orange with a bright green interior and a luscious, tropical
taste.

While enjoying the unusual combination of palm trees set against
snow-capped mountains, you may also enjoy the distinctive specialties of
the nation. *Locro*, a great favorite, is a thick soup made from potatoes
or from kernels of corn of an enormous size, as much as ten times the
size of our usual varieties. In addition there are such things as *ají de
pollo* (chicken with chili peppers) and *camarones con almendras*
(shrimp with an almond sauce). The people are extraordinarily fond
of sweet desserts and eat fairly large amounts of jam, jellies, and preserves. A unique sweet is *mazamorra morada*, a red and purple corn
dessert which unfortunately cannot be duplicated here.

Breakfast may be small but dinner is a large meal. Afternoon tea, a
great institution, is served about 6 P.M., almost the exact time the sun
sets in Quito every day of the year. Naturally, after such a late tea,
supper is even later, certainly not before 9 P.M., and usually much later.

Chicha, a potent, locally made beverage, is drunk by many of the inhabitants, but its ill-mannered taste does not usually appeal to visitors. However, that is hardly the case with the local beers. These are excellent and highly regarded. Two soft drinks the small fry enjoy are *rosero,* made of corn and fruit juices, and *fresco de arroz,* made of rice and fruit juices.

Color-camera fans will be very happy in Ecuador. Of course there are the most wonderful opportunities to get shots of the Indians and their colorful costumes, but the countryside offers much more. The most perfect color picture of Ecuador must certainly be the green palm trees of the country set against the snow-capped mountains, with a sky of Technicolor blue. It's corny, but we love it.

ECUADORIAN TAMALES

CHOCLOTANDAS

4 tablespoons butter
¼ pound cream cheese
4 egg yolks, beaten
1 teaspoon salt

4 egg whites, stiffly beaten
1 cup ground, cooked, or
  canned corn kernels

Cream the butter and cream cheese together until smooth. Add the egg yolks and salt and beat well. Add the egg whites, mixing thoroughly. Add the ground corn and mix well.

Cut parchment paper or aluminum foil into 5-inch squares. Place a heaping tablespoon of the mixture in the center of each and form into thin strips, about 3 inches long and ½ inch wide. Fold over the paper and tie with a string. If aluminum foil is used, the string is unnecessary. Drop into rapidly boiling, salted water and boil for 30 minutes. Serve in the papers in which they were boiled. These tamales make excellent hot hors d'oeuvres. *Makes about 20 tamales.*

POTATO SOUP

AJIACO

4 tablespoons butter
3 large onions, chopped fine
2 tablespoons flour
3 cups beef broth
4 potatoes, diced
⅛ teaspoon saffron
1½ teaspoons salt

Dash of cayenne pepper
3 cups milk, scalded
½ cup cooked green peas
3 eggs
¼ pound cream cheese
1 avocado, peeled and sliced

Melt the butter in a deep saucepan. Add the onions and sauté for 10 minutes. Blend in the flour until smooth. Gradually add the stock, stirring constantly until the boiling point is reached. Add the potatoes, saffron, salt, and cayenne pepper. Cook over low heat for 20 minutes. Add the milk and peas and cook over low heat 5 minutes longer.

Beat the eggs and cream cheese together in a bowl. Gradually add 2 cups of the hot soup, beating constantly to prevent curdling. Return the contents of the bowl to the saucepan, stirring steadily. Correct seasoning. Place a few slices of avocado in each soup plate and pour the soup over it. Serve hot. *Serves 6–8.*

SHRIMP WITH ALMOND SAUCE

CAMARONES CON SALSA DE ALMENDRAS

2 pounds raw shrimp
1½ cups water
1 stalk celery
½ teaspoon pickling spice
2 teaspoons salt
5 slices white bread, trimmed
1½ cups milk
4 tablespoons butter
2 cloves garlic, minced

1½ cups finely chopped onions
1 teaspoon Spanish paprika
½ teaspoon freshly ground black pepper
¼ teaspoon dried ground chili peppers
½ cup olive oil
1 cup finely ground almonds

Combine the shrimp, water, celery, pickling spice, and 1 teaspoon of the salt in a saucepan and bring to a boil. Cook over medium heat 5 minutes. Let the shrimp cool in stock 15 minutes. Strain and reserve stock. Shell shrimp, removing black vein. Soak the bread in the milk 5 minutes. Mash until smooth.

Melt the butter in a skillet and sauté the garlic, onions, paprika, pepper, chili peppers, and remaining salt for 10 minutes. Add the bread and sauté 5 minutes, stirring frequently. Gradually stir in the oil. Mix in the almonds and reserved stock. Add the shrimp. Cook over low heat 5 minutes. *Serves 6.*

As served at the Quito Inter-Continental Hotel.

PORK ROAST

PUERCO HORNEADO

1 teaspoon salt
1 teaspoon saffron
½ teaspoon marjoram
½ teaspoon basil
½ teaspoon ground cumin seed
1 teaspoon freshly ground black
  pepper
3 cloves garlic, minced
2 fillets of pork (4 pounds) or
  loin of pork (6 pounds)

1 cup boiling water
3 tablespoons grated onion
2 tablespoons wine vinegar
¼ teaspoon dried ground chili
  peppers
2 tablespoons chopped parsley
½ cup cold water

Combine the salt, saffron, marjoram, basil, cumin seed, pepper, and garlic. Mix into a paste and rub into the pork. Wrap in wax paper and place in the refrigerator overnight. Place the pork in a roasting pan and roast in a 400° oven for 30 minutes. Reduce the heat to 350°, pour the boiling water over the pork, and roast a total of 25 minutes a pound. Baste frequently.

Remove ½ cup of the pan gravy and combine in a saucepan with the onion, vinegar, chili peppers, parsley, and cold water. Bring to a boil and cook over low heat for 2 minutes. Carve the pork and serve the sauce in a separate sauceboat. The pork is equally good when served cold. *Serves 6–8.*

CHICKEN IN PEPPER SAUCE

AJÍ DE POLLO

½ cup olive oil
2 onions, sliced
2 cloves garlic, minced
2 3½-pound chickens, disjointed
3 teaspoons salt
½ teaspoon freshly ground black
  pepper
2 cups chicken broth
5 tomatoes, peeled and chopped,
  or 1½ cups canned tomatoes

2 onions, chopped fine
4 potatoes, peeled and diced
1 red or green pepper, cut into
  julienne strips
½ teaspoon dried ground chili
  peppers
½ teaspoon marjoram
1 cup fresh bread crumbs
4 hard-cooked eggs, quartered
12 ripe olives

Heat ¼ cup of the olive oil in a large saucepan. Add the sliced onions and garlic and sauté for 5 minutes, stirring frequently. Add the chicken and brown on all sides over high heat. Add 2 teaspoons of the salt, the pepper, and 1 cup of the broth. Cover, reduce the heat, and cook for 1 hour, or until tender.

Heat the remaining oil in a separate saucepan. Add the tomatoes, chopped onions, potatoes, pepper, chili peppers, marjoram, and remaining salt. Cook over high heat for 5 minutes, stirring constantly. Add the remaining broth. Cover and cook over low heat for 20 minutes. Mix in bread crumbs. Add to the chicken. Stir well and correct seasoning. Serve garnished with the hard-cooked eggs and the olives. *Serves 6–8.*

Note: This dish is quite spicy. If desired, reduce the quantity of ground chili peppers to cut down on the spiciness.

VEGETABLE STEW

LOCRO

2 tablespoons butter	½ teaspoon freshly ground black
2 onions, chopped	pepper
2 cloves garlic, minced	4 potatoes, peeled and quartered
½ cup canned tomato sauce	2 cups cooked or canned
½ cup water	pumpkin purée
1 cup fresh or canned corn	¾ cup grated American or
kernels	Gruyère cheese
1 cup fresh or frozen green peas	1 cup milk
1 teaspoon salt	

Melt the butter in a large saucepan. Add the onions and garlic and sauté for 10 minutes, stirring frequently. Add the tomato sauce, water, corn, peas, salt, and pepper. Cover and cook over low heat for 10 minutes. Add the potatoes and pumpkin. Cover and cook for 20 minutes, or until the potatoes are tender. Add the grated cheese and milk and stir carefully but thoroughly. Cook 5 minutes longer. Serve with boiled rice on the side. This makes an excellent luncheon dish. *Serves 6–8.*

SWEET FRITTERS

BUÑUELOS

2 tablespoons butter	⅞ cup sifted flour
½ cup sugar	3 eggs
2 tablespoons grated lemon rind	Vegetable oil for deep-fat
1 cup water	frying

Combine the butter, sugar, lemon rind, and water in a saucepan. Bring to a boil, stirring occasionally. Add the flour all at once, beating hard. Cook until the dough leaves the sides of the pan. Remove from the heat.

Add 1 egg at a time, beating hard after each addition, and until the dough is smooth and shiny. Heat deep oil to 375° in a very deep saucepan. Drop the batter by the teaspoon into the fat. Fry until light brown, approximately 5 minutes. Drain. Prepare the following sauce:

1 cup dark brown sugar	2 tablespoons heavy cream
3 tablespoons flour	1 tablespoon butter
1 cup water	½ teaspoon vanilla extract

Combine the sugar and flour in a saucepan. Add the water, stirring to a smooth paste. Cook over medium heat until the mixture becomes thick, stirring occasionally. Add the cream, butter, and vanilla, mixing well. Pour over the fritters and serve either hot or cold. *Serves 6–8.*

COLD RICE DRINK

FRESCO DE ARROZ

½ cup raw rice	1 cup canned or fresh pineapple,
2 quarts boiling water	cut into ¼-inch cubes
1½ cups sugar	¼ teaspoon cinnamon
1 cup orange juice	4 cloves
¼ cup lemon juice	3 tablespoons grated orange
1 cup canned or fresh	rind
pineapple juice	

Wash the rice in several changes of water. Have the 2 quarts water boiling in a saucepan and add the rice. Cook for 35 minutes, or until extremely soft. Force the rice and liquid through a sieve, or purée in an electric blender. Combine the sugar, orange juice, lemon juice, and pineapple juice in a saucepan. Cook until syrupy, about 10 minutes. Add the strained rice, pineapple cubes, cinnamon, cloves and orange rind. Bring to a boil and remove the cloves. Chill and serve very cold. Sliced strawberries may be added immediately before serving. *Makes about 2 quarts.*

THE GUIANAS

The three areas of the northeastern coast of South America were formerly called the Guianas, and are joined together in this book only for economy of space. Many of their boundaries were settled as recently as the past half century. The Guianas consist of three parts: Guyana (formerly British territory), Surinam (a Dutch area), and the region known as French Guiana.

Georgetown, the capital of Guyana, has a rather unusual personality of its own. Possibly this is owing to the population, which consists of a mixture of Chinese, Indonesians, Negroes, Europeans, and natives. The outstanding spot from a tourist's point of view is Kaieteur Falls, roughly five times higher than our own Niagara.

Guyana produces rice, coffee, coconuts, molasses, and sugar in the food line. There are not too many local food specialties, but *callalu* soup is good, and *broas,* a local cooky, is a favorite. Breadnuts are standard here, and a good soup is made from it. Crabs are exceptional, and a local fish known as *queriman* is cooked in the usual styles of fish cookery. Worthy of mention are such things as *eddoe,* the edible taro leaves, and *casareep,* a liquid seasoning made from cassava. Guavas and soursops are tasty local fruits.

A liquor produced from the juice of the sugar cane is called "shrub." The true liquor specialty of this region is the local Demerara rum, a rum of merely 151 proof! If it ever got that cold in Guyana, it could be used as an anti-freeze for automobiles.

Dutch Guiana, or Surinam, has Paramaribo as its capital. The country itself is a racial mélange consisting of Europeans, Indonesians, Indians, Negroes, natives, and assorted mixtures of these different groups. Like Dutch people the world over, they are happiest when surrounded by the food and liquors of their own country, and Holland beers and liquors are the ones most frequently seen.

Among the local food items of interest are such things as *kwie-kwie* (a swamp fish), *taja,* which resembles a potato, and *paksoi* and *amsoi* (green, leafy vegetables). Otherwise, Dutch food is what the people prefer.

Cayenne is the capital of the French part of the Guianas. French Guiana is actually the worst off of the three parts on all counts. It has the lowest population, the smallest land area, is the poorest in natural resources, and is also undoubtedly the least developed of all.

Incidentally, French Guiana was the location of the formerly notorious penal camp, Devil's Island, whose most famous prisoner was Dreyfus. The Ile du Diable is just a small, rocky island located immediately off the coast of French Guiana, and was almost but not quite escape-proof. Numerous heroic movie actors, particularly in the day of the silent film, made good their escape from the island.

The preferred food and liquor of this portion of the Guianas are naturally as French as the people can afford.

GEORGETOWN RUM SWIZZLE

2 cups finely cracked ice
6 jiggers Demerara rum
½ cup lemon or lime juice
1 cup fresh grapefruit juice
2 tablespoons grenadine
2 tablespoons cherry brandy
½ teaspoon bitters

6 slices fresh pineapple
6 maraschino cherries
6 slices orange
6 slices lemon
6 sprigs mint or 1 teaspoon
  liquid mint flavoring

In a large pitcher—*not* in a cocktail shaker—place the cracked ice, rum, lemon or lime juice, grapefruit juice, grenadine, cherry brandy, and bitters. Using a long swizzle stick between the palms of the hands, agitate the mixture until the pitcher becomes ice cold. In tall highball glasses arrange a pineapple slice, maraschino cherry, orange slice, lemon slice, and a sprig of mint. (If fresh mint is not available, add the liquid mint to the pitcher.) Fill each glass about three fourths full of the liquor and add carbonated water.

Note: Demerara rum is produced locally in British Guiana. It is extremely potent, being about 151 proof.

STUFFED CRABS

1 pound fresh cooked or
  canned crab meat and crab
  shells, if available
1 cup fresh bread crumbs
½ cup melted butter
1 teaspoon salt

¼ teaspoon pepper
Dash of mace
2 tablespoons lime or lemon
  juice
2 pimentos, chopped
2 tablespoons butter

Preheat oven to 375°.

Place the crab meat in a bowl and shred it gently with a fork. Add ¾ cup of the bread crumbs, the melted butter, salt, pepper, mace, lime or lemon juice, and pimentos. Mix well together. Clean the crab shells carefully or butter 6 individual ramekins. Place the mixture in the shells or ramekins. Sprinkle with the remaining bread crumbs and dot with the butter. Bake in 375° oven for 20 minutes, or until delicately browned. *Serves 6.*

PEANUT SOUP, PARAMARIBO

4 tablespoons butter
½ cup flour
8 cups chicken broth

1½ cups peanut butter
1 teaspoon freshly ground black
  pepper

Melt the butter in a saucepan. Add the flour and mix until smooth. Gradually add 6 cups of the broth, stirring constantly until the boiling point is reached. Mix the remaining broth and the peanut butter together in a bowl until smooth. Add to the soup and stir. Add the pepper and mix well. Cook over low heat for 10 minutes, stirring occasionally. Correct seasoning. If there is any leftover cooked chicken available, it may be cut up into small pieces or shreds and sprinkled on top of the soup. Serve hot. *Serves 8–10.*

CALLALU SOUP

2 pounds fresh or 2 packages
   frozen spinach
1 onion, chopped
½ pound smoked ham, cubed
2 quarts water
12 okra, stems removed

12 shrimp, shelled and cleaned
12 shallots or green onions,
   sliced
½ teaspoon freshly ground black
   pepper
⅛ teaspoon thyme

Wash the spinach carefully in many changes of water and remove the stems. Combine the spinach, onion, ham, and water in a saucepan. Cook over medium heat for 20 minutes. Add the okra, shrimp, shallots, pepper, and thyme. Cook 20 minutes longer. Correct seasoning. Serve hot. *Serves 8–10.*

PORK CASSEROLE

HOT POT

12 small pork chops
6 potatoes, peeled and sliced
6 onions, sliced
3½ teaspoons salt
½ teaspoon freshly ground black
   pepper

2 cups boiling water
1 cup sifted flour
½ cup shortening
1 egg, beaten
2 tablespoons ice water

Lightly brown the pork chops in a skillet.

In a heavy casserole arrange alternate layers of the pork chops, potatoes, and onions, sprinkled with 3 teaspoons salt and the pepper. Use half the ingredients for each layer. Add the boiling water. Cover and bake in a 325° oven for 2½ hours.

While the casserole is baking prepare the crust. Sift the flour and remaining salt into a bowl. Cut in the shortening with a pastry blender or two knives. Combine the egg and ice water and add, tossing lightly until a ball of dough is formed. Wrap in wax paper and place in the refrigerator for 45 minutes.

Roll out the dough on a lightly floured surface to fit the top of the casserole. Remove the cover of the casserole and place the dough on top, carefully sealing the edges. Prick the top. Increase the oven temperature to 375° and bake for 25 minutes, or until the top is brown. *Serves 6–8.*

Note: The recipe is of Dutch origin but has become a part of the cuisine of Dutch Guiana.

CHICKEN AND POTATO CASSEROLE

POM

¼ pound (1 stick) butter	1 teaspoon freshly ground black
2 3½-pound chickens, disjointed	pepper
3 onions, chopped	2 teaspoons nutmeg
2 cups canned tomatoes	6 potatoes, peeled and grated
3 celery stalks, sliced	½ cup fresh orange juice
1 tablespoon salt	

Melt the butter in a large saucepan. Add the chicken and brown well on all sides. Add the onions and sauté for 5 minutes. Add the tomatoes, celery, salt, pepper, and nutmeg. Cover and cook over low heat for 1 hour or until the chicken is tender. Remove the chicken and cut the meat from the bones, reserving the sauce.

Mix ¾ cup of the reserved sauce, the grated potatoes, and orange juice together. Line a buttered casserole dish with two thirds of this mixture and place the cut-up chicken meat on top. Pour the remainder of the sauce over it. Cover the top with the remaining third of the potato mixture. Bake in a 350° oven for 1¼ hours. Serve directly from the casserole. *Serves 6–8.*

CHICKEN PILAU

2 4-pound chickens, cut into	1½ cups seedless raisins
quarters	1 cup light cream
2 cups raw rice	¼ teaspoon nutmeg
1 tablespoon salt	3 tablespoons butter

Clean the chickens carefully, place in a large saucepan with water to almost but not quite cover. Cover the saucepan and cook over medium heat while preparing the rice. Wash the rice in several changes of water and place in a separate saucepan with water to cover. Bring to a boil, turn off heat, let soak for 5 minutes, and drain well.

Add the rice and salt to the chicken. Cover and cook over medium heat for 45 minutes. Add the raisins and cook until chicken is tender. Remove the chicken from the saucepan; place it on a heated platter and keep warm. Add the cream, nutmeg, and butter to the rice and stir well. Pack the rice into small cups or molds and turn out onto the platter surrounding the chicken. *Serves 8.*

COOKIES, BRITISH GUIANA STYLE

BROAS

¼ pound (1 stick) butter	1 teaspoon cinnamon
1 cup sugar	2 teaspoons grated lemon or lime
2 cups sifted flour	rind
1 teaspoon baking powder	2 eggs

Preheat oven to 350°.

Cream the butter in a bowl until soft; add the sugar, beating until light and fluffy. Sift the flour, baking powder, and cinnamon together. Add to the butter mixture, beating until well blended. Add the grated rind and stir. Add 1 egg at a time, beating well after each addition. Continue mixing until a ball of dough is formed. Form teaspoonfuls of the dough into balls, and place on a well-buttered baking sheet, allowing about 1 inch between each ball of dough. Bake in a 350° oven for 20 minutes, or until lightly browned. *Makes about 48 cookies.*

PARAGUAY

One of the two countries in South America without a coast line (to save you the trouble of looking it up on a map, the other is Bolivia), Paraguay's development has been hindered by a lack of transportation, although the airplane has helped the situation along to a certain degree. It is a semimythical land to most of us, for it is off the regular tourist path and visited by comparatively few people.

This is a country where the people enjoy eating huge quantities of food, and at very frequent intervals. On arising, most Paraguayans have a cup of *maté*, or Paraguayan tea. This drink closely resembles tea but has a rather bitter taste. Nevertheless, most visitors eventually learn to like the drink and enjoy it as much as coffee. The popularity of *maté* has spread throughout the neighboring countries and is particularly im-

portant in Argentina and Uruguay. The morning cup of *maté* is followed
by a substantial breakfast later in the morning. Lunch is at the customary time, dinner is served between eight and nine in the evening, and
both are meals of many different courses. In the larger communities the
ladies gather for afternoon tea, which consists of a few cakes and much
local gossip.

Asunción, the capital city, has a luxurious hotel for tourists, but,
otherwise, visitors must rough it a trifle, particularly in the outlying
regions. Many people have found this inland country fascinating for
countless other reasons, such as the unbelievably soft air, the colorful
dress of the people, and the unhurried tempo of life. The country is a
great producer of oranges and the atmosphere is always laden with the
odor of orange blossoms as though weddings were constantly in progress.
Bachelors lead nervous lives here, always frightened by the smell of
orange blossoms. Oranges are so plentiful that almost no market exists
for them and, since it is almost impossible to ship them out of the
country owing to the lack of transportation, they are fed to the cattle.
It is difficult, almost requiring a real effort of the will, to starve in
Paraguay because of the tropical fruits and lush vegetation.

There are many good *Paraguayo* dishes, since the people are particularly fond of fine food. Meat stews are a national tradition, and dishes
on the order of the *puchero* are made frequently (for a recipe, see the
section on Argentina). An excellent local specialty is *costillas de cerdo
en vinagre* (pickled and fried spareribs). All sorts of spaghetti and
noodle preparations are appreciated here, and *tallarines con salsa de
hongos* (noodles and mushroom sauce) is not too far removed from the
Italian version. Corn is a regular part of the diet, used in many fashions,
such as in the delicious cheese bread (*chepa*). In addition, there are
many foods of *Guaraní* (native Indian) origin.

In Asunción good meals are obtainable at the hotels and in a few
local restaurants. However, most tourists head for a late evening dinner
that combines good food with Paraguay's delightful music, which is very
listenable and not precisely like that of the rest of South America, although vaguely similar. Most restaurants have a *conjunto*, which really
means a combination, usually consisting of three or four musicians playing
stringed instruments. Sometimes there is a singer, sometimes not. In any
event, it's delightful.

Some adequate local wines are produced, although the best drink of
the country is the *caña*, a light rum. It is used in making all sorts of
mixed drinks, accompanied by various local fruits.

Are you happy? Would you like to be sad at the same time? Follow
our advice: first, go to Paraguay; second, order a drink made with *caña;*
and third, listen to the melancholy songs of the plains, the *Paraguayo*
music.

STUFFED FISH

PESCADO RELLENO

4 tablespoons butter
3 white onions, chopped
1 cup sliced mushrooms
¼ pound ham, minced
12 pitted ripe olives, minced
½ cup dry white wine
2 slices white bread, trimmed
½ cup milk
1 egg, beaten
2 hard-cooked eggs, chopped

3 teaspoons salt
1½ teaspoons freshly ground
 black pepper
1 whole fish (about 4 pounds),
 snapper, whitefish, pompano
 or mackerel
1 teaspoon Spanish paprika
3 tablespoons lemon juice
4 tablespoons olive oil
¾ cup bread crumbs

Melt the butter in a saucepan. Add the onions and mushrooms and sauté for 10 minutes, stirring frequently. Add the ham and olives and sauté for 5 minutes. Add the wine. Cover and cook over low heat for 15 minutes. Remove from heat and let cool for 10 minutes. Soak the bread in the milk for 5 minutes. Squeeze out all the liquid. Mash the bread with a fork and add to the previous mixture. Add the egg, chopped eggs, 1 teaspoon of the salt, and ½ teaspoon of the pepper, and mix well.

Have the fish split but not cut apart, so that it may be stuffed. Remove the central bones. Sprinkle the fish with the remaining salt and pepper, paprika, lemon juice, and olive oil. Stuff the fish with the mixture and fasten the opening carefully with skewers, toothpicks, or thread. Preheat oven to 375°. Place in a buttered baking dish. Sprinkle with the bread crumbs and dot with butter. Bake in a 375° oven for 40 minutes, or until the fish is browned and flaky. Sprinkle a little parsley on the fish and place on a platter. Serve hot or cold. *Serves 4–6.*

PORK STRIPS

GUISADA DE PUERCO

3 pounds boneless leg or shoulder
 of pork
2 cloves garlic, minced
2 cups chopped onions
1½ pounds tomatoes, peeled and
 chopped

2 teaspoons salt
½ teaspoon freshly ground black
 pepper
⅛ teaspoon powdered saffron
¼ cup olive oil
¾ cup water

Trim the fat from the meat. Cut the pork into narrow strips about 2 inches long and ½ inch thick.

In a bowl, mix the garlic, onions, tomatoes, salt, pepper, and saffron. Add the pork, stir well, cover, and let stand 1 hour. Remove and drain the pork strips, reserving the tomato mixture. Heat the oil in a deep skillet until it smokes. Cook the pork over high heat 10 minutes, stirring a few times. Add the tomato mixture and water. Cover and cook over low heat 1 hour. Taste for seasoning. Serve with boiled or fried rice. *Serves 6–8.*

RICE AND MEAT

ARROZ CON CARNE

4 tablespoons olive oil
3 onions, chopped
1 clove garlic, minced
3 pounds beef (cross rib, bottom round, or similar cut), cubed
2 green peppers, sliced
2 teaspoons salt
½ teaspoon freshly ground black pepper

1 teaspoon Spanish paprika
3 cups boiling water
1 Spanish-style sausage, sliced
1 cup rice
3 tablespoons chopped parsley
½ cup sliced stuffed olives

Heat the olive oil in a heavy saucepan. Add the onions, garlic, beef, and green peppers. Cook over high heat until the meat is browned on all sides. Add the salt, pepper, paprika, and water. Cover and cook over low heat for 2 hours.

Add the sausage slices and rice. Mix together gently. Cook over low heat for 30 minutes, stirring occasionally. The rice should be moist but no gravy should remain. Add the parsley and olives and mix together lightly. Correct seasoning and serve. *Serves 6–8.*

NOODLES WITH MUSHROOM SAUCE

TALLARINES CON SALSA DE HONGOS

2 tablespoons olive oil
2 onions, chopped
1 cup tomato sauce
1 tomato, chopped
1 teaspoon salt
½ teaspoon freshly ground black pepper
3 slices bacon, chopped
¼ pound ham, cut into julienne strips

2 sausages (Spanish style, if possible), sliced thin
1 cup chopped mushrooms
1 cup beef broth
1 pound medium noodles, cooked and drained
1 cup grated American, Cheddar, or Parmesan cheese

Heat the olive oil in a saucepan. Add the onions and sauté for 10 minutes, stirring frequently. Add the tomato sauce, tomato, salt, pepper, bacon, ham, and sausages and stir. Cover and cook over low heat for 20 minutes. Mix the mushrooms and stock together and add. Cover and cook over low heat for 15 minutes. Correct seasoning.

Arrange successive layers of cooked noodles, grated cheese, and the sauce in a buttered baking dish. Arrange as many layers as possible, but the top layer should consist of the sauce. Bake in a 375° oven for 25 minutes, or until delicately browned on top. Serve hot, directly from the dish. *Serves 4.*

CHEESE BREAD

CHEPA

⅔ cup shortening	2¼ cups corn meal
2 eggs	¼ teaspoon salt
1½ cups grated American or Cheddar cheese	⅓ cup milk

Preheat oven to 375°.

Cream the shortening. Add the eggs, beating well. Add the cheese and mix until smooth. Combine the corn meal and salt. Add to the cheese mixture, alternately with the milk, mixing steadily. Knead to gether with the hands until well blended. Place the dough in a buttered 9-inch loaf pan. Cover the top with a piece of aluminum foil. Bake in a 375° oven for 35 minutes, or until firm. *Makes one 9-inch loaf.*

RAISIN CAKE

TORTA DE PASA

1 tablespoon cornstarch	2 eggs, beaten
½ cup water	2 cups sifted flour
¾ cup sugar	1½ teaspoons cream of tartar
1¼ cups seedless raisins	1½ teaspoons baking soda
½ cup chopped nuts	½ cup milk
¼ pound (1 stick) butter	1 teaspoon vanilla extract
½ cup dark brown sugar	

Preheat oven to 375°.

Mix the cornstarch and water in a saucepan until smooth. Add ½ cup of the sugar and cook over low heat, stirring constantly until thick, about 5 minutes. Add the raisins and nuts. Mix lightly and set aside while preparing the batter.

Cream the butter. Add the brown sugar and the remaining white sugar, creaming until light and fluffy. Add the eggs, beating well. Sift the flour, cream of tartar, and baking soda together and add alternately

with the milk. Add vanilla. Mix well. Pour half the batter into a buttered
8-inch square pan. Spread the raisin mixture over it and cover with the
remaining batter. Bake in a 375° oven for 25 minutes or until a cake
tester comes out clean. Cool, then turn out of the pan. Cut in squares.
Serves 6-8.

PERU

In the middle of South America's west coast is this land of powerful
contrasts. Here is a country of extremes—barren, icy highlands; fresh,
flower-laden towns with temperate climate; and savage jungles, thick
and impenetrable. For those who enjoy lost cities, there is the fabulous
Inca city of Machu Picchu high up in the Andes, definitely a highlight
of any trip to South America. Nearby is Cuzco, a city more than 10,000
feet above sea level, the ancient capital of the Incas. The life of the Indians in the area is not substantially different from that of their great
ancestors of centuries ago.

Peru is curiously rich and curiously poor. Partly developed but largely
agricultural, it lives in hope of what the future will bring. But the people
are friendly, though formal in manner, and they enjoy good living and
good food. The cuisine is not unlimited, but there are at least a dozen
excellent local specialties.

Everyone in Peru is fond of pickled food, and *seviche* is a great
favorite. It is made from raw fish, but the finished dish has a cooked
taste and is not nearly so exotic as it sounds; and as previously remarked,
even cautious people eat raw oysters and clams. Peru may safely claim
distinction in regard to its soups, for these have been developed to a
greater extent than in almost any other Latin-American country. Most
people eat a thick soup made of vegetables and meat almost every day.
Much more unusual from the American point of view are the *chupes*
(soups made of shrimp, fish, or other ingredients); a recipe for *chupe de
camarones* is supplied. No mention of the food of Peru could possibly
overlook the national snack, *anticuchos* (pieces of beef heart dipped in a
spicy sauce and roasted over a charcoal fire). A tremendous favorite is
the *huancaina* sauce, somewhat spicy but very delicious, which the
Peruvians put over meats, vegetables, and practically anything else.

Partridges and other small game are imaginatively prepared. The
country has some delicious fruit, particularly the *cherimoya*, which is

most enjoyable when eaten fresh and cold, or with sweet cream. Owing
to a large Chinese population, Lima, the capital city, has a fair number
of Chinese restaurants known as *chifas* which serve Chinese food with a
Peruvian twist. Life can be complicated, particularly when selecting
Chinese food from a Spanish menu.

Peruvian wines aren't nearly so good as those produced in Argentina
and Chile, but the local beer is excellent. The popular drink of the people is *chicha,* a fermented liquor made from corn, the taste and odor are
somewhat unappealing. The usual strong drink of the nation is *pisco,* a
cross between gin and brandy that is entitled to consideration as a novel
drink in the world of alcoholic beverages. *Pisco* is made into many different drinks, but the *pisco* sour has been almost unanimously (and
justifiably) acclaimed as the national mixed drink. If your stomach is
strong, we may now consider what might be called, if we wanted to be
polite, an alcoholic potion. This—this—this *creation* is known as *aguardiente anisado.* Its basic ingredient is a crude, unpleasant-tasting alcohol;
you'll note that we are proceeding cautiously, so that those who wish to
may avoid what is coming. Next is added anise flavoring and then
goats' milk for vitamin content! The final product is so delicious that we
had better talk about something else.

PISCO SOUR

6 jiggers *pisco*	½ teaspoon bitters
1 jigger sugar syrup or honey	1 egg white
3 tablespoons lemon juice	Cracked ice

Stir together in a cocktail shaker the *pisco,* sugar syrup or honey, lemon
juice, and bitters. When well mixed, add the egg white and cracked ice.
Shake well. Serve immediately, ice cold. *Serves 6.*

Note: Pisco *is a very pale grape brandy, approximately 100 proof. It
may be imitated by using the lightest possible grape brandy in place of
The Peruvian* pisco. *A California grape brandy is a reasonable substitute.*

TINY CHEESE PIES

EMPANADITAS DE QUESO

1 cup sifted flour	4 tablespoons cream cheese
1 teaspoon baking powder	½ teaspoon salt
2 tablespoons butter	1 teaspoon chili powder
2 egg yolks, beaten	1 egg white
2 tablespoons water	Vegetable oil for deep-fat frying
4 tablespoons cottage cheese	

Sift the flour and baking powder into a bowl. Cut in the butter with a pastry blender or two knives. Add the egg yolks and water and toss lightly with a fork until a soft dough is formed. Add more water if necessary. Combine the cottage cheese, cream cheese, salt, and chili powder, mixing until smooth. Beat the egg white until stiff but not dry and fold into the cheese carefully.

Roll out the dough as thin as possible on a lightly floured surface. Cut into rounds with a 3-inch cooky cutter. Place a teaspoon of the cheese mixture on each round and fold over the dough, sealing the edges carefully with a little water. Press the edges with the tines of a fork, if desired. Heat deep oil to 385° and fry until lightly browned. Drain well. These tiny pies are served as cocktail snacks. *Makes about 24 pies.*

MARINATED FISH

SEVICHE

6 fillets of snapper, sole, or other white-meat fish	1½ cups thinly sliced onions
1 cup dry white wine	1 cup water
1 cup lime or lemon juice	½ cup cider vinegar
2 teaspoons salt	½ teaspoon dried ground chili peppers

This dish must be made with fresh, not frozen, fish.

Wash the fillets, remove any bones, and cut in julienne strips. Marinate in a mixture of the wine, lime or lemon juice, and 1 teaspoon salt for 3 hours.

Soak the onions in the water and remaining salt for 20 minutes. Drain well and squeeze between the hands. Rinse under cold running water and drain again. Soak the onions in the vinegar 1 hour. Drain well and add to the fish with the chili peppers. Chill for 4 hours. Drain and serve on lettuce, garnished with sweet potatoes, if desired. *Serves 8–10 as an appetizer.*

Note: The action of the citrus juice "cooks" the fish.

SHRIMP SOUP

CHUPE DE CAMARONES

6 tablespoons butter
1 cup finely chopped onions
4 cups bottled clam juice
4 cups dry white wine
½ teaspoon white pepper
3 slices white bread, trimmed
  and diced
1 cup milk

2 pounds raw shrimp, shelled
  and deveined
¼ teaspoon dried ground chili
  peppers
¾ cup ground blanched almonds
1 cup heavy cream
½ teaspoon Spanish paprika
2 hard-cooked eggs, chopped

Melt the butter in a saucepan; sauté the onions until soft and lightly browned. Mix in the clam juice, wine, and pepper; bring to a boil and cook over low heat 30 minutes. Soak the bread in the milk and mash smooth; add to the saucepan and cook over low heat 10 minutes. Add the shrimp and chili peppers. Cook 5 minutes. Blend in the almonds, cream, paprika, and eggs. Cook 5 minutes longer. Taste for seasoning— it should be somewhat spicy. *Serves 8–10.*

MEAT ON SKEWERS

ANTICUCHOS

2 pounds sirloin steak
1½ teaspoons salt
½ teaspoon dried ground chili
  peppers
6 peppercorns

¼ teaspoon saffron
3 cloves garlic, minced
1 cup wine vinegar
½ cup water
¼ cup olive oil

Cut the steak into 1-inch cubes. In a bowl, mix together the salt, chili peppers, peppercorns, saffron, garlic, vinegar, and water. Add the meat and marinate overnight in the refrigerator.

Drain the meat; reserve the marinade. Thread the meat on six to eight skewers; brush with the olive oil. Broil as close to the heat as possible for 6 minutes, or to desired degree of rareness, turning and basting frequently with the marinade. *Serves 6–8.*

SAUTÉED BEEF

LOMITO SALTADO

3 tablespoons butter
4 potatoes, peeled and cubed
4 tablespoons olive oil
3 pounds sirloin steak, cut into
   1-inch strips
3 onions, chopped
4 tomatoes, chopped

2 teaspoons salt
½ teaspoon freshly ground black
   pepper
¼ teaspoon dried ground chili
   peppers
2 tablespoons wine vinegar
½ cup fresh or canned peas

Melt the butter and add the potatoes. Fry them for 10 minutes, browning on all sides. Heat the oil in a separate skillet. Place the meat in it and cook over high heat for 3 minutes, shaking the pan frequently. Turn the meat over to sear it on all sides. Remove the steak from the pan and keep warm.

Place the onions in the same skillet; sauté for 5 minutes. Add the tomatoes, salt, pepper, and chili peppers and cook over medium heat for 5 minutes, stirring frequently. Add the steak and potatoes and mix gently. Add the vinegar and stir carefully. Add the peas and cook over low heat for 10 minutes, stirring occasionally. Serve hot. *Serves 6–8.*

STEAK WITH SPICY CHEESE SAUCE

LOMO À LA HUANCAINA

¼ pound cream cheese
4 hard-cooked egg yolks,
   chopped
1 teaspoon salt
½ teaspoon dried ground chili
   peppers or 1 fresh chili
   pepper, minced

½ cup olive oil
¾ cup heavy cream
¼ teaspoon lemon juice
1 cup finely chopped onions
6 club steaks, cut ¾ inch thick
3 hard-cooked eggs, quartered
12 ripe olives

Beat the cream cheese until smooth. Beat in the chopped egg yolks, salt, and chili peppers with a wooden spoon; then beat in the oil, drop by drop. Mix in the cream, lemon juice, and onions. Heat in a saucepan.

Broil the steaks to desired degree of rareness. Arrange on a platter, pour the sauce over them, and garnish with the quartered eggs and the olives. *Serves 6.*

PERUVIAN CRULLERS

PICARONES

1 package active-dry yeast	1¾ cups sifted flour
½ cup lukewarm water	¼ teaspoon mace
½ cup fresh or canned sweet	2 eggs, beaten
potatoes, puréed	3 tablespoons brandy
¼ teaspoon salt	Vegetable oil for deep-fat frying

Combine the yeast and water in a cup and allow to soften for 5 minutes. Mix until smooth. Place the sweet potatoes in a bowl. Add the yeast mixture, salt, flour, and mace and mix well. Add the eggs and brandy, beating well until smooth and creamy. Cover the bowl with a cloth and put in a warm place for 2 hours, or until double in bulk. Heat deep oil to 370° in a deep saucepan. Drop the batter into it by the teaspoonful. Fry for 5 minutes, or until browned on both sides. Sprinkle with powdered sugar and serve with syrup or jelly. *Makes about 50 crullers.*

URUGUAY

Uruguay, a comparatively small country, is known for its rather good, mild climate. The winter months of July and August (their seasons are the reverse of ours) are often gray and damp, however, but the rest of the year is typically pleasant. Montevideo, the capital city, is located near miles of bathing beaches, and when the weather is suitable, the majority of its residents head for one of the many spots for bathing. Punta del Este, a few hours drive from Montevideo, is a popular beach resort with many hotels and elaborate private homes.

The country is a heavy producer of fruit (grapes in particular), grains, olives, and cattle. The national economy is built to a substantial degree on meat; a great deal of it is consumed and also exported as frozen beef, particularly to meat-hungry Great Britain. The *gauchos,* the local cowboys, consume beef in quantities that would amaze anyone, possibly including the *gauchos* themselves. For that matter the per capital consumption of beef in Uruguay is extremely high.

Meal hours and customs follow the usual South American pattern. Teatime is a special ritual, cheerfully honored by the populace who make a point of consuming large numbers of irresistible pastries every afternoon at about 5 P.M. Dinner is usually a meal of many courses, elaborate and substantial, almost never served before nine-thirty in the evening, and often much later.

With its high grape production, it is not surprising to find a serious effort in the direction of wine making. The country produces some white wine, but the reds are superior though not quite up to Chilean standards.

Uruguayans are hearty eaters and appreciate fine food, as their diet indicates. Good soups, on the order of the *pavesa,* for which a recipe is given, are typical. Fish of all sorts are liked, and with its coastline on the south Atlantic, a fair supply is available. The population contains a high percentage of Italian immigrants who have brought their own food habits with them; this accounts for the large number of Italian dishes frequently served here. A good many of Uruguay's restaurants are Italian-owned and -operated, and spaghettis and other *pastas* are standard on every menu.

But beef is *the* dish, prepared as *carbonada criolla, puchero,* or the cowboy specialty, beef barbecued in its own hide (*asado con cuero*). The *gauchos* often exist on only two foods, roast meat and *maté,* the national drink of the country, and for weeks on end during the grazing season eat nothing else. Apparently the beef and the *maté* supply all the needed vitamins, for the cowboys are very healthy specimens. *Maté* closely resembles tea and is made from the leaves of the *Ilex paraguayensis* tree. Although it may be served in a cup, the native fashion is to drink it from a gourd, in which the leaves are steeped in hot water; it is then sipped through a silver tube with a strainer at the lower end. It may be taken *maté amargo* (without sugar) or *maté dulce* (with sugar), and sometimes with orange peelings to add a little extra flavor.

EGG AND SPINACH HORS D'OEUVRES

TORTA PASCUALINA

2 cups sifted flour
3 egg yolks
⅓ cup olive oil
½ cup lukewarm water
2 cups cooked spinach, drained
¾ teaspoon freshly ground black
    pepper

¼ teaspoon nutmeg
¼ cup grated Parmesan cheese
8 eggs
2 teaspoons salt

Sift the flour onto a board; make a well in the center. Place the egg yolks and 3 tablespoons of the olive oil in the center. Gradually work the flour into it, adding enough of the lukewarm water to make a stiff dough. Knead the dough until smooth and elastic. Cover with a cloth and set aside for 10 minutes. Roll out the dough as thin as possible on a lightly floured surface and brush with some of the oil. Cut the dough into four pieces, each large enough to fit an oblong baking dish measuring about 8 by 15 inches. Grease the dish and place two layers on the bottom.

Combine the spinach, pepper, nutmeg, and cheese. Mix well and place evenly over the dough. Make eight evenly spaced depressions in the spinach mixture, using the back of soup spoon. Break an egg into each depression and sprinkle with the salt. Cover with the remaining two layers of dough, sealing the edges carefully. Run a pastry wheel or the handle of a knife over the dough, so as to divide it into eight equal portions with an egg in each. Bake in a 375° oven for 30 minutes, or until lightly browned on top. Serve hot or cold. *Serves 8.*

BEEF BROTH WITH POACHED EGG

PAVESA

2 pounds short ribs of beef
Several beef bones
8 cups water
1 onion
1 stalk celery
1 carrot
2 sprigs parsley
3 teaspoons salt
1 teaspoon freshly ground black pepper
6 eggs
6 slices buttered toast (made from French-style bread, if possible)
¼ cup grated Parmesan cheese

Combine the beef, bones, water, onion, celery, carrot, parsley, salt, and pepper in a deep saucepan. Bring to a boil and skim the top. Cook over medium heat for 2 hours. Strain the soup. Pour 2 cups of the strained soup into a saucepan and poach the eggs in it carefully. Place an egg in each soup plate and return the 2 cups of soup to the balance. Pour the soup over the eggs. Sprinkle the toast with the cheese and place a slice in each soup plate. The meat may be eaten separately. *Serves 6.*

BAKED FISH IN CASSEROLE

CAZUELA DE PESCADO

½ cup olive oil
2 onions, sliced thin
3 tomatoes, peeled and chopped
½ cup water
½ teaspoon saffron
2 teaspoons salt
½ teaspoon freshly ground black pepper
1 bay leaf
6 fish fillets
1 cup boiled potato balls
2 green peppers, sliced thin
½ cup fresh or frozen green peas
3 canned pimentos, sliced thin

Heat the olive oil in a saucepan. Add the onions and sauté for 10 minutes, stirring frequently. Add the tomatoes, water, saffron, salt, pepper, and bay leaf. Cook over low heat for 15 minutes. Place the fillets in a buttered casserole. Arrange the potato balls, green peppers, and peas around the fish. Pour the tomato sauce over the fish and place the sliced pimentos on top. Cover. Bake in a 375° oven for 40 minutes. Serve directly from the casserole. *Serves 6.*

MEAT AND FRUIT STEW

CARBONADA CRIOLLA

3 pounds chuck or rump of beef
2 tablespoons olive oil
4 tablespoons butter
1½ cups diced onions
1½ cups dry white wine
1 tablespoon tomato paste
1 bay leaf
2 teaspoons salt
½ teaspoon freshly ground black
  pepper

½ teaspoon thyme
1 cup beef broth
3 cups peeled cubed sweet
  potatoes
3 pears, peeled and cubed
3 peaches or apples, peeled and
  sliced
3 tablespoons currants or
  seedless raisins
½ cup diced bananas

Cut the meat into 1-inch cubes. Heat the oil and butter in a Dutch oven or heavy casserole; brown the beef in it. Remove the meat. Brown the onions in the fat remaining in the pan. Stir in the wine, tomato paste, bay leaf, salt, pepper, thyme, and broth; return the meat. Bring to a boil, cover, and cook over low heat 1 hour. Add the sweet potatoes; re-cover and cook 30 minutes. Carefully mix in the pears, peaches or apples, and currants. Cook uncovered 10 minutes longer. Taste for seasoning and sprinkle with the bananas. *Serves 6–8.*

TURKEY CASSEROLE

CACEROLA DE PAVO

1 tablespoon salt
1 teaspoon freshly ground
  black pepper
1 teaspoon Spanish paprika
3 cloves garlic, minced
8-pound turkey, disjointed
¾ cup wine vinegar
2 bay leaves

¼ cup olive oil
3 tablespoons butter
2 onions, chopped
1 cup chicken broth
2 pimentos, sliced
12 green olives, sliced
½ cup capers, drained

Combine the salt, pepper, paprika, and garlic. Rub into the turkey pieces thoroughly. Place the turkey in a bowl and pour the vinegar over it. Add the bay leaves and allow the turkey to marinate for 2 hours. Drain.

Heat the olive oil and butter in an earthenware casserole or heavy saucepan. Add the turkey and onions. Cook over high heat until the turkey is well browned on all sides, stirring frequently. Add the broth. Cover and cook over low heat for 1¾ hours, or until the turkey is tender. Add the pimentos, olives, and capers and stir well. Correct seasoning. Serve directly from the casserole. *Serves 8–10.*

CORN BREAD PUDDING

PAN DE MAÍZ

3 tablespoons olive oil	2 cups sifted corn meal
3 onions, chopped	1 teaspoon baking powder
3 tomatoes, chopped	½ pound cottage cheese
¾ cup beef broth	3 tablespoons melted butter
1 teaspoon salt	1½ cups milk

Heat the olive oil in a saucepan. Add the onions and sauté for 5 minutes, stirring frequently. Add the tomatoes and sauté for 10 minutes, again stirring frequently. Add the broth and salt and cook over medium heat for 10 minutes. Preheat oven to 350°.

Sift the corn meal and baking powder into a bowl. Add the cottage cheese and butter and mix well. Add the milk and beat well. Combine with the tomato mixture. Pour into a buttered 8-inch square pan. Bake in a 350° oven for 1 hour, or until lightly set. Turn out onto a platter and serve at once in 1-inch slices. *Serves 6–8.*

MERINGUE DESSERT

POSTRE CHAJA

4 egg whites	5 egg yolks
⅛ teaspoon salt	½ pound (2 sticks) sweet butter
½ teaspoon vinegar	1 tablespoon brandy
1¾ cups sugar	8 slices spongecake or 16 lady
1 teaspoon vanilla extract	fingers
¼ cup water	1 cup strawberries
⅛ teaspoon cream of tartar	2 cups whipped cream

Beat the whites and salt until stiff but not dry. Add the vinegar and gradually add 1 cup of the sugar, spoon by spoon, beating constantly until ⅔ cup of the sugar is used; fold in the remaining ⅓ cup, and the vanilla. Drop by tablespoonfuls onto a buttered baking sheet, or use a pastry bag. Bake in a 250° oven for 30 minutes, or until very delicately browned and dry. Remove from the pan immediately with a spatula and set aside to cool.

Combine the remaining ¾ cup of sugar, the water and cream of tartar in a saucepan. Boil until very syrupy. If a spoon of the mixture is lifted out of the syrup, a thread should form. Beat the egg yolks in a bowl and gradually add the syrup, beating constantly until the mixture is cool and thick. Cream the butter until fluffy and soft and add gradually to the syrup mixture. Add the brandy and mix together.

Place a meringue on each plate and top with a slice of spongecake or 2 lady fingers. Arrange a few strawberries on the spongecake and cover with whipped cream. Place a meringue on top and cover completely with the previously prepared butter cream. Some crumbled meringue may be sprinkled on top. *Serves 8.*

VENEZUELA

Venezuela consists of two principal parts—the tropical, unexplored jungles of the interior and the more modern region bordering the coastline. Far back in the *savannas* (the plains) there are hundreds of miles of territory where no white man has yet been, and where the trees are filled with orchids, and parrots and monkeys scream from the treetops. This description may sound like a Hollywood trailer for a color film about Africa, but then even Hollywood can be right. In the small communities surrounding the wild *savannas* the people eat simple and tasty local dishes based upon what is produced and available in their area, for transportation is poor. Corn forms the basic part of their diet; it is boiled or made into a variety of homemade bread. *Aresancocho,* a meat stew containing many unusual ingredients, is a Venezuelan favorite, and is quite similar to *sancocho,* a recipe for which appears in the Central American section. *Mondongos* are soup-stews on the order of Argentinian *pucheros.*

Nature has been very kind to Venezuela, and the country owns large natural resources of what is known as black gold, or oil. This wealth has permitted the nation to prosper at an amazing pace, and as a result many visitors are surprised to find the capital city, Caracas, a truly modern city with fine homes, hotels, and restaurants. As is true of all big cities, prices of everything are *extremely* high even by our own standards.

Naturally the city folk do not eat the same fare as their country cousins, and their diet is closer to that of other foreign city dwellers than to the diet of their own peasantry.

A good breakfast is eaten almost everywhere in the country—an exception to the usual South American custom. Eggs, homemade bread, and either hot chocolate or coffee start the day. Lunch and dinner are both quite substantial meals of numerous courses. Dinner is often eaten quite late in the evening, extremely late by comparison with our habits.

Beans, root vegetables, stews, corn, and starchy potato tubers (like *apio*, for example) form the basic items of the local diet. If one dish were to be selected as representative of the country, it would have to be *hallacas*, a sort of tamale stuffed with meat. It may be eaten as an hors d'oeuvre or as a main course. In general, fish is available only near the coast line and in the major cities; red snapper is the great favorite.

The outstanding cheese is *queso de mano*, or hand cheese, so called because it is kneaded by hand until the desired elastic quality is obtained. It is much used in Venezuela and deserves to be exported, but owing to the high prices that already prevail in Venezuela, it would have to sell at unwarrantedly high prices here.

As to liquors, a considerable amount of hard liquor is made from corn and sugar cane: there is also *cocuy*, a brandy made from cactus which is not for sissies, or for strong men either, for that matter. Beer is good and is consumed in large quantities, and home brew made from palm trees is popular. Imported wines and liquors are available at very high prices but are not important to the majority of Venezuelans. An exception must be noted in favor of French brandies, for which the country has an extreme fondness. At those prices, too!

MARINATED FRIED FISH

PESCADO EN ESCABECHE

6 slices kingfish, bass, or other firm-fleshed fish
Lemon
2½ teaspoons salt
¾ teaspoon freshly ground black pepper
½ cup flour
2 cups vegetable oil
1 quart cider vinegar

1 pound onions, peeled and sliced
4 sweet red or green peppers, cut julienne
1 teaspoon sugar
¼ cup chopped mustard pickles
2 tablespoons capers
1 zwieback, grated

Wash and dry the fish. Cut the lemon and rub the fish slices with it, then rub the fish with 1½ teaspoons salt and ½ teaspoon pepper. Dip the slices in the flour.

Heat 1 cup oil in a skillet until it bubbles. Brown the fish in it. Drain and place in a deep bowl or wide-mouthed jar.

In a saucepan, combine the vinegar, onions, and peppers. Bring to a boil and cook 5 minutes. Add the remaining 1 cup oil; cook 3 minutes. Remove from the heat and mix in the sugar, pickles, capers, and zwieback crumbs. Pour over the fish. Cover and let marinate in the refrigerator at least 24 hours before serving. The fish may be kept about 2 weeks. Serve cold. *Serves 6.*

FISH AND ALMOND SOUP

SOPA DE PESCADO Y ALMENDRAS

2 tablespoons butter	1 cup ground blanched almonds
1 onion, chopped	1 teaspoon salt
1 pound fillet of sole	½ teaspoon freshly ground black
1 pound shrimp, shelled and	pepper
cleaned	1 teaspoon saffron
¼ pound ham, chopped fine	3 hard-cooked egg yolks,
2 quarts fish stock or 1 quart	chopped
clam juice and 1 quart water	3 tablespoons chopped parsley
½ cup raw rice	

Melt the butter in a saucepan. Add the onion and cook over low heat until soft, but do not allow the onion to brown. Cut the fillet of sole and the shrimp into small pieces. Add to the onion. Add the ham and stock and bring to a boil. Add the rice, almonds, salt, pepper, and saffron and stir. Cook over low heat for 30 minutes. Before serving, add the chopped egg yolks and parsley. Serve with French-style bread. *Serves 8–10.*

VENEZUELAN NATIONAL CORN MEAL DISH

HALLACAS

1½ pounds beef, diced	4 tablespoons chopped parsley
1½ pounds pork, diced	4 teaspoons salt
2 cups water	3 tablespoons vinegar
4 cloves garlic, minced	1 teaspoon sugar
1 cup canned chick-peas	2 teaspoons capers
3 tablespoons olive oil	½ cup seedless raisins
4 tomatoes, chopped	½ cup sliced stuffed olives
4 onions, chopped	3 cups corn meal
2 green peppers, chopped	4 cups boiling water
½ teaspoon dried ground chili	⅓ cup butter
peppers	2 eggs, beaten

Combine the beef, pork, water, and garlic in a saucepan. Bring to a boil and cook over medium heat for 45 minutes. Drain and chop coarsely. Add the chick-peas, mixing lightly. Heat the oil in a large skillet. Add the tomatoes, onions, green peppers, chili peppers, parsley, 2 teaspoons of the salt, vinegar, sugar, and the meat mixture. Cook over low heat for 15 minutes, stirring occasionally. Add the capers, raisins, and olives. Mix lightly. Set aside.

Mix the corn meal with a little cold water. Add to the boiling water in a saucepan, stirring constantly. Add the butter and remaining salt. Cook over low heat for 15 minutes. Remove from the heat and add the eggs, beating until a smooth dough is formed. Butter a large (3-quart) round or square baking dish. Line it with two thirds of the corn-meal mixture and pour the meat mixture into it. Spread the remaining corn meal on top. Cover the dish with a piece of aluminum foil and tie it. Place in a pan of water. Bake in a 350° oven for 1 hour.

In Venezuela the dish is prepared in the form of *tamales*. Banana leaves are used for wrapping the *hallacas*, but aluminum foil or parchment paper will serve as a substitute. Cut 10-inch squares of either paper. Spread about 4 tablespoons of the corn-meal dough in the center and press as thin as possible. Place 2 tablespoons of the meat mixture on the dough and fold over, sealing the edges as well as possible. If the dough breaks, patch it with a little more dough. Fold the paper around the *hallacas* carefully and tie it securely. (If aluminum foil is used, it is not necessary to tie it.) Boil in a large saucepan of salted water for 1½ hours. Serve in the papers. *Serves 8–10.*

ROAST MARINATED LEG OF PORK

CODILLO ASADO

6–8 pound leg of pork	1½ cups grated onions
1 cup wine vinegar	2 cloves garlic, minced
1 cup tomato sauce	2 allspice
½ cup Worcestershire sauce	2 cups Marsala or sweet sherry
2 teaspoons salt	
½ teaspoon freshly ground black pepper	

Prick the leg of pork all over with the point of a knife. Combine all the remaining ingredients but the wine, and marinate the pork in the mixture in the refrigerator for 3 days, basting and turning twice each day.

Drain the pork, and put it in a shallow roasting pan. Roast in a 300°

oven for 30 minutes a pound. Add the wine after 1 hour, and baste frequently. *Serves 8–10.*

As served at the Tamanaco Hotel.

NOODLE AND CHEESE OMELET

TORTILLA DE TALLARINES Y QUESO

6 eggs
1 cup grated Parmesan cheese
1 teaspoon salt
¼ teaspoon freshly ground black pepper

3 cups cooked noodles or spaghetti, broken into very small pieces
4 tablespoons butter

Beat the eggs in a bowl. Add the cheese, salt, pepper, and noodles. Mix well. Melt 2 tablespoons of the butter in a skillet. Pour 2 tablespoons of the mixture into it and fry until brown on both sides. Continue until all of the mixture is used up. Add more butter as required. Keep the little omelets in a warm place until they are all ready to be served. Serve hot. *Serves 6–8.*

AVOCADO-SPINACH SALAD

ENSALADA DE ESPINACA Y AGUACATE

1 pound spinach
2 cups boiling water
2 tablespoons olive oil
2 onions, sliced
½ teaspoon salt

2 avocados, peeled and sliced
2 hard-cooked eggs
Lettuce leaves
½ cup mayonnaise

Wash the spinach until free of sand. Place in a bowl and pour the boiling water over it. Soak for 5 minutes. Drain. Heat the oil in a skillet. Add the onions and salt. Sauté for 5 minutes, stirring occasionally. Place in a chopping bowl. Add the spinach, avocado, and egg. Chop until the mixture is well blended and smooth. Chill for 1 hour. Place the lettuce on individual plates and spoon the avocado mixture over it. Place a tablespoon of mayonnaise on top. *Serves 4–6.*

RICE AND COCONUT PUDDING

ARROZ CON COCO

1 cup rice
3 cups water
1 teaspoon salt
1 cup sugar
¼ cup fresh or dried grated
    coconut

1 cup milk
2 teaspoons grated lemon rind
2 teaspoons cinnamon

Wash the rice in several waters. Combine the water and salt in a sauce-pan and bring to a boil. Add the rice gradually and boil for 15 minutes. Drain. Return the rice to the saucepan and add the sugar, coconut, and milk. Mix well and cook over low heat until creamy and thick, about 15 minutes. Add the lemon rind. Mix lightly. Serve hot or cold, sprinkled with cinnamon. *Serves 4–6.*

WELCOME HOME
we hope your trip was enjoyable and that you have enjoyed trying these new dishes.

Cooking Hints

HELPFUL TIPS

Avocados To keep avocados from turning dark when peeled, place the pit in the center of the dish.

Baking Always have ingredients at room temperature. Butter is creamed more easily; sudden changes in temperature affect baking results.

Coconut Milk To extract the liquid from coconut pulp when making coconut milk or cream, squeeze the liquid and coconut through cheesecloth until the pulp is dry.

Dairy Products Use sweet butter whenever possible.

Deep-Fat Frying Don't crowd the frying basket or kettle; don't use butter, as it burns too quickly.

Dried Fruits To chop raisins and other sticky fruits, heat the knife or food chopper before using.

Fish Remove fish from refrigerator 30 minutes before using.

Herbs Keep herbs and spices well covered, and replace frequently. The flavor of dried herbs may be brought out by soaking for a few moments in hot water, then in cold.

Knives Always use the sharpest possible knives for the cutting and preparation of foods.

Meats Remove from the refrigerator 1 hour before cooking.

Nuts To blanch nuts, cover with cold water, bring to a boil, let soak until skins wrinkle, drain, cover with cold water, and slip the skins off between the fingers. Use a special nut chopper or Mouli grater for grinding nuts, or roll on a board with a rolling pin.

Poultry Season poultry the day before it is to be cooked, if possible. Remove from the refrigerator 1 hour before cooking.

Salad Greens Tear lettuce and other greens into pieces instead of cutting.

Sour Milk If not available, sour milk can be made by adding 2 teaspoons of lemon juice or vinegar to a cup of milk; cook over low heat until milk curdles. Cool and use.

Stock Canned consommé, or bouillon cubes dissolved in hot water, may be substituted for stock. When large quantities are called for, use the canned consommé, as bouillon cubes have a strong flavor when used in quantity.

Yeast Yeast is sold fresh (compressed) or dry in 1-ounce packages.

USEFUL KITCHEN EQUIPMENT *other than normal essentials* (*including some foreign utensils*)

Cake tester	Garlic press	Poultry shears
Casseroles of various sizes	Lettuce basket	Ramekins of various sizes
Chinese or Korean fire pot	MagicMix Food Processor	Salt and pepper mills
Chopping board	Marble slab (for rolling pastry) or	Skewers
Chopsticks	pastry cloth	Soufflé dishes of
Colander	Meat cleaver or	various sizes
Cooky cutter	pounder	Tart pans
Couscousière	Mortar and pestle	Wire whisk
Electric blender	Nut grinder or	Wok or large skillet
Electric mixer	Mouli grater	with sloping sides
Electric skillet	Pastry blender	Wooden spoon for
Flan dish	Pastry brush	mixing
Fondue cooker	Pastry tube	Yogurt maker
Food chopper	Pot de crème dishes	

TEMPERATURE GUIDE, *Fahrenheit*

Very slow oven	225°
Slow oven	250° to 300°
Moderate oven	325° to 375°
Hot oven	400° to 450°
Very hot oven	475° and over

DEEP-FAT FRYING TEMPERATURES, *Fahrenheit*

360° to 375°	Uncooked mixtures; doughnuts, fritters, or shellfish
375° to 385°	Cooked mixtures with coatings; croquettes, etc.
385° to 395°	French-fried potatoes, vegetables, etc.

COOKING MEASUREMENTS

Dash	=	Less than ⅛ teaspoon
3 teaspoons	=	1 tablespoon
2 liquid tablespoons	=	1 ounce
4 tablespoons	=	¼ cup
16 tablespoons	=	1 cup
1 cup	=	½ pint
2 liquid cups	=	1 pound
16 ounces	=	1 pound
4 cups	=	1 quart

CONVERSION TABLE for use outside of the United States (all equivalents are approximate)

WEIGHT

15 grams	=	½ ounce
30 grams	=	1 ounce
50 grams	=	1¾ ounces
75 grams	=	2½ ounces
100 grams	=	3½ ounces
500 grams	=	17 ounces (1 pound, 1½ ounces)
1 kilogram	=	35 ounces (2 pounds, 3 ounces)

LIQUID

1 declitre	=	3½ ounces
1 demilitre	=	⅞ pint
1 litre	=	1¾ pints (35 ounces)
1 American pint	=	16 fluid ounces
1 American cup	=	8 fluid ounces
1 American cup	=	16 fluid ounces
1 teaspoon	=	4.9 cubic centimeters
1 tablespoon	=	14.8 cubic centimeters
1 cup	=	236.6 cubic centimeters

SAMPLE COMPARISONS

Butter (solid fats)	230 grams	= 1 American cup	= ½ pound
Flour	115 grams	= 1 American cup	= ¼ pound
Sugar, granulated	230 grams	= 1 American cup	= ½ pound

For other equivalents, see page 474–75

AMERICAN CAN SIZES

8 oz.	= 1 cup
⋇1 Picnic	= 1¼ cups
⋇1	= 1½ cups
⋇300	= 2 cups
⋇303	= 2 cups
⋇2	= 2½ cups
⋇2¼	= 3½ cups
⋇1 square	= 1 pound

TABLE OF EQUIVALENT WEIGHTS AND MEASURES

Baking powder	1 ounce	=	3½ tablespoons
Beans, dried	½ pound	=	1 cup
Bread crumbs	3 ounces (approx.)	=	1 cup
Butter and solid fats	1 pound	=	2 cups
Butter and solid fats	¼ pound	=	8 tablespoons
Butter and solid fats	¼ pound	=	½ cup
Cheese, cottage	½ pound	=	1 cup
Cheese, cream	½ pound	=	1 cup
Cheese, grated	¼ pound	=	1 cup
Chocolate	1 ounce	=	1 square
Cinnamon	1 ounce	=	4½ tablespoons
Coconut, grated dried	¼ pound	=	1 cup, packed
Consommé	1 can	=	10½ ounces
Corn meal	1 pound	=	3 cups
Cornstarch	4½ ounces	=	1 cup
Cream	½ pint	=	1 cup
Dates, pitted	½ pound	=	1¼ cups
Eggs	2 ounces	=	1 egg
Egg whites	8 to 10	=	1 cup
Flour	1 pound	=	4 cups, sifted
Flour	¼ ounce	=	1 tablespoon
Honey	12 ounces	=	1 cup
Lemon juice	1 lemon	=	2 to 3 tablespoons
Lemon rind, grated	1 lemon	=	2 to 3 teaspoons
Nuts, ground	¼ pound	=	1 cup
Oil	7½ ounces	=	1 cup
Peanut butter	1 pound	=	1¾ cups
Potatoes	1 pound	=	3 average
Raisins	1 pound	=	3 cups
Rice, uncooked	1 pound	=	2 cups
Rice, uncooked	1 cup	=	3 cups, cooked

Sugar, brown	1 pound	=	2¼ cups, packed
Sugar, confectioners'	1 pound	=	3½ to 4 cups, sifted
Sugar, granulated	1 pound	=	2 cups
Tomatoes, fresh	1 pound	=	3 average
Tomato sauce (1 can)	7¾–8 ounces	=	1 cup

A FEW SIMPLE COOKING TERMS

Aspic Clear jelly, variously prepared, used to garnish fancy dishes.

Bake To cook by means of dry heat, usually in an oven.

Barbecue Has many different meanings but generally refers to food roasted outdoors over an open fire; a spicy, smoky sauce.

Baste To brush or spoon liquid over a food while marinating or cooking.

Batter Any combination that includes flour, water, milk, butter, eggs, or the like, used for dipping, coating, or for pancakes, cake, etc.

Beat To mix, using a fork, wire whisk, electric or rotary beater.

Blanch To place in cold water, then bring to a boil. Nuts are blanched by the same method, then placed in cold water and the skin slipped off between the fingers.

Blend To combine several ingredients; to mix together until smooth.

Boil To heat a mixture or liquid until bubbles appear on the surface and vapor rises; also to continue the process thereafter.

Boiling Point The temperature at which a liquid begins to bubble around the edge.

Bouillon Clear soup, usually made from bones, poultry, meat, or fish.

Bouillon Cube Cube containing various solids, usually salted, and to which liquid may be added to produce a bouillonlike liquid.

Braise To brown in a little fat, then cook over low heat in very little liquid in a covered pan.

Broil To cook by direct heat close to the fire or other source of heat.

Brush To spread seasoning, butter, or other coating.

Caramelize To melt sugar slowly over low heat until brown and of a sticky consistency.

Chill To cool foods by placing in the refrigerator.

Chop To cut food into small pieces.

Combine To join two or more ingredients together.

Cream To soften ingredients by beating with a spoon, rotary or electric beater until soft and of creamy texture.

Cube To cut foods into pieces with 6 approximately equal sides; to cut in cubes.

Cut In Shortening To mix shortening with flour by using a pastry blender or two knives until shortening is distributed evenly.

Devilled Seasoned highly.

Dissolve To melt, break up, or liquefy.

Dredge To coat a food well, usually with flour or sugar.

Drippings Fat or juices that cook out of foods.

Dust To sprinkle lightly with a dry coating such as bread crumbs, flour, or sugar.

Flake To separate foods gently with a fork.

Fold In To use a spoon in a gently rolling circular action as a means of combining ingredients.

Fry To cook foods in hot oil or other fat.

Garnish To decorate foods.

Grate To rub food into small pieces on a grater.

Grill To broil foods near open, direct heat.

Grind To put food through a food chopper or mill, to reduce or crush into small pieces, flakes, or powder.

Knead To manipulate or work with the hands, usually a dough, using a folding-back and pressing-forward motion until of the desired consistency.

Lard To insert strips of fat under the skin or into the meat with a larding needle or other pointed instrument, or to cover a food with strips of fat.

Marinade Liquid used for pickling or seasoning by soaking; usually contains vinegar or wine, spices, herbs, and oil.

Marinate To soak in vinegar, wine, or other liquid, usually containing spices, herbs, and oil.

Melt To heat until the ingredient is changed from solid to liquid.

Mince To chop as fine as possible.

Mix To stir ingredients together.

Mortar and Pestle A mortar is a bowl or container in which foods may be ground or crushed; the pestle is a club-shaped utensil used to assist in this process.

Pan Broil To cook in a hot skillet with little or no fat.

Pan Fry To cook foods in a frying pan over direct heat, using some oil or other fat.

Parboil To cook foods partially in water or other liquids.

Pare To remove the outside skin or peel of fruits, vegetables, etc.

Poach To cook in a liquid just below the boiling point.

Preheat To turn on the oven to a selected temperature 10 minutes before it is needed.

Purée Food, usually cooked, forced through a sieve to produce a smooth mixture; to force through a sieve.

Render To melt solid fat away from connective tissue; to clarify fats by melting.

Roast To cook in an oven.

Roll To place on a flat surface and spread thin with a rolling pin.

Roux A smooth mixture of fat and flour, used as a thickening agent.

Sauté To cook or brown over low heat in a little fat, oil, or butter.

Scald To pour boiling liquid over a food, to heat almost to boiling.

Score To cut narrow gashes on the surface of a food.

Sear To brown the surface of a food at high heat.

Sieve A utensil with a perforated bottom used to separate coarse pieces from fine, and as a strainer of liquids.

Sift To separate coarse pieces from fine by shaking through a sieve, thus removing lumps and foreign particles.

Simmer To cook over low heat just below the boiling point.

Skewer To fasten with a wood or metal pin, to hold something in place while cooking; a long wood or metal pin.

Soak To cover a food with liquid until very wet.

Spatula Broad, flexible knife suitable for lifting foods.

Stalk An individual piece; in celery, for example, the various stalks make up a bunch.

Steam To cook by contact with live steam in a covered container or in a perforated container placed over hot water.

Steep To soak in hot liquid below the boiling point.

Stir To mix ingredients together within a container; usually by means of a spoon.

Stock Broth in which meat, poultry, bones, or fish have been cooked, used as base for gravies, sauces, and soups. Substitutes: bouillon cubes dissolved in water; canned consommé; meat extracts. (Where a large quantity is required, canned consommé is preferable to bouillon cubes.)

Truss To secure the body of fowl in such a fashion that it will not move during the cooking process.

Whip To beat a liquid to a froth; to increase the volume of a liquid by beating air into it.

A Glossary for Gourmets

Abaisse A thin, flaky pastry (French).

Abats French term for so-called variety meats: liver, kidneys, lungs, etc.

Abendmahl Supper (German).

Abricotine Apricot brandy (French).

Achaja A Greek wine.

Achiote *See* Annatto.

Adet A brandy.

Advocaat An apéritif, made with brandy; has a characteristic yellow color.

Aemono Fish and vegetables, Japanese style.

Agar-agar Jellylike substance obtained from seaweed; used as a thickening agent in various foods.

Agaric Variety of mushroom.

Agave Mexican cactus plant used in the making of certain Mexican liquors.

Agemono Fried vegetables or fish, Japanese style.

Agnellotti Italian dumplings stuffed with meat and spices.

Aiguillette A long, thin cut of cooked food, such as meat or poultry.

Aillade Sauce containing garlic.

Akala Dark-colored Hawaiian berry.

Aku Malou Air-dried tuna fish.

À la In the manner of (French); used to describe the fashion in which dishes are prepared.

À la carte Prepared to order (French); food not served on a dinner at a fixed price.

Al Dente Italian expression for slightly underdone spaghetti or other similar foods.

Albacore Type of tuna fish.

Ale Beverage resembling beer, but usually somewhat stronger or darker; contains about 4% alcohol.

Alewife Variety of fish particularly known in England.

Alligator Pear An avocado.

Allspice Spice prepared from the dried berry of the pimento tree.

Almond Paste Prepared baking mixture made of sugar, dried eggs, and ground almonds.

Amer Picon Apéritif wine of France.

Amontillado Dry sherry of Spain.

Amoroso Medium sherry of Spain.

Ananas, Crème d' Crème of pineapple, French cordial.

Anchovy Small fish, commonly salted, dried, or packed in oil, used as an appetizer, in cooking, etc.

Anchovy Pear Fruit of a West Indies tree; eaten, pickled, as a relish.

Andouille Sausage or pudding made of pork, popular in parts of France.

Angelica Plant used in flavoring various liqueurs; also candied, and eaten plain or used in baking.

Anglaise, à l' Boiled in plain water.

Angostura Bitters, prepared in the West Indies.

Anise Seeds or oil obtained from a plant and used as a flavoring; also aniseed or aniseed oil.

Anisette French liqueur made from aniseed.

Anjan Siamese food coloring.

Annatto Red, natural dye used for coloring foods, particularly popular on the west coast of South America; also known as achiote.

Antipasto Italian term for the typical appetizer served before a dinner; usually miscellaneous vegetables, fish, cold meats, etc.

Apéritif A light drink, not a whisky, served as a pre-meal drink (French).

Apio South American tuber.

Apple Brandy Cider, with considerable water removed by distillation.

Apple Gin Greenish-yellow gin, flavored with apple.

Apricot Brandy Yellowish brandy flavored with apricots.

Aqua d'Orott Italian cordial made with rose petals.

Aquavit Clear liquor usually with caraway seed flavor; popular in Scandinavian countries.

Arabica Colombian coffee.

Arancini Meat and rice dish popular in Sicily.

Areca Betel nut of Asia.

Aromatics Old term for herbs, spices, and seasoning.

Arrack Strong liquor of the Near East.

Arrowroot Natural starch obtained from a West Indies root plant.

Artichoke, Globe Green vegetable, only moderately popular; head composed of individual leaves, part of each leaf being edible.

Artichoke, Jerusalem Tuber resembling the common potato; not readily prepared since it is irregular and knobby.

Asado Roast meat dish popular in Uruguay and Argentina.

Assam An Indian tea.

Atka Fish Small Pacific Ocean fish.

Attorta Italian almond pastry.

Aubergine Eggplant.

Au Beurre French term for foods served with plain melted butter.

Au Bleu French designation for a fish dish prepared quickly in white wine or water; the fish must be alive immediately before the dish is prepared.

Au Gratin Usually applied to a scalloped dish with a crust of bread crumbs, sometimes mixed with cheese or butter.

Au Jus Any dish containing only its own natural juices.

Au Naturel French term for food served uncooked or otherwise unaltered.

Aurum Italian orange liqueur.

Avocado Green fruit with a thick skin and an oily, rich yellow interior; alligator pear.

Baba Light, buttery yeast cake.

Babassu Nut Oil Oil obtained from the babassu palm; greatly resembles coconut oil.

Bacalao Dried codfish, Spanish style.

Bacardi Well-known Cuban rum.

Bagna Cauda Italian sauce of truffles, garlic, olives, and anchovies.

Bagoong Dried shrimp used in the Philippines.

Baicoli Italian-style sweet pastry.

Bain-Marie French cooking utensil similar to a double boiler in principle, used for cooking food slowly, or for keeping it warm, by surrounding it with hot water.

Baissière Sediment in wine.

Baking Powder Combination of several chemical ingredients used to increase the size of dough and lighten its texture; usually contains cream of tartar and sodium bicarbonate.

Ballotine French term for small balls of meat or poultry used in French-style cookery.

Bannock Flat type of Scotch cake.

Bap Floury, Scotch breakfast roll.

Barcelonas Nuts similar to hazelnuts.

Bar-le-duc French currant jelly.

Baron of Beef Twin sirloins of beef cooked together.

Barquette Boat-shaped pastry.

Barsac A French white wine.

Bavette Type of Italian macaroni that is particularly light and frothy.

Bay Leaf Medium-sized green leaf, often dried, and used for flavoring foods.

Bay Salt A fine, well-flavored salt obtained by evaporating bay water, rather than sea water, in specially-constructed flats; usually has rough crystals.

Bean Curd Soft cakes made from soybeans, used in oriental dishes.

Bean Sprouts Young bean shoots.

Béarnaise Rich sauce, often served with roast meats.

Beaujolais A popular, low-priced wine, usually red, which is best when very young; does not age well.

Béchamel One of the most important French sauces.

Bêche-de-Mer Sea slug, considered a great delicacy by various oriental peoples.

Beignet Any type of fritter.

Bel Paese Medium-soft Italian cheese quite popular in Italy and the United States.

Bĕlachan Siamese shrimp paste.

Benedictine Famous French cordial.

Benzoate of Soda Commonly used food preservative.

Bergamot Herb, formerly much used for flavoring.

Betel Nut Obtained from the betel palm tree; a favorite of the people of Indo-China.

Beurre Fondue Melted butter. (French).

Beurre Noir Literally, black butter; usually refers to a brown butter.

Bifteck Beefsteak (French).

Bitters Liquid containing some alcohol and one or more bitter flavoring ingredients, such as quinine, angostura, etc.

Blackstrap Molasses Poorest grade of molasses.

Blaeberry Edible northern berry.

Blancmange General term used to describe a variety of white puddings.

Blimbing Acidulous fruit of Asia.

Blinis Buckwheat pancakes, usually small of Russian origin.

Bloater Smoked herring.

Blue Points Large, excellent variety of oysters.

Blue Rose A southern rice.

Bluefin Type of tuna fish.

Bombay Duck Dried bummalo fish; popular in India with curried food.

Bonbon General term, but usually refers to small candies, particularly those with icing.

Bonito Similar to but not exactly like tuna fish.

Bordelaise Sauce that presumably originated near Bordeaux, France; made with wine.

Boudin Main-course pudding, usually made with meat or poultry.

Bouillabaisse Famous fish soup or stew of the south of France.

Bouquet Garni French term for a small bundle of herbs fastened together during cooking, to prevent separation and facilitate subsequent removal.

Bourbon Whisky distilled from a mash containing no less than 51% corn grain.

Bourgeoise Family, or home-style, food.

Bourghol Cracked wheat.

Bourride Fish soup or stew, popular in France.

Brazil Nut Extremely oily, rich nut obtained from Brazil; has three angles.

Breadnut A fruit, usually eaten in the West Indies as a substitute for bread.

Bream Type of fish.

Bree Scotch term for soup or stock.

Bressans A cheese, usually made with goat milk.

Brigidini Italian biscuits flavored with aniseed.

Brillat-Savarin Famous writer on food and a gourmet of high repute.

Brinjal Eggplant (India).

Brioche Famous breakfast bread popular in France; made with yeast in a characteristic shape.

Brochan Scotch word for porridge.

Broche, à la Broiled over direct heat on a skewer.

Brochette, en Small pieces of meat, fish, or vegetables roasted on a skewer.

Brodetto Meat, or occasionally fish, served with a considerable amount of sauce or gravy (Italian).

Brose Scotch milk and oatmeal dish.

Brûlé Burned, a French cooking term.

Buccellato An Italian cake.

Buckwheat Herb, commonly used as a food after processing into flour.

Bullace A wild plum.

Burdwan Curried dish popular in India.

Burgol Cracked wheat.

Burgundy Wines produced in the general Burgundy area of France.

Buridda Fish stew of the Italian Riviera; closely resembles the *bourride* of southern France.

Buttermilk Liquid left after butter has been removed during churning.

Byrrh Apéritif popular in France.

Cacciatora Italian term for foods prepared quite simply, "Hunter's Style"; usually a chicken dish with tomatoes and onions.

Cacciucco Italian fish soup.

Caciocavallo Italian cheese of fairly firm consistency, somewhat like *provolone*.

Café Restaurant or bar specializing in drinks; coffee (French).

Café au Lait Coffee and hot milk, half and half.

Caffè Espresso Italian style of coffee-making, involving forcing steam through finely ground coffee; produces a very strong, black coffee.

Café Noir Black coffee (French); usually a demitasse.

Calamondin A citrus fruit.

Calavo Avocados grown in California under a trade name.

Calimyrna Variety of fig.

Calvados French apple brandy.

Calzone Macaroni dish prepared with cheese and meat.

Cambur Variety of banana.

Camembert A very soft, rich white cheese produced in France; often regarded as one of the world's greatest.

Camote Sweet potato.

Canapé Small piece of bread covered with varying ingredients, served as an hors d'oeuvre.

Cannelloni A pasta dish, consisting of squares of dough spread with a meat, poultry, or cheese mixture, covered with a sauce, and baked.

Cannoli Italian dessert made in the shape of a cornucopia.

Capellini d'Angelo Very thin type of Italian macaroni.

Capers Flower buds, pickled and used as a relish or for flavoring.

Capon Castrated male chicken; flavor somewhat superior to that of ordinary chicken.

Caponatina Italian appetizer, usually made with assorted pickled vegetables.

Cappelletti Type of Italian macaroni.

Capsicum Genus of peppers; includes many different types.

Carambola An Asiatic fruit.

Caraway Seeds, used as a spice.

Caraway Oil Obtained from the caraway plant; used as a flavoring agent in liqueurs, bread, cheese, etc.

Cardamom Seasoning ingredient popular in East Indian countries.

Carrageen Edible Irish seaweed.

Casareep West Indian flavoring syrup.

Cashew Nut Grown principally in India; used extensively as a food.

Cassata Italian type of ice cream, usually extremely rich.

Cassis French currant liqueur.

Cassola Fish soup, Italian style.

Caviar Roe of certain varieties of sturgeon; eggs may be black, gray, or gold.

Cayenne Extremely spicy variety of capsicum, the red pepper plant; used as a seasoning.

Celeriac Celery root.

Celery Oil Yellowish oil produced from celery seeds and used as a flavoring.

Celery Salt Celery plant seeds, ground fine and used as a flavoring.

Cèpe Variety of mushroom popular in France.

Ceriman Fruit with a pineapple and banana flavor.

Ceylon Spinach Climbing vegetable plant with thick leaves.

Chablis White Burgundy wine of France.

Champagne Sparkling white wine of the Champagne region of France.

Char Type of fresh-water trout.

Charcuterie Any cold, prepared, cooked meats.

Chartreuse French liqueur; both yellow and green varieties are made.

Chaudfroid Cold meat or poultry covered with a glazed, cold sauce.

Chawanmushi Japanese steamed egg dish, usually with other ingredients added.

Chayote A vegetable, particularly appreciated in Latin and South American countries.

Cheddar A classic English cheese.

Cherimoya Important fruit, particularly in South America, with a white interior and a green exterior.

Cherry Whisky Red liquor.

Chervil Herb with a parsley flavor, commonly used for flavoring.

Cheshire Hard type of English cheese: comes in both red and white.

Chevalier, à la Batter-fried food.

Chianti An Italian wine, typically sold in the familiar straw-covered bottle; usually somewhat rough to the taste.

Chick-pea Starchy pea, much used for food in the Near and Middle East.

Chico A fruit of the Philippines.

Chicory Green plant whose bitter leaves are used in salads; dried root used to flavor coffee.

Chili Peppers Various types of hot red peppers of the capsicum group; may be used fresh, dried, or ground.

Chine Term for two unseparated pork loins.

Chinese Radish Large radishlike vegetable; tastes much like turnip.

Chipolata Small sausages of various types.

Chitterlings Cooked animal intestines, popular in parts of the southern U.S.

Chive Grasslike herb with a mild onion flavor.

Choucroute Sauerkraut (French).

Choux Rich cooked paste made of eggs, butter, and flour.

Choux de Bruxelles Brussels sprouts.

Chowl Indian term for rice.

Chub Variety of fresh-water fish.

Chufa Underground nut resembling a peanut or almond.

Chupatti East Indian wheat cake, used as a bread.

Chutney Spicy Indian relish made from various combinations, but usually containing mangoes, spices, and sugar.

Cider Apple juice, used as a beverage.

Cinnamon A favorite spice available in several styles: whole pieces in stick form, ground, etc.

Cinnamon Oil Oil usually made from cinnamon leaves, used as a flavoring agent.

Citrange Variety of bitter orange.

Citric Acid Acid commonly present in citrus fruits.

Citron Fruit of the citron tree; rind often preserved with sugar.

Claret Another name for the Bordeaux wines of France.

Cloudberry Arctic berry.

Clove Dark red-brown bud used as a spice.

Clove Oil Distilled from the flower buds of the plant, used for flavoring purposes.

Cobnut Type of filbert.

Cockle A shellfish.

Cocoa Chocolate with much of the fat removed in a cooking process; used as a beverage.

Cocotte Individual serving dish, usually ovenproof.

Cognac Brandy manufactured in the Cognac region of France; other brandies may not be called cognac.

Cohune A nut from which an edible oil is obtained.

Cointreau Clear orange-flavored after-dinner liqueur.

Collops Term for small slices of prepared meats, usually sautéed.

Compote Cooked fruits in sweet syrup; use of term limited to fruits that retain their shape in cooking.

Consommé Any clear soup, but usually broth made from meat or poultry.

Coppa Italian variety of salami, usually made with pork products.

Coquille Shell (French); seafood dish served in a shell.

Coriander Seed with a pleasant odor, used for flavoring.

Corn Meal Flour obtained by grinding corn; used for cooking and baking.

Corn Oil Oil obtained by crushing corn; principally used for mayonnaise and salad dressing.

Corn Syrup Obtained by processing crude cornstarch.

Corn Whisky Whisky distilled from a mash containing between 80% and 90% corn.

Cornstarch Starch obtained by a complex process from corn; used for brewing, food, etc.

Coteghino Italian salami containing various starchy legumes, such as beans, etc.; also *cotechino*.

Cottonseed Oil Yellow oil obtained from cottonseed; has many uses for food, canning, etc.

Court Bouillon Liquid in which fish is cooked; usually contains spices, wine, water, etc.

Crawfish A shellfish without claws, but much resembling lobster.

Crayfish A fresh-water shellfish resembling the lobster, but quite small.

Crème de Menthe After-dinner liqueur with a mint flavor.

Creole, à la Term describing foods served with rice and various spices.

Crêpe Thin pancake (French).

Cress Mustard greens.

Croquette Any ground or finely minced mixture, dipped in crumbs or batter and fried.

Croustade Piece of bread fried in butter or oil.

Croûtons Small cubes of fried bread, used to garnish soup or salads.

Cuisson Meat, fish, or poultry stock.

Cumin Seed Aromatic seeds much used for flavoring, particularly in the Near East; also called cumin.

Curaçao Orange-flavored liqueur made in the Dutch West Indies and in Holland.

Curry Powder A combination of various spices, and not a single spice; much used in preparing curries.

Cuscusu Italian variation of *couscous,* made with fish.

Custard Apple A tropical fruit.

Dab Variety of fish.

Damascene Small type of plum.

Damson Variety of plum; customarily used in making jam.

Darjeeling An Indian tea.

Darne A fish slice.

Dato Reddish, tropical fruit obtained from a cactus.

Demitasse A half cup (French); any small cup, but usually refers to after-dinner coffee.

Devonshire Cream Cream prepared by scalding; very rich and thick.

Dewberry Variety of blackberry.

Dhall East Indian lentil.

Diable, à la Food served with a spicy sauce.

Dibs A sweet syrup or wine prepared from grapes or dates in parts of the Near and Middle East.

Dill Green herb used for flavoring; popular in Scandinavian countries.

Dolichos Similar to the string bean, popular in Malaysia.

Dop Secondary type of brandy, usually made by expressing grapeskins.

Drambuie A scotch-whisky cordial flavored with honey.

Drawn Butter Melted butter.

Drupe Fruit with a hard pit or stone, such as peach, cherry, etc.

Dubonnet French apéritif wine.

Duku Fruit popular in Malaysia.

Dulse Edible seaweed.

Durian Fine Indo-Chinese fruit with an objectionable odor.

Dushab Near East syrupy drink made from date wine.

Earthnut Peanut.

Eau de Vie French term for brandy in general.

Edam Famous Dutch cheese, usually made in the shape of a ball.

Elderberry Berry used principally for making wine.

Elver Baby eel; when very young and transparent, considered a great delicacy in Mediterranean countries.

Eminicé Food cut into small pieces, or sometimes chopped fine.

Endive Chicory plant leaves, used principally in salads.

Escabeche Pickled dish containing fish, meat, or poultry; popular in Latin countries.

Escoffier Great French chef; creator of numerous original dishes.

Estouffade Usually a meat dish prepared in a casserole with a sauce.

Etuvée Thick stew, French style.

Faggot Bunch of herbs, such as celery, parsley, etc., tied together for use in cooking.

Fagottino An Italian pastry.

Farci French term for a dish such as poultry, etc., stuffed with a prepared mixture.

Farina General term used to describe any flour.

Farina Dolce Italian flour made from ground chestnuts.

Fennel Herb with a delightful flavor and aroma; particularly used in fish cookery.

Fennel Oil Yellowish oil used principally to flavor gin or other liquors.

Fennel Seed Brownish seed used largely for flavoring.

Fenugreek Herb often used in curry powders.

Fidelini One of the many types of pasta used in Italy.

Filbert Similar to but not identical with the hazelnut.

Fine Champagne Type of French brandy.

Fines Herbes Finely chopped herbs.

Finnan Haddie Smoked haddock; also called *Findon haddock*, after Findon, the Scotch village where it is smoked.

Flageolet A French kidney bean.

Flamande, à la Food served in the Flemish manner.

Flambé Aflame; refers to any dish in the preparation of which a liquor is set afire.

Flan Custard dessert popular with Latin people.

Flensjes Dutch pancake dessert.

Florence Oil A better-quality or live oil.

Flummery Cold oatmeal dessert.

Fondant Cooked, white sugar icing used to decorate cakes.

Fondue Melted-cheese dish of Swiss origin.

Fontina An Italian cheese.

Foratina Variety of macaroni.

Forbidden Fruit A cordial, a liqueur.

Forcemeat Any ground or finely chopped stuffing.

Fra Diavolo Italian term customarily used to describe a lobster dish having a tomato base; "Brother Devil," the Italian bandit.

Fraisia Sweet strawberry liqueur made in France.

Framboise Raspberry (French).

Frappé Iced, or partly frozen.

Friandise Small, dainty fruit or dessert cake or candy.

Fricandeau Large piece or slice of veal larded with fat.

Fricandelle Chopped meat mixture similar to hamburger.

Frit Any fried food (French).

Fritto Misto Mixed fry.

Fumet Strong essence obtained from cooked fish, meat, or poultry.

Galantine Rolled meat or poultry, usually covered with aspic.

Galette Food shaped into a small patty.

Galuska Finger-size dumplings of Hungarian origin.

Game General term used to describe all edible, wild birds and animals not usually raised for food.

Garbure Thick French soup, usually made with vegetables and various other ingredients.

Garni French term for stuffed or decorated food.

Gaufrette Flat, sweet wafer popular in France.

Gelato Any Italian ice cream.

Genipap Acid, tropical fruit.

Gerome A French cheese.

Gervais A rich French cheese.

Ghee Clarified butter; butter with as much water removed as possible.

Gherkin Midget cucumber, used as a relish.

Gin A strong liquor, usually flavored with juniper berries, but may also be made with various other flavoring ingredients.

Ginger Tropical plant whose root is used for flavoring; also candied or preserved.

Ginger Beer English drink with a distinct ginger flavor.

Glace de Viande Meat or fish concentrate used in cooking; prepared by cooking the foods rapidly so as to remove as much moisture as possible.

Glaze Concentrate of fish or meat stock; also, to cover foods with melted jam or other sweetening.

Gnocchi Small boiled or baked Italian dumplings, made from potatoes, semolina, corn meal, or combinations thereof.

Goldwasser Gold water, a German liqueur actually containing gold flakes.

Gorgonzola Italian cheese closely resembling Roquefort.

Granada Tropical fruit somewhat resembling pomegranate.

Granadilla A tropical fruit.

Grappa A potent Italian liquor made from grape pressings.

Gras-double Tripe (French).

Graves Wine of moderate quality produced in a particular part of France.

Grissini Italian breadsticks; may be thin or somewhat thick.

Groats Oats with the husks removed.

Groundnut Peanut.

Gruyère A cheese made in Switzerland or imitated elsewhere; has a characteristic taste and is filled with holes.

Guarana Popular Brazilian soft drink.

Guava Tropical fruit, principally used for making preserves, pastes, or jelly.

Guayaba Tropical fruit best used in preserves.

Gudgeon A type of fresh-water fish found in various parts of Europe.

Guisada A national dish of Spain, usually containing meat and vegetables.

Gula Malacca Sugar made from the coconut palm.

Haggis Scotch national dish; made of a sheep's pluck, and cooked in the lining of a sheep's stomach.

Hallowis Type of edible date.

Herb Any plant whose leaves, roots, or stems are used as a food or for flavoring.

Hock General term for Rhine wines.

Hollandaise Classic sauce made of eggs, butter, and lemon juice.

Holland Gin Famous dry gin manufactured in Holland.

Hominy Finely ground, parched corn. There is also a "Big Hominy."

Hops Blossoms of hop vines grown for beer brewing.

Hors d'Oeuvre General term for an appetizer.

Horseradish. Herb used as a condiment; often combined with sugar, vinegar, or beets.

Hyssop Flowering shrub, generally used near beehives to flavor honey; also a tea.

Imbu A tropical fruit.

Jack Fruit Large fruit of southwestern Asia; largely used as a native food.

Jaggery Palm-tree sugar.

Jantong Flower of the banana.

Jardinière Any dish containing vegetables.

Jereboam Wine bottle holding equivalent of four ordinary bottles.

Jigger Measure of liquor, usually 1½ ounces.

Jimmies Hard crabs.

Jojoto Tropical corn.

Jujube Tropical fruit usually made into jelly or used as a relish.

Julienne Term for various foods cut into thin strips like matches.

Juniper Berry Evergreen plant; berries used for flavoring purposes; commonly used in gin.

Kadanga Flower of southeastern Asia used in desserts.

Kadota Type of fig.

Kaffir African tree producing a starchy food; South African native food.

Kapi Siamese shrimp paste.

Kava Intoxicating beverage made by South Pacific natives.

Kebob Food cooked on a skewer.

Kedgeree Dish containing a combination of rice, eggs, fish, spices, etc.

Kĕladi Tuber popular in Malaysia.

Kelp Dehydrated seaweed, often used for food.

Kipper Split, smoked herring.

Kirsch Clear, cherry-flavored brandy.

Kola Nut Bitter nut of trees grown in Brazil, the West Indies, and Africa; used in preparation of kola (or cola) drinks.

Kosher Food prepared according to Orthodox Jewish rules.

Kumiss Fermented milk drink of Asiatic origin.

Kümmel Liqueur made with caraway seeds and flavored with cumin seeds.

Kumquat Small citrus fruit usually preserved or candied.

Kvass Russian beer.

Lactic Acid Fermented acid, used in pickles, beer, sauerkraut, etc.

Ladies' Fingers Another name for okra.

Lager Any light beer.

Lamprey Edible eel.

Lard Fat obtained from hogs.

Larding Needle Utensil designed to permit the insertion of fat in lean meats.

Lardoon Long, thin piece of bacon or other fat used in the larding process.

Lasagne One of the largest of all the Italian macaroni products.

Lechosa Tropical form of melon, with a perfumed taste.

Leek Edible onionlike plant with flat leaves; flavor comparatively mild.

Legume Starchy vegetable, such as beans, peas, etc.

Lemon Grass Herb used for flavoring.

Lentils Seeds of the lentil plant; a favorite starchy food.

Limburger A soft creamy cheese of German origin with an excellent taste, but having an offensive odor.

Lime Fruit of the lime tree; similar to lemon, but often has a characteristic taste.

Lime Oil Oil obtained from limes; used principally for flavoring.

Limequat A citrus fruit; cross between a lime and a kumquat.

Limu Edible Hawaiian seaweed.

Liqueur Beverage with a high alcoholic content, usually sweet.

Liqueur Brandies Old, thick brandies.

Locksoi Chinese macaroni.

Lodigiano An Italian cheese.

Loganberry Berry obtained by crossing blackberry and raspberry.

Loquat Citrus fruit of little commercial importance.

Love Apple Common tomato.

Lucullus, à la Any dish containing rich ingredients.

Luganica Spicy Italian sausage.

Macaroni General term for most Italian dough products, such as spaghetti, lasagne, etc.

Mace Edible outer covering of nutmeg; used as spice.

Macédoine Mixture of cut-up vegetables or fruit.

Madeleine Molded cake.

Magnum Wine bottle holding the equivalent of two ordinary bottles.

Maitrank German festival wine of May Day.

Maize Another name for corn.

Majorca Type of almond.

Makrut Siamese citrus fruit.

Malmsey Type of sweet Madeira wine.

Maloreddus Italian dumpling colored with saffron.

Malt Germinated, moist barley, used in brewing.

Malt Whisky Whisky distilled from a mash containing not less than 51% malted rye or barley.

Mammee A tropical fruit; often used for ice cream.

Mango Excellent tropical fruit grown in many parts of the world; has many different tropical fruit flavors.

Mangosteen Fine sour-sweet tropical fruit.

Manicotti An Italian macaroni; usually a large noodle stuffed with cheese.

Manju Japanese bean-paste buns.

Manzanilla Light-colored Spanish wine held in high esteem.

Manzano Type of South American banana.

Maraschino Cherry liqueur.

Marble Fat streaks in meat.

Marinara Literally "sailor fashion," but refers to a tomato and onion sauce used for fish and pasta.

Marrons Chestnuts (French).

Marsala Sweet, fairly rich dessert wine produced in Sicily.

Marzipan Crushed almonds combined with sugar; used in baking.

Maté South American beverage resembling tea; of great importance in Argentina, Paraguay, and Uruguay.

Matzoth Unleavened Passover bread of Orthodox Jews.

Methuselah Wine bottle holding the equivalent of eight ordinary bottles.

Meunière Sauce, usually containing butter, lemon juice, and parsley.

Mille-feuille French term for very thin, flaky pastry.

Milt Fish roe.

Minestrone Rich, Italian version of vegetable soup, usually containing some macaroni.

Mirabelle Small French plum with a good flavor.

Mirepoix Vegetables and ham or bacon, diced very small and cooked together in a sauce.

Mirin Japanese wine somewhat resembling sherry.

Miso Japanese flavoring ingredient.

Morel A European type of cherry; also, a distinctive European type of mushroom with a strong taste.

Mornay Sauce whose principal flavor is that of cheese.

Mortadèlla Large Italian-style salami.

Moselle Type of German wine.

Mostacciòlo Sweet Italian cake.

Mousse Cold dish of a frothy nature, usually containing beaten egg whites or whipped cream.

Mousseline Frothy sauce based upon *hollandaise,* but including beaten egg whites or whipped cream.

Mozzarella Soft type of Italian cheese.

Mulberry Edible berry.

Mullet Increasingly important food fish; largest catches made in Florida waters.

Muscat Type of raisin.

Mushimono General Japanese term for steamed foods.

Must Young wine immediately before fermentation.

Mustard Spicy condiment prepared from mustard seeds.

Namplā Siamese sauce made from salted shrimp.

Namprik A Thai sauce prepared with garlic and dried shrimp.

Nartje African citrus fruit.

Nebuchadnezzar The largest of all champagne bottles; holds the equivalent of twenty ordinary bottles.

Nectarine Peach with a smooth, plumlike skin.

Nepal Type of Indian pepper.

Neufchâtel French cheese of a rather soft consistency.

Noggin One quarter pint of alcoholic spirits.

Nori Edible seaweed used in Japanese cookery.

Nutmeg Fruit of a tropical tree used as a spice; *see* Mace.

Olives Fruit of the olive tree; principal types are green (unripe) and black (ripe), with dozens of varieties.

Oloroso Type of Spanish sherry.

Orange Flower Water Liquid containing some essence of distilled orange blossoms; used for flavoring.

Orégano Wild marjoram.

Orgeat Almond- and orange-flavored syrup.

Ortolan Game bird.

Ovar Type of Hungarian cheese.

Palm Kernel Oil Made from palm trees and used in confectionery products and margarine.

Palma A type of rather dry sherry.

Panade Mixture consisting of bread boiled or soaked in a liquid such as milk, stock; etc.; *panada.*

Panettone An Italian cake.

Panforte An Italian cake containing nuts and candied fruits.

Papain Dehydrated juice of the papaya tree; largely used to tenderize meats.

Papelon Crude, raw sugar.

Papillote, en Foods cooked in paper or parchment to retain juices during cooking process.

Paprika Spice of two principal types: Hungarian, strong and sweet; and Spanish, fairly mild.

Parisian Spice Mixture of various spices, usually used in conjunction with salt.

Parmigiana Italian term for a dish made with Parmesan cheese.

Partan A large crab (Scotland).

Passion Fruit Well-flavored fruit grown in various places; makes an excellent beverage.

Pasta General Italian word for macaroni; *pasta asciutta* is used for dry macaroni products.

Pasta e Fagiola Italian term for a dish of beans and macaroni.

Pasticceria Italian word for bakeries and their products.

Pastiera Italian type of sweet pastry, usually eaten at Easter.

Pastina Very small variety of Italian macaroni, customarily used in soup.

Pâté de Foie Gras Smooth paste made of goose livers.

Pawpaw Papaya.

Peanut Oil Oil obtained by crushing peanuts; generally classified as a vegetable oil.

Pectin White substance found in certain plants; used to thicken jellies.

Pekoe Variety of Chinese tea.

Pelardon A French cheese.

Pennoni Type of Italian macaroni.

Peppercorn Whole pepper seed.

Perilla Oriental herb closely resembling mint in flavor.

Periwinkle A shellfish.

Perry Alcoholic beverage prepared from pears.

Persimmon Yellow- to orange-colored fruit, with an extremely distinctive flavor.

Pesto Favorite Genoese flavoring; contains garlic, cheese, nuts, and olive oil.

Petite Marmite Classic French soup.

Petits Fours French term for small, decorated, glazed cakes.

Piccalilli Chopped vegetable relish.

Pigmeo Venezuelan banana.

Pignolias Edible seed of the nut pine.

Pilchard West Coast sardine.

Pimento Mild pepper; also spelled *pimiento.*

Pimento Oil Produced in Jamaica, B.W.I.; has the odor of cloves and nutmeg; also known as *allspice oil.*

Pinza Italian dessert, usually a type of cake.

Pizze Italian word for any flat, baked dough product; type of pie made with tomato sauce, with or without the addition of cheese, salami, etc.; also known as *pizza.*

Plaice Fish resembling sole.

Plantain Large variety of banana, usually inedible before cooking.

Pluck Liver and various other organs of an animal.

Poêlé Dish roasted with butter.

Poi Hawaiian staple food made from taro.

Polenta Italian dish based on corn meal.

Pont l'Evêque Fairly mild French cheese.

Poppy Seeds Edible flower seeds used for flavoring or in baking.

Porter Type of English beer.

Potted Any food preserved in a jar, usually in pounded or ground form.

Printanier Dish or soup made with cut-up spring vegetables.

Prosciutto Italian type of ham particularly suited for an appetizer or hors d'oeuvre; salted and dried.

Provençal Food cooked in the southern French style and containing oil, garlic, onions, etc.

Provola Soft type of Italian cheese.

Provolone Medium to hard type of Italian cheese with a rather smoky taste.

Pulque Alcoholic drink of Mexico made from a cactus plant.

Pumpernickel Dark Germanic bread of heavy texture.

Quenelles Fish or meat ground smooth and formed into balls.

Racahout Sweet drink popular in the Near East.

Ragoût French term for a thick stew.

Rakia Hungarian liqueur.

Rambutan Fruit of southeast Asia.

Raspings Grated bread crusts; often applied to bread crumbs.

Ratafia Bitter almond extract; also a liqueur.

Ravioli Italian specialty; little pockets of dough stuffed with varying ingredients; usually served with a sauce.

Reggiano An Italian cheese.

Rehoboam Wine bottle holding the equivalent of six ordinary bottles.

Rennet Stomach lining of various animals; used largely in cheese making, milk curdling, etc.

Rice, Wild Greenish grain grown in Wisconsin and the Southern states; much appreciated by gourmets.

Ricotta Type of Italian cheese similar to cottage cheese; often used for stuffing macaroni.

Rigatoni Rather large type of Italian macaroni.

Rio Type of Brazilian coffee.

Risotto Italian rice dish; may be served with or without the addition of seafood, etc.

Rissole Ground or chopped meat, fish, or poultry wrapped in pastry, or having a crust.

Rocambole Similar to garlic but slightly milder.

Rosefish A fish, usually caught off the New England coast.

Rosell Tart berry found in Asia and Australia.

Rum Alcoholic drink made from sugar cane.

Rusk Twice-toasted bread or semi-sweet cake.

Rye Whisky Whisky distilled from a mash which contains not less than 51% rye grain.

Sage Gray- to green-colored herb.

Sake Japanese rice wine, but actually similar to beer.

Salami General term for any of various beef, pork, or similar products usually prepared in the familiar long shape.

Salmanasar Wine bottle holding the equivalent of twelve regular bottles.

Salmi Poultry mixture or hash.

Salpicon Various meats or vegetables diced fairly small and used for stuffing or in sauce.

Saltimbocca Classic Italian dish of veal and ham.

Samp Hulled corn.

Sangaree West Indies wine punch.

Sanguinaccio Type of Italian blood sausage.

Santan Coconut milk.

Sarsaparilla Flavoring obtained from smilax roots.

Sassafras Bark and leaves of tree in laurel family used for tea, etc.

Sassafras Oil Distilled oil used for flavoring.

Sauerkraut Fermented cabbage product, usually obtained by action of lactic acid.

Savory Also *savoury;* British preparation usually served after dessert and before coffee, often a spicy or cheese mixture.

Sawi Chinese cabbage.

Sayers Variety of dates.

Scallion Young green onion that has either developed no bulb or a quite small one.

Scaloppine Italian term for thin slices of meat (usually veal) prepared in varying fashions.

Scamozza Type of Italian cheese.

Scampi Type of shellfish similar to large shrimp, usually found only in the Adriatic Sea.

Scungilli Large Italian shellfish, often prepared with various sauces.

Scuppernong A type of grape chiefly found in the southern U.S. and used to make a type of sweet wine.

Semolina Hardest part of the wheat, which is left after the removal of the flour; principally used for making macaroni products.

Sesame Seeds Oily seeds frequently used in cooking and baking; popular in Near Eastern countries.

Sherbet In the United States, a semi-soft frozen confection of water, flavoring, sugar, etc.; in the Near East, a very sweet, cold drink.

Sherry One of the world's most distinctive wines; available in dry, medium, or sweet types.

Shortening Any of a wide variety of edible fats.

Skillet Frying pan.

Sling Cold alcoholic drink, usually made with cracked ice, sugar, liquor, and flavorings.

Sloe Gin Gin flavored with the wild, purple berries of the blackthorn shrub.

Smolt Salmon, about two years old.

Smörgåsbord The Swedish "bread and butter table" consisting of numerous dishes arranged on a table; guests help themselves from cold and hot preparations.

Smørrebrød Danish open-faced sandwiches.

Soba Japanese noodles.

Sorbet Water ice.

Sodium Benzoate Food preservative.

Sorgo Syrup Very sweet, edible product widely used.

Soubise Sauce which is predominantly onion-flavored.

Soufflé Light, frothy dish that increases in size during baking owing to use of egg whites, if a hot soufflé; whipped cream is usually added to a cold soufflé.

Soursop Tart-flavored tropical fruit.

Soy Sauce Favorite Japanese seasoning sauce made from fermented soybeans.

Soybean Oil Edible oil obtained from soybeans.

Spaghetti Most popular type of Italian macaroni; usually the thinner type.

Spaghettini Very thin type of spaghetti.

Sprat Small fish, usually dried; particular favorite of Scandinavian people.

Spring-form Pan Round pan with a removable frame held in place with a spring.

Spumante Descriptive of Italian sparkling wines.

Spumoni Variety of rich, Italian-style ice cream.

Sterlet Young sturgeon.

Stirabout An Irish porridge.

Stracchino Variety of Italian cheese, usually quite soft.

Strega Yellowish Italian liqueur.

Strufoli Italian-style cake.

Sturgeon One of the most prized of all fish; the roe is caviar.

Sunflower Oil Prepared from sunflower seeds; used for shortening, edible oils, etc.

Suribachi Japanese mortar much used in cookery.

Sushi A classic Japanese preparation consisting of rice flavored with vinegar, and served with seafood, shellfish, etc., in small portions.

Sword Bean Type of edible broad bean.

Sybo Green onion or scallion in Scotch usage; also *cibol*.

Tagliarini Narrow Italian noodle.

Tamara Italian mixed spice, usually containing cinnamon, fennel, etc.

Tansy Herb used for flavoring.

Tapioca Starchy food obtained from the cassava plant.

Tarragon Aromatic herb used principally in flavoring vinegar.

Tartaric Acid Natural acid, particularly noticeable in grapes; used in baking powder, various foods, drinks, etc.

Tattie Familiar term for a potato in Scotland.

Tempura Shellfish or vegetables deep-fat fried in the Japanese manner.

Terrapin Edible turtle used for soups, stews, etc.

Thyme Herb commonly used for flavoring.

Timbale Dish containing meat or poultry combined with custard.

Tokay Hungarian wine.

Tomalley Matter in the body of a lobster; also known as *liver of lobster*.

Tomato Paste Paste with a concentrated tomato flavor, usually produced by dehydration.

Torrone Italian nougat-type candy.

Tortellini Variety of Italian macaroni.

Tortilla Flat corn cake; staple food of Mexico.

Tournedos Rather small, thin slices of tenderloin steak.

Travancore An Indian tea.

Treacle Molasses.

Truffle An edible substance, possibly either a fungus or a tuber, which grows underground and has a strong, aromatic effect on food; particularly esteemed in France.

Tufoli Type of Italian macaroni.

Tuna Green tropical fruit obtained from a cactus plant; also the seafood.

Turbot Fish highly regarded by European chefs.

Udon Japanese noodle made of corn flour.

Usquebaugh Spicy Irish whisky or brandy.

Valencia Type of almond.

Vanilla Bean Edible bean of an orchid plant; a very important flavoring source.

Vanillin Active element of the vanilla bean; provides characteristic odor and flavor.

Velouté Creamy, white, thick sauce.

Vermicelli Thinnest of all spaghettis.

Vermouth Apéritif wine, usually prepared with wormwood and other herbs.

Victoria A Brazilian coffee.

Vin Blanc White wine; also any white wine sauce.

Vlattero Greek currant liqueur.

Vodka National alcoholic drink of Russia.

Vol-au-Vent Pastry shell filled with any mixture.

Wasabi Japanese herb with a sharp, spicy flavor.

Water Chestnut Small tuber, with the texture and general shape of a chestnut; popular in oriental cookery.

Wensleydale A British cheese.

Whelk Variety of shellfish.

Widgeon Game bird of the duck family.

Wine Any fermented product obtained from grape juice.

Wintergreen Oil Natural or synthetic product used for flavoring.

Woodruff Leaves of a plant commonly used for flavoring; used to perfume German "May Wine."

Wormwood A bitter herb; formerly used in the manufacture of absinthe.

Yellowtail Type of tuna fish.

Yogurt Cultured milk food of custard-smooth consistency, made from fresh, pasteurized cow's milk to which the yogurt cultures are added; when yogurt is cooked, the action of the cultures is inhibited.

Yokan A Japanese candy.

Zabaglione Also *zabaione;* rich, foamy Italian dessert made with eggs and wine.

Zakuska Russian term for hors d'oeuvres.

Zest Glossy outside skin of an orange or other citrus fruit.

Ziti Rather large type of Italian macaroni.

Zizania Another name for wild rice.

Zuppa Inglese A rich Italian dessert often prepared with liquor.

Index

FOREIGN INDEX

ENGLISH INDEX